THE GLOBAL INFORMAL WORKFORCE

Priorities for Inclusive Growth

Editors
CORINNE C. DELÉCHAT
LEANDRO MEDINA

Cover design: IMF Creative Solutions

Cataloging-in-Publication Data
IMF Library

Names: Deléchat, Corinne, editor. | Medina, Leandro, editor. | International Monetary Fund, publisher.
Title: The global informal workforce : priorities for inclusive growth / editors: Corinne Deléchat, Leandro Medina.
Other titles: Priorities for inclusive growth
Description: Washington, DC : International Monetary Fund, 2021. | Includes bibliographical references.
Identifiers: ISBN 978-1-51357-591-9 (paper) 978-1-51357-744-9 (ePub) 978-1-51357-765-4 (PDF)
Subjects: LCSH: Informal sector (Economics). | Economic development. | Labor market.
Classification: LCC HD2341.G56 2021

Recommended citation: Deléchat, Corinne, and Leandro Medina, eds. 2021. *The Global Informal Workforce: Priorities for Inclusive Growth.* Washington, DC: International Monetary Fund.

ISBN: 978-1-51357-591-9 (paper)
978-1-51357-744-9 (ePub)
978-1-51357-765-4 (PDF)

Please send orders to:

International Monetary Fund, Publication Services
PO Box 92780, Washington, DC 20090, USA
Tel: (202) 623-7430 Fax: (202) 623-7201
E-mail: publications@imf.org
Internet: www.elibrary.imf.org
www.bookstore.imf.org

Table of Contents

Foreword

The informal economy is a globally widespread and pervasive phenomenon: 2 billion workers or 60 percent of the world population participate in the informal sector. Although mostly prevalent in emerging and developing economies, it is also an important part of advanced economies. Whereas workers and firms may choose to operate in the informal sector to avoid taxes or regulations, 85 percent of all informal workers around the world are in precarious employment in small production units, mostly due to lack of opportunities in the formal sector.

This has important macroeconomic consequences. First, informal firms tend to be small, with low productivity, and do not contribute to the tax base. Therefore, countries or regions with higher informality also grow below their potential. Moreover, they do not collect sufficient taxes and cannot provide basic goods and services to the whole population, which reinforces informality. Second, informal workers are more likely to be poor and to earn lower wages compared to their peers in the formal sector, both because they lack social protection and access to credit and because they tend to be less educated. Third, women are more likely than men to be not only in informal employment but also in the most precarious and low-paying categories of informal employment, in part because they lack equal access to education and health services.

This book brings together recent research by IMF staff and academic researchers on the causes, characteristics, and main effects of informality. It advances our understanding of reducing informality as essential for sustainable and inclusive development, because of informality's close but complex links with productivity, poverty, and inequality. This research is all the more relevant in the context of the current COVID-19 pandemic, which has hit particularly hard informal workers in emerging and developing economies. We already know that the pandemic risks erasing the past decade of progress in reducing poverty and inequality, and it is stretching the ability of governments to extend social safety nets to vulnerable informal workers and firms.

Designing and implementing effective policies to address informality requires, first and foremost, our ability to measure it. This is inherently difficult, because participants in the informal economy either do not want to be found or are hard to reach. Another challenge is that informality arises for multiple reasons and can take many different forms within and across countries. This book contributes to the policy debate in three main ways. First, it proposes a novel and consistent measure of the informal economy over time and across countries. Second, it analyzes the drivers and consequences of informality on the economy by analyzing its effects on productivity, labor markets, and gender gaps, as well as its interactions with fiscal policy and financial inclusion. Third, while recognizing that there is no one-size-fits-all solution, the book argues that policies can be effective in reducing informality. Improving access to education, accounting for informality when designing tax and social protection systems, enhancing financial inclusion, and implementing selected structural policies can be effective in promoting greater formalization.

Reducing informality over time is essential for sustained and inclusive development, but this process will inevitably have to be gradual, given the importance of informal activities to the livelihoods of billions of people currently. The analyses and recommendations in this book are a must-read for government officials, researchers, practitioners, and all those interested in designing policies to create a more prosperous world for everyone.

Kristalina Georgieva
Managing Director
International Monetary Fund

Acknowledgments

Producing this book was a collective undertaking by the chapters' authors to take a global look at the causes and consequences of informality, as well as the implications for policies. The book takes its roots in the work done for a chapter of the sub-Saharan African *Regional Economic Outlook* report of May 2017—led by Ali Mansoor and Cemile Sancak—that discussed the policy challenges and opportunities associated with large informal sectors in sub-Saharan Africa. Many people have inspired and supported us in our journey to see this project come to fruition. We are particularly grateful to IMF Managing Director Kristalina Georgieva; Antoinette Sayeh; Abebe Selassie; David Owen; David Robinson; Annalisa Fedelino; Ana Corbacho; and Professor Friedrich Schneider, a world-renowned expert on the informal economy. We also thank Joe Procopio and Rumit Pancholi of the IMF's Communications Department for their excellent work managing all aspects of the production of this book, Devlan O'Connor for copyediting, and Rebekah Young for proofreading. Jacques Treilly provided superb administrative assistance during the many steps needed to bring the book into completion.

Corinne Deléchat
Leandro Medina

Contributors

EDITORS

Corinne Deléchat is a division chief in the IMF's African Department. She is currently leading missions to Senegal as well as the department's analytical groups on inequality and economic diversification. She has also held positions in the Western Hemisphere Department and the Strategy, Policy, and Review Department, leading IMF relations with several emerging markets and low-income countries, and covering financial sector and private capital flow issues, donor coordination, capacity building, and external debt sustainability. Before joining the IMF, she worked at the Swiss Ministry of Economy, where she was in charge of bilateral cooperation to a group of low-income countries, and at the Organisation for Economic Co-operation and Development. Her publications focus on development, financial inclusion, banking, external debt, and international migration. Ms. Deléchat earned an MA and a PhD in economics from Georgetown University and a master's in international economics from the Graduate Institute of International and Development Studies in Geneva.

Leandro Medina is a senior economist in the IMF's Strategy, Policy, and Review Department. Previously, Mr. Medina worked in the IMF's African Department on frontier economy matters, particularly with countries such as Ghana and Mozambique, and a key issue of the *Regional Economic Outlook*, which focused on the size and characteristics of the informal economy in African countries. Before that, Mr. Medina focused on macro-fiscal issues in Southeast Asia in the Fiscal Affairs Department and covered regional policy issues in the Middle East and Central Asia, where he also contributed to the *Regional Economic Outlook*. Before joining the IMF, he worked as an international consultant at the Inter-American Development Bank, participating in portfolio review and policy dialogue missions to Argentina and Uruguay. His research, published in peer-reviewed journals, covers topics in macroeconomics and international finance. He earned a doctorate in economics from The George Washington University.

AUTHORS

Ehtisham Ahmad is a visiting professor at the Grantham Research Institute at the London School of Economics, is a senior fellow at the Chinese Academy of Fiscal Sciences, and was Pao Yu-Kong Professor at Zhejiang University. He directed a program at the London School of Economics on tax and social policy in the presence of informality in Indonesia and Mexico. He is the director of a London School of Economics' program on sustainable urban transitions in China and

Mexico. He previously held senior positions in the IMF's Fiscal Affairs Department, was Special Advisor to the Saudi Finance Minister, and Director of the London School of Economics Development Economics Research Program at STICERD. He has written or edited 13 books and numerous papers and reports on topics in public finance and policy. He holds an MA from the University of Cambridge and an MA and DPhil from the University of Sussex.

Antonio David is a senior economist in the IMF's Western Hemisphere Department. He has previously worked at the IMF's Institute for Capacity Development and African Department. Before that, he was an economist at the World Bank and taught at the University of Essex. His research interests include international macroeconomics, fiscal policy, financial development, and economic growth. He earned a PhD in economics from the University of Cambridge.

Hilary Devine is a research assistant in the IMF's African Department. Her research has covered income inequality in low-income and developing economies, the African Continental Free Trade Area, and private financing for development and international taxation in sub-Saharan Africa. Before joining the IMF, she earned an MA in economics from New York University and a BCA and BSc from Victoria University of Wellington.

Ben Kelmanson is the IMF's Senior Resident Representative in Turkey. Before this, he was IMF Mission Chief for Latvia and Moldova. Previously at the IMF he was Advisor to the First Deputy Managing Director and served in various capacities in the Strategy, Policy, and Review Department, including as Advisor to the Director, as Deputy Chief in the Emerging Markets Division, and in the Low-Income Country Division. Before joining the IMF, he worked for the UK director on the IMF's Executive Board and in HM Treasury in London. He has a BA in economics from the University of Leeds.

Koralai Kirabaeva is a senior economist in the IMF's European Department. An IMF staff member since 2011, she has also worked in the Monetary and Capital Market Department and the Middle East and Central Asia Department. She previously worked in the Financial Markets Department at the Bank of Canada. Her research focuses on macro-financial and structural issues. She holds a PhD in economics from Cornell University.

Lama Kiyasseh is a research officer in the IMF's Research Department, covering global commodity markets. Her research interests include energy economics, infrastructure development, and the drivers of financial inclusion. Her recent work focuses on renewables, the energy transition, and carbon pricing. Before joining the IMF, she examined fiscal policy and macro-financial risks as an economist in Saudi Arabia. She has coauthored multiple IMF working papers and published in the IMF's *World Economic Outlook*, the *Journal of Energy and Development*, and the *Middle East Economic Survey*, among others. She earned an MA in economics from The Johns Hopkins University School of Advanced International Studies and completed Oxford University's Executive Education Program in economic and social development.

Lisa Kolovich is an economist in the IMF's African Department who focuses on São Tomé and Príncipe and gender-related issues. She was previously the team manager for gender research under a joint collaboration between the IMF and the UK Department for International Development that focused on macro issues in low-income countries. Her research examines gender budgeting and fiscal policies initiatives as tools for reducing gender inequality, and she is a contributor to and the editor of the book *Fiscal Policies and Gender Equality*. Before joining the IMF, Ms. Kolovich conducted program evaluations for the US Department of Labor and was a consultant for the World Bank and the Inter-American Development Bank. She holds an MA from the University of Maryland and a PhD from the University of Navarra.

Frederic Lambert is a senior economist in the IMF's Western Hemisphere Department, covering Haiti. He previously worked on the desks for Mexico and Uruguay and on the *Global Financial Stability Report* in the Monetary and Capital Markets Department. Mr. Lambert joined the IMF in 2012 from the Banque de France, where he was head of the International Monetary Relations Division. He earned a PhD in economics from the Stern School of Business at New York University.

Margaux MacDonald is an economist in the IMF's Research Department, where she works on multilateral surveillance issues, including engagement with the G20. She previously worked in the African Department on several IMF program countries and on external sector issues. She has published in the IMF's *World Economic Outlook*, its *Finance & Development* magazine, and in peer-reviewed journals on international macroeconomics and finance, cross-country spillovers from monetary policy, trade, and the role of macroprudential policy on financial inclusion. Her work has been cited by the *Financial Times* and the *Wall Street Journal*. She earned a PhD and an MA in economics from Queen's University and a BBA from St. Francis Xavier University.

Vivian Malta is an economist in the Debt Policy Division of the Strategy, Policy, and Review Department at the IMF. She has previously worked in the Development Issues Unit, where she published several IMF papers on gender and income inequality. Before joining the IMF, she worked as a macroeconomist at the World Bank's office in Brazil and in the financial industry. She earned a PhD in economics from Escola de Pós-Graduação em Economia and a bachelor's degree in industrial engineering from Pontifical

Catholic University of Rio de Janeiro, both in Brazil. During her graduate studies, she spent a year at Columbia University and at the Federal Reserve Bank of New York as a visiting scholar.

Angelica Martínez Leyva is a PhD student at the University of Warwick in England. She was previously a project officer in the Strategy, Policy, and Review Department at the IMF, where she worked on gender and inequality issues. She has earned an MA and BA in economics from the Instituto Tecnólogico Autónomo de México.

Marina Mendes Tavares is an economist in the IMF's Research Department. She was previously an economist in the Strategy, Policy, and Review Department and led the inequality workstream of the IMF and the UK Department for International Development. Before joining the IMF, she worked as an assistant professor at the Instituto Tecnólogico Autónomo de México. Her research interests include macroeconomics, public finance, gender, and inequality. She earned a PhD in economics from the University of Minnesota and an MA from the Instituto de Matemática Pura e Aplicada in Brazil.

Azanaw Mengistu is a financial economist at Fannie Mae. His work focuses on house price modeling and forecasting. He previously worked in the African Department at the IMF, where he was responsible for managing macroeconomic data for five oil-exporting countries. His research interests include financial inclusion, housing finance, trade, and development. He earned degrees in economics and development economics from Georgetown University and The George Washington University.

Manabu Nose is an economist in the IMF's Fiscal Affairs He was previously an economist in the African Department covering countries in southern Africa and in the Fiscal Affairs Department's expenditure policy division. He was also an associate professor at the University of Tokyo. Before joining the IMF, he was an economist at the World Bank and the Japan Bank for International Cooperation. His research analyzes firm productivity, infrastructure and spatial connectivity, and social welfare programs. He earned a PhD in economics from Brown University.

Hector Perez-Saiz is the desk economist in the IMF's African Department E3 division for the Democratic Republic of the Congo. He was previously the desk economist for Equatorial Guinea in the C2 division. Before joining the IMF, he was a principal researcher in the Financial Stability Department at the Bank of Canada, where he studied banking, financial stability, and productivity. His research has been published in the *RAND Journal of Economics*, the *Journal of Financial Stability*, the IMF Working Paper series, IMF Staff Discussion Notes, and the Bank of Canada Working Paper series. Mr. Perez-Saiz earned a PhD in economics from the University of Chicago and an MA in economics from the Toulouse School of Economics.

Delphine Prady joined the IMF in 2016. She is a senior economist in the Fiscal Affairs Department, working on expenditure policy issues with a focus on social spending, energy subsidies, and the digital economy. Before joining the IMF, she worked in the French Treasury; she then was an advisor to social affairs and labor ministers in France and to the French president. She is a graduate of the École normale supérieure in Cachan, France, and earned a doctorate from the Toulouse School of Economics.

Friedrich Schneider studied economics at the University of Konstanz, where he received his PhD in 1977. Now retired, he was a professor of economics and vice director of foreign relations at the Johannes Kepler University Linz and a research professor at the German Institute for Economic Research. He was a board member of the International Institute of Public Finance and a member of the scientific advisory board of Avenir Suisse. He also was the chairman of the Academic Advisory Board of the Zeppelin University in Friedrichshafen, Germany. Since October 2015, he has been a member of the European Academy of Sciences and Arts. His research primarily focuses on the underground economy and illicit work, as well as tax evasion and money laundering. In addition, he has conducted research on political economies, privatization, deregulation, and issues related to environmental economics.

Frederik Toscani is an economist in the IMF's Western Hemisphere Department, covering Brazil. He previously worked on several other Latin American countries in the Western Hemisphere Department as well as in the IMF's Fiscal Affairs Department. His research has focused mainly on issues in labor economics, public economics, and economic growth and has been published in the *Journal of Economic Growth* and the *Journal of Development Economics*. He earned a PhD and MPhil in economics from the University of Cambridge and a BSc in economics from the London School of Economics.

Herve Tourpe is a chief digital advisor in the IMF's Information Technology Department. He leads a team of digital experts in transformative technologies relevant to IMF's member countries, such as fintech, artificial intelligence, blockchain, Big Data, and cloud computing and related cyber risks. A passionate "techno-realist," he strives to provide unbiased and cross-country expertise on technology trends, opportunities, and risks, especially for emerging market economies and low-income countries. He is an expert in national digital strategies, focusing on financial inclusion, sustainable development, digital payment, and central bank digital currencies. He graduated as a software engineer from the *Ecole Supérieure d'Informatique Appliquée de Lorraine* in France.

Arina Viseth is an economist in the IMF's African Department, Western 3 division, serving as the desk economist for Togo. Her other country experience includes Madagascar, Niger, Seychelles, South Sudan, and Uganda. Before joining the IMF, she was a consultant at the World Bank and a part of the trade team working on the World Trade Indicators. She earned a PhD in economics from the University of Delaware and is a Fulbright scholar alumna.

Dong (Frank) Wu is an economist in the IMF's Institute for Capacity Development. He has participated in the development and delivery of various IMF training and technical assistance programs for member countries. In the IMF's area department, he worked on emerging markets and low-income countries for topics, including inflation analysis, macro-financial linkages, external sector assessment, debt sustainability framework, and economic growth. He holds an economics PhD from the University of Maryland.

Rui Xu is an economist in the IMF's Asia and Pacific Department, where she works on Korea and Mongolia. She previously worked in the Institute for Capacity Development and delivered economic training to authorities from Central Asia, Eastern Europe, and the Middle East. Her research interests include growth economics, fiscal rules, monetary policy transmission, and gender inclusion and inequality. She has published in the IMF *Regional Economic Outlook* reports and peer-reviewed journals on issues related to international trade, inequality, volatility in the equity market, fiscal institutions, and fragile states. She earned a PhD and MA in economics from Stanford University and a BSc from The Hong Kong University of Science and Technology.

Abbreviations

AML/CFT	anti–money laundering/combating the financing of terrorism
API	application programming interface
ATM	automated teller machine
CCE	common correlated effects
CDA	currency demand approach
CICO	cash-in/cash-out
CIS	Commonwealth of Independent States
D3	Digitize, Direct, Design
DIY	do it yourself
EU	European Union
FATF	Financial Action Task Force
Findex	Global Financial Inclusion database (World Bank)
fintech	financial technology
FGLS	feasible generalized least squares
G2P	government to person
GMM	generalized method of moments
GSMA	Global System for Mobile Communications Association
ID	identification
ILO	International Labour Organization
IPUMS	International project started by the University of Minnesota Population Center
ISO	International Organization for Standardization
ISR	*impuesto sobre la renta* (Mexican income tax)
IV	instrumental variable
KYC	know your customer
LATE	local average treatment effect
MAR	missing at random
MCAR	missing completely at random
MIMIC	multiple indicators, multiple causes
MMO	mobile money operator
MNAR	missing not at random
MNO	mobile network operator
NOE	nonobserved economy
OECD	Organisation for Economic Co-operation and Development
OLS	ordinary least squares
P2G	person to government
PMM	predictive mean matching method
PPP	purchasing power parity
PUMS	Public Use Microdata Samples
RMSEA	root mean square error of approximation
SDGs	Sustainable Development Goals
SEM	structural equation modeling

SEZ	special economic zone
SIMS	Labor Markets and Social Security Information System
SMS	short message service
SNA	System of National Accounts
TFP	total factor productivity
UN	United Nations
UNESCO	United Nations Educational, Scientific and Cultural Organization
UNICEF	United Nations Children's Fund
USSD	unstructured supplementary service data
VAT	value-added tax
WDI	World Development Indicators (World Bank)
WEF	World Economic Forum
WGI	Worldwide Governance Indicators (World Bank)

INTRODUCTION

What Do We Know About the Informal Economy?

Corinne Deléchat and Leandro Medina

The informal economy has long been at the center of academic and policy debates because of both its pervasiveness and its complex links with development outcomes. The informal economy, comprising activities that have market value and would add to tax revenue and GDP were they recorded, is a widespread global phenomenon. According to the International Labour Organization (ILO; 2018) about 2 billion workers, or 60 percent of the total employed population age 15 years and older, operate in the informal sector. Recent estimates place the size of the informal economy at about one-third of the global economy.

So, what is informality? Informality is a complex and multifaceted phenomenon that is difficult to measure and analyze. By definition, informal activities are not recorded or are underrecorded, and participants do not want to be accounted for. As Kanbur (2009, 2) writes:

> Informality is a term that has the dubious distinction of combining maximum policy importance and political salience with minimal conceptual clarity and coherence in the analytical literature. There is a plethora of definitions, which leads to incoherence in analysis and, at its worst, major policy failures.

Informality covers a large range of situations within and across countries, and it arises for a broad spectrum of reasons. At one end of the spectrum, informality can be the result of a deliberate choice, with individuals and firms deciding to remain outside the formal economy to avoid taxes, social contributions, or compliance with standards and licensing requirements (Schneider 2015; Hassan and Schneider 2016; Williams and Schneider 2016). This choice relates to the often-held but misconceived view that informality is mainly caused by firms and individuals "cheating" on the system to avoid paying taxes. At the other end, informality can exist when some individuals are too poor or too uneducated to access formal employment, public benefits, and financial services, and therefore need to rely on informal activities as a safety net.

Informality can thus take many forms. Not all informal workers are poor, and not all poor workers are in the informal sector. Some workers can be simultaneously or successively employed in the formal and informal sectors. Informal firms range from precarious (hand-to-mouth) one-person operations to thriving small businesses.

The drivers of informality are similarly multifaceted, as highlighted in this book. They vary from low economic development; to inequality of access to health, education, and other basic public goods; to the state of the legal and regulatory environment, notably in labor and product markets; to the design of the tax and social protection system; and to the quality of institutions. In fact, informality can be best understood as a response to a broad set of institutions, which can explain the high persistence of informality, the wide cross-country variations in the size of informal economies, and the equally large within-country variations in types of informality.

This book's chapters advance the discussion on informality by illustrating that the high incidence and persistence of informality, particularly in emerging market and developing economies, is an obstacle to sustainable development because of its close but complex links with economic growth, poverty, and inequality, including gender inequality. Informal firms do not contribute to the tax base and tend to remain small, with low productivity and access to finance. Countries or regions with high informality thus tend to grow less than their potential (La Porta and Schleifer 2008, 2014). Informality also deprives governments of sizable tax revenue that could be used to improve basic public services (the lack thereof, in turn, contributes to informality).

Because informal workers lack formal contracts and social protection and tend to be less educated, they are more likely to be poor and to lack decent work conditions compared with peers in the formal sector. High informality is, moreover, associated with high inequality: workers tend to earn less in the informal sector than formal sector peers with similar skills, and the wage gap between formal and informal workers is higher at lower skill levels. This explains why the large decline in informality in Latin America observed over the past 20 years was associated with significant reductions in inequality.

Informality is also related to gender inequality: in two out of three low- and lower-middle income countries, women are more likely than men to be employed informally and to be in the most precarious and low-paid categories of informal employment. For example, UN Women (2016) finds that the gender wage gap is 28 percent in the informal sector in sub-Saharan Africa, far higher than the 6 percent gap in the formal sector.

The ILO (2018) estimates that, globally, 85 percent of informal workers are precariously employed in small, informal firms, with only 11 percent of informal workers employed in formal firms. Providing workers with decent jobs and facilitating the transition of small firms to formality is thus urgently needed to support inclusive development, as acknowledged in the United Nations' Sustainable Development Goals.[1]

---

[1] Sustainable Development Goal 8 is to "promote sustained, inclusive, and sustainable economic growth, full and productive employment and decent work for all." In particular, Target 8.3 aims to promote development-oriented policies that support productive activities and decent job creation, and to encourage the formalization and growth of micro, small, and medium enterprises, including through access to financial services.

This sense of urgency has only been reinforced by the coronavirus disease 2019 (COVID-19) pandemic. The pandemic has crushed informal activities, particularly in developing countries, where large segments of the population are not covered by existing social protection schemes. The need to provide a lifeline has emerged as an urgent priority for governments. Strict lockdowns destroyed the livelihoods of taxi and minibus drivers, street and market vendors, and bar and restaurant owners depending on daily incomes for survival. Yet countries with thin or nonexistent social safety nets have formulated ad hoc and sometimes innovative cash or in-kind transfer plans in a matter of weeks. Since March 2020, 139 countries and territories around the globe have planned, implemented, or adapted cash transfers to support their citizens (Rawlings, Jean-François, and Macleod 2020).

As discussed in Chapter 10, this crisis like no other can be an opportunity to leverage digital solutions to (1) set up more permanent mechanisms to expand social protection and (2) provide vulnerable individuals or firms with adequate incentives to join a national register as a step toward formalization. Other tools can include a combination of support to small and medium-sized enterprises (incubators, preparation of financial accounts), as well as tax policy, and administration measures (adequate minimal threshold for VAT, simplification of tax payment procedures, incentives to be part of the taxpayer registry).

Gaining a better understanding of the causes and effects of informality is thus central for policymakers to be able to tackle key economic development challenges. However, understanding is complicated by obvious measurement difficulties because participants in the informal sector either do not wish to be accounted for or are difficult to reach. Multiple methods, which can be categorized as either direct or indirect approaches, have been used to measure the size of the informal economy. The direct methods depend mainly on surveys and samples based on voluntary replies, tax audits, or other compliance methods; the results, therefore, are sensitive to the way a questionnaire is formulated or the willingness of respondents to cooperate.

The availability of direct microeconomic data has, nonetheless, much improved. For example, the ILO's 2018 report *Women and Men in the Informal Economy* compiles comparable data on informal employment and employment in the informal sector for more than 100 countries, representing more than 90 percent of the world's employed population age 15 years and older. The indirect approaches, as applied in the first section of this book, suggest the size of the informal economy in total output through alternative measures or indicators, such as the consumption of electricity or the cash in the economy.

Both approaches lead to similar conclusions regarding the size and evolution of informal economies within and across countries: (1) the informal economy is large and represents, on average, one-third of the global economy; (2) informality tends to decline over time and to be lower but still significant in more advanced economies, as compared with lower-income countries (although the declining trend is not universal, and informality has increased over the past decade in several countries, such as Ecuador, Namibia, and Venezuela); (3)

Introduction Figure 1. Size of the Informal Economy

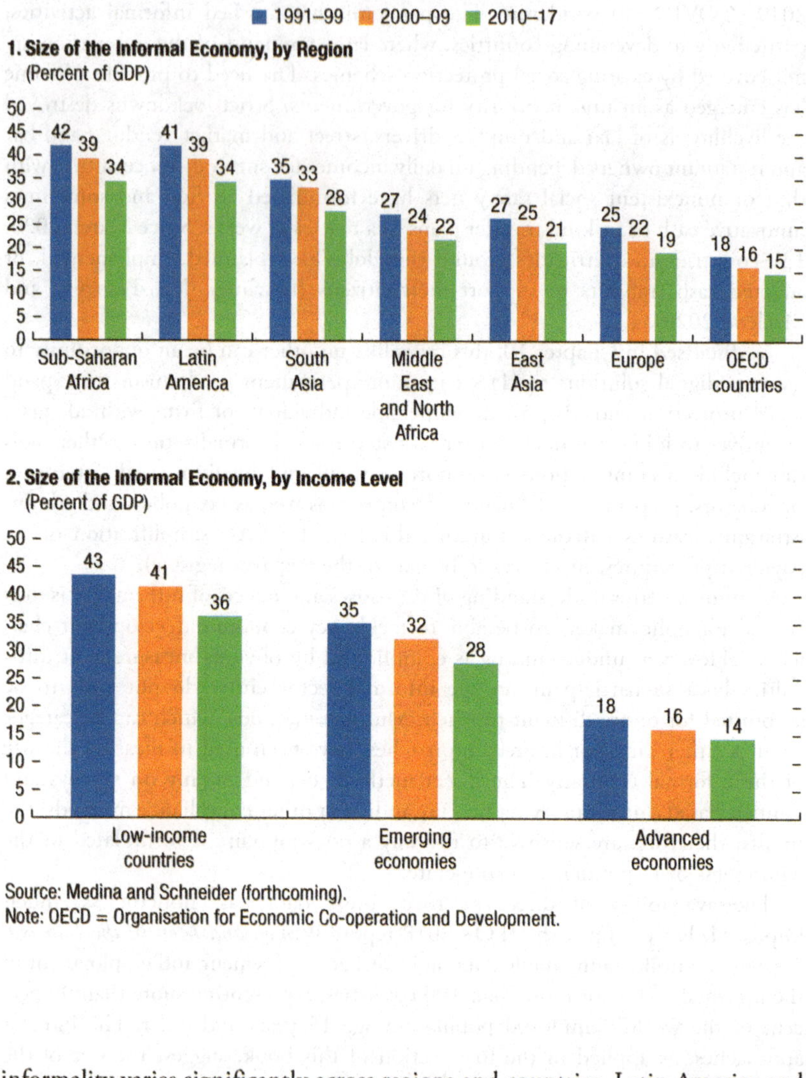

Source: Medina and Schneider (forthcoming).
Note: OECD = Organisation for Economic Co-operation and Development.

informality varies significantly across regions and countries. Latin America and the Caribbean and sub-Saharan Africa stand out as the two regions of the world with the most informality. For low-income countries, the average size of the informal sector remains large at 36 percent (14 percent for advanced economies) (Introduction Figure 1).

The design of effective policies to address informality is complicated by the multiple causes and forms of informality, both across and within countries. Informality is shaped by each country's unique socioeconomic and institutional setting, which means that no one formula can address informality. Nonetheless, the findings presented in this book indicate common guiding principles for policy design. Four broad policies can effectively address the root causes of informality:

- *Improved access to and quality of education is probably the single-most powerful way to lower informality.* Education reforms aimed both at enhancing equality of access and ensuring that students remain in school until the end of the secondary cycle are particularly important. Ample technical and vocational training opportunities will also help.
- *Tax system design should avoid inadvertently increasing incentives for individuals and firms to remain in the informal sector* (Levy 2010). It is generally recognized that simpler value-added and corporate tax systems (with lower rates and no or minimal exemptions and loopholes), as well as low payroll taxes, help reduce informality. Supportive social protection systems, including progressive income taxes and protection for the poorest, help address distributional aspects.
- *Policies to enhance financial inclusion by promoting expanded access to formal (or bank-based) financial services can help lower informality.* For informal firms and entrepreneurs, lack of access to finance is a key constraint, stifling productivity and the growth of their businesses. Countries where access to finance is broader tend to grow faster and have lower income inequality.
- *A range of structural policies can help increase incentives and lower the cost of formalization.* Labor market regulations can be simplified to ensure greater flexibility and facilitate informal workers' entry into formal employment. Competition policy can boost entry of small firms in some sectors by eliminating monopolies. Elimination of excessive regulations and bureaucratic requirements also helps.

Digital platforms, including government-to-person mobile transfers, can support these policies and contribute to inclusive growth by bringing financial accounts to the unbanked, empowering women financially and helping small and medium enterprises grow within the formal sector.

In sum, informality is a widespread and persistent phenomenon that critically affects how fast economies can grow, develop, and provide decent economic opportunities for their populations. Sustainable development requires a reduction in informality over time, but this process is inevitably gradual because the informal sector is currently the only viable income source for billions of people. Informality is best tackled by steady reforms—such as investment in education—and policies that address its underlying causes. Attacks on the sector motivated by the view that it is generally operating illegally and evading taxes are not the answer.

This book, a collection of recent research by IMF staff and renowned academic researchers, takes a fresh look at informality through an economic lens and examines some of the main questions regarding the informal economy: what do we know about the informal economy? What are the main reasons for an individual or a firm to operate in the informal sector? How does informality relate to growth and inequality, including gender inequality? Can tax and social protection systems be designed to avoid pushing workers and firms into the informal sector? Why are individuals often using formal and informal financial services simultaneously, particularly in developing countries? By covering the many facets of informality, this volume provides a unique perspective on this complex phenomenon and contributes to the vast but uneven literature dedicated to the topic.

THE SIZE OF THE INFORMAL ECONOMY AND ITS RELATIONSHIP WITH ECONOMIC DEVELOPMENT

The first section of the book presents new estimations of the size of the informal economy around the world and then discusses its main characteristics and determinants, including the complex relation between informality and GDP per capita.

Chapter 1 uses a novel method to estimate the size of the informal sector in 158 countries over the past 25 years. Leandro Medina and Friedrich Schneider apply the multiple indicators, multiple causes (MIMIC) model, an indirect estimation method based on proxy variables for informality that include data on satellite-measured night lights. MIMIC estimates have been used by recent cross-country studies of informality, including chapters of this book.

In Chapter 2, Ben Kelmanson, Koralai Kirabaeva, and Leandro Medina empirically estimate the drivers of the informal economy in European countries. They find that regulatory quality, poor governance (corruption and weak judicial systems), and tax burden tend to be associated with higher informality, whereas factors such as trade openness and higher productivity are associated with lower informality. The chapter suggests that European countries require comprehensive regulatory and institutional reforms to successfully deal with the informal economy.

Chapter 3, by Dong Frank Wu and Friedrich Schneider, examines long-term determinants of development. They find that informality declines when development increases, but only up to a certain threshold, beyond which informality increases again. The notion of a threshold suggests that potential rewards of shrinking informal sectors are greater at lower development levels and when informality is a large part of the economy. Wu and Schneider also find that education is closely associated with economic development, suggesting that policies directly focused on improving human capital, rather than aimed at reducing the size of the informal sector, best support long-term inclusive growth.

INFORMALITY AND ITS RELATIONSHIP WITH PRODUCTIVITY, LABOR MARKETS, AND GENDER GAPS

The second section of the book focuses on the relationships between informality, productivity, labor markets, and gender gaps.

Chapter 4 by Manabu Nose estimates the allocative efficiency of land and labor in 40 sub-Saharan African countries. Empirical results suggest that improving factor market efficiency, particularly by allocating land to more productive firms, would help sub-Saharan African firms move out of the informal sector and gain significant scale and productivity. Nose finds that improving regulations to formalize land allocation and labor contracts with social insurance benefits effectively supports firm growth when legal capacity is weak.

Chapter 5, by Antonio C. David, Frederic Lambert, and Frederik Toscani, shows that informality dampens unemployment movements over the business cycle in Latin America compared with advanced economies. This is attributable to the presence of dual labor markets, with a well-protected formal labor market and a highly flexible informal one. Countries with higher redundancy costs and cumbersome dismissal regulations exhibit "excess" informality above what would be expected based on income and educational levels. In that regard, David, Lambert, and Toscani find that labor market and tax reforms can greatly affect the informality rate. However, the authors also caution against overoptimism: when GDP per capita is low, informality remains high, as long as demand for formal goods is also low. In other words, a country's productivity, specifically the productivity of its formal sector compared with that of its informal sector, is a key determinant of informality.

Chapter 6, by Arina Viseth, assesses immigration's effect on native employment in the formal and informal sectors in three sub-Saharan African countries. When foreign and native workers are both low skilled, immigration increases labor supply in the formal sector, reducing native employment in that sector and triggering native workers to search for jobs in the informal sector. When both native and foreign workers are highly skilled, immigration increases labor demand in the formal sector, resulting in higher employment and greater economic expansion, which in turn stimulates job creation in the informal sector.

In Chapter 7, Vivian Malta, Lisa Kolovich, Angelica Martínez Leyva, and Marina M. Tavares investigate the factors that can explain the larger presence of women in the informal sector. The authors show the association between female overrepresentation in the informal sector and gender gaps in education, social and legal norms biased against women, and the legal framework. In particular, they find that low education is usually more relevant for women as a driver of informal employment.

INFORMALITY AND FISCAL POLICY

The third section of the book studies the links between informality and fiscal policy.

Chapter 8, by Hilary Devine, assesses the relationship between informality and the quality of political and fiscal institutions in emerging market and developing economies. The analysis finds that political and fiscal institutions matter, in addition to economic development, macroeconomic stability, and measures of human capital. In particular, measures of government accountability, constraints on the executive, and property rights are associated with lower informality. The quality of fiscal institutions matters too: measures of VAT efficiency and fiscal sustainability are also significantly associated with lower informality.

In Chapter 9, Ehtisham Ahmad addresses the two dimensions of informality mentioned earlier: (1) "cheating" by firms to evade taxation on transactions, wages, and profits; and (2) informal workers who live in informal settlements and do not pay taxes but are also excluded from public services and benefits. Ahmad shows that national tax reforms, including to VAT systems, can generate information on "hidden" taxpayers. Subnational reforms include property taxes linked to an accountable provision of the Sustainable Development Goals that can provide incentives for migrant workers to move out of informality.

Chapter 10, by Sonja Davidovic, Soheib Nunhuck, Delphine Prady, and Herve Tourpe, studies how to scale up social protection to reach informal workers and firms during a pandemic using digital technologies. The authors introduce a framework to guide policymakers in building sustainable government-to-person mobile transfer programs. Together with other programs, mobile transfer platforms can strengthen social safety nets, allowing for adequate and effective coverage of vulnerable households and workers.

INFORMALITY AND FINANCIAL INCLUSION

The final section of the book assesses the relationship between the informal economy and the financial sector.

Chapter 11, by Corinne Deléchat, Lama Kiyasseh, Margaux MacDonald, and Rui Xu, analyzes the use of formal versus informal financial services in emerging market and developing economies. The chapter shows that individuals often combine types of financial access (formal and informal), and that this choice is driven by individual characteristics, such as gender and education, but also by country characteristics and policies, including monetary and financial policies. In particular, the chapter finds that strict macroprudential policies (that apply to formal financial services) tend to "leak" by pushing individuals to informal financial services.

The last chapter, by Azanaw Mengistu and Hector Perez-Saiz, studies how the adoption of several financial products affect competition and financial soundness, and thus financial inclusion, in sub-Saharan Africa. Mengistu and Perez-Saiz find that more competition tends to increase the probability of access to these financial products and that this effect is also observed for individuals in the informal economy.

By presenting the reader with this volume, we aim to help close remaining gaps in the academic literature and policy discussions, as well as to provide policymakers and practitioners with empirical evidence, lessons learned, and policy options to address informality and its economic consequences, and thus promote sustainable and inclusive development.

REFERENCES

Hassan, M., and F. Schneider. 2016. "Size and Development of the Shadow Economies of 157 Countries Worldwide: Updated and New Measures from 1999 to 2013." IZA Discussion Paper 10281, Institute of Labor Economics, Bonn, Germany.

International Labour Organization (ILO). 2018. *Women and Men in the Informal Economy: A Statistical Picture*, 3rd ed. Geneva: International Labour Organization.

Kanbur, R. 2009. "Conceptualising Informality: Regulation and Enforcement." IZA Discussion Paper 4186, Institute of Labor Economics, Bonn, Germany.

La Porta, R., and A. Shleifer. 2008. "The Unofficial Economy and Economic Development." *Brookings Papers on Economic Activity* 39–2 (Fall): 275–363.

La Porta, R., and A. Shleifer. 2014. "Informality and Development." *Journal of Economic Perspectives* 28 (3): 109–26.

Levy, S. 2010. *Good Intentions, Bad Outcomes: Social Policy, Informality, and Economic Growth in Mexico.* Washington, DC: Brookings Institution Press.

Medina, L., and F. Schneider. Forthcoming. "Shedding Light on the Shadow Economy: A Global Database." IMF Working Paper, International Monetary Fund, Washington, DC.

Rawlings, L., J. Jean-François, and C. Macleod. 2020. "Using Behavioral Insights to Make the Most of Emergency Social Protection Cash Transfers." *Let's Talk Development* (blog), World Bank, September 8. https://blogs.worldbank.org/developmenttalk/using-behavioral-insights-make-most-emergency-social-protection-cash-transfers.

Schneider, F. 2015. "Size and Development of the Shadow Economy of 31 European and 5 Other OECD Countries from 2003 to 2014: Different Developments?" *Journal of Self-Governance and Management Economics* 3 (4): 7–29.

UN Women. 2016. "Leave No One Behind: A Call to Action for Gender Equality and Women's Economic Empowerment." Report of the UN Secretary-General, United Nations, New York.

Williams, C. C., and F. Schneider. 2016. *Measuring the Global Shadow Economy: The Prevalence of Informal Work and Labour.* Cheltenham, United Kingdom: Elgar.

CHAPTER 1

The Evolution of Shadow Economies through the 21st Century

Leandro Medina and Friedrich Schneider

INTRODUCTION

The shadow economy is, by nature, difficult to measure, because agents engaged in shadow economy activities try to remain undetected. The request for information about the extent of the shadow economy and its developments over time is motivated by its political and economic relevance. Moreover, total economic activity, including official and unofficial production of goods and services, is essential in the design of economic policies that respond to fluctuations and economic development over time and across space. Furthermore, the size of the shadow economy is a core input for estimating the extent of tax evasion and thus deciding how best to control it.

The shadow economy is known by different names, such as the hidden economy, the gray economy, the black economy or lack economy, the cash economy, or the informal economy. All these synonyms refer to some type of shadow economy activities. We use the following definition: the shadow economy includes all economic activities that are hidden from official authorities for monetary, regulatory, and institutional reasons. Monetary reasons include avoiding paying taxes and all social security contributions; regulatory reasons include avoiding governmental bureaucracy or the burden of regulatory framework; and institutional reasons include corruption law, the quality of political institutions, and weak rule of law. For our study, the shadow economy reflects mostly legal economic and productive activities that, if recorded, would contribute to national GDP; therefore, the definition of the shadow economy in this chapter tries to exclude illegal or criminal activities, do-it-yourself activities, or other household activities.[1]

The authors thank Ramdane Abdoun, Maximiliano Appendino, Nazim Belhocine, Claudia Berg, Selim Cakir, Teresa Daban, Suhaib Kebhaj, Julie Kozack, Chris Papageorgiou, Magali Pinat, Martin Sommer, and David Vogel for useful comments.

[1] Overlapping areas include prostitution, illegal construction firms, and so on. Compare, for example, Williams and Schneider (2016), Schneider (2017), and the Estimation Methods section of this chapter, where this problem is tackled.

Empirical research into the size and development of the global shadow economy has grown rapidly (Gerxhani 2003; Feld and Schneider 2010; Schneider 2011, 2015, 2017; Schneider and Williams 2013; Hassan and Schneider 2016; Williams and Schneider 2016). This chapter (1) analyzes the growth of knowledge about the shadow economy in a review covering the past 20 years, concentrating mainly on knowledge about established or new estimation methods; (2) defines or categorizes the shadow economy and new measures of indicator variables, such as the light intensity approach; and (3) presents estimates of the size of the shadow economy for 158 countries over 25 years. We have three concrete goals:

1. To extensively evaluate and discuss the latest developments regarding estimation methods, such as the System of National Accounts (SNA) approach and new micro and macro methods, and the crucial evolution of the macro methodologies—namely the currency demand approach (CDA) and the multiple indicators, multiple causes (MIMIC) model—in tackling the problem of double counting.
2. To present shadow economy estimates for 158 countries from 1991 to 2015 while addressing early criticism. In particular, when using the MIMIC approach, GDP per capita, growth rate of GDP, or first differences in GDP are often used as cause as well as indicator variables. Instead of GDP, we use a light intensity approach as an indicator variable, then run a variety of robustness tests to further assess the validity of our results.[2] We, in addition to MIMIC, use a fully independent method, the predictive mean matching (PMM) method by Rubin (1987), which overcomes these calibration problems. This is one of the first attempts both to include the light intensity approach as an indicator variable within MIMIC and to use a full alternative method, such as PMM.[3]
3. To compare the results of the different estimation methods, showing their strengths and weaknesses, and critically evaluate them.

This chapter is organized as follows. First we draw theoretical considerations and discuss the most important cause variables. Next we discuss methods to estimate the size of the shadow economy. We go on to address the macro methods' shortcomings, introduce the use of night lights (that is, light intensity) as a proxy for the size of an economy, and discuss additional robustness tests. We also cover the econometric results of the MIMIC estimations of the size of the shadow economy for 158 countries and critically evaluate them. Later on we compare the MIMIC results with micro survey results and SNA discrepancy method results before summarizing our findings and providing a conclusion.

---

[2] Furthermore, the discussion on how to calibrate relative MIMIC estimates of the shadow economy has been long and controversial—compare Hashimzade and Heady (2016), Feige (2016a), Schneider (2016), and Breusch (2016).

[3] To the best of our knowledge, both the light intensity approach and the PMM method have been used by Medina, Jonelis, and Cangul (2017) only and only in the context of sub-Saharan Africa.

THEORETICAL CONSIDERATIONS

Individuals are rational calculators who weigh costs and benefits when considering breaking the law. Their decisions to partially or completely participate in the shadow economy are choices overshadowed by uncertainty because they involve a trade-off between gains—if the activities are not discovered—and losses, if the activities are discovered and penalized.

Shadow economic activities, *SE*, thus negatively depend on the probability of detection, *p*, and potential fines, *f*, and positively on the opportunity costs of remaining formal, denoted as *B*. Opportunity costs are positively determined by the burden of taxation, *T*, and high labor costs, *W*—because of labor market regulations, individual income generated in the shadow economy is usually categorized as labor income rather than capital income. Hence, the higher the tax burden and labor costs, the more incentives individuals have to avoid these costs by working in the shadow economy. The probability of detection, *p*, itself depends on enforcement actions, *A*, taken by the tax authority and on the facilitating activities, *F*, individuals undertake to reduce the detection of shadow economic activities. Such calculations suggest the following structural equation:

$$SE = SE\left[\overset{-}{p}\left(\overset{+}{A},\overset{-}{F}\right);\overset{-}{f};\overset{+}{B}\left(\overset{+}{T},\overset{+}{W}\right)\right]$$

Hence, shadow economic activities may be defined as those economic activities and income earned that circumvent government regulation, taxation, or observation. More narrowly, the shadow economy includes monetary and nonmonetary transactions of a legal nature, hence, all productive economic activities that would generally be taxable were they reported to the state (tax) authorities. Such activities are deliberately concealed from public authorities to avoid payment of income, value added, or other taxes and social security contributions or to avoid compliance with certain legal labor market standards, such as minimum wages, maximum working hours, or safety standards and administrative procedures.

The shadow economy thus focuses on productive economic activities that would normally be included in national accounts but that remain underground because of tax or regulatory burdens.[4] Although such legal activities would contribute to a country's value added, they are not captured in national accounts because they are produced in illicit ways. Informal household economic activities

[4] Although classic criminal activities, such as drug dealing, are independent of increasing taxes, and the causal variables included in the empirical models are only imperfectly linked (or causal) to classic criminal activities, the footprints used to indicate shadow economic activities, such as currency in circulation, also apply for classic crime. Hence, macroeconomic shadow economy estimates do not typically distinguish legal from illegal underground activities; instead they represent the whole informal economy spectrum.

such as do-it-yourself projects and neighborly help are typically excluded from analyses of the shadow economy.[5]

What are the determinats of the shadow economy? The size of the shadow economy depends on various elements. The literature highlights specific causes and indicators.[6] Table 1.1 presents the main causes and indicators that determine the shadow economy.

ESTIMATION METHODS

We now describe the methods used to measure the shadow economy,[7] highlighting their advantages and drawbacks.[8] These approaches, including the model-based approach, can be divided into direct or indirect. We then discuss the MIMIC approach in depth, including its shortcomings and a way to overcome them: a structured, hybrid model–based estimation approach combining the CDA and MIMIC models.

Direct Approaches to Estimation

Three direct and micro methods of measuring the shadow economy[9] are briefly presented and critically evaluated: the SNA discrepancy method, representative surveys, and surveys of company managers.[10]

SNA Discrepancy Method

Gyomai and van de Ven (2014) describe this method in detail, starting with a classification for measuring the nonobserved economy:

1. *Underground hidden production.* Activities that are legal and create value but are deliberately concealed from public authorities.

[5] From a social—and maybe even economic—perspective, soft forms of illicit employment such as moonlighting (for example, construction work in private homes) and its contribution to aggregate value added may be assessed positively. For a discussion of these issues, see Thomas (1992) and Buehn, Karmann, and Schneider (2009).

[6] The causes and indicators are only briefly presented here. Compare Schneider (2017) and Williams and Schneider (2016).

[7] Because significant literature is available about various methods to measure a shadow economy, a detailed overview of and list of problems for using these methods (including the MIMIC method) are not discussed here. See, for example, Schneider and Enste (2002); Feld and Schneider (2010); Schneider, Buehn, and Montenegro (2010); Schneider and Williams (2013); Schneider (2015); and Williams and Schneider (2016).

[8] Based on Schneider and Enste (2002), Feld and Schneider (2010), and Williams and Schneider (2016).

[9] The term "shadow economy" here means the nonobserved economy; its measurement will be explained in detail in describing the SNA discrepancy method. Compare here Gyomai and van de Ven (2014), Feld and Schneider (2010), Williams and Schneider (2016), and Schneider (2017).

[10] An extensive critical evaluation is not undertaken here because this is covered in various other studies, including Feld and Schneider (2010), Williams and Schneider (2016), and Schneider (2017).

TABLE 1.1.

Main Causes and Indicators That Determine the Shadow Economy

Causal/Indicator Variable	Theoretical Reasoning	References
Tax and social security contribution burdens	The distortion of the overall tax burden affects labor-leisure choices and may stimulate labor supply in the shadow economy. The bigger the difference is between the total labor cost in the official economy and after-tax earnings (from work), the greater the incentive is to reduce the tax wedge and work in the shadow economy. This tax wedge depends on social security burden/payments and the overall tax burden, making such payments key determinants in the existence of the shadow economy.	Thomas 1992; Johnson, Kaufmann, and Zoido-Lobatón 1998a, 1998b; Giles 1999; Tanzi 1999; Schneider 2003, 2005; Dell'Anno 2007; Dell'Anno, Gomez-Antonio, and Alanon Pardo 2007
Quality of institutions, or corruption	The quality of public institutions is another key factor in the development of the informal sector. In particular, the efficient and discretionary application of the tax code and regulations by the government play crucial roles in the decision to work off the books, even more important than the actual burden of taxes and regulations. A bureaucracy with highly corrupt government officials tends to be associated with larger unofficial activity, whereas good rule of law through secure property rights and contract enforceability increases the benefits of being formal. A certain level of taxation, mostly spent in productive public services, characterizes efficient policies. Production in the formal sector benefits from more provision of productive public services and is negatively affected by taxation, whereas the shadow economy reacts in the opposite way. An informal sector developing as a consequence of the failure of political institutions to promote an efficient market economy, and entrepreneurs going underground because of inefficient public goods provision, may be alleviated if institutions can be strengthened and fiscal policy moves closer to the median voters' preferences.	Johnson, Kaufmann, and Zoido-Lobatón 1998a, 1998b; Friedman and others 2000; Dreher and Schneider 2009; Dreher, Kotsogiannis, and McCorriston 2009; Schneider 2010; Teobaldelli 2011; Schneider and Teobaldelli 2012; Amendola and Dell'Anno 2010; Losby and others 2002; Schneider and Williams 2013; Hassan and Schneider 2016; Williams and Schneider 2016
Regulations	Regulations, for example, labor market regulations or trade barriers, are another factor that reduces freedom (of choice) for individuals in the official economy. They substantially increase labor costs in the official economy and thus provide another incentive to work in the shadow economy: more heavily regulated countries tend to have a larger share of the shadow economy in total GDP. Enforcement, not the overall extent of regulation that is usually not enforced, is the key factor for the burden levied on firms and individuals, inducing them to operate in the shadow economy.	Johnson, Kaufmann, and Shleifer 1997; Johnson, Kaufmann, and Zoido-Lobatón 1998b; Friedman and others 2000; Kucera and Roncolato 2008; Schneider 2011; Hassan and Schneider 2016

(continued)

TABLE 1.1. ***(continued)***

Main Causes and Indicators That Determine the Shadow Economy

Causal/Indicator Variable	Theoretical Reasoning	References
Public sector services	An increase in the shadow economy may reduce state revenues, which, in turn, reduce the quality and quantity of publicly provided goods and services. This may ultimately lead to increasing tax rates for firms and individuals, although deterioration in the quality of public goods (such as public infrastructure) and of the administration would continue. The consequence is an even stronger incentive to participate in the shadow economy. Countries with higher tax revenues achieved by lower tax rates, fewer laws and regulations, a better rule of law, and less corruption should thus have smaller shadow economies.	Johnson, Kaufmann, and Zoido-Lobatón 1998a, 1998b; Feld and Schneider 2010
Tax morale	The efficiency of the public sector also has an indirect effect on the size of the shadow economy because it affects tax morale. Tax compliance is driven by a psychological tax contract that entails rights and obligations not only from taxpayers and citizens but also from the state and its tax authorities. Taxpayers are more inclined to pay their taxes honestly if they receive valuable public services in exchange; however, taxpayers are honest even when the benefit principle of taxation does not hold, that is, for redistributive policies, if such political decisions follow fair procedures. The treatment of taxpayers by the tax authority also plays a role. If taxpayers are treated as partners in a (tax) contract instead of subordinates in a hierarchical relationship, taxpayers will comply with the obligations of the psychological tax contract more easily. Hence, (better) tax morale and (stronger) social norms may reduce the probability of individuals working in the shadow economy.	Feld and Larsen 2005, 2009; Feld and Frey 2007; Kirchler 2007; Torgler and Schneider 2009; Feld and Schneider 2010
Deterrence	Despite the strong focus on deterrence in policies fighting the shadow economy and the unambiguous insights of the traditional economic theory of tax noncompliance, surprisingly little is known from empirical studies about the effects of deterrence. This is because data on the legal background and the frequency of audits are not available internationally; such data are difficult to collect even for Organisation for Economic Co-operation and Development countries. Either the legal background is complicated, differentiating fines and punishment according to the severity of the offense and the noncomplier's true income, or tax authorities do not reveal how intensively auditing is taking place. The little empirical survey evidence available demonstrates that fines and punishment do not exert a negative influence on the shadow economy, while the subjectively perceived risk of detection does. Even so, results are often weak, and Granger causality tests show that the size of the shadow economy can affect deterrence instead of deterrence reducing the shadow economy.	Andreoni, Erard, and Feinstein 1998; Pedersen 2003; Feld and Larsen 2005, 2009; Feld and Schneider 2010

(continued)

TABLE 1.1. ***(continued)***

Main Causes and Indicators That Determine the Shadow Economy

Causal/Indicator Variable	Theoretical Reasoning	References
Development of the official economy	The development of the official economy is another key factor in the shadow economy. The higher (lower) the unemployment quota (GDP growth), the higher (lower) the incentive to work in the shadow economy, if all else is equal.	Schneider and Williams 2013; Feld and Schneider 2010
Self-employment	The higher the rate of self-employment, the more activities can be performed in the shadow economy, if all else is equal.	Schneider and Williams 2013; Feld and Schneider 2010
Unemployment	The higher the rate of unemployment, the higher the probability of working in the shadow economy, if all else is equal.	Schneider and Williams 2013; Williams and Schneider 2016
Size of the agricultural sector	The larger the agricultural sector, the more possibilities to work in the shadow economy, if all else is equal.	Hassan and Schneider 2016
Use of cash	The larger the shadow economy, the more cash will be used, if all else is equal. Mostly measured as M0/M1, M1/M2, or cash per capita outside the banking sector.	Hassan and Schneider 2016; Williams and Schneider 2016
Share of labor force	The larger the shadow economy, the lower the official labor force participation rate, if all else is equal.	Schneider and Williams 2013; Feld and Schneider 2010
GDP per capita (economic growth)[1]	A larger shadow economy is associated with more economic activities moving out of the formal economy, hence, it shows a decrease in economic growth, if all else is equal.	Schneider and Williams 2013

Source: Schneider 2017.

[1]To address criticism of the use of official GDP, this chapter relies on data on light intensity from outer space as a proxy for the "true" economic growth achieved by countries. This approach has been also successfully used by Medina, Jonelis, and Cangul (2017) in the context of sub-Saharan African countries.

2. *Illegal production.* Productive activities that generate goods and services forbidden by law or unlawful when unauthorized.
3. *Informal sector production.* Productive activities conducted by incorporated enterprises in the household sector or by other units that are registered or have fewer employees than specified size and that have some market production.
4. *Production of households for own (final) use.* Productive activities that result in goods or services consumed or capitalized by the households that produced them.
5. *Statistical "underground."* All productive activities that should be accounted for in basic data collection programs but are missed when statistical systems are deficient.

Gyomai and van de Ven (2014) provide a precise definition of nonobserved estimates to reach the goal of exhaustive estimates.

Hidden Activities

As stated in SNA 2008 § 6.40 certain activities may clearly fall in the production boundary of the SNA and also be legal but are deliberately concealed from public authorities to avoid (1) paying income tax, value added, or other payments; (2) paying social security contributions; (3) having to meet certain legal standards, such as minimum wages, maximum hours, and safety or health standards; and (4) complying with certain administrative procedures, such as completing statistical questionnaires or other administrative forms.

Illegal Activities

SNA 2008 § 6.43 describes two kinds of illegal production: (1) the production of goods or services whose sale, distribution, or possession is forbidden by law; and (2) production activities that are usually legal but become illegal when carried out by unauthorized producers, for example, unlicensed medical practitioners.

SNA 2008 § 6.45 indicates that the production boundary encompasses both kinds of illegal production, provided they are genuine production processes whose outputs consist of goods or services for which there is an effective market demand.

With this classification, Gyomai and van de Ven (2014) provide a comprehensive and useful categorization of shadow economy and underground activities. This estimation method is applied by National Statistical Offices and is explained in detail in their handbook for measuring the nonobserved economy (Organisation for Economic Co-operation and Development [OECD] 2010). The authors argue that the nonobserved economy is estimated at three stages during the integrated production of national accounts. First, data sources with identifying biases on reporting on scope are corrected through imputations. Second, upper-bound estimates are used to access the maximum possible amount of nonobserved economy activity for a given industrial activity or product group on the basis of a wide array of available data. And third, special purpose surveys are conducted for areas

Figure 1.1. Classification of the Nonobserved Economy

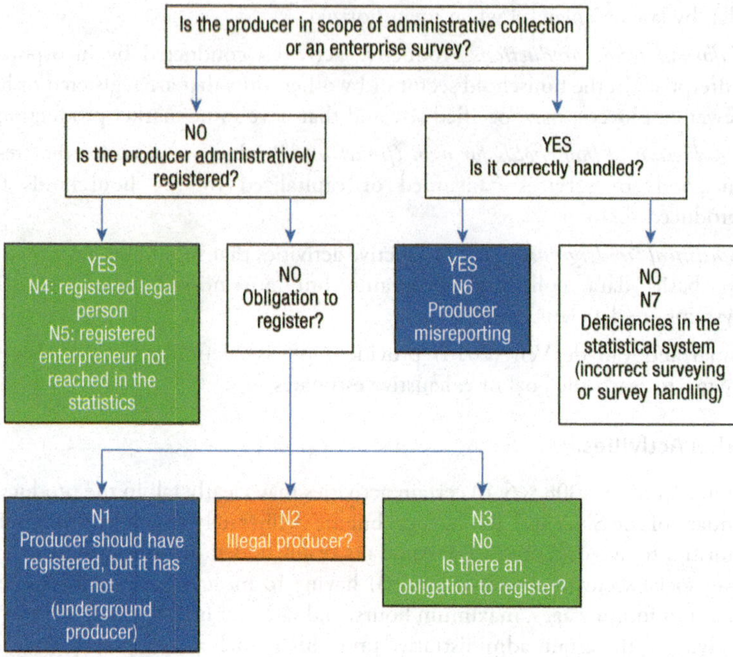

Source: Van de Ven 2017.

where regular surveys provide little guidance and small-scale models built to indirectly estimate areas where direct observation and measurement are not feasible.

Figure 1.1 shows how nonobserved economy producers are classified to reach estimates with the SNA method.

Classification of the nonobserved economy is a careful procedure that considers all possible situations to achieve an exhaustive estimation. The national accounts method to capture all nonobserved economic activities combines several classifications to yield four nonobserved economy categories:

- Economic underground: N1 + N6
- Informal (and own account production): N3 + N4 + N5
- Statistical underground: N7
- Illegal: N2

Much work has been done on the first three categories, but less so on illegal activities; however, the European Union has shown increased interest in accounting for illegal activities since their inclusion has become mandatory with the introduction of the European System of National and Regional Accounts.

In general, discrepancy analysis is performed at a disaggregated level, and the nature of adjustment allows various nonobserved economy categories to be at

TABLE 1.2.

Nonobserved Economy Adjustments, by Informality Type, 2011–12
(Percent of GDP)

Country	Underground N1 + N6	Illegal N2	Informal Sector N3 + N4 + N5	Statistical Underground N7	Total Nonobserved Economy
Austria	2.4 (31.7)	0.2 (2.1)	1.5 (19.4)	3.5 (46.8)	7.5 (100)
Belgium	3.8 (83.8)	...	...	0.7 (16.2)	4.6 (100)
Canada	1.9 (88.2)	0.2 (8.2)	...	0.1 (3.6)	2.2 (100)
Czech Republic	6.3 (77.6)	0.4 (4.5)	1.3 (15.6)	0.2 (2.3)	8.1 (100)
France	3.7 (54.7)	...	2.9 (42.7)	0.2 (2.7)	6.7 (100)
Hungary	3.1 (27.9)	0.8 (7.5)	3.1 (28.6)	3.9 (36)	10.9 (100)
Israel	2.2 (32.6)	...	1.4 (21.8)	3.0 (45.6)	6.6 (100)
Italy	16.2 (92.8)	...	...	1.2 (7.2)	17.5 (100)
Mexico	5.5 (34.7)	...	10.4 (65.3)	...	15.9 (100)
Netherlands	0.8 (36.6)	0.5 (20.1)	0.5 (20.0)	0.5 (23.2)	2.3 (100)
Norway	0.5 (51.5)	0.0 (0.3)	0.5 (43.8)	0.0 (4.4)	1.0 (100)
Poland	12.7 (82.6)	0.9 (6.0)	0.0 (0.0)	1.8 (11.4)	15.4 (100)
Slovak Republic	12.1 (77.3)	0.5 (3.0)	2.9 (18.7)	0.2 (1.0)	15.6 (100)
Slovenia	3.9 (38.2)	0.3 (3.2)	2.8 (27.7)	3.1 (30.9)	10.2 (100)
Sweden	3.0 (100.0)	...	...	...	3.0 (100)
United Kingdom	1.5 (65.6)	...	0.5 (22.9)	0.3 (11.4)	2.3 (100)

Source: Gyomai and van de Ven 2014.
Note: N1 to N7 are classifications in the System of National Accounts; values in parentheses are the percentage of that adjustment type within the total nonobserved economy. Ellipses indicate data not available.

least partly identified. The methodological descriptions countries provide the SNA reveal that country practices in adjusting for nonobserved economies are often quite similar.

Still, substantial differences exist between various OECD countries. Table 1.2 presents nonobserved economy adjustments by informality type for 16 OECD countries from 2011 to 2012. The total nonobserved economy as a percentage of GDP varies considerably.[11] Also the adjustments in the different categories are considerable. This method of discrepancy analysis reveals that some countries have large shadow economies, such as Italy with 17.5 percent of official GDP, followed by Mexico with 15.9 percent, the Slovak Republic with 15.6 percent, and Poland with 15.4 percent. The smallest shadow economy here is in Norway, with 1.0 percent.

Representative Surveys

Representative surveys are often used to get some micro knowledge about the size of the shadow economy and shadow labor markets.[12] These surveys are designed to investigate public perceptions of the shadow economy, actual participation in shadow economy activities, and opinions about shadow practices. As an example,

[11] A comparison with respect to other methods is presented in the "MIMIC Results and Direct Approach Results" section.

[12] Compare, for example, Feld and Larsen (2005, 2009) and Zukauskas and Schneider (2016).

TABLE 1.3.

Undeclared Working Hours as a Proportion of Normal Working Hours, 2015

	(1)	(2)	(3) = (1) × (2)	(4)	(5) = (3) / (4)
Country	Percentage of Friends or Relatives in the Shadow Labor Market	Average Weekly Undeclared Hours Worked by Respondents with Shadow Experience	Average Weekly Undeclared Hours Worked for the Whole Population	Normal Average Weekly Working Hours	Undeclared Hours as a Percentage of Normal Hours
Belarus	29.0	23.5	6.82	39.8	17.1
Estonia	26.0	22.4	5.82	38.9	15.0
Latvia	36.0	20.3	7.31	39.1	18.7
Lithuania	29.0	16.8	4.87	38.1	12.8
Poland	33.0	25.5	8.42	40.7	20.7
Sweden	8.0	18.9	1.51	36.3	4.2

Source: Zukauskas and Schneider 2016.
Note: The values for the experience of friends or relatives in the shadow labor market and average weekly undeclared hours are from a survey, whereas normal average weekly working hours are from the Eurostat database for 2014. In the absence of such data for Belarus, it was estimated as an average of normal working hours for Central and Eastern European countries that belong to the European Union.

the Lithuanian Free Market Institute and its partner organizations for Belarus, Estonia, Latvia, Poland, and Sweden designed surveys to gauge the public's experiences with the shadow labor market. The surveys were administered between May 22 and June 15, 2015. The target audience included local residents ages 18 to 75 years, yielding 6,000 respondents across the six countries. The most important results for our purposes are presented in Tables 1.3 and 1.4.[13]

TABLE 1.4.

Aggregated Shadow Wages as a Proportion of GDP, 2015

	(1)	(2)	(3) = (1) × (2)	(4)	(5) = (3) / (4)
Country	Undeclared Hours Worked per Year (millions)	Average Undeclared Hourly Wage (euros)	Extent of Shadow Market (million euros)	GDP (million euros)	Shadow Employment, Percentage of GDP
Belarus	2,504	7.51	18,816	57,300	32.8
Estonia	289	10.37	2,997	19,963	15.0
Latvia	549	5.03	2,761	23,581	11.7
Lithuania	540	6.62	3,575	36,444	9.8
Poland	11,954	8.24	98,501	410,845	24.0
Sweden	541	13.32	7,206	430,635	1.7

Source: Zukauskas and Schneider 2016.
Note: Undeclared hours worked per year are calculated as follows: Shadow Frequency/100 × Average Undeclared Weekly Hours Worked by Persons Who Performed Shadow Activities × 52 × Total Population of Individuals Ages 18–74 Years. The values for shadow frequency, average undeclared weekly hours, and average undeclared hourly wage are from a survey, whereas the population of individuals ages 18–74 years and GDP at current prices are from the Eurostat database for 2014.

[13] This chapter does not concentrate on various results about the attitudes, which can be seen in detail in Zukauskas and Schneider (2016).

TABLE 1.5.

Size of the Shadow Economy in Baltic Countries, 2009–15
(Percent of GDP)

Year	Estonia	Latvia	Lithuania
2009	20.2	36.6	17.7
2010	19.4	38.1	18.8
2011	18.9	30.2	17.1
2012	19.2	21.1	18.2
2013	15.7	23.8	15.3
2014	13.2	23.5	12.5
2015	14.9	21.3	15.0
Average	17.4	27.8	16.4

Source: Putnins and Sauka 2015, Table 1, 12.

Table 1.3 shows undeclared working hours as a proportion of normal working hours from 2015. Undeclared hours, as a share of normal working hours on the basis of a weekly calculation, vary between 4.2 percent in Sweden and 20.7 percent in Poland. This variation is not unexpected, because the shadow economy in Sweden is much smaller than the one in Poland. If one considers the average weekly undeclared hours worked by respondents with shadow experience, the range is much narrower, ranging between 25.5 hours in Poland and 16.8 hours in Lithuania.

Table 1.4 shows the extent of aggregated shadow wages as a proportion of GDP. Sweden has by far the lowest, with 1.7 percent of GDP as shadow employment; Belarus, the largest, with 32.8 percent, followed by Poland with 24.0 percent.

Surveys of Company Managers

Putnins and Sauka (2015)—and, in a similar way, Reilly and Krstic (2018)—use surveys of company managers as a micro approach to measuring the size of the shadow economy. Both studies combine misreported business income and misreported wages as a percentage of GDP. The method produces detailed information on the structure of the shadow economy, especially in the service and manufacturing sectors. Researchers survey company managers with the premise that these respondents are most likely to know how much business, income, and wages are unreported because of their unique position in dealing with observed and non-observed income.

Putnins and Sauka (2015) and Reilly and Krstic (2018) use a range of survey-designed features to maximize the truthfulness of responses. Their method combines estimations of misreported business income, unregistered or hidden employees, and unreported wages to calculate a total estimate of the size of the shadow economy as a percentage of GDP. This approach is different from most other studies of the shadow economy, which largely focus on either macroeconomic indicators or surveys about households. Putnins and Sauka have developed first results for Estonia, Latvia, and Lithuania. All countries, as Table 1.5 shows, demonstrate a decline in the size of the shadow economy from

2009 to 2015. The largest shadow economy is in Latvia, with a 27.8 percent average from 2009 to 2015, followed by Estonia with 17.4 percent, and Lithuania with 16.4 percent.

Indirect Approaches to Estimation

Indirect approaches, alternatively called indicator approaches, are mostly macroeconomic in nature. These are in part based on a number of approaches, including (1) discrepancy between national expenditure and income statistics, (2) discrepancy between the official and actual labor forces, (3) the "electricity consumption" approach, (4) the "monetary transaction" approach, and (5) the "currency demand" approach. The MIMIC approach will also be discussed extensively here.

Discrepancy between National Expenditure and Income Statistics

If those who work in the shadow economy hid their incomes for tax purposes but not their expenditure, then the difference between national income and national expenditure estimates could be used to approximate the size of the shadow economy. This approach assumes that all components on the expenditure side are measured without error and constructed so that they are statistically independent from income factors.[14]

Discrepancy between Official and Actual Labor Force

If total labor force participation is assumed to be constant, a decline in official labor force participation can be interpreted as an increase in the importance of the shadow economy. Fluctuation in the participation rate might have many other explanations, such as position in the business cycle, difficulty in finding a job, and education and retirement decisions, but these estimates represent weak indicators of the size of the shadow economy.[15]

Electricity Consumption Approach

Kaufmann and Kaliberda (1996) endorse the idea that electricity consumption is the single best physical indicator of overall (official and unofficial) economic activity. Using findings that indicate that electricity use to overall GDP elasticity is close to 1, these authors suggest using the difference between growth of electricity consumption and growth of official GDP as a proxy for growth of the shadow economy. This method is simple and appealing, but its many drawbacks include the fact that (1) not all shadow economy activities require a considerable amount of electricity (for example, personal services) or they may use other energy sources (coal, gas), hence only part of the shadow economy growth is captured;

[14] See, for example, MacAfee (1980) and Yoo and Hyun (1998) for the discrepancy approach.

[15] See, for example, Contini (1981), Del Boca (1981), and O'Neill (1983) for methods to examine the discrepancy between the official and actual labor forces.

and (2) electricity to overall GDP elasticity might significantly vary across countries and over time.[16]

Monetary Transaction Approach

Using Fischer's quantity equation, *Money * Velocity = Prices * Transactions*, and assuming that there is a constant relationship between the money flows related to transactions and the total (official and unofficial) value added, that is, *Prices * Transactions = k (Official GDP + Shadow Economy)*, it is reasonable to derive the equation *Money * Velocity = k (Official GDP + Shadow Economy)*. The stock of money and official GDP estimates are known, and money velocity can be estimated. Thus, as Feige (1979) posited, if the size of the shadow economy as a proportion of the official economy is known for a benchmark year, then the shadow economy can be calculated for the rest of the sample. Although theoretically attractive, this method has several weaknesses: (1) the assumption that *k* would be constant over time seems arbitrary and (2) other factors, such as the development of checks and credit cards, could also affect the desired amount of cash holdings and thus velocity.[17]

Currency Demand Approach

Assuming that informal transactions take the form of cash payments to evade observation by the authorities, an increase in the size of the shadow economy will, consequently, increase demand for currency (Cagan 1958). To isolate this "excess," Tanzi (1980) suggests using a time-series approach in which currency demand is a function of conventional factors, such as the evolution of income, payment practices, and interest rates, as well as factors causing people to work in the shadow economy, such as the direct and indirect tax burden, government regulation, and the complexity of the tax system. Several problems, however, are associated with this method and its assumptions: (1) the CDA may underestimate the size of the shadow economy because not all transactions use cash as a means of exchange, (2) currency demand deposits may increase because of a slowdown in demand deposits rather than an increase in currency used in informal activities, (3) it seems arbitrary to assume equal velocity of money in both the shadow and the formal economies, and (4) the assumption of no shadow economy in a base year is arguable (Cagan 1958; Gutmann 1977; Tanzi 1980, 1983; Schneider 1997; Johnson, Kaufmann, and Zoido-Lobatón 1998b).

MIMIC Approach

This method explicitly considers several causes, as well as the multiple effects, of the shadow economy. The method uses associations between the observable

[16] See, for example, Del Boca and Forte (1982); Portes (1996); and Johnson, Kaufmann, and Shleifer (1997) for examinations of the electricity approach.

[17] See, for example, Feige (1979), Boeschoten and Fase (1984), and Langfeldt (1984).

causes and the effects of an unobserved variable, in this case the shadow economy, to estimate the variable itself (Loayza 1996; also see Vuletin 2008; Schneider 2010, 2015; Feld and Schneider 2010; Slemrod and Weber 2012, Abdih and Medina 2013; and Williams and Schneider 2016).

The Model or Macro MIMIC Approach

The MIMIC model is a special type of structural equation modeling (SEM) that is widely applied in psychometrics and social science research and is based on the statistical theory of unobserved variables developed in the 1970s by Zellner (1970) and Joreskog and Goldberger (1975). The MIMIC model is a theory-based approach to confirm the influence of a set of exogenous causal variables on the latent variable (the shadow economy), as well as the effect of the shadow economy on macroeconomic indicator variables.

At first, it is important to establish a theoretical model explaining the relation between the exogenous variables and the latent variable. Therefore, the MIMIC model is considered to be a confirmatory rather than an explanatory method. The hypothesized path of the relations between the observed variables and the latent shadow economy on the basis of our theoretical considerations is depicted in Figure 1.2.

The pioneers to apply the MIMIC model to measure the size of the shadow economy in 17 OECD countries were Frey and Weck-Hanneman (1984). Following them, scholars such as Buehn, Karmann, and Schneider (2009); Schneider, Buehn, and Montenegro (2010); and Hassan and Schneider (2016) applied the MIMIC model to measure the size of the shadow economy.

Figure 1.2. MIMIC Estimation Procedure

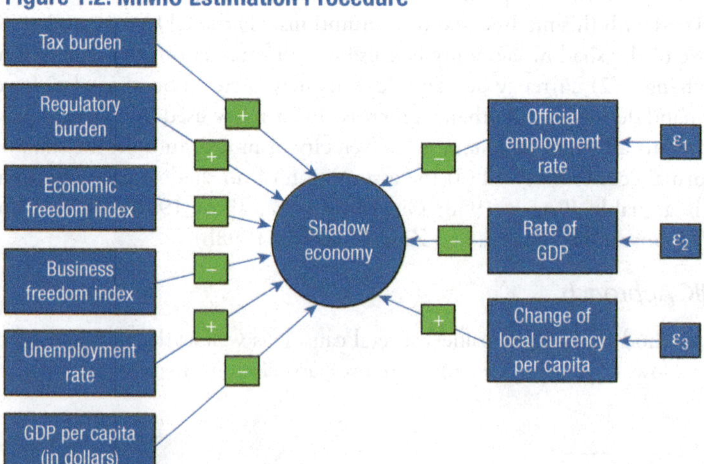

Source: Schneider, Buehn, and Montenegro 2010.
Note: MIMIC = multiple indicators, multiple causes.

Formally, the MIMIC model has two parts: the structural model and the measurement model.

The MIMIC structural and measurement estimation procedures (compare also Figure 1.2) are conducted as follows:

1. Model the shadow economy as an unobservable (latent) variable
2. Describe the relationships between the latent variable and its causes in a structural model: $\eta = \Gamma x + \zeta$
3. Represent the link between the latent variable and its indicators in the measurement model: $y = \Lambda_y \eta + \varepsilon$,

where

η: latent variable (shadow economy)
x: $(q \times 1)$ vector of causes in the structural model
y: $(p \times 1)$ vector of indicators in the measurement model
Γ: $(1 \times q)$ coefficient matrix of the causes in the structural equation
Λ_y: $(p \times 1)$ coefficient matrix in the measurement model
ζ: error term in the structural model
ε: $(p \times 1)$ vector of measurement error in y.

The specification of the structural equation is as follows:

$$[\text{Shadow Economy}] = [\gamma_1, \gamma_2, \gamma_3, \gamma_4, \gamma_5, \gamma_6, \gamma_7, \gamma_8] \times \begin{bmatrix} [\text{Share of Direct Taxation}] \\ [\text{Share of Indirect Taxation}] \\ [\text{Share of Social Security Burden}] \\ [\text{Burden of State Regulation}] \\ [\text{Quality of State Institutions}] \\ [\text{Tax Morale}] \\ [\text{Unemployment Quota}] \\ [\text{GDP per Capita}] \end{bmatrix} + [\zeta]$$

The specification of the measurement equation is as follows:

$$\begin{vmatrix} \text{Employment Quota} \\ \text{Change of Local Currency} \\ \text{Average Working Time} \end{vmatrix} = \begin{vmatrix} \lambda_1 \\ \lambda_2 \\ \lambda_3 \end{vmatrix} \times \begin{vmatrix} \text{Shadow Economy} \end{vmatrix} + \begin{vmatrix} \varepsilon_1 \\ \varepsilon_2 \\ \varepsilon_3 \end{vmatrix},$$

where γi and λi are coefficients to be estimated.

Two steps derive the absolute values:

1. The shadow economy remains an unobserved phenomenon (latent variable), which is estimated using causes of illicit behavior (such as tax burden and regulation intensity) and indicators reflecting illicit activities (such as currency demand and official work time). This procedure produces only relative estimates of the size of the shadow economy.
2. The CDA is used to calibrate the relative estimates into absolute ones by using absolute values of the CDA as starting values for the shadow economy.

The benchmarking procedure used to derive real-world values of shadow economic activities has been criticized (Breusch, 2005a, 2005b). Because the latent variable and its unit of measurement are not observed, SEMs only provide estimated coefficients from which one can calculate an index that shows the dynamics of the unobservable variable. Application of the so-called calibration or benchmarking procedure, regardless which is used, requires experimentation and a comparison of the calibrated values in a wide academic debate. At this stage of research, it is unfortunately unclear which benchmarking method is the best or most reliable.[18]

The economic literature using SEMs is well aware of these limitations. It acknowledges that it is not easy to apply this method to an economic data set but also argues that this does not mean one should abandon the SEM approach. For those following an interdisciplinary approach to economics, SEMs are valuable tools for economic analysis, particularly when studying the shadow economy. Moreover, the objections mentioned should be considered incentives for further research rather than a reason to abandon the method.

Identification Problem with MIMIC Estimates

MIMIC approach estimations "produce" only relative weights. We need another approach to normalize these estimates, and the estimates' validity depends on the reliability of this second approach. Hence it is difficult to draw statistically confirmed conclusions about causal relations in the real world, not only in the model built from these estimates.

Kirchgaessner (2016, 103) correctly argues:

> A necessary condition for testing whether a variable x has a causal impact on a variable y is that the two variables are measured independently. The MIMIC model approach assumes that causal relations exist and, therefore, estimates a linear combination of these (supposedly) causal variables that more or less fits several indicator variables. This linear combination is assumed to be a representation of the unknown variable shadow economy.

This calculation of the shadow economy is not an empirical test of the actual existence of a shadow economy. Neither does the calculation demonstrate that the used causal or explanatory variables have a statically significant effect on the "true" shadow economy. Kirchgaessner (2016, 103) argues further that "significant test statistics in the structural model only show that the used explanatory (or causal) variables contribute significantly to the variance of the constructed variable, shadow economy. We have to assume that this construction represents the shadow economy to make statements about possible causal relations." Hence, these causal variables cannot be used again in subsequent studies to identify policy variables that might reduce or increase the shadow economy. If this is done, a statistically significant relation must automatically or trivially result, argue Feld and Schneider (2016, 115).

---

[18] See Dell'Anno and Schneider (2009) for a detailed discussion on different benchmarking procedures. Compare also the latest discussions and critiques of the MIMIC procedure by Breusch (2016), Feige (2016a, 2016b), Hashimzade and Heady (2016), and Schneider (2016).

To overcome this problem, Kirchgaessner (2016) suggests using other macro approaches, such as the measure of electricity consumption, which devises the size of the shadow economy independently from the causes used in the MIMIC model. Then one can check whether a tax increase leads to a rise in the shadow economy. To conclude, caution is warranted when using shadow economy estimates to test the effect of a tax reduction. This is only possible if the shadow economy series is derived from an approach in which the tax variable has not been used for the construction of the shadow economy.

Structured, Hybrid Model–Based Estimation

Dybka and others' (2017) novel hybrid procedure addresses previous critique of the CDA and MIMIC models by Feige (1996) and Breusch (2016), particularly misspecification in the CDA equations and "vague" transformation of the latent variable obtained through the MIMIC model into interpretable levels and paths of the shadow economy.

Dybka and others' (2017) proposal is based on a new identification method for the MIMIC model, referred to as "reverse standardization." Reverse standardization supplies the MIMIC model with panel-structured information on the latent variable's mean and variance obtained from the CDA estimates, treating this information as given in the restricted full-information maximum likelihood function. This approach does not require the choice of an externally estimated reference point for benchmarking or adopting other ad hoc identifying assumptions (such as unity restriction on a selected parameter in the measurement equation).

Furthermore, the proposed estimation procedure directly addresses the numerical problem of negative variances in the MIMIC estimation, largely disregarded in previous off-the-shelf software. The nonnegativity restriction on variances within the MIMIC framework can materially affect the significance, specification decisions, and measurement results. Paying due respect to the (intuitive) constraint on the nonnegativity of variances may lead to a surprising result of flattening the trajectory of the shadow economy.

Also, the analysis of variance decomposition of *SE* estimated by our hybrid strategy confirms findings from the previous literature by showing that as much as 97.2 to 98.2 percent of *SE* variance in the panel is due to the CDA component (between cross-sections), whereas only the small remaining fraction is due to MIMIC's fine tuning. The latter finding may lead to a legitimate question on the actual contribution of MIMIC models to shadow economy measurement.

First, Dybka and others (2017) estimate and extend a panel version of the CDA equation using both frequent and neglected variables (describing the development of an electronic payment system) and abandon the controversial assumption that the share of the shadow economy in the total economy is zero.

Second, Dybka and others (2017) estimate a MIMIC model by maximizing a (full-information) likelihood function reformulated in two ways: (1) instead of anchoring the index of an arbitrary time period and using arbitrary normalizations or other discretionary corrections, they use the means and variance estimated in the CDA model; and (2) they constrain the parameter vector to explicitly assume away the negative variances of structural errors and measurement errors. Their hybrid model proposes a solution to the long-standing problem of identification in the MIMIC model, which, in many ways, outperforms previous approaches to just-identification. Their approach clearly implies a scale and unit of measurement, avoids obscure ad hoc corrections, and paves the way to the construction of a sensible confidence interval. This new method is a promising approach to overcoming the usual critiques of the CDA and the MIMIC model.

In Table 1.6, statistical offices' shadow economy estimates are compared with the MIMIC estimates derived for this chapter. Macro and adjusted MIMIC values are shown. If we compare the results, we see that within each method the size of the shadow economy varies considerably but is on average much smaller than the macro and adjusted values. The adjusted MIMIC values come close to the values of Dybka and others (2017) for Bulgaria and Switzerland. Values from Dybka and others (2017) and those from the statistical offices are in a similar range for Bulgaria, Israel, Mongolia, Sweden, and the United Kingdom, if using the estimation result of the FGLS44-AR variant. For Croatia, Dybka and others (2017) obtain considerably higher values than those provided by the statistical offices. In the case of Moldova it is the opposite. To summarize, the Dybka and

TABLE 1.6.

Shadow Economy Estimates from Statistical Offices and from Currency Demand Models, 2009–15

		The Size of the Shadow Economy (Percentage of Official GDP)					
Country	Reference Year	Statistical Offices	FGLS	FGLS44	FGLS44-AR	MIMIC Macro	MIMIC Adj.
Bulgaria	2014	9.90	14.40	15.40	9.50	21.60	14.04
Croatia	2015	6.90	13.30	13.70	8.20	22.96	14.92
Czech Republic	2015	10.10	8.40	8.00	5.50	10.47	6.81
Denmark	2012	1.50	7.50	5.60	3.90	15.48	10.06
Hungary	2009	10.90	11.40	10.90	7.00	23.18	15.07
Israel	2014	5.20	8.90	9.00	6.00	19.39	12.60
FYR Macedonia	2012	19.20	13.70	16.00	8.70	...	...
Moldova	2015	23.70	9.90	11.50	7.30	39.68	25.79
Mongolia	2015	15.90	N/A	12.60	7.80	13.20	8.58
Norway	2009	1.00	5.20	4.10	3.20	17.37	11.29
Poland	2014	13.30	9.80	9.90	6.40	18.09	11.76
Sweden	2009	3.00	7.10	5.30	3.70	15.71	10.21
Switzerland	2012	1.30	4.00	4.60	3.40	6.66	4.33
United Kingdom	2009	2.30	5.60	5.60	3.90	11.00	7.15

Sources: Dybka and others 2017, 22, Table 7, for FGLS, FGLS44, and FGLS44-AR; Gyomai and van de Ven 2014 for the data of statistical offices; and authors for macro and adjusted MIMIC values.

Note: FGLS = feasible generalized least square; FGLS44 and FGLS44-AR both are specific FGLS estimations; MIMIC = multiple indicators, multiple causes; N/A = not applicable; . . . = not available.

others (2017) estimation method is promising and most of the values are considerably lower than those obtained using the traditional macro methods of the CDA and MIMIC.

The "Double Counting" Problem

Another problem with macro approaches such as the MIMIC or CDA is that they use causal factors such as tax burden, unemployment, self-employment, and regulation, which are also responsible for people undertaking do-it-yourself activities or asking friends and neighbors for help. Hence, do-it-yourself activities, neighbors' or friends' help, and legally bought material for shadow economy activities are included in these macro approaches. This means that in these macro approaches (including the electricity approach) a "total" shadow economy is estimated that includes do-it-yourself activities, neighbors' help, legally bought material, and smuggling.

In Table 1.7, a decomposition is undertaken for shadow economy activities in Estonia and Germany. Table 1.7 starts with the macro MIMIC estimate, as an average value for 2009 to 2015, of 24.94 percent of GDP for Estonia and 9.37 percent for Germany. Legally bought material for shadow economy or do-it-yourself activities and friends' help is deducted. Then illegal activities are deducted. Furthermore, do-it-yourself activities and neighbors' help are deducted. These subtractions yield a corrected shadow economy roughly two-thirds of the macro size of the shadow economy: 65 percent for Estonia and 64.2 percent for Germany. This correction factor is used to adjust the size of the shadow economy using the MIMIC method. The results for 31 European

TABLE 1.7.

Decomposition of Shadow Economy Activities in Estonia and Germany, 2009–15

(Percentage)

	Estonia		Germany	
Shadow Economy Activities	**Official GDP Average**	**Total Shadow Economy**	**Official GDP Average**	**Total Shadow Economy**
(1) Total shadow economy[1]	24.94	100.00	9.37	100.00
(2) Legally bought material for shadow economy and DIY activities	5.24	21.00	1.79	19.10
(3) Illegal activities[2]	1.75	7.00	0.69	7.40
(4) DIY activities and neighbors' help[3]	1.75	7.00	0.86	9.20
(5) (2) + (3) + (4)	8.73	35.00	3.35	35.70
(6) Shadow economy "corrected" to exclude legal DIY and illegal activities (1) – (5)	16.21	65.00	6.02	64.20

Source: Authors, based on Enste and Schneider (2006) and Buehn and Schneider (2013).

Note: DIY = do-it-yourself.

[1]The total shadow economy is estimated by the multiple indicators, multiple causes model and calibrated by currency demand procedures.

[2]Illegal activities include, for example, smuggling.

[3]DIY activities and neighbors' help do not include legally bought material, which is included in (2).

Figure 1.3. The Size of the Shadow Economy in Selected European Countries, 2017
(Percent of GDP)

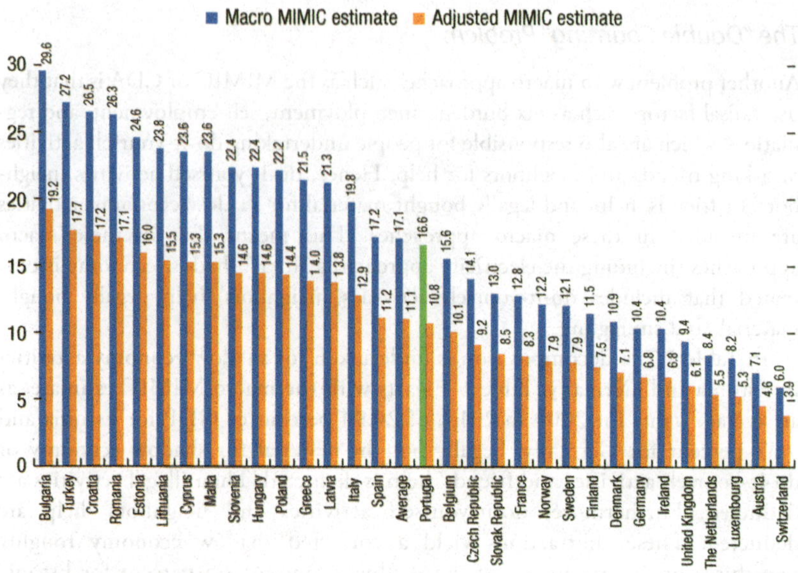

Source: Authors' calculations.
Note: MIMIC = multiple indicators, multiple causes.

countries for 2017 are presented in Figure 1.3. The shadow economy appears considerably smaller, perhaps a more realistic value of its actual size, using a macro method.

MIMIC ESTIMATION RESULTS

In Tables 1.8 through 1.10, each of which includes six specifications, MIMIC estimation results for our entire sample of 158 countries is presented for 1991 to 2015.[19] Table 1.8 shows the estimation results for the entire sample of 158 countries. All cause variables (trade openness, GDP per capita, unemployment, size of government, fiscal freedom, rule of law, control of corruption, and government

[19] The MIMIC regression started with 151 countries. This estimation first generated the coefficients and standard deviations. Following this, during the calibration phase, eight countries were dropped as the time series were not long enough, specifically, Afghanistan, Macao SAR, former Yugoslav Republic of Macedonia, Serbia, St. Lucia, St. Vincent and the Grenadines, Sudan, and Tonga. Moreover, for 15 additional countries, availability of information on the drivers of the shadow economy permitted its estimation economy and therefore the countries were added to the sample, specifically, Austria, Belgium, Ethiopia, Finland, France, Germany, Greece, Ireland, Italy, Mauritania, the Netherlands, Niger, Rwanda, Togo, and the United Kingdom. This completes the list of 158 countries with shadow economy estimates.

TABLE 1.8.

MIMIC Model Estimation Results, All Sample Countries, 1991–2015

	(1)	(2)	(3)	(4)	(5)	(6)
Causes						
Trade openness	−0.086***	−0.085***	−0.137***	−0.086***	−0.086***	−0.113***
GDP per capita	−0.332***	−0.335***	−0.370***	−0.298***	−0.302***	−0.334***
Unemployment rate	0.051**	0.054***	0.069***	0.053**	0.057***	0.069***
Size of government	0.102***	0.102***	0.111***			
Fiscal freedom				−0.131***	−0.134***	−0.147***
Rule of law	−0.049***			−0.060***		
Control of corruption		−0.042***			−0.046**	
Government stability			−0.054***			−0.015
Indicators						
Currency	1	1	1	1	1	1
Labor force participation rate	−0.521***	−0.532***	−0.310***	−0.452***	−0.468***	−0.249***
Growth of GDP per capita	−0.208**	−0.245***	−0.386***	−0.113	−0.144*	−0.157***
Statistical Tests						
RMSEA	0.073	0.073	0.067	0.078	0.078	0.055
Chi-square	513.407	506.430	649.062	508.189	500.667	535.332
No. of observations	1,897	1,892	2,350	1,758	1,757	1,998
No. of countries	151	151	122	144	144	120

Source: Authors.

Note: MIMIC = multiple indicators, multiple causes; RMSEA = root mean square error of approximation.

**$p < 0.05$. ***$p < 0.01$.

stability) have the theoretically expected signs, and most are highly statistically significant. The indicator variables also have the theoretical expected signs and are highly statistically significant. The test statistics are satisfactory.

Table 1.9 shows the estimation results for 105 low-income developing countries. Here the cause variable rule of law is not statistically significant in specification 1, nor is control of corruption in specification 2. These variables are significant and show the expected sign in the other specifications. The indicator variable labor force participation rate is again highly statistically significant.

Results for 26 advanced economies are presented in Table 1.10. Here trade openness is not statistically significant in all specifications, but in all other specifications, except size of government and government stability, most cause variables have the expected signs and are statistically significant.[20] The indicator variables are all statistically significant and have the expected signs.

[20] This is plausible because, in advanced economies, one would already expect strong institutions.

TABLE 1.9.

MIMIC Model Estimation Results, Low-Income Developing Countries, 1991–2015

	(1)	(2)	(3)	(4)	(5)	(6)
Causes						
Trade openness	−0.114***	−0.111***	−0.134***	−0.117***	−0.116***	−0.131***
GDP per capita	−0.282***	−0.287***	−0.337***	−0.244***	−0.245***	−0.291***
Unemployment rate	0.062***	0.059***	0.074***	0.085***	0.085***	0.084***
Size of government	0.111***	0.112***	0.107***			
Fiscal freedom				−0.120***	−0.123***	−0.121***
Rule of law	−0.026			−0.046**		
Control of corruption		−0.029			−0.039*	
Government stability			−0.059***			−0.015
Indicators						
Currency	1	1	1	1	1	1
Labor force participation rate	−0.499***	−0.511***	−0.464***	−0.421***	−0.441***	−0.446***
Growth of GDP per capita	−0.442***	−0.434***	−0.545***	−0.113	−0.462***	−0.433***
Statistical Tests						
RMSEA	0.084	0.087	0.068	0.087	0.086	0.062
Chi-square	309.936	306.792	471.032	302.157	297.420	387.446
No. of observations	1,309	1,304	1,687	1,206	1,205	1,406
No. of countries	105	105	84	98	98	82

Source: Authors.
Note: MIMIC = multiple indicators, multiple causes; RMSEA = root mean square error of approximation.
$*p < 0.1$; $**p < 0.05$; $***p < 0.01$.

TABLE 1.10.

MIMIC Model Estimation Results, Advanced Economies, 1991–2015

	(1)	(2)	(3)	(4)	(5)	(6)
Causes						
Trade openness	0.022	0.031	−0.16139***	0.013	0.025	−0.084
GDP per capita	−0.600***	−0.641***	−0.559***	−0.494***	−0.534***	−0.474***
Unemployment rate	0.099**	0.089*	0.104**	0.056	0.043	0.049
Size of government	−0.151***	−0.158***	−0.122**			
Fiscal freedom				−0.138***	−0.166***	−0.168***
Rule of law	−0.026			−0.084*		
Control of corruption		−0.0972094**			−0.126***	
Government stability			−0.0182766			−0.015
Indicators						
Currency	1	1	1	1	1	1
Labor force participation rate	−0.618***	−0.606***	−0.319***	−0.582***	−0.571***	−0.259***
Growth of GDP per capita	0.279*	0.252*	0.104	−0.113	0.114	0.189*
Statistical Tests						
RMSEA	0.103	0.102	0.117	0.079	0.081	0.083
Chi-square	159.688	164.678	197.819	144.259	152.109	147.310
No. of observations	274	274	416	265	265	359
No. of countries	26	26	25	25	25	22

Source: Authors.
Note: MIMIC = multiple indicators, multiple causes; RMSEA = root mean square error of approximation.
$*p < 0.1$; $**p < 0.05$; $***p < 0.01$.

Alleviation of Potential Shortcomings

Even though the standard MIMIC model of Schneider (2010) and others has been widely used in the literature, it has also been criticized for (1) the use of GDP (GDP per capita and growth of GDP per capita) as both cause and indicator variables; (2) the method relying on another independent study to calibrate from standardized values to estimate the size of shadow economy in percentage of GDP; and (3) the estimated coefficients being sensitive to alternative specifications, the country sample, and time span chosen.[21] Points 2 and 3 will not be discussed in this chapter because they are extensively discussed in Schneider (2016).[22]

Night Lights (or Light Intensity) Approach

This analysis addresses the first criticism as follows: instead of using GDP per capita and growth of GDP per capita as both cause and indicator variables, we use the night lights approach developed by Henderson, Storeygard, and Weil (2012) to independently capture economic activity.[23] They use data on light intensity from outer space as a proxy for "true" economic growth.[24] This approach also uses the estimated elasticity of light intensity with respect to economic growth to produce new estimates of national output for countries deemed to have low statistical capacity. Therefore, by using the night lights approach, we address MIMIC criticisms related to the endogeneity of GDP in a novel way, which is totally independent from problematic GDP measures traditionally used (Medina, Jonelis, and Cangul 2017).

In Tables 1.11 through 1.13, each of which includes six alternative specifications, the MIMIC estimation results using light intensity are shown for 1991 to 2015 for different country samples, depending on data availability. Table 1.11 shows the estimation results for all countries and uses light intensity as an indicator variable. All cause variables (trade openness, unemployment, size of government, fiscal freedom, rule of law, control of corruption, and government stability) have the theoretically expected signs and most are highly statistically significant, except control of corruption. The indicator variables also have the theoretical expected signs and are highly statistically significant. The test statistics are satisfactory.

Table 1.12 shows the estimation results for 103 low-income developing countries. Here, the cause variable unemployment is not statistically significant, nor

[21] See Annex Figure 1.1.1 for an illustration of the traditional MIMIC model.

[22] Light intensity offers many benefits as a proxy for economic activity; however, some weaknesses are worth considering. In rural areas, for example, economic activity can occur in the absence of additional light.

[23] See Annex Figure 1.1.2 for an illustration of the MIMIC model using a night lights approach.

[24] Data on night lights used here have been obtained from the Henderson, Storeygard, and Weil (2012) database.

TABLE 1.11.

MIMIC Model Estimation Results Using Night Lights Instead of GDP, All Sample Countries, 1991–2015

	(1)	(2)	(3)	(4)	(5)	(6)
Causes						
Trade openness	−0.172***	−0.167***	−0.106***	−0.178***	−0.175***	−0.161***
Unemployment rate	0.062**	0.061**	0.008	0.067**	0.068**	0.056**
Size of government	0.106***	0.101***	0.036*			
Fiscal freedom				−0.150***	−0.153***	−0.162***
Rule of law	−0.065**			−0.068**		
Control of corruption		−0.026			−0.035	
Government stability			−0.183***			−0.132***
Indicators						
Currency	1	1	1	1	1	1
Labor force participation rate	−0.457***	−0.503***	−0.478***	−0.226*	−0.244*	−0.230**
Lights (GDP)	−0.346***	−0.372***	−1.838***	−0.275***	−0.289***	−0.661***
Statistical Tests						
RMSEA	0.023	0.027	0.079	0.052	0.053	0.082
Chi-square	125.015	116.891	548.593	158.781	151.930	307.091
No. of observations	1,341	1,336	1,767	1,211	1,210	1,498
No. of countries	148	148	120	139	139	116

Source: Authors.
Note: MIMIC = multiple indicators, multiple causes; RMSEA = root mean square error of approximation.
*$p < 0.1$; **$p < 0.05$; ***$p < 0.01$.

TABLE 1.12.

MIMIC Model Estimation Results Using Night Lights Instead of GDP, Low-Income Developing Countries, 1991–2015

	(1)	(2)	(3)	(4)	(5)	(6)
Causes						
Trade openness	−0.159***	−0.155***	−0.076***	−0.139***	−0.136***	−0.080***
Unemployment rate	0.029	0.029	−0.007	0.047	0.047	0.006
Size of government	0.094**	0.092**	0.026*			
Fiscal freedom				−0.129***	−0.128***	−0.104***
Rule of law	−0.021			−0.009		
Control of corruption		−0.004			−0.009	
Government stability			−0.192***			−0.164***
Indicators						
Currency	1	1	1	1	1	1
Labor force participation rate	−0.419**	−0.427**	−0.518***	−0.311*	−0.313*	−0.323**
Lights (GDP)	−0.636***	−0.657***	−2.389***	−0.694***	−0.704***	−1.426***
Statistical Tests						
RMSEA	0.010	0.014	0.072	0.040	0.040	0.073
Chi-square	89.640	87.740	527.000	113.669	110.397	290.032
No. of observations	957	952	1,304	850	849	1,088
No. of countries	103	103	83	96	96	80

Source: Authors.
Note: MIMIC = multiple indicators, multiple causes; RMSEA = root mean square error of approximation.
*$p < 0.1$; **$p < 0.05$; ***$p < 0.01$.

TABLE 1.13.

MIMIC Model Estimation Results Using Night Lights Instead of GDP, Advanced Economies, 1991–2015

	(1)	(2)	(3)	(4)	(5)	(6)
Causes						
Trade openness	0.132	0.204**	0.229***	0.075	0.108	0.174**
Unemployment rate	–0.352***	–0.360***	–0.410***	–0.300***	–0.295***	–0.340***
Size of government	–0.098	–0.158*	–0.165**			
Fiscal freedom				–0.247***	–0.293***	–0.230***
Rule of law	–0.240***			–0.186**		
Control of corruption		–0.117*			–0.092	
Government stability			–0.064			0.024
Indicators						
Currency	1	1	1	1	1	1
Labor force participation rate	–0.329*	–0.363*	–0.462***	–0.308*	–0.329**	–0.316**
Lights (GDP)	0.467**	0.366*	–0.066	0.553***	0.510***	0.381**
Statistical Tests						
RMSEA	0.068	0.067	0.122	0.052	0.056	0.086
Chi-square	76.456	64.922	136.547	89.160	82.642	113.695
No. of observations	189	189	302	189	189	263
No. of countries	24	24	24	24	24	24

Source: Authors.
Note: MIMIC = multiple indicators, multiple causes; RMSEA = root mean square error of approximation.
$^*p < 0.1$; $^{**}p < 0.05$; $^{***}p < 0.01$.

are rule of law and control of corruption. The indicator variable labor force participation is again statistically significant.

The results for 24 advanced economies are presented in Table 1.13. Here, trade openness is not statistically significant in all specifications, but in all other specifications, most cause variables are statistically significant, except government stability. The indicator variables are all statistically significant and have the expected signs.

Predictive Mean Matching

PMM (Rubin 1987) treats the empirical challenge in the estimation of the size of the shadow economy as a missing data problem: survey-based estimates of the size of the shadow economy are available for several, but not all, countries.[25]

Missing data can result from three mechanisms: (1) missing completely at random (MCAR), (2) missing at random (MAR), or (3) missing not at random (MNAR) (Little and Rubin 2002). PMM analysis assumes that for the shadow economy, the mechanism is MAR. This means that the probability that an observation is missing can depend on observed covariates of nonmissing units and missing units, but it cannot depend on missing data on the size of the shadow economy. In other words, the probability that a country is missing data on its shadow economy can depend on characteristics relevant for the shadow economy,

[25] Forty-nine countries were identified to have survey-based estimates of the size of their informal economies, including nine in sub-Saharan Africa.

but the size of the shadow economy itself should not be a factor. This assumption can be challenged because one can argue that a large shadow economy would be difficult to measure, resulting in missing data. Furthermore, a large shadow economy can be associated with institutional weaknesses and associated capacity constraints that would also make it less likely to be measured. However, available survey data are available for large informal economies as well, such as Burundi and Niger. Therefore, at least in practice, the MAR assumption is somewhat validated but would have to be checked through sensitivity analyses that would operate under MNAR.

The objective is to match the countries where data exist to the those where data are missing using characteristics that would be relevant to the size of the shadow economy.

One challenge inherent in the empirical problem of estimating the size of the shadow economy is that, for many countries, institutional capacity constraints make it hard to estimate. The shadow economy is complex, encompassing many related factors that in any estimation procedure may produce problems of endogeneity and other empirical challenges. A principal constraint in this exercise is that those countries for which some estimation of the shadow economy is available are not similar to countries where this is missing.

PMM circumvents this challenge somewhat by producing multiple data sets using a Bayesian setup. Therefore, where data for similar countries are lacking, the method is able to compensate by taking advantage of the inherent uncertainty associated with a missing data problem.

The other advantage of PMM is that in its actual estimation step, it is nonparametric. It does not suffer from any problems associated with a regular regression method in which dissimilar countries would be estimated (1) using the same covariates and (2) assuming linear extrapolations across covariate distributions that may be different and far apart from one another. The principle of similarity in PMM prevents this fundamental problem: it matches countries lacking data to countries that have data on the basis of their similarity. But how is this similarity itself estimated? This is the crux of the method. Similar to PMM, propensity score matching is also a promising candidate. The constraint with propensity score matching in this case, however, is that not enough similar observations are matched to run separate regressions or even make nonparametric estimates for each group because of the number of estimations required.

The similarity principle for PMM is established using a linear regression. Here, we estimate the following simple ordinary least squares model:

$$Y_{it} = \alpha + \beta_{g_{e0}} * GE_0 + \beta_{rq} * RQ + \beta_c * C + \beta_{\overline{rol}} * \beta * ROL + \beta_{bf} * BF + \beta_{se} * SE + \beta_{HDI} * HDI + \beta_E * E,$$

where Y is the size of the shadow economy as a percentage of GDP, GE is a government effectiveness index, RQ is a regulatory quality index, C is a corruption index, ROL is a rule of law index, BF is a business freedom index, SE is self-employment levels, HDI is the Human Development Index, and E is an education variable.

The distinctive feature of PMM is that this regression is not used to estimate the size of the shadow economy, but rather as a matching tool. For matching, the following seven stages are computed using the SAS Proc MI procedure:[26]

1. A random draw is made from the posterior predictive distribution of the estimated covariate coefficient matrix $\beta.$, resulting in a new covariate coefficient matrix β_{*}.
2. Using $\beta_{*}.$, we predict Y^* for all countries.
3. The algorithm then identifies countries that had an actual *Yi* and whose predicted Y^* are closest to the predicted Y^* of the countries missing the data. Hence matches between Y^*_{iobs} and Y^*_{imiss}: predicted values for the outcome variable originally missing and originally having an estimate of the size of the shadow economy.
4. Each country with missing data is assigned to a group that has similar countries with data from the previous procedure.
5. In each group, the MI procedure randomly selects a match to the countries missing the outcome and assigns the observed outcome from the match to be the estimated outcome variable.
6. Steps 1 to 5 are repeated five times, generating five distinct data sets with imputed values of the shadow economy, mimicking the inherent variability caused by the uncertainty associated with the missing data mechanism.
7. To produce a final estimate, the five data sets for the size of the shadow economy are averaged.[27]

The PMM results are consistent with the rankings produced by the MIMIC method (see Table 1.14), with Spearman's rank correlation at 61 percent and statistical significance at 1 percent. Furthermore, when the MIMIC and PMM samples are divided into three subgroups of shadow economy sizes, specifically "lower than 20 percent of GDP," "between 20 and 30 percent of GDP," and "higher than 30 percent of GDP," more than 60 percent of countries coincide between samples.

Additional Robustness Tests

This section further tests the robustness of the results by fully removing the effects of GDP, dropping both GDP per capita as cause and growth of GDP per capita as indicator.

---

[26] SAS, *STAT 14.1 User's Guide: The MI Procedure*, SAS Institute, 2015. 27

[27] Here, we can weigh these data sets on the basis of a separate estimation procedure that would give certain "matches" more weight. For example, we could separately estimate a propensity score for each country and use the propensity scores to weigh the matches in each data set. For simplicity in this chapter, we use a simple average.

TABLE 1.14.

The Size of the Shadow Economy Using the Predictive Mean Matching Method, 1991–2015

(Percent of GDP)

Less Than 20% GDP				20%–30% GDP				Greater Than 30% GDP			
		Size of Shadow Economy				Size of Shadow Economy				Size of Shadow Economy	
Rank	Country	PMM[1]	MIMIC[2]	Rank	Country	PMM[1]	MIMIC[2]	Rank	Country	PMM[1]	MIMIC[2]
1	Norway	1.0	17.1	32	Kazakhstan	20.0	38.9	60	Lebanon	30.0	31.6
2	Canada	2.2	13.9	33	Jamaica	20.4	34.1	61	Bangladesh	30.3	33.6
3	Netherlands	2.3	10.8	34	Mozambique	20.7	37.2	62	Iran	31.1	17.9
4	United Kingdom	2.3	11.1	35	Colombia	21.3	33.3	63	Côte d'Ivoire	31.1	43.4
5	Sweden	3.0	16.3	36	Kenya	22.1	33.2	64	Zambia	32.7	45.3
6	Belgium	4.6	20.6	37	South Africa	22.7	25.9	65	Burkina Faso	33.1	38.4
7	Israel	6.6	22.0	38	Bulgaria	23.3	29.2	66	Cabo Verde	33.2	35.8
8	France	6.7	14.1	39	Brazil	24.2	37.6	67	Tanzania	33.4	52.2
9	Austria	7.5	8.9	40	Mexico	24.8	31.7	68	Belarus	33.7	44.5
10	Czech Republic	8.1	14.8	41	Azerbaijan	24.8	52.2	69	Angola	33.9	44.0
11	Qatar	8.1	15.9	42	Oman	25.1	19.9	70	Guatemala	34.0	54.7
12	Denmark	8.6	18.6	43	Ecuador	25.2	33.6	71	Gabon	36.3	52.4
13	Japan	8.9	10.4	44	Turkey	25.4	31.4	72	Argentina	36.3	24.1
14	Chile	9.4	16.7	45	Romania	26.0	30.1	73	Chad	37.0	40.1
15	Iceland	9.5	14.2	46	Uganda	26.3	38.7	74	Pakistan	37.3	33.1
16	Lithuania	9.8	25.2	47	Indonesia	26.6	24.1	75	Sierra Leone	37.4	41.5
17	Slovenia	10.2	24.1	48	Bosnia and Herzegovina	27.1	34.2	76	Tunisia	38.0	35.3
18	Hungary	10.9	25.2	49	Kyrgyz Republic	27.5	37.9	77	Cameroon	38.4	32.5
19	Estonia	12.1	28.8	50	The Gambia	27.5	46.9	78	Eswatini	38.5	40.0
20	Uruguay	12.3	42.9	51	Bhutan	27.7	26.9	79	Republic of Congo	39.9	45.1
21	Ukraine	12.9	44.8	52	Algeria	27.9	30.9	80	Togo	40.9	37.3
22	Australia	13.1	12.1	53	Ghana	28.1	42.9	81	Guinea	40.9	39.9
23	Poland	15.4	25.1	54	Albania	28.5	32.7	82	Nigeria	41.4	56.7
24	Slovak Republic	15.6	15.3	55	Kuwait	29.3	19.3	83	Senegal	41.6	43.3
25	Egypt	16.9	34.2	56	Cambodia	29.7	46.0	84	Democratic Republic of the Congo	42.0	46.4
26	Tajikistan	18.3	43.0	57	Nepal	29.8	37.5	85	Zimbabwe	44.0	60.6
27	Croatia	18.7	28.8	58	Mongolia	29.9	17.3	86	India	46.3	23.9
28	Peru	19.0	52.4	59	Moldova	30.0	43.4	87	Comoros	47.6	39.1
29	Armenia	19.5	42.6					88	Central African Republic	49.6	41.9
30	Namibia	19.6	28.1					89	Benin	50.0	53.7
31	Botswana	19.9	30.3					90	Niger	51.5	39.7
								91	Burundi	64.8	36.7

Source: Authors.

Note: MIMIC = multiple indicators, multiple causes; PMM = predictive mean matching.

[1]Average from 1991 to 2015.

[2]Average from 1991 to 2015; results from this chapter's MIMIC estimations.

TABLE 1.15.

MIMIC Model Estimation Results Excluding GDP and GDP per Capita, All Countries, 1991–2015

	(1)	(2)	(3)	(4)	(5)	(6)
Causes						
Trade openness	−0.138***	−0.133***	−0.237***	−0.133***	−0.133***	−0.190***
Unemployment rate	0.113***	0.115***	0.120***	0.099***	0.104***	0.125***
Size of government	0.073***	0.067**	0.086***			
Fiscal freedom				−0.199***	−0.209***	−0.228***
Rule of law	−0.095***			−0.095***		
Control of corruption		−0.041*			−0.048*	
Government stability			−0.024			0.028
Indicators						
Currency	1	1	1	1	1	1
Labor force participation rate	−0.642***	−0.746***	−0.480***	−0.391***	−0.416***	−0.323***
Statistical Tests						
RMSEA	0.032	0.019	0.018	0.062	0.061	0.047
Chi-square	183.492	153.806	250.361	263.345	243.527	331.241
No. of observations	1,901	1,896	2,329	1,761	1,760	1,963
No. of countries	151	151	122	144	144	120

Source: Authors.
Note: MIMIC = multiple indicators, multiple causes; RMSEA = root mean square error of approximation.
$^{*}p < 0.1$; $^{**}p < 0.05$; $^{***}p < 0.01$.

MIMIC estimation results for 1991 to 2015 for different country samples, depending on data availability, are presented in Tables 1.15, 1.16, and 1.17. Results include six alternative specifications per table. These results are consistent with those in the previous sections.

TABLE 1.16.

MIMIC Model Estimation Results Excluding GDP and GDP per Capita, Low-Income Developing Countries, 1991–2015

	(1)	(2)	(3)	(4)	(5)	(6)
Causes						
Trade openness	−0.125***	−0.123***	−0.189***	−0.117***	−0.116***	−0.170***
Unemployment rate	0.099***	0.098***	0.092***	0.098***	0.099***	0.108***
Size of government	0.094***	0.091***	0.082**			
Fiscal freedom				−0.174***	−0.173***	−0.196***
Rule of law	−0.028			−0.041		
Control of corruption		0.001			−0.012	
Government stability			−0.068**			0.0026759
Indicators						
Currency	1	1	1	1	1	1
Labor force participation rate	−0.587***	−0.610***	−0.568***	−0.410***	−0.440***	−0.393***
Statistical Tests						
RMSEA	0.018	0.009	0.054	0.039	0.032	0.054
Chi-square	87.747	81.821	155.224	121.970	115.142	180.803
No. of observations	1,309	1,304	1,670	1,206	1,205	1,384
No. of countries	105	105	84	98	98	82

Source: Authors.
Note: MIMIC = multiple indicators, multiple causes; RMSEA = root mean square error of approximation.
$^{**}p < 0.05$; $^{***}p < 0.01$.

TABLE 1.17.

MIMIC Model Estimation Results Excluding GDP and GDP per Capita, Advanced Economies, 1991–2015

	(1)	(2)	(3)	(4)	(5)	(6)
Causes						
Trade openness	−0.211***	−0.231***	−0.401***	−0.151**	−0.153**	−0.251***
Unemployment rate	0.212***	0.222***	0.192***	0.145**	0.141**	0.174***
Size of government	−0.105	−0.132*	−0.120*			
Fiscal freedom				−0.231***	−0.287***	−0.258***
Rule of law	−0.180***			−0.161**		
Control of corruption		−0.145**			−0.169***	
Government stability			−0.008			0.036
Indicators						
Currency	1	1	1	1	1	1
Labor force participation rate	−0.630***	−0.683***	−0.558***	−0.596***	−0.632***	−0.528***
Statistical Tests						
RMSEA	0.070	0.072	0.095	0.064	0.067	0.116
Chi-square	78.546	75.321	150.647	93.674	98.075	134.892
No. of observations	274	274	408	265	265	351
No. of countries	26	26	25	25	25	25

Source: Authors.
Note: MIMIC = multiple indicators, multiple causes; RMSEA = root mean square error of approximation.
$*p < 0.1$; $**p < 0.05$; $***p < 0.01$.

Results for 158 Countries Using MIMIC

In Table 1.18, the most important results for the 158 countries are shown.[28] The mean value of the size of the shadow economy of the 158 countries is 31.9 percent, and the median is 32.3 percent. The similar values indicate that there is not a strong deviation. The three largest shadow economies are Georgia with 64.9, Bolivia with 62.3, and Zimbabwe with 60.6. The three smallest shadow economies are Switzerland with 7.2, the United States with 8.3, and Austria with 8.9. The average shadow economy comes close to Equatorial Guinea with 31.8 percent and Suriname with 32.2 percent of official GDP.

Figures 1.4 and 1.5 show some disaggregated results. Figure 1.4 presents the shadow economy by region. OECD countries have by far the smallest shadow economies, with values less than 20 percent of GDP. Sub-Saharan Africa and Latin America and the Caribbean have the largest, with average values of 39 percent (both averages from 1991 to 2015). All country groups demonstrate a significant decline in the size of the shadow economy over time; the average decline from 1991 to 2015 was 5.3 percentage points. Figure 1.5 presents the results

[28] For a detailed presentation of MIMIC estimation results over all sample countries and all years from 1991 to 2015, see Annex Table 1.1.1.

TABLE 1.18.

Summary Statistics of the Shadow Economy, 158 Selected Economies, 1991–2015

Economy	Average	Standard Deviation	Median	Minimum	Maximum
Albania	32.72	5.64	32.64	25.41	40.07
Algeria	30.86	5.47	29.62	23.98	38.88
Angola	43.96	6.51	46.30	34.53	52.47
Argentina	24.14	1.91	24.41	20.80	27.18
Armenia	42.59	4.68	43.57	34.56	47.61
Australia	12.06	2.51	12.25	8.10	15.18
Austria	8.93	0.60	8.86	7.69	9.85
Azerbaijan	52.19	7.29	53.67	42.15	64.66
Bahamas	33.52	4.95	35.56	26.20	39.51
Bahrain	19.34	1.33	19.21	16.63	21.11
Bangladesh	33.59	3.17	35.12	27.42	36.71
Belarus	44.52	6.92	47.83	32.29	53.57
Belgium	20.57	1.95	20.93	17.71	23.49
Belize	46.83	4.17	45.38	40.67	53.69
Benin	53.66	3.37	53.52	46.33	56.88
Bhutan	26.93	3.19	27.82	20.28	31.00
Bolivia	62.28	8.27	66.74	45.98	70.57
Bosnia and Herzegovina	34.21	3.46	33.18	29.88	44.45
Botswana	30.30	4.39	31.43	22.10	35.89
Brazil	37.63	2.75	38.47	32.56	41.69
Brunei Darussalam	29.76	1.14	29.84	26.98	31.83
Bulgaria	29.17	5.37	30.72	20.83	35.30
Burkina Faso	38.39	4.78	38.81	29.63	44.75
Burundi	36.74	3.40	37.99	26.87	40.02
Cabo Verde	35.84	5.70	36.02	29.16	43.88
Cambodia	46.04	6.63	45.40	33.85	56.69
Cameroon	32.45	2.25	32.51	28.14	35.60
Canada	13.92	2.80	13.57	9.42	17.61
Central African Republic	41.90	4.61	41.43	36.94	55.96
Chad	40.09	5.92	40.32	28.76	46.60
Chile	16.69	2.60	17.80	12.64	19.74
China	14.67	1.88	15.12	11.74	16.52
Colombia	33.31	4.17	34.95	25.25	39.10
Comoros	39.11	1.89	39.11	35.79	43.22
Democratic Republic of the Congo	46.42	1.73	46.53	41.07	48.00
Republic of Congo	45.10	6.14	47.33	33.18	52.86
Costa Rica	24.46	2.01	24.11	19.24	26.95
Côte d'Ivoire	43.43	2.39	43.63	38.88	46.49
Croatia	28.81	4.82	27.13	21.56	37.33
Cyprus	31.30	2.35	30.77	27.91	34.66
Czech Republic	14.83	2.63	15.80	10.47	18.22
Denmark	15.19	1.36	15.17	12.51	16.69
Dominican Republic	32.37	2.19	32.34	27.60	34.73
Ecuador	33.56	2.75	34.40	28.45	37.02
Egypt	34.24	2.12	35.10	28.88	36.85
El Salvador	45.59	3.84	44.69	40.05	50.78
Equatorial Guinea	31.84	3.26	31.38	27.16	37.27
Eritrea	39.29	4.07	38.65	31.42	46.36
Estonia	23.80	4.23	24.60	27.52	30.51
Eswatini	40.04	2.63	39.55	34.73	43.70
Ethiopia	34.31	4.89	36.39	24.47	40.30
Fiji	32.47	3.36	32.33	25.37	35.77
Finland	13.49	1.84	13.00	10.95	16.32

(continued)

TABLE 1.18. *(continued)*

Summary Statistics of the Shadow Economy, 158 Selected Economies, 1991–2015

Economy	Average	Standard Deviation	Median	Minimum	Maximum
France	14.08	1.60	13.96	11.61	16.60
Gabon	52.43	5.94	53.48	41.60	63.47
The Gambia	46.88	5.36	47.90	35.17	56.73
Georgia	64.87	4.97	65.31	53.07	71.95
Germany	11.97	2.07	12.80	7.75	14.62
Ghana	42.91	2.56	42.62	38.50	46.97
Greece	27.06	1.66	27.08	23.20	29.76
Guatemala	54.74	4.76	53.47	46.88	60.86
Guinea	39.95	1.74	39.70	37.41	43.89
Guinea-Bissau	36.42	5.11	38.61	21.98	42.76
Guyana	31.78	3.27	32.07	26.03	36.27
Haiti	53.28	3.96	54.15	42.14	59.12
Honduras	46.31	4.19	47.36	37.68	50.45
Hong Kong SAR	14.69	1.73	15.36	11.89	16.99
Hungary	25.23	4.11	24.14	20.49	32.03
Iceland	14.20	1.05	14.16	12.45	15.73
India	23.91	3.47	24.84	17.89	27.83
Indonesia	24.11	1.56	24.29	21.05	25.90
Iran	17.88	2.16	18.38	14.52	21.06
Ireland	13.89	2.48	13.36	9.58	17.67
Israel	22.01	1.66	22.26	19.18	23.42
Italy	24.95	1.79	24.49	22.43	27.31
Jamaica	33.02	3.30	33.89	24.97	36.92
Japan	10.41	0.86	10.61	8.19	11.79
Jordan	17.38	2.61	18.26	13.44	20.58
Kazakhstan	38.88	5.64	39.58	30.06	47.35
Kenya	33.18	2.01	33.43	28.68	36.24
Korea	25.70	3.08	26.76	19.83	30.04
Kuwait	19.31	1.72	19.75	15.71	22.07
Kyrgyz Republic	37.92	4.46	38.04	29.95	45.93
Lao P.D.R.	30.25	3.71	30.60	24.10	35.02
Latvia	22.23	4.10	22.05	15.92	28.65
Lebanon	31.58	3.47	33.03	24.63	34.79
Lesotho	31.28	2.83	31.30	24.56	35.17
Liberia	43.24	1.61	43.02	39.95	46.67
Libya	33.62	3.84	34.94	25.86	38.76
Lithuania	25.15	4.75	24.29	17.62	32.49
Luxembourg	10.67	0.60	10.67	9.37	11.97
Madagascar	42.56	2.32	41.67	38.70	47.41
Malawi	38.51	2.29	38.76	33.56	43.66
Malaysia	31.49	2.79	31.10	26.07	35.04
Maldives	27.44	2.70	27.82	20.65	31.50
Mali	38.70	4.81	39.63	29.45	44.71
Malta	29.80	1.74	30.55	26.96	33.12
Mauritania	32.29	4.70	33.39	24.38	38.57
Mauritius	22.57	2.31	22.66	19.23	26.19
Mexico	31.74	2.63	30.99	28.07	38.25
Moldova	43.43	3.00	43.84	37.35	49.08
Mongolia	17.28	2.46	17.68	12.02	21.12
Morocco	34.01	3.93	34.72	27.13	40.42
Mozambique	37.20	4.98	36.57	30.13	46.87
Myanmar	51.39	6.75	49.30	39.86	60.53
Namibia	28.07	3.77	28.82	21.78	32.09

(continued)

TABLE 1.18. *(continued)*

Summary Statistics of the Shadow Economy, 158 Selected Economies, 1991–2015

Economy	Average	Standard Deviation	Median	Minimum	Maximum
Nepal	37.50	2.66	37.35	30.22	40.59
Netherlands	10.77	1.78	10.94	7.83	13.26
New Zealand	11.70	1.47	11.53	8.97	12.93
Nicaragua	42.63	1.89	42.99	38.47	45.20
Niger	39.70	2.61	40.25	34.12	42.76
Nigeria	56.67	4.10	56.95	50.64	66.61
Norway	14.07	1.73	13.77	10.47	16.35
Oman	19.93	2.07	19.90	15.52	23.91
Pakistan	33.10	2.17	33.58	30.28	36.80
Papua New Guinea	34.01	4.12	35.14	23.25	37.81
Paraguay	34.47	2.94	34.54	29.42	40.32
Peru	52.40	7.62	56.43	39.53	59.94
Philippines	39.31	5.35	41.39	28.04	45.40
Poland	25.10	4.56	26.14	16.67	30.21
Portugal	21.88	1.51	22.02	17.82	24.18
Qatar	15.93	2.01	16.65	12.15	19.00
Romania	30.14	4.10	31.12	22.73	34.99
Russian Federation	38.42	5.46	37.68	31.04	48.73
Rwanda	36.25	4.90	38.69	26.68	41.65
Saudi Arabia	16.65	1.97	17.86	13.34	19.15
Senegal	43.35	6.29	41.48	33.68	52.60
Sierra Leone	41.50	6.28	43.17	25.69	50.14
Singapore	11.90	1.36	12.17	9.20	13.76
Slovak Republic	15.33	2.79	16.57	11.18	18.45
Slovenia	24.09	3.10	24.40	17.58	28.17
Solomon Islands	30.41	4.00	30.15	24.90	37.42
South Africa	25.94	3.52	27.64	20.35	29.84
Spain	24.52	1.98	24.04	21.53	27.98
Sri Lanka	45.58	4.67	46.30	35.49	50.22
Suriname	32.22	6.26	35.31	22.46	39.80
Sweden	13.28	2.15	12.60	10.12	16.66
Switzerland	7.24	0.61	7.27	6.16	8.23
Syria	19.58	2.00	19.21	15.65	22.79
Taiwan Province of China	32.50	3.33	33.49	26.88	35.89
Tajikistan	42.99	3.26	43.37	35.42	47.23
Tanzania	52.22	6.18	54.32	38.91	58.43
Thailand	50.63	3.30	50.51	43.12	56.64
Togo	37.31	3.72	37.27	31.49	42.68
Trinidad and Tobago	34.37	5.83	33.09	26.15	43.02
Tunisia	35.31	4.28	36.35	27.16	40.20
Turkey	31.38	2.62	32.03	27.33	34.51
Uganda	38.74	3.93	40.72	31.88	43.25
Ukraine	44.80	5.59	42.90	36.65	57.00
United Arab Emirates	26.54	1.92	27.36	22.02	28.81
United Kingdom	11.08	1.35	11.00	8.32	12.80
United States	8.34	0.82	8.23	7.00	9.23
Uruguay	37.91	9.65	42.20	20.38	48.69
Venezuela	33.81	2.73	32.65	29.64	40.03
Vietnam	18.70	2.27	18.92	14.78	21.75
Yemen	28.34	3.89	28.35	22.94	34.35
Zambia	45.32	7.37	48.52	30.72	52.41
Zimbabwe	60.64	4.21	60.58	52.09	69.08

Source: Authors.

Figure 1.4. The Shadow Economy, by Region
(Average, percent of GDP)

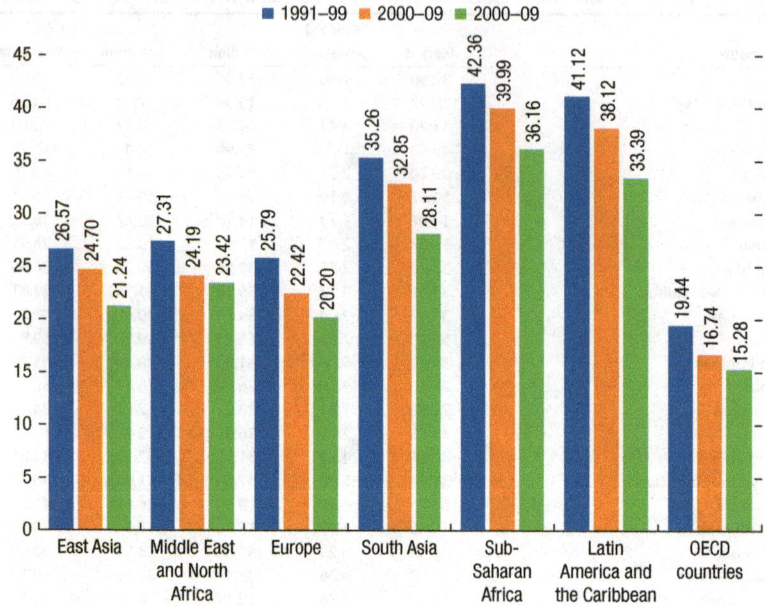

Source: Authors.
Note: OECD = Organisation for Economic Co-operation and Development.

grouped by income. Advanced ecomonies have the smallest shadow economies, and low-income developing countries have the largest.[29,30]

MIMIC RESULTS AND DIRECT APPROACH RESULTS

We first compare the SNA discrepancy method and the MIMIC method (macro and adjusted). Table 1.19 shows the results of 16 OECD countries, averaged from 2011 to 2012. For most countries, the MIMIC results are considerably larger, especially for Belgium, Israel, Mexico, and Norway.

MIMIC and SNA Discrepancy Method Results

It is remarkable that some MIMIC estimates (both macro and adjusted) come very close to the SNA discrepancy estimates. For example, in Austria the

[29] Many countries, specifically those in the Middle East, have recently been affected by massive refugee inflows; unfortunately, our model does not capture this dimension and, therefore, the shadow economy in countries such as Jordan, Lebanon, and Turkey could be underestimated. For the same reason, Syria's most recent five-year results should be taken with caution.

[30] China's results should be taken with caution, because it is partly a market economy and partly a planned economy. The results, therefore, might be capturing the informal economy only partially

Figure 1.5. The Size of the Shadow Economy, by Income Level
(Average, percent of GDP)

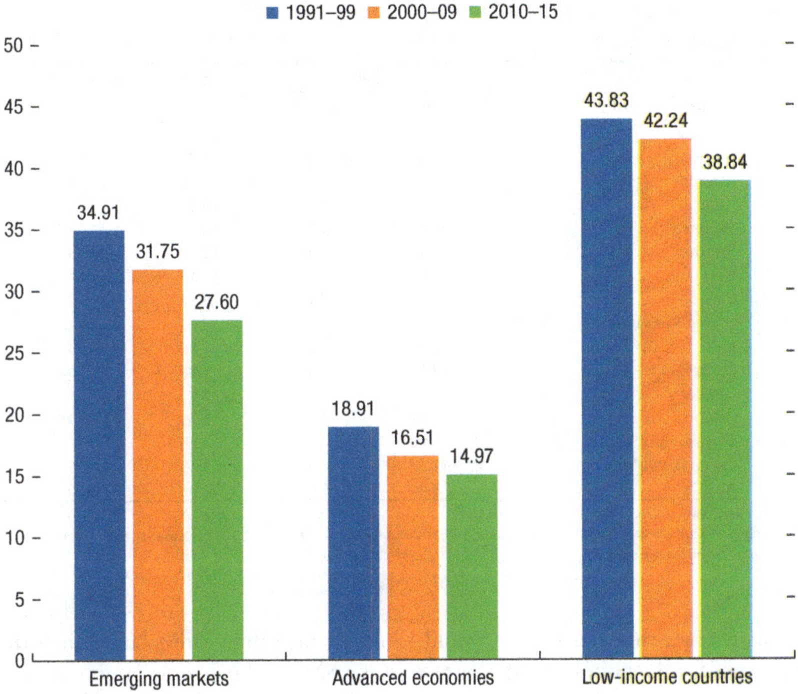

Source: Authors.

nonobserved economy is 7.5 percent of GDP by the SNA discrepancy method and 8.4 percent using the macro MIMIC estimation, whereas the adjusted result is only 5.5 percent—even lower than the SNA discrepancy method. Also somewhat close are the results for the Czech Republic and the Slovak Republic, but the MIMIC macro results are considerably higher than those achieved with the SNA discrepancy method. If one compares the adjusted MIMIC values with the SNA discrepancy method, the differences shrink considerably. Large differences are found for Norway with 9.7 percentage points, Belgium with 7.1 percentage points, and the Slovak Republic with –7.9 percentage points (here the adjusted MIMIC value is lower than that from the National Accounts Statistics), yet some countries show differences less than 3 to 4 percentage points.

We can conclude from Table 1.19 that there are still considerable differences between the macro MIMIC approach and the SNA discrepancy method; however, the variance, especially using the SNA discrepancy method, is large and the MIMIC results for a few countries come close to this calculation of the shadow economy. Hence, the statement by Gyomai and van de Ven (2014) that the

TABLE 1.19.

Macro and Adjusted MIMIC and System of National Accounts Discrepancy Method Estimates for Selected OECD Countries, 2011–12

(Average, percent of GDP)

			MIMIC		Difference (MIMIC – NOE)	
No.	**Country**	**NOE**	**Macro**	**Adjusted**	**Macro – NOE**	**Adjusted – NOE**
2	Norway	1.0	16.48	10.7	15.48	9.7
5	Mexico	15.9	29.89	19.4	13.99	3.5
4	Belgium	4.6	18.00	11.7	13.40	7.1
3	Israel	6.6	19.63	12.8	13.03	6.2
1	Slovenia	10.2	22.53	14.6	12.33	4.4
7	Sweden	3.0	14.49	9.4	11.49	6.4
6	Hungary	10.9	22.07	14.3	11.17	3.4
8	Canada	2.2	10.87	7.1	8.67	4.9
11	United Kingdom	2.3	9.99	6.5	7.69	4.2
14	Italy	17.5	25.00	16.3	7.50	–1.2
12	Netherlands	2.3	8.10	5.3	5.80	3.0
13	France	6.7	11.95	7.8	5.25	1.1
9	Poland	15.4	19.19	12.5	3.79	–2.9
15	Slovak Republic	15.6	11.90	7.7	3.70	–7.9
10	Czech Republic	8.1	11.59	7.5	3.49	–0.6
16	Austria	7.5	8.40	5.5	0.90	–2.0

Sources: Gyomai and van de Ven 2014; and authors.
Note: MIMIC = multiple indicators, multiple causes; NOE = nonobserved economy; OECD = Organisation for Economic Co-operation and Development.

estimates by Schneider (2012) would be on average three times larger than the estimates for the nonobserved economy in the SNA and 6.7 times larger than the relevant underground economy estimates should be reconsidered. Also, their statement that macroeconomic MIMIC models produce a large size for the shadow economy and the differences are likely to be caused largely by unrealistic model assumptions and calibration decisions, at least with the adjusted MIMIC results, should be reconsidered.

Table 1.20 shows a comparison between the SNA discrepancy method and the MIMIC results for eight sub-Saharan African countries from 2010 to 2014. Compared with Table 1.19, Table 1.20 shows the exact opposite result. For most countries, the discrepancy method is considerably higher than the MIMIC results; the same is true when compared with the adjusted MIMIC results. Hence, again, the criticism that the MIMIC estimates are unrealistically high may be untrue, at least for these eight sub-Saharan African countries. In seven out of the eight sub-Saharan African countries, the MIMIC estimation is considerably lower than that obtained using the discrepancy method. For example, in Guinea-Bissau the National Accounts Statistics discrepancy method estimate is 53.4 percent and the MIMIC result is 37.6 percent, a difference of 15.8 percentage points.

In Table 1.6, a comparison of the shadow economy is undertaken using the CDA and MIMIC procedure of Dybka and others (2017) and estimates of the statistical offices obtained from Gyomai and van de Ven (2014), and our values

TABLE 1.20.

System of National Accounts Discrepancy Method and MIMIC Results, Selected Sub-Saharan African Countries, 2010–14

(Average, percent of GDP)

	Methods			Differences	
Country	**National Accounts Statistics**[1]	**MIMIC**	**Adjusted MIMIC**	**MIMIC – National Accounts Statistics**	**Adjusted MIMIC – Adjusted MIMIC**
Mali	55.0	32.3	21.0	−22.7	−34.0
Guinea-Bissau	53.4	37.6	24.4	−15.8	−29.0
Burkina Faso	43.1	31.6	20.5	−11.5	−22.6
Senegal	47.5	37.9	24.6	−9.6	−22.9
Guinea	48.1	39.5	25.7	−8.6	−22.4
Togo	40.1	34.8	22.6	−5.3	−17.5
Benin	55.6	52.1	33.9	−3.5	−21.7
Côte d'Ivoire	34.0	41.9	27.2	7.9	−6.8

Source: Medina, Jonelis, and Cangul 2017; and authors.

Note: Correlation = 0.73; Spearman's rank correlation = 0.857, statistically significant at the 1 percent level.

MIMIC = multiple indicators, multiple causes.

[1]Mostly the discrepancy method is used.

are undertaken. For the European countries we see that the values obtained from statistical offices are considerably lower than the macro and adjusted MIMIC values, however, for Poland the adjusted MIMIC result of 11.8 percent and the Polish statistical office estimate of 13.3 percent come close. This is also true for Moldova and Switzerland.

MIMIC and Micro Survey Methods Results

Figure 1.6 compares the size of the Baltic countries' shadow economies as a percentage of GDP for 2015 with three estimation procedures: the survey of firm managers by Putnins and Sauka (2015) and the representative survey results of Zukauskas and Schneider (2016) are compared with the MIMIC macro and adjusted results here. Adjusted MIMIC results for Estonia are close to those from the other two approaches. The adjusted MIMIC value is 15.3 percent of GDP, the survey of firm managers method yields 14.9 percent, and the pure survey method by Zukauskas and Schneider (2016) is 15.0 percent. Somewhat different results are achieved for Latvia, for which the macro MIMIC estimate of 16.6 percent and the adjusted MIMIC estimate of 10.8 percent are much lower than the 21.3 percent value produced in the survey of firm managers; the pure survey method of Zukauskas and Schneider with 11.7 percent is considerably lower. For Lithuania, the results of the adjusted MIMIC estimates and those of Putnins and Sauka are somewhat close with 12.2 percent and 15.0 percent, and the pure survey results of Zukauskas and Schneider are again lower with 9.8 percent. Again, one clearly sees, applying different survey methods and comparing them with the MIMIC estimations,

Figure 1.6. Size of the Shadow Economy Applying Three Estimation Methods, Baltic Countries, 2015
(Percent of GDP)

Sources: Putnins and Sauka 2015; Zukauskas and Schneider 2016; and authors.
Note: MIMIC = multiple indicators, multiple causes.

that the adjusted MIMIC estimations are close to the other estimations. Only the pure macro MIMIC estimations are considerably higher.

Direct and Indirect Methods: Newer Results

Table 1.21 compares the size of the shadow economies in the Czech Republic and the Slovak Republic using most of the different known estimation methods. The currency demand deposit ratio by Alm and Embaye (2013) gets the largest results with 23.2 percent and 25.1 percent of GDP for the Czech and Slovak Republics, respectively. In second place is the consumption-income gap method by Lichard, Hanousek, and Filer (2014), calculating sizes of 17.6 percent and 22.9 percent. These estimates are considerably lower than the currency demand results but somewhat higher than the deterministic dynamic simulation approach by Elgin and Öztunali (2012) with 16.8 percent and 16.6 percent for the Czech Republic and Slovak Republic, respectively. Consumption-income gap results are also higher than the MIMIC macro approach from Buehn and Schneider (2013) for 2008 with 15.2 percent and 16.0 percent, respectively. The other

TABLE 1.21.

Alternative Estimates of the Shadow Economy for Czech Republic and Slovak Republic
(Percent of GDP)

Estimation Method	Source	Year	Czech Republic	Slovak Republic
Currency demand deposit ratio (panel GMM difference)	Alm and Embaye 2013	2006	23.2	25.1
Consumption-income gap method (switching regression)	Lichard, Hanousek, and Filer 2014	2008	17.6	22.9
Deterministic dynamic general equilibrium model	Elgin and Öztunali 2012	2008	16.8	16.6
MIMIC	Buehn and Schneider 2013	2008	15.2	16.0
Hybrid model of currency demand method	Dybka and others 2017	2008	12.2	N/A
National Statistical Offices discrepancy method	Quintano and Mazzocchi 2010	2008	5.4	13.6
Currency deposit ratio	Alm and Embaye 2013	2000–05	8.0	12.6
Structural model (calibrated to M1)	Ruge 2010	2001	8.2	8.1
Food Engel curves (excluding the self-employed)	Lichard 2012	2008	4.0	6.8
Structural model (calibrated to M2)	Ruge 2010	2001	3.3	3.3

Source: Lichard, Hanousek, and Filer 2014, 23.
Note: GMM = generalized method of moments; MIMIC = multiple indicators, multiple causes; N/A = not available.

results from the hybrid currency demand method, the statistical office discrepancy method, the currency deposit ratio, the Ruge (2010) structural MIMIC models, and the food Engel curves estimation are considerably lower compared with the first four results.

Table 1.20 shows that even using similar approaches, the size of the shadow economy can vary considerably, which again leads to the question of how these results can be evaluated with respect to their plausibility. Table 1.21 demonstrates that the micro approach using household surveys on the consumption-income gap leads to similarly large results as using most macro currency demand or MIMIC approaches. Hence, the question is open why the macro results are seen as unreliably high.

The macro approaches certainly provide upper-bound estimates because they include crime activities, do-it-yourself activities, and voluntary activities in the shadow economy; these are at least partly performed for the same reasons as "pure" shadow economy activities. MIMIC estimations of the size of the shadow economy greatly depend on their starting values. If they are taken from other macro estimates, we have the same problem. A promising approach here is the structured hybrid approach by Dybka and others (2017), who contribute to the CDA and MIMIC method in a new way by avoiding several statistical and econometric problems. One result is that they achieve much smaller shadow economy estimates.

SUMMARY AND CONCLUDING REMARKS

Summary

In this chapter, we first briefly discussed why people work in the shadow economy and the traces that shadow activities leave. Then, we extensively discussed the various methods of estimating a shadow economy, provided a classification of underground activities, and described two conventional methods of estimation.

We also described direct and indirect methods to measure the size of the shadow economy. Acknowledging the drawbacks of such methods, we detailed a structured hybrid approach by Dybka and others (2017) that combines the CDA and MIMIC method. Similarly, the SNA statistical discrepancy method was briefly described. All methods were then used as a benchmark for the MIMIC macro and adjusted methods.

Results from the latest studies were compared in detail, showing that macro MIMIC estimates are sometimes much higher than those from statistical discrepancy methods; however, in eight sub-Saharan African countries we observed the opposite, finding that the discrepancy method leads to considerably higher results than the MIMIC procedures. For several countries, the MIMIC approaches are similar to the other approaches (especially when the MIMIC procedure is adjusted for a double-counting problem), so claims that MIMIC estimates are unrealistically high and rely on unrealistic assumptions, either in calibration or estimation, need to be reconsidered.

Then, we estimated the size and development of the shadow economies of 158 countries from 1991 to 2015 using different methods and alternative specifications. Using a MIMIC method, we are one of the first to (1) use night lights (or light intensity) as an indicator variable instead of GDP, avoiding the problem that GDP is often used as both a cause and an indicator variable; and (2) apply the PMM method, which provides robust results and confirms those of the MIMIC.

The additional robustness tests also clearly show that, in most cases, trade openness, unemployment rate, GDP per capita, size of government, fiscal freedom, rule of law, and control of corruption are highly statistically significant. The results are robust when using the light intensity approach. The results are also robust when dropping GDP and GDP per capita. Again, the results show that trade openness, unemployment rate, size of government, fiscal freedom, rule of law, and corruption are statistically significant. This finding also holds for the subsamples. Hence, these two robustness tests demonstrate that the MIMIC model leads to robust results.

Conclusions from the Estimation Results

MIMIC estimations of 158 countries from 1991 to 2015 produce plausible results comparable with Schneider (2010), Hassan and Schneider (2016), and other studies. Using the lights approach as an indicator variable proved to be an alternative to using GDP per capita or GDP growth rate. Hence, if more or better data from this variable can be obtained, it might be used as an indicator. To avoid the problems of calibrating relative estimates from the MIMIC method we used a newer method, the predictive mean matching method, developed by Rubin (1987). PMM produced plausible results and prevents problems with the usual calibration methods used in Schneider (2010), Hassan and Schneider (2016), and other research. Overall, we again find one stable result: from 1991 to 2015, the size of the shadow economy declined. The continuous decline was interrupted by the 2008 global economic crisis.

Topics for Future Research

Although our analysis has addressed the benefits and drawbacks of several estimation models, methods to allow us to accurately measure the size of the shadow economy should continue to be refined, considering a number of topics for future research. First, there is no superior method. All methods, without exception, have advantages and weaknesses. If possible, one should use multiple methods. Second, much more research is needed on the estimation method and the results for different countries and periods. Third, satisfactory validation of the empirical results should be developed to easily judge the empirical results in their plausibility. We attempted to do so throughout this chapter. Fourth, an internationally accepted definition of "shadow economy" is missing, which is needed to make comparisons easier between countries and methods and to prevent double counting. And last, the link between theory and empirical estimation of the shadow economy is still unsatisfactory. In the best case, theory provides us with derived signs of the causal and indicator variables. A theoretically open question that remains, however, is what are the core causal and core indicator variables?

ANNEX TABLE 1.1.1.

Size of the Shadow Economy, 158 Selected Economies, 1991–2015

1. 1991–2003

No.	Economy	1991	1992	1993	1994	1995	1996	1997	1998	1999	2000	2001	2002	2003
1	Albania	43.18	40.18	39.45	40.07	39.18	37.07	37.59	38.16	36.04	35.3	36.04	33.67	32.64
2	Algeria	34.96	36.14	38.16	38.88	37.64	37.68	37.18	38.28	36.11	34.2	33.58	31.90	29.62
3	Angola	50.17	47.80	55.43	50.48	52.47	46.30	50.48	49.21	48.64	48.8	46.14	48.40	48.86
4	Argentina	25.22	24.41	26.59	26.22	27.18	25.32	25.20	24.00	25.83	25.4	26.94	26.19	25.37
5	Armenia	46.65	49.50	48.63	44.66	47.14	47.48	46.41	45.81	46.85	46.6	47.61	44.11	42.08
6	Australia	15.69	16.63	16.15	15.18	14.42	14.55	13.72	13.29	13.40	13.1	12.50	12.43	12.08
7	Austria	9.03	9.27	9.95	9.65	9.66	9.85	9.57	9.47	9.24	8.8	8.50	8.53	8.70
8	Azerbaijan	54.69	53.67	60.46	64.66	59.95	59.22	58.85	61.13	59.52	60.6	58.29	55.95	54.18
9	Bahamas	35.61	38.96	38.60	39.31	36.81	35.56	34.08	31.13	28.28	26.2	26.86	26.43	28.76
10	Bahrain	22.49	21.83	19.65	19.80	19.64	19.72	19.18	19.37	18.84	18.4	18.76	18.67	18.35
11	Bangladesh	36.34	36.48	37.12	36.71	35.27	35.70	35.78	35.87	35.60	35.6	34.48	35.12	36.65
12	Belarus	52.78	47.83	47.95	49.54	53.57	52.24	51.11	49.32	50.14	48.1	49.39	49.73	48.64
13	Belgium	22.10	22.07	23.31	23.49	23.19	23.41	22.19	22.92	21.63	19.9	19.78	20.93	21.65
14	Belize	50.98	51.65	51.78	52.39	53.69	53.09	52.69	52.60	49.01	43.8	44.59	45.03	42.98
15	Benin	58.78	60.80	58.66	56.88	54.86	52.65	53.47	51.49	51.24	50.2	50.34	49.72	53.24
16	Bhutan	31.24	30.66	30.20	29.64	27.82	31.00	29.94	28.75	27.98	29.4	29.21	29.28	28.18
17	Bolivia	68.09	71.34	71.08	70.39	69.40	66.78	67.31	63.69	68.67	67.1	70.57	68.82	69.01
18	Bosnia and Herzegovina	31.38	32.18	33.43	43.30	44.45	38.53	36.66	33.25	32.87	34.1	33.99	37.34	35.94
19	Botswana	33.57	35.44	36.37	35.89	35.52	35.20	32.98	34.18	32.95	33.4	33.05	32.08	31.43
20	Brazil	40.64	39.67	39.25	38.25	39.61	40.83	40.50	41.69	40.79	39.8	38.65	38.50	38.89
21	Brunei Darussalam	29.84	29.20	29.60	30.73	28.26	26.98	28.48	30.84	31.83	31.1	30.42	29.78	29.52
22	Bulgaria	35.13	34.99	36.05	34.57	32.93	31.45	30.72	32.83	34.60	35.3	34.91	33.45	32.97
23	Burkina Faso	43.42	44.06	44.89	44.75	43.59	43.91	41.76	41.26	38.81	41.4	41.20	41.22	39.34
24	Burundi	26.87	28.78	31.52	32.17	34.62	39.84	38.61	37.99	38.88	39.5	39.36	39.05	40.02
25	Cabo Verde	44.03	44.69	47.21	43.88	43.76	39.60	41.17	38.48	38.25	36.1	35.30	36.05	37.16
26	Cambodia	44.12	45.40	54.06	56.69	54.55	55.11	53.95	53.24	51.95	50.1	49.80	49.35	49.66
27	Cameroon	35.14	35.48	37.91	34.86	33.00	35.60	34.03	33.37	33.58	32.8	33.06	32.94	31.96

(continued)

ANNEX TABLE 1.1.1. ***(continued)***

Size of the Shadow Economy, 158 Selected Economies, 1991–2015

1. 1991–2003

No.	Economy	1991	1992	1993	1994	1995	1996	1997	1998	1999	2000	2001	2002	2003
28	Canada	19.31	19.52	18.92	17.61	16.59	16.59	15.15	14.65	13.79	13.4	13.52	14.15	14.25
29	Central African Republic	39.80	43.28	43.64	41.94	39.84	42.26	39.11	38.70	41.43	42.6	41.84	40.28	43.12
30	Chad	45.92	45.75	48.86	46.23	46.18	46.31	46.04	44.36	46.60	46.2	45.23	40.32	42.04
31	Chile	19.83	19.62	19.82	19.51	18.61	19.06	18.03	18.77	19.74	18.9	18.53	18.34	17.80
32	China	17.47	17.03	16.86	16.43	15.86	16.07	16.07	16.13	16.52	16.5	16.33	15.82	15.12
33	Colombia	35.69	34.53	34.95	35.41	35.24	37.30	36.19	37.46	38.98	39.1	37.26	37.97	35.87
34	Comoros	39.97	35.79	35.89	40.15	39.87	41.56	40.77	43.22	42.93	39.6	39.11	39.31	37.86
35	Democratic Republic of the Congo	48.08	49.10	49.27	46.08	45.76	46.36	47.56	47.85	46.97	48.0	47.71	47.74	46.28
36	Republic of Congo	50.40	50.74	52.82	52.08	49.00	47.53	51.09	52.86	52.17	48.2	48.41	48.24	47.33
37	Costa Rica	28.63	26.72	26.47	26.71	26.72	26.95	26.18	23.82	23.99	23.9	25.70	25.09	24.11
38	Côte d'Ivoire	46.29	48.39	48.25	44.53	41.05	38.88	42.53	40.37	41.53	43.2	43.64	43.68	46.49
39	Croatia	30.70	32.85	34.93	35.91	37.33	35.64	32.64	34.22	34.60	32.0	30.91	29.06	27.13
40	Cyprus	36.22	34.72	35.29	34.09	27.91	28.94	28.96	30.51	30.13	28.7	28.40	29.31	31.62
41	Czech Republic	18.42	17.77	18.18	18.22	16.81	16.05	16.70	16.31	17.15	16.8	15.80	16.75	17.08
42	Denmark	17.08	17.03	18.06	16.69	16.15	16.50	15.17	15.54	15.16	14.6	14.23	14.77	14.94
43	Dominican Republic	35.84	35.85	35.62	34.73	34.41	33.57	34.07	32.24	32.49	32.1	33.59	33.68	31.94
44	Ecuador	35.84	35.47	36.03	36.98	35.69	34.54	36.58	34.75	37.02	34.4	36.05	35.81	36.42
45	Egypt	36.02	35.57	36.51	36.82	36.85	35.28	35.99	35.47	35.83	35.1	35.49	35.70	35.16
46	El Salvador	52.74	52.96	52.82	49.56	48.33	50.78	47.93	47.80	46.88	46.3	46.03	44.19	43.53
47	Equatorial Guinea	37.64	37.54	38.10	37.27	35.97	32.71	33.10	33.47	32.69	32.8	30.75	32.06	30.82
48	Eritrea	37.57	48.92	44.07	36.69	38.65	33.54	31.42	34.25	38.16	40.3	36.28	35.68	39.56
49	Estonia	23.54	26.04	29.13	29.79	30.51	30.22	27.01	26.79	27.59	27.7	26.16	25.39	24.77
50	Eswatini	43.99	42.74	44.13	43.61	41.48	41.42	43.70	42.81	42.55	41.4	39.55	38.44	37.55
51	Ethiopia	38.29	37.77	36.71	37.55	38.05	36.39	36.22	37.83	39.82	40.3	37.98	38.79	39.30
52	Fiji	38.88	38.44	38.40	35.64	34.81	32.50	35.63	35.77	32.90	33.6	32.84	31.17	31.74
53	Finland	16.52	17.11	17.00	16.32	15.74	15.91	14.51	13.77	13.39	12.5	12.46	13.00	12.71
54	France	14.96	15.58	16.76	16.60	16.20	16.28	16.01	15.34	14.92	13.8	13.31	14.72	14.58

(continued)

ANNEX TABLE 1.1.1. ***(continued)***

Size of the Shadow Economy, 158 Selected Economies, 1991–2015

1. 1991–2003

No.	Economy	1991	1992	1993	1994	1995	1996	1997	1998	1999	2000	2001	2002	2003
55	Gabon	48.72	50.91	48.21	43.95	43.84	44.23	41.60	43.10	49.15	48.0	56.07	55.82	57.40
56	The Gambia	50.65	49.38	49.46	53.55	56.73	55.31	54.35	51.61	48.35	45.1	42.36	51.76	42.85
57	Georgia	61.47	65.31	65.01	63.70	71.95	71.33	69.35	71.27	70.10	67.3	66.86	67.53	64.90
58	Germany	13.26	13.78	14.28	14.18	14.06	14.62	13.97	13.72	13.32	12.9	12.48	13.01	13.18
59	Ghana	46.07	46.12	47.71	46.18	44.98	46.97	44.65	45.70	44.58	41.9	42.62	42.66	42.60
60	Greece	28.79	28.46	29.35	28.92	29.76	28.63	28.91	28.23	27.82	26.1	26.46	27.01	26.17
61	Guatemala	63.95	63.38	61.90	60.18	59.76	60.86	58.75	57.45	54.66	51.5	54.44	55.29	56.06
62	Guinea	41.22	41.34	41.16	41.88	41.75	42.03	41.32	39.73	40.14	39.7	39.12	38.09	39.01
62	Guinea-Bissau	30.64	30.50	32.41	30.82	30.73	27.98	21.98	42.76	37.78	39.6	39.88	41.71	42.40
64	Guyana	36.55	35.01	34.54	34.18	33.53	31.45	32.07	31.70	32.40	33.6	33.86	34.17	35.83
65	Haiti	42.14	46.75	44.87	55.79	50.18	52.83	50.89	57.19	54.69	55.4	56.61	59.12	56.05
66	Honduras	53.74	51.79	49.64	49.83	48.89	49.12	46.96	48.10	50.41	49.6	50.45	49.28	49.36
67	Hong Kong SAR	15.75	15.69	15.48	15.31	15.56	16.13	15.36	16.84	16.93	16.6	16.54	16.99	16.61
68	Hungary	31.89	32.26	33.69	32.03	30.18	29.18	28.35	27.11	26.57	25.1	24.70	24.14	24.19
69	Iceland	15.03	15.81	16.01	15.72	15.73	15.54	14.92	14.64	14.41	14.3	14.05	14.64	14.57
70	India	28.43	27.96	28.02	26.50	26.67	25.69	27.07	26.96	27.83	26.7	26.62	26.48	24.84
71	Indonesia	26.99	26.18	26.38	25.59	24.62	23.64	23.49	21.78	24.33	23.7	24.05	25.43	25.90
72	Iran	19.13	19.54	20.42	20.85	21.06	20.65	20.07	20.35	19.88	18.9	19.89	18.39	17.02
73	Ireland	18.36	18.30	18.11	17.67	16.75	16.69	15.51	14.76	13.82	13.4	12.92	13.23	13.76
74	Israel	25.02	24.83	24.05	23.18	23.42	22.26	23.38	23.18	22.91	21.9	22.82	22.81	23.32
75	Italy	29.14	28.52	28.31	27.15	24.80	24.18	25.13	24.14	24.54	22.7	23.55	23.46	24.28
76	Jamaica	36.02	32.72	32.76	31.25	31.18	33.89	36.11	34.82	35.76	36.4	35.23	35.76	34.57
77	Japan	10.35	10.46	10.67	10.80	10.85	10.72	10.61	10.91	11.22	11.2	11.31	11.79	11.57
78	Jordan	21.12	19.75	20.27	20.58	19.81	19.91	19.92	19.93	19.76	19.4	19.29	19.34	18.26
79	Kazakhstan	43.62	43.41	44.49	42.63	46.08	47.35	45.99	45.66	44.61	43.2	42.73	40.89	39.58
80	Kenya	34.75	35.01	31.63	32.21	31.68	34.08	34.68	36.24	35.46	34.3	34.45	35.34	35.92
81	Korea	29.13	29.23	29.14	28.35	27.48	28.03	26.97	30.04	28.49	27.5	27.37	26.76	27.41

(continued)

ANNEX TABLE 1.1.1. ***(continued)***

Size of the Shadow Economy, 158 Selected Economies, 1991–2015

1. 1991–2003

No.	Economy	1991	1992	1993	1994	1995	1996	1997	1998	1999	2000	2001	2002	2003
82	Kuwait	18.55	21.40	20.35	19.83	19.39	19.03	19.18	19.22	20.66	20.1	20.67	20.91	18.79
83	Kyrgyz Republic	35.75	38.76	41.83	44.44	45.93	43.02	41.83	41.65	41.94	41.2	40.35	43.00	39.05
84	Lao People's Democratic Republic	36.16	35.88	35.62	35.02	35.00	33.96	33.70	32.10	32.04	30.6	30.66	30.80	31.33
85	Latvia	20.07	24.44	25.29	24.79	28.65	28.07	26.96	27.44	27.07	26.7	25.18	25.12	23.71
86	Lebanon	36.68	35.85	34.93	33.96	33.03	32.23	33.07	33.27	34.54	34.1	34.47	34.23	34.79
87	Lesotho	35.12	35.37	35.76	34.37	35.17	32.57	34.58	32.02	32.97	31.3	31.51	29.85	30.58
88	Liberia	42.08	43.89	44.70	45.25	45.55	46.67	45.12	45.95	44.64	43.2	42.23	41.84	43.02
89	Libya	34.24	36.22	35.75	35.07	34.68	36.26	36.26	38.21	36.20	35.1	36.24	34.94	31.83
90	Lithuania	21.15	23.78	26.36	28.76	32.49	32.22	30.90	31.27	30.88	31.1	29.31	28.45	27.01
91	Luxembourg	11.07	11.43	11.37	11.24	11.40	11.97	11.38	10.90	10.37	9.8	10.18	10.32	10.71
92	Madagascar	40.40	41.06	41.06	41.22	40.90	44.34	41.95	41.67	40.21	39.6	41.16	47.41	45.47
93	Malawi	39.40	40.32	40.19	43.66	39.25	39.91	40.17	38.55	37.52	40.3	40.34	41.99	39.41
94	Malaysia	37.47	37.30	36.79	35.04	33.22	30.58	30.37	32.10	31.63	31.1	32.27	32.65	32.03
95	Maldives	28.11	28.29	27.35	26.75	31.50	30.21	30.98	30.22	30.60	30.3	29.39	28.93	27.73
96	Mali	44.15	45.15	45.28	42.78	43.40	43.36	41.10	44.71	42.22	42.3	39.63	39.70	38.10
97	Malta	31.54	30.61	31.40	31.03	30.88	33.12	31.65	30.61	29.72	27.1	30.66	30.15	30.99
98	Mauritania	36.00	36.59	35.26	36.38	33.39	31.80	35.57	36.45	36.09	36.1	37.39	38.57	38.27
99	Mauritius	25.83	25.61	25.94	26.19	25.86	25.43	24.12	22.90	24.01	23.1	21.67	22.14	22.66
100	Mexico	33.06	33.53	36.34	35.81	38.25	36.63	33.70	32.62	31.44	30.1	31.20	30.99	30.84
101	Moldova	38.89	43.96	44.53	48.96	49.08	47.10	44.20	42.98	46.30	45.1	45.23	46.53	45.50
102	Mongolia	18.83	20.65	19.53	21.12	20.12	19.54	19.15	18.81	18.87	18.4	18.88	18.01	17.68
103	Morocco	36.59	38.18	40.33	38.96	40.42	35.91	38.68	35.70	37.28	36.4	36.48	35.25	34.72
104	Mozambique	43.14	44.97	44.79	46.87	42.39	41.06	40.67	41.11	40.14	40.3	39.03	36.57	36.60
105	Myanmar	63.83	61.85	61.55	60.53	59.12	58.63	57.67	57.77	53.59	52.6	49.77	47.66	43.64
106	Namibia	31.84	31.86	32.12	31.96	32.09	31.57	31.89	31.45	31.88	31.4	31.32	29.14	28.82
107	Nepal	43.39	40.59	40.88	39.15	39.97	40.59	39.59	38.68	38.04	36.8	37.20	37.71	37.35
108	Netherlands	13.21	13.13	13.38	13.26	13.00	12.80	11.79	11.51	10.92	10.5	10.40	11.33	11.75

(continued)

ANNEX TABLE 1.1.1. *(continued)*

Size of the Shadow Economy, 158 Selected Economies, 1991–2015

1. 1991–2003

No.	Economy	1991	1992	1993	1994	1995	1996	1997	1998	1999	2000	2001	2002	2003
109	New Zealand	14.97	14.62	13.85	12.92	12.70	12.75	12.78	12.93	12.13	11.5	10.85	11.36	11.36
110	Nicaragua	44.54	44.75	44.82	44.71	44.74	42.70	42.99	43.01	43.23	45.2	43.76	43.50	43.68
111	Niger	38.66	43.09	42.70	41.65	40.80	40.23	41.28	39.04	42.00	41.9	40.06	40.25	41.63
112	Nigeria	56.95	58.17	58.82	66.61	62.21	61.09	60.69	62.33	59.87	57.9	57.64	59.93	57.19
113	Norway	16.25	17.30	17.17	16.35	15.77	14.84	13.44	13.77	14.04	12.7	12.73	15.20	15.42
114	Oman	23.41	22.56	22.42	22.42	21.99	20.72	20.11	19.88	20.04	18.9	18.82	19.82	20.17
115	Pakistan	37.55	34.92	34.40	34.90	34.48	32.81	34.58	34.63	35.35	36.8	35.12	34.97	33.58
116	Papua New Guinea	41.96	38.86	34.34	32.09	33.64	30.63	35.36	34.44	34.63	36.1	36.43	37.08	37.34
117	Paraguay	34.63	35.39	33.95	32.29	30.67	32.67	34.54	34.87	37.79	39.8	39.65	40.32	37.60
118	Peru	59.87	59.25	61.00	58.50	58.52	59.63	57.08	58.23	59.94	59.9	58.47	56.43	56.65
119	Philippines	45.43	45.39	45.53	45.40	45.04	42.21	43.50	43.79	44.43	43.3	43.02	42.16	41.39
120	Poland	33.10	32.70	31.96	30.21	29.54	28.40	27.60	26.14	26.70	26.2	26.90	26.69	26.42
121	Portugal	23.28	23.66	24.40	24.18	23.62	23.01	22.81	21.88	22.02	21.4	21.79	21.70	22.36
122	Qatar	16.41	15.40	15.80	17.65	16.68	18.21	17.02	16.65	17.21	19.0	18.32	17.74	18.31
123	Romania	36.03	35.13	34.80	34.99	33.40	31.12	31.65	32.18	34.45	34.4	32.33	32.51	33.03
124	Russian Federation	39.73	31.49	41.53	45.04	45.65	46.83	48.73	47.72	42.05	41.91	40.81	40.78	40.08
125	Rwanda	39.72	39.59	39.61	39.91	41.09	41.65	38.69	40.25	41.23	40.3	41.14	39.01	38.52
126	Saudi Arabia	18.90	17.93	18.07	17.86	18.03	17.98	18.62	19.15	18.22	18.4	18.33	18.79	17.96
127	Senegal	52.64	52.30	53.39	51.60	50.08	52.60	51.87	47.48	45.97	45.1	44.05	41.48	41.95
128	Sierra Leone	38.20	41.77	43.17	43.67	44.51	46.36	46.60	45.96	48.49	48.6	50.14	47.76	45.34
129	Singapore	13.69	13.38	13.13	12.56	12.17	12.76	12.26	13.56	12.86	13.1	13.40	13.76	13.00
130	Slovak Republic	17.19	19.45	19.27	18.28	17.92	18.45	17.17	17.85	17.41	17.6	17.23	17.15	16.57
131	Slovenia	27.41	28.59	29.47	28.16	28.17	27.02	26.54	25.01	25.88	25.2	25.00	24.50	24.40
132	Solomon Islands	30.60	29.61	29.41	25.84	25.71	24.90	25.79	24.97	27.51	33.4	36.36	37.42	36.16
133	South Africa	29.87	31.12	31.25	29.84	27.66	29.05	28.68	28.62	29.19	28.4	27.78	27.64	28.15
134	Spain	27.49	28.04	28.69	27.98	27.37	26.13	25.96	24.78	24.47	22.7	23.02	23.13	23.05
135	Sri Lanka	52.94	51.87	50.43	49.94	50.22	48.67	48.28	47.07	46.3	44.6	46.29	46.85	46.19

(continued)

ANNEX TABLE 1.1.1. ***(continued)***

Size of the Shadow Economy, 158 Selected Economies, 1991–2015

1. 1991–2003

No.	Economy	1991	1992	1993	1994	1995	1996	1997	1998	1999	2000	2001	2002	2003
136	Suriname	36.49	38.08	39.36	38.26	37.60	39.11	37.28	37.94	38.13	39.8	36.42	36.36	35.31
137	Sweden	15.54	17.01	17.85	16.66	15.40	16.40	15.07	14.87	13.74	12.6	12.10	12.93	12.91
138	Switzerland	7.56	8.08	8.23	8.23	8.08	8.05	7.83	7.33	7.27	6.8	7.07	7.34	7.78
139	Syria	24.23	21.90	20.58	19.13	18.80	18.35	18.72	17.27	18.88	19.3	19.47	18.83	19.16
140	Taiwan Province of China	38.43	37.66	36.72	35.65	35.24	35.89	34.97	35.31	33.62	33.61	34.32	34.17	33.49
141	Tajikistan	35.42	47.43	46.64	46.53	45.92	47.23	45.21	46.97	45.51	43.2	44.02	43.98	42.62
142	Tanzania	60.32	59.95	58.11	57.47	54.69	55.35	56.10	57.87	58.43	58.3	57.09	55.25	53.90
143	Thailand	55.72	54.05	54.34	53.11	51.84	50.05	51.98	55.43	56.64	52.6	54.17	51.36	50.51
144	Togo	38.45	40.70	50.52	42.68	40.48	36.69	32.17	34.52	35.24	35.1	37.73	37.75	36.86
145	Trinidad and Tobago	43.72	44.75	44.26	43.02	41.56	40.18	38.91	37.03	37.98	34.4	35.73	34.27	33.09
146	Tunisia	42.00	40.08	39.60	39.42	38.85	38.92	39.42	40.20	38.46	38.4	36.35	37.74	37.24
147	Turkey	35.99	35.89	35.30	34.51	32.84	32.95	31.01	32.03	33.26	32.1	32.75	33.74	32.07
148	Uganda	41.79	41.88	42.66	43.25	41.36	40.93	41.69	42.35	40.72	43.1	41.56	43.23	41.67
149	Ukraine	38.96	41.79	44.06	48.12	48.92	51.76	56.31	57.00	51.91	52.2	49.06	47.06	45.29
150	United Arab Emirates	27.74	28.05	28.50	27.47	27.00	26.76	26.98	27.72	28.54	26.4	28.15	27.81	27.46
151	United Kingdom	13.65	13.93	13.37	12.80	12.13	11.95	11.29	10.98	11.11	10.8	10.66	11.19	11.23
152	United States	10.12	10.00	9.69	9.23	8.91	8.90	8.23	8.00	7.82	7.6	8.01	8.54	8.40
153	Uruguay	47.99	46.04	46.91	44.92	47.52	48.69	42.96	42.20	45.21	46.1	46.57	46.33	43.18
154	Venezuela	32.02	31.12	31.12	31.69	32.21	29.64	35.08	35.57	38.18	36.0	38.26	38.70	40.03
155	Vietnam	22.24	21.39	22.17	21.75	21.23	20.59	21.31	20.18	19.98	19.2	19.73	19.22	18.92
156	Yemen	35.03	34.24	34.02	34.35	30.83	29.39	29.80	30.17	28.35	27.4	26.48	27.20	25.42
157	Zambia	54.17	50.68	50.91	51.39	51.33	52.41	51.74	51.61	49.86	48.9	48.85	47.71	48.40
158	Zimbabwe	57.35	62.24	59.35	56.29	57.27	54.05	56.16	52.09	56.43	59.4	56.12	58.32	61.83
	Average	*34.51*	*34.82*	*35.22*	*34.89*	*34.50*	*34.14*	*33.81*	*33.83*	*33.78*	*33.26*	*33.17*	*33.14*	*32.73*

(continued)

ANNEX TABLE 1.1.1. ***(continued)***

Size of the Shadow Economy, 158 Selected Economies, 1991–2015

2. 2004–15

No.	Economy	2004	2005	2006	2007	2008	2009	2010	2011	2012	2013	2014	2015	Average
1	Albania	31.72	30.89	29.58	28.53	27.12	26.91	26.10	25.41	25.52	25.68	25.78	26.21	32.72
2	Algeria	27.76	24.93	24.44	24.21	24.07	25.90	25.89	27.37	26.94	25.98	25.74	23.98	30.86
3	Angola	46.81	43.84	41.23	37.13	35.26	36.25	36.54	36.49	36.60	35.92	34.53	35.25	43.96
4	Argentina	24.32	23.21	22.63	21.93	21.87	22.97	21.64	20.80	21.62	21.57	22.02	24.99	24.14
5	Armenia	43.57	41.03	41.38	39.47	35.39	41.04	40.14	38.46	35.52	34.56	34.78	35.96	42.59
6	Australia	12.11	12.25	11.66	9.32	8.96	9.39	9.14	8.87	9.83	9.95	8.89	8.10	12.06
7	Austria	8.72	8.86	8.34	7.69	7.78	9.65	9.07	8.47	8.40	8.68	8.39	9.01	8.93
8	Azerbaijan	52.45	50.01	48.02	45.32	43.70	44.82	44.20	43.71	43.30	42.26	42.15	43.66	52.19
9	Bahamas	29.23	27.92	27.50	27.37	30.82	37.73	37.77	38.57	37.62	39.51	38.92	38.55	33.52
10	Bahrain	17.64	17.54	18.12	18.79	18.16	20.33	20.30	21.01	21.11	20.03	19.21	16.63	19.34
11	Bangladesh	36.50	34.95	34.13	32.93	31.32	31.47	30.78	28.79	28.97	28.22	27.42	27.60	33.59
12	Belarus	46.72	46.77	44.64	42.10	38.69	39.70	38.17	33.03	32.29	34.07	34.12	32.37	44.52
13	Belgium	21.12	21.11	20.74	18.27	18.28	18.74	18.80	17.71	18.28	18.81	18.06	17.80	20.57
14	Belize	44.56	43.74	41.18	41.87	40.67	47.13	45.51	45.45	45.38	44.08	44.69	42.29	46.83
15	Benin	55.49	56.38	55.79	52.75	53.52	56.63	54.49	55.12	53.64	50.71	46.33	48.28	53.66
16	Bhutan	27.26	27.15	25.91	25.87	24.63	26.04	24.19	23.40	22.26	21.81	21.06	20.28	26.93
17	Bolivia	66.74	65.64	61.77	59.97	54.65	58.40	55.06	51.82	49.64	48.18	46.93	45.98	62.28
18	Bosnia and Herzegovina	33.57	32.72	33.48	33.11	30.97	33.13	33.18	32.60	32.59	31.38	31.19	29.88	34.21
19	Botswana	30.57	30.12	27.85	26.52	27.06	28.46	26.44	25.03	24.44	22.85	22.10	23.99	30.30
20	Brazil	37.29	38.47	37.62	37.05	35.16	36.90	34.55	33.06	32.71	32.56	33.01	35.22	37.63
21	Brunei Darussalam	29.96	30.39	29.94	30.55	29.04	29.80	28.88	28.34	28.16	30.00	31.81	30.44	29.76
22	Bulgaria	30.58	28.63	26.78	23.70	22.77	24.08	23.42	22.39	22.12	22.37	21.60	20.83	29.17
23	Burkina Faso	38.69	37.25	36.21	38.30	36.40	35.64	33.29	32.06	31.12	31.12	30.53	29.63	38.39
24	Burundi	39.75	38.08	35.96	38.89	38.23	37.95	38.64	37.86	37.04	36.93	36.25	35.68	36.74
25	Cabo Verde	36.02	34.86	30.32	29.94	29.16	31.48	30.83	29.59	29.52	29.20	29.26	30.23	35.84
26	Cambodia	46.74	43.69	40.92	41.76	41.02	42.88	42.31	40.30	38.08	36.56	34.92	33.85	46.04
27	Cameroon	32.06	31.37	30.44	30.43	30.26	32.51	31.93	31.20	30.52	29.63	28.14	28.93	32.45

(continued)

ANNEX TABLE 1.1.1. *(continued)*

Size of the Shadow Economy, 158 Selected Economies, 1991–2015

2. 2004–15

No.	Economy	2004	2005	2006	2007	2008	2009	2010	2011	2012	2013	2014	2015	Average
28	Canada	13.77	13.57	12.92	12.87	12.02	12.26	10.71	10.46	11.28	11.21	10.05	9.42	13.92
29	Central African Republic	42.12	41.58	39.12	38.15	38.88	38.23	37.54	36.94	37.85	52.64	55.96	50.71	41.90
30	Chad	35.03	34.26	35.01	36.35	37.11	37.11	34.11	35.14	33.90	34.30	31.20	28.76	40.09
31	Chile	16.86	16.16	15.67	15.10	14.09	14.47	14.06	12.96	12.64	12.79	12.72	13.16	16.69
32	China	14.31	14.14	13.84	13.82	12.79	12.83	12.13	12.03	12.41	12.25	11.74	12.11	14.67
33	Colombia	35.30	33.98	31.79	30.89	29.82	31.24	30.71	27.60	27.34	26.77	25.99	25.25	33.31
34	Comoros	38.78	37.92	37.45	38.08	39.21	40.02	39.05	38.63	38.61	36.63	36.44	40.92	39.11
35	Democratic Republic of the Congo	46.64	46.53	47.09	44.51	44.06	46.36	44.19	44.81	45.98	45.65	41.07	46.95	46.42
36	Republic of Congo	46.31	44.52	41.81	45.64	43.27	40.65	36.40	36.43	37.13	36.28	33.18	35.05	45.10
37	Costa Rica	24.00	23.06	22.12	22.20	21.30	24.33	24.60	24.72	23.76	23.81	23.41	19.24	24.46
38	Côte d'Ivoire	45.62	44.55	43.84	44.39	43.94	42.81	42.15	43.63	43.47	41.06	38.94	42.40	43.43
39	Croatia	26.10	24.96	23.80	22.50	21.56	25.27	25.60	24.64	25.26	25.28	24.48	22.96	28.81
40	Cyprus	30.74	30.77	29.90	29.03	28.77	31.64	31.39	32.71	33.32	34.66	32.69	32.20	31.30
41	Czech Republic	15.75	14.46	13.14	11.53	11.18	13.52	12.97	11.68	11.50	11.79	10.76	10.47	14.83
42	Denmark	14.55	13.75	12.66	12.51	13.01	16.33	16.17	15.26	15.48	15.24	14.13	14.70	15.19
43	Dominican Republic	32.34	32.95	30.78	32.24	31.26	33.10	30.71	30.48	30.58	29.02	27.60	27.97	32.37
44	Ecuador	33.84	32.67	32.14	31.40	31.04	34.32	32.07	29.71	29.19	28.45	28.50	30.18	33.56
45	Egypt	33.92	33.47	33.07	30.80	28.88	30.30	30.50	32.91	33.64	34.37	34.96	33.32	34.24
46	El Salvador	42.21	42.74	42.34	40.93	40.05	45.73	44.69	42.77	42.72	41.78	41.30	42.60	45.59
47	Equatorial Guinea	29.77	30.15	29.27	27.70	27.16	27.87	28.76	28.37	28.55	29.92	32.20	31.38	31.84
48	Eritrea	39.42	39.86	41.13	41.61	46.36	44.45	44.88	41.38	37.33	38.18	36.09	36.53	39.29
49	Estonia	23.15	21.26	19.00	17.84	19.42	24.60	22.99	19.67	18.34	17.97	17.52	18.49	23.80
50	Eswatini	39.19	38.69	38.02	38.27	38.48	38.17	38.97	40.28	36.44	35.57	34.73	40.94	40.04
51	Ethiopia	36.97	36.13	33.87	32.41	31.68	31.41	30.10	27.65	26.84	26.21	24.47	25.10	34.31
52	Fiji	27.94	28.57	30.42	32.33	29.84	33.48	32.06	29.64	29.48	31.19	28.97	25.37	32.47
53	Finland	12.29	11.97	11.26	10.98	10.95	13.11	12.54	12.19	12.59	13.08	12.12	13.30	13.49
54	France	14.00	13.96	13.31	12.88	11.61	13.89	13.11	11.81	12.08	12.41	12.12	11.65	14.08

(continued)

ANNEX TABLE 1.1.1. *(continued)*

Size of the Shadow Economy, 158 Selected Economies, 1991–2015

2. 2004–15

No.	Economy	2004	2005	2006	2007	2008	2009	2010	2011	2012	2013	2014	2015	Average
55	Gabon	58.13	55.41	59.63	58.68	60.07	63.47	58.02	54.75	53.50	52.52	53.48	52.01	52.43
56	The Gambia	38.90	45.77	48.19	47.90	45.28	39.78	35.17	48.57	42.64	40.95	43.81	43.64	46.88
57	Georgia	66.10	66.91	63.79	64.55	67.93	68.46	64.73	60.86	58.67	56.57	54.10	53.07	64.87
58	Germany	12.80	12.61	11.41	10.56	9.59	11.69	10.88	9.05	8.85	9.22	8.17	7.75	11.97
59	Ghana	42.90	43.16	41.68	41.51	41.41	40.61	40.03	40.64	40.99	39.25	38.50	39.37	42.91
60	Greece	25.29	25.99	24.90	24.23	23.20	25.32	26.15	27.08	28.39	27.78	27.11	26.45	27.06
61	Guatemala	53.47	53.12	50.46	49.68	50.47	53.26	52.23	51.76	50.62	50.48	47.82	46.88	54.74
62	Guinea	38.77	37.54	37.41	38.30	38.94	42.16	43.89	39.60	37.51	38.32	38.18	41.58	39.95
62	Guinea-Bissau	41.51	40.07	40.40	39.20	38.51	38.61	37.54	34.13	39.01	38.69	38.75	34.94	36.42
64	Guyana	34.65	36.27	31.85	29.65	31.58	30.65	28.73	27.52	26.35	26.16	26.03	26.09	31.78
65	Haiti	54.67	55.02	56.53	58.25	54.15	53.72	52.93	52.30	52.49	51.84	51.21	56.38	53.28
66	Honduras	47.36	44.37	42.68	41.14	40.97	45.48	44.90	41.96	42.12	42.37	39.51	37.68	46.31
67	Hong Kong SAR	15.52	14.45	13.74	13.11	13.01	13.81	12.79	12.22	12.29	12.15	11.89	12.39	14.69
68	Hungary	22.88	22.52	21.05	21.40	20.58	23.18	22.82	21.87	22.26	21.63	20.78	20.49	25.23
69	Iceland	13.78	13.26	13.14	12.69	12.56	14.12	14.16	13.74	13.38	13.31	13.07	12.45	14.20
70	India	23.87	23.44	22.06	21.03	21.68	22.27	20.65	19.71	18.99	18.11	18.33	17.89	23.91
71	Indonesia	25.18	24.82	24.87	25.13	23.40	24.29	23.44	22.65	22.22	21.92	21.05	21.76	24.11
72	Iran	16.01	16.63	16.34	14.52	14.60	15.73	15.60	14.93	15.79	16.17	16.14	18.38	17.88
73	Ireland	13.52	13.08	12.59	12.55	12.45	13.36	11.78	12.49	11.40	11.14	9.93	9.58	13.89
74	Israel	22.43	21.84	21.11	21.80	20.37	21.50	20.48	19.40	19.85	19.90	19.39	19.18	22.01
75	Italy	24.17	24.62	23.81	22.43	23.51	27.31	26.13	24.54	25.53	24.49	24.33	22.97	24.95
76	Jamaica	32.20	33.19	30.71	30.61	30.42	35.55	36.92	35.43	36.28	26.49	26.33	24.97	33.02
77	Japan	11.09	10.91	10.35	10.14	9.21	10.39	9.93	9.89	9.73	9.28	8.69	8.19	10.41
78	Jordan	16.09	14.91	14.71	13.66	13.44	14.91	14.96	15.38	15.00	14.64	14.20	15.16	17.38
79	Kazakhstan	38.41	36.39	35.12	34.21	32.66	34.65	33.03	31.61	31.92	30.77	30.06	32.82	38.88
80	Kenya	34.64	33.32	32.27	33.35	32.93	33.62	31.54	29.92	30.11	29.99	28.68	33.43	33.18
81	Korea	26.23	26.03	26.37	24.89	23.86	23.13	22.97	20.81	20.96	21.27	20.36	19.83	25.70

(continued)

ANNEX TABLE 1.1.1. ***(continued)***

Size of the Shadow Economy, 158 Selected Economies, 1991–2015

2. 2004–15

No.	Economy	2004	2005	2006	2007	2008	2009	2010	2011	2012	2013	2014	2015	Average
82	Kuwait	17.63	16.33	15.85	15.71	16.45	18.98	19.75	19.81	19.86	20.55	22.07	21.72	19.31
83	Kyrgyz Republic	37.73	38.04	37.52	34.72	33.34	34.10	34.32	33.06	34.26	31.35	29.95	30.78	37.92
84	Lao P.D.R.	30.35	29.31	28.08	27.52	27.37	28.33	26.53	25.78	25.29	25.73	24.10	25.00	30.25
85	Latvia	22.05	19.93	18.13	17.04	18.27	21.16	20.41	18.67	17.32	16.68	15.92	16.62	22.23
86	Lebanon	31.71	32.10	33.05	31.39	28.09	26.02	24.63	25.51	25.67	27.96	29.06	29.16	31.58
87	Lesotho	31.05	31.86	30.89	30.07	28.68	29.85	28.81	28.20	27.79	26.71	24.56	32.32	31.28
88	Liberia	41.31	42.47	39.95	42.71	43.09	43.45	41.57	41.52	42.23	42.37	42.45	43.67	43.24
89	Libya	31.29	29.51	28.30	27.02	25.86	27.88	27.05	38.76	32.79	34.75	37.91	38.27	33.62
90	Lithuania	25.69	23.88	22.38	20.58	20.28	24.29	23.13	20.86	19.32	18.30	17.62	18.65	25.15
91	Luxembourg	10.67	10.72	10.33	9.37	9.65	11.01	10.37	10.34	10.80	10.65	10.39	10.38	10.67
92	Madagascar	39.87	40.98	41.34	42.68	38.70	43.33	44.98	45.02	44.30	46.27	44.84	45.29	42.56
93	Malawi	38.76	38.76	39.40	37.34	36.75	38.01	36.39	37.29	36.05	35.09	34.28	33.56	38.51
94	Malaysia	30.59	29.77	29.21	31.23	30.03	31.71	30.17	29.82	29.78	29.84	26.41	26.07	31.49
95	Maldives	26.83	27.82	30.09	27.92	24.85	25.80	25.28	24.39	24.49	24.21	23.41	20.65	27.44
96	Mali	41.00	39.04	36.21	36.86	35.08	36.67	33.28	34.22	31.49	31.40	30.88	29.45	38.70
97	Malta	31.92	30.84	28.69	26.96	27.30	30.55	29.19	28.06	27.25	27.15	28.08	29.43	29.80
98	Mauritania	36.50	33.26	27.78	27.81	28.67	29.90	28.39	27.03	25.42	24.45	24.38	25.75	32.29
99	Mauritius	23.06	23.05	22.49	20.85	19.24	21.18	20.83	19.67	19.24	20.28	19.62	19.23	22.57
100	Mexico	29.81	29.47	28.53	30.65	29.82	32.65	31.15	30.25	29.52	30.05	29.14	28.07	31.74
101	Moldova	42.90	41.60	43.84	41.50	40.89	45.06	43.52	41.05	40.84	39.26	37.35	39.68	43.43
102	Mongolia	17.31	17.22	16.77	16.89	15.90	16.37	16.35	13.69	13.69	13.04	12.02	13.20	17.28
103	Morocco	33.92	34.30	32.27	30.94	28.68	30.93	29.37	28.98	29.83	29.79	29.18	27.13	34.01
104	Mozambique	36.36	35.16	34.26	33.53	33.16	32.84	31.50	31.37	30.13	31.46	31.71	30.98	37.20
105	Myanmar	43.91	39.86	48.41	46.38	48.89	49.30	48.60	47.56	45.49	43.93	43.30	50.99	51.39
106	Namibia	28.68	28.21	26.00	25.11	23.96	24.54	24.79	23.46	22.85	22.85	22.23	21.78	28.07
107	Nepal	36.86	37.60	36.24	36.59	37.09	38.02	36.48	35.70	35.98	33.46	33.42	30.22	37.50
108	Netherlands	11.36	11.12	10.94	10.55	9.58	8.90	8.60	8.09	8.11	8.44	8.75	7.83	10.77

(continued)

ANNEX TABLE 1.1.1. ***(continued)***

Size of the Shadow Economy, 158 Selected Economies, 1991–2015

2. 2004–15

No.	Economy	2004	2005	2006	2007	2008	2009	2010	2011	2012	2013	2014	2015	Average
109	New Zealand	11.07	11.53	11.72	10.57	10.76	11.66	11.62	10.19	10.33	10.09	9.33	8.97	11.70
110	Nicaragua	43.72	41.78	42.11	41.40	41.79	42.91	42.76	40.90	40.12	38.47	38.58	39.51	42.63
111	Niger	42.76	42.33	40.95	41.45	39.27	38.94	35.85	36.51	35.77	35.48	35.74	34.12	39.70
112	Nigeria	56.72	55.84	51.95	54.96	53.06	53.98	52.80	51.51	51.56	51.70	50.64	52.49	56.67
113	Norway	13.52	12.90	11.29	11.03	10.47	14.37	14.05	13.63	13.32	13.64	13.35	15.07	14.07
114	Oman	19.90	20.38	19.55	18.18	15.52	16.83	16.76	17.65	18.25	19.07	21.07	23.91	19.93
115	Pakistan	33.87	31.19	30.94	30.84	30.49	31.28	30.28	30.91	31.12	30.62	30.29	31.62	33.10
116	Papua New Guinea	35.67	37.81	37.24	35.29	35.14	33.83	32.20	28.49	27.07	26.32	23.25	35.16	34.01
117	Paraguay	36.34	35.42	35.19	33.96	32.34	36.18	31.72	30.65	33.87	30.78	29.42	31.66	34.47
118	Peru	53.50	54.68	51.36	48.83	46.08	47.70	43.04	40.42	39.73	39.53	40.18	41.53	52.40
119	Philippines	39.87	36.50	36.18	36.37	35.08	37.02	34.63	33.90	33.61	31.71	29.30	28.04	39.31
120	Poland	25.84	25.32	24.18	23.51	21.65	21.56	20.93	19.33	19.04	18.86	18.09	16.67	25.10
121	Portugal	22.26	22.68	22.69	22.05	20.74	21.67	20.79	20.37	20.24	20.38	19.29	17.82	21.88
122	Qatar	16.67	17.25	15.33	15.36	15.39	16.69	14.56	12.72	12.28	12.15	12.31	13.08	15.93
123	Romania	30.57	30.49	28.88	27.03	25.44	28.23	26.76	25.41	25.14	23.97	22.73	22.94	30.14
124	Russian Federation	37.68	36.41	35.47	34.59	32.6	36.79	33.70	32.03	31.88	32.21	31.04	33.72	38.42
125	Rwanda	36.16	39.23	37.79	35.44	32.73	32.48	31.50	29.53	28.47	27.56	26.68	28.05	36.25
126	Saudi Arabia	17.38	16.63	16.27	15.03	13.76	15.07	14.37	13.97	13.34	13.60	13.88	14.70	16.65
127	Senegal	40.00	37.74	39.84	37.16	36.06	39.37	38.36	40.20	37.59	37.21	35.91	33.68	43.35
128	Sierra Leone	43.88	43.45	42.96	40.92	40.87	40.60	39.34	36.12	32.36	25.69	26.47	34.18	41.50
129	Singapore	11.74	11.13	10.88	11.51	10.72	11.87	10.72	10.13	9.90	10.15	9.90	9.20	11.90
130	Slovak Republic	15.37	14.50	13.52	12.15	11.52	13.47	12.84	11.96	11.81	11.75	11.64	11.18	15.33
131	Slovenia	23.25	22.70	20.94	17.96	17.58	22.24	22.54	22.18	22.89	23.02	21.49	20.21	24.09
132	Solomon Islands	36.03	36.04	35.32	32.52	30.25	32.56	30.15	27.38	27.08	26.88	27.44	30.89	30.41
133	South Africa	26.58	25.44	21.33	21.81	20.35	23.41	23.23	22.08	22.20	21.47	21.33	21.99	25.94
134	Spain	23.47	23.32	22.96	22.67	21.53	24.24	23.91	23.65	24.08	24.35	24.04	22.01	24.52
135	Sri Lanka	45.63	45.93	46.17	47.55	46.35	48.85	41.88	39.33	37.53	38.14	37.02	35.49	45.58

(continued)

ANNEX TABLE 1.1.1. ***(continued)***

Size of the Shadow Economy, 158 Selected Economies, 1991–2015

2. 2004–15

No.	Economy	2004	2005	2006	2007	2008	2009	2010	2011	2012	2013	2014	2015	Average
136	Suriname	33.21	31.42	29.60	27.57	26.38	26.89	25.18	23.00	23.14	22.46	22.65	23.80	32.22
137	Sweden	12.06	12.32	11.14	10.12	10.30	12.71	11.45	11.08	11.89	12.31	11.88	11.74	13.28
138	Switzerland	7.54	7.30	6.96	6.34	6.16	7.06	6.76	6.62	6.66	6.56	6.39	6.94	7.24
139	Syria	17.98	17.15	16.53	15.65	20.81	19.21	19.39	21.50	22.18	22.79	22.24	19.53	19.58
140	Taiwan, Province of China	32.04	31.43	31.45	31.32	30.12	28.89	28.22	28.00	28.02	28.01	26.88	28.97	32.50
141	Tajikistan	43.52	44.48	43.37	42.19	41.20	42.80	42.13	41.59	38.80	39.63	36.54	37.73	42.99
142	Tanzania	53.00	51.40	54.32	48.78	47.18	49.49	46.73	44.08	44.29	44.04	40.45	38.91	52.22
143	Thailand	49.45	48.70	48.24	48.11	47.84	51.22	48.65	47.88	46.67	46.74	47.25	43.12	50.63
144	Togo	38.24	38.93	38.14	37.27	38.40	37.53	35.90	35.12	35.09	34.16	33.52	31.49	37.31
145	Trinidad and Tobago	31.56	30.23	27.41	27.43	26.15	30.04	29.85	28.11	28.92	29.36	29.90	31.40	34.37
146	Tunisia	34.43	33.98	31.49	29.27	27.16	29.12	27.83	33.85	31.97	32.94	33.08	30.90	35.31
147	Turkey	30.80	29.77	29.47	30.38	29.14	32.33	30.21	27.65	28.03	27.33	27.45	27.43	31.38
148	Uganda	40.34	39.18	38.25	36.41	34.46	34.88	34.87	34.63	32.28	32.46	32.75	31.88	38.74
149	Ukraine	41.96	42.08	40.89	38.71	36.65	43.53	42.15	39.19	39.65	39.99	39.95	42.90	44.80
150	United Arab Emirates	27.53	27.99	28.81	27.36	26.77	25.54	25.09	23.92	23.11	22.44	22.02	24.26	26.54
151	United Kingdom	11.43	11.39	10.44	10.78	9.83	11.00	10.33	10.06	9.91	9.57	8.81	8.32	11.08
152	United States	8.43	7.86	7.47	8.00	7.76	9.18	8.71	8.23	7.83	7.66	7.04	7.00	8.34
153	Uruguay	40.74	39.93	39.92	31.94	30.20	30.72	27.32	25.68	23.25	22.49	20.59	20.38	37.91
154	Venezuela	36.21	33.05	32.16	31.55	31.13	35.15	33.50	32.65	32.12	31.74	32.65	33.63	33.81
155	Vietnam	18.40	17.18	17.64	17.13	16.99	17.4	17.18	16.09	15.79	15.82	15.06	14.78	18.70
156	Yemen	24.38	23.46	23.18	23.29	23.31	22.94	23.57	32.07	31.98	31.07	27.61	28.81	28.34
157	Zambia	47.60	49.01	48.52	45.54	43.22	42.17	34.47	36.61	33.38	30.83	30.72	32.99	45.32
158	Zimbabwe	63.50	63.16	60.58	60.42	61.66	69.08	65.62	63.89	63.69	64.55	65.85	67.00	60.64
	Average	*31.79*	*31.24*	*30.41*	*29.69*	*28.98*	*30.56*	*29.42*	*28.77*	*28.33*	*28.05*	*27.44*	*27.78*	*31.77*

Source: Authors.

Annex Figure 1.1.1. Estimation of the Shadow Economy Using the MIMIC Model

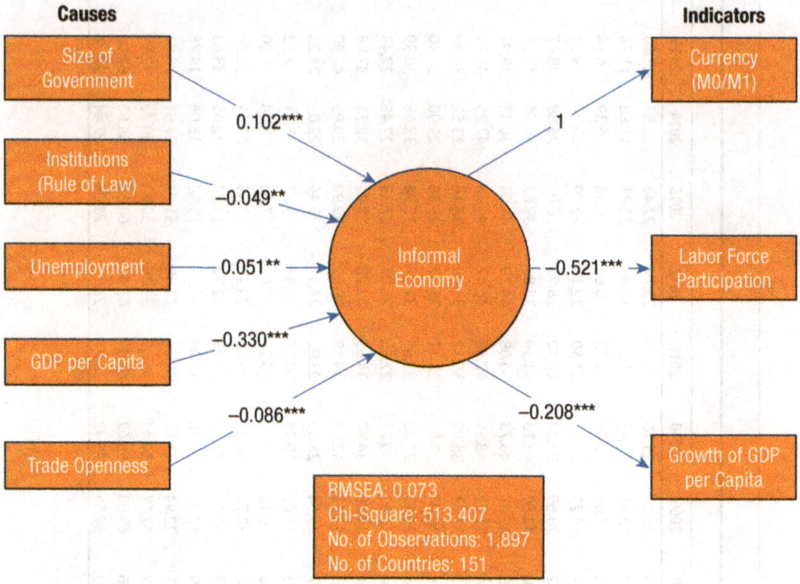

Source: Authors.
Note: MIMIC = multiple indicators, multiple causes; RMSEA = root mean square error of approximation. $^{**}p < 0.05$; $^{***}p < 0.01$.

Annex Figure 1.1.2. MIMIC Estimation Using the Night Lights Approach

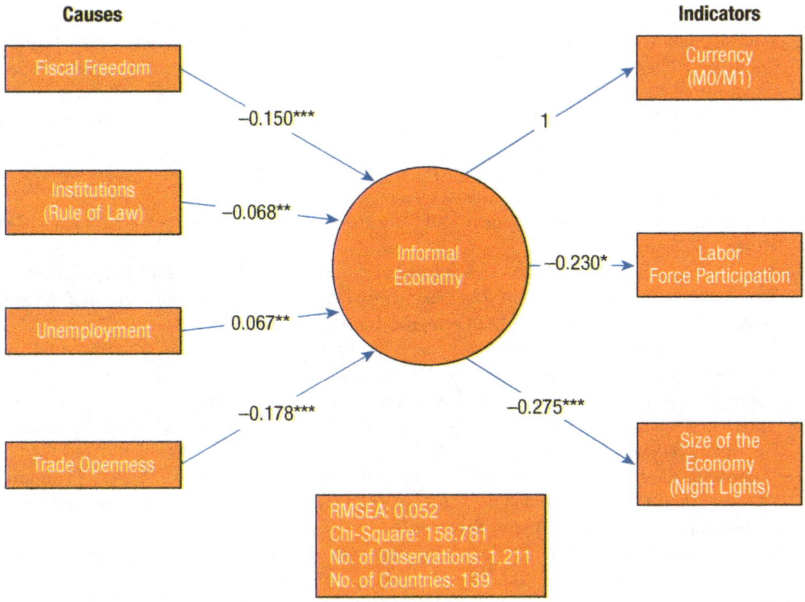

Source: Authors.
Note: MIMIC = multiple indicators, multiple causes; RMSEA = root mean square error of approximation.
$^*p < 0.1$; $^{**}p < 0.05$; $^{***}p < 0.01$.

REFERENCES

Abdih, Y., and L. Medina. 2013. "Measuring the Informal Economy in the Caucasus and Central Asia." IMF Working Paper 13/137, International Monetary Fund, Washington, DC.

Alm, J., and A. Embaye. 2013. "Using Dynamic Panel Models to Estimate Shadow Economies around the World, 1984–2006." Working Paper 1303, Tulane University, Department of Economics, New Orleans, Louisiana.

Amendola, A., and R. Dell'Anno. 2010. "Institutions and Human Development in the Latin America Shadow Economy." *Estudios en Derecho y Gobierno* 3 (1): 9–25.

Andreoni, J., B. Erard, and J. Feinstein. 1998. "Tax Compliance." *Journal of Economic Literature* 36 (4): 818–60.

Boeschoten, W. C., and M. M. G. Fase. 1984. *The Volume of Payments and the Informal Economy in the Netherlands, 1965–1982*. Dordrecht, Netherlands: M. Nijhoff.

Breusch, T. 2005a. "The Canadian Underground Economy: An Examination of Giles and Tedds." *Canadian Tax Journal* 53: 367–91.

Breusch, T. 2005b. "Estimating the Underground Economy Using MIMIC Models." Department of Economics Working Paper 0607, Johannes Kepler University of Linz, Linz, Austria.

Breusch, T. 2016. "Estimating the Underground Economy Using MIMIC Models." *Journal of Tax Administration* 2 (1).

Buehn, A., A. Karmann, and F. Schneider. 2009. "Shadow Economy and Do-It-Yourself Activities: The German Case." *Journal of Institutional and Theoretical Economics* 165 (4): 701–22.

Buehn, A., and F. Schneider. 2013. "Size and Development of Tax Evasion in 38 OECD Countries: What Do We (Not) Know?" Department of Economics Discussion Paper, University of Linz, Linz, Austria.

Cagan, P. 1958. "The Demand for Currency Relative to the Total Money Supply." *Journal of Political Economy* 66: 302–28.

Contini, B. 1981. "Labor Market Segmentation and the Development of the Parallel Economy: The Italian Experience." *Oxford Economic Papers* 33: 401–12.

Del Boca, D. 1981. "Parallel Economy and Allocation of Time." *Micros (Quarterly Journal of Microeconomics)* 4: 13–18.

Del Boca, D., and F. Forte. 1982. "Recent Empirical Surveys and Theoretical Interpretations of the Parallel Economy in Italy." In *The Underground Economy in the United States and Abroad*, edited by V. Tanzi. Lexington, MA: Lexington Books.

Dell'Anno, R. 2007. "The Shadow Economy in Portugal: An Analysis with the MIMIC Approach." *Journal of Applied Economics* 10: 253–77.

Dell'Anno, R., M. Gomez-Antonio, and A. Alanon Pardo. 2007. "Shadow Economy in Three Different Mediterranean Countries: France, Spain and Greece—A MIMIC Approach." *Empirical Economics* 33: 51–84.

Dell'Anno, R., and F. Schneider. 2009. "A Complex Approach to Estimate Shadow Economy: The Structural Equation Modelling." In *Coping with the Complexity of Economics*, edited by M. Faggnini and T. Looks. Berlin: Springer.

Dreher, A., and F. Schneider. 2009. "Corruption and the Shadow Economy: An Empirical Analysis." *Public Choice* 144 (2): 215–77.

Dreher, A., C. Kotsogiannis, and S. McCorriston. 2009. "How Do Institutions Affect Corruption and the Shadow Economy?" *International Tax and Public Finance* 16 (4): 773–96.

Dybka, P., M. Kowalczuk, B. Olesinski, M. Rozkrut, and A. Torój. 2017. "Currency Demand and MIMIC Models: Towards a Structured Hybrid Model-Based Estimation of the Shadow Economy Size." Discussion paper presented at the 5th International Conference on the Shadow Economy, Tax Evasion and Informal Labor, Warsaw School of Economics, Institute of Econometrics, July 27–30.

Elgin, C., and O. Öztunali. 2012. "Shadow Economies around the World: Model Based Estimates." Boğaziçi University Working Paper, 2012/05, Istanbul, Turkey.

Enste, D., and F. Schneider. 2006. "Umfang und Entwicklung der Schattenwirtschaft in 145 Ländern." In *Jahrbuch Schattenwirtschaft 2006/07*, edited by F. Schneider and D. Enste. Berlin: LIT Publishing.

Feige, E. L. 1979. "How Big Is the Irregular Economy?" *Challenge* 22 (5): 5–13.

Feige, E. L. 1996. "Overseas Holdings of U.S. Currency and the Underground Economy." In *Exploring the Underground Economy*, edited by S. Pozo, 5–62. Kalamazoo, MI: W.E. Upjohn Institute for Employment Research.

Feige, E. L. 2016a. "Reflections on the Meaning and Measurement of Unobserved Economies: What Do We Really Know about the 'Shadow Economy'?" *Journal of Tax Administration* 2 (2).

Feige, E. L. 2016b. "Professor Schneider's Shadow Economy (SSE): What Do We Really Know? A Rejoinder." *Journal of Tax Administration* 2 (2).

Feld, L. P., and B. S. Frey. 2007. "Tax Compliance as the Result of a Psychological Tax Contract: The Role of Incentives and Responsive Regulation." *Law and Policy* 29 (1): 102–20.

Feld, L. P., and C. Larsen. 2005. "Black Activities in Germany in 2001 and 2004: A Comparison Based on Survey Data." Research Unit Study 12, Rockwool Foundation, Copenhagen.

Feld, L. P., and C. Larsen. 2009. *Undeclared Work, Deterrence and Social Norms: The Case of Germany*. Berlin: Springer.

Feld, L., and F. Schneider. 2010. "Survey on the Shadow Economy and Undeclared Earnings in OECD Countries." *German Economic Review* 11 (2): 109–49.

Feld, L., and F. Schneider. 2016. "Reply to Gebhard Kirchgaessner." *German Economic Review* 18 (1): 112–17.

Frey, B., and H. Weck-Hanneman. 1984. "The Hidden Economy as 'Unobserved Variable.'" *European Economic Review* 26: 33–53.

Friedman, E., S. Johnson, D. Kaufmann, and P. Zoido-Lobatón. 2000. "Dodging the Grabbing Hand: The Determinants of Unofficial Activity in 69 Countries." *Journal of Public Economics* 76 (4): 459–93.

Gerxhani, K. 2003. "The Informal Sector in Developed and Less-Developed Countries: A Literature Survey." *Public Choice* 114 (3–4): 295–318.

Giles, D. E. A. 1999. "Measuring the Hidden Economy: Implications for Econometric Modelling." *Economic Journal* 109 (3): 370–80.

Gutmann, P. M. 1977. "The Subterranean Economy." *Financial Analysts Journal* 34 (1): 24–27.

Gyomai, G., and P. van de Ven. 2014. "The Non-Observed Economy in the System of National Accounts." Statistics Brief 18, Organisation for Economic Co-operation and Development, Paris.

Hashimzade, N., and C. Heady. 2016. "Reflections on the Meaning and Measurement of Unobserved Economies: An Editorial Comment." *Journal of Tax Administration* 2 (2).

Hassan, M., and F. Schneider. 2016. "Size and Development of the Shadow Economies of 157 Worldwide Countries: Updated and New Measures from 1999 to 2013." *Journal of Global Economics* 4: 3.

Henderson, V. J., A. Storeygard, and D. N. Weil. 2012. "Measuring Economic Growth from Outer Space." *American Economic Review* 102 (2): 994–1028.

Johnson, S., D. Kaufmann, and A. Shleifer. 1997. "The Unofficial Economy in Transition." *Brookings Papers on Economic Activity*, Fall.

Johnson, S., D. Kaufmann, and P. Zoido-Lobatón. 1998a. "Corruption, Public Finances and the Unofficial Economy." World Bank Policy Research Working Paper 2169, World Bank, Washington, DC.

Johnson, S., D. Kaufmann, and P. Zoido-Lobatón. 1998b. "Regulatory Discretion and the Unofficial Economy." *American Economic Review* 88 (2): 387–92.

Joreskog, K., and A. S. Goldberger. 1975. "Estimation of a Model with a Multiple Indicators and Multiple Causes of a Single Latent Variable." *Journal of American Statistical Association* 70: 631–39.

Kaufmann, D., and A. Kaliberda. 1996. "Integrating the Unofficial Economy into the Dynamics of Post Socialist Economies: A Framework of Analyses and Evidence." In *Economic Transition in Russia and the New States of Eurasia*, edited by B. Kaminski. London: M. E. Sharpe.

Kirchgaessner, G. 2016. "On Estimating the Size of the Shadow Economy." *German Economic Review* 18 (1): 99–111.

Kirchler, E. 2007. *The Economic Psychology of Tax Behaviour.* Cambridge: Cambridge University Press.

Kucera, D., and L. Roncolato. 2008. "Informal Employment: Two Contested Policy Issues." *International Labor Review* 147 (3): 321–48.

Langfeldt, E. 1984. "The Unobserved Economy in the Federal Republic of Germany. In *The Unobserved Economy*, edited by E. L. Feige. Cambridge: Cambridge University Press.

Lichard, T., J. Hanousek, and R. K. Filer. 2014. "Hidden in Plain Sight: Using Household Data to Measure the Shadow Economy." Prague CEPR Discussion Paper 10483, Prague.

Lichard, T. 2012. "Shadow Economy in the Czech Republic, Russia, Slovakia and Ukraine: Food Engel Curve Approach." Unpublished report.

Little, R. J. A., and D. B. Rubin. 2002. *Statistical Analysis with Missing Data*, 2nd edition. Hoboken, NJ: John Wiley & Sons, Inc.

Loayza, N. V. 1996. "The Economics of the Informal Sector: A Simple Model and Some Empirical Evidence from Latin America." *Carnegie-Rochester Conference Series on Public Policy* 45: 129–62.

Losby, J. L., J. F. Else, M. E. Kingslow, E. L. Edgcomb, E. T. Malm, and V. Kao. 2002. "Informal Economy Literature Review." Aspen Institute, Microenterprise Fund for Innovation, Effectiveness, Learning and Dissemination, Washington DC, and ISED Consulting and Research, Newark, DE.

MacAfee, K. 1980. "A Glimpse of the Hidden Economy in the National Accounts." *Economic Trends* 136: 81–87.

Medina, L., A. Jonelis, and M. Cangul. 2017. "The Informal Economy in Sub-Saharan Africa: Size and Determinants." IMF Working Paper 17/156, International Monetary Fund, Washington, DC.

O'Neill, D. M. 1983. "Growth of the Underground Economy 1950–81: Some Evidence from the Current Population Survey." In *Study for the Joint Economic Committee*, US Congress Joint Committee Print. Washington, DC: US Government Printing Office.

Organization for Economic Co-operation and Development (OECD). 2010. *Measuring the Non-observed Economy: A Handbook.* Paris: OECD.

Pedersen, S. 2003. "The Shadow Economy in Germany, Great Britain and Scandinavia: A Measurement Based on Questionnaire Service." Study 10, Rockwool Foundation Research Unit, Copenhagen.

Portes, A. 1996. "The Informal Economy." In *Exploring the Underground Economy*, edited by S. Pozo. Kalamazoo, MI: W.E. Upjohn Institute for Employment Research.

Putnins, T., and A. Sauka. 2015. "Measuring the Shadow Economy Using Company Managers." *Journal of Comparative Issues* 43 (2): 471–90.

Quintano, C., and P. Mazzocchi. 2010. "Some Alternative Estimates of Underground Economies in 12 New EU Member States." *International Economic Journal* 24 (4): 413–35.

Reilly, B., and G. Krstic. 2018. "Shadow Economy: Is an Enterprise Survey a Preferable Approach?" *Panoeconomicus* 66 (5): 589–610.

Rubin, D. B. 1987. *Multiple Imputation for Nonresponse in Surveys.* Hoboken, NJ: Wiley.

Ruge, M. 2010. "Determinants and the Size of the Shadow Economy – A Structural Equation Model." *International Economic Journal* 24 (4): 382–404.

Schneider, F. 1997. "The Shadow Economies of Western Europe." *Journal of the Institute of Economic Affairs* 17 (3): 42–48.

Schneider, F. 2003. "The Shadow Economy." In *Encyclopedia of Public Choice*, edited by C. K. Rowley and F. Schneider. Dordrecht, Netherlands: Kluwer Academic Publishers.

Schneider, F. 2005. "Shadow Economies around the World: What Do We Really Know?" *European Journal of Political Economy* 21 (4): 598–642.

Schneider, F. 2010. "The Influence of Public Institutions on the Shadow Economy: An Empirical Investigation for OECD Countries." *European Journal of Law and Economics* 6 (3): 441–68.

Schneider, F., ed. 2011. *Handbook on the Shadow Economy*. Cheltenham, UK: Elgar.

Schneider, F. 2015. "Schattenwirtschaft und Schattenarbeitsmarkt: Die Entwicklungen der vergangenen 20 Jahre." *Perspektiven der Wirtschaftspolitik* 16 (1): 3–25.

Schneider, F. 2016. "Comment on Feige's Paper 'Reflections on the Meaning and Measurement of Unobserved Economies: What Do We Really Know about the Shadow Economy?'" *Journal of Tax Administration* 2 (2): 82–92.

Schneider, F. 2017. "Estimating a Shadow Economy: Results, Methods, Problems, and Open Questions." *Open Economics* 1 (1): 1–29.

Schneider, F., A. Buehn, and C. E. Montenegro. 2010. "New Estimates for the Shadow Economies All over the World." *International Economic Journal* 24 (4): 443–61.

Schneider, F., and D. Enste. 2002. *The Shadow Economy: Theoretical Approaches, Empirical Studies, and Political Implications.* Cambridge: Cambridge University Press.

Schneider, F., and C. C. Williams. 2013. *The Shadow Economy*. London: IEA.

Schneider, F., and D. Teobaldelli. 2012. "Beyond the Veil of Ignorance: The Influence of Direct Democracy on the Shadow Economy." CESifo Working Paper Series 3749, CESifo.

Slemrod, J., and C. Weber. 2012. "Evidence of the Invisible: Toward a Credibility Revolution in the Empirical Analysis of Tax Evasion and the Informal Economy." *International Tax and Public Finance* 19 (1): 25–53.

Tanzi, V. 1980. "The Underground Economy in the United States: Estimates and Implications." *Banca Nazionale del Lavoro* 135: 427–53.

Tanzi, V. 1983. "The Underground Economy in the United States: Annual Estimates, 1930–1980." *IMF Staff Papers* 30: 283–305.

Tanzi, V. 1999. "Uses and Abuses of Estimates of the Underground Economy." *Economic Journal* 109 (3): 338–47.

Teobaldelli, D. 2011. "Federalism and the Shadow Economy." *Public Choice* 146 (3): 269–89.

Thomas, J. J. 1992. *Informal Economic Activity*. London School of Economics Handbooks in Economics. London: Harvester Wheatsheaf.

Torgler, B., and F. Schneider. 2009. "The Impact of Tax Morale and Institutional Quality on the Shadow Economy." *Journal of Economic Psychology* 30 (3): 228–45.

van de Ven, P. 2017. "The Non-Observed Economy in the System of National Accounts." First published in OECD Statistics Brief, June 2014, No. 18; then presented at a workshop about informal economy in the OECD, Paris.

Vuletin, G. J. 2008. "Measuring the Informal Economy in Latin America and the Caribbean." IMF Working Paper 08/102, International Monetary Fund, Washington, DC.

Williams, C. C., and F. Schneider. 2016. *Measuring the Global Shadow Economy: The Prevalence of Informal Work and Labour.* Cheltenham, UK: Elgar.

Yoo, T., and J. K. Hyun. 1998. "International Comparison of the Black Economy: Empirical Evidence Using Micro-Level Data." Paper presented at the 1998 Congress of the International Institute of Public Finance, Córdoba, Argentina.

Zellner, A. 1970. "Estimation of Regression Relationships Containing Unobservable Independent Variables." *International Economic Review* 11 (3): 441–54.

Zukauskas V., and F. Schneider 2016. "Microbased Results of Shadow Labor Market in the Baltic States, Poland and Sweden." *Applied Economics: Systematic Research* 10 (2): 117–33.

CHAPTER 2

Europe's Shadow Economies: Estimating Size and Outlining Policy Options

Ben Kelmanson, Koralai Kirabaeva, and Leandro Medina

INTRODUCTION

Informality has declined across Europe but remains significant, especially in emerging market economies. As a share of formal GDP, shadow economies have been broadly stable, although on a slightly declining trend over the past 20 years, with the exception of the global financial crisis. On average, shadow economies are around 15 to 25 percent of GDP in the European Union. For advanced European economies, the shadow economy averages 15 to 20 percent, whereas it is more prevalent in emerging market economies, amounting to around 30 to 40 percent of GDP and a much larger share still in some Commonwealth of Independent States (CIS) countries (Schneider 2015; Hassan and Schneider 2016; Medina and Schneider 2018; Kelmanson and others 2019).

Although shadow activities can act as a source of supplemental or otherwise unavailable income, they exist partly because of inefficiencies and other factors in the broader economy. Such activities have significant economic and social implications across several dimensions. Shadow economy activity often goes untaxed and therefore weakens public revenues, resulting in suboptimal provision of public goods. Larger shadow economies tend to be associated with high and persistent unemployment rates and low labor force participation (Schneider 2013). Having a large number of workers in the shadow economy makes it more difficult for a country to target effective labor policies. Operating informally tends to limit firms' growth below the efficient scale of production, impeding productivity and innovation. The costs of the shadow economy also include lowering provision of and access to financing, reducing human and physical capital accumulation, and undermining growth prospects. Large shadow economies can distort economic indicators, possibly leading to misdiagnoses and flawed policy choices. Although

This chapter provides an overview of results and policy recommendations from Kelmanson and others (2019) and presents updated estimates of the shadow economies in Europe, with the sample period extended to 2019.

it is too early to assess the effect of the coronavirus disease 2019 (COVID-19) on the shadow economy in Europe, governments should consider its size and nature when designing policy responses.

The size of the shadow economy tends to be smaller in more developed countries, both as the share of GDP and as a share of employment. The share of shadow economic activity is strongly negatively associated with income per capita across different country samples and time periods. In more advanced economies, the shadow economy is dominated by tax evasion and undeclared labor in registered firms (Schneider and Buehn 2012). In contrast, developing economies tend to have a relatively higher share of informal workers (Oviedo 2009).

ESTIMATES OF THE SHADOW ECONOMY IN EUROPE

The hidden nature of informal activity makes it—by definition—challenging to measure accurately. Alternative concepts of the shadow economy encompass a wide range of phenomena. Some definitions focus on hidden output (Gerxhani 2004), and others on hidden employment (Hussmanns 2004; Perry 2007). Although unregistered firms hide all their output, registered firms may choose to hide a fraction of their output to reduce tax liability. We follow the definition of the shadow economy used by Schneider and others (Schneider and Williams 2013; Schneider 2014; Hassan and Schneider 2016) as being mostly legal and productive economic activities deliberately hidden from official authorities that, if recorded, would contribute to GDP (excluding illegal or criminal activities and do-it-yourself, charitable, or household activities). We use "informality" interchangeably with "shadow economy."

We update the estimates of the size of shadow economies from Kelmanson and others (2019) for 47 European countries, extending the period from 2016 to 2019, using the multiple indicators, multiple causes (MIMIC) model. In MIMIC the size of the shadow economy is represented by a latent variable (an index), with its causes and indicators observed and measured. This latent variable is used in a system of two equations: (1) as the dependent variable with its causes as the explanatory variables and (2) as the explanatory variable for the indicators of informality. The equations are simultaneously estimated, and the fitted values of the latent variable are used to estimate the size of the shadow economy as a share of GDP.[1] Causal variables are productivity (GDP per worker), tax revenues, trade volume, and agriculture value added, and indicator variables are GDP growth, labor force participation rate, and investment.[2]

The share of the shadow economy remains significant in many European countries, ranging from less than 10 percent to about 40 percent of GDP (Figure 2.1).

[1] Kelmanson and others (2019) discuss other estimation methods, as well as strengths and weaknesses of the MIMIC approach.

[2] Kelmanson and others (2019) also use *government effectiveness* as an alternative input variable.

Figure 2.1. The Size of the Shadow Economy in European Countries, 2019
(Percent of GDP)

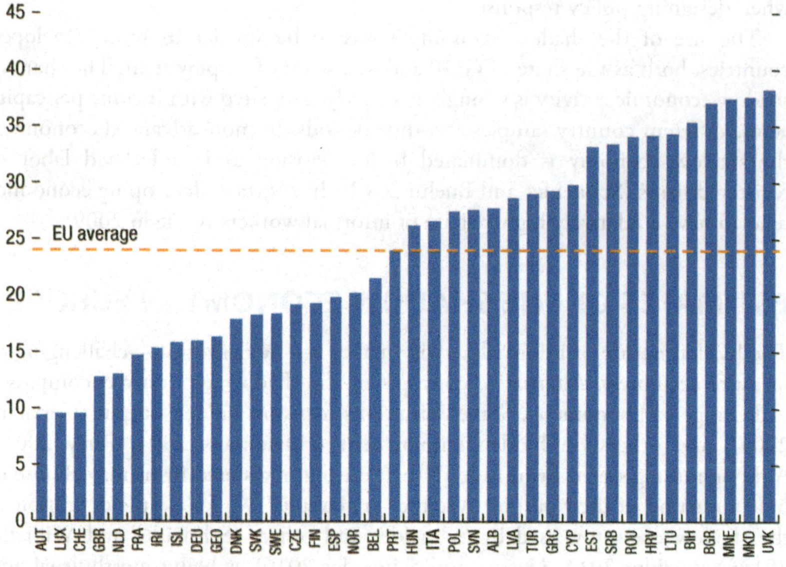

Source: IMF staff calculations.
Note: Data labels use International Organization for Standardization country codes.

The average size of the shadow economy in the European Union[3] is 23 percent and in the euro area is close to 22 percent. Emerging economies tend to have larger shadow economies, around 33 percent on average. In many CIS countries, the shadow economy is around 35 to 40 percent of GDP and even higher in some cases.

Although the average size of the shadow economy in Europe remained broadly stable until the global financial crisis, the dynamics were heterogeneous across countries. The shadow economy has grown since the early 2000s in some Balkan and CIS countries and declined in others, such as Germany, the former Yugoslav Republic of Macedonia, and the Slovak Republic.

Shadow economies tended to peak around 2008 to 2010 at the time of the global financial crisis and then decline to around precrisis levels. Most countries experienced an uptick in shadow activity of around 1 to 2 percent of GDP (Figure 2.2).

The shadow economy appears to be weakly countercyclical in most countries. For example, for the euro area, the correlations between shadow economy and

[3] The United Kingdom is included in the analysis because it was a part of the European Union in 2019.

Figure 2.2. The Size of the Shadow Economy in Europe, the Euro Area, and the European Union, 2000–19
(Percent of GDP)

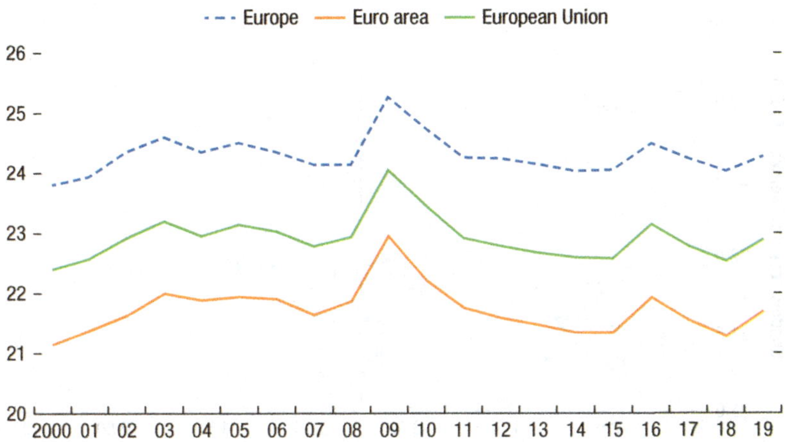

Source: IMF staff calculations.

output gap estimates are negative (Figure 2.3); however, a few countries (Czech Republic, Greece, Slovenia, Spain) show a positive correlation.[4]

Estimates of the shadow economy here are broadly in line with the literature. The estimates are close to Hassan and Schneider (2016)[5] but less volatile, reflecting a greater contribution from institutional factors and economic structure (for example, trade openness and share of agriculture), which tend to change slowly over time. Schneider (2015) has lower averages for EU and euro area countries (17.8 percent and 15.8 percent for 2015, respectively), although the sample is missing the Slovak Republic. The estimates of Medina and Schneider (2018) for 2017 EU and euro area averages are 16.0 percent and 15.5 percent, respectively. For 2015 estimates are 16.7 percent and 14.7 percent, respectively.

The estimates for the CIS group appear to be more sensitive to estimation specifications, with the divergence especially pronounced in the early 2000s; however, the recent dynamics are broadly similar. Medina and Schneider (2018) estimate the shadow economy in CIS countries to be 39.2 percent on average in 2017 (40.6 percent in 2016). The difference in the estimates for the CIS economy could be affected by data limitations as well as changes in data-collection methodology and data-processing techniques from the late 1990s to the early

[4] Output gap estimates are from the IMF's World Economic Outlook database, October 2019.

[5] We used estimates for 2000 from Hassan and Schneider (2016) as initial values in our analysis. Their paper has the most comprehensive coverage of the European countries. Schneider (2015) covers only EU economies, and Medina and Schneider (2018) are missing several emerging European countries in their sample.

Figure 2.3. Shadow Economy and Output Gap Estimates of the Euro Area, 1999–2019
(Percent of GDP)

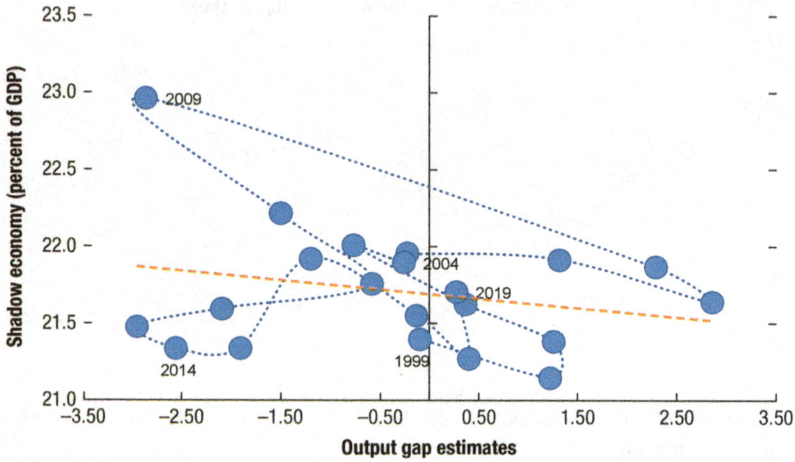

Source: IMF staff calculations.

2000s.[6] Also, while the absolute values of the MIMIC estimations can be sensitive to the sample and variables used, the relative ranking is more robust (Table 2.1).

There is also a trade-off between sample homogeneity and sample size. Focusing on European economies allows us to capture more relevant factors in

TABLE 2.1.

Various MIMIC Estimations of the Size of the Shadow Economy in Europe, 2013, 2016, and 2019
(Percent of GDP)

	2013			2016		2019
	Updated Results	Kelmanson and Others 2019	Hassan and Schneider 2016	Updated Results	Kelmanson and Others 2019	Updated Results
Sample average	28.1	28.5	30.1	28.4	28.5	28.1
Europe (excluding CIS)	24.1	24.8	25.2	24.5	24.8	24.3
Advanced economies	20.0	20.7	20.5	20.4	20.7	20.2
Emerging market economies	33.6	34.1	33.9	33.7	34.0	33.6
European Union	22.7	23.4	23.2	23.1	23.5	22.9
Euro area	21.3	22.2	22.6	21.9	22.3	21.7
CIS	41.3	40.9	51.6	41.3	40.8	40.8

Sources: Hassan and Schneider 2016; Kelmanson and others 2019; and IMF staff estimates.
Note: CIS = Commonwealth of Independent States; MIMIC = multiple indicators, multiple causes.

[6] For those reasons, we chose not to report the estimates for the CIS countries in Annex 2.1.

our estimations; however, such focus comes at the expense of the country sample: fewer than 50 countries compared with more than 150 countries in the papers by Schneider and his coauthors. Possibly for this reason, for some countries (especially several advanced economies) the updated estimates appear to be higher than in previous literature, and for some emerging market economies, lower.

DETERMINANTS OF THE SHADOW ECONOMY

A broad literature has explored the determinants of the shadow economy, covering institutional and macroeconomic factors. Kelmanson and others (2019) identified determinants of the shadow economy more relevant for European countries.

We find the following to be important macroeconomic explanatory factors for the evolution of the shadow economy in Europe, including productivity (GDP per worker), government effectiveness, tax revenues, trade volume as a percentage of GDP, and agriculture value added as a percentage of GDP. Institutional factors are also important, notably weak institutional quality (such as excessive regulatory burden), inefficiency of government institutions, weak rule of law, and widespread corruption.

- Regulatory quality is negatively associated with the size of shadow economies. Regulatory burden suppresses entrepreneurial freedom, imposes higher entry costs, and results in more bureaucracy (Dabla-Norris, Gradstein, and Inchauste 2008).
- Weak governance, including corruption and weak judicial systems, are important determinants of the size of the shadow economy, especially in interaction with regulation and other variables. The effect of regulation and financial constraints on informality is stronger with better rule of law (Dabla-Norris, Gradstein, and Inchauste 2008) and when governance levels exceed certain thresholds (for more details, see Oviedo 2009).
- Tax burden and tax administration are also factors that explain the size of the shadow economy. The higher the overall tax burden and the less systematic the monitoring and enforcement, the stronger the incentive for tax evasion and underreporting of wages (Schneider and Williams 2013; Hassan and Schneider 2016). We also find government effectiveness to be negatively associated with the size of the shadow economy.

Similar to prior literature, we find the following macroeconomic factors to have an effect:

- Trade openness is negatively associated with the size of the shadow economy (Torgler and Schneider 2007). Trade is relatively transparent and easier to tax and, therefore, more difficult to conceal for tax and other purposes.
- Countries with higher productivity (GDP per worker) typically have a better allocation of resources within the economy and thus smaller informal sectors (Porta and Shleifer 2008). Productivity could also act as a proxy for a country's development, which is generally correlated with taxation capacity

and demand for public goods and services. As with national income, the relationship between productivity and the size of the shadow economy is endogenous, with causation going both ways. As expected, we find a negative relationship between productivity and the size of the shadow economy.

- Informal work is prevalent in agriculture and related sectors (along with lower enforcement). Contrary to some literature findings (Vuletin 2008; Schneider 2014), we find agriculture value added per GDP to be negatively related to the shadow economy in Europe.[7]
- Shadow economies are associated with lower human capital, with informal workers having fewer skills and less education (Porta and Shleifer 2008; Dabla-Norris, Gradstein, and Inchauste 2008). Human capital accumulation and entrepreneurial talent are held back by lower levels of innovation and productivity in countries with larger shadow economies. Similar to the literature, we find a negative relationship between human capital and the size of the shadow economy.
- Migration and remittances play a dual role with respect to the shadow economy. Migrant workers, like informal workers, tend to reside in rural areas, to have less education, and to be employed more in labor-intensive (less-productive) activities compared with workers in the formal sector. Shadow economic activity and migration also play a similar poverty-reducing role, providing a safety net for the poor. As a result, migration and remittances can be viewed as substitute activities and are therefore negatively related. On the other hand, remittances can encourage informality by providing the capital, or a safety net, to encourage remittance recipients to choose less-secure informal work (Ivlevs 2016). For example, in Moldova some women and young people in families with household members working abroad choose informal employment rather than a formal job (Ganta 2012). In this case, remittances positively contribute to the size of the shadow economy. The ultimate sign of the relationship between the two phenomena depends on which of these two effects is stronger. We find a negative relationship between remittances (share of GDP) and the size of the shadow economy. This suggests that migration and informality can be viewed as substitutes, even though the two phenomena likely have common determinants: weak institutional factors, low human capital, and low productivity.[8]

[7] This is contrary to some literature findings (Vuletin 2008; Schneider 2014); however, the literature focuses predominantly on developing countries. Because about half this sample comprises advanced economies with more developed institutions, including taxation systems, this result could be a function of more efficient—and formalized—agriculture sectors in advanced Europe dominating the sample. In this case, the larger agricultural sector offers more employment opportunities, and we would expect a negative relationship with the size of the shadow economy.

[8] Imposing country fixed effects significantly reduces the explanatory power of these variables, because most do not exhibit strong time variation. Thus, when we control for institutional factors, countries that are more dependent on remittances (and, correspondingly, have higher levels of migration) have smaller shadow economies.

For the full sample, macroeconomic factors appear to be more important than institutional factors. We would expect this given the more highly developed institutions in advanced economies. For emerging economies, however, institutional factors play a stronger role, although productivity is still important. This is also to be expected, given that institutions in many emerging market economies are less developed and, in line with the literature, suggests that institutional elements, such as regulatory quality and government effectiveness, help drive informality.

POLICY OPTIONS

In seeking to identify policy options to address the shadow economy, it is useful to group determinants into two broad categories: (1) "exit" factors and (2) "exclusion" factors[9] (Perry 2007; Oviedo 2009). Exit factors from the formal economy tend to lead to voluntary informal employment, with shadow workers typically earning similar or higher incomes relative to comparable formal workers and enjoying more employment flexibility. In contrast, exclusion factors from the formal economy tend to result in forced informal employment when workers are unable to find formal work. The difference mostly depends on whether, as a result, workers are better off with a formal, compared with an informal, job. In most countries, exit and exclusion factors are present to a varying degree.[10] Where informal activity is driven more by exclusion factors, workers tend to rely on their jobs to provide their income subsistence. Those workers typically have lower skills and less education and are less productive.

Improving Regulation and Institutional Quality

Given the inverse relationship between institutional quality and shadow economic activity, efforts to strengthen institutions can have a dual effect, reducing the shadow economy while also supporting the achievement of development goals. It is well recognized that better institutions foster more equitable and sustainable growth in the long term. More effective governance serves the well-being of broader parts of society, mitigating exit and exclusion factors. Regulatory and institutional reforms are critical to tackling bottlenecks in the business climate,

[9] Exit factors include burdensome and costly regulation, such as high entry costs; trade barriers; complex and excessive taxation and poor tax administration; administrative barriers, including excessive paperwork; corruption; low monitoring and enforcement; smaller benefits to formal employment and registration; low quality of public goods and services (infrastructure, social protection); and individual preference for self-employment. Exclusion factors include lack of opportunities in the formal sector, especially for certain demographics (for example, young or old workers) or ethnic groups; low productivity; low skills; and low human capital.

[10] According to the study based on the 2013 Eurobarometer survey, 24 percent of undeclared workers are driven by exclusion factors, 45 percent by exit factors, and 31 percent by a combination of factors, although the composition varies across countries (Williams and Kayaoglu 2020).

strengthening the rule of law, improving government effectiveness, and combating corruption.

- *Reducing regulatory and administrative barriers.* Lower regulatory burden will lower the cost incentive for participating in the shadow economy. Examples of successful reforms include simplifying registration and licensing processes (for example, automatic licensing in Georgia), creating one-stop-shop registration (Estonia), and reducing registration fees and statutory requirements (USAID 2005).
- *Increasing transparency and engagement.* Adopting measures to promote transparency (for example, though mandatory public electronic auctions for public procurement) and public administration (for example, by improving court system efficiency) can improve the perception of government effectiveness and the link between revenues and expenditure, increasing voluntary compliance. Possible measures include the public identification of tax evaders and targeted public relations campaigns. Adopting industry-based strategies can also be helpful, through continued engagement with industry bodies, advisory programs, clear communication in areas of noncompliance, follow-up audit programs, and prosecution of the worst offenders.
- *Improving governance.* Many emerging market economies still lag behind advanced EU economies in the quality of their judicial systems and property rights, and institutional quality improvement has been uneven across countries (IMF 2017). Although initial conditions (such as resource allocation) and external factors (for example, EU accession) play an important role, reforms focused on improving public administration, transparency, and accountability help form positive feedback.[11]

Taxation-Related Policies

Improving tax administration, reducing regulatory burdens, and enhancing transparency would reduce incentives for informal activities driven by exit factors. Actions aimed at boosting revenues can also be helpful in reducing the shadow economy. The scope for improvement in tax administration varies across Europe; however, many countries face challenges with process automation, organizational structure, and operational performance.[12] Successful policy actions can include increasing tax compliance and promoting electronic payments:

- *Increasing tax compliance* may be achieved by improving registration, audit, and collection. Registration can be strengthened by facilitating the information exchange between government agencies. For example, in most EU countries, firms and workers have a single common business ID for social security, unemployment, and tax agencies (Oviedo 2009). The tax base can

[11] See IMF (2017) for country examples of institution-building paths.

[12] See IMF (2016) for how to improve tax administration efficiency and for country experiences in improving tax administration.

be broadened by gradually eliminating existing distortionary exemptions. Simplifying tax and social benefits systems, if not necessarily tax rates, will reduce tax-compliance costs.

- *Promoting electronic payments* can help increase collections and reduce value-added tax fraud. Several countries have recently obliged businesses to record payments and money transfers through fiscal devices. According to Schneider and others (2013), increasing electronic payments by an average of 10 percent annually for at least four consecutive years can reduce the size of the shadow economy by up to 5 percent. Promoting electronic payments and limiting the use of cash would likely help with shadow activities in which one side of the transaction (typically a consumer) does not benefit from not reporting the transaction (and may not even be aware of contributing to the expansion of the shadow economy through cash payment). Electronic payments may have a more limited effect, where both sides of the transaction benefit from not reporting.

Labor Market Reforms and Human Capital Development

In countries with high labor migration, and where the shadow economy can act as a social safety net, policy actions should focus on improving incentives for informal workers to move into the formal sector. When informal activities are driven primarily by exclusion factors, a sole focus on enforcement and compliance may result in informal workers seeking employment abroad and driving shadow firms out of business. In such circumstances, encouraging private sector job creation and fostering skill formation would help bring firms and workers out of the shadows and promote more inclusive growth.

Policy actions aimed at improving human capital will improve job-search capacity and the earnings potential of informal workers. The relevant labor market and education policies include the following:

- Increasing hiring and firing flexibility in countries with overly restrictive labor laws (for example, labor market reforms in the Slovak Republic), while enforcing effective labor laws elsewhere to maintain a level playing field across enterprises and encourage lawful behavior.
- Strengthening enforcement and monitoring (for example, enforced obligation to register all new workers in Bulgaria).
- Making the labor market more inclusive by developing and implementing customized employment and training measures for the target groups most in danger of social exclusion (for example, young people).
- Creating a favorable employment environment for returning migrants, providing special training, and recognizing practical skills gained abroad.

CONCLUSION

To successfully combat the shadow economy, comprehensive reforms, carefully designed for each country based on its most relevant determinants, are necessary. Measures can vary from regulatory and institutional reforms to tax policies and administration. The menu of policies most relevant for emerging market economies would include reducing regulatory and administrative burdens, promoting transparency, and improving government effectiveness, as well as improving tax compliance, automating procedures, and promoting electronic payments. In addition, a well-designed policy set should address incentives for informal workers to transition to the formal sector, especially in countries that rely more on remittances and where the shadow economy provides a social safety net. Furthermore, policy actions focused on encouraging private sector job creation and fostering human capital development would help bring firms and workers out of the shadows and promote more inclusive growth.

Unlike previous recessions, during the COVID-19 pandemic shadow economies are likely to shrink dramatically in line with the contraction of nonessential services, although some restricted activities may be pushed into the shadows. Workers in the shadow economy are particularly vulnerable because they fall outside the government's support perimeter. Some advanced economies may experience some formalization of informal activities in order for enterprises to benefit from government stimulus measures. Although government benefits provide an incentive for transition to a formal sector, the eligibility conditions may be too restrictive (for example, requirements to be a taxpayer in the previous year, to demonstrate evidence of the lockdown's effect on business). Also, closures and restrictions may have incentivized some activities to operate informally. Taking into account the size and nature of shadow activities and employment in specific jurisdictions will be important when designing policy responses to the pandemic.[13]

---

[13] An IMF research note by Diez and others (2020) reviews COVID-19 crisis responses and the costs of expanding transfers to informal workers in emerging market and developing economies. An International Labour Organization (2020) brief on the COVID-19 crisis and the informal economy discusses the immediate policy responses to address the consequences of the pandemic for the informal economy. Williams and Kayaoglu (2020) analyze the distribution of undeclared workers by industry and discuss policy options.

ANNEX 2.1. MIMIC ESTIMATION RESULTS FOR EUROPEAN SHADOW ECONOMIES

ANNEX TABLE 2.1.1.

Shadow Economy Estimates, Europe, 2000–06

(Percentage of GDP)

Country	2000	2001	2002	2003	2004	2005	2006
Albania	27.8	28.2	28.0	28.0	28.2	28.3	28.1
Austria	9.3	8.9	9.2	9.4	9.3	9.7	9.5
Belgium	20.8	21.1	21.5	21.7	21.4	21.6	21.2
Bosnia and Herzegovina	34.1	34.3	35.4	34.7	35.3	34.4	33.9
Bulgaria	36.9	37.2	37.9	37.5	36.8	36.8	36.2
Croatia	33.4	33.5	32.8	34.1	33.7	34.3	33.8
Cyprus	28.6	28.5	28.9	29.7	29.9	30.0	30.3
Czech Republic	18.9	19.0	19.5	19.6	19.2	19.2	19.3
Denmark	17.7	17.4	18.1	18.4	18.2	18.3	18.0
Estonia	33.1	34.0	33.8	33.8	33.2	33.5	33.5
Finland	18.1	19.0	19.3	19.7	19.8	19.5	19.6
France	14.3	14.4	14.8	15.2	15.1	15.1	15.1
Germany	15.7	15.5	16.2	16.5	15.9	16.6	16.3
Greece	28.1	28.7	29.3	29.7	30.1	29.8	30.5
Hungary	25.1	25.6	26.8	27.2	26.4	27.2	26.8
Iceland	15.9	15.7	15.9	16.3	16.6	16.5	16.3
Ireland	14.3	14.9	15.2	15.6	15.4	15.8	15.7
Italy	25.6	25.7	26.4	26.6	26.6	27.2	26.6
Kosovo	37.8	36.7	39.2	38.9	38.9	38.7	38.3
Latvia	28.5	28.4	28.5	29.2	28.5	28.6	29.1
Lithuania	33.7	34.2	34.1	34.5	34.6	33.9	33.9
Luxembourg	9.4	9.4	9.2	9.6	9.6	9.6	9.7
FYR Macedonia	38.2	39.1	38.6	37.5	37.0	37.8	38.3
Montenegro	36.8	36.3	37.4	38.8	37.9	37.7	36.7
Netherlands	12.6	12.7	13.1	13.3	13.5	13.2	12.9
Norway	19.1	19.8	20.7	21.5	20.6	20.1	19.7
Poland	27.6	27.6	28.5	28.5	26.8	27.4	27.5
Portugal	23.3	23.7	24.1	24.4	24.5	24.8	24.2
Romania	34.4	34.1	34.6	33.7	33.3	34.5	34.2
Serbia	33.0	32.3	33.4	33.4	32.9	33.9	34.1
Slovak Republic	19.2	18.8	18.9	19.0	19.0	18.9	18.6
Slovenia	27.1	27.6	27.3	28.5	27.9	27.5	27.6
Spain	18.9	19.1	19.5	19.6	19.8	20.0	20.1
Sweden	17.9	18.0	18.4	18.6	18.3	19.0	18.3
Switzerland	9.2	9.5	9.6	9.8	9.6	9.6	9.6
Turkey	29.5	29.2	28.7	28.8	28.7	29.0	29.0
United Kingdom	12.3	12.5	12.6	12.9	12.8	13.2	12.8

Source: IMF staff calculations.

ANNEX TABLE 2.1.2.

Shadow Economy Estimates, Europe, 2007–13

(Percentage of GDP)

Country	2007	2008	2009	2010	2011	2012	2013
Albania	27.4	27.7	28.1	27.7	27.2	27.6	27.6
Austria	9.2	9.2	10.0	9.5	9.1	9.1	9.2
Belgium	21.1	21.3	22.7	21.6	21.5	21.0	21.3
Bosnia and Herzegovina	35.4	35.8	37.4	36.7	36.2	36.5	36.3
Bulgaria	36.2	35.5	38.3	38.5	37.9	37.3	36.9
Croatia	34.1	34.0	35.5	35.7	35.5	35.7	35.0
Cyprus	29.7	29.8	31.2	30.9	30.8	31.0	30.6
Czech Republic	19.3	19.6	20.2	20.1	18.9	18.5	18.3
Denmark	17.9	18.2	18.9	18.3	17.9	17.4	17.7
Estonia	32.0	33.3	34.9	33.2	31.5	31.6	32.0
Finland	18.7	18.8	20.2	19.4	19.2	19.2	19.2
France	15.0	15.1	16.2	15.3	14.7	14.6	14.7
Germany	16.0	15.6	16.6	15.9	15.2	15.4	15.1
Greece	30.1	30.2	31.4	30.9	30.2	29.5	29.3
Hungary	26.1	26.0	26.9	26.8	25.9	25.5	25.6
Iceland	16.6	16.3	16.1	15.7	15.3	15.2	15.6
Ireland	15.6	15.9	16.1	15.6	15.4	15.5	15.4
Italy	26.4	26.7	28.3	27.4	26.7	26.2	26.0
Kosovo	38.2	37.0	37.4	37.0	36.7	37.4	37.9
Latvia	29.3	30.3	30.6	28.2	28.9	28.5	28.4
Lithuania	34.5	34.2	36.4	35.4	34.4	33.7	34.0
Luxembourg	9.4	9.6	9.8	9.8	9.8	9.4	9.5
FYR Macedonia	37.2	34.8	37.6	37.5	37.4	38.0	37.8
Montenegro	36.0	35.4	37.6	38.5	37.7	37.8	37.7
Netherlands	12.9	13.3	13.8	13.1	13.4	13.4	13.2
Norway	19.9	19.8	21.2	20.4	20.5	21.2	21.2
Poland	26.3	27.3	28.2	27.7	26.8	27.2	26.8
Portugal	24.3	24.3	25.7	25.1	24.6	24.5	23.5
Romania	34.9	34.8	36.0	35.0	33.4	33.9	33.8
Serbia	34.2	33.9	34.6	34.5	34.1	34.3	33.7
Slovak Republic	18.0	17.8	18.9	19.1	18.3	18.1	17.4
Slovenia	27.5	27.7	28.9	28.5	27.5	27.7	27.9
Spain	19.8	20.5	21.6	20.8	20.5	20.2	19.9
Sweden	17.8	17.6	18.9	18.2	18.0	18.3	18.8
Switzerland	9.5	9.3	9.6	9.5	9.4	9.5	9.3
Turkey	29.6	29.3	29.4	28.6	27.9	28.2	28.6
United Kingdom	13.1	12.5	13.2	12.8	12.3	12.6	12.5

Source: IMF staff calculations.

ANNEX TABLE 2.1.3.

Shadow Economy Estimates, Europe, 2014–19

(Percentage of GDP)

Country	2014	2015	2016	2017	2018	2019
Albania	27.1	27.5	27.6	27.1	27.4	27.7
Austria	9.3	9.4	9.6	9.4	9.3	9.4
Belgium	21.4	21.4	22.4	22.1	21.7	21.5
Bosnia and Herzegovina	36.6	36.4	37.1	36.8	36.5	35.4
Bulgaria	36.9	36.8	37.2	36.8	36.8	37.1
Croatia	35.5	34.5	33.9	33.5	33.7	34.2
Cyprus	30.2	29.9	29.6	29.2	29.2	29.8
Czech Republic	18.2	18.4	19.5	19.4	19.0	19.2
Denmark	17.4	18.0	18.8	18.1	17.9	18.0
Estonia	31.7	32.2	33.7	33.7	33.6	33.2
Finland	19.4	19.9	20.6	20.2	19.0	19.3
France	14.4	14.2	15.2	14.8	14.4	14.8
Germany	15.2	16.0	16.7	16.0	15.7	16.0
Greece	28.7	28.7	29.0	28.3	27.8	29.4
Hungary	25.3	25.2	26.1	26.2	25.9	26.2
Iceland	15.8	15.8	15.4	16.1	16.1	15.9
Ireland	15.1	15.4	15.2	15.1	15.3	15.3
Italy	26.4	26.0	27.7	27.1	26.0	26.6
Kosovo	37.8	38.5	38.2	38.3	38.8	38.3
Latvia	28.1	27.5	27.9	27.2	27.8	28.7
Lithuania	34.5	34.4	34.7	34.0	34.2	34.4
Luxembourg	9.3	9.4	9.8	9.6	9.5	9.6
FYR Macedonia	37.0	37.0	37.3	37.9	37.9	37.6
Montenegro	37.4	37.6	38.0	38.2	38.0	37.5
Netherlands	12.9	12.6	13.0	12.4	12.9	13.0
Norway	20.9	20.7	19.8	19.9	19.6	20.2
Poland	27.2	28.0	28.2	26.9	27.5	27.5
Portugal	23.3	23.1	24.0	23.5	23.2	24.0
Romania	33.7	33.1	34.3	34.6	33.8	34.2
Serbia	33.4	33.0	33.0	33.0	32.8	33.5
Slovak Republic	16.8	17.2	17.2	17.4	17.5	18.3
Slovenia	27.7	27.4	28.4	28.3	26.8	27.7
Spain	19.7	19.4	20.0	19.7	19.1	19.9
Sweden	18.7	18.6	19.4	19.1	18.3	18.5
Switzerland	9.5	9.7	9.9	9.8	9.8	9.6
Turkey	28.7	28.6	30.1	29.2	28.5	29.1
United Kingdom	12.7	12.9	12.7	12.3	12.5	12.7

Source: IMF staff calculations.

REFERENCES

Dabla-Norris, E., M. Gradstein, and G. Inchauste. 2008. "What Causes Firms to Hide Output? The Determinants of Informality." *Journal of Development Economics* 85 (1): 1–27.

Diez, F., R. Duval, C. Maggi, Y. Ji, I. Shibata, and M. Tavares. 2020. "COVID-19 Policy Responses to Support Informal Workers in EMDEs." IMF Research Note, International Monetary Fund, Washington, DC.

Ganta, V. 2012. "The Impact of International Labour Migration on the Republic of Moldova." CARIM-East Research Report 2012/32, Migration Policy Centre, Florence, Italy.

Gerxhani, K. 2004. "The Informal Sector in Developed and Less Developed Countries: A Literature Survey." *Public Choice* 120 (3–4): 267–300.

Hassan, M., and F. Schneider. 2016. "Size and Development of the Shadow Economies of 157 Worldwide Countries: Updated and New Measures from 1999 to 2013." *Journal of Global Economics* 4 (3): 1–14.

Hussmanns, R. 2004. "Measuring the Informal Economy: From Employment in the Informal Sector to Informal Employment." Working Paper 53, Policy Integration Department, Bureau of Statistics, International Labour Office, Washington, DC.

International Labour Organization (ILO). 2020. "COVID-19 Crisis and the Informal Economy: Immediate Responses and Policy Challenges." ILO Brief, Geneva, May.

International Monetary Fund (IMF). 2016. "Effective Government for Stronger Growth." In *Regional Economic Outlook: Europe.* Washington, DC, November.

International Monetary Fund (IMF). 2017. "Reforming the Judiciary: Learning from the Experience of Central, Eastern and Southeastern Europe." In *Regional Economic Outlook: Europe.* Washington, DC, November.

Ivlevs, A. 2016. "Remittances and Informal Work." *International Journal of Manpower* 37 (7): 1172–90.

Kelmanson, M. B., K. Kirabaeva, L. Medina, M. Mircheva, and J. Weiss. 2019. "Explaining the Shadow Economy in Europe: Size, Causes and Policy Options." IMF Working Paper 19/278, International Monetary Fund, Washington, DC.

Medina, L., and F. Schneider. 2018. "Shadow Economies around the World: What Did We Learn over the Last 20 Years?" IMF Working Paper 18/17, International Monetary Fund, Washington, DC.

Oviedo, A. M. 2009. "Economic Informality: Causes, Costs, and Policies—A Literature Survey of International Experience." Background paper prepared for Turkey Country Economic Memorandum *Informality: Causes, Consequences, Policies.* World Bank, Washington, DC.

Perry, G., ed. 2007. *Informality: Exit and Exclusion.* Washington, DC: World Bank.

Porta, R. L., and A. Shleifer. 2008. "The Unofficial Economy and Economic Development." NBER Working Paper 14520, National Bureau of Economic Research, Cambridge, MA.

Schneider, F. 2013. "Size and Development of the Shadow Economy of 31 European and 5 Other OECD Countries from 2003 to 2013: A Further Decline." Unpublished report, Department of Economics, Johannes Kepler University, Linz, Austria.

Schneider, F. 2014. "The Shadow Economy: An Essay." Unpublished report, Department of Economics, Johannes Kepler University, Linz, Austria.

Schneider, F. 2015. "Size and Development of the Shadow Economy of 31 European and 5 Other OECD Countries from 2003 to 2014: Different Developments?" *Journal of Self-Governance and Management Economics* 3 (4): 7–29.

Schneider, F., and A. Buehn. 2012. "Shadow Economies in Highly Developed OECD Countries: What Are the Driving Forces?" IZA Discussion Paper 6891, Institute for the Study of Labor, Bonn, Germany.

Schneider, F., and C. C. Williams. 2013. *The Shadow Economy.* London: IEA.

Schneider, F., A. T. Kearney, and Visa Europe. 2013. "The Shadow Economy in Europe, 2013." A. T. Kearney, Chicago.

Torgler, B., and F. Schneider. 2007. "What Shapes Attitudes toward Paying Taxes? Evidence from Multicultural European Countries." *Social Science Quarterly* 88 (2): 443–70.

USAID. 2005. "Removing Barriers to Formalization: The Case of Reform and Emerging Best Practice." USAID.

Vuletin, G. J. 2008. "Measuring the Informal Economy in Latin America and the Caribbean." IMF Working Paper 08/102, International Monetary Fund, Washington, DC.

Williams, C. C., and A. Kayaoglu. 2020. "The Coronavirus Pandemic and Europe's Undeclared Economy: Impacts and Policy." *South East European Journal of Economics and Business* 15 (1): 80–92.

CHAPTER 3

Nonlinearity between the Shadow Economy and Economic Development

Dong Frank Wu and Friedrich Schneider

INTRODUCTION

The shadow economy has been labeled with many names, such as the informal economy, the hidden economy, the black economy, and the underground economy. Although existing studies provide a broad range of definitions or descriptions, most are similar. This chapter follows the definition proposed in Chapter 1 because it uses that chapter's authors' estimated data for the size of the shadow economy:

> The shadow economy includes all economic activities that are hidden from official authorities for monetary, regulatory, and institutional reasons. Monetary reasons include avoiding paying taxes and all social security contributions; regulatory reasons include avoiding governmental bureaucracy or the burden of regulatory framework; and institutional reasons include corruption law, the quality of political institutions, and weak rule of law. For our study, the shadow economy reflects mostly legal economic and productive activities that, if recorded, would contribute to national GDP.

One of the most intensively studied topics in economics is the cause of the shadow economy around the world. Although our understanding of potential shadow economy drivers has improved substantially in the past two decades, questions regarding its long-term behavioral pattern are still open to debate (Schneider and Enste 2000; La Porta and Shleifer 2008; Feld and Schneider 2010; Williams and Schneider 2016). For example, does the size of the shadow economy converge to a certain level, or does it have a robust long-term linear relationship with its determinants? This chapter aims to fill the gap in the literature by investigating the long-term relationship between the shadow economy and its key determinants.

We identify a U-shaped relationship between the size of the shadow economy[1] and the level of economic development, using a panel data set covering 158

[1] Here the size of the shadow economy is expressed as the percentage ratio of the shadow economy to official GDP.

countries from 1996 to 2015. We take into account a wide range of the shadow economy's determinants and adopt various regression specifications to test the robustness of the nonlinearity between the shadow economy and GDP per capita.[2] Our results reveal that, after controlling for key economic, policy, and institutional variables, less-developed economies witness a negative relationship between the size of the shadow economy and GDP per capita; however, when GDP per capita exceeds a threshold, the size of the shadow economy increases with per capita income. These findings are consistent with economic intuition that economic development may have two opposite effects on the size of the shadow economy.

On the one hand, economic development, characterized by productivity improvement and technology advance, may support the long-term expansion of the shadow economy because advanced development means a high level of human capital, which helps individuals make a living. When less constrained by financial pressures, some people prefer informal jobs to gain more work flexibility or to reach a better work-life balance, especially if the wage difference between the formal and informal sectors is negligible. In addition, technology innovation can support the shadow economy by providing more convenient jobs and reliable decentralized payment systems.[3]

On the other hand, economic development can help downsize the shadow economy by offering high-quality public goods and services. Advanced economic development is normally characterized by strong institutional capacity and better social infrastructure, which help absorb firms and individuals from the informal sector or encourage them to stay formal. Two competing forces jointly determine the net effect of economic development on the shadow economy: at a low level, the downsizing effect associated with economic development plays a dominant role—people join or switch to the formal sector to enjoy more benefits of economic growth, thus the shadow economy shrinks. At a high level, more household members obtain enough financial freedom to consider informal jobs to pursue diverse goals. Thus, there is a gradual resurgence of the informal sector.

The U-shaped curve,[4] as Figure 3.1 displays, discloses a different development pattern than most studies, which assume or identify a linear relationship between the size of the shadow economy and its determinants. The finding of nonlinearity implies that the shadow economy is able to coexist with different levels of development and that the shadow economy does not disappear in the long term.

---

[2] GDP per capita is used here as proxy for economic development.

[3] Going forward, new waves of the digital economy, data sharing, and the gig economy are expected to boost the shadow economy. Also, blockchain technology and cryptocurrencies can be used to pay workers in the informal sector.

[4] The following sections examine the nonlinearity with rigorous econometric methods. In addition, the nonlinear relationship may not necessarily be symmetric around the turning point. Investigation of the asymmetric nonlinearity is left to future research.

Figure 3.1. Nonlinear Relationship between the Shadow Economy and GDP per Capita

(Average, constant 2011 international dollars)

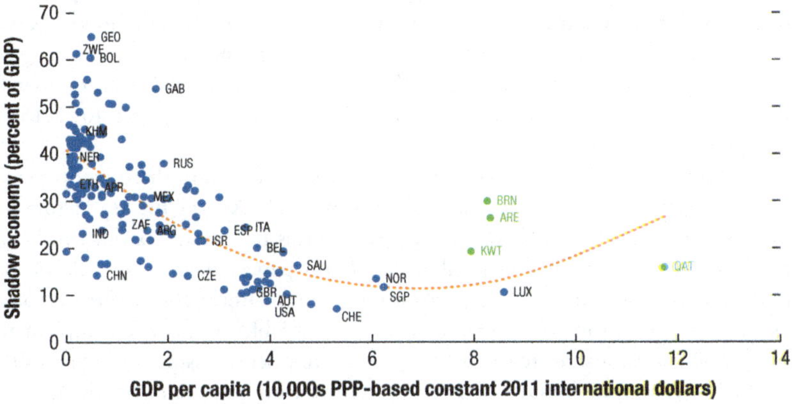

Sources: Medina and Schneider 2018; and World Bank data.
Note: GDP per capita is the average value of constant 2011 international dollars from 1996 to 2015 based on purchasing power parity. Data labels use International Organization for Standardization country codes.

This is contrary to the inference of a linear relationship, which predicts a shrinking trend or the final disappearance of the shadow economy. One question from Figure 3.1 is related to the observation that the average GDP per capita for most countries lies at the downward part of the U-shaped curve, while only a few countries lie on the upslope, including four oil-exporting countries. This chapter examines the robustness of the relationship by using an alternative measure of GDP per capita, which moves the four countries downward on the curve, and by dropping the four countries.

This chapter also seeks to identify factors that could boost GDP per capita. Consistent with the growth literature, we find that educational attainment plays a vital role in improving GDP per capita, especially having a college degree or higher. This result helps shed some light on a possible mechanism of a U-shaped pattern at the micro level. From the individual perspective, people work to make themselves better off. When development is low, education helps build labor productivity; skilled workers with a college education or higher choose to stay in the formal sector to enjoy benefits from high productivity and the social security net. When the economy advances to a new level at which skilled workers' income becomes high enough and one household member can easily cover a family's daily expenses, demand for work flexibility or other desirable perks of informal work is likely to increase. Hence, the size of shadow economy reverses its downtrend.

LITERATURE REVIEW

There is a considerable amount of economic research on the shadow economy, with a particular focus on its estimated size and causes.[5] The estimation approaches include survey-based methods, observable-variable methods, and model-based methods.[6] One of the latest examples is Medina and Schneider (2018), using the multiple indicators, multiple causes (MIMIC) approach to find that the estimated average size of the shadow economy in 158 countries from 1991 to 2015 is 31.9 percent relative to GDP.

The causes of the shadow economy can be categorized into three groups: economic, policy related, and regulatory and institutional.[7] Among the key factors are access to financing, political stability, public services provision, tax burden, labor market regulations, and institutional quality. Many papers identify potential determinants of the shadow economy by assuming a simple linear effect, whereas some take advantage of various interactions among the variables to revise or complement early findings. Almost all research, explicitly or implicitly, assumes or agrees that the shadow economy should be expected to shrink with economic growth, upgraded financial and public services, improved institutional quality, and effective regulation.

One related question is whether this shrinking trend is a long-term, irreversible phenomenon. Suppose that all countries keep strengthening their capacity in supervision and regulation, providing efficient public services, and reducing their institutional weaknesses. Is it then reasonable to predict that the shadow economy will continue shrinking until it disappears or becomes negligible?

This is the first attempt to investigate the nonlinear long-term trend of the shadow economy. Our major contribution includes the revelation of a U-shaped relationship between the shadow economy and level of development, using GDP per capita as proxy for development. Although some research already uses GDP per capita, its purpose is to control for the level of development (for example, La Porta and Shleifer 2008). We allow for a U-shaped relationship by including squared GDP per capita. Our main results disclose the significance of the squared GDP per capita term, and the following regressions support its robustness.

Furthermore, this chapter explores possible long-term factors for level of development. It is not surprising to find that educational attainment plays a vital role, especially those who hold college degrees and higher. Even so, our finding regarding this variable contrasts with earlier work. Buehn and

---

[5] A recent survey is by Elgin and Erturk 2019.

[6] For a detailed discussion, see Medina and Schneider 2018; see also Gerxhani 2003; Kirchgaessner 2016; and Adair 2017. See Medina and Schneider (2018) for a detailed discussion, as well as Gerxhani (2003); Adair (2017); and Kirchgaessner (2016).

[7] For details, see La Porta and Shleifer 2008, 2014; Schneider 2014; and Williams and Schneider 2016. Regarding the effect of the shadow economy on economic development, see the dual view proposed by Lewis 1954 and advocated by La Porta and Shleifer 2008, 2014; Feld and Larsen 2009; and Feld and Schneider 2010.

Farzanegan (2013) find, by interacting education and institutional quality in the regression model, that higher educational attainment can decrease the shadow economy in a strong institutional environment. This finding suggests that the educational effect on informality depends on institutional quality. When the quality of institutions is high enough, Buehn and Farzanegan (2013) imply, educational achievement contributes to the decline of the shadow economy. The issue with this conclusion is the estimated effect of institutional quality on the shadow economy. As Buehn and Farzanegan (2013) show, the institution has a positive effect on the size of the shadow economy, and the effect declines with education because of the same interaction item, which contradicts economic intuition and is hard to explain.

In addition, our finding is contrary to Elgin and Erturk (2016), who support the negative relationship. The regression in Elgin and Erturk (2016) uses a longer time series on the size of the shadow economy while relying only on fixed-effect dummies to control for all other factors. In addition, Elgin and Erturk (2016) set up a model to capture the underlying mechanism, which assumes the value of total factor productivity (TFP) is constant. Instead the model implies the size of the shadow economy depends on the relative TFP values between the formal and informal sectors. If informal sector productivity catches up to that of the formal sector, the informal tends to grow, which is consistent with our finding.

We focus on the long-term determinants of the size of the shadow economy, whereas Elgin and Birinci (2016) explore the nonlinear effect of the shadow economy on economic growth. One difference is the direction of the effect; Elgin and Birinci (2016) aim to identify one new factor of growth. Furthermore, there is no direct inference between the two studies' findings. Elgin and Birinci (2016) find an inverted U between the shadow economy and growth of GDP per capita. Given that growth of GDP per capita has no simple monotone relationship with the level of GDP per capita, it is hard to derive from these findings a relationship between the shadow economy and GDP per capita and thus to judge whether this work is consistent with theirs. One key finding of Elgin and Birinci (2016), though, is that the informal sector has positive spill-over effects on TFP growth.

METHOD AND DATA

In this section, we set up a framework for comprehensive econometric analysis to identify the nonlinear relationship between the size of the informal economy and GDP per capita.

Empirical Method

First, we conduct several regressions with different estimators. The benchmark cross-sectional regression is based on the following setting:

$$SE_i = \beta_0 + \beta_1 y_i + \beta_2 y_i^2 + \sum_{k=3}^{n} \beta_k x_{k,i} + \varepsilon_i, \qquad (1)$$

where SE_i is the percentage ratio of the shadow (or informal) economy relative to GDP of country i; y_i stands for GDP per capita for country i; $x_{k,i}$ represents other control variables; and ε_i denotes the error term. The inclusion of the squared GDP per capita term in the regression is to check for the potential existence of a nonlinear relationship between the size of the informal economy and GDP per capita.

Subsequently, we calculate the cross-sectional regression using variables constructed as 20-year averages. Then we conduct the robustness check with four settings:

1. Dummy variables are used to control for country group effects, complemented by separate regressions on each country group.
2. Regressions on variables of 10-year averages are conducted to further confirm the original findings.
3. The panel regression method with a 5-year average is adopted to continue checking the validity of the empirical results. The method includes regressions with one-period and two-period lagged variables to control for endogeneity.
4. Regressions are conducted to control for other potential economic and institutional factors.

For the panel regression, the equation is set up as follows:

$$SE_{it} = \beta_0 + \beta_1 y_{it} + \beta_2 y_{it}^2 + \sum_{k=3}^{n} \beta_k x_{k,it} + \theta_i + \delta_t + \varepsilon_{it}, \quad (2)$$

where dummies of θ_i and δ_t are inserted to reflect the country and time effects. Both the fixed effect and random effect estimators are reported here.

Data

We collect annual cross-country panel data covering 158 countries or regions from 1996 to 2015.[8] In our regressions, the variables are 20-, 10-, or 5-year averages. Variables constructed as 20- and 10-year averages are used in the cross-sectional regressions, and the 5-year average variables are fed into the panel data regressions.

The size of the shadow economy relative to GDP is borrowed from Medina and Schneider (2018), who revise the standard MIMIC approach by using light intensity instead of GDP as an indicator variable. By limiting GDP to being only a cause (and not also an effect) variable, this revision improves the estimation results. To make the study's findings reliable, we also use the shadow economy data from Elgin and Oztunali (2012) as a robustness check.[9] Elgin and Oztunali (2012) estimate the shadow economy based on a deterministic dynamic general equilibrium model. As the empirical results will show, the two estimated series are highly correlated.

[8] Most of the key time series are from 1990 to 2015, except for the World Bank Worldwide Governance Index, which starts from 1996. Therefore, our regressions change the sample period to 1996 to 2015.

[9] The estimated size of the shadow economy from Elgin and Oztunali (2012) spans 1950 to 2014.

The choice of control variables is based on the existing empirical literature, including GDP per capita, the political stability index, growth of GDP per capita, consumer price index inflation, trade openness, financial depth, tax burden, education-related variables, and capital stock:

- GDP per capita comes from the World Bank World Development Indicators (WDI) database, and two measurements are used to ensure the robustness of the results: one is constant 2011 international dollars based on purchasing power parity (PPP), and the other is constant 2010 US dollars. This latter series is the main series used to establish this chapter's major finding.
- The index of political stability, used to control for institutional differences, is extracted from the database of the World Bank Worldwide Governance Indicators (WGI). Its original values range from –2.5 to 2.5, which we change here into 0 to 100.
- The noninstitutional variables of GDP per capita growth, consumer price index inflation, trade openness, financial depth, and tax burden are also from the WDI. GDP per capita growth is calculated with national currency, and the lowest GDP per capita growth occurs in Libya in 2011. Inflation is measured with consumer price index data and expressed in percentages. Trade openness is defined as the sum of exports and imports of goods and services as a percentage of GDP. Financial depth is measured as the ratio of domestic credit to private sector credit provided by financial corporations,[10] such as through loans, nonequity securities, and trade credit. Tax burden is captured by the ratio of taxes and mandatory contributions payable to commercial profits.
- The regression, aiming to explore the determinants of GDP per capita, also uses data on educational attainment from the WDI and total capital stock from the IMF. Three educational variables are constructed: the percentages of people completing primary school only, completing high school only, and completing college and higher.[11] The IMF Investment and Capital Stock Dataset includes three measurements of capital stock, namely public capital, private capital, and public-private partnership capital. We calculate total capital stock as the sum of the 20-, 10-, or 5-year time series.

EMPIRICAL RESULTS

This section presents empirical findings on the nonlinear interaction between the shadow economy and GDP per capita.

[10] Financial corporations include monetary authorities, deposit money banks, and other financial corporations, such as finance and leasing companies and insurance corporations.

[11] For most countries, data on completion of high school or higher are available only after 2012. This is why the number of observations for high-school-or-higher educational attainment is so small compared with that of primary school attainment.

Here endogeneity can come from two main possible sources: (1) the effect of informal activities on the formal sector, through households' or firms' decisions, may imply that institution and economic variables on the right side of the regression equation are influenced by the size of the shadow economy;[12] and (2) the measurement error embedded in the estimated size of the shadow economy may also lead to the two-way causality between regressors and dependent variables. We adopted various specifications to check the sensitivity of the results and to ensure that endogeneity has been effectively mitigated.

Findings of the Benchmark Model

The results of the benchmark static cross-sectional regression are reported in Table 3.1, which uses each country as one observation by taking a 20-year average on all relevant time series.

The first column reports the regression results using the estimated shadow economy size from Medina and Schneider (2018) and GDP per capita in PPP-based international dollars, while the second column reports the regression on GDP per capita in 2010 US dollars. The third column reports the results of regressing the estimated informality numbers from Elgin and Oztunali (2012) on

TABLE 3.1.

Nonlinearity between the Shadow Economy and GDP Per Capita, 1996–2015
(Average)

Dependent Variable	Shadow Economy[1]		Shadow Economy[2]		Shadow Economy2[3]	
GDP_PPP$	–5.314***	(1.142)			–5.246***	(1.214)
(GDP_PPP$)^2	0.352***	(0.110)			0.348***	(0.112)
GDP_2010$			–5.611***	(1.238)		
(GDP_2010$)^2			0.398***	(0.123)		
Institutional Factor						
Political Stability	–0.129**	(0.0570)	–0.114*	(0.0585)	–0.0848	(0.0567)
Noninstitutional Factors						
GDP growth	–0.310	(0.367)	–0.362	(0.363)	0.00131	(0.376)
Inflation	0.109	(0.113)	0.115	(0.115)	0.0514	(0.122)
Openness	0.0168	(0.0114)	0.00458	(0.0109)	0.00981	(0.0117)
Financial depth	–0.0581**	(0.0278)	–0.0479*	(0.0279)	–0.0624**	(0.0271)
Constant	45.23***	(2.613)	43.82***	(2.689)	44.26***	(2.626)
R^2	0.574		0.569		0.556	
No. of observations	152		152		147	
F-test	44.03		56.07		43.69	

Sources: Authors.
Note: Standard errors appear in parentheses. PPP = purchasing power parity.
$^*p < .10$; $^{**}p < .05$; $^{***}p < .01$.
[1]Estimated shadow economy size from Medina and Schneider 2018 and GDP per capita in PPP-based international dollars.
[2]Estimated shadow economy size from Medina and Schneider 2018 and GDP per capita in 2010-based US dollars.
[3]Estimated shadow economy size from Elgin and Oztunali 2012 and GDP per capita in PPP-based international dollars.

[12] See Annex Table 3.1.2 for the correlation matrix.

PPP-based GDP per capita. All three regressions identify, at the 1 percent significance level, the positive coefficient for the squared shadow economy size and thus support the existence of the U-shaped relationship between the shadow economy and GDP per capita. That is, the shadow economy shrinks with the increase of GDP per capita until it reaches a threshold; after that point, the shadow economy and GDP per capita are positively related and the shadow economy size grows with GDP per capita.

The benchmark regression uses the indicator of political stability from the WGI to proxy for institutional factors, which is motivated by Elbahnasawy, Ellis, and Adom (2016). The coefficient for political stability is consistently negative, implying that institutional factors help contain the expansion of the shadow economy.

In addition, the estimated negative coefficient of financial depth reveals that financial development is instrumental in dampening the activities of the shadow economy, which is consistent with the findings of World Bank Enterprise Surveys.[13]

Further Investigation of the Nonlinear Relationship

Which factors determine the long-term value of GDP per capita and thus indirectly influence the size of the shadow economy? The classic production function implies that physical capital, human capital, and technology are three fundamental variables. In addition, Barro (2013) argues that inflation is negatively related to economic growth. Guided by the existing literature, the regression equation of GDP per capita is set as the following:

$$\begin{aligned} y_i = {} & \beta_0 + \beta_1 * college_i + \beta_2 * HighSch + \beta_3 * PrimSch \\ & + \beta_4 * inflation + \beta_5 * CapStock + \varepsilon_i \end{aligned} \quad (3)$$

The results in Table 3.2 reveal that educational attainment, especially college and graduate degrees, contributes to the increase of GDP per capita. It is not surprising to see that bachelor's degrees and higher are significant and more important than high school and primary school diplomas in boosting GDP per capita. College and postgraduate education help employees reach higher productivity, and the skill-complementary technology trend in recent decades has created a constant demand for skilled labor, as Acemoglu (2002) shows. In addition, the regression confirms that inflation is detrimental to GDP per capita, supporting existing studies on the long-term negative relationship between inflation and economic growth.

Then what is the economic intuition behind the implied long-term relationship between education and the shadow economy? The formal sector is more productive than the informal sector, and firms tend to move out of the informal sector to hire skilled workers when more people become well educated, thus reducing the size of the shadow economy; however, when education reaches a certain

[13] La Porta and Shleifer (2014) highlight the role of financial access, one important aspect of financial development. The study compares perceived obstacles to doing business reported by informal and formal entrepreneurs and lists access to financing as the top factor for firm owners to decide whether to stay formal.

TABLE 3.2.

Long-Term Determinants of GDP Per Capita, 1996–2015
(Average)

Dependent Variable	GDP_PPP$	
College	0.0787**	(0.0309)
High school	0.00682	(0.0132)
Primary school	0.0196*	(0.0110)
Inflation	−0.0868***	(0.0311)
Capital stock	−0.000232	(0.00014)
Constant	1.796*	(0.976)
R^2	0.306	
No. of observations	70	
F-test	13.86	

Source: Authors.
Note: Standard errors appear in parentheses. PPP = purchasing power parity.
*$p < .10$; **$p < .05$; ***$p < .01$.

level as GDP per capita hits a threshold, further attainment not only pushes up GDP per capita but also reverses the declining trend of the shadow economy. This reversal could be attributed to growing productivity leading to an increase in informal sector salaries. When household revenue exceeds a critical level, financial pressure becomes less intense. Some family members may become more willing to take temporary, unregistered assignments, rather than formal full- or part-time positions, in exchange for flexibility, which leads to the expansion of the shadow economy.

The R^2 value indicates that education, capital stock, and inflation can explain about 30.6 percent of GDP per capita; a large share of GDP per capita remains unexplained in the regression. In addition, capital stock's effect on GDP per capita is not significantly different from zero in the long term.

Robustness Checks

Besides the initial robustness regressions in Table 3.1, this subsection continues to conduct robustness checks to test the observed U-shaped relationship between the shadow economy and GDP per capita. Specifically, we implement four types of tests:

1. We explore the robustness of the U-shaped relationship with an additional control variable, tax burden, and then within different country groups, which include regressions with country group dummies and separate estimations for each country group.
2. We use 10-year averages to run the benchmark regression to check the results' consistency.
3. We calculate 5-year averages and run panel regressions with different estimators to check if the same relationship exists.
4. We test the robustness of the result by dropping the four oil-exporting countries on the upward part of the U curve.

Robustness Check Controlling for Tax Burden and for Country Groups

This subsection investigates the robustness of the results by controlling for tax burden and for different country groups. One motivation for firms to remain unregistered and in the informal sector is to avoid taxes.[14] A potential question is whether, in the long term and at the national level, the tax burden is a factor affecting a firm's decision to stay informal or whether it has any implication for long-term nonlinearity. In the regression, we add the ratio of corporate tax to corporate profit as proxy for a firm's tax burden. The first column of Table 3.3 shows a positive but nonsignificant coefficient for the tax variable, whereas the two GDP per capita variables remain significant.

To check whether the nonlinear relationship significantly exists within different country groups, the chapter divides the countries with two criteria. We borrow the definition of advanced economy from the October 2017 *World Economic Outlook* and split the 158 countries into advanced economies and nonadvanced economies. This chapter also follows the World Bank's country income classification, using 2015 gross national income per capita, to group all countries or regions into three categories: low-income countries with annual income of less than $1,025, middle-income countries with annual income from $1,026 to $12,475, and high-income countries with income of $12,476 or higher.[15]

The second and third columns of Table 3.3 present the regression results with country group dummies. One advantage of this method is to use all the observations instead of regressing on a subsample of the data. The nonlinear relationship remains significant even with the dummies.

To further investigate the robustness of the U-shaped relationship for each country group, we run separate regressions for country groups of advanced economies, nonadvanced economies, high-income countries, and non–high-income countries. Table 3.4 shows that the squared GDP per capita remains significant for advanced economies, nonadvanced economies, and high-income countries. In contrast, non–high-income countries demonstrate a significant linear relationship between the shadow economy and GDP per capita. The negative linear relationship for non–high-income countries stems from this group lying far from the threshold, where observations suggest a predominantly downward relationship.

That the R^2 values for advanced economies and high-income countries are higher than 50 percent while those for nonadvanced economies and non–high-income countries are lower than 50 percent implies that nonlinearity is mainly driven by advanced economies and high-income countries whose GDP per capita lies around the threshold.

[14] Recent research provides empirical and quantitative evidence to support the negative correlation between taxes and the informal sector and attributes it to high-quality institutional factors (Friedman and others 2000) or public turnover and public trust in government (Elgin and Solis-Garcia 2012). The appearance of the negative correlation is likely attributable to the failure of the analysis to identify or control for other determinants.

[15] See Annex Table 3.1.4 for the country list of each group.

TABLE 3.3.

Robustness Check for Nonlinear Relationship between the Shadow Economy and GDP: AEs and Non-AEs

	Shadow Economy					
Dependent Variable	**With Tax Burden**		**With Dummy for AEs**		**With Dummies for HICs and LICs**	
GDP_PPP$	−5.301***	(1.143)	−4.562***	(1.181)	−3.769**	(1.474)
(GDP_PPP$)^2	0.352***	(0.110)	0.286**	(0.111)	0.239*	(0.125)
Institutional Factor						
Political stability	−0.129**	(0.0571)	−0.112*	(0.0574)	−0.111*	(0.0591)
Noninstitutional Factors						
GDP growth	−0.301	(0.372)	−0.271	(0.377)	−0.270	(0.357)
Inflation	0.109	(0.113)	0.103	(0.115)	0.0985	(0.118)
Openness	0.0172	(0.0114)	0.0149	(0.0117)	0.0156	(0.0119)
Financial depth	−0.0577**	(0.0281)	−0.0439	(0.0303)	−0.0546*	(0.0277)
Tax burden	0.00461	(0.0184)	0.0107	(0.0186)	−0.000863	(0.0200)
Dummy						
AEs			−3.987*	(2.251)		
HICs					−3.749	(2.867)
LICs					2.123	(2.144)
Constant	44.91***	(3.062)	43.39***	(3.112)	43.31***	(3.297)
R^2	0.574		0.581		0.580	
No. of observations	152		152		152	
F-test	39.33		38.50		32.17	

Source: Authors.

Note: Standard errors appear in parentheses. AEs = advanced economies; HICs = high-income countries; LICs = low-income countries; PPP = purchasing power parity.

*$p < .10$; **$p < .05$; ***$p < .01$.

Robustness Check with 10-Year Averages

In the previous subsections, all regressions were conducted with variables of 20-year averages to explore the long-term nonlinear relationship. One associated question is whether this nonlinear relationship remains unchanged if empirical analysis concentrates on shorter time horizons, such as a 10- or 5-year average. This subsection conducts analysis based on two 10-year averages, whereas the next one uses four separate 5-year averages.

We run separate regressions for 1996 to 2005 and 2006 to 2015 and summarize the results in Table 3.5. Despite the changes in coefficient values between these two decades, the nonlinear relationship remains as expected, which indicates that the identified nonlinear relationship is stable in the medium term. This finding provides support to the results of the benchmark model.

Robustness Check with 5-Year Averages

This subsection of robustness checks employs panel data regressions with 5-year averages. These results are shown in Tables 3.6 through 3.8. Following the growth literature, the 5-year averages are used to smooth the cyclical elements contained in the time series. Both the fixed effect and the random effect estimators are listed

TABLE 3.4.

Robustness Check for Nonlinear Relationship between the Shadow Economy and GDP: AEs and Non-AEs without Dummies

	Shadow Economy				
Dependent Variable	**For AEs**	**For Non-AEs**	**For HICs**	**For Non-HICs**	**For Non-HICs**
GDP_PPP$	−8.954***	−4.081***	−6.728***	−4.549	−3.345*
	(2.771)	(1.302)	(2.309)	(5.626)	(1.773)
(GDP_PPP$)^2	0.555**	0.249*	0.426**	0.590	
	(0.224)	(0.126)	(0.179)	(2.331)	
Institutional Factor					
Political stability	−0.152*	−0.0977	−0.125	−0.107	−0.110
	(0.0876)	(0.0651)	(0.0865)	(0.0774)	(0.0737)
Noninstitutional Factors					
GDP growth	−1.938**	−0.239	−2.589***	−0.194	−0.187
	(0.936)	(0.366)	(0.824)	(0.421)	(0.407)
Inflation	0.774	0.0764	1.151*	0.0680	0.0636
	(0.821)	(0.121)	(0.672)	(0.139)	(0.130)
Openness	0.0450**	0.0176	0.0317**	0.0175	0.0186
	(0.0171)	(0.0182)	(0.0127)	(0.0256)	(0.0254)
Financial depth	0.0258	−0.0869**	−0.0234	−0.0792	−0.0829
	(0.0276)	(0.0428)	(0.0289)	(0.0563)	(0.0506)
Constant	45.65***	44.22***	45.11***	44.50***	44.32***
	(8.057)	(2.867)	(7.061)	(3.016)	(3.181)
R^2	0.623	0.310	0.517	0.155	0.155
No. of observations	34	118	49	103	103
F-test	5.202	10.80	9.271	2.988	3.500

Source: Authors.
Note: Standard errors appear in parentheses. AEs = advanced economies; HICs = high-income countries; LICs = low-income countries; PPP = purchasing power parity.
$^*p < .10$; $^{**}p < .05$; $^{***}p < .01$.

in Table 3.6, although the Hausman test suggests that the random effect estimator may be inconsistent.

One concern with the panel regression is endogeneity. To check the effect of endogeneity, panel data regressions are conducted with one- and two-period lags (Tables 3.7 and 3.8). All panel regression results support the U-shaped relationship identified previously. These checks clearly demonstrate that all results are robust after undertaking the usual tests.

Robustness Check Controlling for the Four Oil-Exporting Countries

This subsection aims to isolate the effect of some outliers and check the robustness of the U-shaped curve. As Figure 3.1 suggests, one valid concern is that the four

TABLE 3.5.

Robustness Check for Nonlinear Relationship between the Shadow Economy and GDP

	Shadow Economy			
Dependent Variable	**10-Year Average of 1996–2005**		**10-Year Average of 2006–15**	
GDP_PPP$	−6.510***	(1.358)	−5.088***	(1.062)
$(GDP\_PPP\$)^2$	0.458***	(0.137)	0.306***	(0.0853)
Institutional Factor				
Political stability	−0.112**	(0.0548)	−0.109*	(0.0573)
Noninstitutional Factors				
GDP growth	−0.109	(0.184)	−0.569	(0.437)
Inflation	0.0696	(0.0581)	−0.0922	(0.158)
Openness	0.0148	(0.0115)	0.0102	(0.00988)
Financial depth	−0.0610**	(0.0302)	−0.0585**	(0.0250)
Constant	47.09***	(2.679)	45.05***	(2.695)
R^2	0.601		0.55	
No. of observations	144		149	
F-test	55.83		35.91	

Source: Authors.

Note: Standard errors appear in parentheses. PPP = purchasing power parity.

$*p < 0.10$; $**p < 0.05$; $***p < 0.01$.

TABLE 3.6.

Robustness Check for Nonlinear Relationship between the Shadow Economy and GDP: Panel Regression

	Shadow Economy (5-Year Average)			
Dependent Variable	**Robust Fixed Effect**		**Robust Random Effect**	
GDP_PPP$	−11.59***	(1.640)	−8.755***	(1.141)
$(GDP\_PPP\$)^2$	0.838***	(0.215)	0.656***	(0.157)
Institutional Factor				
Political stability	−0.0559*	(0.0336)	−0.0418	(0.0292)
Noninstitutional Factors				
GDP growth	0.0261	(0.0659)	−0.000569	(0.0512)
Inflation	0.0704***	(0.0221)	0.0846***	(0.0185)
Openness	−0.0476***	(0.0148)	−0.0308***	(0.00995)
Financial depth	−0.0136	(0.0119)	−0.0278**	(0.0122)
Constant	52.02***	(3.032)	46.89***	(2.079)
No. of observations	558		558	
F-test	25.50			

Source: Authors.

Note: Standard errors appear in parentheses. PPP = purchasing power parity.

$*p < 0.10$; $**p < 0.05$; $***p < 0.01$.

oil-exporting countries lying on the upward part of the curve, namely Brunei Darussalam, Kuwait, Qatar, and United Arab Emirates, may play a disproportionately large role in determining the nonlinear relationship. One way to check is to switch to another measurement of GDP per capita. With GDP per capita measured by

TABLE 3.7.

Robustness Check for Nonlinear Relationship between the Shadow Economy and GDP: Panel Regression with One-Period Lags

	Shadow Economy (5-Year Average)			
Dependent Variable	**Robust Fixed Effect with Lags**		**Robust Random Effect with Lags**	
GDP_PPP$(−1)	−9.444***	(1.391)	−7.814***	(0.934)
(GDP_PPP$(−1))^2	0.665***	(0.173)	0.565***	(0.122)
Institutional Factor				
Political stability(−1)	−0.00467	(0.0391)	−0.0272	(0.0289)
Noninstitutional Factors				
GDP growth(−1)	−0.317***	(0.0847)	−0.331***	(0.0723)
Inflation(−1)	0.0770***	(0.0191)	0.0828***	(0.0172)
Openness(−1)	−0.0159	(0.0138)	−0.00515	(0.00957)
Financial depth(−1)	−0.00410	(0.0118)	−0.0223*	(0.0123)
Constant	43.24***	(2.817)	42.13***	(1.717)
No. of observations	414		414	
F-test	27.36			

Source: Authors.
Note: Standard errors appear in parentheses. PPP = purchasing power parity.
*$p < .10$; ***$p < .01$.

TABLE 3.8.

Robustness Check for Nonlinear Relationship between the Shadow Economy and GDP: Panel Regression with Two-Period Lags

	Shadow Economy (5-Year Average)			
Dependent Variable	**Robust Fixed Effect with Lags**		**Robust Random Effect with Lags**	
GDP_PPP$(−2)	−4.636***	(1.754)	−6.294***	(1.138)
(GDP_PPP$(−2))^2	0.717***	(0.210)	0.465***	(0.139)
Institutional Factor				
Political stability(−2)	0.0281	(0.0459)	−0.0401	(0.0337)
Noninstitutional Factors				
GDP growth(−2)	−0.104	(0.0853)	−0.221***	(0.0774)
Inflation(−2)	0.0776***	(0.0221)	0.0641***	(0.0150)
Openness(−2)	−0.0251	(0.0181)	−0.00326	(0.00999)
Financial depth(−2)	−0.0105	(0.0130)	−0.0285	(0.0182)
Constant	33.29***	(3.822)	39.51***	(1.837)
No. of observations	266		266	
F-test	6.587			

Source: Authors.
Note: Standard errors appear in parentheses. PPP = purchasing power parity.
***$p < .01$.

constant 2010 US dollars, these four countries move to the downward part of the U curve in Figure 3.2. When this measurement of level of development is used, the regression outcome in Table 3.9 supports the U-shaped relationship.

Figure 3.2. Nonlinear Relationship between the Shadow Economy and GDP Per Capita, 1996–2015
(Average, constant 2010 US dollars)

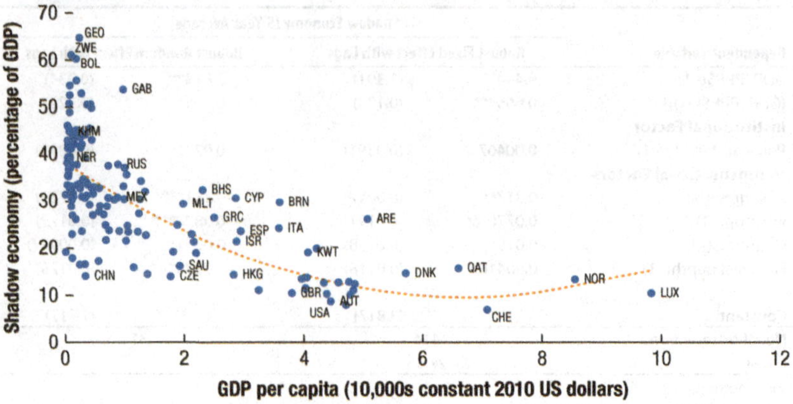

Sources: Medina and Schneider 2018; and World Bank.
Note: GDP per capita is the average value of constant 2011 international dollars from 1996 to 2015 based on purchasing power parity. Data labels use International Organization for Standardization country codes.

Another way to check the effect of these four oil-exporting countries, which may be convincing, is to do the regression with the same measurement while dropping the outliers. The results are summarized in Table 3.9 and the same U curve is still identified, although at a less significant level than before.

Labor Market and Policy Implications

One view on the shadow economy is that labor market rigidity makes job search and matching lengthy and costly for firms. Firms may thus be reluctant to register newly hired workers with the authorities or to stay formal. This, in turn, may cause workers, especially migrant workers, to be less interested in formal jobs. Thus, it is important to control for the institutional effect of labor market rigidities when examining the determinants of the shadow economy. In response, we use the indicator of labor market flexibility from the World Economic Forum Global Competitiveness Index to control for the institutional factors of the labor market. The indicator is on a scale of 1 to 7, with high values meaning more flexibility. The results are summarized in Table 3.10. Labor market flexibility helps reduce the size of the shadow economy in the long term, although not significantly. Meanwhile, the coefficient of squared GDP per capita remains significant to support the U-shaped curve.

It is arguable that not only institutional factors but also the labor force composition of the market can influence the size of the shadow economy. For

TABLE 3.9.

Robustness Check for Nonlinear Relationship between the Shadow Economy and GDP: Alternate Measure of GDP Per Capita, 1996–2015

(Average)

	Shadow Economy			
Dependent Variable	**Using GDP Per Capita in 2010 US Dollars**		**Using GDP per Capita in PPP-Based US Dollars and Dropping the Four Oil-Exporting Countries**	
GDP_PPP$			–5.391***	(1.294)
(GDP_PPP$)^2			0.256*	(0.154)
GDP_2010$	–5.611***	(1.238)		
(GDP_2010$)^2	0.398***	(0.123)		
Institutional Factor				
Political stability	–0.114*	(0.0585)	–0.129**	(0.0569)
Noninstitutional Factors				
GDP growth	–0.362	(0.363)	–0.251	(0.379)
Inflation	0.115	(0.115)	0.117	(0.112)
Openness	0.00458	(0.0109)	0.0205	(0.0124)
Financial depth	–0.0479*	(0.0279)	–0.0452	(0.0282)
Constant	43.82***	(2.689)	44.48***	(2.603)
R^2	0.569		0.585	
No. of observations	152		148	
F-test	64.94		64.94	

Source: Authors.
Note: Standard errors appear in parentheses. PPP = purchasing power parity.
*p < 0.10; **p < 0.05; ***p < 0.01.

TABLE 3.10.

Robustness Check for Nonlinear Relationship between the Shadow Economy and GDP: Labor Market Indicator, 1996–2015

(Average)

	Shadow Economy	
Dependent Variable	**With Labor Market Indicator**	
GDP_PPP$	–6.086***	(1.310)
(GDP_PPP$)^2	0.413***	(0.124)
Institutional Factor		
Political stability	–0.125**	(0.0614)
Noninstitutional Factors		
GDP growth	–0.594	(0.573)
Inflation	0.0480	(0.128)
Openness	0.0179	(0.0121)
Financial depth	–0.0544*	(0.0292)
Labor market	–0.205	(1.606)
Constant	47.81***	(7.582)
R^2	0.578	
No. of observations	139	
F-test	34.75	

Source: Authors.
Note: Standard errors appear in parentheses. PPP = purchasing power parity.
*p < 0.10; **p < 0.05; ***p < 0.01.

example, Goldin (1994) finds a U-shaped curve between female labor participation and economic development. Female participation declines initially with economic development and then picks up after a turning point. If the estimated trend in Goldin (1994) is true, it is reasonable to predict that more women tend to work informally with economic development. Differences between men's and women's involvement in the shadow economy is an interesting topic for further investigation with data availability.

To set out appropriate and effective measures to tackle the ramifications of the shadow economy, it is necessary first to have a comprehensive, current view of how the shadow economy affects economic growth and social welfare.[16] First, the existence of the shadow economy poses a severe threat to fiscal revenue collection and thus undermines the government's ability to provide adequate public goods and services. Second, empirical evidence shows that firms in the shadow economy are smaller and less productive than those in the formal sector. Third, authorities have limited access to information related to the shadow economy, which weakens their efforts to implement economic monitoring and management. Fourth, the shadow economy keeps evolving and adapts to new developments; it is thus crucial for policymakers to regularly update their knowledge. Even so, the shadow economy does play a positive role by improving some workers' welfare. For example, the informal sector provides temporary low-paid jobs when the economy does not have a well-established social safety net. Also, the informal sector helps the economy maintain an untapped reservoir of labor supply. When a positive shock to demand emerges, the economy can quickly increase production by making use of the extra labor supply in the shadow economy.

Views are mixed on the shadow economy, and this chapter's finding provides another reason for policymakers to be cautious. If the long-term trend of the shadow economy can be reversed with economic development, then it is key to be aware of the current economic state and remain alert to policy effectiveness. If an economy is less developed or experiences a catch-up phase, its shadow economy is expected to downsize. In this period, authorities can attract more firms and workers out of the shadow economy by promoting financial development, containing inflation, stabilizing the political situation, and expanding educational spending. By contrast, when the economy has reached the threshold GDP per capita and starts to show the positive relationship between GDP per capita and the shadow economy, authorities should make working in the formal sector more beneficial by, for example, reducing labor market rigidities to improve market efficiency and simplifying tax-compliance procedures with recent technology innovations.

Our results, which show the importance of the level of economic development, indicate that taking harsh measures to dramatically reduce or even to eradicate the

[16] La Porta and Shleifer (2008, 2014) comprehensively summarize views of the role of the shadow economy.

shadow economy is not a first-best solution. The appropriateness of policy depends on the level of economic development. Authorities might consider the following policy recommendations:

1. Strengthen capacity in data collecting and processing to assess the current relationship between the shadow economy and level of development. Exploiting all available data sources is crucial, especially given the rapid growth of the digital economy, and relevant government agencies must work collectively to cross-check data quality. The authorities should be able to measure the effect of policy accurately and thus keep adjusting to achieve the better outcomes.
2. Streamline administrative procedures to reduce firms' and households' compliance costs and make public goods and services more accessible by taking advantage of technology innovations. The growing digital economy makes it advantageous and convenient for workers to stay in the informal sector. In response, the associated government agencies should revise their policy measures to create a business-friendly environment and ensure that firms and workers can obtain these advantages and stay in or move to the formal sector.
3. Expand education, not only to improve human capital but also to teach workers about the role of the shadow economy and promote healthy social norms that will positively influence economic behavior. It is important that all firms and households be advised on the merits and risks of the shadow economy, take a positive attitude toward formal jobs, and understand the importance of transparency for economic monitoring and policy design.

CONCLUSION

This chapter reveals a long-term U-shaped relationship between GDP per capita and the size of the shadow economy using a data set of 158 countries. Furthermore, the chapter examines the possible long-term determinants of GDP per capita and finds that the share of the population with a bachelor's degree or higher promotes average productivity, which is consistent with existing literature.

The U-shaped pattern between the shadow economy and GDP per capita is worth further investigation. One possible direction is whether the nonmonotonic relationship before and after the threshold is symmetric. Although a long-term nonlinearity in the shadow economy is identified here using the quadratic regression equation, the relationship between GDP per capita and the size of the shadow economy may be asymmetric. One possible scenario is that a shadow economy may accelerate in productivity when the country's development exceeds a certain stage, resulting from industrial advancement in the formal sector and technological innovation.

ANNEX 3.1. SUPPLEMENTARY TABLES

TABLE 3.1.1.

Economy Names and ISO Codes

Economy	ISO Code	Economy	ISO Code	Economy	ISO Code
Albania	ALB	Gabon	GAB	Netherlands, The	NLD
Algeria	DZA	Gambia	GMB	New Zealand	NZL
Angola	AGO	Georgia	GEO	Nicaragua	NIC
Argentina	ARG	Germany	DEU	Niger	NER
Armenia	ARM	Ghana	GHA	Nigeria	NGA
Australia	AUS	Greece	GRC	Norway	NOR
Austria	AUT	Guatemala	GTM	Oman	OMN
Azerbaijan	AZE	Guinea	GIN	Pakistan	PAK
Bahamas	BHS	Guinea-Bissau	GNB	Papua New Guinea	PNG
Bahrain	BHR	Guyana	GUY	Paraguay	PRY
Bangladesh	BGD	Haiti	HTI	Peru	PER
Belarus	BLR	Honduras	HND	Philippines	PHL
Belgium	BEL	Hong Kong	HKG	Poland	POL
Belize	BLZ	Hungary	HUN	Portugal	PRT
Benin	BEN	Iceland	ISL	Qatar	QAT
Bhutan	BTN	India	IND	Romania	ROM
Bolivia	BOL	Indonesia	IDN	Russia	RUS
Bosnia and Herzegovina	BIH	Iran	IRN	Rwanda	RWA
Botswana	BWA	Ireland	IRL	Saudi Arabia	SAU
Brazil	BRA	Israel	ISR	Senegal	SEN
Brunei Darussalam	BRN	Italy	ITA	Sierra Leone	SLE
Bulgaria	BGR	Jamaica	JAM	Singapore	SGP
Burkina Faso	BFA	Japan	JPN	Slovak	SVK
Burundi	BDI	Jordan	JOR	Slovenia	SVN
Cabo Verde	CPV	Kazakhstan	KAZ	Solomon Islands	SLB
Cambodia	KHM	Kenya	KEN	South Africa	ZAF
Cameroon	CMR	Korea	KOR	Spain	ESP
Canada	CAN	Kuwait	KWT	Sri Lanka	LKA
Central African Republic	CAF	Kyrgyz Rep.	KGZ	Suriname	SUR
Chad	TCD	Laos	LAO	Swaziland	SWZ
Chile	CHL	Latvia	LVA	Sweden	SWE
China	CHN	Lebanon	LBN	Switzerland	CHE
Colombia	COL	Lesotho	LSO	Syrian Arab Rep.	SYR
Comoros	COM	Liberia	LBR	Taiwan	TWN
Democratic Republic of the Congo	COD	Libya	LBY	Tajikistan	TJK
Congo Rep	COG	Lithuania	LTU	Tanzania	TZA
Costa Rica	CRI	Luxembourg	LUX	Thailand	THA
Côte d'Ivoire	CIV	Madagascar	MDG	Togo	TGO
Croatia	HRV	Malawi	MWI	Trinidad and Tobago	TTO
Cyprus	CYP	Malaysia	MYS	Tunisia	TUN
Czech	CZE	Maldives	MDV	Turkey	TUR
Denmark	DNK	Mali	MLI	Uganda	UGA
Dominican Rep.	DOM	Malta	MLT	Ukraine	UKR
Ecuador	ECU	Mauritania	MRT	United Arab Emirates	ARE

(continued)

TABLE 3.1.1. *(continued)*

Economy Names and ISO Codes

Economy	ISO Code	Economy	ISO Code	Economy	ISO Code
Egypt	EGY	Mauritius	MUS	United Kingdom	GBR
El Salvador	SLV	Mexico	MEX	United States	USA
Equatorial Guinea	GNQ	Moldova	MDA	Uruguay	URY
Eritrea	ERI	Mongolia	MNG	Venezuela	VEN
Estonia	EST	Morocco	MAR	Vietnam	VNM
Ethiopia	ETH	Mozambique	MOZ	Yemen	YEM
Fiji	FJI	Myanmar	MMR	Zambia	ZMB
Finland	FIN	Namibia	NAM	Zimbabwe	ZWE
France	FRA	Nepal	NPL		

Source: International Organization for Standardization.
Note: ISO = International Organization for Standardization.

TABLE 3.1.2.

Correlations of Variables, 1996–2015

	Description	1	2	3	4	5	6
1. Shadow economy	Size of the shadow economy, % of GDP, from Medina and Schneider 2018	1					
2. Shadow economy[2]	Size of the shadow economy, % of GDP, from Elgin and Oztunal 2012	0.945***	1				
3. GDP_ PPP$	GDP per capita, 10,000s of PPP-based constant US dollars	−0.670***	−0.676***	1			
4. GDP_2010$	GDP per capita, 10,000s of 2010-based constant US dollars	−0.682***	−0.683***	0.901***	1		
5. Political stability	Index of political stability and absence of violence and terrorism, from the WGI database	−0.608***	−0.556***	0.583***	0.618***	1	
6. GDP growth	Growth of GDP per capita, %	0.147***	0.224***	−0.239***	−0.242***	−0.0900**	1
7. Inflation	CPI inflation, %	0.254***	0.239***	−0.303***	−0.339***	−0.318***	0.146***
8. Openness	Trade openness, the sum of exports and imports of goods and services, % of GDP	−0.308***	−0.315***	0.427***	0.345***	0.394***	0.0295
9. Financial depth	Credit to the private sector, % of GDP	−0.562***	−0.591***	0.536***	0.630***	0.483***	−0.236***
10. Tax burden	Tax and mandatory contributions as a share of commercial profit, %	0.207***	0.200***	−0.251***	−0.177***	−0.189***	−0.0216
11. Capital stock	Capital stock in billions of constant 2011 international dollars	−0.0568	−0.0223	−0.0620	−0.0379	−0.100**	0.0750*
12. Labor market	Flexibility of labor market on a scale of 1–7 (best)	−0.205***	−0.225***	0.311***	0.234***	0.243***	−0.00701

(continued)

TABLE 3.1.2. *(continued)*

Correlations of Variables, 1996–2015

	Description	7	8	9	10	11	12
1. Shadow economy	Size of the shadow economy, % of GDP, from Medina and Schneider 2018						
2. Shadow economy[2]	Size of the shadow economy, % of GDP, from Elgin and Oztunal 2012						
3. GDP_PPP$	GDP per capita, 10,000s of PPP-based constant US dollars						
4. GDP_2010$	GDP per capita, 10,000s of 2010-based constant US dollars						
5. Political stability	Index of political stability and absence of violence and terrorism, from the WGI database						
6. GDP growth	Growth of GDP per capita, %						
7. Inflation	CPI inflation, %	1					
8. Openness	Trade openness, the sum of exports and imports of goods and services, % of GDP	−0.155***	1				
9. Financial depth	Credit to the private sector, % of GDP	−0.340***	0.278***	1			
10. Tax burden	Tax and mandatory contributions as a share of commercial profit, %	0.0693*	−0.222***	−0.200***	1		
11. Capital stock	Capital stock in billions of constant 2011 international dollars	0.0532	−0.0381	0.00406	−0.0469	1	
12. Labor market	Flexibility of labor market on a scale of 1–7 (best)	−0.180***	0.397***	0.246***	−0.207***	−0.223***	1

Sources: Elgin and Oztunali 2012; Medina and Schneider 2018; IMF, Investment and Capital Stock Dataset; World Bank, World Development Indicators; World Bank, Worldwide Governance Indicators; and World Economic Forum, Global Competitiveness Index.

Note: The correlation matrix is calculated with 958 annual observations; educational variables are not included because of their small numbers of observations; CPI = consumer price index; PPP = purchasing power parity; WGI = World Bank Worldwide Governance Indicators.

*$p < .10$; **$p < .05$; ***$p < .01$.

TABLE 3.1.3.

Summary Statistics of Variables, 1996–2015
(Average)

Variable	Description	Mean	Standard Deviation	Minimum	Maximum	No. of Observations
Shadow economy	Size of the shadow economy, % of GDP, from Medina and Schneider 2018	31.016	12.788	6.160	71.332	3,160
Shadow economy[2]	Size of the shadow economy, % of GDP, from Elgin and Oztunal 2012	31.536	12.192	7.924	67.801	2,888
GDP_PPP$	GDP per capita, 10,000s of PPP-based constant US dollars	1.667	1.960	0.026	12.935	3,099
GDP_2010$	GDP per capita, 10,000s of 2010-based constant US dollars	1.280	1.831	0.012	11.197	3,099
Political stability	Index of political stability and absence of violence and terrorism, from the WGI database	48.39	18.49	0.35	85.20	2,652
GDP growth	Growth of GDP per capita, %	2.55	5.90	−62.23	140.50	3,107
Inflation	CPI inflation, %	7.24	12.29	−4.01	198.52	2,987
Openness	Trade openness, the sum of exports and imports of goods and services, % of GDP	88.11	55.44	0.17	531.74	3,045
Financial depth	Credit to the private sector, % of GDP	46.93	45.16	0.49	312.12	2,932
Tax burden	Tax and mandatory contributions as a share of commercial profit, %	48.08	39.79	8.00	339.10	1,607
College	People completing college, % of population ages 25+ years	17.22	9.21	0.00	36.95	165
High school	People completing high school, % of population ages 25+ years	38.81	18.41	0.96	82.46	164
Primary school	People completing primary school, % of population ages 25+ years	31.50	14.86	3.02	78.77	571
Capital stock	Capital stock in billions of constant 2011 international dollars	4,839.89	1,762.20	218.00	8,543.00	3,010
Labor market	Flexibility of labor market on a scale of 1–7 (best)	4.51	0.62	2.41	6.39	1,301

Sources: Elgin and Oztunali 2012; Medina and Schneider 2018; IMF, Investment and Capital Stock Dataset; World Bank, World Development Indicators; World Bank, Worldwide Governance Indicators; and World Economic Forum, Global Competitiveness Index.

Note: CPI = consumer price index; PPP = purchasing power parity; WGI = World Bank Worldwide Governance Indicators.

TABLE 3.1.4.

Analytical Categorization of the Global Economy

Advanced Economies	Non–Advanced Economies		High-Income Countries	Non–High-Income Countries	
				Middle-Income Countries	
Australia	Albania	Kuwait	Australia	Albania	Peru
Austria	Algeria	Kyrgyz Republic	Austria	Algeria	Philippines
Belgium	Angola	Lao P.D.R.	The Bahamas	Angola	Romania
Canada	Argentina	Lebanon	Bahrain	Argentina	Russian Federation
Cyprus	Armenia	Lesotho	Belgium	Armenia	Solomon Islands
Czech Republic	Azerbaijan	Liberia	Brunei Darussalam	Azerbaijan	South Africa
Denmark	Bahamas, The	Libya	Canada	Bangladesh	Sri Lanka
Estonia	Bahrain	Madagascar	Chile	Belarus	Suriname
Finland	Bangladesh	Malawi	Croatia	Belize	Eswatini
France	Belarus	Malaysia	Cyprus	Bhutan	Syrian Arab Rep.
Germany	Belize	Maldives	Czech Republic	Bolivia	Tajikistan
Greece	Benin	Mali	Denmark	Bosnia and Herzegovina	Thailand
Iceland	Bhutan	Mauritania	Estonia	Botswana	Tunisia
Ireland	Bolivia	Mauritius	Finland	Brazil	Turkey
Israel	Bosnia and Herzegovina	Mexico	France	Bulgaria	Ukraine
Italy	Botswana	Moldova	Germany	Cabo Verde	Venezuela
Japan	Brazil	Mongolia	Greece	Cambodia	Vietnam
Korea, Rep. of	Brunei Darussalam	Morocco	Hong Kong SAR	Cameroon	Yemen
Latvia	Bulgaria	Mozambique	Hungary	China	Zambia
Lithuania	Burkina Faso	Myanmar	Iceland	Colombia	
Luxembourg	Burundi	Namibia	Ireland	Congo, Rep.	
Malta	Cabo Verde	Nepal	Israel	Costa Rica	Low-Income Countries
Netherlands, The	Cambodia	Nicaragua	Italy	Côte d'Ivoire	Benin
New Zealand	Cameroon	Niger	Japan	Dominican Republic	Burkina Faso
Norway	Central African Republic	Nigeria	Korea, Rep. of	Ecuador	Burundi
Portugal	Chad	Oman	Kuwait	Egypt	Central African Republic
Singapore	Chile	Pakistan	Latvia	El Salvador	Chad
Slovak Republic	China	Papua New Guinea	Lithuania	Equatorial Guinea	Comoros
Slovenia	Colombia	Paraguay	Luxembourg	Fiji	Congo, Dem. Rep. of
Spain	Comoros	Peru	Malta	Gabon	Eritrea
Sweden	Congo, Dem. Rep. of	Philippines	Netherlands, The	Georgia	Ethiopia

(continued)

TABLE 3.1.4. ***(continued)***

Analytical Categorization of the Global Economy					
Advanced Economies	**Non–Advanced Economies**		**High-Income Countries**	**Non–High-Income Countries**	
Switzerland	Congo, Rep. of	Poland	New Zealand	Ghana	Gambia, The
United Kingdom	Costa Rica	Qatar	Norway	Guatemala	Guinea
United States	Côte d'Ivoire	Romania	Oman	Guyana	Guinea-Bissau
	Croatia	Russian Federation	Poland	Honduras	Haiti
	Dominican Republic	Rwanda	Portugal	India	Liberia
	Ecuador	Saudi Arabia	Qatar	Indonesia	Madagascar
	Egypt, Arab Rep. of	Senegal	Saudi Arabia	Iran	Malawi
	El Salvador	Sierra Leone	Singapore	Jamaica	Mali
	Equatorial Guinea	Solomon Islands	Slovak Republic	Jordan	Mozambique
	Eritrea	South Africa	Slovenia	Kazakhstan	Nepal
	Ethiopia	Sri Lanka	Spain	Kenya	Niger
	Fiji	Suriname	Sweden	Kyrgyz Republic	Rwanda
	Gabon	Eswatini	Switzerland	Lao P.D.R.	Senegal
	Gambia, The	Syrian Arab Rep.	Taiwan Province of China	Lebanon	Sierra Leone
	Georgia	Taiwan Province of China	Trinidad and Tobago	Lesotho	Tanzania
	Ghana	Tajikistan	United Arab Emirates	Libya	Togo
	Guatemala	Tanzania	United Kingdom	Malaysia	Uganda
	Guinea	Thailand	United States	Maldives	Zimbabwe
	Guinea-Bissau	Togo	Uruguay	Mauritania	
	Guyana	Trinidad and Tobago		Mauritius	
	Haiti	Tunisia		Mexico	
	Honduras	Turkey		Moldova	
	Hong Kong SAR	Uganda		Mongolia	
	Hungary	Ukraine		Morocco	
	India	United Arab Emirates		Myanmar	
	Indonesia	Uruguay		Namibia	
	Iran	Venezuela		Nicaragua	
	Jamaica	Vietnam		Nigeria	
	Jordan	Yemen		Pakistan	
	Kazakhstan	Zambia		Papua New Guinea	
	Kenya	Zimbabwe		Paraguay	

Sources: IMF, October 2017 *World Economic Outlook*; and World Bank data.

Note: Income economy groups are based on the World Bank definition. The group of advanced economies is consistent with the IMF's October 2017 *World Economic Outlook*.

REFERENCES

Acemoglu, D. 2002. "Technical Change, Inequality, and the Labor Market." *Journal of Economic Literature* 40 (1): 7–72.

Adair, P. 2017. "Non-Observed Economy vs. the Shadow Economy in the EU: The Accuracy of Measurements Methods and Estimates Revisited." Paper presented at the 4th OBEGEF Interdisciplinary Insights on Fraud and Corruption conference, Porto, Portugal, November.

Barro, R. J. 2013. "Inflation and Economic Growth." *Annals of Economics and Finance* 14 (1): 121–44.

Buehn, A., and M. R. Farzanegan. 2013. "Impact of Education on the Shadow Economy: Institutions Matter." *Economics Bulletin* 33 (3): s2052–63.

Elbahnasawy, N. G., M. A. Ellis, and A. D. Adom. 2016. "Political Instability and the Informal Economy." *World Development* 85 (C): 31–42.

Elgin, C., and S. Birinci. 2016. "Growth and Informality: A Comprehensive Panel Data Analysis." *Journal of Applied Economics* 19: 271–92.

Elgin, C., and F. Erturk. 2016. "Is Informality a Barrier to Convergence?" *Economics Bulletin* 36 (4): 2556–68.

Elgin, C., and F. Erturk. 2019. "Informal Economies around the World: Measures, Determinants and Consequences." *Eurasian Economic Review* 9 (2): 221–37.

Elgin, C., and O. Oztunali. 2012. "Shadow Economies around the World: Model Based Estimates." Department of Economics Working Paper 2012/05, Boğaziçi University, Istanbul.

Elgin, C., and M. Solis-Garcia. 2012. "Public Trust, Taxes and the Informal Sectors." *Boğaziçi Journal Review of Social, Economic and Administrative Studies* 26 (1): 27–44.

Feld, L. P., and C. Larsen. 2009. "Undeclared Work in Germany 2001–2007: Impact of Deterrence, Tax Policy, and Social Norms—An Analysis Based on Survey Data." Springer, Berlin.

Feld, L. P., and F. Schneider. 2010. "Survey on the Shadow Economy and Undeclared Earnings in OECD Countries." *German Economic Review* 11 (2): 109–49.

Friedman, E., S. Johnson, D. Kaufmann, and P. Zoido-Lobaton. 2000. "Dodging the Grabbing Hand: The Determinants of Unofficial Activity in 69 Countries." *Journal of Public Economics* 76 (3): 459–93.

Gerxhani, K. 2004. "The Informal Sector in Developed and Less-Developed Countries: A Literature Survey." *Public Choice* 114 (3–4): 295–318.

Goldin, C. 1994. "The U-Shaped Female Labor Force Function in Economic Development and Economic History." NBER Working Paper 4707, National Bureau of Economic Research, Cambridge, MA.

Kirchgaessner, G. 2016. "On Estimating the Size of the Shadow Economy." *German Economic Review* 18 (1): 99–111.

La Porta, R., and A. Shleifer. 2008. "The Unofficial Economy and Economic Development." *Brookings Papers on Economic Activity* 392 (Fall): 275–363.

La Porta, R., and A. Shleifer. 2014. "Informality and Development." *Journal of Economic Perspectives* 28 (3): 109–26.

Lewis, W. A. 1954. "Economic Development with Unlimited Supplies of Labor." *Manchester School of Economic and Social Studies* 22 (2): 139–91.

Medina, L., and F. Schneider. 2017. "Shadow Economies around the World: What Did We Learn over the Last 20 Years?" Discussion Paper, University of Linz, Linz, Austria.

Medina, L., and F. Schneider. 2018. "Shadow Economies around the World: What Did We Learn Over the Last 20 Years?" IMF Working Paper 18/17, International Monetary Fund, Washington, DC.

Schneider, F. 2014. "The Shadow Economy: An Essay." Unpublished report, Department of Economics, Johannes Kepler University, Linz, Austria.

Schneider, F., and D. H. Enste. 2000. "Shadow Economies: Size, Causes, and Consequences." *Journal of Economic Literature* 38 (1): 77–114.

Williams, C. C., and F. Schneider. 2016. *Measuring the Global Shadow Economy: The Prevalence of Informal Work and Labor*. Cheltenham, UK: Elgar.

CHAPTER 4

The Effect of Regulatory Policy on Firm Growth in Sub-Saharan Africa

Manabu Nose

INTRODUCTION

After a decade of strong growth, buoyed by a supercycle of global commodity prices and surging investments in natural resources, economic growth in sub-Saharan Africa has recently faltered. The sustained decline in global commodity prices and a prolonged slowdown of growth among the region's main trading partners (China, in particular) have weighed on Africa's convergence toward higher incomes.

The recent slowdown in economic performance reminds us that sub-Saharan Africa continues to lack a competitive industrial base. Despite rapid urbanization driven by fast population growth, Africa has in fact *deindustrialized* since the mid-1970s (Jedwab, Christiaensen, and Gindelsky 2017). Africa's growth contributed little to formal manufacturing industries, leaving the sector dominated by small and informal firms. The manufacturing share of employment stands well below the global average at 8 percent, and manufacturing output, measured by a percentage of GDP, has declined from 15 percent in the mid-1970s to around 10 percent in 2020. On the basis of data from the Groningen Growth and Development Centre, Rodrik (2016) finds that African countries are underindustrialized at all income levels, whereas industrialization in Asia has progressed as income has grown.

Another reason Africa did not grow in conformity with a neoclassical growth convergence model is the large informal economy. Average productivity of the informal sector in sub-Saharan Africa is only about 20 percent of the formal sector (IMF 2017). Few informal firms grow out of informality, dragging on the region's productivity.

At the same time, sub-Saharan Africa's population is expected to more than double over the next three decades, growing from 1.2 billion in 2020 to nearly 2.5 billion in 2050. With an ample young population entering the labor force, firms will realize significant productivity dividends if they manage to reallocate factor inputs more efficiently (Hsieh and Klenow 2009; IMF 2017; Restuccia and Rogerson 2017).

Whereas stronger labor and business regulations should induce firms to formally register, recent studies have shown that developing countries achieve little formalization by regulating small and informal firms (de Andrade, Bruhn, and McKenzie 2014; Benhassine and others 2018). In fact, labor market regulation and taxation may be a cause of informality. As De Soto (1989) describes, informal firms' choice to operate informally is rational when the cost of formal registration outweighs the benefits (see also Maloney 2004). If informality in sub-Saharan Africa's economies is the equilibrium outcome of firms weighing costs versus benefits, factor market reforms should improve market efficiency. However, product and factor markets in the region are still at the infancy stage because of weak state capacity (Besley and Persson 2011), wage rigidities, or market domination by state- and foreign-owned enterprises (Bai, Hsieh, and Song 2016).

How efficient are factor markets in sub-Saharan Africa compared to those in developing Asia? How can policymakers in the region design formal and informal sector regulations to support firm growth and reduce informality?

Using data on firm balance sheets from a World Bank Enterprise Survey, this chapter quantifies the degree and determinants of factor allocative efficiency in labor and land for 40 sub-Saharan African countries. Next, it estimates the effects of factor allocative efficiency on firm age, size, and productivity using a pooled country sample, then verifies findings through a single country case (Nigeria) using firm panel data. In identifying the effect, the endogeneity of factor allocations is addressed by the instrumental variable (IV) regression using subnational institutions as the exogenous variation.

The empirical findings on labor allocation can be summarized as follows. Efficiency of labor allocation is significantly explained by the strength of formal and informal sector regulations, but the correlation can be either positive or negative depending on the country's legal capacity. The inspection of informal activities often depends on firm size, with larger firms attracting more attention from regulators (size-dependent regulatory policy); such an imbalance is detrimental for productive firms' growth in weak institutional context. For this reason, when legal capacity is weak, the formalization of labor contracts with social insurance benefits is found to be more effective than regulation in supporting firm growth. In contrast, as legal capacity develops, stronger informal sector regulation becomes more effective in accelerating the reallocation of workers to productive formal activities. This finding underscores that regulatory design needs to match local legal capacity to improve factor allocative efficiency in sub-Saharan Africa.

As for land allocation efficiency, ethnic fractionalization in sub-Saharan Africa is associated with conflict and thus less optimal land allocation across firms, as typically found in development literature. Moreover, land use is often dictated by custom or local authority rather than by legally binding contract. Regression results confirm that improvement in factor allocative efficiency through reallocation of land and workers would allow firms to grow and survive longer in the formal sector. The IV regression result highlights that marginal firms operating in a weak institutional environment can reap especially large benefits from the introduction of formal labor contracts, which allows productive firms to attract workers.

Last, the chapter further explores whether factor reallocation contributes to firm growth through credit and taxation channels. The result indicates that sub-Saharan Africa could increase access to credit and corporate tax revenues by addressing factor misallocation, which may further support firm growth.

STYLIZED FACTS

Firm Size, Age, and Productivity

As typically found in the literature (for example, Hsieh and Klenow 2014), balance sheet data from a World Bank Enterprise Survey show that enterprises in sub-Saharan Africa remain small during their life cycles. Midsized and large firms are conspicuously absent in Africa compared to developing Asia, making firm-size distribution highly skewed. On average, African firms are only one-third of the size of Asian firms, and most are young and unproductive (Annex Table 4.1). A Kolmogorov-Smirnov test supports that the distributions of firm age, size, and productivity in sub-Saharan Africa and Asia are statistically distinct (Figure 4.1).

Land and Labor Markets

Lack of access to land can prevent firms from scaling up business operations and using land as collateral to obtain loans. As land size increases, firm size also significantly increases in both sub-Saharan Africa and developing Asia (Figure 4.2). Whereas large parts of sub-Saharan Africa are land abundant, land with access to utilities and transport to markets is scarce. Land title systems are weak, and land rental markets are severely underdeveloped. Secure property rights and removal of restrictions on land markets are critical as the population grows and land use intensifies (Dihn and others 2012; Holden and Otsuka 2014).

In many parts of sub-Saharan Africa, land use is governed by custom and land-use rights are allocated locally by village chiefs. Land ownership is often inherited, and land transfers are severely restricted (Restuccia and Santaeulalia-Llopis 2017). Given weak institutions and pervasive corruption, political connections also affect access to land. Such weak regulatory and institutional situations raise a concern that land is not allocated to the most productive firms.

Labor markets in sub-Saharan Africa are dominated by subsistence agriculture and informal employment. The share of wage earners in the region's labor force is small, which leads to stagnant productivity growth. Pervasive informality in sub-Saharan Africa complicates effective regulation design because many small firms do not comply with law. Governments have weak capacity to enforce regulations and seek informal payments (that is, bribes) from small firms for granting business licenses, land, or utility access. Business owners may thus remain informal to avoid costly regulatory requirements. From a worker's perspective, formal employment is attractive only if labor regulation is enforced, mandating that firms pay social benefits such as pension, insurance, or severance payments under a contract (Almeida and Carneiro 2012).

Minimum Wage and Firm Productivity

In addition to the provision of social insurance, labor codes often stipulate a wage floor for formal sector jobs. Considering that a minimum wage prevents downward wage adjustments below the statutory floor, workers with marginal productivity below the minimum wage are induced to participate in the formal sector.

Figure 4.1. Firm Growth in Sub-Saharan Africa and Developing Asia

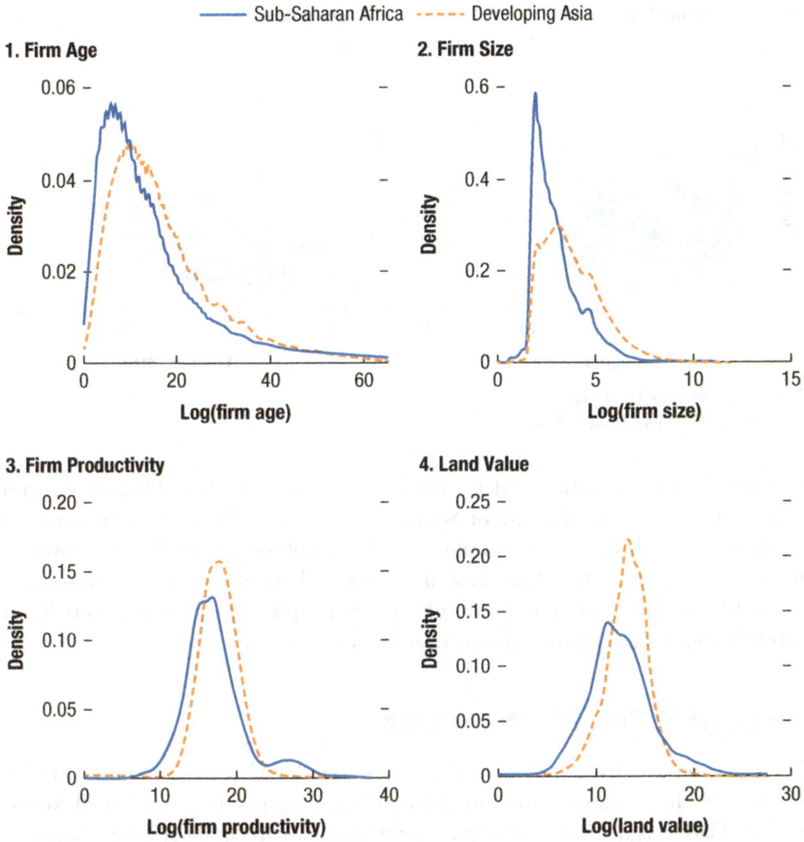

Source: World Bank Enterprise Survey.
Note: Firm productivity is defined as real output per employee. Both firm productivity and land value are in 2005 international dollars. For all panels, the Kolmogorov-Smirnov test *p* value is 0.00.

International Labour Organization data show that statutory minimum wages in sub-Saharan Africa are generally lower than in developing Asia, and that noncompliance with minimum wage law is common (Bhorat, Kanbur, and Stanwix 2017).

How does minimum wage affect firm size and productivity? The law of supply and demand suggests that firms will cut labor if the minimum wage is set above the market-clearing wage. If the minimum wage is instead below the equilibrium level, raising the minimum wage could increase formal employment. The evidence on employment effects in developing countries is quite mixed (Neumark and Corella 2019). When a country's minimum wage law is not enforced, previous studies found a small or statistically nonsignificant disemployment effect of higher minimum wage. When informal employment is large, the enforcement of the minimum wage could benefit workers by providing higher wages and

Figure 4.2. Land Size and Firm Size in Sub-Saharan Africa and Developing Asia

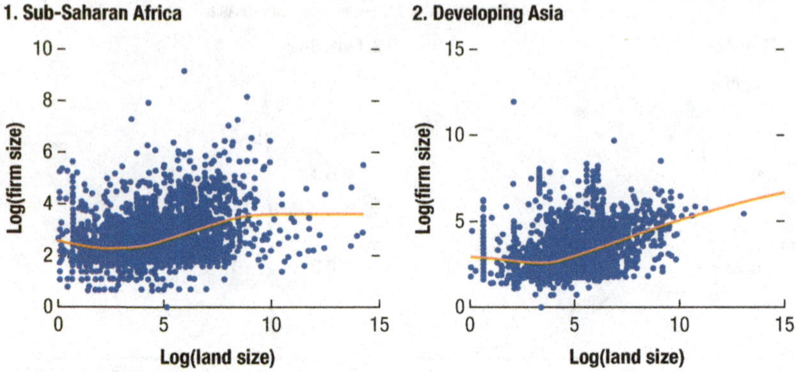

Source: World Bank Enterprise Survey.
Note: For both panels, bandwidth = 0.8.

mandated social benefits under formal labor contracts (see Dinkelman and Ranchhod [2012] for the case of South Africa). If social insurance benefits for workers outweigh the cost of employment for employers, formal sector employment will expand. Our data show a positive relationship between minimum wages (defined in level or as a ratio of GDP per capita) and firm productivity in sub-Saharan Africa, whereas the correlation is not clear in Asia.[1]

THEORETICAL FRAMEWORK

Based on these stylized facts, a dual-economy model with two margins of informality (at the extensive and intensive margins) explains how formal versus informal labor regulations determine employment size in equilibrium (Galiani and Weinschelbaum 2012; Ulyssea 2018). This section summarizes the key hypotheses and discusses the possible effect of heterogeneity by state legal capacity.[2]

The theoretical framework describes how formal versus informal taxes distort labor allocation that distinguishes formal and informal employment. This distinction affects policy prioritization: for which conditions should the government either provide an incentive to formalize labor contracts with social insurance or restrict informal contracts through stricter inspections.

In this framework, the optimization of a firm and its workers determines the equilibrium outcome. A payroll tax is levied on firms as mandated benefits to hire workers, while firms pay penalties for informal activities (if detected). Enforcement of formal regulation (payroll tax) and intensity of informal sector inspections (tax

[1] The previous literature shows a negative effect of minimum wage hikes on firm size in many Asian countries. See Neumark and Corella (2019) for a comprehensive survey and Nose (2020a) for a detailed study on Vietnam.

[2] See Nose (2020b) for theoretical details (https://sites.google.com/site/econnose/).

collection by the authority) are size dependent. That is, formal regulations are rigorously applied to large firms that face pressure from a labor union to offer competitive social security benefits. Likewise, informal sector inspection would be stricter for large businesses that are more visible to tax regulators and have more difficulty avoiding inspections. Size-dependent regulatory policies lead to factor misallocation: when large (productive) firms are taxed more strictly, they use fewer workers than less-productive firms.

As in Olley and Pakes (1996), a less-than-perfect correlation between productivity and factor use indicates a misallocation of factors across firms. Later in the empirical analysis section, the allocative efficiency index is estimated as the correlation between firm productivity and factor use.

The model analysis derives comparative statics to interpret the effect of labor regulations on employment size. First, an increase in formal labor regulation increases the cost of hiring formal labor, and firms may substitute with informal labor. Regulation simultaneously creates workers' incentive for formal employment by securing mandated benefits. The equilibrium outcome is ambiguous, depending on the elasticity of labor demand and supply, to an increase in payroll tax. If labor demand elasticity is high, stronger regulation may decrease formal sector employment in the equilibrium; yet if labor demand elasticity is low and labor supply elasticity is high, formal sector employment will increase. Labor supply would be more elastic in countries with a large informal sector.

Stricter informal sector inspections and penalties increase the cost of hiring informal labor, thereby creating an incentive to formalize labor contracts. Workers may also prefer to shift to the formal sector after an increase in informal tax. The efficiency of informal sector regulation depends on the enforcement of penalties. If state legal capacity is weak, informal sector regulation would be applied ad hoc, which may distort labor allocation and could be negative for firm growth.

The model also analyzes labor demand and supply responses to the minimum wage hike. When the minimum wage is initially set below the market wage, there is an excess demand for labor. As the minimum wage increases closer to the market-clearing wage, labor supply increases and the formal sector expands. If the minimum wage is raised above the market wage, firms may retrench formal labor demand because of higher labor costs, contracting formal employment.

DATA

This chapter uses a World Bank Enterprise Survey that samples formal manufacturing and service firms with at least five employees in low- and middle-income countries.[3] The sample uses 23,000 firms in 40 sub-Saharan African countries and about 29,000 firms in 14 developing Asian countries (see Annex 4.2 for the country sample).

[3] Because the World Bank Enterprise Survey covers formal firms, labor regulations such as social insurance benefits largely determine factor allocative efficiency. A comprehensive analysis using each country's census data is needed to represent small firms.

The Enterprise Survey is conducted using stratified sampling procedures based on industry group (using the two-digit International Standard Industrial Classification), average sales, firm size, and geographical location. The aggregate-level analysis uses cross-sectional firm balance sheet data for countries surveyed from 2006 until 2017. Later in the case study, Enterprise Survey panel data for Nigeria are used to examine the role of factor markets in determining firm productivity at the micro level.

Summary statistics are provided in Annex Table 4.1. Spatial distributions of firm size and productivity are also provided in Annex 4.3. For the pooled firm sample in the 40 sub-Saharan African countries, the average firm size is 58 employees, only one-third of the average size in Asia. Annex 4.3 shows that the average firm size is less than 31 in many sub-Saharan African countries. Value added per employee and land value show larger variance and spatial variations in sub-Saharan Africa, with wide disparity in the region's firm productivity and land values. Land ownership and access to credit are about 20 percent and 12 percent smaller in sub-Saharan Africa than in Asia, respectively. More foreign-owned firms exist in the sub-Saharan Africa sample, with 81 percent being manufacturing firms and the rest in the service sector.

EMPIRICAL ANALYSIS

The empirical analysis tests the hypotheses related to labor regulations but also considers the role of land allocation in reducing informality and promoting firm growth.

Aggregate-Level Analysis

The aggregate-level analysis estimates factor market efficiency for sub-Saharan Africa and examines its effect on firm growth.

Degree of Factor Misallocations

As the first step, the efficiency of labor and land allocations are estimated based on the correlation between firm productivity and factor allocation, following Olley and Pakes (1996). Models of heterogeneous firms predict that productive firms yield more output by using larger factor inputs. The correlation between labor and land allocations and firm productivity is computed for each district in a country.

Following the approach of Hsieh and Klenow (2009), real output total factor productivity (TFPQ) is used as firms' productivity measure. The allocative efficiency index is the correlation between the TFPQ and factor use (s_{isj}) for firm i within sector s in district j. The correlation is weighted by firm i's share of production in each sector-district group to define the firm-level measure of misallocation, M_{isj}:

$$M_{isj} = w_{isj,t-3} \times \rho\left(TFPQ_{isj}, s_{isj}\right). \tag{1}$$

The weight w_{isj} is firm *i*'s past market share at three years before each survey year *t*. The allocation measure is transformed to the standardized *z*-score. As M_{isj} gets larger in positive values, factors are allocated more efficiency to productive firms. Smaller positive or negative values of M_{isj} indicate factor misallocation that results in less output compared to the output under an efficient allocation.

Annex 4.4 shows the spatial distribution of the land allocation and labor allocation indices. Land allocation is negative in most sub-Saharan African countries, but worse in southern Africa. Labor allocation has more variation across sub-Saharan African countries, showing that some countries have a more efficient labor market.

Determinants of Factor Allocative Efficiency

Which policies or institutions determine the variation in factor allocative efficiency? Since the seminal contribution by Easterly and Levine (1997), ethnic fractionalization has been found to shape bad policies, conflicts, and inefficient resource allocation in sub-Saharan Africa. Local socioeconomic hierarchies in the region define who gets access to land. Ethnic fractionalization often creates land-related disputes, making land allocation inefficient.

The subnational ethnic fractionalization index developed by Alesina and Zhuravskaya (2011) is used here as the measurement. For each district *j* of country *c*, the fractionalization index captures the probability that two randomly drawn individuals belong to different groups: $F_{jc} = \sum_{m=1}^{M_c} \pi_{mjc}\left(1 - \pi_{mjc}\right)$, where π_{mjc} stands for the fraction of group *m* in district *j* of country *c*.

Figure 4.3 examines how ethnic fractionalization and land allocative efficiency are correlated in sub-Saharan Africa compared to developing Asia. The figure uses the sampling weight to compute average land allocative

Figure 4.3. Determinants of Land Allocative Efficiency in Sub-Saharan Africa and Developing Asia

1. Land Allocation in Sub-Saharan Africa

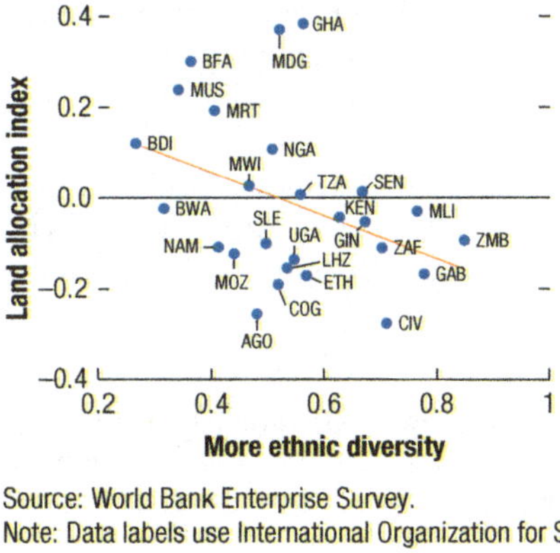

2. Land Allocation in Asia

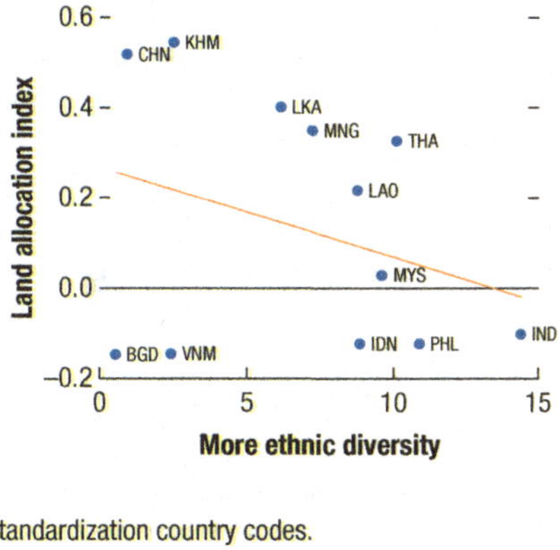

Source: World Bank Enterprise Survey.
Note: Data labels use International Organization for Standardization country codes.

efficiency and land-ownership variables at the country level. The figure shows that land allocation tends to be less efficient in countries with more ethnic fractionalization.

Figure 4.4 shows the relationship between labor allocative efficiency and the country's regulatory quality. The variable is constructed based on firms' responses to a World Bank Enterprise Survey on business environment, defined by the intensity of regulatory action to enforce labor codes (r_{isj}) and the frequency of tax inspections to regulate informal activities (t_{isj}), in each sector-district pair where firms operate. The regulatory environment is district specific, thus the average regulatory action in each district j is computed by taking its average for firms within the same sector: $R_j = E_s\left(r_{-isj}\right)$. Tax administration varies by sector, thus the average tax inspection is computed similarly but for firms within the same district j: $T_s = E_j\left(t_{-isj}\right)$. In both expressions, $-i$ indexes peer firms (all except own firm) that operate in the same sector (to compute R_j) or in the same district (to compute T_s).

The analysis accounts for heterogeneity in the legal capacity to design proper regulatory and tax inspection frameworks. Firms are grouped into those operating in districts with weak or strong state capacity.[4] Weak state capacity is defined as ineffective contract enforcement accompanied by widespread informal activity. In an area with weak legal capacity, workers would perceive less value in mandated social security, considering the benefits may not be legally enforced. In such a context, stricter formal regulatory action is needed to enforce the labor code, which may improve the efficiency of labor allocation. In contrast, if strong legal capacity is already in place, additional formal regulation may be too burdensome for businesses. In that context, stricter monitoring of "off the books" informal labor may create an efficiency gain.

As expected, panels 1 and 2 in Figure 4.4 indicate that stricter formal labor regulation improves the efficiency of labor allocation only in the weak state-capacity group, whereas intensive regulatory actions create a burden for private businesses in the strong state-capacity group.

Panels 3 and 4 give the opposite picture: stricter inspection efforts *decrease* labor allocative efficiency for the weak state-capacity group, presumably because inspection agencies under weak institutional environments demand informal payments from small firms. The correlation is slightly positive for the strong state-capacity group for which inspection efforts improve compliance and reduce informality, making the labor market more efficient.

These descriptive patterns imply that ethnic fragmentation and weak regulatory capacity, as typically observed in sub-Saharan Africa, drive factor misallocation in the region. This descriptive pattern is confirmed by the linear

[4] The World Bank Enterprise Survey asks firms' perceptions on the severity of corruption in their business. Based on this measure, the proportion of firms facing corruption for each district is computed. Each district is categorized into the weak state-capacity group when the district's corruption level is above the regional average corruption level.

Figure 4.4. Interaction between Regulatory Quality and Labor Allocative Efficiency in Sub-Saharan Africa

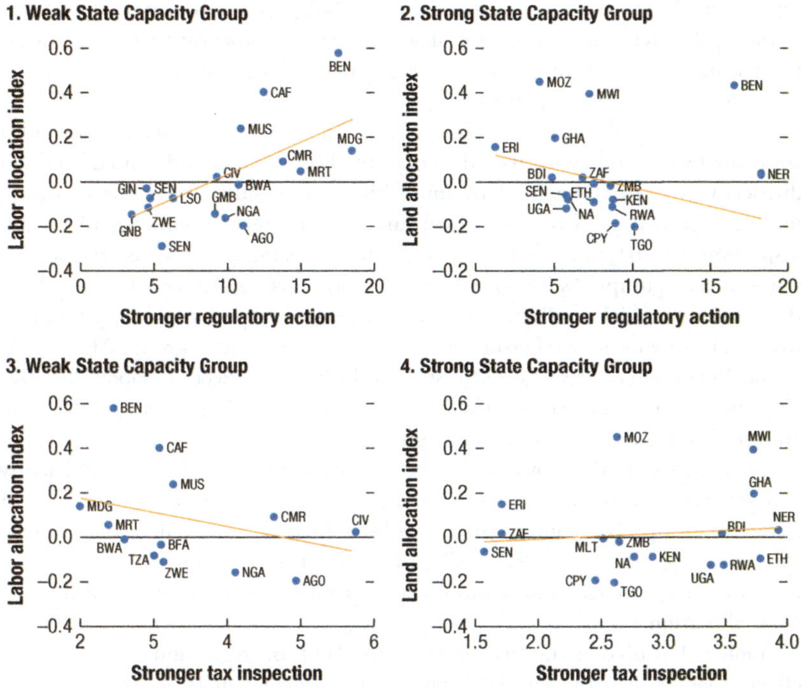

Source: World Bank Enterprise Survey.
Note: The strong state capacity group consists of countries in which the proportion of firms finding corruption a major obstacle is greater than the regional average, whereas the weak state capacity group consists of countries with below-average corruption. Data labels use International Organization for Standardization country codes.

regression that estimates the determinants of factor allocative efficiency in Table 4.1:

$$M_{isjck} = \delta_0 + \delta_1 Z_{sjck} + \delta_2 x_{isjck} + \kappa_s + \mu_k + \varepsilon_{isjck}$$

$$Z_{sjck} = \begin{cases} F_{jck} & \text{for land allocation index} \\ (R_{jck}, T_{sck}), & \text{for labor allocation index} \end{cases} \tag{2}$$

where i indexes firms, s indexes sector, j indexes district, c indexes country, and k indexes region (western, central, eastern, and southern sub-Saharan Africa dummies). M stands for either the land or the labor allocation index, and x controls for firm-level variables such as machines and equipment investments, managers' work experience, and firm-ownership dummies (for example, state-owned enterprise or foreign enterprise). Country-level variables such as real GDP per capita growth, the ratio of private credit to GDP, judicial efficiency (the quality of the legal system, including judicial administration, processing time, and court regulations to enforce contracts), and trade openness are also included.[5] κ_s and μ_k are sector and region fixed effects.

In column 1, the negative coefficient of the ethnic fractionalization index confirms lower land-allocative efficiency (for both owned and rented land) in districts where ethnic fractionalization is higher. In column 2, a labor allocation index is regressed on two institutional variables (stronger formal regulations and inspection efforts) along with other controls, separately for weak and strong state-capacity groups. As found in Figure 4.4, stronger regulatory action improves the efficiency of labor allocation in the weak state-capacity group, whereas it worsens labor allocative efficiency in the strong state-capacity group. Also, stronger tax inspection efforts worsen (or statistically have no effect on) labor allocative efficiency in the weak state-capacity group, whereas it improves the allocative efficiency in the strong state-capacity group.

Coefficients of other covariates indicate that land tends to be more efficiently allocated for firms with more capital, more experienced managers, and foreign or state ownership. For country-level variables, financial deepening and judicial efficiency support efficient factor allocations, whereas fast GDP growth does not necessarily improve factor allocation. Trade openness is also associated with better labor allocation.

Table 4.1 is used as the first stage for the IV-Tobit regression to identify the effect of factor allocative efficiency on firm performance in Table 4.4.

Effect of Land Market and Regulations on Firm Size

Table 4.2 shows reduced-form estimates that regress firm size on land value, labor regulation, and inspection actions to test our theoretical hypotheses. Columns 3 and 6 restrict the sample to places where the minimum wage is set below the market-clearing wage.[6]

Columns 1 to 3 estimate the effect of higher land value on firm size. The ownership of higher-value land significantly increases firm size, considering firms can reap scale benefits by relaxing collateral constraints. The effect is positive regardless of the minimum wage.[7]

Estimates in columns 4 and 5 show that formal regulations increase firm size whereas stronger inspections have an insignificant effect. Column 6 tests the

---

[5] Laeven and Woodruff (2007) show that in Mexico, improvement in the quality of the legal system supports firm growth by reducing the business risk faced by firm owners.

[6] The market-clearing wage is defined as the employees' average monthly earnings from the ILOSTAT. For countries where ILOSTAT does not provide data, mean wage data from Table 1 of Bhorat, Kanbur, and Stanwix (2017) are used.

[7] The effect of land value on firm size becomes insignificant for rented land, because it cannot serve as collateral for borrowing.

TABLE 4.1.

Determinants of Factor Allocative Efficiency in Sub-Saharan Africa

	(1) Land Allocation Index		(2) Labor Allocation Index		
	Owned	Owned or Rented			
Ethnic diversity index	−0.660*** [0.102]	−0.437*** [0.047]			
Stronger regulatory action			0.000 [0.002]	0.006** [0.002]	−0.008*** [0.002]
Stronger inspection efforts			0.009 [0.008]	−0.011 [0.011]	0.030*** [0.009]
Ln(capital investment)	0.022*** [0.004]	0.011*** [0.001]	0.004*** [0.001]	0.005*** [0.001]	0.004*** [0.001]
Ln(manager experience)	0.074*** [0.019]	0.068*** [0.007]	0.038*** [0.005]	0.028*** [0.009]	0.044*** [0.008]
Foreign ownership	0.059** [0.029]	0.126*** [0.018]	0.123*** [0.014]	0.138*** [0.020]	0.116*** [0.021]
State ownership	0.315** [0.134]	0.138** [0.056]	0.023 [0.033]	0.022 [0.044]	0.061 [0.055]
GDP per capita growth	−0.035*** [0.008]	−0.020*** [0.003]	−0.012*** [0.003]	−0.017*** [0.004]	−0.005 [0.004]
Private credit/GDP	0.110 [0.139]	0.236*** [0.075]	0.134** [0.053]	0.218** [0.100]	0.062 [0.074]
Judicial efficiency	0.260 [0.188]	0.511*** [0.113]	0.011 [0.091]	0.250* [0.147]	−0.252** [0.115]
Trade openness	−0.283** [0.116]	−0.105** [0.041]	0.092* [0.048]	0.165** [0.070]	0.095* [0.048]
Constant	0.047 [0.171]	−0.190*** [0.072]	−0.211*** [0.080]	−0.373*** [0.116]	−0.082 [0.083]
No. of observations	6,707	19,962	15,169	6,927	8,242
R^2	0.059	0.056	0.040	0.071	0.044
Sample	All	All	All	Weak state capacity group	Strong state capacity group
Sectoral and regional fixed effects	Yes	Yes	Yes	Yes	Yes

Source: Author.
Note: Standard errors clustered at the sampling strata level appear in brackets.
*$p < 0.10$; **$p < 0.05$; ***$p < 0.01$.

effect of stronger regulation on firm size when the sample only covers countries where the minimum wage is set below market-clearing wage. The effect is ambiguous in theory, depending on labor demand and supply elasticity to regulation changes. The result shows that stronger regulation has a positive effect on firm size, suggesting that labor demand shrinks less in response to stronger regulations, whereas formalization of workers increases more.

Columns 2, 3, 5, and 6 show that an increase in the minimum wage (relative to per capita income) reduces firm size on average, but with a small magnitude, showing the limited disemployment effect of the minimum wage; however, a higher

TABLE 4.2.

Direct Effect of Land and Labor Regulations in Sub-Saharan Africa (Reduced Form)

	Ln(Firm Size)					
	(1)	(2)	(3)	(4)	(5)	(6)
Ln(land value)	0.039***	0.031***	0.033***			
	[0.002]	[0.003]	[0.004]			
Stronger regulatory action				0.015***	0.014***	0.011**
				[0.004]	[0.005]	[0.004]
Stronger inspection efforts				0.023	−0.003	0.014
				[0.020]	[0.023]	[0.023]
Ln(capital investment)	0.062***	0.083***	0.079***	0.045***	0.045***	0.046***
	[0.008]	[0.009]	[0.008]	[0.004]	[0.004]	[0.004]
Ln(manager experience)	0.222***	0.253***	0.236***	0.260***	0.262***	0.254***
	[0.024]	[0.026]	[0.030]	[0.016]	[0.018]	[0.019]
Foreign ownership	0.786***	0.747***	0.795***	0.772***	0.767***	0.804***
	[0.068]	[0.060]	[0.067]	[0.040]	[0.039]	[0.042]
State ownership	1.075***	0.968***	0.944***	0.450***	0.393***	0.368***
	[0.154]	[0.175]	[0.193]	[0.104]	[0.110]	[0.112]
Minimum wage/GDP per capita		−0.014***	3.027**		−0.007***	2.443**
		[0.002]	[1.443]		[0.002]	[0.970]
GDP per capita growth	0.007	0.009	0.016	0.028***	0.024*	0.026**
	[0.011]	[0.019]	[0.018]	[0.008]	[0.014]	[0.013]
Private credit/GDP	0.897***	0.825***	0.738***	0.626***	0.274	0.245
	[0.254]	[0.246]	[0.237]	[0.179]	[0.210]	[0.202]
Judicial efficiency	−0.632*	−0.25	0.007	−0.266	−0.236	−0.02
	[0.345]	[0.603]	[0.644]	[0.311]	[0.403]	[0.384]
Trade openness	−0.519***	−0.568**	-0.580**	−0.465***	−0.376***	−0.403***
	[0.175]	[0.252]	[0.239]	[0.122]	[0.133]	[0.123]
Constant	2.077***	1.797***	1.512***	2.152***	2.338***	2.058***
	[0.243]	[0.426]	[0.458]	[0.187]	[0.216]	[0.226]
No. of observations	7,997	6,023	5,598	19,237	15,414	14,417
Sample	All	All	Minimum wage below market wage	All	All	Minimum wage below market wage
Sectoral and regional fixed effects	Yes	Yes	Yes	Yes	Yes	Yes

Source: Author.

Note: Standard errors clustered at the sampling strata level appear in brackets.

*$p < .10$; **$p < .05$; ***$p < .01$.

minimum wage significantly increases firm size when the sample is restricted only to firms where the minimum wage is set below market-clearing wage. This implies that the initial level of the minimum wage is significantly lower than market-clearing wage, thus, raising the minimum wage simply attracts more labor.

Other covariates show that firms with more capital and experienced managers tend to be larger. Foreign-owned firms or state-owned enterprises are also larger than local private firms. Income growth and financial deepening also support firm growth, whereas judicial efficiency has no direct effect on firm size. Larger trade openness appears to adversely affect small firms for surviving market competition.

Effect of Factor Allocative Efficiency on Firm Size and Survival

What are the consequences of land and labor misallocations? Figure 4.1 and Annex Table 4.1 show that sub-Saharan African firms are significantly smaller (in employees), less productive, and less long-lived than Asian firms. Here we use the established factor allocation index and analyze its effect on firm size and age in sub-Saharan Africa.

To study factors that affect firm size and age, we run the following Tobit regression:

$$y_{isjck} = \max\left(0, \alpha_0 + \alpha_1 M_{isjck} + \alpha_2 x_{isjck} + \kappa_s + \mu_k + \varepsilon_{isjck}\right). \tag{3}$$

The same explanatory variables as used in equation (2) are included as control variables. Table 4.3 shows the effect of factor allocative efficiency on firm size (in columns 1 to 4) and firm age (in columns 5 to 8). Columns 1 and 5 show the effect of the allocative efficiency of owned land, whereas columns 2 and 6 show the result for the allocative efficiency of both owned and rented land. The results in columns 2 and 6 show that an increase in land allocative efficiency by 1 standard deviation significantly increases firm size (by 32 percent) and survival (by 11 percent), both significant at the 1 percent level.

Higher labor allocative efficiency also significantly increases firm size for both strong and weak state capacity groups (columns 3, 4, 7, and 8). The negative and significant square term of the labor allocation index indicates that the effect of labor allocative efficiency on firm size and age is concave, that is, the positive effect is particularly large when initial labor allocation is inefficient. As a labor market develops to achieve efficient labor allocation, the marginal effect gets smaller.

Other covariates show similar results as found in the reduced-form regression in Table 4.2.

Instrumental Variable Results: Heterogeneity in Effects of Factor Allocative Efficiency on Firm Performance

In identifying an allocative efficiency index, one faces an endogeneity problem for potential reverse causality. That is, firm performance could affect allocative efficiency. Firms whose land and labor allocations are affected by regulation and ethnic fractionalization are marginally productive in the local market (Imbens 2010). The decision to reallocate factors of production varies with firm productivity. An IV-Tobit regression estimates the local average treatment effect (LATE) of factor allocative efficiency on firm performance.

TABLE 4.3.

Firm Performance and Factor Allocative Efficiency in Sub-Saharan Africa (Ordinary Least Squares Tobit)

	Ln(Firm Age)							
	(1)	(2)	(3)	(4)	(5)	(6)	(7)	(8)
Land allocation index (owned)	0.574***				0.205***			
	[0.066]				[0.035]			
Land allocation index (owned or rented)		0.315***				0.113***		
		[0.065]				[0.022]		
Labor allocation index			1.380***	1.479***			0.243***	0.202***
			[0.132]	[0.139]			[0.046]	[0.045]
Labor allocation index squared			−0.295***	−0.303***			−0.074***	−0.058***
			[0.052]	[0.050]			[0.022]	[0.022]
Ln(capital investments)	0.074***	0.047***	0.051***	0.047***	0.009***	0.006***	0.005***	0.006***
	[0.010]	[0.004]	[0.004]	[0.004]	[0.003]	[0.001]	[0.002]	[0.002]
Ln(manager experience)	0.217***	0.267***	0.176***	0.201***	0.558***	0.561***	0.523***	0.527***
	[0.023]	[0.015]	[0.023]	[0.023]	[0.016]	[0.010]	[0.017]	[0.015]
Foreign ownership	0.776***	0.683***	0.590***	0.683***	0.083***	0.061***	0.067**	0.062***
	[0.068]	[0.040]	[0.052]	[0.041]	[0.028]	[0.019]	[0.027]	[0.022]
State ownership	1.060***	0.506***	0.222**	0.445***	0.482***	0.252***	0.116**	0.303***
	[0.157]	[0.097]	[0.088]	[0.114]	[0.083]	[0.043]	[0.051]	[0.070]
GDP per capita growth	0.017	0.017**	0.030***	0.032**	0.014**	0.009**	0.036***	−0.002
	[0.012]	[0.007]	[0.012]	[0.013]	[0.007]	[0.004]	[0.006]	[0.006]
Private credit/GDP	0.666**	0.615***	0.132	1.098***	0.348***	0.184***	0.115	0.364***
	[0.259]	[0.159]	[0.185]	[0.267]	[0.094]	[0.062]	[0.102]	[0.086]
Judicial efficiency	−0.345	−0.367	−1.657***	0.741**	−0.326	−0.598***	−1.055***	−0.268*
	[0.403]	[0.258]	[0.395]	[0.351]	[0.207]	[0.111]	[0.198]	[0.156]
Trade openness	−0.424**	−0.337***	−0.451**	−0.815***	−0.119	−0.294***	−0.615***	−0.131**
	[0.194]	[0.106]	[0.190]	[0.155]	[0.084]	[0.043]	[0.073]	[0.057]
Constant	2.069***	2.228***	3.387***	2.007***	1.214***	1.504***	2.158***	1.305***
	[0.259]	[0.144]	[0.225]	[0.216]	[0.126]	[0.076]	[0.132]	[0.091]
No. of observations	7,687	22,295	6,927	8,242	7,539	21,770	7,253	8,861
Sample	All	All	Weak state capacity group	Strong state capacity group	All	All	Weak state capacity group	Strong state capacity group
Sectoral and regional fixed effects	Yes	Yes	Yes	Yes	Yes	Yes	Yes	Yes

Source: Author.

Note: Standard errors clustered at the sampling strata level appear in brackets.

*$p < .10$; **$p < .05$; ***$p < .01$.

As defined in equation (2), different IVs are used in the first-stage regression. The subnational-level ethnic diversity index is the only IV for the land allocation index that influences firms' access to land. The ethnic fractionalization index comes from census data near 2000, thus it offers predetermined ethnic diversity for each district before the World Bank conducted the Enterprise Survey.

The model is overidentified by using two IVs for the labor allocation index: the average level of regulatory action taken by subnational governments toward peer firms in the same district (R_j) and the average inspection efforts taken toward peer firms to regulate tax evasion in the same sector (T_s). The first variable captures the average level of formal regulatory measures to formalize labor contracts, whereas the second variable is the intensity of informal sector monitoring, that is, the penalty or cost of noncompliance (*informal tax*) (Olken and Singhal 2011).

The identifying assumption is that average regulatory situations for a peer group affect own-firm performance only through the factor allocation. The rationale for the exclusion restriction is that when looking at the same district across sectors (for R_j) or the same sector across districts (for T_s), government regulatory actions toward peer firms affect factor allocation in the same labor market but have limited effect on own firms' production.

Table 4.4 shows IV Tobit estimates that are the LATE of the land and labor allocation index for marginally productive firms. In the lower panel of Table 4.4, the first-stage F-statistics are sufficiently high for all specifications (p value = 0.00), showing that ethnic fractionalization and regulations are valid instruments for the land and labor allocation indices.

Columns 1, 2, 5, and 6 show that land allocation matters for marginal firms to grow and survive longer (significant at 1 percent). In columns 2, 3, 5, and 6, the positive square term and negative linear term of the labor allocation index suggest that the effect of labor allocative efficiency is convex: the effect exponentially increases as a labor market develops and labor allocation gets more efficient. The convex LATE of labor allocative efficiency is different from the concave effect found by the OLS Tobit regression in Table 4.3 for the average firm. This suggests large heterogeneity in the effect of labor allocative efficiency. The marginal effect of labor allocation index on firm size is much larger for firms operating in countries with weak state capacity. Both OLS and IV-Tobit estimates find that overall, efficient labor allocation contributes to firm growth and longer survival.

Effect of Factor Allocations on Credit Access and Tax Contributions

We further investigate whether better factor allocation helps firm growth through credit access and tax contributions. Better land allocation, when land acts as a collateral, as well as more efficient labor allocation, may help firms obtain credit and grow faster. With stronger labor and tax regulations, labor contracts would be more formalized and firms' tax contributions to the government may increase.

TABLE 4.4.

Firm Performance and Factor Allocative Efficiency in Sub-Saharan Africa (IV Tobit)

	Ln(Firm Age)							
	(1)	(2)	(3)	(4)	(5)	(6)	(7)	(8)
Land allocation index (owned)	0.408***				0.416***			
	[0.114]				[0.072]			
Land allocation index (owned or rented)		0.288***				0.569***		
		[0.089]				[0.062]		
Labor allocation index			−0.708	−3.856***			−1.412***	−0.935*
			[0.790]	[0.805]			[0.435]	[0.561]
Labor allocation index squared			1.684***	1.722**			0.124	1.312**
			[0.618]	[0.715]			[0.347]	[0.531]
Constant	2.213***	2.354***	3.091***	1.366***	1.375***	1.729***	1.824***	1.252***
	[0.125]	[0.069]	[0.247]	[0.211]	[0.077]	[0.047]	[0.135]	[0.156]
First Stage: F-Statistics for Excluded Instrumental Variables (*p* value)								
Land allocation index (owned)	174.5				165.8			
	[0.00]				[0.00]			
Land allocation index (owned or rented)		298.2				287.9		
		[0.00]				[0.00]		
Labor allocation index			24.8	49.5			22.4	46.8
			[0.00]	[0.00]			[0.00]	[0.00]
Labor allocation index^2			8.2	13.3			7.1	11.0
			[0.00]	[0.00]			[0.00]	[0.00]
No. of observations	6,707	19,962	6,927	8,242	6,564	19,462	6,687	8,050
Sample	All	All	Weak state capacity group	Strong state capacity group	All	All	Weak state capacity group	Strong state capacity group
Sectoral and regional fixed effects	Yes	Yes	Yes	Yes	Yes	Yes	Yes	Yes
Basic controls included	Yes	Yes	Yes	Yes	Yes	Yes	Yes	Yes

Source: Author.

Note: Standard errors clustered at the sampling strata level appear in brackets. Basic controls include country and firm characteristics as included in the ordinary least squares Tobit regression in Table 4.3.

$*p < .10$; $**p < .05$; $***p < .01$.

Figure 4.5. The Effect of Land and Labor Allocative Efficiency on Firm Performance in Sub-Saharan Africa
(Percentage points)

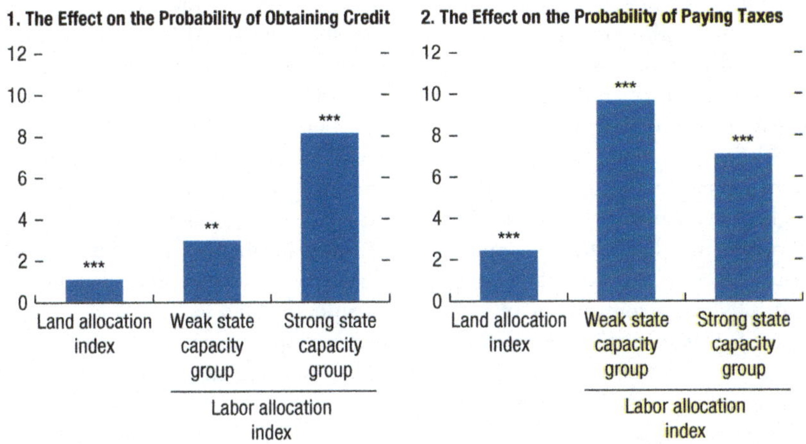

Source: Author.
Note: The bars capture the coefficient of each allocation index on the probabilities of obtaining credit and paying taxes.
$^{**}p < .05$; $^{***}p < .01$.

Figure 4.5 reports the effects of land and labor allocative efficiency on firms' access to credit (loans from banks or other financial institutions) and on tax contributions (percentage of sales reported for tax payments).

The result suggests that firms perform better as factor allocation becomes more efficient. The increase in land and labor allocation indices by 1 standard deviation increases the probability of obtaining credit by about 1 and 6 percentage points, respectively. The effect is larger at about 8 percentage points where state capacity is strong.

The estimate also shows that improvement in factor allocative efficiency would accelerate the formalization of industries through higher tax contributions. In weak institutional regions, an improvement in labor allocative efficiency through stronger regulation increases tax contributions by about 10 percentage points, which is larger than the same effect in strong-institution regions by about 2 percentage points. If land is allocated more to productive firms, they can expand for longer periods with more chance to obtain a credit line from a bank, increasing their tax contributions.

Panel Data Analysis: Case Study for Nigeria

Here we examine whether the aggregate-level findings on firm growth can be confirmed for a single country, using firm panel data from Nigeria. Nigeria panel data from the World Bank Enterprise Survey include basic financial accounts; we may therefore estimate TFPQ using Levinsohn and Petrin's (2003) method. Firm-level analysis within Nigeria better identifies policy effects, because time-invariant factors can be removed using panel data structure.

Nigeria is the most populous country in sub-Saharan Africa, composed of more than 250 ethnic groups and endowed with the 10th largest oil reserves in the world.[8] However, the GDP per capita (in constant 2011 international dollars based on purchasing power parity) is ranked 133 of 191 countries (IMF 2018b), with the poverty rate increasing in recent years. Poverty is most prevalent in the northern part of the country, with the state of Jigawa's headcount poverty rate the highest at 78 percent (Nwude 2013; World Bank 2015), whereas the southern part near the Niger Delta is wealthy from its oil endowment. The quality of governance has been low: in the Transparency International Corruption Perceptions Index, Nigeria scores as one of the most corrupt countries in the world (ranked 148 of 180 countries). Furthermore, underdeveloped areas in the north are plagued by conflicts (for example, Islamist extremist insurgency by Boko Haram), again leading to weak state capacity.

The land tenure system and land rental market are underdeveloped in Nigeria. The land allocation index for Nigerian states computed using equation (1) is mapped in Annex Figure 4.4.3. Many states in the northwest and the southeast are scored at negative or small positive values, suggesting inefficiency in land allocation.

Annex Figure 4.4.4 similarly shows that the labor allocation index is negative or close to zero in the northwestern Nigerian states. Figure 4.6 shows that labor allocative efficiency is negatively correlated with tax inspection by the local government (World Bank 2014). Despite slight improvements in business conditions, the World Bank's Ease of Doing Business Index scores most Nigerian states lower than the sub-Saharan African average. Multiple layers of regulatory requirements lead to high start-up costs.

Nigeria's fiscal regime also entails the extensive use of tax incentives and exemptions, eroding the fairness of tax treatments and leading to tax evasion. Nigeria was the first sub-Saharan African country to explore a contributory social insurance system, but social security coverage has been limited with weak regulatory capacity, leading to high tax noncompliance and the accumulation of tax arrears (IMF 2005, 2018a). As a result, the current regulatory system is little trusted by the private sector, making firms operate informally and distorting the labor allocation.

In such a context, the following panel regression estimates the effect of land and labor allocative efficiency on firm size in Nigeria:

$$y_{isjt} = \alpha_0 + \alpha_1 M_{isjt} + \alpha_2 X_{isjt} + \lambda_i + \kappa_s + \mu_t + \varepsilon_{isjt}, \quad (4)$$

[8] Central Intelligence Agency, "World Factbook," https://www.cia.gov/library/publications/the-world-factbook/.

Figure 4.6. Labor Misallocation and Tax Inspection in Nigeria

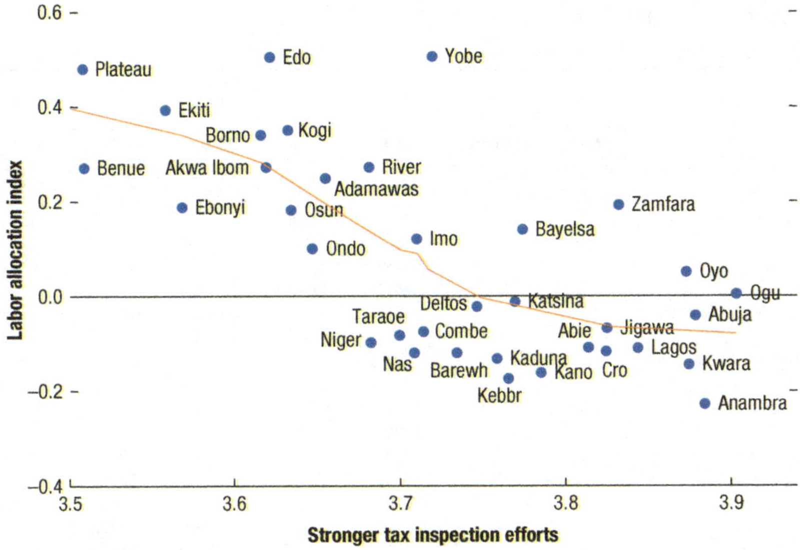

Source: World Bank Enterprise Survey, Nigeria panel data, 2007–14.
Note: Bandwidth = 0.8.

where M_{isjt} is the factor market efficiency index for firm i in sector s and state j at time t (t= 2007/09 or 2014). X_{isjt} controls for firm and state characteristics, such as the distance to the capital city Abuja, urbanization rate, and the suitability of land for agriculture from Gershman and Rivera (2018). λ_i, κ_s, and μ_t are firm, sector, and year fixed effects.

At the bottom of Table 4.5, the Breusch and Pagan Lagrange multiplier (LM) test supports the random effect specification rather than the pooled OLS regression, whereas the Hausman test supports the fixed effect rather than the random effect model.

In Table 4.5, both random and fixed effect estimates confirm that landholding with higher land value and efficient factor allocations significantly increases firm size in Nigeria. The coefficients get smaller in magnitude under the fixed effect model, but the effects remain significant. Stronger inspection efforts significantly constrain firm growth, whereas the effect of formal regulation has no effect under the fixed effect model. Estimates for other control variables show that firm size gets larger as firms locate in urbanized areas with land suitable for nonagricultural activities.

TABLE 4.5.

Determinants of Firm Size in Nigeria

(Fixed versus random effect regressions)

	Ln (Firm Size)							
	(1)		(2)		(3)		(4)	
	RE Model	FE Model	RE Model	FE Model	RE Model	FE Model	RE Model	FE Model
Ln(land value, owned or rented)	0.022*** [0.006]	0.022*** [0.007]						
Stronger regulatory action			0.006** [0.003]	0.000 [0.003]				
Stronger inspection efforts			−0.215*** [0.065]	−0.199*** [0.070]				
Land allocation index					0.109*** [0.028]	0.057** [0.028]		
Labor allocation index							0.205*** [0.044]	0.129*** [0.036]
Ln(capital investment)	0.012* [0.006]	0.001 [0.007]	0.021*** [0.005]	0.009 [0.006]	0.023*** [0.006]	0.010 [0.006]	0.018*** [0.006]	0.008 [0.006]
Ln(manager experience)	0.058 [0.039]	0.029 [0.045]	0.054 [0.039]	0.027 [0.045]	0.048 [0.042]	0.018 [0.051]	0.069* [0.040]	0.038 [0.048]
Foreign ownership	0.277** [0.117]	0.173 [0.142]	0.269** [0.119]	0.158 [0.144]	0.210* [0.119]	0.161 [0.138]	0.318*** [0.120]	0.239* [0.143]
State ownership	0.195* [0.107]	0.164 [0.123]	0.139 [0.110]	0.13 [0.126]	0.245** [0.111]	0.148 [0.125]	0.171 [0.113]	0.107 [0.125]
Ln(distance to Abuja)	0.212*** [0.066]		0.209*** [0.066]		0.209*** [0.065]		0.204*** [0.065]	
Urbanization rate	0.668*** [0.188]		0.685*** [0.187]		0.687*** [0.186]		0.724*** [0.183]	
Land suitability for agriculture	−0.094 [0.062]		-0.112* [0.062]		−0.097 [0.061]		−0.104* [0.060]	
Constant	1.124** [0.440]	2.402*** [0.135]	2.097*** [0.521]	3.339*** [0.315]	1.217*** [0.441]	2.473*** [0.147]	1.289*** [0.436]	2.493*** [0.147]
No. of observation	1,499	1,499	1,499	1,499	1,374	1,374	1,415	1,415
R^2 (overall)	0.135	0.054	0.139	0.049	0.170	0.077	0.192	0.097
Sector dummies	Yes	Yes	Yes	Yes	Yes	Yes	Yes	Yes
Diagnostic Tests								
Breusch and Pagan Lagrange multiplier test	220.61 [0.000]			212.38 [0.000]		130.46 [0.000]		158.96 [0.000]
Hausman test	73.42 [0.000]			101.28 [0.000]		74.43 [0.000]		77.77 [0.000]

Source: Author.

Note: Robust standard errors appear in brackets. FE = fixed effect; RE = random effect.

*$p < .10$; **$p < .05$; ***$p < .01$.

CONCLUSIONS

Despite a long period of strong growth, pessimistic development prospects dominate in sub-Saharan Africa because of its heavy reliance on natural resources and low competitiveness. This chapter examined the roots of the region's weak industrial performance by examining the efficiency of the factor market and its role in firm growth.

This chapter first estimated the allocative efficiency of land and labor in 40 sub-Saharan African countries following Olley and Pakes (1996), which suggests significant factor misallocations in the region. Factor market distortions stem primarily from fragile institutional environments, including conflict among diverse ethnic groups, customary land systems, and weakly enforced regulations. Estimated factor allocation indices suggest ample scope for improving land and labor efficiencies through factor reallocations to more productive firms.

On the basis of predictions from a dual-economy model with two margins of informality, the chapter tested whether sub-Saharan African firms could achieve significantly more scale and productivity gains by improving factor market efficiency.

IV regression confirms that African firms face significant factor misallocation from ethnic fractionalization and regulatory actions. Given that the allocation of land is often informally determined and land disputes among ethnic groups are common in sub-Saharan Africa, access to land is limited for productive firms. Under limited enforcement of labor regulations, workers are unwilling to continue formal business at a large scale. In low-income sub-Saharan Africa where corruption is widespread, stricter monitoring of small enterprises by tax inspectors increases "informal tax," which often outweighs the benefits of running a formal business.

Based on first-stage results, the IV-Tobit regressions using pooled data of 40 sub-Saharan African countries and Nigerian panel data show that factor reallocation would allow firms to survive longer and achieve better growth, with an especially large policy effect (LATE) for marginally productive firms. The results also suggest that access to credit and tax contributions could increase if factor misallocation were addressed, which may further support firm growth in sub-Saharan Africa.

From a policy perspective, the results imply that the effect of regulatory reforms on factor market efficiency and firm growth depends on local legal capacity. There is no one size fits all, but regulation design needs to match local legal capacity. Stricter monitoring of informal activities does not always support firm growth in sub-Saharan Africa. Formalizing labor contracts with mandated benefits is more effective in supporting firm growth when legal capacity is weak. As legal capacity develops, stronger informal sector monitoring becomes more effective in accelerating the reallocation of workers to productive formal activities.

As it stands, high informality in sub-Saharan Africa could be the equilibrium outcome of informal firms' rational choice to stay in the informal sector. This may reflect that the informal sector provides small African firms with safety nets, whereas the costs outweigh the benefits of operating formal businesses. In this regard, a natural way to reduce informality in sub-Saharan Africa is to introduce simple formal sector or informal sector regulations, as they fit the local context, to achieve more efficient land and labor allocations and support the growth of formal micro entrepreneurs.

ANNEX 4.1. SUMMARY STATISTICS

ANNEX TABLE 4.1.1.

Cross-Country Pooled Firm Data: Sub-Saharan Africa versus Developing Asia

Variables	Source	Definition	Sub-Saharan Africa					
			Number	Mean	Median	Standard Deviation	Minimum	Maximum
Firm-Level Variables								
Firm size	World Bank Enterprise Survey	No. of employees	23,000	58.1	13.3	392.7	1.0	45,000.0
Firm age	World Bank Enterprise Survey	Years after starting business	22,364	14.3	11.0	11.7	0.0	65.0
Ln(value added/ employee)	World Bank Enterprise Survey, *World Economic Outlook*	Log of sales minus labor and input costs (including electricity, raw materials and intermediate goods, and fuels) (in 2011 international $) divided by the number of employees	22,248	9.88	9.53	2.75	–7.23	24.41
Ln(land value, owned)	World Bank Enterprise Survey, *World Economic Outlook*	Net book values of land and buildings (in 2011 international $)	7,307	8.56	10.51	6.33	0.00	25.60
Ln(land value, owned or rented)	World Bank Enterprise Survey, *World Economic Outlook*	Log of annual expenditure on purchases, repurchases, and renting of land and building (in 2011 international $)	23,000	4.79	0.00	6.37	0.00	28.91
Percent owned land	World Bank Enterprise Survey	Percent of land owned by the firm	18,594	43.75	0	48.51	0	100
Ln(capital investment)	World Bank Enterprise Survey, *World Economic Outlook*	Purchase or repurchase of equipment (in 2011 international $)	23,000	5	8.69	6.30	0.00	28.92
Ln(manager experience)	World Bank Enterprise Survey	Chief executive officer's work experience in the same sector (in years)	22,604	2.49	2.48	0.69	0.00	4.33
State ownership	World Bank Enterprise Survey	Dummy: owned by government	22,702	0.02	0	0.15	0	1
Foreign ownership	World Bank Enterprise Survey	Dummy: owned by private foreign individuals or companies	22,683	0.16	0.00	0.36	0.00	1.00
Have credit access	World Bank Enterprise Survey	Dummy: firm has a line of credit or loan	22,605	0.21	0	0.41	0	1
Heavy industry	World Bank Enterprise Survey	Sector dummy	23,000	0.14	0	0.35	0	1
Wholesale and retail	World Bank Enterprise Survey	Sector dummy	23,000	0.19	0	0.39	0	1
Country-Level Variables								
GDP per capita growth	WDI	Percent (in real growth)	23,000	3.44	2.94	2.78	–3.39	12.53
Private credit/GDP	International Financial Statistics	Percentage	23,000	0.20	0.16	0.16	0.02	0.83
Judiciary efficiency	Doing Business	Distance to frontier (rescaled to 0–1; larger score is closer to frontier and thus more efficient)	23,000	0.53	0.53	0.10	0.26	0.67
Trade openness	World Development Indicators	(Export + Import)/GDP	23,000	23,000	0.66	0.64	0.23	0.28

(continued)

ANNEX TABLE 4.1.1. ***(continued)***

Cross-Country Pooled Firm Data: Sub-Saharan Africa versus Developing Asia

			Developing Asia					
Variables	**Source**	**Definition**	**Number**	**Mean**	**Median**	**Standard Deviation**	**Minimum**	**Maximum**
Firm-Level Variables								
Firm size	World Bank Enterprise Survey	No. of employees	29,609	180.3	31.3	2,079.4	0.0	170,666.7
Firm age	World Bank Enterprise Survey	Years after starting business	29,115	17.1	14.0	11.5	0.0	65.0
Ln(value added/employee)	World Bank Enterprise Survey, *World Economic Outlook*	Log of sales minus labor and input costs (including electricity, raw materials and intermediate goods, and fuels) (in 2011 international $) divided by the number of employees	27,272	9.46	9.56	2.17	−2.60	19.80
Ln(land value, owned)	World Bank Enterprise Survey, *World Economic Outlook*	Net book values of land and buildings (in 2011 international $)	13,802	11.20	12.73	4.90	0.00	26.93
Ln(land value, owned or rented)	World Bank Enterprise Survey, *World Economic Outlook*	Log of annual expenditure on purchases, repurchases, and renting of land and building (in 2011 international $)	29,665	5.43	0.00	6.53	0.00	26.01
Percent owned land	World Bank Enterprise Survey	Percent of land owned by the firm	22,587	62.32	100.00	47.36	0	100.00
Ln(capital investment)	World Bank Enterprise Survey, *World Economic Outlook*	Purchase or repurchase of equipment (in 2011 international $)	29,665	7.03	9.54	6.27	0.00	23.07
Ln(manager experience)	World Bank Enterprise Survey	Chief executive officer's work experience in the same sector (in years)	28,432	2.60	2.71	0.65	0.00	4.26
State ownership	World Bank Enterprise Survey	Dummy: owned by government	29,598	0.01	0	0.11	0	1
Foreign ownership	World Bank Enterprise Survey	Dummy: owned by private foreign individuals or companies	29,600	0.07	0.00	0.26	0.00	1.00
Have credit access	World Bank Enterprise Survey	Dummy: firm has a line of credit or loan	26,827	0.33	0	0.47	0	1
Heavy industry	World Bank Enterprise Survey	Sector dummy	29,665	0.35	0	0.48	0	1
Wholesale and retail	World Bank Enterprise Survey	Sector dummy	29,665	0.16	0	0.37	0	1
Country-Level Variables								
GDP per capita growth	WDI	Percent (in real growth)	29,665	5.19	5.16	1.71	2.01	11.65
Private credit/GDP	International Financial Statistics	Percentage	29,665	0.56	0.50	0.33	0.13	1.21
Judiciary efficiency	Doing Business	Distance to frontier (rescaled to 0–1; larger score is closer to frontier and thus more efficient)	22,575	0.43	0.33	0.16	0.27	0.72
Trade openness	World Development Indicators	(Export + Import)/GDP	29,665	0.66	0.49	0.36	0.40	1.79

Sources: IMF 2018b; IMF, International Financial Statistics database; IMF, African Department database; World Bank, Ease of Doing Business Index; World Bank, Enterprise Survey; and World Bank, World Development Indicators.

ANNEX 4.2. COUNTRY SAMPLE

Sub-Saharan Africa (40 Countries)

Sub-Saharan African countries include Angola, Benin, Botswana, Burkina Faso, Burundi, Cabo Verde, Cameroon, Central African Republic, Chad, Republic of Congo, Côte d'Ivoire, The State of Eritrea, Kingdom of Eswatini, The Federal Democratic Republic of Ethiopia, Gabon, The Gambia, Ghana, Guinea, Guinea-Bissau, Kenya, Kingdom of Lesotho, Liberia, Republic of Madagascar, Malawi, Mali, Islamic Republic of Mauritania, Mauritius, Republic of Mozambique, Namibia, Niger, Nigeria, Rwanda, Senegal, Sierra Leone, South Africa, United Republic of Tanzania, Togo, Uganda, Zambia, and Zimbabwe.

Developing Asia (14 Countries)

Developing Asia includes Bangladesh, Cambodia, People's Republic of China, India, Indonesia, Lao People's Democratic Republic, Malaysia, Mongolia, Myanmar, Nepal, Philippines, Sri Lanka, Thailand, and Vietnam.

ANNEX 4.3. SPATIAL DISTRIBUTION OF FIRM PERFORMANCE IN SUB-SAHARAN AFRICA AND DEVELOPING ASIA

Annex Figure 4.3.1. Firm Size in Sub-Saharan Africa and Developing Asia

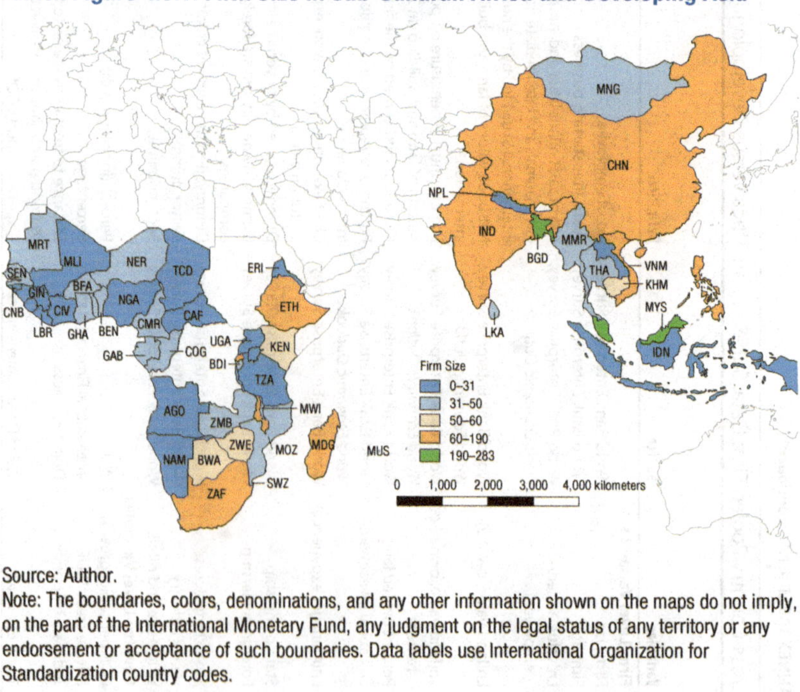

Source: Author.
Note: The boundaries, colors, denominations, and any other information shown on the maps do not imply, on the part of the International Monetary Fund, any judgment on the legal status of any territory or any endorsement or acceptance of such boundaries. Data labels use International Organization for Standardization country codes.

Annex Figure 4.3.2. Productivity in Sub-Saharan Africa and Developing Asia

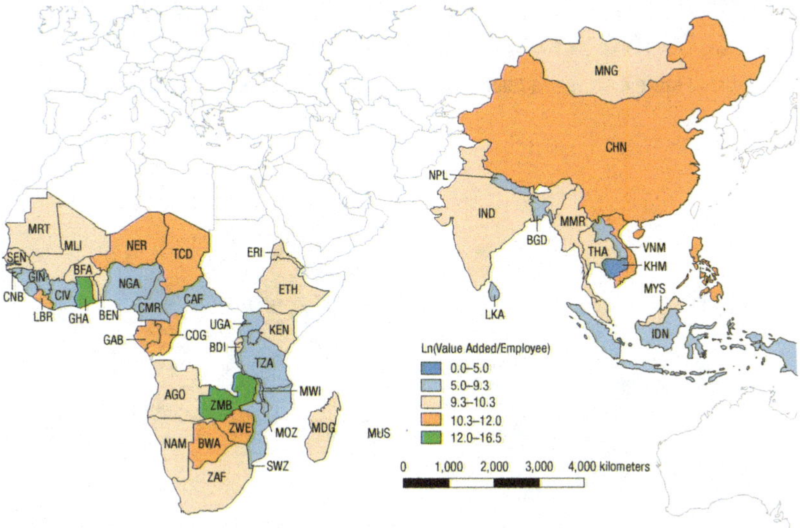

Source: Author.

Note: The boundaries, colors, denominations, and any other information shown on the maps do not imply, on the part of the International Monetary Fund, any judgment on the legal status of any territory or any endorsement or acceptance of such boundaries. Data labels use International Organization for Standardization country codes.

ANNEX 4.4. SPATIAL DISTRIBUTION OF FACTOR ALLOCATIVE EFFICIENCY IN SUB-SAHARAN AFRICA, DEVELOPING ASIA, AND NIGERIA

Annex Figure 4.4.1. Land Allocation in Sub-Saharan Africa and Developing Asia

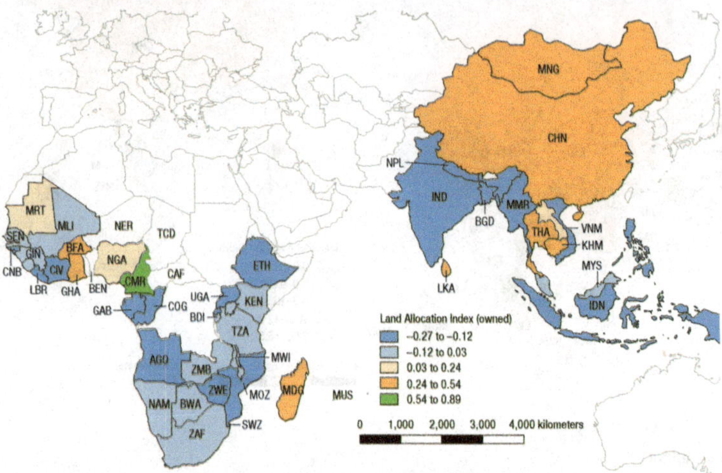

Source: Author.
Note: The boundaries, colors, denominations, and any other information shown on the maps do not imply, on the part of the International Monetary Fund, any judgment on the legal status of any territory or any endorsement or acceptance of such boundaries. Data labels use International Organization for Standardization country codes.

Annex Figure 4.4.2. Labor Allocation in Sub-Saharan Africa and Developing Asia

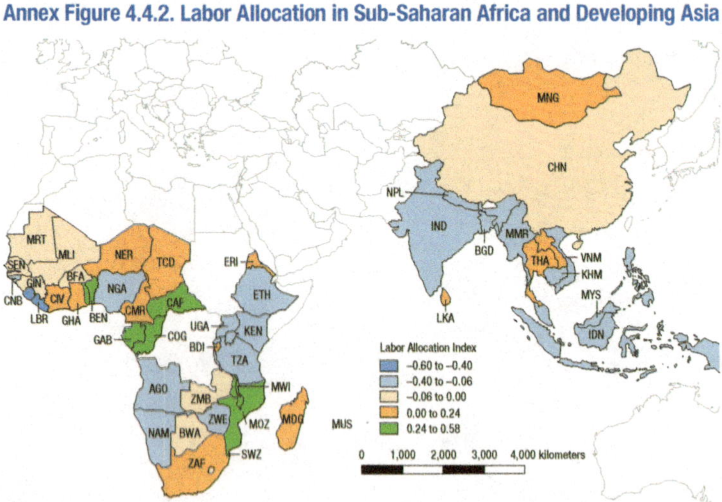

Source: Author.
Note: The boundaries, colors, denominations, and any other information shown on the maps do not imply, on the part of the International Monetary Fund, any judgment on the legal status of any territory or any endorsement or acceptance of such boundaries. Data labels use International Organization for Standardization country codes.

Annex Figure 4.4.3. Land Allocation in Nigeria

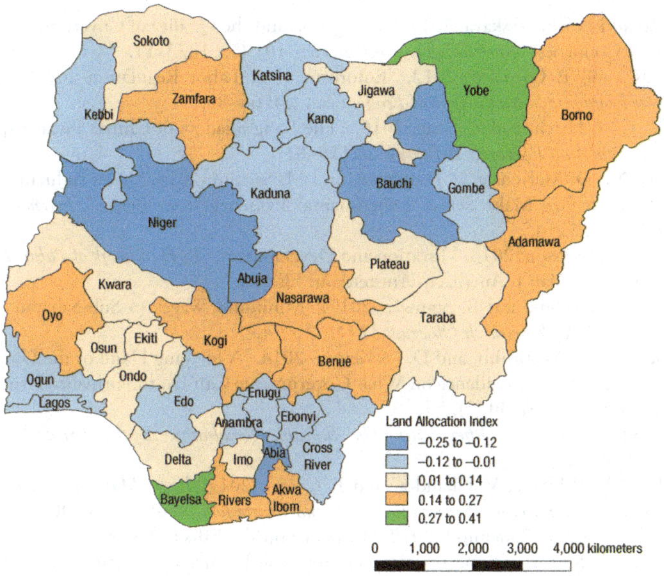

Source: Author.

Annex Figure 4.4.4. Labor Allocation in Nigeria

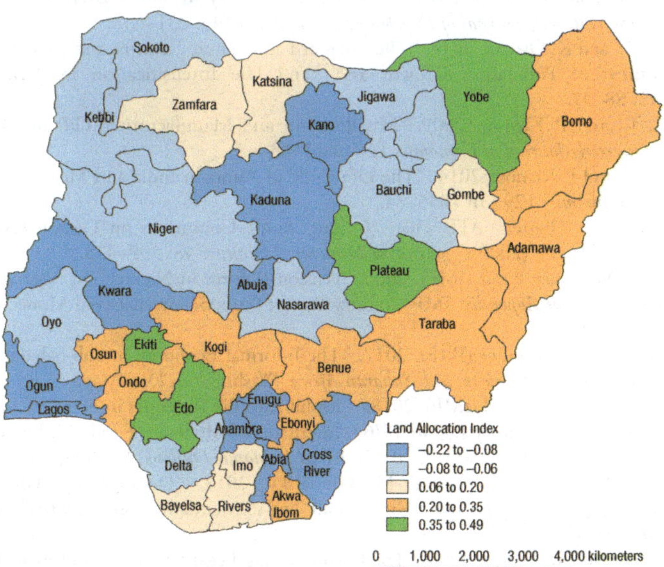

Source: Author.

REFERENCES

Alesina, A., and E. Zhuravskaya. 2011. "Segregation and the Quality of Government in a Cross Section of Countries." *American Economic Review* 101 (5): 1872–11.

Almeida, R., and P. Carneiro. 2012. "Enforcement of Labor Regulation and Informality." *American Economic Journal: Applied Economics* 4 (3): 64–89.

Bai, C.-E., C.-T. Hsieh, and Z. Song. 2016. "The Long Shadow of China's Fiscal Expansion." *Brookings Papers on Economic Activity* Fall: 129–81.

Benhassine, N., D. McKenzie, V. Pouliquen, and M. Santini. 2018. "Does Inducing Informal Firms to Formalize Make Sense? Experimental Evidence from Benin." *Journal of Public Economics* 157: 1–14.

Besley, T., and T. Persson. 2013. "Taxation and Development." In *Handbook of Public Economics* vol. 5, edited by Alan J. Auerbach. Amsterdam: Elsevier.

Bhorat, H., R. Kanbur, and B. Stanwix. 2017. "Minimum Wages in Sub-Saharan Africa: A Primer." *World Bank Research Observer* 32 (1): 21–74.

de Andrade, G. H., M. Bruhn, and D. McKenzie. 2014. "A Helping Hand or the Long Arm of the Law? Experimental Evidence on What Governments Can Do to Formalize Firms." *World Bank Economics Review* 30 (1): 54.

De Soto, H. 1989. *The Other Path: The Invisible Revolution in the Third World.* New York: Basic Books.

Dihn, H. T., V. Palmade, V. Chandra, and F. Cossar. 2012. *Light Manufacturing in Africa: Targeted Policies to Enhance Private Investment and Create Jobs.* Washington, DC: World Bank.

Dinkelman, T., and V. Ranchhod. 2012. "Evidence on the Effect of Minimum Wage Laws in an Informal Sector: Domestic Workers in South Africa." *Journal of Development Economics* 99 (1): 27–45.

Easterly, W., and R. Levine. 1997. "Africa's Growth Tragedy: Policies and Ethnic Divisions." *Quarterly Journal of Economics* 112 (4): 1203–50.

Galiani, S., and F. Weinschelbaum. 2012. "Modeling Informality Formally: Households and Firms." *Economic Inquiry* 50 (3): 821–38.

Gershman, B., and D. Rivera. 2018. "Subnational Diversity in Sub-Saharan Africa: Insights from a New Dataset." *Journal of Development Economics* 133: 231–63.

Holden, S. T., and K. Otsuka. 2014. "The Roles of Land Tenure Reforms and Land Markets in the Context of Population Growth and Land Use Intensification in Africa." *Food Policy* 48: 88–97.

Hsieh, C.-T., and P. Klenow. 2009. "Misallocation and Manufacturing TFP in China and India." *Quarterly Journal of Economics* 124 (4): 1403–48.

Hsieh, C.-T., and P. Klenow. 2014. "The Life Cycle of Plants in India and Mexico." *Quarterly Journal of Economics* 129 (3): 1035–84.

Imbens, G. 2010. "Better LATE Than Nothing: Some Comments on Deaton (2009) and Heckman and Urzua (2009)." *Journal of Economic Literature* 48: 399–423.

International Monetary Fund (IMF). 2005. "Pension Reform in Nigeria." In *Nigeria: Selected Issues and Statistical Appendix.* IMF Country Report 05/303, International Monetary Fund, Washington, DC.

International Monetary Fund (IMF). 2017. "The Informal Economy in Sub-Saharan Africa." In *Regional Economic Outlook: Sub-Saharan Africa*. Washington, DC, May.

International Monetary Fund (IMF). 2018a. "Mobilizing Tax Revenues in Nigeria." In *Nigeria: Selected Issues.* IMF Country Report 18/64, International Monetary Fund, Washington, DC.

International Monetary Fund (IMF). 2018b. *World Economic Outlook*. Washington, DC, April.

Jedwab, R., L. Christiaensen, and M. Gindelsky. 2017. "Demography, Urbanization and Development: Rural Push, Urban Pull and ... Urban Push?" *Journal of Urban Economics* 98: 6–16.

Laeven, L., and C. Woodruff. 2007. "The Quality of the Legal System, Firm Ownership, and Firm Size." *Review of Economics and Statistics* 89 (4): 601–14.

Levinsohn, J., and A. Petrin. 2003. "Estimating Production Functions Using Inputs to Control for Unobservables." *Review of Economic Studies* 70: 317–41.

Maloney, W. 2004. "Informality Revisited." *World Development* 32 (7): 1159–78.

Neumark, D., and L. F. Corella. 2019. "Do Minimum Wages Reduce Employment in Developing Countries? A Survey and Exploration of Conflicting Evidence." NBER Working Paper 26462, National Bureau of Economic Research, Cambridge, MA.

Nose, M. 2020a. "Minimum Wage, Market Imperfection, and Production Efficiency: Panel Event Study Analysis in Vietnam." Paper presented at International Institute of Public Finance Annual Congress, Reykjavik, August 21.

Nose, M. 2020b. "The Effect of Regulatory Policy on Firm Growth in Sub-Saharan Africa." The University of Tokyo, Tokyo.

Nwude, C. 2013. "The Politics of Minimum Wage in Nigeria: The Unresolved Issues." *Asian Journal of Empirical Research* 3 (4): 477–92.

Olken, B., and M. Singhal. 2011. "Informal Taxation." *American Economic Journal: Applied Economics* 3: 1–28.

Olley, S., and A. Pakes. 1996. "The Dynamics of Productivity in the Telecommunications Equipment Industry." *Econometrica* 64 (6): 1263–97.

Restuccia, D., and R. Rogerson. 2017. "The Causes and Costs of Misallocation." *Journal of Economic Perspectives* 31 (3): 151–174.

Restuccia, D., and R. Santaeulalia-Llopis. 2017. "Land Misallocation and Productivity." NBER Working Paper 23128, National Bureau of Economic Research, Cambridge, MA.

Rodrik, D. 2016. "An African Growth Miracle?" *Journal of African Economies* 27 (1): 1–18.

Ulyssea, G. 2018. "Firms, Informality, and Development: Theory and Evidence from Brazil." *American Economic Review* 108 (8): 2015–47.

World Bank. 2014. "Doing Business in Nigeria 2014: Understanding Regulations for Small and Medium-Size Enterprises." World Bank, Washington, DC.

World Bank. 2015. "More, and More Productive, Jobs for Nigeria: A Profile of Work and Workers." World Bank, Washington, DC.

CHAPTER 5

Informality and Labor Market Dynamics in Latin America

Antonio C. David, Frederic Lambert, and Frederik Toscani

INTRODUCTION

This chapter has three goals: we first present stylized facts on labor markets in Latin America from a comparative perspective to motivate and ground the subsequent work. Second, we empirically analyze the cyclical behavior of Latin American labor markets. Last, we sketch a small open-economy dynamic stochastic general equilibrium model, which can replicate the stylized facts and empirical results laid out previously.[1] The importance of informality, as both a structural and cyclical feature, is stressed throughout.

Labor markets in Latin America tend to be characterized by low labor productivity, high informality, and a rigid regulatory environment, which contribute to strong duality between well-protected formal sector jobs and unprotected informal sector jobs.

To study the cyclical behavior of Latin American labor markets, we decompose changes in the unemployment rate into demand and supply factors to show how labor productivity, informality, and the participation rate adjust to limit unemployment movements during the business cycle.[2] On the basis of the decompositions, this chapter argues that beyond the unemployment rate, information on formal job creation and changes in the informality rate are necessary to understand slack in Latin American labor markets.

The authors thank Bas Bakker, John Bluedorn, Valentina Flamini, Jaime Guajardo, Jorge Roldos, Antonio Spilimbergo, and Alejandro Werner for their comments. Genevieve Lindow provided outstanding research assistance.

[1] For additional details about the empirical work, see David, Lambert, and Toscani (2019). Details of the modeling framework can be found in Lambert, Pescatori, and Toscani (2020).

[2] In this chapter, South America includes Argentina, Bolivia, Brazil, Chile, Colombia, Ecuador, Guyana, Paraguay, Peru, Suriname, Uruguay, and Venezuela. Central America includes Belize, Costa Rica, El Salvador, Guatemala, Honduras, Nicaragua, and Panama. Although Mexico behaves similarly to South American economies in certain aspects, it is included in the Central America group because of its close integration with the US economy and lower exposure to the commodity cycle.

Next, we reexamine the link between changes in unemployment and changes in output by estimating the Okun's law relationship and explore the cross-country variation in coefficients to gain insights about how structural features of the labor market affect its cyclical behavior. Unemployment has reacted much less to changes in GDP in Latin America than it would have in advanced economies. We argue that this is the product of structural characteristics in the region's labor markets. Although we do not find a direct link between most labor market institutions and the cyclical behavior of labor markets conditional on informality, these institutions may still influence the "structural" level of informality, thereby indirectly affecting the cyclical behavior of the labor market.

In the last part of the chapter, we draw on the empirical findings to develop a theoretical framework that allows us to study the role of labor market frictions in more detail. Specifically, we build a small open-economy dynamic stochastic general equilibrium model with two sectors, formal and informal, which can replicate the negative relationships between labor informality rate and per capita GDP, both at business cycle frequency and in a cross-section of countries, and between the Okun's coefficient and the level of labor informality. The model is calibrated to Colombia.

The results show that labor market and tax reforms play an important role in changing the informality rate but also caution against overoptimism—with low GDP per capita, informality will remain relatively high because there is insufficient demand for formal goods. From a quantitative perspective, we find that higher productivity in the formal sector is key to explaining the difference between Colombia and countries with significantly lower informality. We use the model to study how labor informality and labor market frictions mediate the cyclical response of the economy to shocks, including commodity price shocks, which are particularly relevant in many Latin American countries. Informality is shown to play an important role as a shock absorber with the informal-formal margin limiting movements in the employed-unemployed margin.

This chapter adds to a vast literature studying the nexus of labor market institutions, informality, and unemployment in emerging market and developing economies. Notable references include the reviews of the effect of labor market institutions in emerging market and developing economies by Freeman (2010) and Betcherman (2014), as well as a recent paper by Duval and Loungani (2018) on the design of labor market institutions in emerging market and developing economies. Kugler (2019) provides a comprehensive overview of the effect of labor market institutions in Latin America by surveying the microeconomic literature. Perry and others (2007) provide a detailed study of informality in Latin America. Additional papers studying the role of informality over the business cycle include Bosch and Esteban-Pretel (2012), Castillo and Montoro (2012), Restrepo-Echavarria (2014), and Leyva and Urrutia (2020). The modeling framework presented in this chapter builds on Anand and Khera (2016) and Munkacsi and Saxegaard (2017).

STYLIZED FACTS

Labor Productivity

The median value in 2017 for output per worker in South America was about 30 percent of the median advanced economy (20 percent in Central America). Strong employment growth in the early 2000s was accompanied by lackluster productivity growth in both Central and South America before the global financial crisis. Growth rates, however, were strong from 2008 to 2011 as commodity prices recovered quickly and many South American countries' terms of trade peaked. Country-level data do not reveal any strong patterns, but the volatility of labor productivity growth stands out starkly, with all countries except Chile and Peru achieving positive productivity growth in only two out of the four periods (Figure 5.1).

Figure 5.1. Labor Productivity Level and Growth across Latin American Regions and Countries

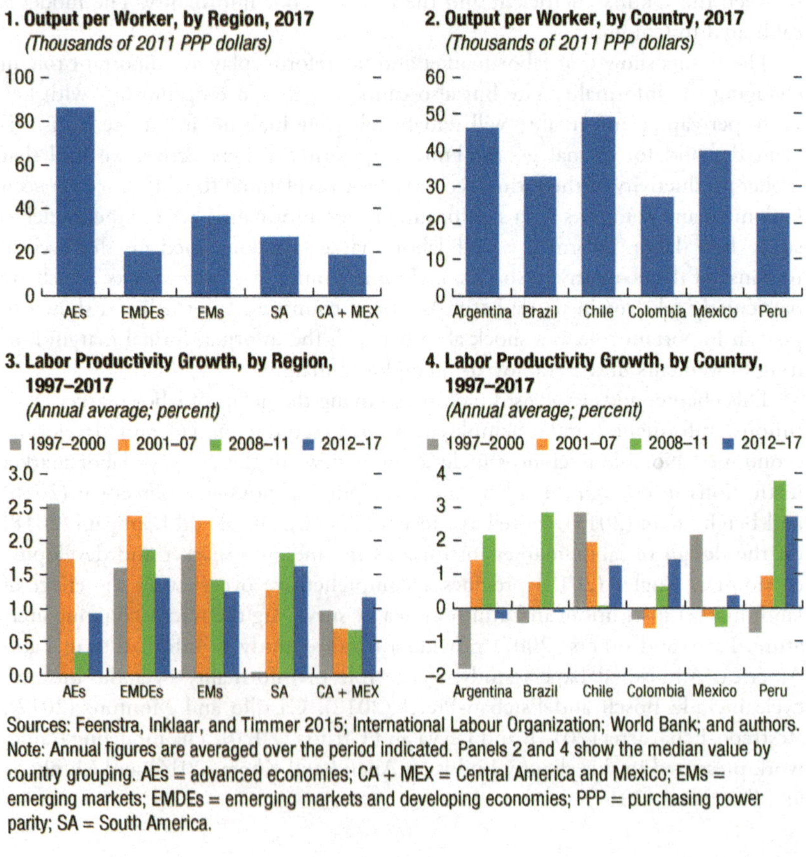

Sources: Feenstra, Inklaar, and Timmer 2015; International Labour Organization; World Bank; and authors.
Note: Annual figures are averaged over the period indicated. Panels 2 and 4 show the median value by country grouping. AEs = advanced economies; CA + MEX = Central America and Mexico; EMs = emerging markets; EMDEs = emerging markets and developing economies; PPP = purchasing power parity; SA = South America.

Informality

Informality in Latin America is high, accounting for more than 50 percent of total employment. Latin America, however, is not an outlier—the level of informality in South and Central America is broadly comparable to that in other emerging market and developing economies. Informality in advanced economies is significantly lower (Figure 5.2).[3]

Even within Latin America, the degree of heterogeneity is large, with labor informality ranging from around 30 to 70 percent among the largest economies. Panel 2 of Figure 5.2 presents a scatterplot of GDP per capita against the labor informality rate. It shows that, in line with standard predictions, labor informality has generally decreased as countries' incomes have risen (except for Mexico, where, despite higher GDP per capita, informality has actually increased); yet, even for the same level of income, countries show differences in labor informality, suggesting that other factors are also at play. Mexico and Peru, but also Argentina, do worse than other countries do in their levels of development.

Figure 5.2. Informal Employment as a Proportion of Total Employment, by Region and Country

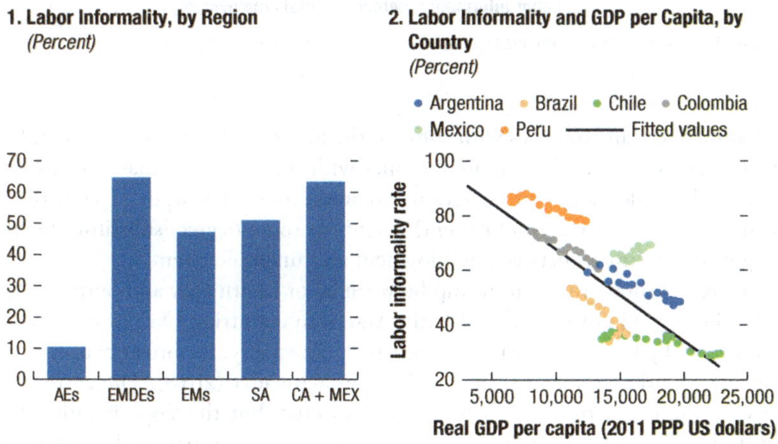

Sources: International Labour Organization; and Inter-American Development Bank's Labor Markets and Social Security Information System.
Note: AEs = advanced economies; CA + MEX = Central America and Mexico; EMs = emerging markets; EMDEs = emerging markets and developing economies; PPP = purchasing power parity; SA = South America.

[3] Cross-sectional labor informality data come from the International Labour Organization (we focus on the share of informal employment in total nonagricultural employment). Time-series labor informality data for Latin American countries come from the Inter-American Development Bank's Labor Markets and Social Security Information System. Data are harmonized across countries. The working-age population is defined to be between 15 and 64 years old.

Figure 5.3. Labor Informality and Output Informality in Latin America

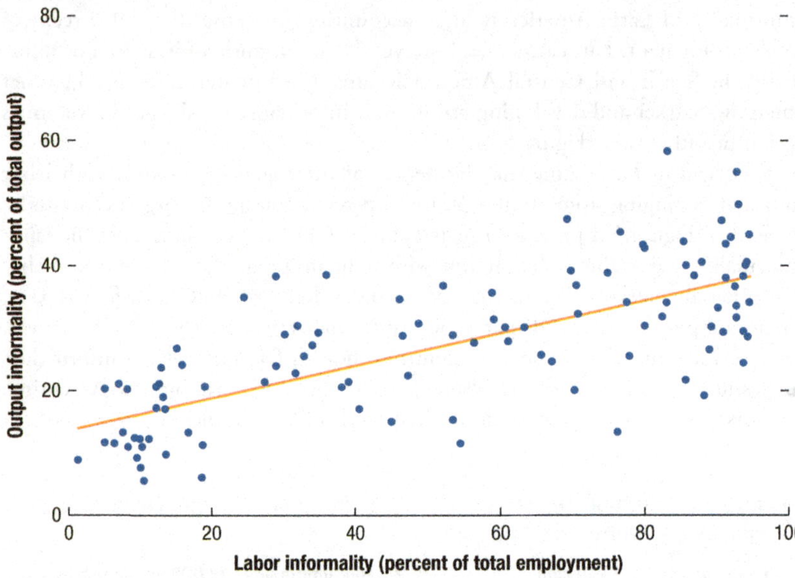

Sources: International Labour Organization; and Medina and Schneider 2018.

Latin American countries with some of the lowest and most stable unemployment rates (Mexico and Peru) are the ones with the most informality relative to their levels of development, suggesting that the second margin of adjustment (formal versus informal employment) might, to some degree, substitute for the margin of adjustment between employment and unemployment.

Figure 5.3 shows the relationship between labor informality and output informality in a broad cross-section of Latin American countries. Output informality is substantially harder to measure than labor informality; for broad country coverage, we use the estimates from Medina and Schneider (2018). The correlation between the two series is high (0.75), as expected, but the slope is rather flat. Given the informal sector's lower productivity, even in countries with labor informality rates higher than 70 or even 80 percent, output informality tends to be around 40 percent.

Labor Market Institutions

Labor market institutions are multidimensional and not easily described by any one set of indicators. Nevertheless, to provide an overview of the situation in Latin America, we focus on key perceptions-based indicators and indicators aimed at quantifying laws and regulations.

Panels 1 and 2 in Figure 5.4 show two key perceptions-based indicators from the World Economic Forum's (2018) executive survey on labor markets. Whereas the flexibility of wages is similar in the whole of Latin America compared to other country groups, hiring and firing practices in South America are perceived to be substantially more rigid than nearly everywhere else.

With this in mind, panels 3 and 4 in Figure 5.4 show summary indicators of employment protection laws and regulations constructed by the Organisation for Economic Co-operation and Development (OECD) and the International Labour Organization, respectively. It is perhaps surprising that the

Figure 5.4. Labor Market Rigidity, by Economic Development Level and Region

1. Flexibility of Wage Determination, 2017
(Median)

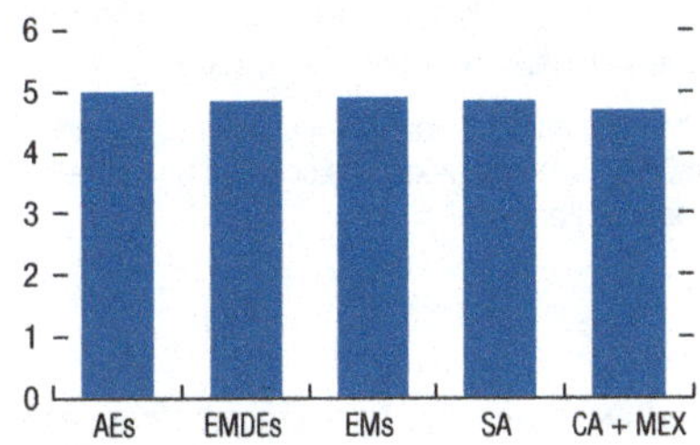

Source: WEF 2018.

2. Flexibility of Hiring and Firing Practices, 2017
(Median)

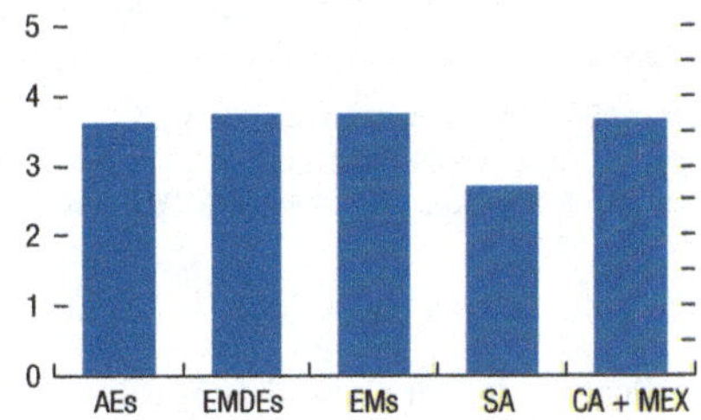

Source: WEF 2018.

3. Index of Strictness of Employment Protection, 2013
(Regular contracts, individual, and collective dismissals; average)

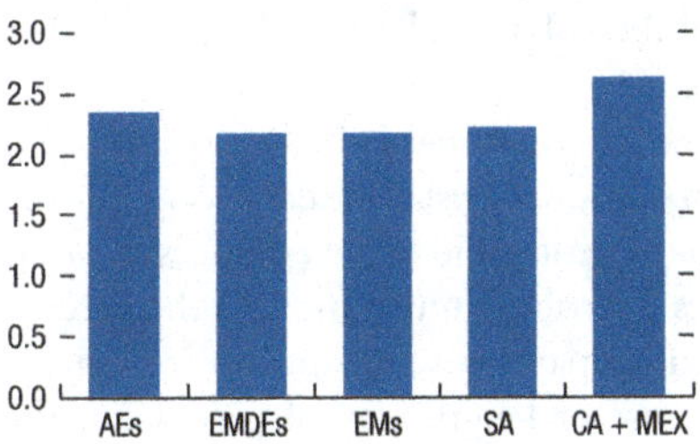

Source: OECD, employment protection legislation indicators.

4. Employment Protection Legislation, 2010
(Regular contracts, individual dismissals; average)

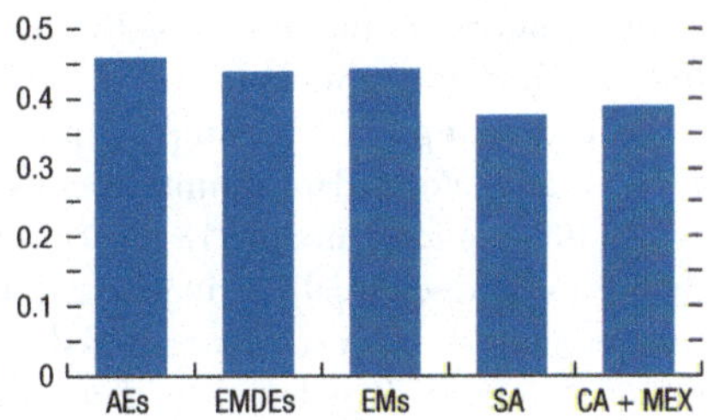

Source: International Labour Organization, EPLex Employment Protection Legislation Database.

5. Is Third-Party Approval for Dismissal of One Worker Required?
(1 = yes, 0 = no; average, 2017)

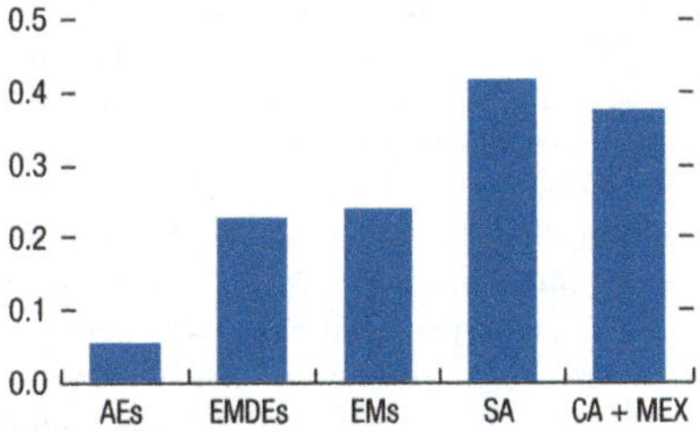

Source: World Bank, Doing Business indicators.

6. Are Fixed-Term Contracts Prohibited for Permanent Tasks?
(1 = yes, 0 = no; average, 2017)

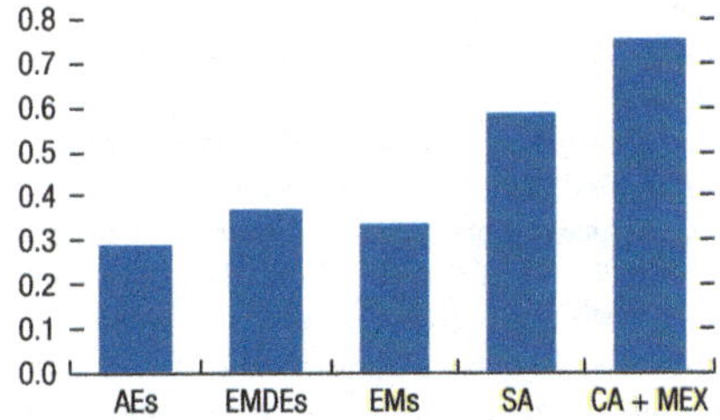

Source: World Bank, Doing Business indicators.

Figure 5.4. Labor Market Rigidity, by Economic Development Level and Region

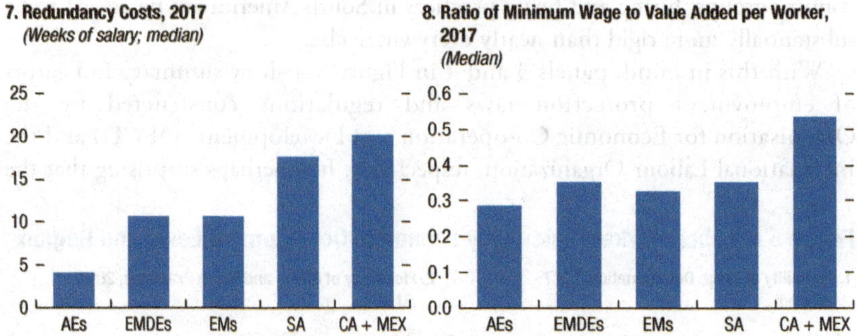

Source: World Bank, Doing Business indicators.

Source: World Bank, Doing Business indicators.

Note: AEs = advanced economies; CA + MEX = Central America and Mexico; EMs = emerging markets; EMDEs = emerging markets and developing economies; OECD = Organisation for Economic Co-operation and Development;SA = South America; WEF = World Economic Forum

indicators do not show that South America has stronger employment protection legislation than other countries. This raises two possibilities: (1) employment legislation is not de jure rigid in South America, but certain aspects of implementation, perhaps related to the legal system, make it de facto rigid; or (2) the aggregate indices hide more specific factors of the legislative framework, which in practice are more important for the flexibility of the labor market than other (offsetting) elements included in the index.

By correlating each subcomponent of the International Labour Organization, OECD, and World Bank Employment Protection Legislation data sets with the World Economic Forum's 2018 perceptions of hiring and firing practices, we find that hiring and, especially, firing procedures contribute much more to the perception of rigidness than severance or redundancy pay per se (results not reported). Other factors, such as length of notice period or length of trial period (on the hiring side), do not affect perceived flexibility at all.[4]

[4] From the OECD indicators, specifically, stricter "notification procedures," "definition of justified or unfair dismissal," "compensation following unfair dismissal," and "possibility of reinstatement following unfair dismissal" are significantly negatively correlated with perceptions of a more flexible labor market. From the International Labour Organization indicators, stricter rules on "valid grounds for dismissals," "prohibited grounds for dismissals," "procedural requirements for dismissals," and "[more] redress [possibilities]" are significantly negatively correlated with perceptions of a more flexible labor market. Finally, from the World Bank indicators, "fixed-term contracts prohibited for permanent tasks," "third-party notification if one worker is dismissed," "third-party approval if one worker is dismissed," "retraining or reassignment [obligations before dismissal]," "priority rules for redundancies or reemployment," and "severance pay for redundancy dismissal (weeks of salary)" are significantly negatively correlated with perceptions of a more flexible labor market.

Panels 5 and 6 in Figure 5.4 thus focus on hiring and firing procedures and compare Latin America to other regions. Panel 7 shows redundancy costs.[5] Although this is not the case for all relevant dimensions, the three indicators shown here highlight that Latin American labor markets do exhibit noticeable rigidities in some key dimensions. Dismissal of even one worker often requires third-party approval, permanent contracts are often mandatory for permanent tasks, and redundancy costs are higher than in advanced economies or other

Figure 5.5. Labor Market Rigidities for the Largest Economies in Latin America

1. Is Third-Party Approval for Dismissal of One Worker Required?
(1 = yes, 0 = no; 2017)

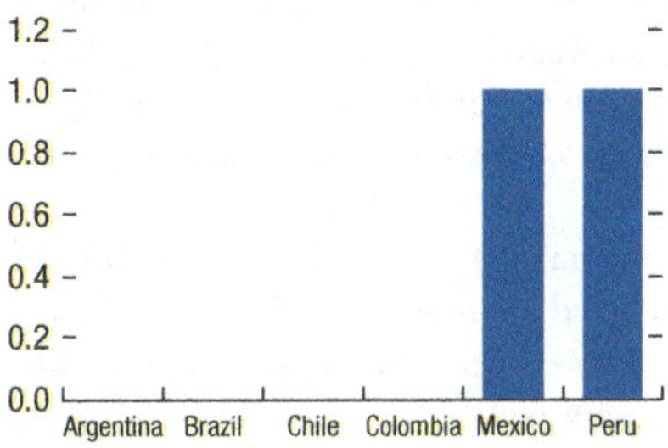

Source: World Bank, Doing Business indicators.

2. Are Fixed-Term Contracts Prohibited for Permanent Tasks?
(1 = yes, 0 = no; 2017)

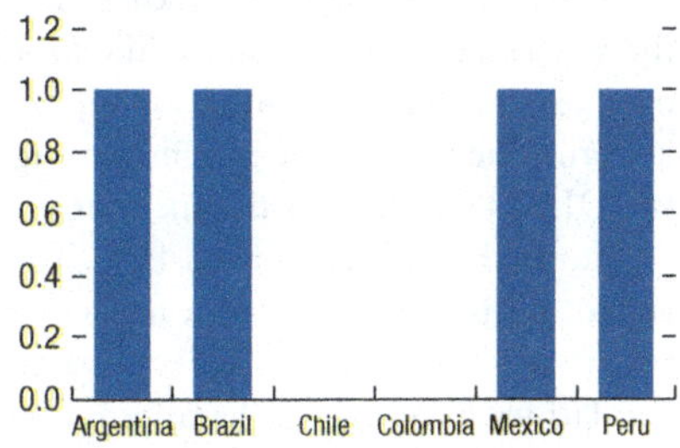

Source: World Bank, Doing Business indicators.

3. Redundancy Costs, 2017
(Weeks of salary)

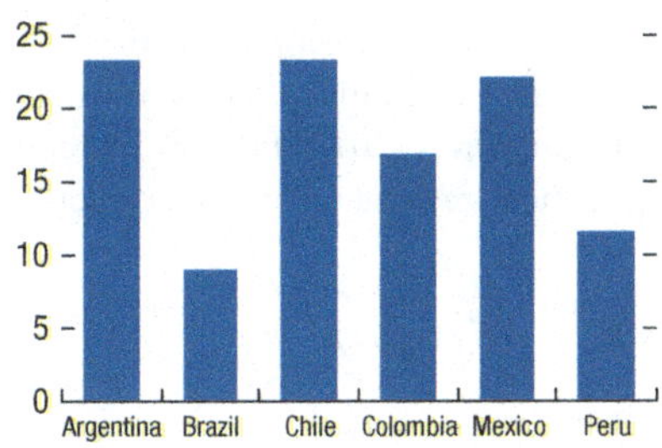

Source: World Bank, Doing Business indicators.

4. Minimum Wage Ratios per Worker

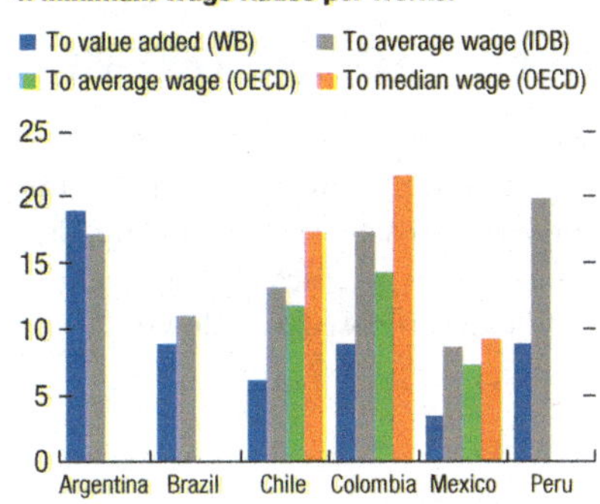

Sources: Inter-American Development Bank's Labor Markets and Social Security Information System; OECD, Employment Protection Legislation indicators; and World Bank, Doing Business indicators.
Note: IDB = Inter-American Development Bank; OECD = Organisation for Economic Co-operation and Development; WB = World Bank.

[5] The World Bank data have the broadest country coverage, which makes World Bank measures preferred for the regressions in subsequent parts of this chapter.

emerging market and developing economies. These indicators suggest strong *de facto* job protection for formal, permanent jobs.

Panel 8 in Figure 5.4 shows the ratio of minimum wage to value added per worker, gauging how binding the minimum wage is. The cross-country comparison provides little evidence that the minimum wage is more binding in South America than in other regions, but Central America stands out as having a high ratio.

Figure 5.5 reproduces panels 5 through 8 of Figure 5.4 on hiring and firing procedures, redundancy costs, and minimum wage at the country level for the largest economies in Latin America. Cross-country comparisons suggest that those countries with persistently high informality (Mexico and Peru, as discussed) have cumbersome hiring and firing procedures. Argentina, however, has the highest redundancy costs and a high minimum wage.

As panel 4 of Figure 5.5 shows, the choice of denominator greatly determines the assessment of how binding the minimum wage is. The minimum wage is low in Brazil and Mexico, whereas it appears high in Colombia and, to a lesser degree, in Peru. The ratio of the minimum wage to the median wage is not available from the OECD for three of the six countries.

Summarizing the stylized facts, we note that (1) informality is a major feature of Latin American labor markets and (2) there is some evidence that countries with higher informality also have more rigid employment protection legislation, although de facto employment protection is a difficult concept to measure. The remainder of the chapter explores these findings through several empirical exercises.

DECOMPOSING UNEMPLOYMENT DYNAMICS

We now use a simple approach to decompose changes in unemployment for the largest countries in Latin America into changes in labor supply and demand.[6] A similar approach was implemented by Hijzen and others (2017) for OECD economies. More specifically, changes in unemployment relative to a reference period can be decomposed as follows:[7]

$$u - u^* \approx -(y - y^*) + (z - z^*) + (part - part^*) + (wap - wap^*) \qquad \text{(1a)},$$

[6] In this section, we use labor force, working-age population, employment, and unemployment data from the International Labour Organization. Output data are from the IMF's World Economic Outlook database, and informality data are from the Inter-American Development Bank.

[7] Alternatively,

$$u \approx -ln(1-u) = -ln\left(\tfrac{L}{LF}\right) = -\ln(Y) + \ln\left(\tfrac{Y}{L}\right) + \ln(\rho) + ln(wap) \qquad \text{(1b)}$$

$$u \approx -\ln(L_F) + \ln\left(\tfrac{L_F}{L}\right) + \ln(\rho) + ln(wap),$$

where u is the unemployment rate, LF is the labor force, L is the number of persons employed, L_F is the number of formal employees, Y is output, ρ is the labor force participation rate defined as LF/wap, and wap is the working-age population.

Figure 5.6. Decomposed Changes in Unemployment in Latin America
(Percent)

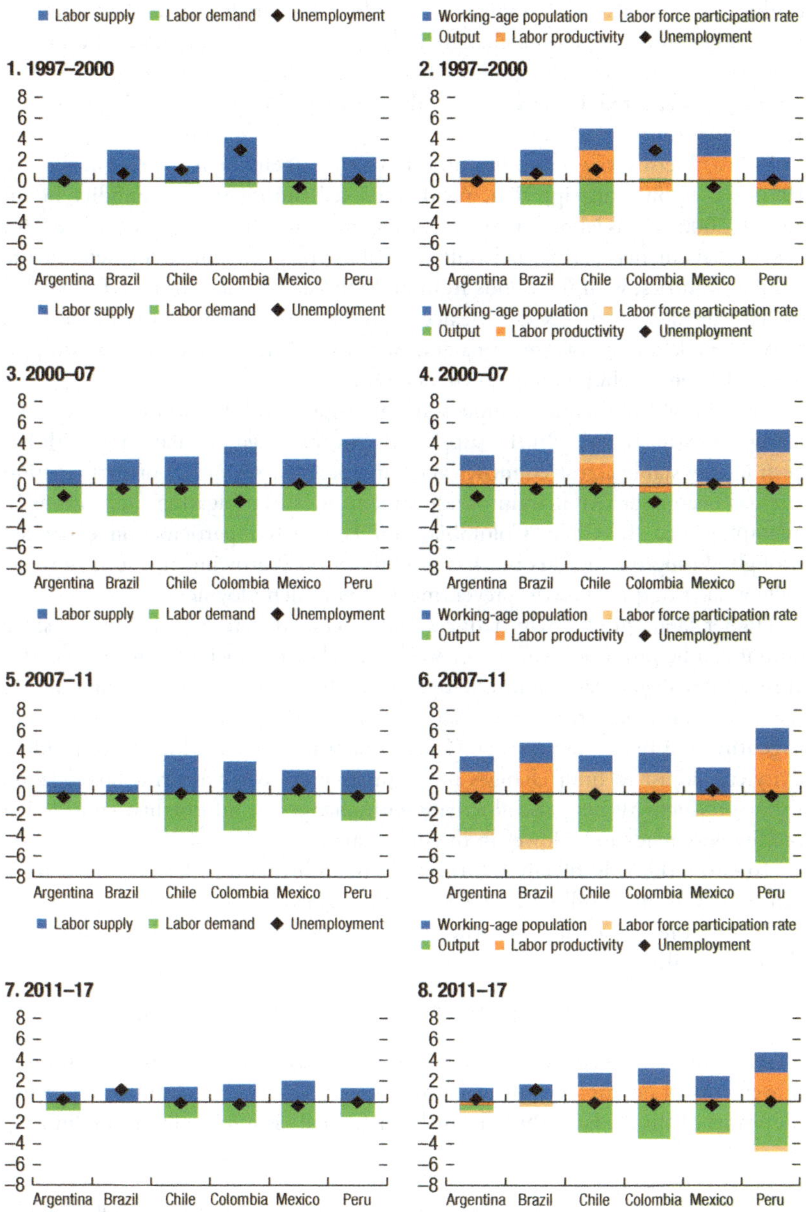

Source: Authors.

where u denotes the unemployment rate, and y, z, $part$, and wap are the logarithms of GDP, labor productivity, the labor force participation rate, and working-age population (* indicates the value of a variable at the beginning of the period). In this equation, changes in labor demand correspond to the sum of changes in output and changes in labor productivity, whereas changes in labor supply are captured by changes in the participation rate and the working-age population.

In broad terms, the decomposition shows that unemployment rose in the late 1990s as supply outstripped demand, then fell during the commodity boom period (2000–11) as labor demand picked up more than labor supply (Figure 5.6). The global financial crisis had only a limited effect on unemployment in the sample countries, with the trends from 2000 to 2007 similar to those from 2007 to 2011 in all countries except Mexico. In recent years, unemployment has been broadly stable, except in Argentina and Brazil, where it rose after a sharp drop in demand, even as labor supply growth slowed.

More insightful than the simple split into supply and demand is a look at the margins of adjustment. On the supply side, working-age population growth has been largely stable across countries and time periods; yet the labor participation rate has been an active margin of adjustment, mostly mitigating fluctuations in unemployment. In Chile, Colombia, and Peru, labor participation expanded strongly during boom years but has recently stopped growing and seen substantially weaker output growth, preventing a rise in unemployment.

Higher labor productivity reduces labor demand here, given that the same output can be produced with fewer workers. Labor productivity growth has also greatly limited fluctuations in unemployment (see, for example, Mexico during the global financial crisis, where labor productivity growth was negative, and Argentina and Brazil since 2011). One mechanism through which labor productivity can adjust to limit changes in unemployment is when firms hoard labor. Labor productivity may also fluctuate with changes in informality, considering productivity tends to be lower in the informal sector.

To show the role of labor formality and informality, the decomposition can be rewritten as follows, where l_F is the logarithm of formal employment and f is the logarithm of the ratio of formal to total employment (labor formality):[8]

$$u - u^* \approx -(l_F - l_F^*) + (f - f) + (part - part^*) + (wap - wap^*) \quad (2)$$

As Figure 5.7 shows, labor informality has played a crucial role in limiting movements in unemployment in Latin America. Consider Colombia, for example (panel 4). In the late 1990s, labor formality fell (as informality rose), limiting

[8] The formal and informal margins operate separately from the labor force participation margin, given that the labor force comprises unemployed, formally employed, and informally employed workers.

Figure 5.7. Decomposing Changes in Unemployment in Latin America: The Role of Informality, 1997–2017
(Percent)

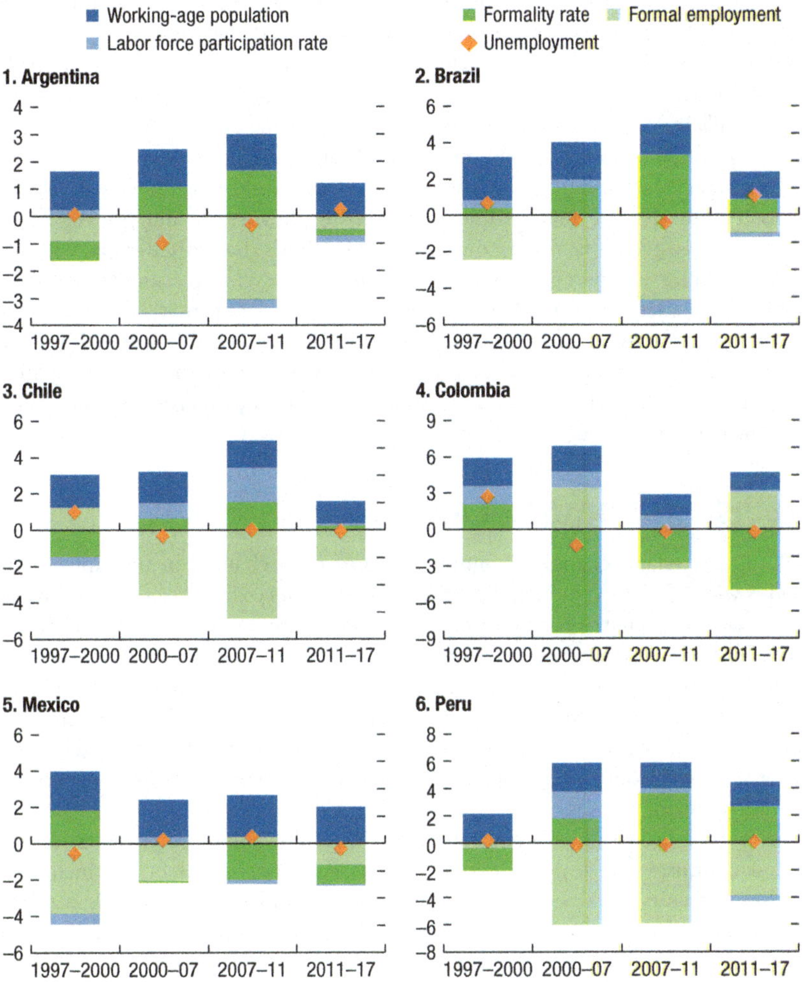

Source: Authors.

the rise in unemployment during a difficult economic time when labor demand was weak and the labor force participation rate rose. During the boom of the early 2000s, informality fell sharply, only to resume its role as a shock absorber during the global financial crisis. In the years since 2011, informality has again fallen significantly, implying that the unemployment rate did not fall as much as it would have otherwise.

Similar countercyclical properties of informality can be observed in Argentina, Chile, and Peru (Figure 5.7, panels 1, 3, and 6). Chile from 2007 to 2011 shows how a strong increase in formal labor demand was met, in roughly equal shares, with increased participation and a reduction in informality for a stable unemployment rate. The two recent periods in Brazil and Mexico (panels 2 and 5) are interesting to examine for the lack of adjustment along the informality margin: in Brazil, informality continued to fall from 2011 to 2017, even as unemployment increased strongly. Meanwhile in Mexico, informality has increased since the early 2000s, although the unemployment rate has been low and even decreasing in recent years.

Changes in informality and labor force participation have, however, overall helped limit the rise in unemployment during downturns and growth slowdowns. More generally, the decomposition highlights the limited average annual fluctuations in unemployment over the business cycle, stressing the need to look at broader labor market outcomes to assess labor market slack when studying Latin American countries. On the basis of the decompositions, we suggest using a combination of formal employment growth, the informality rate, and the unemployment rate to study the cyclical properties of labor markets in Latin America.

REVISITING OKUN'S LAW

Okun's law relates changes in output to short-term changes in unemployment and is widely used to study cyclical relations between economic activity and labor markets. To compare observed fluctuations in unemployment over the business cycle in Latin America and the Caribbean with those in other emerging market and developing economies and in advanced economies, we present estimates of Okun's law for a broad panel of countries and then explore the cross-country variation of estimated coefficients to gain insights about how key structural characteristics or labor market policies affect labor markets' responsiveness to output growth.

We use a heterogeneous panel approach that allows slope coefficients to vary across countries and deals with possible cross-sectional dependency by including common factors in the estimation. The sample includes both emerging markets and advanced economies. The general empirical specification is summarized in equation (3) for $i = 1, \ldots, N$ countries; and $t = 1, \ldots, T$ time periods.[9]

$$u_{i,t} - u_{i,t-1} = \beta_i(y_{i,t} - y_{i,t-1}) + \vartheta_{i,t} \tag{3}$$

$$\vartheta_{i,t} = \alpha_i + \sum_{m=1}^{p} \lambda_{i,m} f_{m,t} + \varepsilon_{i,t},$$

[9] We also consider an alternative specification in which variables are expressed as "gaps" (deviations from trend), calculated using the Hodrick-Prescott filter with a smoothing parameter of 6.25. The results obtained are quantitatively close to the ones reported in Table 5.1.

where $u_{i,t}$ is the unemployment rate, $y_{i,t}$ is the log of output (real GDP), $f_{m,t}$ are common factors that affect all countries and change over time, and α_i are country-specific fixed effects capturing country characteristics that do not change over time. These common factors are not directly observable, and their factor loadings (λ_i) can be country specific.

One reason accounting for such factors may be important when estimating Okun's law is the possibility that, for example, technological changes that are common across countries could affect the relationship between unemployment and output. $\varepsilon_{i,t}$ is the error term, which is assumed to be white noise. A caveat regarding this specification is that changes in unemployment can lead to changes in future output, posing a possible endogeneity issue.

Standard panel estimators usually treat the slope coefficients (β) as homogeneous across countries and frequently require stationarity of the variables included in the analysis, which might not be appropriate assumptions for macroeconomic panels. In addition, estimators traditionally used in panel data analysis require the assumption of cross-sectional independence throughout panel members. In the presence of cross-sectionally correlated error terms, these methods do not produce consistent estimates of the parameters of interest and can lead to incorrect inference (Kapetanios, Pesaran, and Yamagata 2011).

To address these potential problems, we use the common correlated effects (CCE) estimator proposed by Pesaran (2006). This estimator uses cross-sectional averages of the dependent and independent variables as proxies for unobserved common factors in the regressions (equation 3). The CCE yields consistent and efficient estimates, and its small sample properties do not seem to be affected by residual serial correlation of the error terms. Kapetanios, Pesaran, and Yamagata (2011) show that the CCE performs well when variables included in the model are nonstationary, and they advocate the use of this estimator irrespective of the order of the data's integration. Eberhardt and Presbitero (2015) apply this approach to examine the link between debt and growth.

Baseline Results

Table 5.1 presents the results obtained when estimating different versions of Okun's law using the CCE estimator with annual data for 127 countries from 1990 to 2017 (the panel is unbalanced, and data availability varies by country). We exclude from the sample countries with fewer than 20 years of data. The unemployment rate series (expressed as a percentage of the total labor force) comes from the World Bank World Development Indicators database, and the real GDP series in constant local currency units comes from the IMF's World Economic Outlook database.

Specification 1 presents the results of a model with no lags of the change in real GDP; the coefficient β is around –0.12 and is statistically significant at the 1 percent level. Including up to four additional lags of the change in GDP (specifications 2 to 5) does not change the contemporaneous coefficient much.

TABLE 5.1.

Okun's Coefficient Heterogeneous Panel Estimates, 1990–2017

	Δ Unemployment				
	(1)	**(2)**	**(3)**	**(4)**	**(5)**
Δ GDP_t	−0.125***	−0.115***	−0.124***	−0.122***	−0.126***
	(0.0152)	(0.0169)	(0.0174)	(0.0173)	(0.0185)
Δ GDP_{t-1}		−0.0330***	−0.0386***	−0.0387***	−0.0372***
		(0.00989)	(0.0111)	(0.0118)	(0.0122)
Δ GDP_{t-2}			0.0187*	−0.00683	−0.000180
			(0.0110)	(0.0114)	(0.0138)
Δ GDP_{t-3}				0.0341***	0.0202*
				(0.0109)	(0.0110)
Δ GDP_{t-4}					0.0282***
					(0.00984)
Constant	0.0600	0.0239	−0.0159	0.0966	0.205
	(0.0867)	(0.107)	(0.106)	(0.106)	(0.144)
No. of observations	3,399	3,379	3,355	3,331	3,307
No. of countries	127	127	127	127	127

Source: Authors.
Note: Standard errors appear in parentheses.
$^*p < 0.1$; $^{***}p < 0.01$.

Moreover, only the first lag of the change in GDP appears to be statistically significant in a robust manner.[10,11]

Ball, Leigh, and Loungani (2017) obtain average estimates for β of around −0.40 for a sample of 20 advanced economies, but these authors point to significant cross-country variation in estimates.[12] This suggests that unemployment responds less to output fluctuations in low-income developing countries. This conclusion is confirmed by average estimates for country income groups (Figure 5.8). We also present the sum of coefficients for changes in GDP in specification 2. Coefficient estimates are larger in absolute value for advanced economies relative to all other groupings (including South and Central America with Mexico). Coefficients for Latin America and the Caribbean are somewhat larger than for emerging markets more broadly.

Okun's Coefficients and Labor Institutions

We now examine the cross-country variation of estimated coefficients to key structural labor market characteristics and institutions (focusing on specification 2

[10] As a robustness check, we also estimate the specification using quarterly data and obtain similar estimates. Nevertheless, the country and time-series coverage of the regressions is significantly reduced.

[11] We undertake a similar exercise using the employment rate as the dependent variable. Results are available on request.

[12] Ahn and others (2019) also consider the cyclical sensitivity of unemployment for a broad sample of emerging market and developing economies using more traditional panel data methods with interaction effects. They obtain results consistent and quantitatively similar to the ones discussed in this chapter.

Figure 5.8. Unemployment's Responsiveness to GDP Changes, by Region and Country
(Percent)

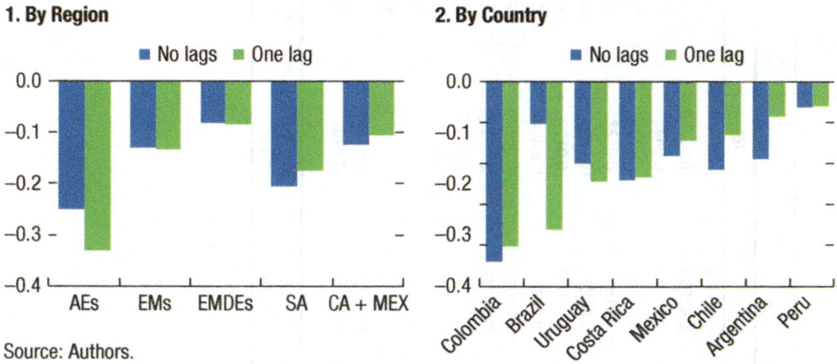

Source: Authors.
Note: AEs = advanced economies; CA + MEX = Central America and Mexico; EMs = emerging markets; EMDEs = emerging markets and developing economies; SA = South America.

in Table 5.1). More restrictive institutions can create distortions that would prevent the efficient allocation of labor, possibly leading to adverse effects on productivity (Freeman 2010; Duval and Loungani 2018). Restrictive institutions can also impede adjustment to shocks by reducing churning and turnover in the labor market. Nevertheless, institutions can also play a neutral or positive role by reducing information asymmetries and solving coordination problems (Freeman 2010).

More precisely, we estimate the following specification, where $X_{j,i}$ is a vector of control variables capturing institutional features of labor markets (including informality):

$$\beta_i = c + \sum_{j=1}^{k} \gamma_j X_{j,i} + \varepsilon_i.$$

Outlier-robust regressions of Okun's coefficients reported in Table 5.2 show that once we control for informality, most indicators capturing labor market institutions are not statistically significant, with the exception of the indicator capturing wage flexibility. To provide a sense of the variables' relative economic importance, specification 6 demonstrates that a 1 standard deviation increase in informality increases Okun's coefficient by 0.10 point and that a 1 standard deviation increase in wage flexibility increases the coefficient by 0.03 point.

In addition to a measure of hiring and firing practices and redundancy costs, we include in the regressions a dummy capturing whether third-party approval is required to dismiss one worker as well as a dummy indicating whether fixed-term contracts are prohibited for permanent tasks (both variables come from the World Bank's Doing Business Indicators database). Moreover, we consider the restrictiveness of employment protection legislation as measured by the International Labour Organization's Employment Protection Legislation Database (higher

TABLE 5.2.

Okun's Coefficient, Informality, and Labor Market Institutions

	(1)	(2)	(3)	(4)	(5)	(6)	(7)
Informality	0.00368***	0.00368***	0.00366***	0.00363***	0.00355***	0.00354***	0.00353***
	(0.000487)	(0.000518)	(0.000537)	(0.000595)	(0.000593)	(0.000644)	(0.000843)
Wage flexibility		0.0419**	0.0398*	0.0404*	0.0446*	0.0442*	0.0829***
		(0.0203)	(0.0230)	(0.0234)	(0.0233)	(0.0235)	(0.0276)
Hiring and firing			0.00448	0.00575	0.0150	0.0128	−0.0118
			(0.0271)	(0.0284)	(0.0288)	(0.0291)	(0.0350)
Dismissal approval				0.00642	0.00929	0.0122	−0.000733
				(0.0434)	(0.0433)	(0.0444)	(0.0527)
Fixed-term contract					0.0604*	0.0621*	0.0640
					(0.0322)	(0.0326)	(0.0409)
Redundancy costs						0.000456	0.000285
						(0.00135)	(0.00169)
Employment protection							−0.0276
							(0.190)
Constant	−0.314***	−0.518***	−0.525***	−0.533***	−0.619***	−0.614***	−0.686***
	(0.0275)	(0.0984)	(0.110)	(0.114)	(0.119)	(0.120)	(0.160)
No. of observations	93	90	90	90	90	89	65
R^2	0.385	0.414	0.412	0.409	0.432	0.440	0.475

Source: Authors' calculations.

Note: Standard errors appear in parentheses. Outlier-robust regressions follow Li (1985).

*$p < 0.1$; **$p < 0.05$; ***$p < 0.01$.

values of the indicator reflect more restrictive regulations). Country coverage for the latter indicator is somewhat more limited. Results suggest that labor market institutions are more likely to affect Okun's coefficient indirectly, if at all (that is, to the extent that institutions affect the level of informality).

These results say nothing about whether it would be desirable for unemployment to be more sensitive to the cycle. As highlighted by Ahn and others (2019), in the absence of unemployment insurance or an adequate social safety net, unemployment becoming more responsive to growth could indeed reduce, rather than increase, welfare. Yet informality has economic implications that go beyond its role in dampening the cyclicality of unemployment (Levy Algazi 2018), which makes it worth analyzing in more detail.

A MODEL OF LABOR INFORMALITY AND THE BUSINESS CYCLE

This section briefly presents a dynamic stochastic general equilibrium model that is consistent with the empirical patterns of informality at both the business cycle and long-term frequencies. The details of the model are laid out by Lambert, Pescatori, and Toscani (2020).

Our modeling framework builds on Anand and Khera (2016) and Munkacsi and Saxegaard (2017). The model includes a representative household that consumes formal and informal goods and supplies labor, perfectly competitive intermediate goods producers, monopolistic competitive wholesale final goods producers, retailers, capital producers, and a public sector (government and a monetary authority). Formal and informal firms (which produce formal and informal goods, respectively) face different frictions in terms of entry costs, hiring costs, and payroll taxes (although informal goods can only be consumed by domestic households, formal goods can also be exported and consumed by the government).

We specify the utility function such that there is a zero-income effect on the consumption of the informal goods. This captures the so-called demand channel of informality as laid out by La Porta and Shleifer (2014), among others. Entrepreneurs who want to modernize their businesses need to generate sufficient sales to cover the fixed costs of investment. When income is low, demand for formal goods may be too low to cover fixed costs. Demand for low-quality, cheap informal goods therefore expands the informal sector at the cost of the formal sector.

This mechanism is important to allow the model to generate a decreasing, concave relationship between informality and GDP per capita. Formal sector total factor productivity (TFP) is the key model parameter that allows us to match the shape of the curve as it is in the data; however, changes in aggregate TFP create a slope that is too "flat"—informality does not fall sufficiently fast as GDP per capita increases. This result model suggests that the gap between formal and informal sector TFP (that is, the rise in formal TFP and simultaneous

Figure 5.9. The Relationship between Labor Informality and Okun's Coefficient

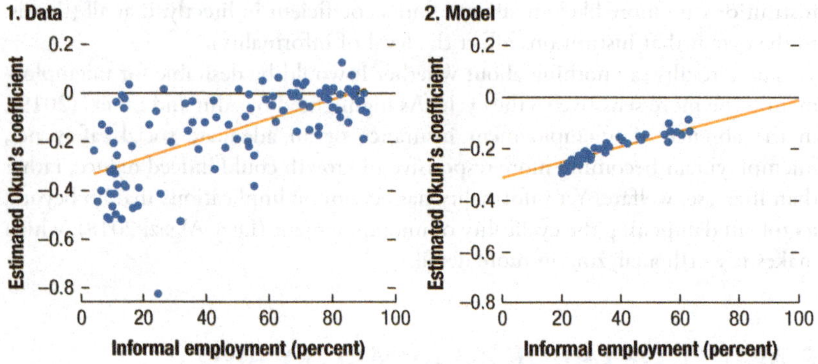

Source: Authors' calculations.

stagnation of informal TFP), more than the rise in aggregate TFP, is the main driver of the decline in labor market informality.

Labor informality is countercyclical in the model, as in the data, and the absolute value of the Okun's coefficient estimated from data simulated by the model decreases with labor informality (Figure 5.9). To the best of our knowledge, these three facts (decreasing relationship between labor market informality and per capita GDP, countercyclical informality, and lower responsiveness of unemployment to GDP when informality is high) could not be jointly captured in most existing models.

We use our modeling framework to study both the effect of structural reforms on informality in the steady state and the role of informality and labor market frictions in business cycle dynamics. In particular, we calibrate the model to replicate the Colombian economy (the parameters that determine business cycle moments are estimated using a simulated method of moments) and then focus on how informality reacts to and mediates shocks over the business cycle. We find that labor market reforms are not enough to substantially reduce labor informality in the absence of an increase in formal sector productivity but are key to reduce the steady state unemployment rate.

Regarding the model dynamics, impulse response functions for both TFP and commodity price shocks display the expected reactions of macroeconomic variables (to illustrate, Figure 5.10 shows the reaction to a positive commodity price shock). Unemployment, labor informality, and output informality are shown to be countercyclical. A higher level of informality (when all else is equal, and conditional on TFP or commodity price shocks) is found to mitigate business cycle fluctuations in GDP and, especially in consumption and unemployment, confirms the role of informality as a "buffer." This is an important consideration given that higher levels of informality are also associated with a smaller welfare state.

Figure 5.10. Impulse Response Function for the Reaction to a Positive Commodity Price Shock

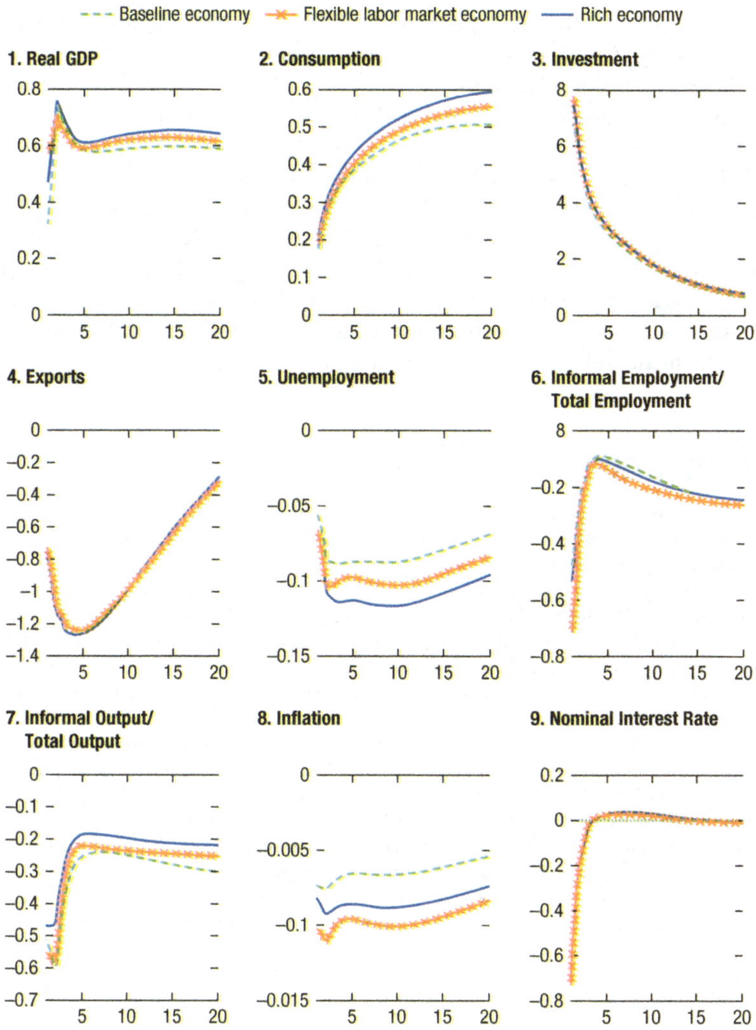

Source: Authors' calculations.

CONCLUSION

This chapter emphasizes the role of informality in the dynamics of labor markets in Latin America. A decomposition of changes in unemployment during several subperiods highlights the countercyclical role of informality (David, Pienknagura, and Roldos 2020). An econometric analysis of Okun's law shows that the formal and informal adjustment margin reduce the importance of the employment and unemployment margin. This result implies that, in economies with prevalent informality, reporting only the unemployment and job creation rates (as is standard in advanced economies) may not be sufficient to capture labor market slack. To gauge the cyclical position of Latin American labor markets, reporting the informality rate is more informative.

Model simulations suggest that a country's productivity and, notably, the productivity of its formal sector compared to that of the informal sector are key determinants of informality. Although both lower labor market frictions and higher formal sector labor productivity are important, reductions in informality will always be bounded absent productivity gains. In contrast, higher formal sector labor productivity has no direct effect on the unemployment rate, whereas labor market reform aimed at reducing frictions is key in that regard. Over the business cycle, informality acts as an important shock absorber in the model—consistent with the empirical findings discussed earlier—limiting fluctuations in unemployment and macroeconomic aggregates.

REFERENCES

Ahn, J., Z. An, J. Bluedorn, G. Ciminelli, Z. Koczan, D. Malacrino, D. Muhaj, and P. Neidlinger. 2019. "Work in Progress: Improving Youth Labor Market Outcomes in Emerging Markets and Developing Economies." IMF Staff Discussion Note 19/02, International Monetary Fund, Washington, DC.

Anand, R., and P. Khera. 2016. "Macroeconomics Impact of Product and Labor Market Reforms on Informality and Unemployment in India." IMF Working Paper 16/47, International Monetary Fund, Washington, DC.

Ball, L., D. Leigh, and P. Loungani. 2017. "Okun's Law: Fit at 50?" *Journal of Money, Credit and Banking* 49 (7): 1413–41.

Betcherman, G. 2014. "Labor Market Regulations. What Do We Know about Their Impacts in Developing Countries?" Policy Research Working Paper 6819, World Bank, Washington, DC.

Bosch, M., and J. Esteban-Pretel. 2012. "Job Creation and Job Destruction in the Presence of Informal Markets." *Journal of Development Economics* 98 (2): 270–86.

Castillo, P. B., and C. Montoro. 2012. "Dinámica Inflacionaria en Presencia de Informalidad en Mercados Laborales." *Economia Chilena* 15 (1): 33–47.

David, A., F. Lambert, and F. Toscani. 2019. "More Work to Do? Taking Stock of Latin American Labor Markets." IMF Working Paper 19/55, International Monetary Fund, Washington, DC.

David, A., S. Pienknagura, and J. Roldos. 2020. "Labor Market Dynamics, Informality, and Regulations in Latin America." IMF Working Paper 20/19, International Monetary Fund, Washington, DC.

Duval, R., and P. Loungani. 2018. "Designing Labor Market Institutions in Emerging and Frontier Economies: Evidence and IMF Advice." IMF Staff Discussion Note 19/04, International Monetary Fund, Washington, DC.

Eberhardt, M., and A. F. Presbitero. 2015. "Public Debt and Growth: Heterogeneity and Non-Linearity." *Journal of International Economics* 97 (1): 45–58.

Feenstra, R. C., R. Inklaar, and M. P. Timmer. 2015. "The Next Generation of the Penn World Table." *American Economic Review* 105 (10): 3150–82.

Freeman, R. B. 2010. "Labor Regulations, Unions, and Social Protection in Developing Countries: Market Distortions or Efficient Institutions?" *Handbook of Development Economics*, vol. 5, edited by T. P. Schultz and J. Strauss. Amsterdam: Elsevier.

Hijzen, A., A. Kappeler, M. Pak, and C. Schwellnus. 2017. "Labour Market Resilience: The Role of Structural and Macroeconomic Policies." OECD Economics Department Working Paper 1406, Organisation for Economic Co-operation and Development, Paris.

International Labour Organization. 2018. *Women and Men in the Informal Economy: A Statistical Picture*, 3rd ed. Geneva: International Labour Office.

Kapetanios, G., M. H. Pesaran, and T. Yamagata. 2011. "Panels with Nonstationary Multifactor Error Structures." *Journal of Econometrics* 160 (2): 326–48.

Kugler, A. 2019. "Impacts of Labor Market Institutions and Demographic Factors on Labor Markets in Latin America." IMF Working Paper 19/155, International Monetary Fund, Washington, DC.

La Porta, R., and A. Shleifer. 2014. "Informality and Development." *Journal of Economic Perspectives* 28 (3): 109–26.

Lambert, F., A. Pescatori, and F. Toscani. 2020. "Labor Market Informality and the Business Cycle." IMF Working Paper (forthcoming).

Levy Algazi, S. 2018. *Under-Rewarded Efforts: The Elusive Quest for Prosperity in Mexico*. Washington, DC: Inter-American Development Bank.

Leyva, G., and C. Urrutia. 2020. "Informality, Labor Regulation, and the Business Cycle." *Journal of International Economics* 126: 103340.

Li, G. 1985. "Robust Regression." In *Exploring Data Tables, Trends, and Shapes*, edited by D. C. Hoaglin, C. F. Mosteller, and J. W. Tukey, 281–340. New York: Wiley.

Medina, L., and F. Schneider. 2018. "Shadow Economies around the World: What Did We Learn over the Last 20 Years?" IMF Working Paper 18/17, International Monetary Fund, Washington, DC.

Munkacsi, Z., and M. Saxegaard. 2017. "Structural Reform Packages, Sequencing, and the Informal Economy." IMF Working Paper 17/125, International Monetary Fund, Washington, DC.

Perry, G., W. Maloney, P. Fajnzylber, O. S. Arias, A. D. Mason, and J. Saavedra-Chanduvi. 2007. *Informality: Exit and Exclusion*. Washington, DC: World Bank.

Pesaran, M. H. 2006. "Estimation and Inference in Large Heterogeneous Panels with Multifactor Error Structure." *Econometrica* 74 (4): 967–1012.

Restrepo-Echavarria, P. 2014. "Macroeconomic Volatility: The Role of the Informal Economy." *European Economic Review*, 70 (C): 454–69.

World Economic Forum. 2018. "The Global Competitiveness Report 2017–18." Insight Report, World Economic Forum, Geneva.

CHAPTER 6

Immigration and Employment: Substitute versus Complementary Labor in Selected African Countries

Arina Viseth

INTRODUCTION

Academic and policy circles have focused on the effect of immigration on advanced economies' labor markets, yet this issue is particularly relevant in emerging market and developing economies because of their large informal sectors.[1] Most of the jobs in emerging market and developing economies are in the informal sector. For example, the informal economy contributes between 25 and 65 percent of GDP (IMF 2017) and accounts for 85.8 percent of total employment in sub-Saharan Africa (International Labour Organization 2018).

Against this background, we ask the following questions:

- How does immigration in emerging market and developing economies affect native employment, including sectoral composition (formal versus informal employment) and type of employment (self-employment versus wage employment) in each sector?
- How is this effect different when foreign workers have complementary versus substitute skills compared with those of native workers?

The answers to these questions have important implications for emerging market and developing economies' productivity, especially as African economies continue to combat the economic effect of the coronavirus disease 2019 (COVID-19) pandemic while reopening borders and open spaces (at the time of writing).[2] On the one hand, by importing skills where the need for human

[1] In the formal sector, firms are licensed, are regulated, pay taxes, and must follow specific rules and regulations governing their employees. In the informal sector, workers are not guaranteed the same protections and benefits.

[2] The current context highlights the importance of studying how immigration would affect informal employment. In previous crises, the informal sector helped cushion the economic fallout on the formal sector through continuous supply to the domestic economy, sustaining incomes and consumption for the majority of households. In the current crisis, however, informal workers are the most vulnerable to employment and income losses.

capital is high, economies could find that immigration increases labor demand, stimulates job creation, and enhances productivity in formal and informal sectors. On the other hand, by changing the sectoral composition of the labor force toward more informality, immigration could reduce productivity. As the current consensus indicates, the informal sector tends to perpetuate low-productivity jobs (Ardagna and Lusardi 2008; La Porta and Shleifer 2008; Banerjee and Duflo 2011; De Paula and Scheinkman 2011), although early studies have found the opposite (De Soto 1989, 2000).

According to the concept of demand and supply, the effect of immigration on the receiving economy's labor market depends on whether immigrants and native workers substitute or complement one another. If immigrant and native workers have substitute skills, immigration increases labor supply, resulting in lower wages and less employment of native workers. If immigrant and native workers have skills that complement one another, immigration increases labor demand, resulting in higher wages and more employment of native workers.

To understand the effect of immigration in the context of a segmented labor market, we start with a modified version of the Rivera-Batiz (1981) model. Our modified model's main assumptions are (1) both formal and informal sectors hire foreign workers, (2) foreign and native workers could have either substitute or complementary skill sets, (3) wages are flexible, and (4) labor markets are closed markets. Assuming foreign and native workers have substitute skills, immigration increases labor supply, reducing native employment in that sector and triggering native workers to search for jobs in the informal sector. As a result, some native workers become self-employed in the informal sector out of necessity. When foreign and native workers have complementary skills, immigration leads to an increase of labor demand in the formal sector, resulting in higher employment and economic expansion, which, in turn, stimulates further activities and job creation in the informal sector.

To empirically estimate the employment effect of immigration in Africa, we use census and household survey data from three sub-Saharan African countries—Cameroon, Ghana, and South Africa—from 2005 to 2011. We selected the countries on the basis of data available on the informal sector. A "foreign worker" is defined as a person born outside the country.[3] Stylized facts reveal that immigration from outside the African continent (interregional immigration) brings workers with skills complementary to those of natives, whereas immigration within the African continent (intraregional) brings workers with skills that substitute for those of natives. We rely on those stylized facts and test the channels assumed to be operating in the theoretical framework, distinguishing between complementary and substitutive skill sets.

Results validate the theoretical framework. Whereas interregional immigration increases total native employment, intraregional immigration reduces it. Results also suggest interregional immigration tends to promote wage employment

[3] This definition of "foreign worker" is standard in the literature (Borjas 2003; Mishra 2007).

(formal and informal), whereas intraregional immigration generates more necessity-driven informal self-employment.

We make the following contributions to the existing literature. First, we estimate the effect of immigration in the context of a segmented labor market in sub-Saharan Africa, assessing the effect on total employment, sectoral allocation (employment in the formal versus the informal sector), and type of employment in each sector (self-employment versus wage employment). Second, we distinguish between two skill sets associated with foreign workers, complementary or substitute to skills of native workers, using data on immigration outside of and within sub-Saharan Africa. Third, we apply the national framework adopted by Borjas (2003) at the continental level, using cross-country data on Cameroon, Ghana, and South Africa and defining skill groups by level of education and years of experience in a particular sub-Saharan African country.

Using cross-country data allows us to consider the sub-Saharan African region as one single segmented labor market, hence accounting for the possible native move within the sub-Saharan African region that follows immigration, given that frontiers in the region are often porous. In particular, this approach implies workers of the same education and years of experience are not perfectly substitutable across countries, reflecting the diverse quality of education in the region. Because this approach asks how immigration of workers from a certain skill group affects native workers from that same skill group, it also implies that immigrants' skills are substitutable to those of native workers. We assume this holds through migrant social networks, which reduce possible disparities in the skills required, by providing immigrants with information on employment opportunities and the labor market in destination countries (Banerjee 1984).

The rest of this chapter provides an overview of the literature, lays the theoretical framework, describes the empirical framework and stylized facts, presents the results and conducts a sensitivity analysis, and concludes with policy recommendations.

LITERATURE REVIEW

A common approach adopted in the literature is the area or local labor market approach. The popularity of the area approach stems from its simplicity; it relies on immigrants clustering in particular geographic locations. The typical study defines a city, state, or region as a closed labor market and correlates a measure of native economic outcome (wage, employment) on the relative quantity of immigrants in that location. Studies often focus on the United States and Europe and include Altonji and Card (1989, 1991), Schoeni (1997), Card (2001, 2007), and Card and Lewis (2007) for the US labor market; Pischke and Velling (1997) and Glitz (2012) for Germany; and Winter-Ebmer and Zweimüller (1996) for Austria.

Although this approach is intuitively appealing, a well-known drawback arises from endogeneity issues, including native workers and firms responding to immigration by moving out of the specific location and immigrants selecting themselves into the specific location. As a result, the area approach could not confirm the expected results from the standard labor supply and demand model.

To answer this drawback, other studies use natural experiments or cases of unexpected migration prompted by exogenous factors (such as political events or natural disasters). For example, Card (1990) examines the influx of Cuban immigrants to Miami during the 1980 Mariel boatlift. His findings show that this migration had only small wage and employment effects on natives.

An alternative is the national labor market approach, as pioneered by Borjas (2003). Borjas (2003) exploits variations across skill groups, where skills are defined by education and experience. This approach asks how immigrants of a particular skill group affect native workers' labor market outcomes in that skill group. Although native workers within the same skill group are perfectly substitutable, they cannot easily move to other skill groups at a certain time. In this approach, the assumption of closed labor markets in the basic textbook theory is therefore more plausible.

Borjas' (2003) findings are in line with the standard labor supply and demand model, that is, when immigrants and natives are substitute workers, immigration is likely to harm the natives' labor market outcomes. Since the publication of Borjas' paper, many have followed the national labor market approach, including Bond and Gaston (2011) for Australia; Borjas and Monras (2017) for the United States, the European Union, and the former Soviet Union; and Maani and Tse (2017) for New Zealand. Some authors have also tried to account for adjustment mechanisms to immigration. Recent studies include Lewis (2011, 2013), who examines changes in technology, as well as Peri and Sparber (2009) and Ottaviano, Peri, and Wright (2013), who investigate changes in native task specialization.

Only a few publications analyze the labor market effect of immigration in emerging market and developing economies and how natives adjust to immigration. Those include Del Carpio, Ozden, and Testaverde (2015) for Malaysia; Bryant and Rukumnuaykit (2013) for Thailand; and Tumen (2016) for Turkey. Del Carpio, Ozden, and Testaverde (2015) use survey data for Malaysia and examine native responses to immigration on multiple extensive margin choices, using variation across states and over time. The authors find that natives do adapt to immigration shocks. Following the area approach, Bryant and Rukumnuaykit (2013) use survey data on Thailand and find that immigration negatively affects native wages with a magnitude stronger than in advanced economies. However, the authors did not find evidence of any effect of immigration on native employment or native migration.[4] Using survey data on the forced immigration from Syria to Turkey, Tumen (2016) analyzes the effect of Syrian refugees in Turkey and examines labor market outcomes, including formal and informal employment, unemployment, wages, and price indices. Tumen's paper exploits the quasi-experimental regional variation in refugee concentration before and after the inflows (and, as such, belongs to the area approach literature) and finds that the Syrian refugee influx reduced informal employment, but also prices. The author interprets those

[4] Internal migration is the migration of native-born workers to other geographic locations as a response to immigration in a particular location.

results as reflecting labor-cost advantages in informal labor-intensive sectors, which reduce the consumer prices of items produced in the informal sector relative to items produced in the formal sector.

Applying Borjas' (2003) national approach, Sparreboom, Mertens, and Berger (2019) use census and household survey data on Ghana, Rwanda, and South Africa to estimate the employment, unemployment, and wage effects of immigration. Sparreboom, Mertens, and Berger (2019) are the first to publish a cross-country study to examine the effect of immigration in sub-Saharan African labor markets using Borjas' (2003) method. The authors find that the effect is likely negative for workers with less education and that the complementarity of workers helps explain the results in some countries but not in all. Their study, however, does not consider the informal sector.

THEORETICAL FRAMEWORK

The labor market in emerging market and developing and receiving economies is often characterized by a large informal sector, which calls for a theoretical framework with a segmented labor market. To this end, our theoretical model is based on Rivera-Batiz (1981), who describes the labor market effect of immigration in the context of a two-sector segmented labor market. As in Rivera-Batiz (1981), our focus is in the short to medium term, with fixed nonlabor input (in other words, capital does not respond to immigration) and closed labor markets.

However, to apply our model to emerging market and developing economies, we made three adjustments. First, whereas the Rivera-Batiz (1981) model assumes that only the informal sector hires foreign labor, we assume both formal and informal sectors use domestic and foreign labor. There is no reason to assume only the informal sector would hire foreign workers when the need for skilled labor is high. Second, whereas the Rivera-Batiz (1981) model assumes binding wages and unemployment are characteristics of the formal sector, we assume both sectors have flexible wages and full employment. Labor unions are often weak in emerging market and developing economies, resulting in low bargaining power.[5] Third, whereas the Rivera-Batiz (1981) model assumes domestic and foreign labor have substitute skill sets, we also consider cases in which domestic and foreign labor have complementary skill sets.

The formal sector produces an importable good X_f through a short-term production function F_f using both domestic and foreign workers, N_f and S, respectively.

$$X_f = F_f(N_f + S) \quad F_f' > 0, \quad F_f'' < 0$$

The offer curve of foreign labor is defined as follows:

$$W_S = G(S, Z) \quad G_S > 0 \quad G_Z > 0,$$

[5] Although labor unions are not weak in South Africa, the South African authorities have recently discussed with the IMF ways to promote a more flexible labor market (IMF 2020).

where W_S is the wage paid to foreign labor S, and Z is the average income of the foreign worker's origin country, assumed to be set exogenously.

Total consumption C_f is the difference between what is produced, X_f, and exported, E_f:

$$C_f = X_f - E_f$$

Consumption is a function of real income, Y, and the international price ratio $P^r = P_f / P_i$, where P_f is the price of export goods and P_i is the price of imports.

$$C_f = C_f(P^r, Y) \quad C_{fp} > 0, \quad C_{fy} > 0,$$

where C_{fp} is the partial derivative of C_f with respect to P^r, and C_{fy} is the partial derivative of C_f with respect to Y.

Real income Y is equal to the budget constraint:

$$Y = P_f C_f + P_i C_i$$

Profits in the formal sector, Π, is defined by the following:

$$\Pi = P^r . F_f(N_f + S) - W_f N_f - W_S S = P^r . F_f(N_f + S) - W_f N_f - S . G(S, Z)$$

The first order conditions for profit maximization with respect to N_i and S are, respectively,

$$P^r . F_f' = W_f \tag{1}$$

$$P^r . F_f' = W_S \tag{2}$$

The equilibrium conditions (1) and (2) are shown in Figure 6.1. The marginal product curve $P^r . F_f'$ is the labor demand curve. The domestic labor supply curve is LS_0. The total labor supply curve to the sector that includes foreign as well as native workers is LS_1.

The equilibrium wage is W_1, employment of domestic labor is ON_1, and employment of foreign labor is $L_1 - N_1$.

The intersectoral allocation of total labor L^* is determined by workers who compare the expected wage in the formal sector with the current wage in the informal sector.

Figure 6.1 shows that immigration results in lower wages, from W_0 to W_1, reducing native employment from N_0 to N_1 and forcing some native workers to become unemployed or move to the informal sector, including choosing informal self-employment for necessity reasons.

The Rivera-Batiz (1981) model assumes that all labor—foreign and domestic—is of one type, either low skilled or high skilled, yet foreign and domestic workers' skill sets could complement one another. When skills are complementary, there would be two labor markets to consider: the low-skilled labor market and the high-skilled labor market.

Assume, for simplicity, that all foreign workers fall into the high-skilled category. In the high-skilled formal labor market, then, the arrival of high-skilled

Figure 6.1. The Effect of Immigration on the Formal Sector: Substitute Skill Sets

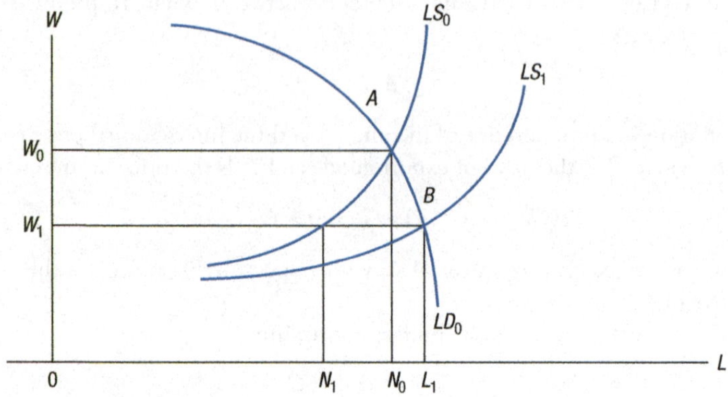

Source: Rivera-Batiz 1981.

immigrant workers would have a similar effect on employment as described in Figure 6.1. An increase in labor supply would reduce wages and native employment, triggering native workers to either become unemployed or search for jobs in the informal sector.

In the low-skilled formal labor market, the arrival of high-skilled immigrant workers would complement the low-skilled labor, inducing higher productivity. As a result, labor demand for low-skilled native workers would increase, raising wages and employment to W_2 and N_2 (Figure 6.2). Higher employment of

Figure 6.2. The Effect of Immigration on the Formal Sector: Complementary Skills Sets

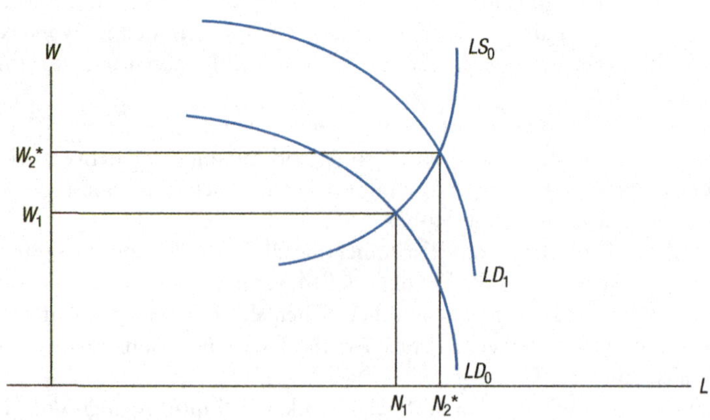

Source: Rivera-Batiz 1981.

TABLE 6.1.

The Expected Short-Term Employment Effects of Immigration

	Complementary Labor			Substitute Labor		
Total Employment	+			–		
Formal Employment	+	Self-Employment Rate	+	–	Self-Employment Rate	–
		Wage Employment Rate	+		Wage Employment Rate	–
Informal Employment	+	Self-Employment Rate	+	+	Self-Employment Rate	+
		Wage Employment Rate	+		Wage Employment Rate	+

Source: Author.

low-skilled workers in the formal sector would likely support an expansion of economic activity, which, in turn, could create positive spillovers and stimulate economic activity in the informal sector, creating more jobs in that sector.[6]

Table 6.1 summarizes the expected short-term employment effects of immigration.

EMPIRICAL FRAMEWORK

We examine the effect of immigration on native total employment rate, which we further decompose into native formal employment rate and native informal employment rate. We then examine the effect of immigration on self-employment versus wage employment within each sector (formal and informal).

Stylized Facts

The sub-Saharan Africa region is an interesting case study for four reasons: (1) the region has one of the largest informal economies in the world (Figure 6.3);[7] (2) the region needs skills and could benefit from immigration; (3) although immigration still accounts for a small proportion of the population (1 to 4 percent), immigration is both interregional and intraregional, with each type likely to bring different skills (Figure 6.4); and (4) sub-Saharan Africa's workers are among the most entrepreneurial in the world (Figure 6.5).

Our study uses census and household survey data from the Public Use Microdata Samples (PUMS) of the Decennial Censuses and Surveys, obtained

[6] The labor market outcomes derived here would remain similar should immigration be low skilled. If immigrant workers were low skilled, the low-skilled formal labor market would see less employment and lower wages among native workers, triggering native workers to either become unemployed or search for jobs in the informal sector. The high-skilled formal labor market would benefit from low-skilled immigration, supporting economic activities and creating positive spillovers in the informal sector.

[7] Although South Africa's informal sector is not as large as the rest of sub-Saharan Africa's, the informal sector has been a rational response to the formal labor market's rigidity.

Figure 6.3. The Informal Economy, by Region, Income Level, and Type of Economy

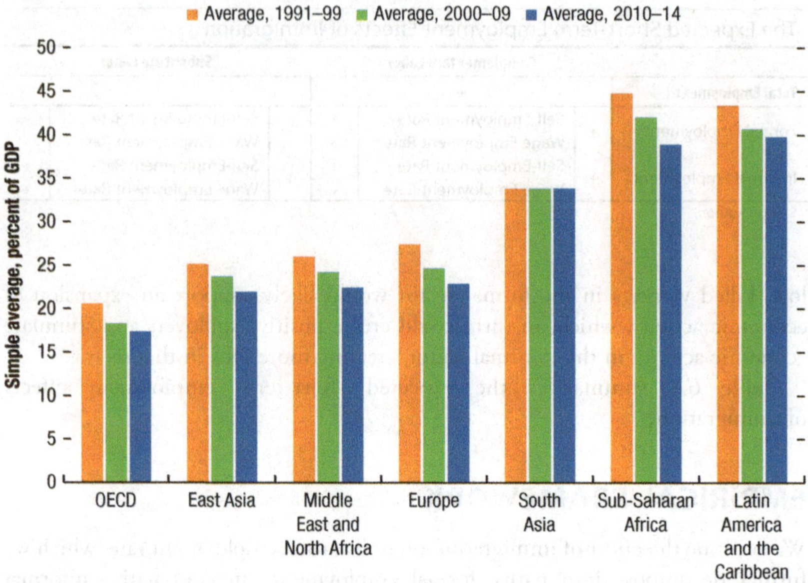

Source: IMF 2017.
Note: OECD = Organisation for Economic Co-operation and Development.

Figure 6.4. Number of Sub-Saharan African Migrants, 1960–2013
(Millions of people)

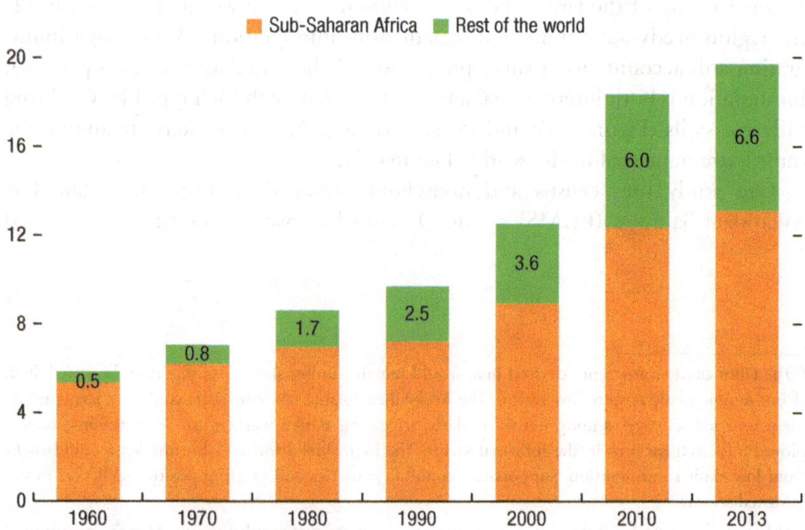

Source: Gonzalez-Garcia and others 2016.

Figure 6.5. Percentage of Population 18–64 Years of Age Who Are Nascent Entrepreneurs

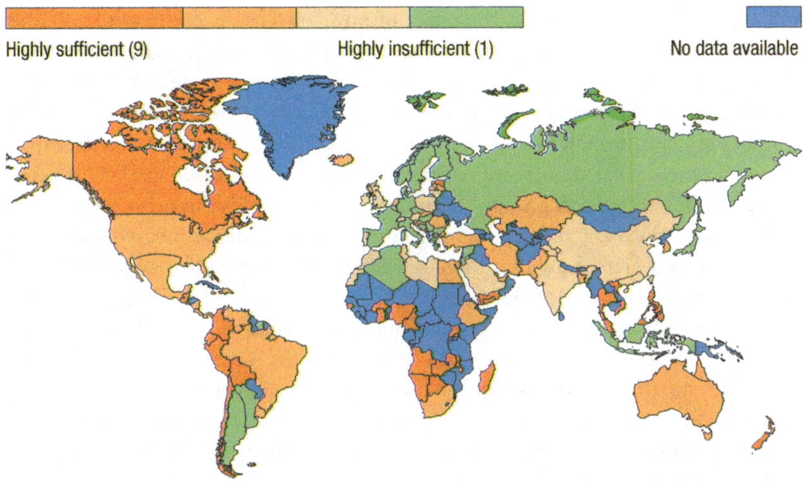

Source: Global Entrepreneurship Research Association 2018.
Note: The Global Entrepreneurship Research Association scores countries on a nine-point Likert scale with 1 being "highly insufficient" and 9 being "highly sufficient." The boundaries, colors, denominations, and any other information shown on the maps do not imply, on the part of the International Monetary Fund, any judgment on the legal status of any territory or any endorsement or acceptance of such boundaries.

from the IPUMS[8]-International project started by the Minnesota Population Center. Because of data availability on the informal sector and employment, we focus our analysis on Cameroon, Ghana, and South Africa. Panel 1 of Annex Figures 6.1 through 6.3 captures the main stylized facts, summarized from Viseth (2020).

In all three countries, interregional immigrants are relatively more educated than intraregional immigrants, and intraregional immigrants tend to match native workers' education profiles. These features allow us to test the hypothesis of complementarity versus substitutability between immigrant and native workers' skills sets, as described in the theoretical framework. In all three countries, the informal sector is also large. Except for South Africa, the informal sector dominates the economies, accounting for more than 80 percent of employment in Cameroon and Ghana. In South Africa, the informal sector is smaller than the formal sector but still significant, accounting for about 12 percent of employment (excluding private households). In all three countries, informal workers tend to be less educated than formal workers.

[8] IPUMS is the world's largest collection of publicly available individual-level census data and provides census and survey data integrated across time and space.

Model Specifications

Borjas (2003) exploits variations across skill groups and time, defined by education and experience, and identifies the effect of immigration on native workers' labor market outcomes. By conducting an analysis at the national level and not focusing on one geographic area, Borjas' (2003) approach addresses some of the drawbacks raised by the area approach, such as natives moving out of areas where immigration is taking place. Although this approach does not consider adjustments to the capital stock, the theoretical framework's assumption of a closed labor market, as represented by the various skill groups,[9] becomes more plausible than previous methods. Borjas (2003) finds a significant and negative effect of immigration on native wages.

Our stylized facts show that there are variations across skills, which we use to follow Borjas' (2003) method. Our empirical strategy applies Borjas (2003) to sub-Saharan Africa but at the regional level, using cross-sectional data and defining skill groups by education and experience in each country. With the sub-Saharan Africa region as a unit of analysis, this definition implies that workers with the same education and experience are different across countries. We assume this is the case, because within sub-Saharan Africa the quality of education is likely different from country to country.

We also assume that a foreign worker is perfectly substitutable to a native worker of the same education and experience in the considered country, because of migrants' networks. Migrants' networks have been shown to reduce asymmetries of information regarding labor market rules, institutions, and employment opportunities, making job search more efficient for immigrants (Waldinger 1997; Elliott 2001) and providing formal education and training required for immigrants to obtain a job in the host country (Drever and Hoffmeister 2008).

The term "immigrant" is defined as an individual who is foreign born. To account for the two types of immigration, interregional and intraregional, we use two definitions of immigrant: (1) foreign born outside the considered country and outside the sub-Saharan Africa region (interregional immigrant) and (2) foreign born outside the considered country but within the sub-Saharan Africa region (intraregional immigrant).

The effect of immigration on the total employment rate of native-born workers is expressed as follows:

$$Y_{cij} = \eta . Z_{cij} + C_c + I_i + J_j + \varepsilon_{ijt},$$

where Y_{cij} is the employment rate of a native born in country *c*, with education *i* and experience *j*.

$Z_{cij} = M_{cij} / N_{cij}$ is the immigrant supply shock or the immigrant share of the working-age population and measures the percentage increase in the labor supply of skill group *cij* caused by immigration.

[9] Workers are said to be perfectly substitutable within, but not across, skill groups.

The η coefficient is the parameter of interest. If η is statistically significant, the coefficient will provide information on the direction and magnitude of change in the total native employment rate from an immigration-induced labor supply shock.

We allow for linear fixed effects to control for the systematic differences in the total native employment outcome caused by differences in country characteristics, education, and experience.

C is a vector of fixed effects reflecting the characteristics of the country in consideration, which controls for total native employment differences across countries. The country fixed effects vector captures, among other factors, quality of education and the structure of the labor market (gender, labor market flexibility, labor market segmentation, and economic activity).

I and *J* are vectors of fixed effects indicating the group's educational attainment and work experience, respectively, which control for differences in total native employment across education and experience groups.

The effect of immigration on the sector composition of native-born workers is expressed as follows:

$$Y_{cij} = \eta . Z_{cij} + C_c + I_i + J_j + \varepsilon_{ijt},$$

where Y_{cij} is the share of population working in either the formal sector or the informal sector.

$Z_{cij} = M_{cij} / N_{cij}$ is the immigrant supply shock (that is, the immigration share of the working-age population) and measures the percentage increase in the labor supply of skill group *cij* from immigration.

Again, we allow for linear fixed effects.

Compared with the previous two specifications, the specification for the effect of immigration on the type of employment of native-born workers is another variable that determines employment type.

Because self-employment depends on access to capital as much as skills, we add the access to capital variable as a determinant of employment type. IPUMS categorizes individuals as owners of a dwelling if the individual has acquired his or her housing unit with a mortgage or other lending arrangement. We use this information as a proxy for access to capital, A_{cij}, which is calculated as the share of individuals who own a dwelling, standing for those with access to capital among the working-age population:

$$Y_{cij} = \eta . Z_{cij} + A_{cij} + Cc + I_i + J_j + \varepsilon_{ijt},$$

where Y_{cij} is either the share of the population working as self-employed or wage employed in the informal sector, or the share of the population working as self-employed or wage employed in the formal sector.

$Z_{cij} = M_{cij} / N_{cij}$ is the immigrant supply shock (that is, the immigration share of the working-age population) and measures the percentage increase in the labor supply of skill group *cij* from immigration.

A_{cij} is proxy for access to capital (that is, the share of the working-age population of individuals who have acquired their housing unit with a mortgage or other lending arrangement).

Again, we allow for linear fixed effects.

Data

Our period of analysis is 2010. Following the literature (Borjas 2003; Mishra 2007), when 2010 was not available we proxied with the closest census and survey data: the 2010 Cameroon data are proxied by the 2005 census and survey data. The 2010 South Africa census and survey data are proxied by the 2011 census and survey data.

To define a foreign-born worker, we use data indicating the country of birth for Ghana and South Africa. Because country of birth is not available for Cameroon, we use data on Cameroonian citizenship as a proxy for country of birth. We pick the countries of birth to differentiate between foreign-born within sub-Saharan Africa and foreign-born outside sub-Saharan Africa.

Individuals are divided into seven groups of education and eight groups of experience. Educational attainment is categorized by (1) no schooling, (2) some primary school completed, (3) primary school completed, (4) lower secondary general or lower secondary technical education completed, (5) secondary general education completed, (6) some college or postsecondary technical education, and (8) college completed.

Following Borjas (2003), "work experience" is defined as the number of years that have elapsed since the person left school. We measure experience by current age minus the entry age (*AT*) into the labor market for the typical worker (Age – *AT*). Entry age is assumed to be 17 years for the first four categories, 19 years for those with secondary general completed, 21 years for people with some college or postsecondary technical education, and 23 years for college graduates. We restrict the sample to individuals with experience ranging from 1 to 40 years to focus on the individuals in the working-age and healthy life expectancy group 18 to 57 years old.[10] This approach gives us eight experience groups of five-year intervals.

As specified in Borjas (2003), because women typically enter and leave employment more often than men, particularly around child-rearing, defining experience on the basis of age and entry age may not be relevant. This resulted in Borjas (2003) restricting the analysis to men, including women only as a specification test to determine the sensitivity of the results. We follow Borjas (2003) accordingly, focusing on men and including women as a specification test.

By using the sub-Saharan Africa region as our unit of analysis, our empirical strategy controls for the possibility that native workers move across countries

[10] According to the World Health Organization, healthy life expectancy at birth is estimated to be 54 years old in Africa.

following immigration. Because migrants' networks may result in immigrants self-selecting into the considered country, we use past distribution of immigration as defined by the previous decade or the 1990s' immigrant distribution (or closest to the 1990s when data are not available).[11] We use the 1987 Cameroonian census and survey data, the 1984 Ghanaian census and survey data, and the 1996 South African census and survey data in the construction of our immigration variable.

RESULTS

Our empirical results largely validate the theoretical framework.

Basic Results

Table 6.2 shows that in the case of complementary skill sets or interregional immigration, immigration stimulates production and increases labor demand for native workers, resulting in higher native employment. In the case of substitute skill sets or intraregional immigration, immigrants and native workers compete for the same jobs, resulting in a decline of the native labor supply. Although some women are likely to be misclassified because of gaps in their labor experience, results are similar across genders.[12]

Tables 6.3 and 6.4 show how labor is allocated across formal and informal sectors following immigration. Interregional immigration has a positive, although not statistically significant, effect on native formal employment (Table 6.4). As immigrants enter the formal sector, production and labor demand increases,

TABLE 6.2.

The Effect of Immigration on Native Total Employment-to-Population Ratios

	Specification I: Interregional Immigration	Specification II: Intraregional Immigration
Male employment	2.626**	−1.488***
	(1.274)	(0.352)
Female employment	5.398***	−1.575***
	(1.392)	(0.298)

Source: Author.

Note: Standard errors appear in parentheses and have been corrected for heteroskedasticity using White's correction. There are 168 observations. The total number of country-education-experience cells is 3 × 7 × 8 = 168. Regressions are weighted by the sample size of the country-education-experience cell. Specification I defines an immigrant as foreign-born outside sub-Saharan Africa; specification II defines immigrant as foreign-born outside Country C and within sub-Saharan Africa. All specifications include fixed effects.

$^{**}p < 0.05$; $^{***}p < 0.01$.

---

[11] The use of a past instrument is common in the literature and assumes that past immigration inflows are good predictors of contemporary immigrant inflows and uncorrelated with current unobserved labor demand shocks. See, for example, Card (2001) and Mishra (2007).

[12] On informality and gender gaps in sub-Saharan Africa, see Malta and others (2019).

TABLE 6.3.

The Effect of Immigration on the Share of Population Working in the Formal Sector

	Specification I: Interregional Immigration	Specification II: Intraregional Immigration
Male employment	0.256	−2.638***
	(1.217)	(0.306)
Female employment	2.745	−0.505
	(2.301)	(0.452)

Source: Author.

Note: Standard errors appear in parentheses and have been corrected for heteroskedasticity using White's correction. There are 168 observations. The total number of country-education-experience cells is 3 × 7 × 8 = 168. Regressions are weighted by the sample size of the country-education-experience cell. Specification I defines an immigrant as foreign-born outside sub-Saharan Africa; specification II defines immigrant as foreign-born outside Country C and within sub-Saharan Africa. All specifications include fixed effects.

***$p < 0.01$.

TABLE 6.4.

The Effect of Immigration on the Share of Population Working in the Informal Sector

	Specification I: Interregional Immigration	Specification II: Intraregional Immigration
Male employment	2.160*	1.122***
	(1.219)	(0.433)
Female employment	16.743	21.277***
	(19.875)	(7.039)

Source: Author.

Note: Standard errors appear in parentheses and have been corrected for heteroskedasticity using White's correction. There are 168 observations. The total number of country-education-experience cells is 3 × 7 × 8 = 168. Regressions are weighted by the sample size of the country-education-experience cell. Specification I defines an immigrant as foreign-born outside sub-Saharan Africa; specification II defines immigrant as foreign-born outside Country C and within sub-Saharan Africa. All specifications include fixed effects.

*$p < 0.10$; ***$p < 0.01$.

resulting in more native employment in that sector. The expansion of the formal sector induced by interregional immigration, then, has positive productivity spillovers in the informal sector, resulting in higher informal employment (Table 6.5). Intraregional immigration, conversely, decreases formal employment (Table 6.4). As immigrants enter the formal sector, they compete with native workers for the same jobs, resulting in some natives being unemployed in the formal sector or finding employment in the informal sector (Table 6.5). Results are broadly similar across gender, although the effect on female employment tends to be stronger.

Calculating elasticities, we estimate that (1) a 10 percent increase in interregional immigration leads to a 0.4 percent increase in informal employment, and (2) a 10 percent increase in intraregional immigration would lead to a 0.2 percent increase in informal employment.

Although both types of immigration lead to a positive effect on native employment in the informal sector, examining how the types of informal employment are affected reveals two different processes (Tables 6.5 to 6.8). The positive effect

TABLE 6.5.

The Effect of Immigration on the Share of Population Working as Self-Employed in the Formal Sector

	Specification I: Interregional Immigration		Specification II: Intraregional Immigration	
	Male	Female	Male	Female
Self-employment	–4.003***	–3.160***	–0.251	–0.097
	(0.931)	(0.853)	(0.457)	(0.451)
Access to capital	0.245***	0.242***	–0.209***	0.216***
	(0.025)	(0.025)	(0.028)	(0.028)

Source: Author.

Note: Standard errors appear in parentheses and have been corrected for heteroskedasticity using White's correction. There are 168 observations. The total number of country-education-experience cells is 3 × 7 × 8 = 168. Regressions are weighted by the sample size of the education-experience-country cell. Specification I defines an immigrant as foreign-born outside sub-Saharan Africa; specification II defines immigrant as foreign-born outside Country C and within sub-Saharan Africa. All specifications include fixed effects.

***$p < 0.01$.

of interregional immigration on informal employment is driven by wage employment. This indicates that positive productivity spillovers from the formal sector lead to more hiring in the informal sector.

The effect of interregional immigration on self-employment is the only result that does not have the expected sign (Table 6.5). This result may indicate that expansion in the formal sector has likely increased competition, driving smaller businesses out and resulting in a negative effect on self-employment. The positive effect of intraregional immigration on informal employment is driven by self-employment (Table 6.7). As native workers are driven out of the formal sector into the informal sector, they become self-employed. Results confirm the importance of access to capital, with better access to capital shown to increase native self-employment in both formal and informal sectors.

TABLE 6.6.

The Effect of Immigration on the Share of Population Working as Wage-Employed in the Formal Sector

	Specification I: Interregional Immigration		Specification II: Intraregional Immigration	
	Male	Female	Male	Female
Wage employment	1.933***	4.003***	–0.353	0.151
	(0.764)	(0.871)	(0.283)	(0.253)
Access to capital	0.088***	0.190***	0.094***	0.223***
	(0.020)	(0.026)	(0.023)	(0.223)

Source: Author.

Note: Standard errors appear in parentheses and have been corrected for heteroskedasticity using White's correction. There are 168 observations. The total number of country-education-experience cells is 3 × 7 × 8 = 168. Regressions are weighted by the sample size of the education-experience-country cell. Specification I defines an immigrant as foreign-born outside sub-Saharan Africa; specification II defines immigrant as foreign-born outside Country C and within sub-Saharan Africa. All specifications include fixed effects.

***$p < 0.01$.

TABLE 6.7.

The Effect of Immigration on the Share of Population Working as Self-Employed in the Informal Sector

	Specification I: Interregional Immigration		Specification II: Intraregional Immigration	
	Male	Female	Male	Female
Self-employment	0.206	1.593	0.847*	0.721
	(0.734)	(1.146)	(0.468)	(0.751)
Access to capital	0.118***	0.197***	0.140***	0.227***
	(0.028)	(0.042)	(0.031)	(0.047)

Source: Author.

Note: Standard errors appear in parentheses and have been corrected for heteroskedasticity using White's correction. There are 168 observations. The total number of country-education-experience cells is 3 × 7 × 8 = 168. Regressions are weighted by the sample size of the education-experience-country cell. Specification I defines an immigrant as foreign-born outside sub-Saharan Africa; specification II defines immigrant as foreign-born outside Country C and within sub-Saharan Africa. All specifications include fixed effects.

$^{*}p < 0.10$; $^{***}p < 0.01$.

TABLE 6.8.

The Effect of Immigration on the Share of Population Working as Wage-Employed in the Informal Sector

	Specification I: Interregional Immigration		Specification II: Intraregional Immigration	
	Male	Female	Male	Female
Wage employment	0.305***	0.346***	−0.105**	−0.077*
	(0.118)	(0.094)	(0.054)	(0.046)
Access to capital	−0.003	0.010***	−0.105*	0.011***
	(0.003)	(0.003)	(0.054)	(0.003)

Source: Author.

Note: Standard errors appear in parentheses and have been corrected for heteroskedasticity using White's correction. There are 168 observations. The total number of country-education-experience cells is 3 × 7 × 8 = 168. Regressions are weighted by the sample size of the education-experience-country cell. Specification I defines an immigrant as foreign-born outside sub-Saharan Africa; specification II defines immigrant as foreign-born outside Country C and within sub-Saharan Africa. All specifications include fixed effects.

$^{*}p < 0.10$; $^{**}p < 0.05$; $^{***}p < 0.01$.

Calculating elasticities, we find that (1) a 10 percent increase in interregional immigration raises informal wage employment by 0.5 percentage points, and (2) a 10 percent increase in intraregional immigration leads to an increase in informal self-employment by 1.9 percentage points.

Table 6.9 summarizes the expected effects of immigration on native men's employment.

Our results also provide empirical evidence that necessity-driven self-employment needs to be distinguished from transformational self-employment. This distinction was identified in Schoar (2010), who argues that necessity-driven self-employment cannot automatically lead to transformational self-employment solely on the basis of, for example, greater access to capital. The author shows that to support more transformational self-employment, other factors and policy measures are needed, including product and labor market deregulation.

TABLE 6.9.

Summary of Results

	Interregional Migration			Intraregional Migration		
	+			−		
Formal Employment Rate of Native Men	+	Self-Employment Rate	−	−	Self-Employment Rate	−
		Wage Employment Rate	+		Wage Employment Rate	−
Informal Employment Rate of Native Men	+	Self-Employment Rate	+	+	Self-Employment Rate	+
		Wage Employment Rate	+		Wage Employment Rate	−

Source: Author.

Note: Cells shaded in gray indicate statistically not significant; cells shaded in blue indicate statistically significant.

Specific Skill Groups Results

Because the inflows of immigrants in our sample include a large proportion of high school dropouts,[13] we assess whether the results were driven by a specific group of high school dropouts and estimate regressions specifically for native workers with at least a high school diploma (Table 6.10).

TABLE 6.10.

The Effect of Immigration on Employment, Sector Allocation, and Type of Employment among Individuals Who Are at Least High School Graduates

	Interregional Immigration	Intraregional Immigration
Total employment	−0.089	0.721
	(0.981)	(2.928)
Formal employment	2.172	−1.441
	(1.535)	(3.585)
Informal employment	−2.338**	2.431
	(0.911)	(1.969)
Formal self-employment	−0.974***	−2.296***
	(0.314)	(0.893)
Formal wage employment	1.042	−2.233
	(1.209)	(2.872)
Informal self-employment	−1.952***	0.503
	(0.483)	(0.984)
Informal wage employment	−0.227*	−0.036
	(0.135)	(0.229)

Source: Author.

Note: Standard errors appear in parentheses and have been corrected for heteroskedasticity using White's correction. There are 168 observations. The total number of country-education-experience cells is 3 × 8 × 3 = 72. Regressions are weighted by the sample size of the education-experience-country cell. The regressions include country, education, and experience effects. The regressions also include interactions between education and experience fixed effects and interactions between education and country fixed effects.

$*p < 0.10$; $**p < 0.05$; $***p < 0.01$.

[13] The high school dropout categories are defined by those with (1) no schooling, (2) some primary school completed, (3) primary school completed, and (4) lower secondary general or lower secondary technical education completed.

The findings indicate that our basic results may have been driven by the particular group of high school dropouts. Whereas results regarding intraregional immigration and sector allocation tend to go in the same direction as the basic results, interregional immigration is shown to have a negative effect on informal employment (both self-employment and wage employment). Interpretation of the basic results should therefore be considered within the context of sub-Saharan Africa, where immigration is largely composed of high school dropouts.

CONCLUSION AND POLICY RECOMMENDATIONS

We assess the effect of immigration on native employment in receiving emerging market and developing economies, using data on three sub-Saharan African countries. First, results confirm what standard textbooks predict. That is, the direction of the effect depends on the degree of substitutability or complementarity between immigrants and native workers. Should native workers be less skilled, immigration that brings higher-skilled workers increases native employment, whereas immigration that brings lower-skilled workers reduces native employment. Our results corroborate immigration studies of advanced economies such as Borjas (2003), who finds that low-skilled immigration hurts low-skilled native workers. Second, we find evidence that immigration shifts native employment between the formal and the informal sectors in receiving emerging market and developing economies.

Although both interregional and intraregional immigration positively affect informal employment, each prompts a shift to informal employment for a different reason. With interregional immigration, the informal sector is found to be where jobs are created, because the boost in native employment generated by immigration translates into more informal wage employment. With intraregional immigration, the informal sector is found to be where low-productivity jobs perpetuate.

Given our findings, receiving emerging market and developing economies should enhance efforts to increase complementarity between immigrant and native workers. Policy recommendations include (1) investing more in education and training—and ensuring the quality of the education system; (2) better targeting active labor market policies, especially in regions that receive large inflows of immigrants whose skill profiles match those of native workers; (3) reducing gender gaps to improve women's education and labor force participation; and (4) strengthening the business environment and access to capital to help firms expand. Access to finance is important, but our findings show that it may not be enough to promote self-employment and job creation. Any policy that promotes employment in Africa should aim to yield sustained, inclusive growth, which implies an increase in the demand for formal labor. The degree of regulation of labor and product markets, as well as the political environment, could be equally important factors to enable self-employment to generate innovation and jobs for others.

ANNEX 6.1. MAIN STYLIZED FACTS

Annex Figure 6.1. Main Stylized Facts for Cameroon

(Percent)

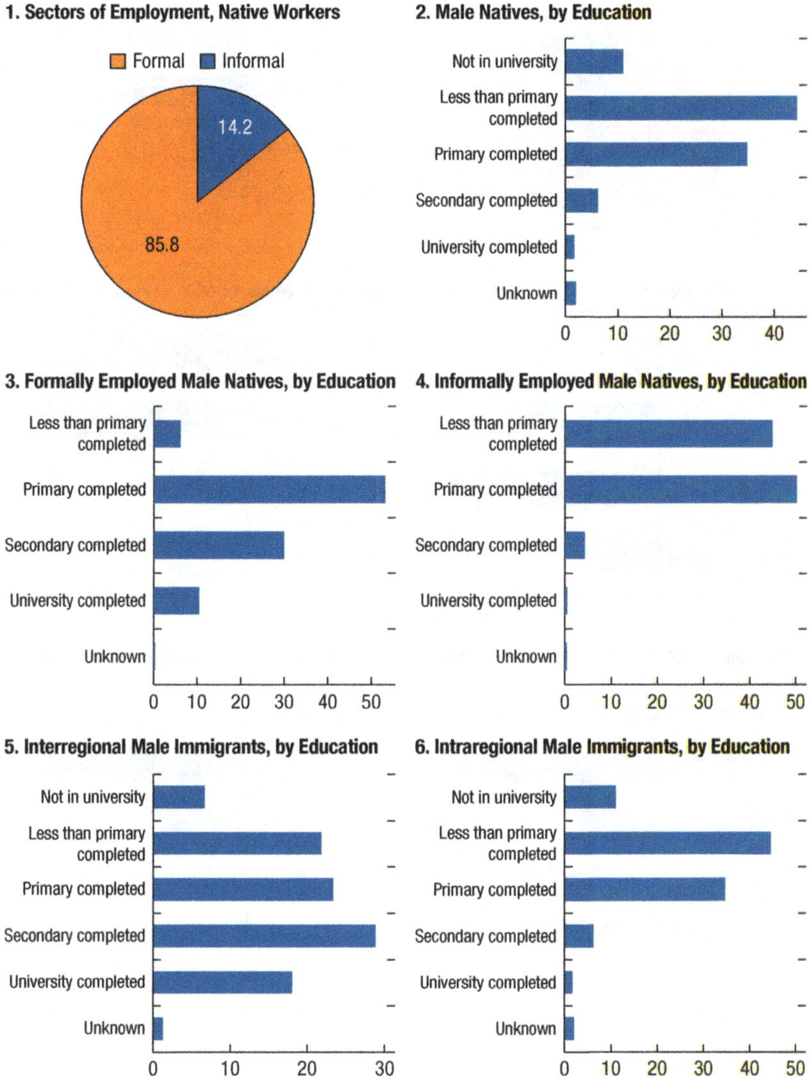

Source: Cameroon census and survey data 2005.

Annex Figure 6.2. Main Stylized Facts for Ghana

(Percent)

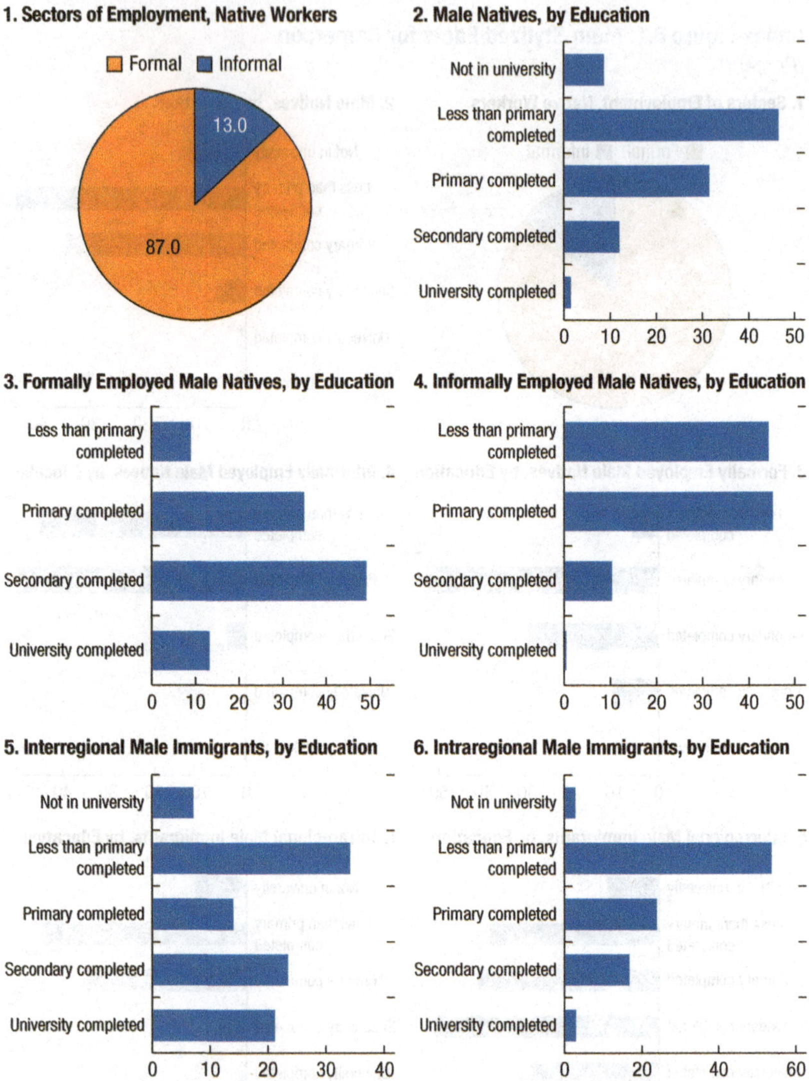

Source: Ghana census and survey data 2010.

Annex Figure 6.3. Main Stylized Facts for South Africa
(Percent)

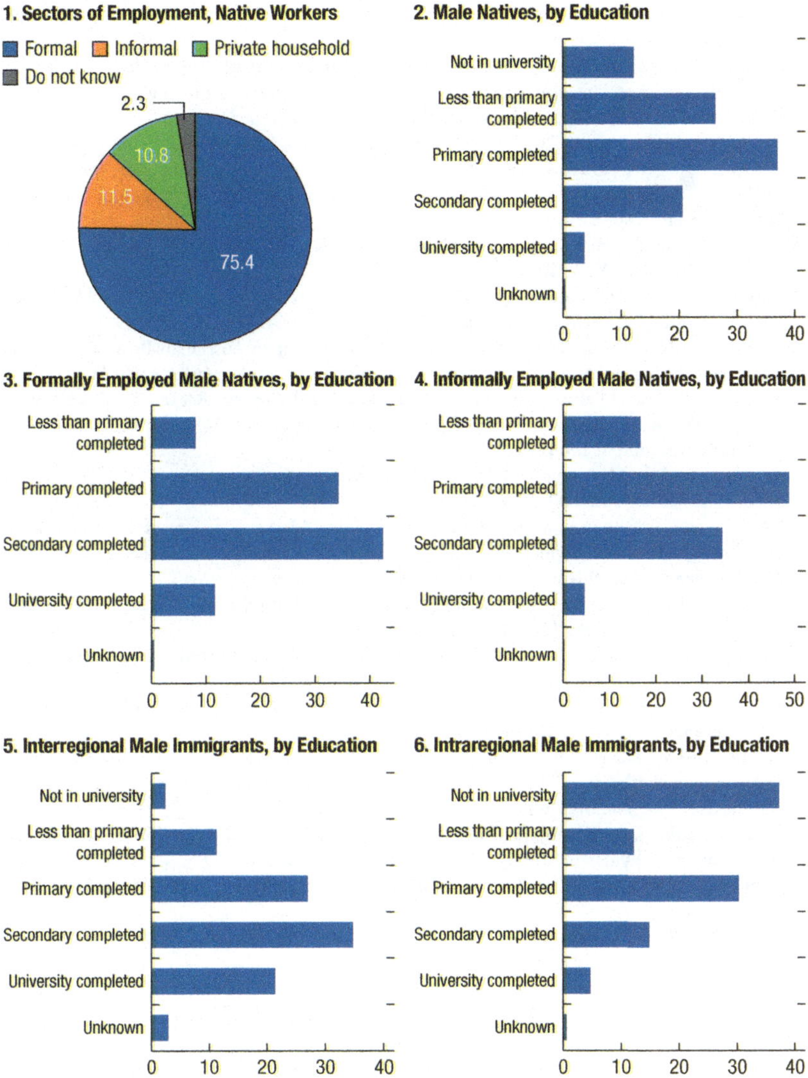

Source: South Africa census and survey data 2010.

REFERENCES

Altonji, J., and D. Card. 1989. "The Effects of Immigration on the Labor Market Outcomes of Natives." NBER Working Paper 3123, National Bureau of Economic Research, Cambridge, MA.

Altonji, J., and D. Card. 1991. "The Effects of Immigration on the Labor Market Outcomes of Less-Skilled Natives." In *Immigration, Trade and the Labor Market*, edited by J. M. Abowd and R. B. Freeman. Cambridge, MA: National Bureau of Economic Research.

Ardagna, S., and A. Lusardi. 2008. "Explaining International Differences in Entrepreneurship: The Role of Individual Characteristics and Regulatory Constraints." In *International Differences in Entrepreneurship*, edited by J. Lerner and A. Schoar. Chicago: University of Chicago Press.

Banerjee, A., and E. Duflo. 2011. *Poor Economics: A Radical Rethinking of the Way to Fight Global Poverty*. New York: Perseus.

Banerjee, B. 1984. "Information Flow, Expectations and Job Search: Rural-to-Urban Migration Process in India." *Journal of Development Economics* 15 (1–3): 239–57.

Bond, M., and N. Gaston. 2011. "The Impact of Immigration on Australian-Born Workers: An Assessment Using the National Labour Market Approach." *Economic Papers* 30 (3): 400–13.

Borjas, G. 2003. "The Labor Demand Curve Is Downward Sloping: Reexamining the Impact of Immigration on the Labor Market." NBER Working Paper 9755, National Bureau of Economic Research, Cambridge, MA.

Borjas., G., and J. Monras 2017. "The Labour Market Consequences of Refugee Supply Shocks." *Economic Policy* 32 (91): 361–413.

Bryant, J., and P. Rukumnuaykit. 2013. "The Labour Market Impacts of Immigration to Developing Countries: Evidence from a Registration Campaign in Thailand." *Journal of Development Studies* 49 (6): 785–800.

Card, D. 1990. "The Impact of the Mariel Boatlift on the Miami Labor Market." *Industrial and Labor Relations Review* 43 (2): 245–57.

Card, D. 2001. "Immigrant Inflows, Native Outflows, and the Local Market Impacts of Higher Immigration." *Journal of Labor Economics* 19 (1): 22–64.

Card, D. 2007. "How Immigration Affects U.S. Cities." Discussion Paper 11/07, Center for Research and Analysis of Migration, London.

Card, D., and E. Lewis. 2007. "The Diffusion of Mexican Immigrants During the 1990s: Explanations and Impacts." In *Mexican Immigration to the United States*, edited by G. Borjas. Cambridge, MA: National Bureau of Economic Research.

De Paula, A., and J. A. Scheinkman. 2011. "The Informal Sector: An Equilibrium Model and Some Empirical Evidence from Brazil." *Review of Income and Wealth* 57 (s1): S8–S26.

De Soto, H. 1989. *The Other Path: The Invisible Revolution in the Third World*. New York: Harper and Row.

De Soto, H. 2000. *The Mystery of Capital: Why Capitalism Triumphs in the West and Fails Everywhere Else*. New York: Basic Books.

Del Carpio, X., C. Ozden, and M. Testaverde. 2015. "Local Labor Supply Responses to Immigration." *Scandinavian Journal of Economics* 117 (2): 493–521.

Drever, A. I., and O. Hoffmeister. 2008. "Immigrants and Social Networks in a Job-Scarce Environment: The Case of Germany." *International Migration Review* 42 (2): 425–48.

Elliott, J. R. 2001. "Referral Hiring and Ethnically Homogeneous Jobs: How Prevalent Is the Connection and for Whom?" *Social Science Research* 30 (3): 401–25.

Glitz, A. 2012. "The Labor Market Impact of Immigration: A Quasi-Experiment Exploiting Immigrant Location Rules in Germany." *Journal of Labor Economics* 30 (1): 175–213.

Global Entrepreneurship Research Association. 2018. *Global Entrepreneurship Monitor: 2017/2018 Global Report*. London: London Business School.

Gonzalez-Garcia, J., E. Hitaj, M. Montfort, and A. Viseth. 2016. "Sub-Saharan African Migration: Patterns and Spillovers." IMF Spillover Notes 9, International Monetary Fund, Washington, DC.

International Labour Office (ILO). 2018. *Women and Men in the Informal Economy: A Statistical Picture*, 3rd edition. Geneva: International Labour Organization.

International Monetary Fund (IMF). 2017. *Regional Economic Outlook: Sub-Saharan Africa—Restarting the Growth Engine*. Washington, DC, May.

International Monetary Fund (IMF). 2020. "South Africa: 2019 Article IV Consultation." IMF Staff Country Report 20/33, International Monetary Fund, Washington DC.

La Porta, R., and A. Shleifer. 2008. "The Unofficial Economy and Economic Development." *Brookings Papers on Economic Activity* Fall: 275–352.

Lewis, E. 2011. "Immigration, Skill Mix, and Capital Skill Complementarity." *Quarterly Journal of Economics* 126 (2): 1029–69.

Lewis, E. 2013. "Immigration and Production Technology." *Annual Review of Economics* 5: 165–91.

Maani, S., and M. Tse. 2017. "The Impact of Immigration on Earnings and Employment: Accounting for Effective Immigrant Work Experience." *Australian Journal of Labour Economics* 20 (1): 291–317.

Malta, V., L. Kolovich, L. Martinez, and M. Tavares. 2019. "Informality and Gender Gaps Going Hand in Hand." IMF Working Paper 19/112, International Monetary Fund, Washington, DC.

Mishra, P. 2007. "Emigration and Wages in Source Countries: Evidence from Mexico." *Journal of Development Economics* 82 (1): 180–99.

Ottaviano, G., G. Peri, and G. Wright. 2013. "Immigration, Offshoring, and American Jobs." *American Economic Review* 103 (5): 1925–59.

Peri, G., and C. Sparber. 2009. "Task Specialization, Immigration, and Wages." *American Economic Review* 1 (3): 135–69.

Pischke, J., and J. Velling. 1997. "Employment Effects of Immigration to Germany: An Analysis Based on Local Labor Markets." *Review of Economics and Statistics* 79 (4): 594–604.

Rivera-Batiz, F. 1981. "The Effects of Immigration in a Distorted Two-Sector Economy." *Economic Inquiry* 19: 626–39.

Schoar, A. 2010. "The Divide between Subsistence and Transformational Entrepreneurship." In *Innovation Policy and the Economy*, volume 10, edited by J. Learner and S. Stern. Cambridge, MA: National Bureau of Economic Research.

Schoeni, R. F. 1997. "The Effects of Immigration on the Employment and Wages of Native Workers: Evidence from the 1970s and 1980s." Working Paper, RAND, Santa Monica, CA.

Sparreboom, T., J. Mertens, and S. Berger. 2019. "The Labour Market Impact of Immigration in Three Sub-Saharan African Economies." *Journal of International Migration and Integration* 21: 1225–1248.

Tumen, S. 2016. "The Economic Impact of Syrian Refugees on Host Countries: Quasi-Experimental Evidence from Turkey." *American Economic Review: Papers and Proceedings* 106 (5): 456–60.

Viseth, A. 2020. "Immigration and Employment: Substitute versus Complementary Labor in Selected African Countries." IMF Working Paper 20/149, International Monetary Fund, Washington, DC.

Waldinger, R. 1997. "Social Capital or Social Closure? Immigrant Networks in the Labor Market." Working Paper 26, Lewis Center for Regional Policy Studies, Los Angeles.

Winter-Ebmer, R., and J. Zweimüller. 1996. "Immigration and the Earnings of Young Native Workers." *Oxford Economic Papers* 48(3): 473–91.

CHAPTER 7

The Close Relationship between Informality and Gender Gaps in Sub-Saharan Africa

Vivian Malta, Lisa Kolovich, Angelica Martínez Leyva, and Marina M. Tavares

INTRODUCTION

Women are disproportionately overrepresented in the informal economy in more than 90 percent of countries in sub-Saharan Africa. Women's average share of informal employment in the region's nonagricultural sector is 83 percent, whereas for men the share is 72 percent. When the agricultural sector is included, these shares rise to 94 percent and 89 percent, respectively (International Labour Organization [ILO] 2018).[1]

Informal employment is often characterized by job instability, a lack of social protection, lower earnings, and higher gender gaps. UN Women (2016) finds that the gender wage gap in sub-Saharan Africa is 28 percent for the informal sector, far higher than the 6 percent gap for the formal sector. Although some of the wage gap can be explained by observable differences, such as job characteristics, number of hours worked, and skills required for the job, gender wage gaps can also reflect gender discrimination—a wage premium for male workers

The authors thank Claudia Berg, Anna Fruttero, Roland Kangni Kpodar, Michel Lazare, Monique Newiak, and Tito Nicias Teixeira da Silva Filho for their comments. This chapter is based on the authors' IMF Working Paper 19/112, "Informality and Gender Gaps Going Hand in Hand." This chapter is part of a research project on macroeconomic policy in low-income countries supported by the UK Department for International Development. The research results and conclusions expressed herein are those of the authors and do not necessarily reflect the views of the Department for International Development, the IMF, its executive board, or its management.

[1] ILO (2018) distinguishes employment in the informal sector from informal employment. Employment in the informal sector (or in the informal economy) is a concept based on the characteristics of an enterprise or an employee's place of work. Examples of the informal sector are unincorporated private economic units and economic units not registered to a relevant national institution or with no formal bookkeeping. Informal employment, in contrast, is job based and defined by the employment relationship and protections associated with the job. Examples of informal employment are own-account workers and employers in the informal sector and employees who are not subjected to national labor legislation, income taxation, or social protection or are not entitled to employment benefits. Here we use both terms interchangeably.

that cannot be explained after controlling for observable individual and job characteristics.

In this chapter, we investigate the factors that can explain the larger presence of women in the informal sector, including differences in education, social norms, and the legal framework. We adopt two approaches. First, using cross-country data, we show the association between women's overrepresentation in the informal sector and gender differences in education, social norms, and legal barriers. Second, using microdata from Senegal, we use probit regression models to analyze possible factors behind disproportionate female employment in the informal sector.

We focus on Senegal because of its similarity to other sub-Saharan African countries and the high quality of its microdata. Employment in Senegal's informal sector is 91 percent, versus the 92 percent regional average (ILO 2018). The country's informal sector share of GDP (40 percent) is close to the sub-Saharan African average (38 percent) (IMF 2017e), as is its ratio of employment between women and men in the informal sector (ILO 2018).

As in other studies, this cross-country analysis indicates a high association between the disproportionate presence of women in the informal sector and gender gaps in education, limited access to reproductive health care, and higher rates of early marriage.[2] Education is critical in explaining women's participation in the informal sector: women tend to receive less education than men, and formal jobs often require more skills and education than informal jobs.

Using microdata from Senegal and a probit regression model to assess the determinants of working in the informal sector, our estimations find that women in urban areas are 8.5 percentage points more likely to work in the informal sector than men, all else held constant. For these women, each additional child increases her probability of being in the informal sector by 1.4 percent. In contrast, being married or having children reduces a man's likelihood of working in the informal sector. For each additional child in the household, an employed man's likelihood of being in the informal sector decreases by 0.6 percent. Furthermore, attaining primary and secondary education is usually more important for women than for men in leaving informal employment. Completing secondary education decreases an employed woman's chances of being in the informal sector by 61 percent (in comparison with 54 percent for men).

Lower levels of education, traditional gender roles, and gender-biased laws may curtail women's possibilities of working in the formal sector. Although informal jobs may offer certain appealing features, such as employment closer to home and greater flexibility, the informal sector can be a poverty trap for women. Female workers may remain in activities requiring fewer skills and providing lower earnings, which can lead to fewer incentives to invest in young girls' education, creating perpetual gaps between men and women.

[2] See Malta and others (2019) for a more complete literature review on women's participation in the informal sector.

Several laws in sub-Saharan Africa still restrict women's economic possibilities and competitiveness. In many countries in the region, women cannot get a job without their husband's permission, make decisions for the household, travel outside the country the same way as men, administer marital property, perform the same jobs as men, or open a bank account. Furthermore, in more than half of the countries in sub-Saharan Africa, women's access to finance is not protected by law, and in several, inheritance and property rights are not the same as men's (World Bank 2018).

Governments have a range of policy options to tackle discrimination and women's overrepresentation in the informal economy, such as investing in the physical and human capital needed for high-quality education, removing discriminatory barriers from the legal framework, providing family planning to women and families that desire it, and improving infrastructure.[3] Our analysis concludes with policy recommendations to address these options for fighting gender inequality.

GENDER GAPS IN THE INFORMAL SECTOR

The informal economy is large worldwide, particularly in emerging market and developing economies. According to the ILO (2018), 70 percent of employment in these economies is informal, contrasting with only 18 percent in advanced economies.

Informal work is an even larger share in sub-Saharan Africa, corresponding to 92 percent of total employment. IMF (2017b) estimates that the informal sector in sub-Saharan Africa accounted for 38 percent of GDP between 2010 and 2014 (Figure 7.1, panel 1). Country by country, however, sub-Saharan Africa demonstrates wide variation in the size of the informal economy (Figure 7.1, panel 2). For example, in Mauritius, the informal sector is small, hovering around 20 percent of GDP, comparable to Organisation for Economic Co-operation and Development countries. Yet in Nigeria, the informal economy accounts for more than 60 percent of GDP. In sub-Saharan Africa as a whole, informal jobs are concentrated in the agricultural sector, whereas most formal jobs are in the services sector (Figure 7.1, panel 3).

Most informal workers in the region are own-account workers, and this is true for both men and women. According to the ILO (2018), after own-account workers, male informal workers tend to be employees (32 percent), whereas female informal workers tend to be contributing family workers (24 percent), defined as those "who hold self-employment jobs in an establishment operated by a related person, with a too-limited degree of involvement in its

[3] Fabrizio and others (2020), using an overlapping generation model calibrated to low-income developing countries, simulates the effect of reducing education gaps, improving infrastructure, and proving women with cash transfers on women's labor force participation and output, as well as gender inequality.

operation to be considered a partner."[4] This means that these women—although employed—are not fully independent and do not control the family business.

Even when agricultural activities are excluded, informality dominates in all sub-Saharan African countries, and on average, women work more often in the informal sector. In fact, informality is, on average, 10 percentage points higher for female workers in the non-agriculture sectors than for their male counterparts (ILO 2018; see Figure 7.1, panel 4).

In sub-Saharan Africa, these larger gender gaps in the informal sector are associated with greater gender inequality. Figure 7.2 shows this relationship between gender gaps in the informal sector and the World Economic Forum's 2018 Global Gender Gap Index score. The index is a weighted average of four indicators: (1) educational empowerment, (2) legal empowerment, (3) financial access, and (4) health and survival perspectives. Higher levels of gender equality (that is, higher index values) are associated with lower rates of women in informal employment.

Figure 7.1. Informality around the World and in Sub-Saharan Africa

1. Size of Informal Economy, by Region, 1991–2014

(Share of GDP, percentage points)

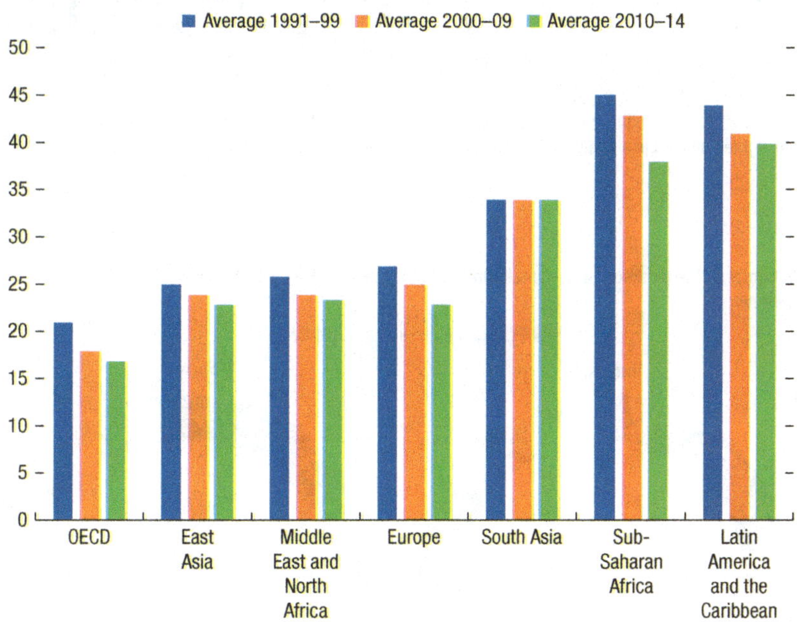

Sources: IMF 2017b; and authors.

Note: OECD = Organisation for Economic Co-operation and Development.

[4] Definitions of workers' groups are from the ILO, "Current Guidelines," available at https://www.ilo.org/global/%20statistics-and-databases/statistics-overview-and-topics/status-in-employment/current-guidelines/lang--en/index.htm/.

2. Size of Informal Economy, by Sub-Saharan African Country
(Share of GDP, percentage points, 2010–14 average)

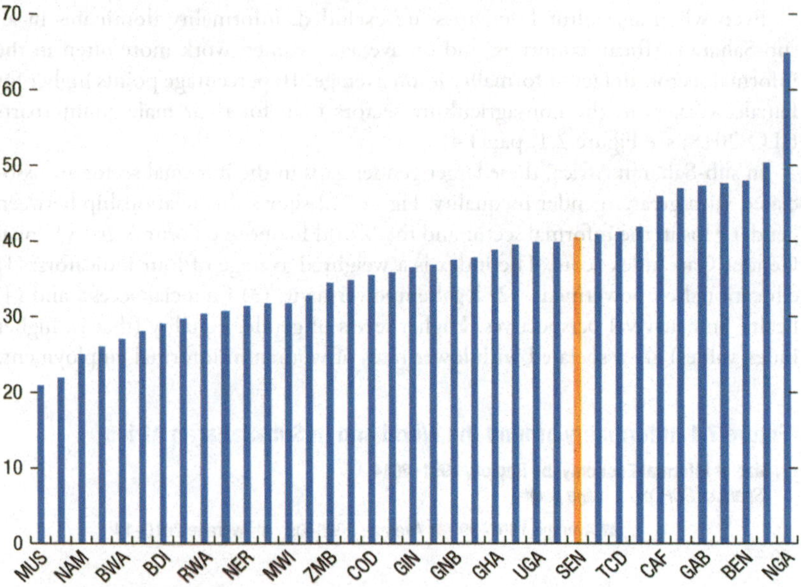

Sources: IMF 2017b; and authors.
Note: Data labels use International Organization for Standardization country codes. Senegal is highlighted as the case study in this chapter.

3. Sectoral Composition of Informal and Formal Employment in Sub-Saharan Africa
(Percent)

Sources: International Labour Organization statistics; and IMF staff calculations.

4. Informal Employment (Non-agriculture)
(Percent)

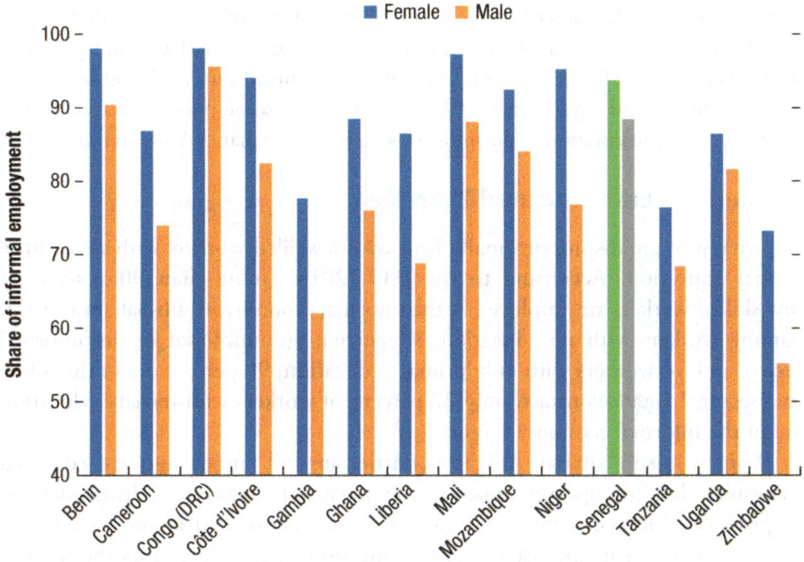

Source: International Labour Organization statistics.
Note: Latest available year for each country.

Figure 7.2. Informality and Gender Inequality in Sub-Saharan African Countries, 2018

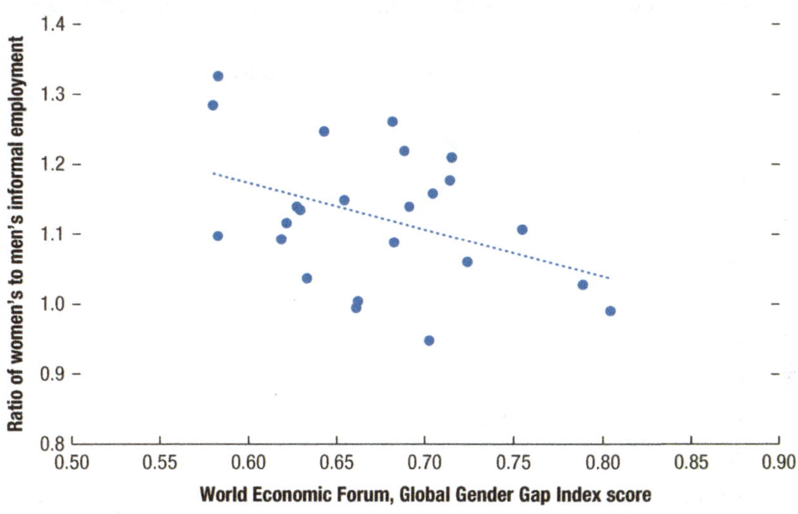

Source: IMF staff estimates based on International Labour Organization and World Economic Forum statistics.
Note: Each dot in the figure indicates a country. Informal employment in the agricultural sector is not included in the ratio.

Women tend to work more in the informal sector than men for several reasons. Factors such as difficult or unsafe commutes, poverty, and discrimination can all affect women's labor market outcomes. Here, we examine three of the most prevalent factors: lower levels of education (often due to early marriage and pregnancy), social norms (a preference for flexible employment due to unpaid care work and household responsibilities), and legal barriers. We now investigate some possible factors behind women's overrepresentation in the informal sector in sub-Saharan Africa in more detail.

Women Are Less Educated Than Men

Informal jobs are disproportionally held by low-skilled workers with no or little formal education. According to the ILO (2018), more than 90 percent of low-skilled workers are employed in the informal economy in sub-Saharan Africa. Among workers with no education, 95 percent are employed in the informal sector, and for workers with only primary education, 90 percent are in the informal sector. In stark contrast, only 27 percent of workers with tertiary education are in the informal economy (Figure 7.3).

Women in sub-Saharan African countries are still, on average, less educated than men, despite improvements over the previous two decades. The gender gap in primary education completion rates has been eliminated in most countries; however, gender gaps persist in higher education. Figure 7.4 shows the ratio of average years of education between women and men for 22 sub-Saharan African countries. In years of schooling, women's average is only 70 percent that of men's. In countries such as Chad and Guinea, the ratio is around 30 percent.

Figure 7.3. Informal Employment as a Share of Total Employment, by Education
(Percent)

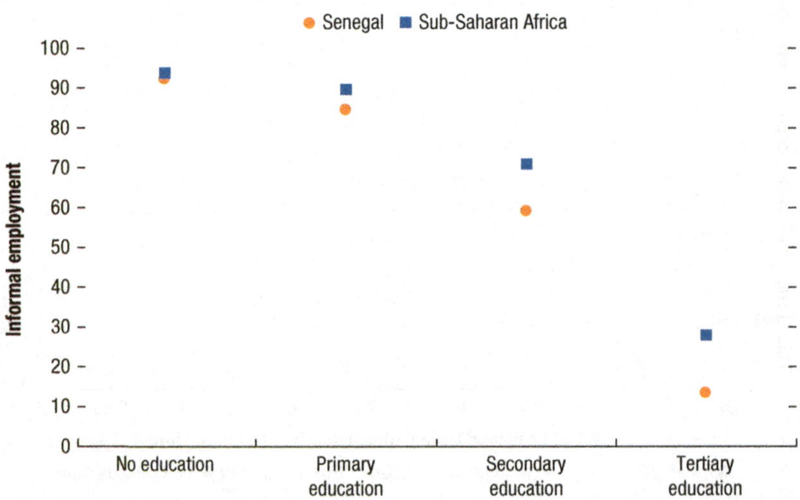

Sources: International Labour Organization 2018; and *Enquête de Suivi de la Pauvreté au Sénégal*: ESPS II, 2011 (Senegal household survey, 2011).

Figure 7.4. Gender Gaps in Education in Sub-Saharan Africa

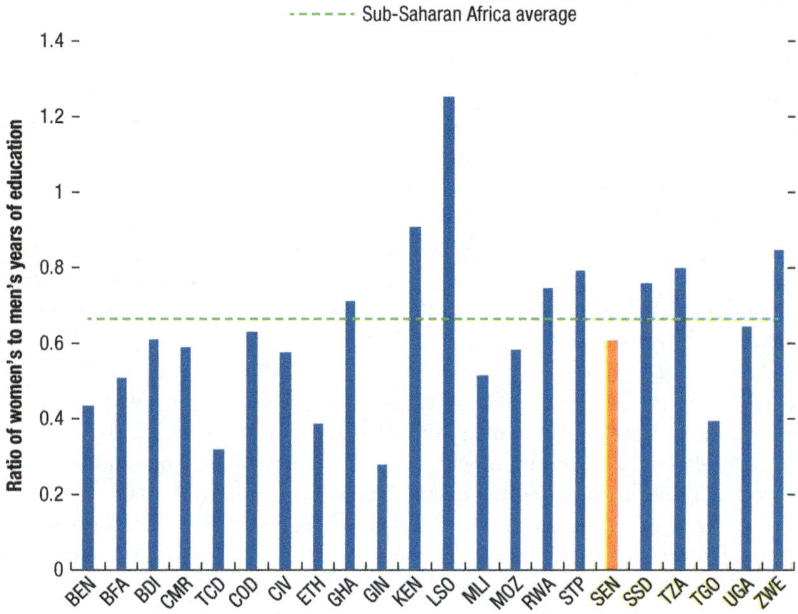

Source: World Bank statistics.
Note: Data are from the latest available year for each country. Data labels use International Organization for Standardization country codes. Senegal is highlighted as the case study in this chapter.

Incomplete education, in turn, leads to output (GDP) losses. Patrinos (2008) concludes that if a girl were to complete the level of education from which she dropped out (either primary or secondary), her lifetime earnings equivalent would increase up to 68 percent of annual gross domestic product, depending on the country and education level.[5] GDP loss caused by incomplete secondary school education is estimated at 48 percent for Kenya, 32 percent for Tanzania, 35 percent for Uganda, and 24 percent for Senegal.

Although these losses are calculated in terms of these girls' own generations, benefits from girls' education go beyond their own life cycles: educating future mothers improves not only their individual employment opportunities but also their children's health, cognitive skills, grades, educational attainment, and future employment opportunities. Women's education generates a virtuous cycle of human capital formation and economic prosperity.

Secondary education, specifically, provides large returns for women. According to Psacharopoulos and Patrinos (2004), women's return on secondary education (18.4 percent) is higher than their returns on primary education (12.8 percent) and postsecondary education (10.8 percent). Furthermore, the study shows that

[5] The 68 percent is the estimation for secondary education in Burundi.

Latin American and sub-Saharan African countries have the highest returns on education in the world.

Girls may drop out of secondary education because of the high opportunity costs of schooling at this stage of life. That is, girls may be required to work for a family business or in other jobs, help with household chores, and take care of younger children. Moreover, early marriage and early childbearing happens when girls would be in secondary education. Early marriage is one of the main reasons that girls drop out of school, preventing the full development of their human capital potential (World Bank 2012). This, in turn, often leads to work in low-paying jobs in the informal sector. For example, Herrera and Sahn (2015) estimate that in Madagascar, early childbearing increases the probability of dropping out of school by 42 percent and decreases the chances of completing secondary school by 44 percent.

Access to family planning and reproductive health care are also linked to female school enrollment. In fact, in countries where more family planning needs are met, more girls are in secondary school. There is a strong correlation between the secondary education enrollment ratio between girls and boys and access to reproductive health care in sub-Saharan Africa (Malta and others 2019).

Gender gaps in education should also be analyzed under the urban-rural divide. Educational attainment in rural areas of sub-Saharan Africa is significantly lower than in urban areas. For example, according to the 2011 Senegal household survey,[6] boys and girls between the ages of 10 and 14 years living in rural regions have approximately 1.5 years fewer education than those living in urban areas. The urban-rural divide only increases as we look at boys and girls ages 15 to 19 years, with students living in urban areas having completed approximately twice as many years of education as those living in rural areas.

Figures 7.5 and 7.6 show years of education in rural and urban Senegal by gender and age group, with the youngest age group being 10 to 14 years old and the oldest being 75 to 79 years old. Gender gaps in years of education are larger in urban than in rural areas (1.3 versus 0.7 years, on average). However, in percentage terms, women complete much less education than men in rural areas of Senegal; the difference in urban areas averages 31 percent (vertical axis), whereas in rural areas it increases to 57 percent.

Sub-Saharan African countries with wider gender disparities in education also have more women working in informality. Figure 7.7 plots the relation between gender gaps in informal employment and secondary education in 14 sub-Saharan African countries. The correlation of –0.53 shows a negative linear relationship between gender gaps in informal employment and gender gaps in secondary education.

Despite the gender gaps in education, women in Senegal who do work in the formal sector have similar years of education compared with men. According to

[6] *Enquête de Suivi de la Pauvreté au Sénégal*: ESPS II, 2011, is the latest available comprehensive household survey in Senegal containing individual and household data on social and economic characteristics.

Figure 7.5. Education, by Age and Gender: Rural Senegal

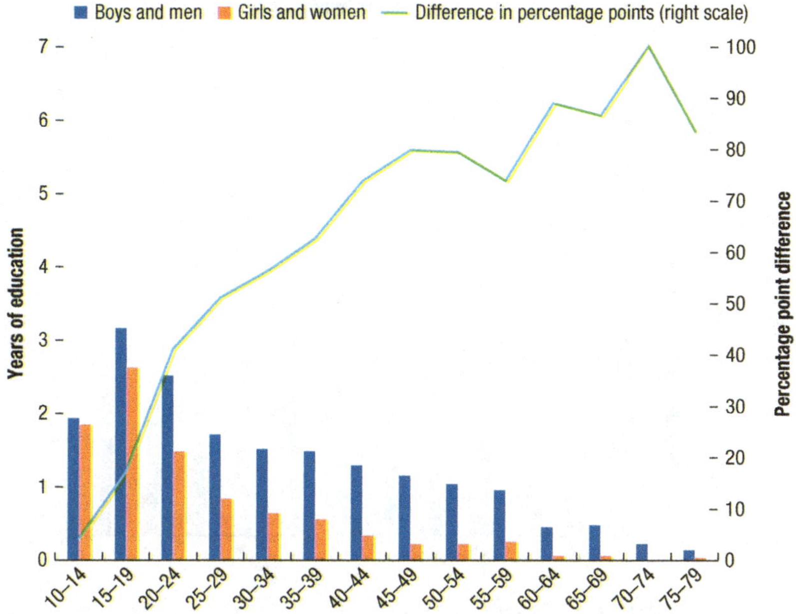

Source: *Enquête de Suivi de la Pauvreté au Sénégal*: ESPS II, 2011 (Senegal household survey, 2011).

the 2011 Senegal household survey, women working in the formal sector have on average 6.0 years of education, not much lower than men's average of 6.5 years. In the informal sector, female workers have on average 1.3 years of education whereas male workers have 1.9 years.

Social Norms Curtail Women's Competitiveness

Social norms, such as traditional gender roles, reduce women's competitiveness in the formal labor market. Gender roles that impose significantly larger burdens on women prevent them from joining the labor force. Moreover, if women do enter the labor force, they often need to look for flexible opportunities to maintain the "double shift" of work inside and outside the home.

Unpaid care work and household responsibilities fall disproportionally on women and girls, starting from an early age (United Nations Children's Fund 2016). For instance, in Senegal, women (both inside and outside the labor force) spend on average six times more time than men taking care of family and doing household chores.[7] Even when women are employed, they still spend considerably more time completing household activities than men. According to Wodon and Blackden (2006), in Benin, working women spend 208 minutes a day on household chores,

[7] Our findings on women's versus men's hours of domestic labor are calculated using the 2011 Senegal household survey.

Figure 7.6. Education, by Age and Gender: Urban Senegal

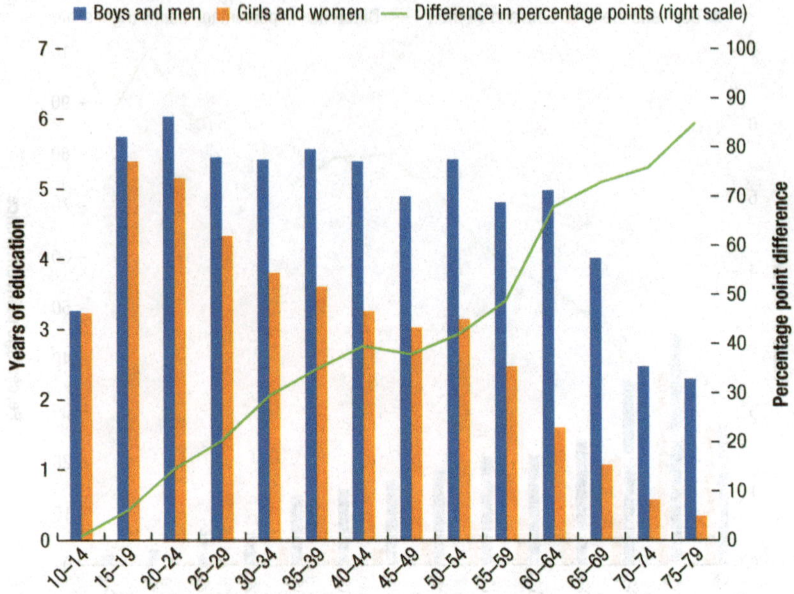

Source: *Enquête de Suivi de la Pauvreté au Sénégal* : ESPS II, 2011 (Senegal household survey, 2011).

Figure 7.7. Correlation of Informality and Education in Sub-Saharan African Countries

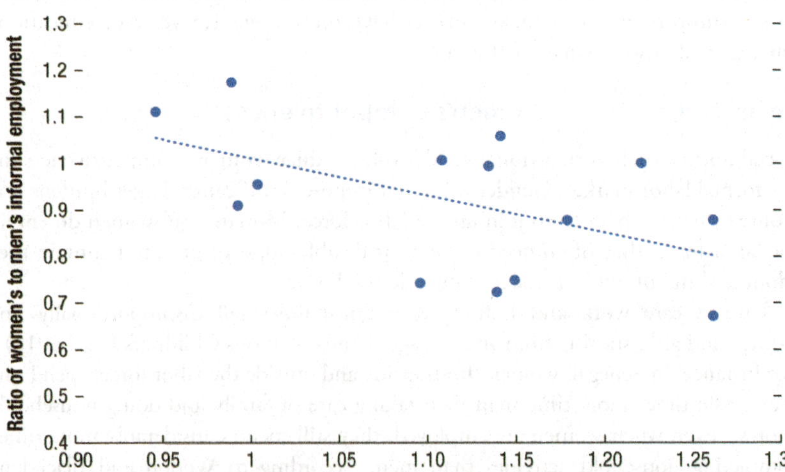

Source: IMF staff estimates based on International Labour Organization and United Nations statistics.
Note: Each dot in the figure indicates a country. Informal employment in the agricultural sector is not included in the ratio.

whereas men spend 67 minutes. In South Africa, these numbers are 228 minutes for women and 75 minutes for men, and in Mauritius, 277 minutes for women and 73 minutes for men. The substantially larger amount of time spent on domestic activities diminishes not only women's productivity at work but also their competitiveness in the labor market.

Early marriage, early childbearing, and lack of family planning impose further constraints on women's abilities to compete in the labor market. As noted, early marriage is one of the main reasons for school dropouts, impeding women from fully developing their human capital potential and thus increasing their probability of working in poorly remunerated jobs in the informal sector.

Girls marrying young is associated with higher levels of informal employment. Figure 7.8 uses data from 57 countries (24 in sub-Saharan Africa) and shows the relationship between early marriage and informal employment. Countries where girls marry before the age of 18 years is more common and tend to have higher rates of informal employment for women relative to men (the correlation between these two variables is 0.54).

Women who have had children young face additional time constraints, impairing their human capital formation, which further reduces their competitiveness in the labor market. Herrera, Sahn, and Villa (2016) find that women who had their first child during adolescence work largely in low-quality informal

Figure 7.8. Correlation of Girls' Early Marriage and Informality, Worldwide
(Percent)

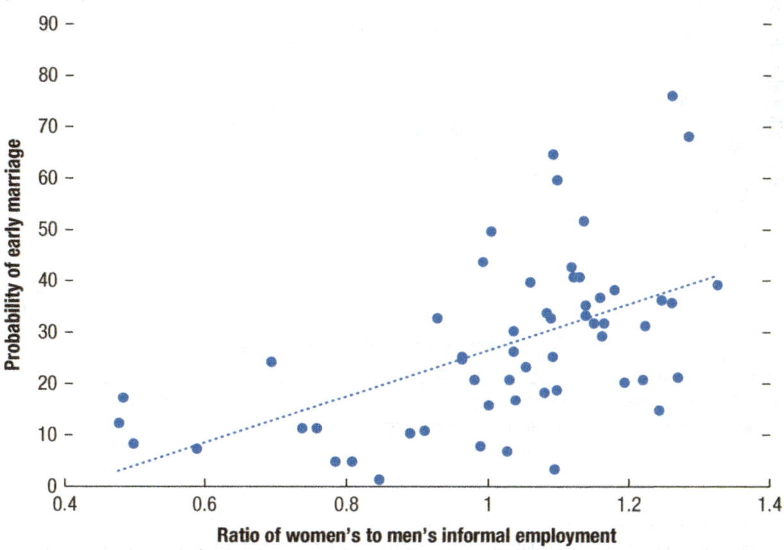

Source: IMF staff estimates based on the International Labour Organization and United Nations statistics.
Note: Each dot in the figure indicates a country. Informal employment in the agricultural sector is not included in the ratio. Early marriage is before the age of 18 years.

jobs. Figure 7.9 shows that in sub-Saharan African countries, unattended family planning needs are associated with more women working in the informal sector relative to men. Given that women in sub-Saharan Africa carry most of the burden of unpaid care work, higher fertility rates and numbers of children pose further obstacles to the labor market.[8] Figure 7.10 shows that high fertility rates are associated with low incomes.[9]

Given the strong effect of young marriage and childbearing, countries that better attend to family planning needs have more girls in secondary school. Figure 7.11 shows a strong correlation between the ratio of women and men with secondary education and access to family planning in sub-Saharan Africa. Countries in which more women's family planning needs are satisfied through modern methods have more girls currently enrolled in secondary school.

The combination of low education, gender roles, early pregnancy, and early marriage can create a poverty trap for women and girls. Expectations play a

Figure 7.9. Gender Gaps in Informality, by Girls' Early Marriage, Worldwide
(Percent)

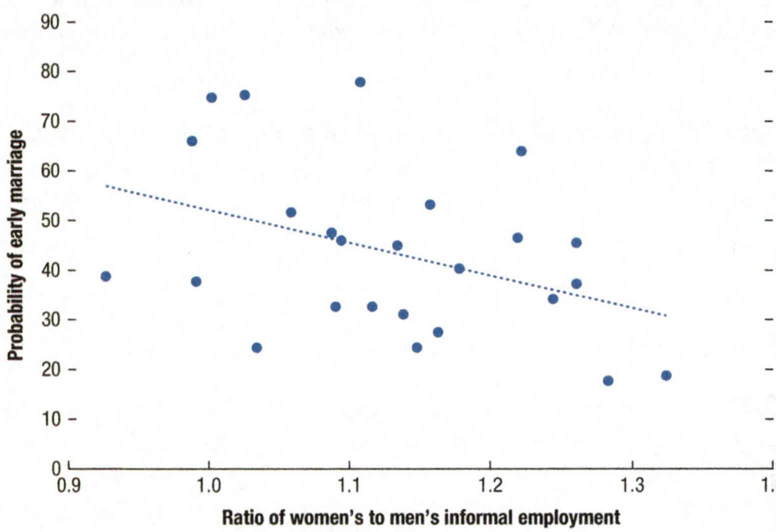

Source: IMF staff estimates based on International Labour Organization and United Nations statistics.
Note: Each dot in the figure indicates a country. Informal employment in the agricultural sector is not included in the ratio. Early marriage is before the age of 18 years.

[8] Bloom and others (2009) estimate a large negative effect of the fertility rate on labor force participation using cross-country panel data.

[9] See the 2018 IMF Country Report on Nigeria for a discussion on how high fertility rates can lower economic growth (IMF 2018b).

Figure 7.10. GDP Per Capita, by Fertility, Worldwide

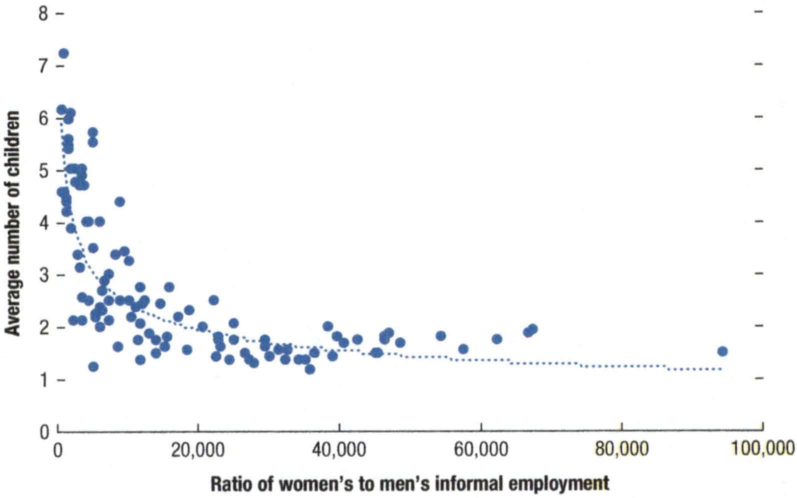

Source: IMF staff estimates based on World Bank data.
Note: Each dot in the figure indicates a country. Purchasing power parity dollars are dollars adjusted for purchasing power parity.

large role in economic outcomes, and this is no different for women in poor employment conditions. Parents expecting lower returns from their daughters in the labor market have fewer incentives to keep their girls in school. Girls with less education and fewer professional opportunities may not prioritize improving their skills and will choose to stay out of the labor force or to seek flexible jobs that allow them to reconcile the demands of work inside and work outside the home. This cycle can leave women trapped in informal and lower-paying jobs.

Legal Frameworks Impose Barriers for Working Women

Legal barriers may impose additional constraints for women trying to pursue a career that includes working in the formal sector or being a successful entrepreneur. The World Bank's "Women, Business, and the Law" data set provides information on legal rights and restrictions in 189 countries, covering 47 countries in sub-Saharan Africa. Our analysis draws on several indicators, of which we highlight four:[10]

[10] See Malta and others (2019) for a more complete discussion on the various legal barriers that exist in the region.

Figure 7.11. Correlation of Reproductive Health Care and Secondary Education in Sub-Saharan African Countries
(Percent)

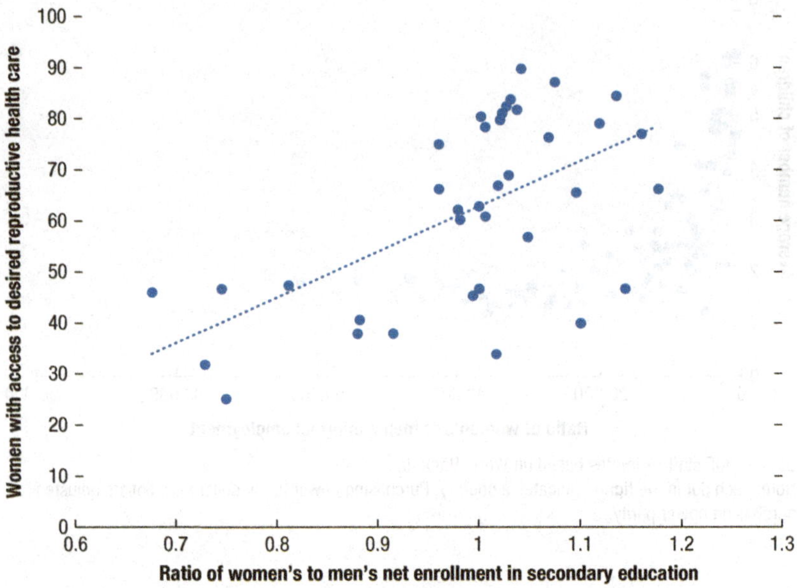

Source: IMF staff estimates based on International Labour Organization and United Nations statistics.
Note: Each dot in the figure indicates a country.

1. *Women's access to institutions.* Sub-Saharan Africa ranks sixth out of six groups for women's ability to access institutions.[11] The "access to institutions" indicator measures women's legal ability to make their own choices and to transform their choices into economic outcomes. If laws prevent women from interacting with public authorities or with the private sector in the same way as men, then their agency and *Women's access to institutions* economic activities will be limited, pushing them out of formality. For this indicator, sub-Saharan African countries outperform only Middle Eastern and North African countries (World Bank 2018).
2. *Women's access to property.* Property rights for women are still compromised in many sub-Saharan African countries. In eight countries, only husbands can legally administer marital property. In nine, married women may not have equal ownership rights and female and male surviving spouses do not have equal inheritance rights.

[11] The six groupings are high-income countries: Europe and Central Asia, Latin America and the Caribbean, East Asia and the Pacific, sub-Saharan Africa, South Asia, and the Middle East and North Africa.

3. *Women's access to credit.* In the vast majority of sub-Saharan African countries, discrimination on the basis of gender or marital status is not prohibited in access to finance.
4. *Women's access to equality under the law.* Women's working opportunities and conditions are many times impaired by law. In 27 sub-Saharan African countries, women are legally barred from performing the same jobs as men. Workplace protection and parental benefits in the region are also weaker than the global average.[12] Many sub-Saharan African countries do not have laws that prohibit or invalidate child or early marriage, criminalize domestic violence, or address sexual harassment. Yet some countries have improved over the previous decade. Since the first Women, Business and the Law report in 2010, 31 out of the 47 sub-Saharan African countries have improved gender equality in their legal frameworks. Countries with considerable legal advancements include Democratic Republic of the Congo, Guinea, Mauritius, Rwanda, São Tomé and Príncipe, and Zambia.

CASE STUDY: SENEGAL

We now further investigate the relationship between gender and informal employment in Senegal. In addition to presenting relevant stylized facts for the country, we use probit regression models to estimate the probability of Senegalese workers, particularly women, being employed in the informal sector. For this purpose, we use microdata from the 2011 Senegal household survey.

We define a formal worker as a paid worker who declares having a formal contract with the employer (11.9 percent), having affiliation through the employer to a social security system (7.7 percent), or both. In sum, 14.3 percent of all workers are formal workers under this classification.

The Context of Senegal

Senegal's sectoral division is similar to that of other low-income sub-Saharan African countries. Employment is concentrated in the agricultural sector, accounting for almost half of total employment. The second-largest sector is industry, and the smallest is services. Senegal's economic structure resembles that of a country beginning a structural transformation.[13]

[12] Ensuring that all boys and girls have access to high-quality pre-primary childhood education by 2030 is one of the Sustainable Development Goals. Countries considering options to increase access to childcare and thus female labor force participation include Austria (IMF 2017a), Egypt (IMF 2018a), and the former Yugoslav Republic of Macedonia (IMF 2019).

[13] For a review of the literature on structural transformation, see Herrendorf, Rogerson, and Valentinyi (2014).

Education

Gender gaps for both enrollment in and completion of primary education have closed, and even reversed, in Senegal (IMF 2018c). According to UNESCO (data accessed from the World Bank Data website), from 1999 to 2016, gross enrollment in primary education jumped from 59 percent to 88 percent for girls, whereas for boys, the rates improved from 71 percent to 78 percent. Primary education completion rates rose from 33 percent for girls and 43 percent for boys in 2000 to 64 percent and 54 percent in 2016. However, according to the United Nations Development Programme (data also accessed from the World Bank Data website), the average was only 2.8 years of education in 2015, lower than the average for the West African Economic and Monetary Union (3.0 years) and sub-Saharan Africa (5.1 years).

More progress is needed, because girls' completion of secondary education and enrollment in tertiary education remain substantially lower than boys'. Senegal's Demographic and Health Survey 2012–13 reported that, in 2012, the average completion rate in secondary education was only 13 percent for girls compared with 21 percent for boys. The women's completion rate for tertiary education doubled from 4 percent in 2006 to 8 percent in 2016; however, the men's rate is still much higher, having increased from 8 percent to 13 percent. Despite these gender gaps, the women who work in the formal sector in Senegal are on average almost as educated as the men.

Social Norms

Women's labor force participation increased from 34 percent in 2000 to 41 percent in 2016. Furthermore, according to the ILOSTAT, the ratio of unemployed young women to unemployed young men (from 15 to 24 years old) dropped from 1.7 to 1.1 between 2000 and 2017.

Women in Senegal rarely work part-time, even when employed in the informal sector. One benefit of the informal sector is the possibility of working flexible hours and days. This is especially valuable for women, who are almost always responsible for the bulk of unpaid care work. As a result, women could prefer a job that requires fewer hours or offers greater flexibility over a job that offers better security, compensation, or other benefits.

Using the household survey data, we calculate the share of men and women working full and part time in the formal and informal sectors. Table 7.1 confirms that Senegalese women are more likely than men to work part-time (20 percent versus 7 percent), although the majority of both women and men work full-time. On average, urban women work 43 hours per week in the formal sector and 48 hours per week in the informal sector. Thus, Senegalese women do not seem to benefit from the part-time flexibility more often given by the informal sector.

Gender gaps vary across the distribution of income. Female Senegalese workers from the top income groups are more often informal workers than their male counterparts, but that statistic does not hold for lower-income groups. At the top

TABLE 7.1.

Part-Time Workers in Rural and Urban Senegal, by Formal and Informal Sector
(Percent average)

	Rural		Urban		All	
	Formal	Informal	Formal	Informal	Formal	Informal
Male	8.4	8.1	7.9	5.4	8.2	7.2
Female	25.1	20.8	16.4	19.5	19.0	20.2

Source: *Enquête de Suivi de la Pauvreté au Sénégal*: ESPS II 2011 (Senegal Household Survey 2011).

40 percent of the income distribution, female workers are on average 9 percentage points more often in the informal sector than male workers (82 percent versus 73 percent). In contrast, at the bottom 40 percent of the income distribution, the difference falls from 9 percent to 0. This could be partially explained by education gaps, which are larger among richer households: at the top 40 percent of the income distribution, the gap is 0.92 years of education, whereas at the bottom 30 percent, the gap is 0.60 years.

Legal Barriers

Gender discrimination in the Senegalese legal framework is worse than in sub-Saharan Africa as a whole. World Bank (2018) calculates that Senegal scores below the sub-Saharan African average in women's legal rights (Figure 7.12), particularly for the indicators "using property" (related to asset ownership), "going to court," "getting a job," "building credit," and "accessing institutions." Legal restrictions still prevent women who are not pregnant or nursing from performing the same jobs as men. Moreover, sexual harassment is not recognized as a criminal offense, and the constitution does not formally recognize, nor does it prohibit, discrimination against women that may result from customary laws.

The Senegalese family code allows for early marriage, setting the minimum age for girls at 16 years. However, household survey data show that Senegalese women tend to marry earlier than men, and these women receive less education. Twenty-three percent of female adolescents ages 15 to 19 years are already married, whereas among males the same age, only 2 percent are married. Married female adolescents have on average one-third fewer years of education than unmarried ones (2.6 years versus 3.9 years), suggesting that early marriage might have substantial negative effects on educational outcomes.

Women own few assets, and their ownership is not protected by law. The Senegalese family code also gives husbands the power to make all decisions for the household. As a further complication, the system of inheritance described in the family code also gives advantages to men. This hampers women's ability to own land or equipment, reducing their competitiveness in the labor market.

Senegal, however, scores above the sub-Saharan Africa average in areas such as "providing incentives to work" and "protecting women from violence." Women working in the formal sector have a legal guarantee of an equivalent position after

Figure 7.12. Legal Equality for Women in Sub-Saharan Africa and Senegal

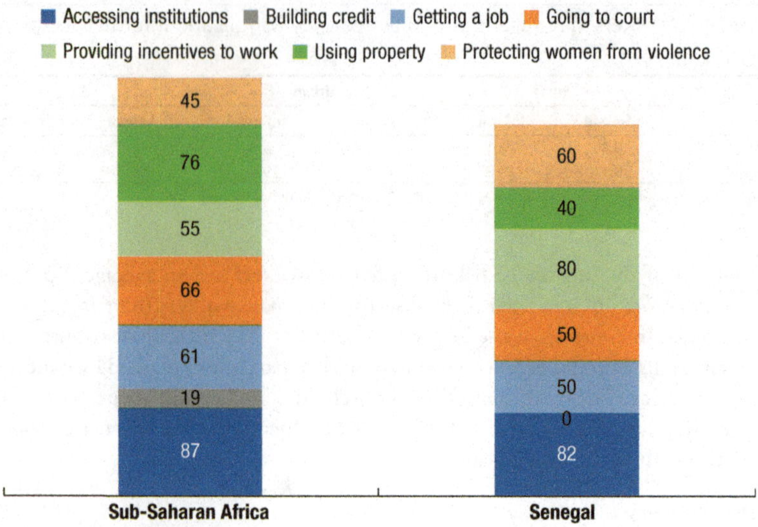

Source: World Bank 2018.
Note: Data are based on the World Bank's *Women, Business and the Law* score.

maternity leave, and the government provides parents in the workforce with child allowances. In addition, Senegal has made progress in passing legislation against domestic violence.

Empirical Analysis

We further examine factors that could determine whether a worker is formal or informal. Using the 2011 Senegal household survey, we construct probit models to quantify the probability of Senegalese workers between the ages of 15 and 64 years being formal or informal. We examine the marginal effects of seven variables on the probability of being an informal worker: gender, educational attainment, head of household status, marital status, number of children in the household, decile in the income distribution, and age group, controlling for urban or rural regions. We run probit models using the entire household sample as well as urban and rural areas separately, as is standard in the literature. For each of these three specifications, we run models including all workers, female workers only, and male workers only.[14]

[14] Annex Table 7.1.1 presents the coefficients and standard errors of the marginal effects of the resulting nine probit models. Annex Table 7.1.2 presents these results, including the controls for urban and rural regions and the *z*-tests for all variables.

Our results indicate that women are more likely to be in the informal sector than men. Being a female worker increases by 3.4 percentage points the probability of being employed in the informal sector, and this coefficient is significant at the 1 percent level. In urban areas, this discrepancy is even higher: all else constant, a working woman is 8.5 percentage points more likely to be in the informal sector than a working man (Annex Table 7.1.1).

Getting an education has the largest positive effect on the probability of being a formal worker, and it is usually more important for women. Primary, secondary, and tertiary education have the largest marginal effects on the probability of being in the informal sector, except for primary education in rural areas. Paid workers who completed primary education are 16.4 percent less likely to be in the informal sector. Urban female paid workers who completed primary education, in particular, are 31.2 percent less likely to be in the informal sector compared with a reduction of 22.5 percent for their male counterparts. However, for rural regions, a primary school diploma is less relevant in shifting a worker from the informal to the formal sector. Primary school completion decreases the probability of being informal by 7.2 percent for men and 4.6 percent for women.[15]

In other words, the likelihood of being in the informal sector decreases as educational attainment increases. Workers who have earned a secondary diploma are on average 55.5 percent less likely to be in the informal sector. Among urban residents, the decrease is 60.4 percent. The importance of secondary education is larger for women than for men: 61.0 percent versus 53.8 percent, respectively. In urban areas, these numbers rise to 66.4 for women and 57.1 for men. Individuals with tertiary education are 72.9 percentage points less likely to be working in the informal sector. For the urban sample, the tertiary education premium is higher for women (69.4 percent) than for men (68.6 percent).[16]

Chi-squared tests confirm that women generally have larger coefficients (in absolute terms) in primary and secondary education in both urban and rural areas, indicating that primary and secondary education are more important for women than for men in reducing their probability of working in the informal sector.

Men enjoy bonuses from being married and from fatherhood. In Senegal, married men have on average a 2.1 percent lower probability of being in the informal sector when compared with single men, and this rate rises to 10.2 percent when considering only urban areas. For each additional child in the household, the likelihood of a working man being in the informal sector decreases by 0.6 percent, whereas for women in urban areas, each additional child increases her

[15] The discrepancy between informally employed urban and rural workers might result from the limited size of the formal sector in rural areas. In rural Senegal, only 6.7 percent of workers have a primary school diploma, whereas in urban areas, this percentage increases to 21.7.

[16] Only 22 observations in the sample of 163,490 correspond to female workers with tertiary education; thus, the estimations suffer from small sample bias.

probability of being in the informal sector by 1.4 percent.[17] Given that women in Senegal have on average five children, the effect of having children on labor informality can be sizable.

Being the head of the household reduces the probability of being an informal worker, particularly for women. The probability of a Senegalese worker being an informal worker is 2.5 percent lower when he or she is head of the household, and 5.3 percent lower if he or she is head of the household in an urban area. When subsamples of women and men are separated, only the women show a significant coefficient (at the 5 percent level) for head of the household, increasing the probability of being a formal worker by 2.8 percent. A higher income increases the probability of being a formal worker for men more than for women. For each decile a working man's household climbs in Senegal's income distribution, the chance of him being in the informal sector decreases by 1.6 percent (3.1 percent in urban areas), whereas for a working woman, this reduction is smaller, at 0.6 percent (1.6 percent in urban areas). This divergence is in line with the larger gender gaps in informality at the top of the income distribution.

CONCLUSION AND POLICY RECOMMENDATIONS

Women are disproportionately overrepresented in the informal economy in sub-Saharan Africa, where they experience less stability, reduced social protection, lower productivity, lower earnings, and more discrimination. We offer evidence that countries with more informality among female workers, on average, have larger gender gaps in education, satisfy fewer family planning needs, and have higher incidences of early marriage. We further demonstrate how legal frameworks create constraints for women. That is, laws in sub-Saharan Africa reduce women's economic possibilities and competitiveness by reducing their access to property, jobs, and credit.

The combination of low education, traditional gender roles, legal constraints, early pregnancy, and early marriage can trap women in the informal sector. Parents expecting lower returns from their daughters in the labor market have fewer incentives to keep them in school. Girls with less education and those who are tasked with the work associated with traditional gender roles have fewer chances of joining the formal labor market. Early pregnancy and early marriage further restrict their labor force opportunities. This cycle can leave women trapped in informal or less-attractive jobs.

Using microdata from Senegal, we confirm that women are more likely to be in the informal sector than men. We also find that primary and secondary education are usually more relevant to shifting women out of informality than men.

[17] Correll, Benard, and Paik (2007), using a randomized control trial in the United States, find that mothers are perceived as less competent, are less likely to be promoted, and have lower wages than fathers. Bear and Glick (2016) examine how reframing mothers as "breadwinners" can reduce the motherhood penalty.

Furthermore, being married or having children implies a lower probability of being an informal worker for men—but the effect is opposite for women. Larger incomes also decrease the probability of being in the informal sector more for men than for women.

Governments have a role to play in diminishing these inequalities and ensuring men and women can compete equally in the labor market. Policymakers may choose to focus on the following findings:

- Increasing girls' educational attainment can substantially diminish the probability of women being employed in the informal sector. More high-quality years of education lead to higher salaries and thus better living standards for families. Governments should improve the access to, the quality of, and the effectiveness of their education systems. Costs can be much lower in countries where the physical infrastructure is in place, but for reasons such as social stigma, early marriage and childbearing, and discrimination, girls abandon school before completion of secondary education. Policymakers can provide parents with incentives to keep their daughters at school, for instance, by making targeted cash transfers to those who keep their girls home until they complete primary and secondary education.[18] Prohibiting child marriage and disseminating information on women's health also helps prevent girls from dropping out, especially in rural areas.
- Changing the legal framework to enshrine gender equality is financially costless. Governments should expunge these legal differences not only because they violate the basic principle of equality between individuals before the law but also because, economically, they create distortions and wrong incentives. Sustainable growth cannot be achieved with half of the population lacking access to institutions, assets, credit, freedom of mobility, and freedom of choice. Enforcement of property rights—including inheritance rights—is particularly relevant, especially in countries where small agricultural plots are the most common site of economic activity, and thus where land ownership is highly valuable. Moreover, enforcing women's legal rights by combating domestic violence, sexual harassment, and child marriage improves women's living standards and breaks the cycle of gender inequality.
- Meeting demands for family planning is imperative. Policymakers can run education campaigns and provide high-quality health care and information to young women interested in learning about reproductive health care. Disseminating knowledge and creating an atmosphere where women learn about and have access to family planning, sexual education, and modern contraceptives can pave the way to a healthier, more informed, and more prosperous generation of women.

[18] See, for example, IMF staff reports on Guatemala (2016a), Jordan (2017c), Morocco (2017d), Nigeria (2016b), and Pakistan (2016c), which discuss targeted cash transfers to increase female enrollment.

- Investing in infrastructure reduces time spent on home production and provides safe transportation options for women. Women's disproportionately high participation in the informal labor sector is linked to the reduced number of available hours to dedicate to work outside their homes. Often, their choices are to find an informal job close to home or to not participate in the labor market. However, governments can invest in infrastructure for access to water and energy to reduce the time women spend in home production and to allow them to safely travel to and from workplaces and schools.[19]
- Addressing social norms that economically disadvantage women is necessary. Policymakers should enforce equal rights and opportunities. Social norms have changed in urban areas of many sub-Saharan African countries, but gender inequalities still prevail in rural areas. In this context, policy recommendations include enforcing civil laws where customary laws reduce women's freedom and power, combating domestic violence, and promoting and encouraging a more equal division of labor at home by developing education campaigns and introducing paternity leave.
- Mitigating discrimination in the formal labor market can help equalize opportunities. Governments can support gender equality through changes in the legal framework (that is, passing laws against gender discrimination and sexual harassment), as well as by provision of childcare subsidies or childcare facilities and parental leave. These policies can have positive spillovers to the informal sector. Fiscal policies such as tax breaks or subsidies for families with young children and generous parental leave (provided by the government, not the private sector) can encourage women to enter the labor force, especially the formal sector. Making sure the tax system, particularly income tax, does not penalize secondary wage earners is also important. Access to credit and assets is paramount in promoting equal opportunity of entrepreneurship between men and women—and this is helpful for both formal and informal sectors. Spillovers from reduced gender discrimination in social norms and curtailed education gaps also positively affect all working women, along with girls who wish to one day participate in the labor force.

Implementation barriers should not prevent policymakers from working on gender equality measures. Some of our policy recommendations have vast empirical basis in the literature, such as "increasing education generates better salaries and living standards." Although other channels and causal links between gender inequality and informality might be challenging to prove, governments should pursue equal opportunities for men and women and eliminate economic distortions related to gender inequality.

[19] See, for example, Mexico City's and Bolivia's efforts to create safe transportation options (Kolovich 2018) along with IMF staff reports such as Chile (2015), India (2017b), and Jordan (2017c).

ANNEX 7.1.

ANNEX TABLE 7.1.1.

Marginal Effects from Probit Regressions

Independent Variables	All Workers	Female Workers	Male Workers	Urban Workers	Urban Female Workers	Urban Male Workers	Rural Workers	Rural Female Workers	Rural Male Workers
Female	0.0340***			0.0850***			0.0088*		
	(0.0050)			(0.0113)			(0.0049)		
No education	0.0336***	0.0197**	0.0376***	0.0634***	0.0269	0.0803***	0.0186***	0.0175*	0.0153**
	(0.0062)	(0.0090)	(0.0084)	(0.0135)	(0.0189)	(0.0187)	(0.0056)	(0.0095)	(0.0066)
Primary education	−0.1640***	−0.2010***	−0.1506***	−0.2547***	−0.3120***	−0.2248***	−0.0656***	−0.0461**	−0.0720***
	(0.0115)	(0.0216)	(0.0138)	(0.0177)	(0.0301)	(0.0221)	(0.0111)	(0.0191)	(0.0132)
Secondary education	−0.5553***	−0.6098***	−0.5384***	−0.6044***	−0.6643***	−0.5707***	−0.4577***	−0.6073***	−0.4364***
	(0.0311)	(0.0582)	(0.0365)	(0.0267)	(0.0478)	(0.0314)	(0.0645)	(0.1530)	(0.0664)
Tertiary education	−0.7285***	−0.6551***	−0.7625***	−0.6990***	−0.6939***	−0.6862***	−0.7793***		−0.7899***
	(0.0611)	(0.1610)	(0.0415)	(0.0367)	(0.1131)	(0.0220)	(0.1503)		(0.1504)
Head of household	−0.0249***	−0.0279**	−0.0063	−0.0530***	−0.0361	−0.0292	−0.0190**	−0.0239	−0.0031
	(0.0071)	(0.0131)	(0.0087)	(0.0155)	(0.0230)	(0.0210)	(0.0074)	(0.0177)	(0.0071)
Married	−0.0213***	0.0071	−0.0392***	−0.0477***	0.0173	−0.1016***	−0.0000	0.0079	−0.0013
	(0.0062)	(0.0082)	(0.0090)	(0.0134)	(0.0166)	(0.0212)	(0.0059)	(0.0088)	(0.0069)
No. of children	−0.0020	0.0036	−0.0059**	−0.0007	0.0139**	−0.0084	−0.0033**	−0.0011	−0.0049***
	(0.0019)	(0.0027)	(0.0025)	(0.0047)	(0.0067)	(0.0064)	(0.0014)	(0.0022)	(0.0018)
Income decile (1 to 10)	−0.0116***	−0.0060***	−0.0161***	−0.0254***	−0.0165***	−0.0310***	−0.0055***	−0.0020	−0.0081***
	(0.0011)	(0.0016)	(0.0014)	(0.0029)	(0.0039)	(0.0042)	(0.0009)	(0.0015)	(0.0010)
Urban	−0.0735***	−0.0560***	−0.0836***						
	(0.0052)	(0.0076)	(0.0070)						
Age: 15–19 years	−0.0054	−0.0090	−0.0002	−0.0272	−0.0258	−0.0367	−0.0123	−0.0167	−0.0065
	(0.0116)	(0.0171)	(0.0147)	(0.0403)	(0.0465)	(0.0593)	(0.0088)	(0.0159)	(0.0096)
Age: 20–24 years	−0.0353***	−0.0372*	−0.0338*	−0.0840**	−0.0614	−0.1109*	−0.0380***	−0.0395*	−0.0337**
	(0.0132)	(0.0196)	(0.0176)	(0.0405)	(0.0478)	(0.0585)	(0.0125)	(0.0204)	(0.0153)
Age: 25–29 years	−0.0669***	−0.0806***	−0.0529***	−0.1354***	−0.1183**	−0.1531***	−0.0624***	−0.0720***	−0.0446***
	(0.0145)	(0.0236)	(0.0167)	(0.0408)	(0.0496)	(0.0575)	(0.0147)	(0.0251)	(0.0136)
Age: 30–34 years	−0.0910***	−0.0793***	−0.1027***	−0.1971***	−0.1776***	−0.2136***	−0.0622***	−0.0364*	−0.0872***
	(0.0144)	(0.0216)	(0.0192)	(0.0419)	(0.0516)	(0.0580)	(0.0135)	(0.0206)	(0.0170)

(continued)

ANNEX TABLE 7.1.1. *(continued)*

Marginal Effects from Probit Regressions

Independent Variables	All Workers	Female Workers	Male Workers	Urban Workers	Urban Female Workers	Urban Male Workers	Rural Workers	Rural Female Workers	Rural Male Workers
Age: 35–39 years	−0.0909***	−0.0685***	−0.1145***	−0.2104***	−0.1688***	−0.2410***	−0.0511***	−0.0306	−0.0805***
	(0.0153)	(0.0218)	(0.0213)	(0.0428)	(0.0543)	(0.0583)	(0.0145)	(0.0198)	(0.0210)
Age: 40–44 years	−0.0801***	−0.0535***	−0.1081***	−0.1948***	−0.1544***	−0.2228***	−0.0401***	−0.0125	−0.0792***
	(0.0152)	(0.0193)	(0.0224)	(0.0441)	(0.0520)	(0.0615)	(0.0121)	(0.0146)	(0.0188)
Age: 45–49 years	−0.0931***	−0.0330*	−0.1576***	−0.2184***	−0.0834*	−0.3211***	−0.0473***	−0.0192	−0.0865***
	(0.0163)	(0.0194)	(0.0243)	(0.0449)	(0.0494)	(0.0602)	(0.0138)	(0.0183)	(0.0199)
Age: 50–54 years	−0.0739***	−0.0323*	−0.1167***	−0.1898***	−0.1065**	−0.2508***	−0.0322**	−0.0051	−0.0687***
	(0.0161)	(0.0190)	(0.0243)	(0.0460)	(0.0522)	(0.0635)	(0.0126)	(0.0139)	(0.0201)
Age: 55–59 years	−0.0821***	−0.0408*	−0.1209***	−0.2491***	−0.1451**	−0.3100***	−0.0080	0.0143	−0.0359**
	(0.0184)	(0.0224)	(0.0270)	(0.0502)	(0.0574)	(0.0676)	(0.0114)	(0.0120)	(0.0181)
Age: 60–64 years	−0.0433*	−0.0233	−0.0655**	−0.1286**	0.0008	−0.2244***	−0.0232	−0.0381	−0.0201
	(0.0260)	(0.0397)	(0.0274)	(0.0536)	(0.0596)	(0.0748)	(0.0268)	(0.0461)	(0.0213)
Pseudo R^2 of the probit model	0.2435	0.2209	0.2588	0.2212	0.2326	0.2159	0.1021	0.0919	0.1218
No. of observations	47,169	19,367	27,802	19,069	7,583	11,486	28,100	11,783	16,316

Source: Authors.

Note: Standard errors appear in parentheses. We included "no education," complete "primary education," complete "secondary education," and complete "tertiary education" in the regressions, omitting incomplete "primary education." The dependent variable was informal worker (binary variable).

***$p < 0.01$; **$p < 0.05$; *$p < 0.1$.

ANNEX TABLE 7.1.2.

Marginal Effects of Probit Regressions (Including *Z*-Tests and All Control Variables)

Independent Variables	All Workers	Female Workers	Male Workers	Urban Workers	Urban Female Workers	Urban Male Workers	Rural Workers	Rural Female Workers	Rural Male Workers
Female	0.0340***			0.0850***			0.0088*		
Standard error	(0.0050)			(0.0113)			(0.0049)		
z	6.76			7.51			1.82		
P > *z*	0.000			0.000			0.069		
No education	0.0336***	0.0197**	0.0376***	0.0634***	0.0269	0.0803***	0.0186***	0.0175*	0.0153**
Standard error	(0.0062)	(0.0090)	(0.0084)	(0.0135)	(0.0189)	(0.0187)	(0.0056)	(0.0095)	(0.0066)
z	5.42	2.19	4.50	4.70	1.42	4.30	3.32	1.85	2.31
P > *z*	0.000	0.028	0.000	0.000	0.155	0.000	0.001	0.065	0.021
Primary education	–0.1640***	–0.2010***	–0.1506***	–0.2547***	–0.3120***	–0.2248***	–0.0656***	–0.0461**	–0.0720***
Standard error	(0.0115)	(0.0216)	(0.0138)	(0.0177)	(0.0301)	(0.0221)	(0.0111)	(0.0191)	(0.0132)
z	–14.26	–9.31	–10.91	–14.41	–10.37	–10.18	–5.92	–2.41	–5.46
P > *z*	0.000	0.000	0.000	0.000	0.000	0.000	0.000	0.016	0.000
Secondary education	–0.5553***	–0.6098***	–0.5384***	–0.6044***	–0.6643***	–0.5707***	–0.4577***	–0.6073***	–0.4364***
Standard error	(0.0311)	(0.0582)	(0.0365)	(0.0267)	(0.0478)	(0.0314)	(0.0645)	(0.1530)	(0.0664)
z	–17.88	–10.48	–14.74	–22.64	–13.9	–18.15	–7.09	–3.97	–6.57
P > *z*	0.000	0.000	0.000	0.000	0.000	0.000	0.000	0.000	0.000
Tertiary education	–0.7285***	–0.6551***	–0.7625***	–0.6990***	–0.6939***	–0.6862***	–0.7793***		–0.7899***
Standard error	(0.0611)	(0.1610)	(0.0415)	(0.0367)	(0.1131)	(0.0220)	(0.1503)		(0.1504)
z	–11.92	–4.07	–18.37	–19.05	–6.13	–31.12	–5.18		–5.25
P > *z*	0.000	0.000	0.000	0.000	0.000	0.000	0.000		0.000
Head of household	–0.0249***	–0.0279**	–0.0063	–0.0530***	–0.0361	–0.0292	–0.0190**	–0.0239	–0.0031
Standard error	(0.0071)	(0.0131)	(0.0087)	(0.0155)	(0.0230)	(0.0210)	(0.0074)	(0.0177)	(0.0071)
z	–3.54	–2.13	–0.72	–3.42	–1.57	–1.39	–2.56	–1.35	–0.44
P > *z*	0.000	0.033	0.472	0.001	0.117	0.165	0.010	0.176	0.660
Married	–0.0213***	0.0071	–0.0392***	–0.0477***	0.0173	–0.1016***	–0.0000	0.0079	–0.0013
Standard error	(0.0062)	(0.0082)	(0.0090)	(0.0134)	(0.0166)	(0.0212)	(0.0059)	(0.0088)	(0.0069)
z	–3.42	0.87	–4.34	–3.57	1.05	–4.8	–0.01	0.90	–0.2
P > *z*	0.001	0.383	0.000	0.000	0.295	0.000	0.994	0.370	0.845

(continued)

ANNEX TABLE 7.1.2. *(continued)*

Marginal Effects of Probit Regressions (Including *Z*-Tests and All Control Variables)

Independent Variables	All Workers	Female Workers	Male Workers	Urban Workers	Urban Female Workers	Urban Male Workers	Rural Workers	Rural Female Workers	Rural Male Workers
No. of children	–0.0020	0.0036	–0.0059**	–0.0007	0.0139**	–0.0084	–0.0033**	–0.0011	–0.0049***
Standard error	(0.0019)	(0.0027)	(0.0025)	(0.0047)	(0.0067)	(0.0064)	(0.0014)	(0.0022)	(0.0018)
z	–1.06	1.37	–2.32	–0.14	2.07	–1.31	–2.29	–0.52	–2.69
P > *z*	0.289	0.171	0.020	0.886	0.038	0.189	0.022	0.604	0.007
Income decile (1 to 10)	–0.0116***	–0.0060***	–0.0161***	–0.0254***	–0.0165***	–0.0310***	–0.0055***	–0.0020	–0.0081***
Standard error	(0.0011)	(0.0016)	(0.0014)	(0.0029)	(0.0039)	(0.0042)	(0.0009)	(0.0015)	(0.0010)
z	–10.74	–3.68	–11.55	–8.6	–4.21	–7.45	–6.45	–1.32	–8.47
P > *z*	0.000	0.000	0.000	0.000	0.000	0.000	0.000	0.186	0.000
Urban	–0.0735***	–0.0560***	–0.0836***						
Standard error	(0.0052)	(0.0076)	(0.0070)						
z	–14.25	–7.33	–11.96						
P > *z*	0.000	0.000	0.000						
Age: 15–19 years	–0.0054	–0.0090	–0.0002	–0.0272	–0.0258	–0.0367	–0.0123	–0.0167	–0.0065
Standard error	(0.0116)	(0.0171)	(0.0147)	(0.0403)	(0.0465)	(0.0593)	(0.0088)	(0.0159)	(0.0096)
z	–0.47	–0.52	–0.02	–0.68	–0.55	–0.62	–1.39	–1.05	–0.68
P > *z*	0.637	0.600	0.988	0.499	0.580	0.536	0.165	0.293	0.495
Age: 20–24 years	–0.0353***	–0.0372*	–0.0338*	–0.0840**	–0.0614	–0.1109*	–0.0380***	–0.0395*	–0.0337**
Standard error	(0.0132)	(0.0196)	(0.0176)	(0.0405)	(0.0478)	(0.0585)	(0.0125)	(0.0204)	(0.0153)
z	–2.67	–1.89	–1.92	–2.07	–1.28	–1.89	–3.05	–1.93	–2.2
P > *z*	0.008	0.058	0.055	0.038	0.199	0.058	0.002	0.053	0.028
Age: 25–29 years	–0.0669***	–0.0806***	–0.0529***	–0.1354***	–0.1183**	–0.1531***	–0.0624***	–0.0720***	–0.0446***
Standard error	(0.0145)	(0.0236)	(0.0167)	(0.0408)	(0.0496)	(0.0575)	(0.0147)	(0.0251)	(0.0136)
z	–4.61	–3.42	–3.16	–3.32	–2.38	–2.66	–4.24	–2.86	–3.29
P > *z*	0.000	0.001	0.002	0.001	0.017	0.008	0.000	0.004	0.001
Age: 30–34 years	–0.0910***	–0.0793***	–0.1027***	–0.1971***	–0.1776***	–0.2136***	–0.0622***	–0.0364*	–0.0872***
Standard error	(0.0144)	(0.0216)	(0.0192)	(0.0419)	(0.0516)	(0.0580)	(0.0135)	(0.0206)	(0.0170)
z	–6.3	–3.67	–5.34	–4.71	–3.44	–3.69	–4.6	–1.77	–5.11
P > *z*	0.000	0.000	0.000	0.000	0.001	0.000	0.000	0.077	0.000

(continued)

ANNEX TABLE 7.1.2. ***(continued)***

Marginal Effects of Probit Regressions (Including Z-Tests and All Control Variables)

Independent Variables	All Workers	Female Workers	Male Workers	Urban Workers	Urban Female Workers	Urban Male Workers	Rural Workers	Rural Female Workers	Rural Male Workers
Age: 35–39 years	−0.0909***	−0.0685***	−0.1145***	−0.2104***	−0.1688***	−0.2410***	−0.0511***	−0.0306	−0.0805***
Standard error	(0.0153)	(0.0218)	(0.0213)	(0.0428)	(0.0543)	(0.0583)	(0.0145)	(0.0198)	(0.0210)
z	−5.92	−3.14	−5.38	−4.92	−3.11	−4.14	−3.53	−1.55	−3.84
P > z	0.000	0.002	0.000	0.000	0.002	0.000	0.000	0.121	0.000
Age: 40–44 years	−0.0801***	−0.0535***	−0.1081***	−0.1948***	−0.1544***	−0.2228***	−0.0401***	−0.0125	−0.0792***
Standard error	(0.0152)	(0.0193)	(0.0224)	(0.0441)	(0.0520)	(0.0615)	(0.0121)	(0.0146)	(0.0188)
z	−5.29	−2.77	−4.83	−4.42	−2.97	−3.62	−3.32	−0.85	−4.21
P > z	0.000	0.006	0.000	0.000	0.003	0.000	0.001	0.394	0.000
Age: 45–49 years	−0.0931***	−0.0330*	−0.1576***	−0.2184***	−0.0834*	−0.3211***	−0.0473***	−0.0192	−0.0865***
Standard error	(0.0163)	(0.0194)	(0.0243)	(0.0449)	(0.0494)	(0.0602)	(0.0138)	(0.0183)	(0.0199)
z	−5.72	−1.7	−6.48	−4.86	−1.69	−5.34	−3.42	−1.05	−4.35
P > z	0.000	0.089	0.000	0.000	0.091	0.000	0.001	0.296	0.000
Age: 50–54 years	−0.0739***	−0.0323*	−0.1167***	−0.1898***	−0.1065**	−0.2508***	−0.0322**	−0.0051	−0.0687***
Standard error	(0.0161)	(0.0190)	(0.0243)	(0.0460)	(0.0522)	(0.0635)	(0.0126)	(0.0139)	(0.0201)
z	−4.59	−1.7	−4.8	−4.13	−2.04	−3.95	−2.55	−0.37	−3.41
P > z	0.000	0.088	0.000	0.000	0.041	0.000	0.011	0.713	0.001
Age: 55–59 years	−0.0821***	−0.0408*	−0.1209***	−0.2491***	−0.1451**	−0.3100***	−0.0080	0.0143	−0.0359**
Standard error	(0.0184)	(0.0224)	(0.0270)	(0.0502)	(0.0574)	(0.0676)	(0.0114)	(0.0120)	(0.0181)
z	−4.47	−1.82	−4.48	−4.96	−2.53	−4.59	−0.7	1.19	−1.99
P > z	0.000	0.068	0.000	0.000	0.011	0.000	0.486	0.233	0.047
Age: 60–64 years	−0.0433*	−0.0233	−0.0655**	−0.1286**	0.0008	−0.2244***	−0.0232	−0.0381	−0.0201
Standard error	(0.0260)	(0.0397)	(0.0274)	(0.0536)	(0.0596)	(0.0748)	(0.0268)	(0.0461)	(0.0213)
z	−1.67	−0.59	−2.39	−2.4	0.01	−3	−0.87	−0.83	−0.94
P > z	0.095	0.557	0.017	0.016	0.990	0.003	0.386	0.409	0.346
Dakar	−0.0344***	−0.0194*	−0.0407***	−0.0378***	−0.0022	−0.0568***	−0.1024***	−0.1284***	−0.0903***
Standard error	(0.0078)	(0.0110)	(0.0105)	(0.0132)	(0.0186)	(0.0177)	(0.0179)	(0.0320)	(0.0218)
z	−4.39	−1.77	−3.86	−2.88	−0.12	−3.2	−5.73	−4.01	−4.15
P > z	0.000	0.077	0.000	0.004	0.904	0.001	0.000	0.000	0.000

(continued)

ANNEX TABLE 7.1.2. ***(continued)***

Marginal Effects of Probit Regressions (Including *Z*-Tests and All Control Variables)

Independent Variables	All Workers	Female Workers	Male Workers	Urban Workers	Urban Female Workers	Urban Male Workers	Rural Workers	Rural Female Workers	Rural Male Workers
Diourbel	−0.0476***	−0.0747***	−0.0066	−0.0986***	−0.0894***	−0.0984***	−0.0243**	−0.0477**	0.0029
Standard error	(0.0173)	(0.0252)	(0.0187)	(0.0188)	(0.0269)	(0.0253)	(0.0119)	(0.0187)	(0.0124)
z	−2.75	−2.97	−0.36	−5.24	−3.33	−3.89	−2.04	−2.55	0.23
P > *z*	0.006	0.003	0.722	0.000	0.001	0.000	0.041	0.011	0.815
Kaffrine	−0.2032***	−0.1858***	−0.2086***				−0.1481***	−0.1413***	−0.1506***
Standard error	(0.0138)	(0.0202)	(0.0186)				(0.0109)	(0.0165)	(0.0146)
z	−14.72	−9.18	−11.23				−13.62	−8.59	−10.33
P > *z*	0.000	0.000	0.000				0.000	0.000	0.000
Kaolack	−0.0333***	−0.0227	−0.0403***				−0.0329***	−0.0267**	−0.0369***
Standard error	(0.0105)	(0.0150)	(0.0146)				(0.0087)	(0.0134)	(0.0114)
z	−3.16	−1.51	−2.76				−3.78	−1.99	−3.24
P > *z*	0.002	0.130	0.006				0.000	0.046	0.001
Kedougou	−0.0160*	−0.0041	−0.0256**	−0.1490***	−0.1062***	−0.1764***			
Standard error	(0.0094)	(0.0135)	(0.0129)	(0.0253)	(0.0404)	(0.0314)			
z	−1.71	−0.3	−1.99	−5.88	−2.63	−5.61			
P > *z*	0.087	0.761	0.047	0.000	0.009	0.000			
Louga	−0.0358***	−0.0708***	−0.0154	−0.2204***	−0.2991***	−0.1507***			
Standard error	(0.0088)	(0.0146)	(0.0115)	(0.0205)	(0.0332)	(0.0254)			
z	−4.06	−4.85	−1.34	−10.74	−9.01	−5.94			
P > *z*	0.000	0.000	0.180	0.000	0.000	0.000			
Saint Louis	−0.0409***	−0.0541***	−0.0344***	−0.0888***	−0.0818***	−0.0928***	−0.0134*	−0.0316**	−0.0050
Standard error	(0.0086)	(0.0150)	(0.0107)	(0.0176)	(0.0271)	(0.0226)	(0.0075)	(0.0155)	(0.0083)
z	−4.76	−3.6	−3.2	−5.05	−3.02	−4.11	−1.79	−2.04	−0.6
P > *z*	0.000	0.000	0.001	0.000	0.003	0.000	0.073	0.042	0.550
Sedhiou	0.0414***	0.0371**	0.0419***				0.0225***	0.0238***	0.0210***
Standard error	(0.0109)	(0.0162)	(0.0145)				(0.0058)	(0.0089)	(0.0074)
z	3.81	2.30	2.89				3.85	2.68	2.83
P > *z*	0.000	0.022	0.004				0.000	0.007	0.005

(continued)

ANNEX TABLE 7.1.2. ***(continued)***

Marginal Effects of Probit Regressions (Including *Z*-Tests and All Control Variables)

Independent Variables	All Workers	Female Workers	Male Workers	Urban Workers	Urban Female Workers	Urban Male Workers	Rural Workers	Rural Female Workers	Rural Male Workers
Thies	−0.0446***	−0.0353***	−0.0519***	−0.0669***	−0.0365*	−0.0863***	−0.0299***	−0.0306***	−0.0315***
Standard error	(0.0082)	(0.0114)	(0.0114)	(0.0165)	(0.0214)	(0.0229)	(0.0074)	(0.0117)	(0.0096)
z	−5.46	−3.09	−4.55	−4.07	−1.7	−3.76	−4.05	−2.62	−3.28
$P > z$	0.000	0.002	0.000	0.000	0.088	0.000	0.000	0.009	0.001
Pseudo R^2 of the probit model	0.2435	0.2209	0.2588	0.2212	0.2326	0.2159	0.1021	0.0919	0.1218
No. of observations	47,169	19,367	27,802	19,069	7,583	11,486	28,100	11,783	16,316

Source: Authors.

Note: Standard errors appear in parentheses. We included "no education," complete "primary education," complete "secondary education," and complete "tertiary education" in the regressions, omitting incomplete "primary education." The dependent variable was informal worker (binary variable).

$^{***}p < 0.01$; $^{**}p < 0.05$; $^{*}p < 0.1$.

REFERENCES

Bear, J. B., and P. Glick. "Breadwinner Bonus and Caregiver Penalty in Workplace Rewards for Men and Women." *Social Psychological and Personality Science* 8 (7): 780–88.

Bloom, D. E., D. Canning, G. Frink, and J. E. Finlay. 2009. "Female Labor Force Participation, and the Demographic Dividend." *Journal of Economic Growth* 14 (2): 79–101.

Correll, S. J., S. Benard, and I. Paik. 2007. "Getting a Job: Is There a Motherhood Penalty?" *American Journal of Sociology* 112 (5): 1297–38.

Fabrizio, S., A. Fruttero, D. Gurara, L. Kolovich, V. Malta, M. M. Tavares, and N. Tchelishvili. 2020. "Women in the Labor Force: The Role of Fiscal Policies." IMF Staff Discussion Note 20/03, International Monetary Fund, Washington, DC.

Herrendorf, B., R. Rogerson, and Á. Valentinyi. 2014. "Growth and Structural Transformation." In *Handbook of Economic Growth*, volume 2, edited by P. Aghion and S. N. Durlauf. Amsterdam: Elsevier.

Herrera, C., and D. E. Sahn. 2015. "The Impact of Early Childbearing on Schooling and Cognitive Skills among Young Women in Madagascar." Food and Nutrition Policy Program Working Paper 247, Cornell University, Ithaca, NY.

Herrera, C., D. Sahn, and K. Villa. 2016. "Early Fertility and Labor Market Segmentation: Evidence from Madagascar." Paper presented at the Annual Meeting of the Agricultural and Applied Economics Association, Boston, MA, July 31–August 2.

International Labour Organization (ILO). 2018. *Women and Men in the Informal Economy: A Statistical Picture*, 3rd edition. Geneva: International Labour Organization.

International Monetary Fund (IMF). 2015. "Chile: Staff Report for the 2015 Article IV Consultation." International Monetary Fund, Washington, DC.

International Monetary Fund (IMF). 2016a. "Guatemala: Staff Report for the 2016 Article IV Consultation." International Monetary Fund, Washington, DC.

International Monetary Fund (IMF). 2016b. "Nigeria: Staff Report for the 2016 Article IV Consultation." International Monetary Fund, Washington, DC.

International Monetary Fund (IMF). 2016c. "Pakistan: Staff Report for the 2015 Article IV Consultation." International Monetary Fund, Washington, DC.

International Monetary Fund (IMF). 2017a. *Austria: 2016 Article IV Consultation*. IMF Country Report 17/26, International Monetary Fund, Washington, DC.

International Monetary Fund (IMF). 2017b. "India: Staff Report for the 2017 Article IV Consultation." International Monetary Fund, Washington, DC.

International Monetary Fund (IMF). 2017c. "Jordan: Staff Report for the 2017 Article IV Consultation." International Monetary Fund, Washington, DC.

International Monetary Fund (IMF). 2017d. "Morocco: Staff Report for the 2017 Article IV Consultation." International Monetary Fund, Washington, DC.

International Monetary Fund (IMF). 2017e. *Regional Economic Outlook: Sub-Saharan Africa—Restarting the Growth Engine.* Washington, DC, May.

International Monetary Fund (IMF). 2018a. *Arab Republic of Egypt: Selected Issues*. IMF Country Report 18/15, International Monetary Fund, Washington, DC.

International Monetary Fund (IMF). 2018b. *Nigeria: Selected Issues*. IMF Country Report 18/64, International Monetary Fund, Washington, DC.

International Monetary Fund (IMF). 2018c. *Senegal: Selected Issues*. IMF Country Report 19/28, International Monetary Fund, Washington, DC.

International Monetary Fund (IMF). 2019. *Former Yugoslav Republic of Macedonia: 2018 Article IV Consultation*. IMF Country Report 19/32, International Monetary Fund, Washington, DC.

Kolovich, L. 2018. *Fiscal Policies and Gender Equality*, edited by L. Kolovich. Washington, DC: International Monetary Fund.

Malta, V., L. Kolovich, A. Martinez, and M. Mendes Tavares. 2019. "Informality and Gender Gaps Going Hand in Hand." IMF Working Paper 19/112, International Monetary Fund, Washington, DC.

Patrinos, H. 2008. "Returns to Education: The Gender Perspective." In *Girls' Education in the 21st Century: Gender Equality, Empowerment, and Economic Growth*, edited by M. Tembon and L. Fort. Washington, DC: World Bank.

Psacharopoulos, G., and H. A. Patrinos. 2004. "Returns to Investment in Education: A Further Update." *Education Economics* 12 (2): 111–34.

UN Women. 2016. "Leave No One Behind: A Call to Action for Gender Equality and Women's Economic Empowerment." Report of the UN Secretary-General, United Nations, New York.

United Nations Children's Fund (UNICEF). 2016. "Girls Spend 160 Million More Hours than Boys Doing Household Chores Everyday." Press release, October 7. https://www.unicef.org/press-releases/girls-spend-160-million-more-hours-boys-doing-household-chores-everyday.

Wodon, Q., and C. M. Blackden. 2006. "Gender, Time Use, and Poverty in Sub-Saharan Africa." Working Paper 73, World Bank, Washington, DC.

World Bank. 2012. *World Development Report 2012: Gender Equality and Development.* Washington, DC: World Bank.

World Bank. 2018. *Women, Business and the Law 2018*. Washington, DC: World Bank.

CHAPTER 8

How Institutions Shape the Informal Economy

Hilary Devine

INTRODUCTION

A large body of literature has investigated interrelations between the informal sector and institutions. Yet no consensus has emerged on the exact determinants of or transmission channels through which this association arises. Ongoing work has investigated why the informal economy is large and persistent in many developing countries and what the barriers to formalization are (Loayza and Meza-Cuadra 2018; Afonso, Neves, and Pinto 2020).

One strand of this literature analyzes how the size of the informal economy relates to institutional settings, including taxation, regulatory burdens, corruption, law and order, and governance, as well as how informality reflects and responds to the business cycle—an important aspect in designing policy responses to the current coronavirus disease 2019 (COVID-19) crisis.

A second strand of the literature explores the relationship between informality and institutions in the context of democratic or political environment (Aruoba 2010; Elgin 2010; Teobaldelli and Schneider 2013; Elbahnasawy, Ellis, and Adom 2016). Better institutions and government policies are clearly linked to higher tax revenues and lower informality, with some recent studies finding a negative relationship between measures of institutional quality and the size of the informal economy (Torgler and Schneider 2009; Aruoba 2010; Elgin 2010).Yet limited research shows the direction of causality (Elgin 2010; Mazhar 2015; Elbahnasawy, Ellis, and Adom 2016; Elgin, Elveren, and Bourgeois 2020).

Institutional settings are influenced by the political environment and can foster polices that lead to the development of, or a reduction in, the informal economy. For example, countries with low political turnover have been found to have, on average, a higher tax burden as well as a smaller informal economy (Elgin 2010). This implies that changes in political environment and political stability, even toward more democratic regimes, could be associated with an increase in the size of the informal economy, if the reforms create greater political instability (Elbahnasawy, Ellis, and Adom 2016).

This chapter draws on this previous work to address the question, "Are institutional settings and changes in institutions significantly different in countries with decreasing or low informality, as compared with those with high or increasing informality?" Therefore, the chapter focuses on drawing a link between institutions and their effect on informal activity and identifying the direction of causality using political cycles to control for changes in institutional settings. We explore the literature to analyze how changes in institutional settings lead to changes in the size of the informal sector.

To model our hypothesis and account for endogeneity between institutional variables and the informal economy, we use a dynamic panel data set and several methods to determine the direction of causality between measures of institutional settings as determinants of the size of the informal economy. Given the difficulty in finding credible instruments to account for the considerable endogeneity between the size of the informal economy and institutions, we use the generalized method of moments (GMM) estimator with lags based on the political cycles in the data to identify changes in variables. We undertake two robustness checks comparing alternative specifications to measure the effect of political changes and an alternative measure of the change in the informal economy. In addition, we also compare two methods for measuring the size of the informal economy to check the robustness of our results. We use both the multiple indicators, multiple causes (MIMIC) model developed by Medina and Schneider (2018) and the dynamic general equilibrium (DGE) model from Elgin and Oztunali (2012). We find that, even when political turnover is controlled for, institutional settings affect the size of the informal economy. Institutional indicators such as tax administration, business environment, corruption, and government accountability are significantly related to the size of the informal economy.

The remainder of this chapter is structured as follows. We present stylized facts, review existing work on informality and institutions, and briefly assess how the informal economy is measured. Next, we outline the method and the data used in our analysis, present and describe the results, and conclude with policy recommendations.

STYLIZED FACTS

We briefly present stylized facts on the size of the informal economy over time and how well it correlates to our institutional and political variables. The informal economy includes all economic activities hidden from official authorities for regulatory and institutional reasons and is defined as a percentage of official GDP. Informal economic activities are legal and productive activities that would be included in GDP if recorded (Medina and Schneider 2018). Two methods for measuring the informal economy are presented in Figure 8.1 showing the similarity of the two measures for emerging market and developing economies and for advanced economies (Box 8.1). The figure illustrates that although informality has been on a downward trend since the 1980s, it remains a significant share of the official GDP of emerging market and developing economies.

Figure 8.1. Size of the Informal Economy
(Percentage of official GDP)

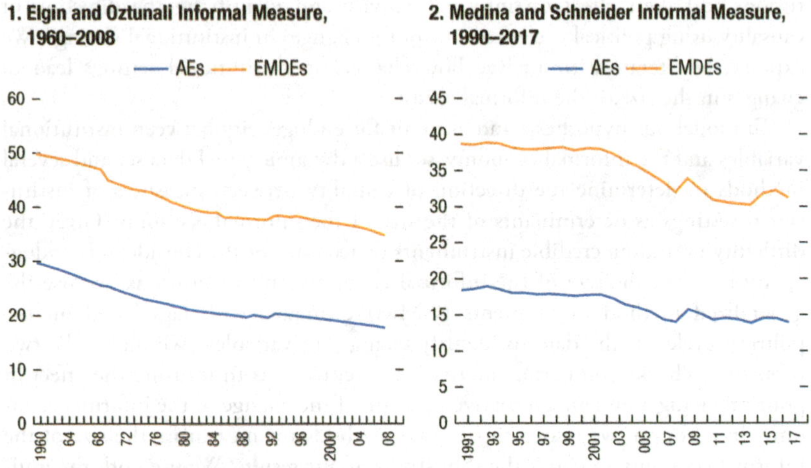

Sources: Elgin and Oztunali 2012; Medina and Schneider 2018; and author.
Note: AEs = advanced economies; EMDEs = emerging market and developing economies.

Box 8.1. Measuring Informality

By its nature, the informal economy is difficult to measure. Informality has been defined as activity that is legal but hidden from public authorities (Schneider, Buehn, and Montenegro 2010). Various methods are used to derive and measure the informal economy through both surveys and model-based estimates.

The informal economy is typically measured through household, labor force, and firm-based surveys. Surveys can be more robust than model-based estimates, because they do not rely on calibration and assumptions. However, they are infrequently conducted and have varied definitions and methods across countries, limiting their usefulness for cross-country panel analysis.

Model-based estimates use indirect measures that derive the size of the informal economy from various indicators as proxies. Proxies include the currency-demand approach (as in Ardizzi and others 2014); the electricity-demand approach (as in Schneider and Enste 2000); the multiple indicators, multiple causes model (Schneider, Buehn, and Montenegro 2010); and the dynamic general equilibrium model (as in Ihrig and Moe 2004; Elgin and Oztunali 2012; and Orsi, Raggi, and Turino 2014). These measures all have strengths and weaknesses.

Source: Author.

To facilitate our analysis, we compare emerging market and developing economies where informality is increasing and decreasing. We define decreasing informality as the informal economy falling as a percentage of official GDP for five consecutive years or longer, to enable us to compare institutional changes preceding or during these periods. From this, we identify a high-informality group whose informal economy has increased for five or more consecutive years between 1991 and 2017, 64 out of 126 countries. The second group is countries where informality has decreased or remained the same as a percentage of official GDP, 100 out of 164 countries. The decreasing group demonstrates a steady and ongoing reduction in the size of its informal economies, whereas the sustained size of the informal economy is steady or growing across all years in the increasing group (Figure 8.2). Both groups after 2005 show a decrease, which is much steeper for those with more informality to start with.

Selected indicators for emerging market and developing economies with increasing or decreasing informal sectors show better institutional settings are associated with decreasing informal sectors (Figure 8.2). Figure 8.2 shows the sample is split

Figure 8.2. Periods of Sustained Increasing or Decreasing Informality, 1990–2017

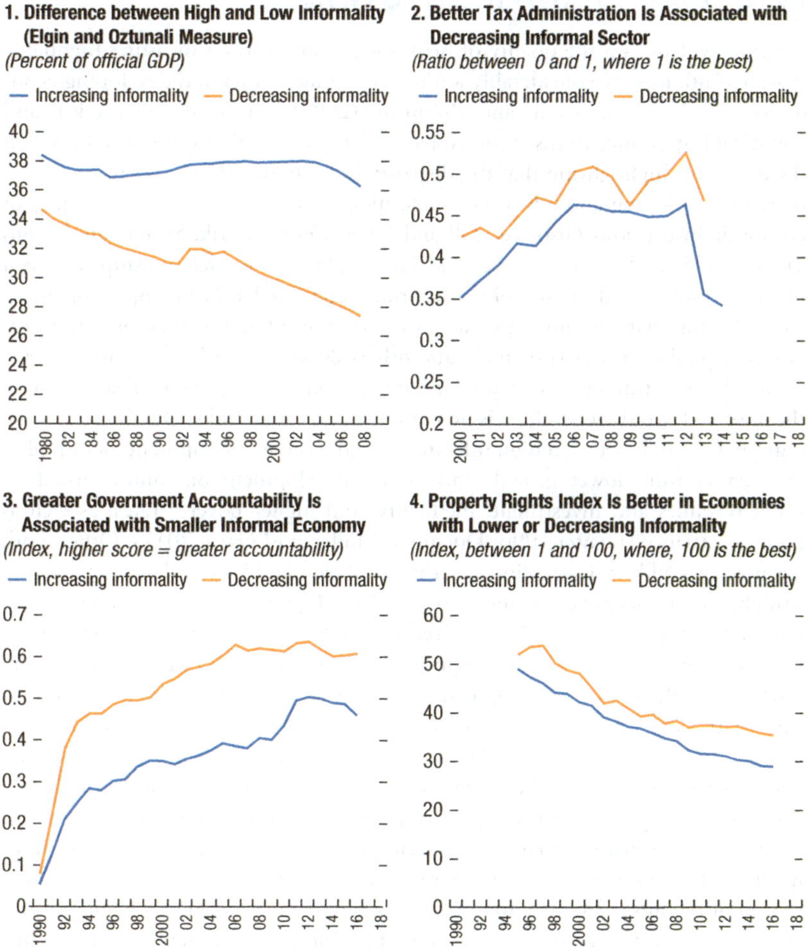

Source: Author.

between countries where informality is increasing or decreasing, comparing the correlation between governance indicators of these two groups. Better tax administration measured using C-efficiency value-added tax (VAT) is associated with smaller or decreasing informal sectors, indicating that less efficient or more onerous tax administration may drive entrepreneurs into informal activity. Government accountability also shows a marked difference between economies with increasing informality and those with an informal sector: as informality decreases, government accountability increases, indicating that more transparent government policy and actions may help shrink the informal economy. Property rights are associated with a similar pattern, although the difference is not as pronounced.

INFORMALITY AND INSTITUTIONS

Existing evidence on the quality of institutions using various measures highlights that institutions vary considerably among emerging market and developing economies. Acemoglu, Johnson, and Robinson (2005) outline the theoretical and empirical importance of institutions, particularly on the allocation of resources in the economy, highlighting that the disparity in economic development outcomes between developing and advanced economies is related to the varying quality of economic institutions (also see Hall and Jones 1999; Rodrik, Subramanian, and Trebbi 2004; Lederman, Loayza, and Soares 2005). This relationship has been further explored, and the size of the informal economy has been empirically related to institutional determinants such as taxation, burden of regulations, and provision of public services (Friedman and others 2000; Schneider and Enste 2000).

Yet the literature on informality and institutions remains inconclusive: despite the observed correlations, there is no consensus on causal links. One body of work examines the link between high informality and level of development, with higher informality from lower growth and poorer development outcomes caused by lower revenues and investment, inequality, and higher poverty rates, as well as poor governance (Loayza 1996; Docquier, Müller, and Naval 2017). Other work has investigated how institutional settings, policies, and lack of development lead to higher informality in emerging market and developing economies (Dabla-Norris, Gradstein, and Inchauste 2008; Dreher and Schneider 2010; Mazhar 2015; Loayza 2016). Although neither hypothesis is incorrect, Loayza and Meza-Cuadra (2018) note the level of development and poor productivity are not sufficient to explain the cross-country differences in the size of the informal economy we observe. Our chapter therefore focuses on this second argument, drawing a link between institutions and their effect on informal activity to seek a causal link, using political cycles to control for changes in institutional settings.

We focus on institutional settings that encompass policy decisions by governments and investigate how they might affect the degree and the level of formalization of the informal economy. We investigate three areas: (1) fiscal institutions and tax burden; (2) regulatory burden and business environment; and (3) political environment, including corruption.

Fiscal institutions and tax burden are key reasons many join the informal economy; that is, the heavy burden of tax and tax administration drives entrepreneurs involved in legitimate and legal activities into informal operations.

The business environment and regulatory burdens' effect on informality is similar to that of taxation, whereby the imposition of heavy-handed regulations and unnecessary transaction costs can drive businesses into informal activity. Regulatory burden also includes factors such as property rights and the ability to enforce contracts; the possibility of being unable to enforce contracts or ownership rights in an unbiased court system may also drive activity into the informal sector.

The third group of institutional indicators covers political and governance variables, including corruption, government accountability, and constraints on the executive.[1] These indicators capture the potential for political agents to misuse or misdirect resources toward low-productivity and low-growth activities, such as rent seeking. Political environment includes not only government resources but also political power: corruption at all levels of government can misuse and misdirect resources, creating a greater incentive for workers to join the informal economy.

Fiscal Institutions and Tax Burden

Strong fiscal institutions are an indicator of better fiscal and economic outcomes (Alesina and others 1999; Glaeser and others 2004; Dabla-Norris and others 2010). Better fiscal institutions are associated with effective collection of revenues, stronger management of public expenditures, and budget planning, which provide greater fiscal space and support macroeconomic sustainability and resilience (Deléchat and others 2015). Better-managed fiscal positions that allow for provision of public goods and support economic development, without heavy-handed taxation, have been found to be linked to a smaller informal economy (Loayza 1997; Loayza, Oviedo, and Servén 2006; Kuehn 2007).

Fiscal Management

Poor fiscal management is associated with negative economic consequences, including larger fiscal deficits and, over time, increased debt (Elgin and Uras 2013). It can also crowd out private sector investment, resulting in lower growth. However, developing strong fiscal institutions, including efficient tax systems and strong expenditure management, has been shown to be important in controlling the informal economy (Costa, Garcia-Cintado, and Usabiaga 2019). Institutional settings and the modalities of checks and balances on expenditures; taxation; and the distribution of expenditure toward development objectives, investment, or redistribution of wealth are core functions of government and often mishandled or abused (Cortellese 2015). Disclosure of public expenditure and public involvement

[1] Constraints on the executive is an index from the Polity IV Database and measures institutionalized constraints on the decision-making powers of the executive branch, presented as a scale of 1 (worst) to 7 (best).

in spending decisions can limit tax evasion, fostering improvements in compliance and governance, including accountability of officials (Perry and others 2007).

A large informal sector can complicate fiscal consolidation efforts. A recent study examining fiscal consolidation in Greece after the global financial crisis shows the informal sector can distort the effect of fiscal policy (Dellas and others 2019). The large informal sector in Greece limited the decrease in total output usually associated with large fiscal consolidation; however, this was at the expense of tax revenue collection needed for procyclical policies. The design of tax systems and of fiscal adjustment measures could also be related to the size of the informal sector. Our hypothesis is that countries with strong fiscal institutions should, on average, have smaller informal sectors. We include a measure of the budget balance, an index created by the International Country Risk Guide capturing the likelihood of large deficits or surplus. We expect a negative relationship between budget balance and the size of the informal economy.

Tax Burden

The tax burden is often cited as a strong deterrent against entry into the formal economy or as a reason to remain informal, as discussed in Chapter 9. Although the evidence is mixed on whether the tax burden drives firms out of the formal sector or it is the size of the informal sector that places a higher burden on those who pay, a negative correlation between tax rates and size of the informal economy has been found empirically (Kuehn 2007; Elgin 2010).

Tax administration is often a barrier to informal businesses becoming part of the formal economy. As a result, nonpayment of taxes by large sections of the economy also means that emerging market and developing economies often cannot raise necessary revenues. C-efficiency, a measure of tax collection, is the ratio of actual revenue collection to potential revenue, indicating collection and administrative efficiency (Ueda 2017). Increases in revenue collection in emerging market and developing economies have been driven by increases in C-efficiency rather than increases in tax rates (Keen 2013). Therefore, we expect a higher C-efficiency VAT ratio to be associated with a smaller informal economy. Because VAT is the main source of tax revenues for many emerging market and developing economies (Coady 2018), we include measures of tax administration (C-efficiency VAT) as well as measures of the tax burden (tax revenues as percentage of GDP) to capture this relationship, anticipating a negative relationship with the size of the informal economy.

Regulatory Burden and Business Environment

Informality is more common where the regulatory or administrative burden is larger; informal activity is undertaken to avoid potentially heavy compliance costs. The regulatory burden covers both compliance (including labor, safety laws, and product standards) and bureaucratic rules and procedures that are costly in time or money and can lead to evasion in the informal sector (De Soto 1989; Loayza 1996; Krakowski 2005).

Regulatory Burden

Regulatory burden also covers the effectiveness of governments for which compliance and enforcement of regulations are required. Johnson, Kaufmann, and Zoido-Lobaton (1998) demonstrate that the effectiveness of government and administration of regulations are key determinants of the size of the informal sector. Johnson, Kaufmann, and Zoido-Lobaton (1998) highlight that fewer regulations and a more business-friendly environment are correlated with a smaller informal sector; however, how regulations are administered appears to be as important as the regulations themselves. We include a measure from the World Bank Worldwide Governance Indicators (Kaufmann, Kraay, and Mastruzzi 2010) that captures as an index the quality of regulation across counties, expecting a negative relationship with the size of the informal sector.

Business Environment

Distinct from regulatory burden, the rules that govern the business environment are often more tacit, relying on networks and relationships in addition to formal rules and regulations (Klovienė 2012). Goel and Nelson (2016) note that incentives to remaining in informal sectors (that is, not formalizing) are different from those to joining the informal sector (that is, newly entering). The study finds robust determinants of the informal sector size, including business startup costs, property registration costs, and complexity of bureaucracy. In addition to indicators that measure formal regulation and quality, we also include several indicators, including property rights, private credit, and contract viability, to capture this negative relationship with the size of the informal economy.

Political Environment

Two key strands of the existing literature, salient to our definition of institutional settings, relate to changes in the political environment and governance and corruption. Consensus on their association with informality and the direction of causality is still limited.

Changes in Political Regime

Our key contribution is to evaluate institutional settings and their interactions with political economy and the informal sector. Policy changes resulting from the political process determine institutional settings and thereby affect economic actors' decisions to participate in the formal or informal sector. "Institutions" can be long-term rules underpinning political and economic activity, but they are not immune to changes resulting from the political cycle—particularly fiscal rules, which can adapt with political direction and budget cycles.

Institutional change is not well explored in relation to the informal economy. Elgin (2015) constructs a theoretical model whereby two political parties can alternate in office and are only able to set economic polices while in office. In Elgin's model, if the incumbent remains in power and is able to increase taxes to invest in public goods, the formal sector benefits most from public investment. A corollary is that the smaller the informal sector, the greater the political stability.

Elgin (2010) further explores the relation between political turnover and informality: once the political cycle is controlled for, the empirical relation between the tax burden and the informal economy disappears. Therefore, we include political turnover in our model, incorporating a lag in our panel data set to capture average political cycles in emerging market and developing economies. This control allows us to estimate the relation between the informal economy and institutional quality separately from the political cycle.

Governance and Corruption

Governance and corruption have been empirically shown to be significantly associated with the size of the informal economy (Sarte 2000; Choi and Thum 2005; Dreher and Schneider 2010). Corruption can be either complement or substitute to informal sector participation, depending on whether corruption is interpreted as a tax on operations to avoid formal economy taxes and other obligations (complements) or whether firms and individuals join the informal sector to avoid corruption and the cost of bribery (substitutes).

Corruption is broadly defined but varies considerably across countries in how it manifests and who it benefits. Bribes and payments to bureaucrats affect informal sector participants differently than high-level corruption by the executive (Ang 2020). Bribes and payments made to bureaucrats influence informality directly and may deter entry into the formal market to avoid these costly interactions. Corruption by the executive and high-level officials resulting in theft or misallocation of resources may not affect informal sector participants directly but may deter them from paying taxes, and the resulting lack of public services and infrastructure may reduce the incentive to participate in the formal sector. To capture this difference, we use several measures in our analysis to explore whether changes in corruption and governance lead to changes in the informal sector's size. We include measures of bureaucratic quality, corruption, and government accountability, as well as constraint on the executive, to test this relationship with the size of the informal economy.

MEASURES OF INFORMALITY

For robustness, we use the two most widely used measures of informality—MIMIC and DGE models—for comparison in our analysis.

Multiple Indicators, Multiple Causes Model

MIMIC is a structural equation model applied to indirectly measure the size of the informal economy through seven causes and three indicators: fiscal freedom, rule of law, unemployment, trade openness, currency (M0/M1), labor force participation, and size of economy from night lights satellite data.[2] The informal sector is difficult to measure. This form of estimation is therefore attractive, considering that it uses multiple indicators to capture informal activity. Although earlier

[2] By estimating light density from satellite data, night lights provide an alternative estimate of economic activity to official GDP, which may only estimate, at best, part of the informal economy.

versions of MIMIC have been criticized for using GDP growth or GDP per capita growth in estimates, later iterations have overcome this objection by using the independently observed night lights metric as an alternative activity measure (Medina and Schneider 2018). Night lights are a widely used and cited proxy for economic activity, given their country coverage and long time period. However, the indicator has some limitations, including its need for independent survey-based estimates to calibrate model outputs and its sensitivity to model specifications.

Dynamic General Equilibrium Model

DGE models are an increasingly common method to estimate the size of the informal economy (Ihrig and Moe 2004; Aruoba 2010; Elgin and Oztunali 2012). Such models are constructed based on households' choice to allocate their labor between formal and informal employment, considering the capital households own and the technology of the formal and informal sectors. The model's time variation is partly determined by comparing the output of the informal to the official formal sector. This model provides a long time series for 1950 through 2016 and large country coverage for panel models. As with MIMIC and other model-based approaches, the DGE relies on assumptions and requires independent observations (usually from surveys) to calibrate.

Figure 8.3 shows measures of the informal sector on a country and year basis and highlights the strong correlation between both measures with limited outliers. As shown in Figures 8.1 and 8.3, there is a strong correlation between the Elgin and Oztunali (2012) and the Medina and Schneider (2018) measures. We use both of these measures, which are available for long time periods, to explore the relationship between the size of the informal economy and institutional settings.

Figure 8.3. Measures of Informal Economy, Medina and Schneider and Elgin and Oztunali, 1990–2017

(Percent of official GDP)

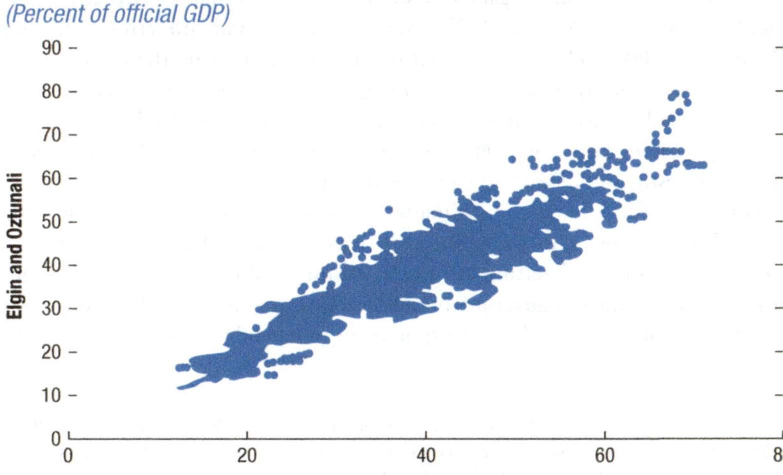

Sources: Elgin and Oztunali 2012; Medina and Schneider 2018; and author.

MODEL AND DATA

Inherent endogeneity exists between institutions and informality, and finding a suitable and credible instrument is difficult.[3] We adopt a dynamic system GMM model (Arellano and Bond 1991; Arellano and Bover 1995; Blundell and Bond 1998) that uses lagged variables to account for changes in institutional quality and the size of the informal economy.

We compare two measures of informality, as outlined in Annex Tables 8.3.1 and 8.3.2. This comparison has the advantage of using both independent measures from Elgin and Oztunali (2012) and Medina and Schneider (2018), which have different theoretical underpinnings, therefore helping us reduce endogeneity. Data on institutional settings are collected from a wide variety of sources, with variables, definitions, and sources included in Annex Tables 8.1.1 and 8.1.2.

Model

The link between institutional settings and the informal economy has been established by many (Schhneider and Enste 2000; Oviedo, Thomas, and Karakurum-Özdemir 2009; Loayza 2016). However, the challenge is to disentangle the direction of causality between institutions and informality. The model to present our estimation is outlined as follows:

$$Informal_{it} = f(Informal_{it-x}, institutional\,quality_{it}, control\,variables, \mu_{it}) \qquad (1)$$

The dependent variables are the extent of the informal economy in country *i* (measured as the share of the informal economy in country *i*'s official GDP); we include institutional quality variables in country *i* and vectors of control variables that affect the informal economy and institutions, and μ_i represents the error term.

Our hypothesis is that strengthening institutions and improving institutional quality, controlling for the political cycle, reduces the size of the informal economy as firms formalize and engage in more productive formal activity. Our calculations use system GMM with Windmeijer robust standard error correction (Windmeijer 2005). The use of lagged instruments to capture the persistence of the informal economy addresses the endogeneity problem and modeling issues, including unobserved country effects that may create omitted variable bias (Roodman 2009). Equation (1) is estimated both in levels and in first differences for efficient estimates of the model without endogeneity.

As in Elgin (2010) and in Elbahnaswy, Ellis, and Adom (2016), we also consider political turnover, or the political cycle. In the model we assume that any changes in institutional setting are made within or alongside political election cycles, that is, changes in governments and leadership or an incumbent advancing a political agenda. Rather than incorporate an independent variable, we use this

[3] Typically used instruments are latitude (Friedman and others 2000; Dreher and Schneider 2010), a variable for presidential versus parliamentary regimes (Lederman, Loayza, and Soares 2005; Elgin 2010), and legal system (LaPorta and others 1999; Elgin 2010).

premise to integrate the political cycle into our panel, lagging our institutional quality variables by the average length of election cycles in emerging market and developing economies (four years). This controls for political instability and its effect on institutional settings.

Data

In the regressions, we include several control variables, including GDP per capita, inflation, trade restrictions, and measure of human capital. GDP per capita is correlated with economic development, and we expect a negative relationship with informality. Although there is correlation between less-developed economies and larger informal sectors, Loayza and Meza-Cuadra (2018) notes there is not always a one-to-one relationship. Some countries have higher or lower informality than predicted by their development, indicating other determinants of informality.

Trade restrictions are also controlled for, because they indicate a shift toward domestic activity and larger informal sectors as domestic demand increases. Trade restrictions also limit international competition, meaning there is a lower opportunity cost to being informal (Elbahnasawy, Ellis, and Adom 2016). We use an index of trade restrictions that includes tariff and nontariff barriers, trade taxes, and numbers of trade agreements, in which the highest index value denotes the least amount of restrictions, so that we expect a negative relationship with informality.

As a control we include inflation, which is positively correlated with informal economy and an important factor in the interaction between informality and institutions (Aruoba 2010). Koreshkova (2006) and Aruoba (2010) observe quantitatively and theoretically the relationship between tax evasion and inflation, whereby low inflation, increased tax base, and lower informality are observed. Inflation is also a proxy for the quality of macroeconomic management and macroeconomic stability.

Human capital is a measure from Penn World Tables[4] that combines a measure of average years of schooling with an assumed rate of return to education. A higher share of lower-skilled workers in a country is associated with a larger informal economy (Docquier, Müller, and Naval 2017; Elgin and others 2019). As LaPorta and Shleifer (2008) note, although informality provides employment and wages, the informal sector is associated with fewer worker skills and low productivity compared with the formal sector. We therefore expect a negative relationship with higher informality.

RESULTS

Table 8.1 presents the results of the system GMM estimations for our institutional quality measures. The main results for measures of fiscal and tax burden

[4] Version 9.1 of Penn World Tables is used here.

TABLE 8.1.

System GMM Estimations, Medina and Schneider Informality, 1990–2017

	1	2	3	4	5	6	7	8	9	10	11	12	13
L. Medina informal	0.807***	0.722***	0.794***	0.805***	0.766***	0.775***	0.781***	0.807***	0.817***	0.814***	0.782***	0.808***	0.809***
	(0.012)	(0.027)	(0.015)	(0.014)	(0.014)	(0.016)	(0.017)	(0.012)	(0.014)	(0.014)	(0.017)	(0.012)	(0.013)
Real GDP per capita	−0.030***	−0.118**	−0.026***	−0.037***	−0.039***	−0.056***	−0.049***	−0.030***	−0.030***	−0.028***	−0.046***	0.031***	−0.034***
	(0.009)	(0.049)	(0.009)	(0.009)	(0.009)	(0.012)	(0.013)	(0.009)	(0.009)	(0.009)	(0.013)	(0.009)	(0.009)
Trade restrictions	−0.016***	−0.004	−0.014**	−0.009*	0.002	−0.016**	−0.009	−0.017***	−0.012**	−0.011**	−0.009	−0.014***	−0.013**
	(0.005)	(0.015)	(0.006)	(0.005)	(0.005)	(0.007)	(0.008)	(0.005)	(0.006)	(0.005)	(0.008)	(0.005)	(0.005)
Inflation	0.108***	0.071	0.089**	0.074*	0.071*	0.122***	0.077	0.110***	0.110***	0.106***	0.088*	0.112***	0.103***
	(0.034)	(0.089)	(0.040)	(0.039)	(0.038)	(0.045)	(0.053)	(0.034)	(0.039)	(0.039)	(0.053)	(0.034)	(0.035)
Human capital	−2.530***	−1.826*	−2.213***	−2.349***	−1.396***	−2.696***	−2.527***	−2.556***	−2.410***	−2.225***	−2.363***	−2.466***	−2.714***
	(0.302)	(1.042)	(0.394)	(0.354)	(0.362)	(0.478)	(0.559)	(0.305)	(0.358)	(0.361)	(0.559)	(0.313)	(0.319)
Fiscal and Tax Burden													
C-efficiency VAT		−1.527*											
		(0.807)											
Tax revenues			−0.022										
			(0.014)										
Risk budget balance				−0.134***									
				(0.025)									
Business and Regulatory Environment													
Contract viability					−0.373***								
					−0.038								
Property rights						−0.019***							
						(0.005)							
Regulatory quality							−0.170						
							(0.217)						
Private credit								−0.002					
								(0.003)					
Political and Legal Environment													
ICRG bureaucracy									0.004				
									(0.071)				
Corruption										−0.156***			
										(0.050)			
Rule of law											−0.199		
											(0.242)		
Government integrity													
Government accountability												−0.218**	
												−0.094	
Executive constraint													−0.023
													(0.031)
Constant	4.311***	3.125	2.564***	4.134***	3.579**	1.537	3.882***	4.367***	3.715***	3.592***	3.607**	4.251***	4.054***
	(1.565)	(2.019)	(0.978)	(1.478)	(1.802)	(2.088)	(1.307)	(1.545)	(1.298)	(1.174)	(1.452)	(1.604)	(1.083)
No. of observations	2,501	722	1,883	1,961	1,961	1,760	1,493	2,501	1,961	1,961	1,493	2,397	2,293
No. of countries	100	61	95	84	84	98	100	100	84	84	100	96	95
Year dummies	Yes	Yes	Yes	Yes	Yes	Yes	Yes	Yes	Yes	Yes	Yes	Yes	Yes
No. of instruments	36	32	44	42	42	37	33	44	42	42	33	44	44
AR(2) *p* values	0.0	0.0	0.0	0.0	0.0	0.0	0.0	0.0	0.0	0.0	0.0	0.0	0.0
AR(1) *p* values	0.874	0.138	0.111	0.558	0.659	0.262	0.282	0.827	0.768	0.774	0.353	0.971	0.914

Source: Author.

Note: Standard errors appear in parentheses. GMM = generalized method of moments; ICRG = International Country Risk Guide; VAT = value-added tax. *$p < 0.10$, **$p < 0.05$, ***$p < 0.01$.

(columns 2 through 4) show that C-efficiency VAT and risk of budget balance are negative and significant at the 10 percent and 1 percent levels, respectively. This indicates that even when political cycles are controlled for, institutional settings are directly related to the size of the informal economy. However, the size of tax revenues is not significant when the political cycle is controlled for. This interesting result indicates that it may be tax administration, rather than the tax rates or the tax burden, that affects choice to participate in the informal sector. Care, however, should be taken with interpretations of the C-efficiency VAT measure, considering that there are limited observations.

Institutional quality measures for the business and regulatory environment (columns 5 to 8) show that contract viability and property rights are both negative and significant at a 1 percent level. Regulatory quality and private credit coefficients are both negative but are not significant, indicating that these may be relevant only contemporaneously, rather than for longer term political turnover or as barriers to entering the formal economy.

The institutional quality for political and legal environment (columns 9 to 13) show that corruption and government accountability are negative and significant at the 1 percent and 5 percent levels, respectively. This indicates that higher corruption (Elgin 2010; Dreher and Schneider 2010) and greater government accountability are associated with smaller informal sectors. The results indicate that institutional quality matters even when political turnover is considered, and improvements in institutions reduce the size of the informal economy over time.

As a further robustness check, we use a measure of the informal economy developed by Elgin and Oztunali (2012). The results are in Annex 8.3 and are consistent with those for Medina and Schneider (2018) presented in Tables 8.1 and 8.2.

Table 8.2 presents results using the random effects logit model, which allows us to identify the marginal effects of institutional change from the probability of change in the size of the informal economy as a percentage of official GDP. We use the same institutional quality variables as in the systems GMM estimation to investigate the effect.

Fiscal and tax burden variables are presented in columns 2 to 4. Tax revenues as a percentage of GDP and the risk of budget balance are both negative and significantly related to the size of the informal economy.

Indicators for business and regulatory environment (columns 5 to 8) show that contract viability and private credit are both negatively and strongly significantly linked to the size of the informal economy. Indicators of political and legal environment (columns 9 to 13) show that corruption and government accountability are negatively and significantly related to the size of the informal economy, although the marginal effect on the size of the informal economy is only significant at the 10 percent level.

We undertake robustness checks to test the validity of our results (Annex 8.2). The first check addresses the strength of including a lag in the panel to account for the effect of political cycles on institutional quality and indicates that our main results are robust. Such a check demonstrates that when government

TABLE 8.2.

Random Effects Logit, Medina and Schneider Informality, 1990–2017

	1	2	3	4	5	6	7	8	9	10	11	12	13
L. Medina informal	3.419***	3.213***	3.579***	3.441***	3.333***	3.546***	3.437***	3.407***	3.453***	3.430***	3.435***	3.342***	3.238***
	(0.119)	(0.208)	(0.131)	(0.133)	(0.133)	(0.129)	(0.136)	(0.119)	(0.132)	(0.132)	(0.136)	(0.122)	(0.124)
Real GDP per capita	−0.0352***	−0.143***	−0.0395***	−0.0376***	−0.0396***	−0.0404***	−0.0338***	−0.0349***	−0.0378***	−0.0346***	−0.0336***	−0.0496***	−0.0502***
	(0.00996)	(0.0386)	(0.0105)	(0.0109)	(0.0105)	(0.0118)	(0.0110)	(0.0100)	(0.0107)	(0.0104)	(0.0111)	(0.0136)	(0.0138)
Trade restrictions	−0.00836*	−0.00160	−0.0123**	−0.0110**	−0.00726	−0.00936*	−0.00930	−0.0127**	−0.0110**	−0.0114**	−0.00878	0.00774	−0.00837*
	(0.00477)	(0.00829)	(0.00528)	(0.00525)	(0.00534)	(0.00521)	(0.00572)	(0.00496)	(0.00524)	(0.00523)	(0.00562)	(0.00493)	(0.00502)
Inflation	0.0369	0.0258	0.0105	0.00921	0.0766	0.0403	0.066	0.0756	0.0114	0.00283	0.0648	−0.0496	0.0559
	(0.0512)	(0.0991)	(0.0573)	(0.0565)	(0.0600)	(0.0569)	(0.0618)	(0.0525)	(0.0563)	(0.0569)	(0.0616)	(0.0519)	(0.0524)
Human capital	−0.0269	−0.528*	−0.0328	−0.0867	−0.168	−0.0237	−0.0526	−0.0446	−0.126	−0.0719	−0.0692	0.0599	−0.0871
	(0.124)	(0.279)	(0.143)	(0.140)	(0.142)	(0.133)	(0.143)	(0.126)	(0.149)	(0.140)	(0.141)	(0.135)	(0.144)
Fiscal and Tax Burden													
C-efficiency VAT		−0.208											
		(0.618)											
Tax revenues			−0.0187**										
			(0.00906)										
Risk budget balance				−0.0369**									
				(0.0176)									
Business and Regulatory Environment													
Contract viability					−0.270***								
					(0.0560)								
Property rights						−0.00135							
						(0.00408)							
Regulatory quality							−0.147						
							(0.136)						
Private credit								−0.00848***					
								(0.00252)					
Political and Legal Environment													
ICRG bureaucracy									−0.0858				
									(0.0917)				
Corruption										−0.142*			
										(0.0781)			
Rule of law											−0.132		
											(0.135)		
Government accountability												−0.108*	
												(0.0652)	
Executive constraint													−0.0296
													(0.0356)
Constant	−2.206***	−1.952***	−2.201***	−2.370***	−2.616***	−2.318***	−2.147***	−2.185***	−2.281***	−1.976***	−2.106***	−2.179***	−2.022***
	(0.304)	(0.561)	(0.331)	(0.414)	(0.365)	(0.348)	(0.408)	(0.303)	(0.354)	(0.376)	(0.397)	(0.305)	(0.312)
No. of observations	2,421	721	2,088	1,947	1,947	2,139	1,776	2,421	1,947	1,947	1,776	2,224	2,049
No. of countries	100	61	95	84	84	99	100	100	84	84	100	96	95

Source: Author.

Note: Standard errors appear in parentheses. ICRG = International Country Risk Guide; VAT = value-added tax.

*$p < 0.10$; **$p < 0.05$; ***$p < 0.01$.

turnover is accounted for, institutional changes still matter for the size of the informal economy. Political and legal environment indicators, other than rule of law, are no longer significant once government turnover is controlled.

Our second check addressed the robustness of the logit model by using an alternative measure of the decrease in the size of the informal economy, using a standard deviation decrease rather than an indicator of the sustained decrease in the informal economy. Results for tax revenues and risk of budget balance are both significant, as are those for regulatory quality. All measures of political and legal environment, except for government accountability, are significant at the 10 percent level or higher, indicating that the marginal changes in these variables are significant for changes in the informal economy.

These two robustness check results do not change our underlying results, confirming that once political changes are controlled for, institutional factors are still important determinants for participation in, and therefore size of, the informal economy.

CONCLUSION

This chapter links changes in the size of the informal economy to changes in institutional setting and political cycle to capture why the informal economy is so large and persistent in emerging market and developing economies. Following from previous work, we use political turnover to help explain the variation in institutional settings. One of our key contributions is to build the political cycle into our panel to explain changes in institutions and in the size of the informal sector. The analysis shows that, controlling for political cycles, institutions still matter. Indicators of the quality of fiscal institutions, the business and regulatory environment, and the political and legal environment are found to be significant. Our robustness checks help confirm our results that political turnover is relevant to institutions and the size of the informal sector and needs to be controlled for in empirical analysis. Changes in institutional variables also affect informality and are robust to alternative definitions of changes in informality. These results highlight that structural reforms to enhance the quality of fiscal institutions, the business and regulatory environment, and the political and legal environment can all be effective in reducing informality over time.

ANNEX 8.1. SUMMARY STATISTICS AND VARIABLES

ANNEX TABLE 8.1.1.

Summary Statistics

Variables	No. of Observations	Mean	Standard Deviation	Minimum	Maximum
Dependent Variables					
Medina informal	3,267	35.3	10.9	11.0	70.5
Elgin informal	2,208	37.2	11.4	11.5	80.3
Explanatory Variables					
Real GDP per capita	3,346	4.3	7.7	31.3	10,193
Trade restrictions	3,345	48.4	16.2	11.0	92
Inflation	3,326	0.4	4.7	0	5
Human capital	3,158	6.4	2.8	0	13
Government turnover	3,072	8.2	8.7	1	46
C-efficiency VAT	779	0.5	0.2	0	1
Tax revenues	2,744	14.7	7.7	0	53
Risk budget balance	2,574	5.6	1.9	0	10
Contract viability	2,574	1.7	1.4	0	4
Property rights	2,624	39.4	17.7	0	90
Regulatory quality	2,268	–0.4	0.7	–2.6	1.5
Private credit	3,402	28.8	27.3	0	167
Bureaucratic quality	2,574	1.7	0.9	0	4
Corruption	2,574	2.4	1.0	0	5
Rule of law	2,268	–0.5	0.7	–2.2	1.5
Government integrity	2,628	32.2	15.0	0.0	90.0
Government accountability	3,107	0.5	0.8	–1.6	2.0
Executive constraint	2,820	4.5	2.0	1.0	7.0

Source: Author.
Note: VAT = value-added tax.

ANNEX TABLE 8.1.2.

Variables and Data Sources

Variables	Details	Time Span	Source
L. Medina informal	Size of the informal economy as a percent of official GDP, as estimated in Medina and Schneider (2018).	1991–2017	Medina and Schneider (2017)
Elgin informal	Size of the informal economy as a percent of official GDP, as estimated in Elgin and Oztunali (2012).	1960–2008	Elgin and Oztunali (2012)
Real GDP per capita	Growth of real GDP per capita in US dollars.	1960–2017	Elgin and Oztunali 2012
Trade restrictions	Range from 0 to 100, where lower values suggest greater economic restrictions, components, hidden import barriers, mean tariff rate taxes on international trade, and capital controls. Index has been reversed for analysis.	1970–2017	KOF Swiss Economic Institute, the KOF Globalization Index
Inflation	Index based on annual average Consumer Price Index growth; 1 = negative growth, 2 = 0 to 5 percent growth, 3 = 5 to 10 percent growth, 4 = 10 to 15 percent growth, 5 = 15+ percent growth.	1960–2017	IMF, World Economic Outlook database
Human capital	Human capital index based on average years of schooling from Barro and Lee (2013) and assumed rate of return to education based on Mincer equation estimates around the world (Psacharopoulos 1994).	1960–2018	Penn World Tables, 9.1

(continued)

ANNEX TABLE 8.1.2. ***(continued)***

Variables and Data Sources

Variables	Details	Time Span	Source
Government turnover	Number of years the incumbent executive's political party has held executive office.	1975–2015	World Bank Database of Political Institutions
C-efficiency VAT	C-efficiency VAT ratio is the share of the VAT in GDP divided by the standard VAT rate.	2000–2016	IMF, Fiscal Affairs Department Tax Rate database
Tax revenues	General government tax revenues, based on percent of fiscal year GDP.	1960–2017	IMF, World Economic Outlook Database
Risk budget balance	Central government budget balance (including grants) for a given year in the national currency is expressed as a percentage of the estimated GDP, ranging from high 10 to low –30. The higher the points, the lower the risk.	1990–2016	International Country Risk Guide
Contract viability	Risk of contract modification or cancellations and possible appropriation of assets.	1990–2016	International Country Risk Guide
Property rights	Index 1–100 measuring degree to which a country's laws protects private property rights and the degree to which its government enforces those laws.	1990–2017	Heritage Foundation
Regulatory quality	Regulatory quality captures perceptions of the ability of the government to formulate and implement sound policies and regulations that permit and promote private sector development, on a scale of –2.5 (worst) to 2.5 (best).	1995–2017	World Bank Governance Indicators
Private credit	Domestic credit to private sector as a percent of GDP.	1960–2017	World Bank, World Development Indicators
Bureaucratic quality	Institutional strength and quality of the bureaucracy limits the ability for political interference. The scale ranges from 0 (worst) to 4 (best).	1990–2017	International Country Risk Guide
Corruption	Measure of corruption that distorts the political system. Scale is from 1 (worst) to 6 (best).	1990–2017	International Country Risk Guide
Rule of law	Rule of law captures perceptions of the extent to which agents have confidence in and abide by the rules of society, in particular, the quality of contract enforcement, property rights, the police, and the courts; scale is from –2.5 (worst) to 2.5 (best).	1996–2017	World Bank Governance Indicators
Government integrity	Transparency International's Corruption Perceptions Index; a 10-point scale in which a score of 10 indicates very little corruption and a score of 0 indicates a very corrupt government.		Heritage Foundation
Government accountability	Measure of government accountability and requirements for justification for its actions and decisions, composite index.	1960–2017	Polity IV Project; Marshall, Gurr, and Jaggers 2017
Executive constraint	Institutionalized constraints on the decision-making powers of the executive branch on a scale of 1 to 7.	1960–2017	Polity IV Project; Marshall, Gurr, and Jaggers 2017

Source: Author.
Note: VAT = value-added tax.

ANNEX 8.2. ROBUSTNESS CHECKS

We undertake robustness checks to check the validity of our results. The first, presented in Annex Table 8.2.1, addresses the lag included in the panel to account for the effect of political cycles on institutional quality and informality. For this check, we remove the lag and add an additional variable, as in Elbahnasawy, Ellis, and Adom (2016): a time-varying indicator of political turnover that measures the years since the most recent regime change with the same institutional quality variables used in the systems GMM. This gives robust results for fiscal and tax burdens, and business and regulatory environment indicators. Negative and significant results are reported for C-efficiency VAT, tax revenues, risk of budget balance and contract viability, property rights regulatory quality, and private credit. The results for political and legal environments are not significant, although they give the correct sign. This indicates that our main results are robust, and the implication of including the lag on the basis of political cycles is twofold: when government turnover is accounted for, institutional changes still matter for the size of the informal economy. Additionally, political and legal environment indicators, other than rule of law, are no longer significant once government turnover is controlled.

The second check, presented in Annex Table 8.2.2, verifies the robustness of the logit test by using an alternative measure of the decrease in the size of the informal economy. In this model, rather than using an indicator of the sustained reduction of the informal economy, we use the standard deviation decrease in the informal economy away from a five-year average (for example, 2005–09 or 2010–15). The purpose is to capture a "natural rate" of informal activity. Advanced economies with the best institutions still record an informal economy averaging 16 percent of official GDP (Medina and Schneider 2018), indicating that although informal activities can be minimized, they do not disappear at high levels of development.

We use standard deviations away from the emerging market and developing economy average instead of a growth measure to capture the change for the logit. Standard deviations above or below the average indicate a growing or shrinking informal economy. The results are presented in Annex Table 8.2.2. Both tax revenues and risk of budget balance are significant, as is regulatory quality, based on these measures. All measures of political and legal environment are significant at the 10 percent level or higher, indicating that the marginal changes in these variables are significant for changes in the informal economy. These two robustness check results do not change our underlying results, confirming that once political changes are controlled for, institutional factors are still important determinants for participation in, and therefore size of, the informal economy.

ANNEX TABLE 8.2.1.

System GMM Estimation, Medina and Schneider Informality, 1990–2017: Robustness Check, Alternate Political Turnover Variables with No Election Lag

	1	2	3	4	5	6	7	8	9	10	11	12	13
L.Medina informal	0.778***	0.652***	0.763***	0.780***	0.786***	0.755***	0.780***	0.784***	0.783***	0.784***	0.771***	0.778***	0.778***
	(0.014)	(0.031)	(0.015)	(0.015)	(0.015)	(0.015)	(0.017)	(0.014)	(0.015)	(0.015)	(0.017)	(0.014)	(0.014)
Real GDP per capita	−0.026***	−0.203***	−0.023**	−0.020**	−0.023**	−0.041***	−0.034***	−0.027***	−0.024**	−0.024**	−0.029**	−0.026***	−0.026***
	(0.010)	(0.050)	(0.010)	(0.010)	(0.010)	(0.012)	(0.012)	(0.010)	(0.010)	(0.010)	(0.012)	(0.010)	(0.010)
Trade restrictions	−0.026***	−0.034**	−0.029***	−0.020***	−0.018***	−0.029***	−0.033***	−0.028***	−0.021***	−0.022***	−0.037***	−0.025***	−0.027***
	(0.005)	(0.015)	(0.006)	(0.006)	(0.006)	(0.006)	(0.007)	(0.005)	(0.006)	(0.006)	(0.007)	(0.005)	(0.005)
Inflation	0.087**	0.033	0.072*	0.064	0.044	0.114***	0.121***	0.102***	0.066	0.069*	0.112**	0.086**	0.089**
	−0.037	(0.074)	(0.040)	(0.040)	(0.042)	(0.041)	(0.045)	(0.037)	(0.040)	(0.040)	(0.044)	(0.037)	(0.037)
Human capital	−2.466***	−4.715***	−2.335***	−2.519***	−2.125***	−2.139***	−1.957***	−2.589***	−2.572***	−2.566***	−2.245***	−2.466***	−2.431***
	(0.358)	(1.175)	(0.423)	(0.378)	(0.416)	(0.444)	(0.518)	(0.360)	(0.384)	(0.392)	(0.515)	(0.358)	(0.359)
Government turnover	−0.081***	−0.167*	−0.071**	−0.066*	−0.064*	−0.074*	−0.101**	−0.071**	−0.071**	−0.070**	−0.062	0.064*	−0.134***
	(0.030)	(0.100)	(0.034)	(0.034)	(0.034)	(0.038)	(0.044)	(0.030)	(0.034)	(0.034)	(0.044)	(0.036)	(0.048)
Fiscal and Tax Burden													
C-efficiency VAT		−3.481***											
		(0.791)											
Tax revenues			−0.072***										
			(0.015)										
Risk budget balance				−0.072***									
				(0.028)									
Business and Regulatory Environment													
Contract viability					−0.094**								
					(0.040)								
Property rights						−0.021***							
						(0.005)							
Regulatory quality							−0.762***						
							(0.212)						

(continued)

ANNEX TABLE 8.2.1. *(continued)*

System GMM Estimation, Medina and Schneider Informality, 1990–2017: Robustness Check, Alternate Political Turnover Variables with No Election Lag

	1	2	3	4	5	6	7	8	9	10	11	12	13
Private credit								−0.008***					
								(0.003)					
Political and Legal Environment													
ICRG bureaucracy									−0.063				
									(0.095)				
Corruption										−0.020			
										(0.059)			
Rule of law											−1.435***		
											(0.232)		
Government accountability												−0.149	
												(0.176)	
Executive constraint													−0.088
													(0.063)
Constant	−2.018***	−3.526***	−2.152***	−1.841***	−2.004***	−2.552***	−1.000**	−2.022***	−2.428***	−3.426***	−1.066**	−1.967***	−1.903***
	(0.290)	(0.794)	(0.338)	(0.423)	(0.324)	(0.366)	(0.427)	(0.290)	(0.355)	(0.434)	(0.435)	(0.299)	(0.304)
No. of observations	2,171	709	1,787	1,854	1,854	1,836	1,558	2,171	1,854	1,854	1,558	2,171	2,171
No. of countries	95	61	90	81	81	94	95	95	81	81	95	95	95
Year dummies	Yes	Yes	Yes	Yes	Yes	Yes	Yes	Yes	Yes	Yes	Yes	Yes	Yes
No. of instruments	45	38	48	48	48	45	41	48	48	48	41	48	45
AR(2) *p* values	0.0	0.0	0.0	0.0	0.0	0.0	0.0	0.0	0.0	0.0	0.0	0.0	0.0
AR(1) *p* values	0.545	0.995	0.159	0.495	0.493	0.485	0.018	0.523	0.474	0.475	0.015	0.580	0.545
Hansen *p* values	0.527	0.905	0.761	0.167	0.176	0.134	0.481	0.879	0.218	0.203	0.380	0.845	0.527

Source: Author.

Note: Standard errors appear in parentheses. GMM = generalized method of moments; ICRG = International Country Risk Guide; VAT = value-added tax.

*$p < 0.10$; **$p < 0.05$; ***$p < 0.01$.

ANNEX TABLE 8.2.2.

Random Effects Logit, Medina and Schneider Informality, 1990–2017: Robustness Check, Alternative Dependent Variable Change in Informality													
	1	**2**	**3**	**4**	**5**	**6**	**7**	**8**	**9**	**10**	**11**	**12**	**13**
L. Medina informal	2.959***	5.984***	2.940***	2.902***	2.932***	2.516***	3.027***	2.956***	2.921***	2.946***	2.947***	2.931***	2.785***
	(0.271)	(0.383)	(0.298)	(0.314)	(0.316)	(0.262)	(0.381)	(0.273)	(0.316)	(0.313)	(0.372)	(0.279)	(0.293)
Real GDP per capita	−0.273***	−0.126*	−0.328***	−0.327***	−0.347***	−0.323***	−0.388***	−0.277***	−0.348***	−0.337***	−0.415***	−0.289***	−0.303***
	(0.0772)	(0.0701)	(0.0896)	(0.0913)	(0.0943)	(0.103)	(0.121)	(0.0781)	(0.0960)	(0.0926)	(0.128)	(0.0944)	(0.0980)
Trade restrictions	−0.0320*	−0.00396	−0.0276	−0.0233	−0.0226	−0.0336*	−0.0585**	−0.0337*	−0.0193	−0.0317	−0.0551**	−0.0319*	−0.0324*
	(0.0177)	(0.0155)	(0.0191)	(0.0209)	(0.0213)	(0.0193)	(0.0238)	(0.0184)	(0.0201)	(0.0202)	(0.0239)	(0.0185)	(0.0197)
Inflation	0.162	0.132	0.141	0.248*	0.276*	0.198	0.219	0.157	0.204	0.19	0.290**	−0.177	0.212*
	(0.113)	(0.174)	(0.120)	(0.135)	(0.143)	(0.124)	(0.143)	(0.115)	(0.132)	(0.134)	(0.148)	(0.116)	(0.121)
Human capital	−0.838	−0.0166	−0.882	−0.646	−1.245	−0.0365	−0.614	−0.826	−0.788	−0.415	−0.423	0.388	−0.254
	(0.697)	(0.513)	(0.766)	(0.842)	(0.977)	(0.707)	(0.937)	(0.701)	(0.795)	(0.825)	(0.913)	(0.786)	(0.843)
Fiscal and Tax Burden													
C-efficiency VAT		−0.927											
		(1.056)											
Tax revenues			−0.358**										
			(0.153)										
Risk budget balance				−0.0162*									
				(0.00943)									
Business and Regulatory Environment													
Contract viability					−0.151								
					(0.134)								
Property rights						−0.00641							
						(0.0118)							
Regulatory quality							−2.133***						
							(0.566)						
Private credit								0.00371					
								(0.0112)					

(continued)

ANNEX TABLE 8.2.2. *(continued)*

Random Effects Logit, Medina and Schneider Informality, 1990–2017: Robustness Check, Alternative Dependent Variable Change in Informality

	1	2	3	4	5	6	7	8	9	10	11	12	13
Political and Legal Environment													
ICRG bureaucracy									−0.841***				
									(0.311)				
Corruption										−0.381*			
										(0.231)			
Rule of law											−3.687***		
											(0.639)		
Government accountability												0.0934	
												(0.346)	
Executive constraint													−0.348*
													(0.211)
Constant	0.0526	−2.095*	0.613	1.400	−0.359	1.862	4.391**	0.0466	1.361	2.079	3.140	0.993	2.420
	(1.469)	(1.099)	(1.466)	(1.864)	(1.948)	(1.345)	(2.025)	(1.475)	(1.652)	(1.920)	(1.992)	(1.541)	(1.645)
No. of observations	2,503	721	2,129	2,016	2,016	2,139	1,776	2,503	2,016	2,016	1,776	2,302	2,120
No. of countries	100	61	95	84	84	99	100	100	84	84	100	96	95

Source: Author.

Note: Standard errors appear in parentheses. ICRG = International Country Risk Guide; VAT = value-added tax.

$*p < 0.10$; $**p < 0.05$; $***p < 0.01$.

ANNEX 8.3. ALTERNATIVE RESULTS USING ELGIN AND OZTUNALI (2012)

ANNEX TABLE 8.3.1.

System GMM Estimation, Elgin and Oztunali Informality, 1990–2008

	1	2	3	4	5	6	7	8	9	10	11	12	13
L. Elgin informal	0.958***	1.088***	0.967***	0.946***	0.936***	0.965***	0.961***	0.964***	0.944***	0.946***	0.961***	0.961***	0.958***
	(0.007)	(0.030)	(0.011)	(0.010)	(0.010)	(0.016)	(0.018)	(0.007)	(0.010)	(0.010)	(0.018)	(0.007)	(0.007)
Real GDP per capita	–0.001	0.004*	0.000	–0.001	0.000	–0.003***	–0.003	–0.001	–0.001	–0.001	–0.003	0.000	0.000
	(0.000)	(0.002)	(0.001)	(0.001)	(0.001)	(0.001)	(0.002)	(0.000)	(0.001)	(0.001)	(0.002)	(0.001)	(0.000)
Trade restrictions	–0.005**	0.006	–0.004	–0.003	–0.001	–0.005	–0.005	–0.007***	–0.004	–0.004	–0.005	–0.004	–0.002
	(0.002)	(0.009)	(0.003)	(0.003)	(0.003)	(0.004)	(0.006)	(0.002)	(0.003)	(0.003)	(0.006)	(0.002)	(0.002)
Inflation	0.036**	–0.057	0.040**	0.019	0.020	0.015	0.030	0.043***	0.027	0.028	0.032	0.037***	0.021
	(0.014)	(0.040)	(0.017)	(0.018)	(0.017)	(0.023)	(0.030)	(0.014)	(0.017)	(0.017)	(0.030)	(0.014)	(0.013)
Human capital	–0.600***	–3.244***	–0.762***	–0.615***	–0.067	–0.780**	–1.929***	–0.618***	–0.788***	–0.792***	–1.908***	–0.577***	–0.808***
	(0.146)	(0.799)	(0.209)	(0.207)	(0.218)	(0.355)	(0.432)	(0.145)	(0.201)	(0.205)	(0.430)	(0.162)	(0.141)
Fiscal and Tax Burden													
C-efficiency VAT		–0.533											
		(0.513)											
Tax revenues			–0.016**										
			(0.008)										
Risk budget balance				–0.032***									
				(0.012)									
Business and Regulatory Environment													
Contract viability					–0.110***								
					(0.015)								
Property rights						0.008***							
						(0.002)							
Regulatory quality							–0.143						
							(0.124)						
Private credit								0.006***					
								(0.001)					

(continued)

ANNEX TABLE 8.3.1. ***(continued)***

System GMM Estimation, Elgin and Oztunali Informality, 1990–2008

	1	2	3	4	5	6	7	8	9	10	11	12	13
Political and Legal Environment													
ICRG bureaucracy									−0.028				
									(0.028)				
Corruption										−0.010			
										(0.022)			
Rule of law											−0.151		
											(0.152)		
Government accountability												−0.093**	
												(0.039)	
Executive constraint													−0.023**
													(0.011)
Constant	2.583***	3.645	2.676***	3.223***	2.254***	2.432**	5.232***	2.308***	3.488***	3.422***	5.150***	2.399***	2.994***
	(0.422)	(2.287)	(0.601)	(0.602)	(0.608)	(1.070)	(1.204)	(0.424)	(0.616)	(0.619)	(1.199)	(0.449)	(0.411)
No. of observations	1,625	219	1,049	1,226	1,226	907	602	1,625	1,226	1,226	602	1,557	1,481
No. of countries	101	55	95	85	85	98	101	101	85	85	101	97	96
Year dummies	Yes	Yes	Yes	Yes	Yes	Yes	Yes	Yes	Yes	Yes	Yes	Yes	Yes
No. of instruments	27	23	35	33	33	28	24	35	33	33	24	35	35
AR(2) *p* values	0.0631	0.747	0.0358	0.0552	0.0758	0.00271	0.488	0.0418	0.0696	0.0639	0.457	0.0545	0.00118
AR(1) *p* values	0.907	0.968	0.225	0.880	0.895	0.257	0.892	0.873	0.864	0.893	0.880	0.904	0.120
Hansen *p* values	0.416	0.331	0.426	0.723	0.736	0.182	0.244	0.059	0.298	0.784	0.902	0.472	0.565

Source: Author.

Note: Standard errors appear in parentheses. GMM = generalized method of moments; ICRG = International Country Risk Guide; VAT = value-added tax.

*$p < 0.10$; **$p < 0.05$; ***$p < 0.01$.

ANNEX TABLE 8.3.2.

Random Effects Logit, Medina and Schneider Informality, 1990–2008

	1	2	3	4	5	6	7	8	9	10	11	12	13
L. Medina Informal	4.288***	5.368***	4.210***	4.190***	4.194***	4.094***	3.926***	4.275***	4.131***	4.168***	3.952***	4.315***	4.235***
	(0.173)	(0.552)	(0.193)	(0.185)	(0.191)	(0.195)	(0.229)	(0.173)	(0.185)	(0.187)	(0.229)	(0.178)	(0.179)
Real GDP per capita	0.00551	−0.199*	0.00507	0.00675	0.00113	−0.0168	−0.0202	0.00624	−0.000163	0.00644	−0.0192	−0.00993	−0.00734
	(0.0155)	(0.113)	(0.0164)	(0.0160)	(0.0171)	(0.0189)	(0.0195)	(0.0153)	(0.0160)	(0.0153)	(0.0194)	(0.0219)	(0.0216)
Trade restrictions	−0.000455	0.0141	0.000486	−0.00136	0.00725	−0.000384	−0.0127	−0.00152	−0.00236	−0.00224	−0.0116	−0.00277	−0.00314
	(0.00717)	(0.0197)	(0.00825)	(0.00759)	(0.00788)	(0.00803)	(0.00988)	(0.00723)	(0.00764)	(0.00765)	(0.00978)	(0.00751)	(0.00751)
Inflation	0.315***	0.691***	0.306***	0.279***	0.150**	0.321***	0.287***	0.336***	0.287***	0.232***	0.305***	0.325***	0.321***
	(0.0679)	(0.211)	(0.0769)	(0.0727)	(0.0760)	(0.0774)	(0.0908)	(0.0700)	(0.0722)	(0.0739)	(0.0906)	(0.0696)	(0.0698)
Human capital	−0.246	−0.132	−0.193	−0.150	−0.0127	−0.524**	−0.726***	−0.291	−0.313	−0.199	−0.550**	−0.159	−0.225
	(0.190)	(0.560)	(0.222)	(0.206)	(0.210)	(0.217)	(0.276)	(0.194)	(0.215)	(0.205)	(0.260)	(0.213)	(0.223)
Fiscal and Tax Burden													
C-efficiency VAT		−0.417											
		(1.399)											
Tax revenues			−0.00734										
			(0.0141)										
Risk budget balance				−0.0254									
				(0.0571)									
Business and Regulatory Environment													
Contract viability					−0.418***								
					(0.0667)								
Property rights						0.0200***							
						(0.00579)							
Regulatory quality							1.019***						
							(0.240)						
Private credit								0.00412					
								(0.00325)					

(continued)

ANNEX TABLE 8.3.2. ***(continued)***

Random Effects Logit, Medina and Schneider Informality, 1990–2008													
	1	2	3	4	5	6	7	8	9	10	11	12	13
Political and Legal Environment													
ICRG bureaucracy									0.261**				
									(0.119)				
Corruption										0.416***			
										(0.0988)			
Rule of law											0.863***		
											(0.219)		
Government accountability												–0.0986	
												(0.120)	
Executive constraint													–0.0144
													(0.0492)
Constant	–3.242***	–6.132***	–3.339***	–3.095***	–2.914***	–3.541***	–1.454**	–3.288***	–3.321***	–4.016***	–1.829***	–3.292***	–3.067***
	(0.421)	(1.208)	(0.459)	(0.525)	(0.464)	(0.504)	(0.657)	(0.423)	(0.467)	(0.514)	(0.633)	(0.425)	(0.429)
No. of observations	1,637	449	1,306	1,377	1,377	1,280	995	1,637	1,377	1,377	995	1,569	1,507
No. of countries	101	60	96	85	85	98	101	101	85	85	101	97	96

Source: Author.

Note: Standard errors appear in parentheses. ICRG = International Country Risk Guide; VAT = value-added tax.

$^{*}p < 0.10$; $^{**}p < 0.05$; $^{***}p < 0.01$.

REFERENCES

Acemoglu, D., S. Johnson, and J. Robinson. 2005. "Institutions as the Fundamental Cause of Long-Run Growth." In *Handbook of Economic Growth*, edited by P. Aghion and S. Durlauf. Amsterdam: Elsevier.

Afonso, O., P. Neves, and T. Pinto. 2020. "The Non-Observed Economy and Economic Growth: A Meta-Analysis." *Economic Systems* 44 (1): 100746.

Alesina, A, R. Hausmann, R. Hommes, and E. Stein. 1999. "Budget Institutions and Fiscal Performance in Latin America." *Journal of Development Economics*, 59 (2): 253–73.

Ang, Y. 2020. "Unbundling Corruption: Revisiting Six Questions on Corruption." *Global Perspectives* 1 (1): 12036.

Ardizzi, G., C. Petraglia, M. Piacenza, and G. Turati. 2014. "Measuring the Underground Economy with the Currency Demand Approach: A Reinterpretation of the Methodology, With an Application to Italy." *Review of Income and Wealth* 4: 747–72.

Arellano, M., and S. Bond. 1991. "Some Tests of Specification for Panel Data: Monte Carlo Evidence and an Application to Employment Equations." *Review of Economic Studies* 58 (2): 277–97.

Arellano, M., and O. Bover. 1995. "Another Look at the Instrumental Variable Estimation of Error-Components Models." *Journal of Econometrics* 68 (1): 29–51.

Aruoba, S. 2010. "Informal Sector, Government Policy and Institutions." Paper 324, Presented at the Society for Economic Dynamics 2010 Meeting, Montreal, Canada, July 8–10.

Barro, R., and J. Lee. 2013. "A New Dataset of Educational Attainment in the World, 1950–2010." *Journal of Development Economics* 104: 184–98.

Blundell, R., and S. Bond. 1998. "Initial Conditions and Moment Restrictions in Dynamic Panel Data Models." *Journal of Econometrics* 87 (1): 115–43.

Choi, J., and M. Thum. 2005. "Corruption and the Shadow Economy." *International Economic Review* 46 (3): 817–36.

Coady, D. 2018. "Creating Fiscal Space." *Finance and Development* 55 (4): 24–27.

Cortellese, F. 2015. "Definition of Informal Economy and Estimation of Tax Evasion for European Countries: The Impact of Financial Crisis on Tax Evasion Estimation." Unpublished report, Universidad Autónoma de Madrid, Madrid.

Costa, C., Jr., A. Garcia-Cintado, and C. Usabiaga. 2019. "Fiscal Adjustments and the Shadow Economy in an Emerging Market." *Macroeconomic Dynamics* 1–35.

Dabla-Norris, E., M. Gradstein, and G. Inchauste. 2008. "What Causes Firms to Hide Output?" *Journal of Development Economics* 85 (1–2): 1–27.

Dabla-Norris, E., R. Allen, L. Zanna., E. Prakash, E. Kvintradze, V. Lledo, I. Yackovlev, and S. Gollwitzer. 2010. "Budget Institutions and Fiscal Performance in Low-Income Countries." IMF Working Paper 10/80, International Monetary Fund, Washington, DC.

De Soto, H. 1989. *The Other Path: The Invisible Revolution in the Third World*. New York: Harper and Row.

Deléchat, C., E. Fuli, D. Mulaj, G. Ramirez, and R. Xu. 2015. "Exiting from Fragility in Sub-Saharan Africa: The Role of Fiscal Policies and Fiscal Institutions." IMF Working Paper 15/268, International Monetary Fund, Washington, DC.

Dellas, H., D. Malliaropulos, D. Papageorgiou, and E. Vourvachaki. 2019. "Fiscal Multipliers with an Informal Sector." Unpublished report, Economic Analysis and Research Department, Bank of Greece, Athens.

Docquier, F., T. Müller, and J. Naval. 2017. "Informality and Long⊠Run Growth." *Scandinavian Journal of Economics* 119 (4): 1040–85.

Dreher, A., and F. Schneider. 2010. "Corruption and the Shadow Economy: An Empirical Analysis." *Public Choice* 144 (1–2): 215–38.

Elbahnasawy, N., M. Ellis, and A. Adom. 2016. "Political Instability and the Informal Economy." *World Development* 85 (C): 31–42.

Elgin, C. 2010. "Political Turnover, Taxes, and the Shadow Economy." Unpublished report, University of Minnesota, Minneapolis.

Elgin, C. 2015. "Informal Economy in a Dynamic Political Framework." *Macroeconomic Dynamics* 19 (3): 578–617.

Elgin, C., and O. Oztunali. 2012. "Shadow Economies around the World: Model-Based Estimates." Department of Economics Working Paper 5, Boğaziçi University, Istanbul.

Elgin, C., and B. Uras. 2013. "Public Debt, Sovereign Default Risk, and Shadow Economy." *Journal of Financial Stability* 9 (4): 628–40.

Elgin, C., A. Elveren, and J. Bourgeois. 2020. "Informality, Inequality, and Profit Rate." *Applied Economics Letters*, July 20.

Elgin, C., A. Kose, F. Ohnsorge, and S. Yu. 2019. "Shades of Grey: Measuring the Informal Economy Business Cycles." Unpublished report, International Monetary Fund, Washington, DC. https://www.imf.org/-/media/Files/Conferences/2019/7th-statistics-forum/session-ii-yu.ashx.

Feenstra, R., R. Inklaar, and M. Timmer. 2015. "The Next Generation of the Penn World Table." *American Economic Review* 105 (10): 3150–82.

Friedman, E., S. Johnson, D. Kaufmann, and P. Zoido-Lobaton. 2000. "Dodging the Grabbing Hand: The Determinants of Unofficial Activity in 69 Countries." *Journal of Public Economics* 76 (3): 459–93.

Glaeser, E., R. La Porta, F. Lopes-de-Silanes, and A. Shleifer. 2004. "Do Institutions Cause Growth?" *Journal of Economic Growth* 9 (3): 271–303.

Goel, R., and M. Nelson. 2016. "Shining a Light on the Shadows: Identifying Robust Determinants of the Shadow Economy." *Economic Modelling* 58: 351–64.

Hall, R., and C. Jones. 1999. "Why Do Some Countries Produce So Much More Output per Worker than Others?" *Quarterly Journal of Economics* 114 (1): 83–116.

Heritage Foundation. "The Heritage Foundation Database." Washington, DC.

Ihrig, J., and K. S. Moe. 2004. "Lurking in the Shadows: The Informal Sector and Government Policy." *Journal of Development Economics* 73 (2): 541–57.

International Country Risk Guide (ICRG) Researchers. 2013. "International Country Risk Guide." ICRG.

International Monetary Fund (IMF). 2020a. Fiscal Affairs Department Tax Rate Database, Washington, DC.

International Monetary Fund (IMF). 2020b. World Economic Outlook Database, Washington, DC.

Johnson, S., D. Kaufmann, and P. Zoido-Lobaton. 1998. "Regulatory Discretion and the Unofficial Economy." *American Economic Review* 88 (2): 387–92.

Kaufmann, D., A. Kraay, and M. Mastruzzi. 2010. "The Worldwide Governance Indicators: Methodology and Analytical Issues." Policy Research Working Paper 5430, World Bank, Washington, DC.

Keen, M. 2013. "The Anatomy of the VAT." *National Tax Journal* 66 (2): 423–46.

Klovienė, L. 2012. "Institutional Factors as Criteria for Business Environment Identification." *Economics and Management* 17 (4): 1245–51.

KOF Swiss Economic Institute. 2020. KOF Globalization Index. https://kof.ethz.ch/en/forecasts-and-indicators/indicators/kof-globalisation-index.html.

Koreshkova, T. 2006. "A Quantitative Analysis of Inflation as a Tax on the Underground Economy." *Journal of Monetary Economics* 53: 773–96.

Krakowski, M. 2005. "Determinants of the Informal Economy: The Importance of Regional Factors." HWWA Discussion Paper 313, Hamburg Institute of International Economics, Hamburg, Germany.

Kuehn, Z. 2007. "Tax Rates, Governance, and the Informal Economy in High-Income Countries." Unpublished report, Universidad Carlos III de Madrid, Madrid.

LaPorta, R., F. Lopez-de-Silanes, A. Shleifer, and R. Vishny. 1999. "The Quality of Government." *Journal of Law, Economics and Organization* 15 (1): 222–79.

LaPorta, R., and A. Shleifer. 2008. "The Unofficial Economy and Economic Development." *Brookings Papers on Economic Activity* 47 (1): 123–35.

Lederman, D., N. Loayza, and R. Soares. 2005. "Accountability and Corruption: Political Institutions Matter." *Economics and Politics* 17 (1): 1–35.

Loayza, N. 1996. "The Economics of the Informal Sector: A Simple Model and Some Empirical Evidence from Latin America." *Carnegie-Rochester Conference Series on Public Policy* 45 (1): 129–62.

Loayza, N. 1997. "The Economics of the Informal Sector: A Simple Model and Some Empirical Evidence from Latin America." Policy Research Working Paper Series 1727, World Bank, Washington, DC.

Loayza, N. 2016. "Informality in the Process of Development and Growth." *World Economy* 39 (12): 1856–916.

Loayza, N., and C. Meza-Cuadra. 2018. "A Toolkit for Informality Scenario Analysis." World Bank. http://www.worldbank.org/informality.

Loayza, N., A. Oviedo, and L. Servén. 2006. "The Impact of Regulation on Growth and Informality: Cross-Country Evidence." In *Linking the Formal and Informal Economy*, edited by B. Guha-Khasnobis, R. Kanbur, and E. Ostrom. UNU-WIDER Studies in Development Economics. New York: Oxford University Press.

Marshall, M., T. Gurr, and K. Jaggers. 2017. "Polity IV Project: Dataset." http://www.systemicpeace.org/inscr/p4manualv2016.pdf.

Mazhar, U. 2015. "Does Regulatory Discretion Increase the Unofficial Economy? Evidence from Panel Data." *Acta Oeconomica* 65 (1): 129–41.

Medina, L., and F. Schneider. 2018. "Shadow Economies around the World: What Did We Learn over the Last 20 Years?" IMF Working Paper 18/17, International Monetary Fund, Washington, DC.

Orsi, R., D. Raggi, and F. Turino. 2014. "Size, Trend, and Policy Implications of the Underground Economy." *Review of Economic Dynamics* 17 (3): 417–36.

Oviedo, A., M. Thomas, and K. Karakurum-Özdemir. 2009. "Economic Informality: Causes, Costs, and Policies—A Literature Survey." Working Paper 167, World Bank, Washington, DC.

Perry, G. E., W. F. Maloney, O. S. Arias, P. Fajnzylber, A. Mason, and J. Saavedra-Chanduvi. 2007. *Informality: Exit and Exclusion.* Washington, DC: World Bank.

Psacharopoulos, G. 1994. "Returns to Investment in Education: A Global Update." *World Development* 22: 1325–43.

Rodrik, D., A. Subramanian, and F. Trebbi. 2004. "Institutions Rule: The Primacy of Institutions over Geography and Integration in Economic Development." *Journal of Economic Growth* 9: 131–65.

Roodman, D. 2009. "A Note on the Theme of Too Many Instruments." *Oxford Bulletin of Economics and Statistics* 71 (1): 135–58.

Sarte, P. 2000. "Informality and Rent-Seeking Bureaucracies in a Model of Long-Run Growth." *Journal of Monetary Economics* 46 (1): 173–97.

Schneider, F., and D. H. Enste. 2000. "Shadow Economies: Size, Causes, and Consequences." *Journal of Economic Literature* 38: 77–114.

Schneider, F., A. Buehn, and C. E. Montenegro. 2010. "New Estimates for the Shadow Economies All over the World." *International Economic Journal* 24 (4): 443–61.

Teobaldelli, D., and F. Schneider. 2013. "The Influence of Direct Democracy on the Shadow Economy." *Public Choice* 157 (3): 543–67.

Torgler, B., and F. Schneider. 2009. "The Impact of Tax Morale and Institutional Quality on the Shadow Economy." *Journal of Economic Psychology* 30 (3): 228–45.

Ueda, J. 2017. "The Evolution of Potential VAT Revenues and C-efficiency in Advanced Economies." IMF Working Paper 17/158, International Monetary Fund, Washington, DC.

Windmeijer, F. 2005. "A Finite Sample Correction for the Variance of Linear Efficient Two-Step GMM Estimators." *Journal of Econometrics* 126 (1): 25–51.

World Bank. 2020a. World Bank Database of Political Institutions. Washington, DC.

World Bank. 2020b. World Development Indicators. Washington, DC.

CHAPTER 9

National and Subnational Tax Reforms to Address Informality

Ehtisham Ahmad

Tax design can help address two types of informality that affect emerging market and developing economies. The first relates to general incentives to "cheat" on formal taxes or contributions, facilitated by hard-to-tax smaller businesses interacting with large enterprises, with segmentation of the tax bases. Incomplete information flows can seriously affect the general government revenue position and ability to finance basic services and public investments. The second concerns the popular perception of the informal sector as poor migrants and marginalized groups in metropolitan areas, often living in shanty towns with limited access to public services, such as education or health care, and extremely vulnerable to pandemics, such as coronavirus disease 2019 (COVID-19).

THE RELATIONSHIP BETWEEN INFORMALITY AND TAX POLICY

The presence of people willing to work without contracts facilitates informality of the first kind, enabling firms to hide payroll taxes that add to the cost of doing business by disguising transaction volumes, wages, and profits. Informal workers often lack rights to formal benefits, access to public services, and ability to attract credit.

Informality as "cheating" typically arises when firms have both an incentive to evade taxes and the ability to do so. Such opportunities typically originate as well-meaning government measures to provide investment incentives or social benefits through exemptions or preferences in the tax system or segmentation of tax administration between large taxpayers and a residual small taxpayer regime that may be delegated to lower levels of government. The resulting provisions create discontinuities that generate rents, as well as breaks in the information chain. Often, these provisions do not achieve either distributional or investment

This chapter draws on an article prepared for the Group of Twenty-Four, "Political Economy of Tax Reforms," which was presented at the IMF/World Bank 2019 Spring Meetings (Ahmad 2018a), as well as at an ongoing, joint London School of Economics and Coalition for Urban Transitions research program on financing sustainable development in China and Mexico (Ahmad and others 2020).

objectives and seriously hamstring revenue generation. Examples are found in Pakistan over the past 30 years (Ahmad and Mohammed 2018) and in Mexico before its 2013 reforms.

Standard prescriptions to enhance distributional outcomes, or to encourage investments and ease administration, often generate counterproductive outcomes. Redistributional policies may increase incentives to cheat and reduce revenues while generating negative consequences for the informal sector and the poorest groups. Adverse effects include complicating the value-added tax (VAT) with multiple rates or exemptions, as well as a VAT applied only to large taxpayers. VATs that exempt natural resource investments and special economic zones (SEZs) also create incentives to cheat, as seen in the Nigerian petroleum sector (Petroleum Revenue Special Task Force [PRSTF] 2012).

Other complex measures, such as payroll taxation on formal sector workers, in replicating Bismarckian social protection instruments, also increase the cost of doing business and create double taxation of labor, thus encouraging informality. Further, means-tested benefits, including the globally popular conditional cash transfers, generate severe disincentive effects and often create poverty traps. In Chiapas, the poorest state in Mexico, such unintended effects prompted abolition of the *Oportunidades*,[1] the conditional cash transfer program that has been copied by many other countries worldwide.

National Tax Reforms to Discourage Informality

National tax measures affect incentives facing firms and workers, hence informality and revenue potential. The design and administration of a tax system influences the cost of doing business and prices, affecting both producers and households. This in turn affects the distribution of income and spending. Insights from optimal tax theory, as well as the simpler theory of reform, provide directions for welfare-enhancing reforms (Ahmad and Stern 1991) that can be used in conjunction with the structural measures to consolidate tax bases and information generation.

Several countries have triggered structural reforms by shifting from taxes that increase business costs to more efficient sources of revenue, such as the VAT, that do not distort production decisions or tax exports. Policies that raise minimum general revenues while reducing the cost of doing business have centralized the main tax handles. Reform has not always been easy, as in seen in China in 1993/94 (Ahmad, Rydge, and Stern 2013) and Mexico in 2013 (Ahman 2015), and focused on consolidating national taxes, particularly the VAT. Neither addressed the subnational need for own-source revenues, permitting control over rates. Shared revenues are like transfers and do not generate appropriate incentives at the subnational level.

Emerging market and developing economies can err by expecting one instrument, such as the VAT or the corporate income tax, to simultaneously generate revenues, encourage investment, and address income distribution.

[1] The Mexican budget for 2019 by the Obrador government.

Transplanting from Organisation for Economic Co-operation and Development countries a formal social security system financed by payroll taxes similarly adds to the costs of doing business and could thus increase both types of informality—the incentives to cheat, as well as the incentives facing workers to remain in the informal sector. As seen in China (Ahmad 2018b), a tax reform "package" is needed, covering a range of taxes and transfers to offset gainers and losers at subnational levels. The package should include tax measures that minimize distortions and reduce the costs of doing business, as well as public investment and social spending designed to motivate sustainable and inclusive growth.

As part of any reform package, an integrated VAT is critical. A "clean" VAT free of loopholes and exemptions generates complete information on the production chain, thus reducing the ability to hide transactions and informal employment. Integration of the VAT base was a critical element in the 2013 Mexican reforms and helped prevent both perverse incentives and evasion, not just for the VAT but for excises, payroll taxes, and income taxes.

Given that wide-ranging tax reforms generate both gainers and losers, political economy considerations require either joint implementation of taxes and transfers (as with the Chinese 1993/94 reforms) or simultaneous offsetting tax reforms (as with the 2013 Mexican reforms). China and Mexico offer the most significant examples of systemic tax reforms in major emerging market economies in the past three decades, with major revenue and structural consequences. Both country's reforms were based on introducing or fixing the VAT and offer lessons for emerging market economies in an increasingly global world. As argued in this chapter, reforms in China and Mexico helped reduce informality and cheating by firms, consequently raising the revenues needed to anchor spending for basic needs.

Subnational Own-Source Taxation for Sustainable Development Goals and Addressing Informality

At the subnational level, broad-based access to basic services generates incentives for informal workers to move to the formal sector. Such services constitute the core of the UN Sustainable Development Goals (SDGs) and are also critical in addressing the global pandemic and building back better. Own-source local revenues to finance the SDGs are critical in ensuring accountable policymaking. These own-source revenues are also the basis to access other financing mechanisms, including municipal bonds and capital markets, to ensure adequate infrastructure investments needed for sustainable growth.

Well-designed clean, compact, and connected cities can become sustainable employment hubs and engines of economic growth, provided that adequate local supplies of public goods are available to the entire population. Yet, if most productive activity and employment opportunities are concentrated in a few metropolitan areas (as in Dakar, Guangzhou, Mexico City, Mumbai, or Santiago de Chile), megacities will continue to attract migrants in search of better living conditions. The result is growing informal settlements as well as urban sprawl—the opposite of the clean and compact cities needed for sustainable development.

Badly designed cities, financed by land value capture, contain islands of wealth but also generate urban sprawl, congestion, pollution, and inequalities. Poorer households are often evicted from rapidly appreciating areas and are pushed into slums in the outskirts of town. Furthermore, land value capture often involves eviction through land grabs, facilitated by vested interests, to build low-density villas or golf courses that ultimately pay little tax.

Standard prescriptions concerning property taxation can also be counterproductive and contribute to the increase in informality, typically seen in metropolitan areas such as Cairo, Karachi, and Mexico City. The typical property tax, based on ownership and accurate valuation, further discriminates against poor migrant squatters or tenants who cannot prove residence to access public services. Moreover, enforced titling on communal land can break down social cohesion and the risk-sharing mechanisms critical in countries with weak or no social protection mechanisms.

Property Tax as a Cornerstone of Sustainable Development

A typical model of property taxation, based on ownership titles and accurate valuation, as in the United States, does not work well in emerging market economies. Ownership titles are often unclear, and accurate valuation is difficult to obtain in a timely manner. Even in the United Kingdom, this type of model was abandoned by former Prime Minister Margaret Thatcher. The political economy constraint in countries like India, where the tax was introduced in the late 1800s, is even more problematic—the taxation of fixed- or low-income households living in rapidly appreciating properties that have often not been revalued for decades.

Yet property taxation remains critical for equitable and sustainable development, even if aggregate revenue potential is limited to 2 to 3 percent of GDP and is dwarfed relative to broad-based taxes, such as the VAT. Even if 1 or 2 percent of GDP could be generated locally, as opposed to the typical collection of about 0.25 percent of GDP in many developing countries, including in Latin America and India, this would be significant in financing basic services, because such taxation also helps facilitate access to credit for local investments and infrastructure. If linked to basic services, a beneficial property tax would generate incentives for better governance.

The alternative "beneficial" property tax could be based on simple identification of occupancy, size of property, and location, but with rates linked to basic services. The linkage with basic services is critical in overcoming political resistance, developing a theme suggested by Alfred Marshall (1890). The identification of size, location, and occupancy is straightforward and sidesteps the problems with ownership and valuation. The use of satellite imagery and blockchain technology are promising new methods of administration that can further simplify application. Using simulations for Chinese cities, Ahmad and others (2020) illustrate the effects of a simple area-based property tax yielding

2 percent of GDP. Such revenue can finance basic education, provide poorer households with education stipends, and support social housing. Appropriately designed property taxation allows informal households better access to public services and can play a pivotal role in addressing health crises, such as with the pandemic.

Proposals for a beneficial property tax for Mexico suggest a significant short-term revenue potential of about 1.5 percent of GDP rather than the 0.25 percent of GDP currently generated by the traditional property tax. The beneficial property tax could also lead to reductions in inequality and become an anchor for the post-pandemic "building back better" agenda for the informal workers in metropolitan areas and those who returned home in the lagging southern states (Ahmad and Viscarra 2020).

THE RELATIONSHIP BETWEEN FORMAL SOCIAL PROTECTION AND INFORMALITY

Informality as cheating arises when firms and workers have an incentive to hide transactions from tax administrators and the design of the tax and information system makes it easy for them to do so. Measures to address investment or distributional objectives often create discontinuities that encourage informality.

One such example is the argument by Levy (2008) that inappropriately designed formal social protection systems can raise the cost of doing business and increase incentives for firms to hide profits, turnover, and outlays on labor (see also Antón, Hernández, and Levy 2013). Firms then shift workers to temporary and informal contracts. Both forms of evasion lead to inefficient outcomes and reduce growth. The social protection system thus constitutes, as Levy writes, "good intentions, bad outcomes."

NATIONAL TAX REFORMS IN MEXICO TO BLOCK RENT-SEEKING

Levy's recommendation for Mexico was to shift from high payroll tax on firms (which adds to the cost of doing business) to the VAT, which, when well designed, is neutral to production and exports. However, Mexico, before its 2013 reforms, did not have a VAT capable of generating sufficient revenues to replace the payroll tax. Since the early 1980s, when Mexico introduced its VAT, successive governments aimed to provide incentives for investment, production, and redistribution by reducing rates in sensitive or "border" regions outside the tax-free maquiladora zone and providing exemptions and domestic zero rating.

The base for the Mexican VAT (as well as the income and other major taxes) was further split as the small taxpayer system (REPECOS) was allocated to the state level. With the federal government granting gap-filling transfers to meet state deficits, states had no incentive to pursue hard-to-tax groups. A study for the

Mexican Tax Administration estimated over 90 percent evasion of the REPECOS (Fuentes Castro and others 2011). The net result was that the ratio of non-oil tax to GDP was about 10 percent for general government, or similar to Pakistan—well below the average for Latin American and Caribbean countries or about 15 percent of GDP. The C-efficiency of the Mexican VAT was also not dissimilar to that of the Pakistani VAT, and at about 25 percent was among the lowest in the world (Antón, Hernández, and Levy 2013). An inefficient VAT could not therefore replace the distorting payroll tax.

The Mexican income tax (ISR) also suffered from base erosion. Many beneficiaries of exemptions or preferences were large firms with political connections. Once given, provisions and tax breaks become virtually impossible to remove—a pattern that resonates in other emerging market contexts (and in advanced economies as well). The Mexican government initially followed Latin America's widespread attempts to implement a gross asset tax, called the minimum asset tax, in Mexico. As with the ISR, the incidence was on the largest taxpayers, who could maintain their preferences, and it did not have much of an effect on addressing the poor revenue collections.

Stand alone reforms to specific taxes had not been successful, presaging the reform efforts to follow. To remove preferences and deductions, governments must confront powerful vested interests. Reform thus becomes complicated if some parties can use state interests to block measures in the senate. In 2007, the Mexican government was not able to overcome senate opposition to address loopholes in either the ISR or the VAT. An indirect mechanism was consequently chosen—a minimum tax in the VAT mode credited against the ISR through a single-rate business tax, *Impuesto Empresarial a Tasa Única* (IETU), which replaced the minimum assets tax. It worked initially but soon began to be affected by the distortions and exemptions that were the problem in the ISR in the first place.

Passage of the IETU reform was facilitated by a Chinese-style stop-loss provision and a rationalization of intergovernmental transfers to ensure that no state lost revenues because of the reforms. The "reform package" consequently had sufficient support to be approved by Mexico's congress. Although the single business-tax rate had some disincentive effects, the underlying value-added design did not disadvantage investments as much as a turnover tax would have.

A later attempt in 2010 also failed to close VAT loopholes by providing households with additional benefits through the *Oportunidades* conditional cash transfer. First, many of the losers from a VAT reform are urban households, and conditional cash transfer provides benefits mainly to poor rural households, making it an inappropriate compensation mechanism for many energy price and tax reforms. Second, the main losers in a VAT reform tend to be firms with vested interests and possibly some states, given Mexico's revenue-sharing system. The interactions between the VAT loopholes and the provisions in the ISR present formidable incentives to evade taxes and engage in informal activities, but such incentives cannot be addressed by conditional cash transfers to poor rural households.

Other problems with conditional cash transfers became apparent in Mexico and are relevant for countries considering both tax reforms and energy price adjustments. The principal problem is that conditional cash transfers create a poverty trap that encourages informality and reduces mobility. Poverty rates and uptake of *Oportunidades* rose simultaneously for 20 years in Chiapas. Conditional cash transfers were finally abolished in 2019 (by a left-wing government, although the Peña Nieto administration had attempted a significant overhaul in 2014).

As stressed by some academics, a turnover tax is offered as a third-best option for countries that have difficulty with revenue generation (Best and others 2015). This was never an option in Mexico, because the government knew that such a tax would add to the cost of doing business and would adversely affect Mexico's competitive position with its trading partners.

The Mechanisms of Tax Evasion by Mexican Firms

Firms use two mechanisms for evading or avoiding taxes. In the first mechanism, firms avoid VAT or ISR by remaining below the annual turnover threshold or by splitting into smaller firms. This is the typical case discussed in the literature and formalized in Keen and Mintz (2004). The revenue losses from such reconstitution are likely to be small, prompting a strong recommendation from international agencies that countries raise the registration threshold to reduce burdens on the tax administration (IMF and others 2015). Yet small traders and small and medium enterprises exercise enormous political power in countries such as Pakistan and are an obstacle to meaningful reforms—unless losses might be shown to offset by a rationalization of income taxes, as in Singapore (Ahmad 2018a). Rationalization, however, requires the establishment of an arm's length tax administration that does not impose additional costs of doing business, especially on small firms.

The second tax evasion mechanism, and by far the more important element in Levy's (2008) view, is outright evasion by larger firms, which also have much greater political clout than smaller traders in a more advanced economy such as Mexico's.

The principal channels for rent-seeking are twofold:

1. Incentives to cheat are generated through tax systems that encourage pricing discontinuities and arbitrage. Such systems may charge multiple VAT rates for the same goods, implement exemptions for border regions, and privilege *maquiladoras* through creation of SEZs. Together with loopholes in direct taxes, high marginal rates that add to the cost of doing business, and domestic zero-rating, such incentives encourage and reward rent-seeking.
2. Exemptions from the VAT lead to absence of information on transactions, creating silos of tax information within tax groups and across tax instruments. Breaks in the value-added chain and presumptive mechanisms to estimate VAT liability, when used extensively as in Pakistan, prevent the self-policing aspects of the VAT from operating. Such breaks are exacerbated by weak or

ineffective administration for components of the tax system. In Mexico, the weakness was the REPECOS system that strongly encouraged informality.

Before Mexico's 2013 VAT reform, both channels for rent-seeking operated in tandem, as summarized in Figure 9.1.

Figure 9.1 identifies several tax evaders under the pre-2014 regime:

- REPECOS and adjusters. The REPECOS tax regime was for small businesses with turnover below Mex$2 million. Few REPECOS firms paid any tax in Mexico. Although the VAT has no legal registration threshold, turnover below Mex$2 million became the de facto threshold. Smaller firms were effectively ignored by the Mexican Tax Adminstration, but this group of taxpayers also includes the "adjusters," who legally reduce turnover to stay under the REPECOS threshold.
- *Enanos*, or "ghosts." Many so-called *enanos* firms are too large to be eligible for REPECOS but pretend to be eligible regardless. Furthermore, because the enforcement of REPECOS is weak, businesses know that if they at least pay some REPECOS dues, the state governments and the Mexican Tax Administration will likely be satisfied. These firms are the ghosts identified by Kanbur and Keen (2014).

Figure 9.1. Incentives to Cheat in Mexico

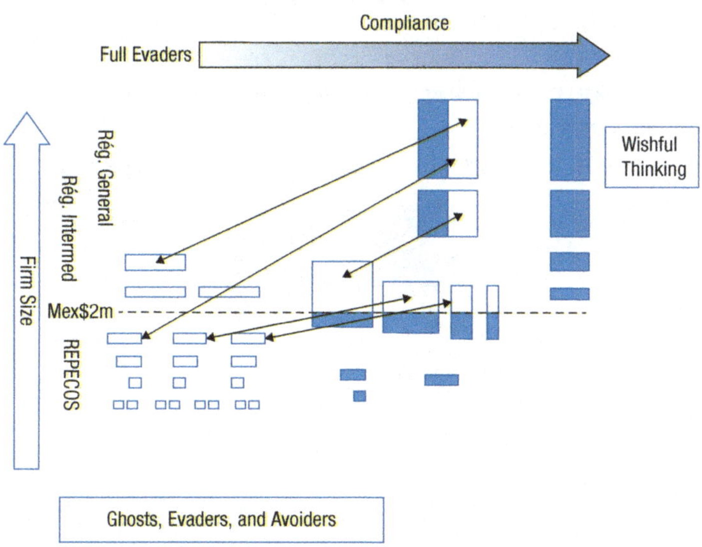

Source: Ahmad 2018a.

Note: The rectangles represent firms, and the size of the rectangle represents the size of the firm. Rég. general = the regular tax regime applying to large taxpayers; Rég. intermed = the tax regime for intermediate-size taxpayers; REPECOS (*Regimen de Pequeños Contribuyentes*) = the small firms subject to administration by the states. Academics and some international agencies think of large taxpayers as compliant and honest, which is wishful thinking.

- Larger firms. As argued by Levy (2008), middle- and large-size firms often hide transactions, turnover, employment, and profits by trading with the *enanos*, truly REPECOS-eligible small firms, and other rent-seekers. Larger firms can thereby reduce payroll and profit taxes by avoiding the VAT chain.
- "Honest" firms. International agencies often assume some firms are not able to evade taxation because they are either run by multinationals or too large to do so undetected. Yet, large firms are often the best-connected "vested interests." Moreover, multinationals are better able to avoid taxation than most large domestic firms, for example, by moving corporate headquarters to low-tax jurisdictions, such as Ireland or Luxembourg, if not The Bahamas or Panama. However, we maintain the "honest" firm categorization in Figure 9.1 for completeness (the dark blue squares to the right—whereas the "true" characterization is in the white and blue squares immediately to the left).

All possible forms of VAT fraud are greatly facilitated by the existence of the *maquiladora* tax system, particularly by its lack of transparency. This allows firms to hide and disguise taxable activities, including within the rest of the country, and the ever-widening definition allows more and more firms to take advantage.

Figure 9.2 summarizes the revenue losses created by interaction between the *maquiladora* system (that is, SEZs) and the VAT. The figure depicts a standard carousel fraud. Businesses that import inputs can pass the input credits to another

Figure 9.2. The *Maquiladora* Sink Holes: Potential Reliance on Special Economic Zones

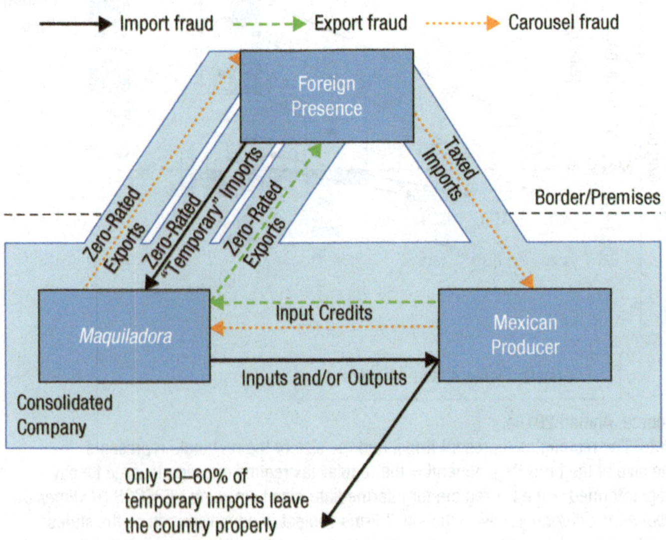

Source: Ahmad 2018a.

Mexican firm, which can then export and claim the input credits. This fraud is greatly facilitated by the ability of *maquiladoras* to operate as part of a group of firms both within Mexico and abroad, with few reporting requirements to the Mexican authorities. Figure 9.2 also depicts a more straightforward export fraud in which a pair of related firms, one a *maquiladora*, collude to claim an input credit for a transaction that never occurred.

Figure 9.2 depicts the most pernicious fraud as well. Under the *maquiladora* system, bonded imports do not incur a VAT liability, provided that the transformed outputs are reexported. These inputs or their resulting transformed outputs are then passed to another Mexican company, which sells them in the domestic market without ever having paid VAT on the imported inputs. Customs data show that only an estimated 50 to 60 percent of the inputs imported under this system ever leave Mexico.

A comparison of the profits declared to the Mexican Tax Administration versus those implied by the economic census (which may itself be an underestimate) indicates the possible extent of underdeclarations and their components and support the Levy (2008) hypothesis. The analysis also shows that both the incentives and the ability to cheat exist for firms of all sizes. Small and medium enterprises do not appear to have a monopoly on cheating the tax administration. As firms fail to declare turnover and profits, they push workers into informal contracts to further disguise the scale of their operations. Thus, one type of informality, cheating, thrives on and perpetuates the traditional definition of informality—workers without formal benefits.

The Mexican Tax Reform Package of 2013

The political economy of Mexico's 2013 package of tax reforms was instructive—with all main taxes reformed together rather than treated separately. Because these reforms were designed to close loopholes, the interactions between a reformed VAT and income taxes were particularly important. In addition to the elimination of policy loopholes, the principal administrative reform was thus to replace REPECOS and the intermediate tax regime by a new *Régimen de Incorporación Fiscal* (RIF) integrated with the regular tax system. This required small taxpayers below the Mex$2 million threshold to use a simple cash-flow electronic accounting package (provided by the Mexican Tax Administration) and issue electronic invoices.

All taxpayers were accordingly brought under the Mexican Tax Administration's registration, compliance, and audit. Anomalies in the VAT itself were removed, as were border-region rates, whereas the standard rate was retained. The goal of the reform was to bring the whole value chain under the Mexican Tax Administration's supervision. The income tax was rationalized, but its rate structure was maintained.

With the full VAT in operation and electronic tracking of invoices, the ability of firms to engage in hidden transactions was effectively eliminated. Mexico thus had little need to maintain the IETU minimum tax, and it was abolished, reducing administrative burdens on taxpayers. The only additional tax introduced was a carbon tax or petroleum excise, above an adjustment of petroleum prices toward world prices.

The political economy of the reform was important, and the losers with respect to one major tax were offset by gainers on others. The reform was supported by all parties, because the package would enhance the basis for long-term growth, minimize the effect on poor households by excluding unprocessed food from the VAT, and create a basic minimum pension that would not generate labor market disincentives or a poverty trap, ensuring that the most vulnerable, especially in urban areas, would not be affected by relative price changes. Furthermore, the reform maintained VAT information flows, because unprocessed food does not enter the middle of the production chain. The only compensatory measure was the basic pension for those older than 65 years who did not have alternative occupational pensions. The typical recommendation to facilitate the adjustment in energy prices through *Oportunidades* was not implemented.[2]

Outcomes for the 2013 reforms exceeded expectations. Despite the period of low growth affecting much of Latin America, largely attributable in Mexico to depressed petroleum prices, the 2013 tax reform offset most of the fall in petroleum revenues, raising over 4 percent of GDP by 2016 with no increase in the rates of the major tax instruments.

NATIONAL TAX REFORMS IN CHINA

China is of interest because its tax and structural reforms were closely linked. After Deng Xiaoping introduced the Responsibility System in the late 1970s, both total revenues collected and the proportion shared upward with the central government fell precipitously, yet incentives for producers improved. Yet, because China did not have a central tax administration, the total tax-to-GDP ratio fell from 25 percent to about 10 percent by 1992/93 (Ahmad, Rydge, and Stern 2013), despite attempts to encourage local officials to share revenue with the central government (Gao 1995). The central share of tax revenues, which had been about 55 percent of total revenues at the start of the Responsibility System reform, fell to well under 30 percent by 1993 (Figure 9.3) as local governments sought to protect local interests in the face of falling revenue collections.

In the absence of modern fiscal institutions and instruments, the structural changes generated a fiscal crisis. The plummeting tax-to-GDP ratio, as well as the decline in the share going to the central government, seriously compromised the central government's ability to maintain macroeconomic stability, ensure redistribution, and meet the fundamental responsibilities of a nation-state. By 1993/94, China needed a major tax reform to consolidate the structural reforms initiated

[2] *Oportunidades* had a negative effect on incentives to participate in the labor market, generated no reduction in poverty in the poorest state, and had been open to diversion of funds in key states (as seen during 2012). *Oportunidades* was replaced in 2014 by *Prospera*, which focused on training and supporting small business to encourage participation in the labor market. *Prospera* was abolished by the administration of President Obrador in 2019.

Figure 9.3. China's Evolution of Tax/GDP Ratios and Central-Local Shares

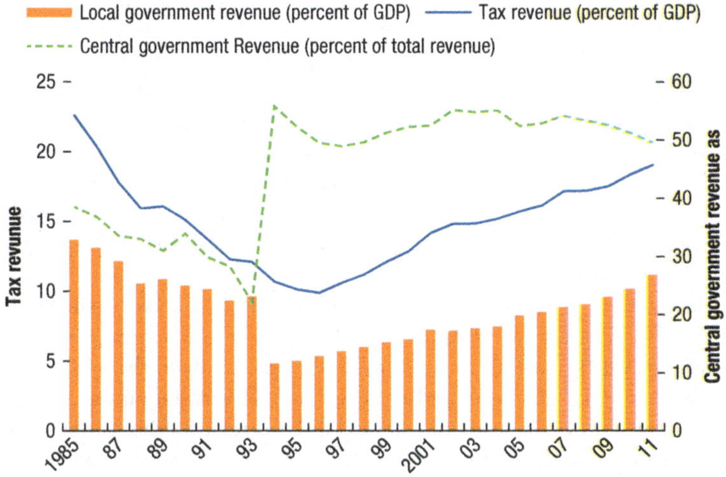

Source: Ahmad, Rydge, and Stern 2013.

by the Responsibility System and to strengthen the central government's ability to maintain macroeconomic stability, redistribution, and public investment (Ahmad, Gao, and Tanzi 1995; Ahmad, Rydge, and Stern 2013).

The 1993/94 Fiscal Reform Package: Consolidating Structural Reforms

The establishment of the (central) State Administration of Taxation, along with central revenue-raising powers, was facilitated by the introduction of an investment-type VAT in 1994. However, a package of tax administration and policy reforms was needed to minimize losses and share benefits across rich and poor provinces alike. The key elements of the reform "package" include the following:

- Preventing losses among local governments through a hold harmless clause guaranteed all provinces 1993 levels of revenues in absolute terms in perpetuity.
- Providing a share of the (increasing) revenues from the VAT with the provinces that generated the value added—mainly benefiting the richer ones.
- Introducing a modern equalization framework enabled all provinces to provide similar services with similar effort. The version adopted in China was based on a simplified version of the Australian model and benefited the poorer provinces.

The most innovative component of the reform package was a revenue-return policy to return additional funds to where they were generated, that is, the better-connected provinces, but on a gradually decreasing basis. This measure was critical in concentrating resources toward production hubs, leveraging existing connectivity to generate investment, exports, and employment in the short term.

The VAT that China initially implemented applied only to manufacturing and imports, because of both administrative constraints and the need to leave at least one tax handle in provincial hands (namely the local business tax on services). Furthermore, the VAT was the investment type; that is, the VAT on capital purchases could not be offset against the VAT due on sales. This, again, was to meet revenue targets, and this formulation of the VAT was simpler for China's nascent tax administration to enforce. Almost 15 years later, in the aftermath of the 2008 global economic crisis, there was pressure to reduce the cost of doing business and protect Chinese competitiveness. The investment-type VAT was converted to a consumption-type VAT, with VAT on capital purchases permitted to be offset against VAT on sales.

China conducted a further reform in 2015, similar to the reforms in Mexico in 2013/14,[3], to integrate the subnational local business tax on services with the VAT. This reform aimed to reduce the costs of doing business, with the VAT on service inputs being offset against sales and exports. The VAT integration was also needed to create an integrated economic area—and to remove the borders around Shenzhen, a successful SEZ, to facilitate development of regional links needed for a high-tech zone. Business tax integration with the VAT was expected to reduce revenues, given the additional input tax offsets and refunds, yet revenues increased. As in Mexico, expanding the VAT to cover the full value chain made tax evasion more difficult for firms, thus improving compliance, including for income taxes.

Effects of the Chinese Tax Reform Package on Informality

In China, as in Mexico, major tax reforms designed to reduce the cost of doing business and revenue loss centralized the wide-area tax policy framework and integrated tax administration. The consequence has been a loss of simple subnational tax handles, constraining subnational access to credit and ability to finance basic services and essential investments. Cities have continued to rely on land value capture, particularly land sales, to finance investment.

Shenzhen is an example of a successful SEZ. Yet the borders around Shenzhen were removed after VAT reforms in 2015, because the central government began refunding VAT on exports regardless of whether the export was from an SEZ. At the same time, Shenzhen suspended the land sales model, because it became clear that younger families could no longer afford to live in the metropolitan area and were being forced into the informal sector.

Information generated by the VAT is also an important tool for monitoring investment and production of natural resources, including petroleum. Again, international financial institutions typically recommend that VAT should not apply on capital goods in the petroleum sector, especially because this is to be refunded promptly on exports and is not a source of additional revenues. This practice, however, means that complete information on operations of the petroleum sector is not

[3] The Mexican tax policy package was enacted at the end of 2013—and the integration of the small taxpayer regime was undertaken during 2014.

collected. As demonstrated in the landmark Ribadu Committee Report (PRSTF 2012) on the Nigerian petroleum sector, revenue losses could be averted if complete records were available and the VAT and treasury single accounts would play a role.

The more appropriate mechanism, especially in countries with prevalent informality, may well be what is practiced in China—to apply VAT on capital and other inputs in the petroleum sector to be offset against VAT liability on outputs, or zero-rated when exports are verified. As recommended in the Ribadu report (PRSTF 2012), tax systems must also track the flow of funds, including between petroleum companies' and governments' financial information management systems.

Whereas distributional effects depend on combinations of taxes and social policies, a simple VAT design with minimal exemptions reduces the need for compensatory measures. For instance, as in Mexico, excluding unprocessed basic staples (wheat, rice, corn) was designed to protect the poor (as also argued by Ahmad and Stern [1991] in the context of India and Pakistan). In the final analysis, the best "safety net" available in Mexico is a combination of the nondistortionary minimum pension (65 years and older), that did not affect incentives to participate in the labour market, together with sustained job creation, especially in the lagging regions of southern Mexico. Similar issues arise with job creation in the western regions of China, and the absence of subnational own-source revenues is a major constraint to the "rebalancing" sought in China, especially in response to the pandemic. Mexico will face similar constraints, and connectivity investments are not likely to be sufficient, even if necessary.

Effects of the Chinese Tax Reform Package on Sustainable Development

The success of the 1993/94 Chinese reform is striking. In addition to the strengthening of the fiscal space, more than 750 million people were taken out of poverty, 500 million moved from rural to urban areas, and 150 million moved to the historic as well as new coastal hubs (for example, Shenzhen). However, now Chinese cities face difficulty financing sustainable basic spending. Local government land sales have led to urban sprawl and generated off-budget financing vehicles that created rent-seeking opportunities (Wang, Wu, and Ye 2018). Sprawl, in turn, has accentuated spatial inequalities, with adverse effects on the formal employment of migrant households (as is typically seen around megacities in emerging market economies, including in Africa). Although smaller interior cities also engage in land sales, lower appreciation rates make them less attractive to investors than metropolitan areas.

National investment in connectivity infrastructure is necessary for developing less well-off regions, but as the Chinese example illustrates, it is not sufficient to ensure balanced development or convergence. Firms are unlikely to move to smaller cities that lack adequate infrastructure and agglomeration economies, including availability of workers with the requisite skills. Workers may still want to migrate to megacities, drawn to better services and higher-paying jobs. Thus, the pressure of migration to megacities continues, with the likelihood that informal settlements will grow even larger.

BENEFICIAL PROPERTY TAXES FOR SUBNATIONAL SERVICE PROVISION

Property taxes have long been regarded as the main source of finance for local spending, particularly in the United States. High property taxes in the US context are synonymous with good public service delivery. In most US cities, property taxes are linked closely with property values that reflect the quality of public education and other basic services.

A robust property tax system is also the foundation for ratings that govern municipal bond issuance for infrastructure investments. Mobility, as a key feature of political competition models, is significant: taxpayers will move to jurisdictions that provide better education, even if the property tax rates are higher. However, for the US-style property tax system to work, property titles must be clearly delineated. Furthermore, municipalities must be capable of real-time adjustment of property values.

Such conditions, however, do not exist in many parts of the world. The property tax is thus moribund in much of Africa, Latin America, and Asia. Experiments in China, in Shanghai and Chongqing, to introduce versions of US-style property tax have not been successful, given the political difficulty of taxing fixed-income households in potentially expensive areas, as well as defining property titles and valuations.

In emerging market and developing economies, with few exceptions, the "standard" property tax has been dismal in raising revenues. In Africa, only Mauritius (briefly) and South Africa exceeded 1 percent of GDP, and the Latin American average is just 0.3 percent of GDP. An additional problem is that the standard property tax is typically based on the US ownership and valuation model that discriminates against informal sector people who seldom own properties that they occupy. Informal migrants typically cannot use ad hoc contracts as proof of residence to qualify for loans and credit for purchase of assets or improvement of property, or even to access public services.

Given difficulties in establishing ownership and making timely valuations, the United Kingdom abandoned the ownership and valuation model of recurrent taxation of housing in the early 1990s and moved toward a "banded system" linked to the cost of local services or benefits provided by local councils. However, ownership and valuation were retained for business premises, which tend to have a more robust market, and all property sales.

In Mexico, rate setting at the state level with administration at the local level has also generated severe disincentive effects. Local administrations have no accountability, and proximity to taxpayers generates opportunities for rent-seeking and favoring friends and relatives. The property tax is largely dysfunctional, with collections below the dismal Latin American and Caribbean average of 0.3 percent of GDP (Ahmad, Brosio, and Pöschl 2015). In India, although the tax has been in force since the late 1870s, collections are lower than in Mexico. In both countries, this tax just does not work very well (Rao 2012). Like in the United Kingdom, reforming a long-standing tax requires strong leadership to initiate change—or a crisis like the pandemic.

China experimented in Shanghai and Chongqing with variants of the US-type recurrent property tax, but neither city was successful. The problem is not only a lack of information on who owns which property or what the market valuations might be, but also the political economy conundrum of fixed- and low-income households living in expensive neighborhoods.

Local governments in China rely mainly on shared revenues and transfers, as well as land sales in some cases, and there has been telescoping budgetary pressures at the lowest levels of government as additional functions are devolved. And local government borrowing was not permitted, except through local government financing vehicles. As mentioned above, land sales typically accrue to off-budget accounts of local government financing vehicles, are not particularly transparent, and are open to rent-seeking, often circumventing national constraints on debt issuance. The incentives from increased subnational budget pressures and poor information on the local government financing vehicles led to a huge increase in unregulated subnational debt, particularly after the 2008–10 global financial crisis, when local governments played a key role in countercyclical policies on behalf of the central government.

China introduced a municipal bond system in 2015 to reduce the growing problem of subnational debt. However, because there are no effective own-source revenues, the measure has not succeeded in reducing subnational risks. To be sustainable, a municipal bond system requires effective own-source revenue that allows a local government to set rates at the margin, even if a band is set by the national legislature. A band for some property sales taxes has already been centrally legislated: provinces choose a range within the band, then cities pick a rate. This mechanism could serve as own-source revenue if it were applied to a more substantive base, such as recurrent beneficial property taxation—even if, as in China, all administration is centralized.

A Beneficial Property Tax Linked to Public Services

An attractive alternative to the US-type property tax model is to bypass the valuation system altogether and link property-based tax to area and location, as well as the cost of public services. Such a Marshallian "benefit-tax" proposal can help governments overcome political resistance and link taxes paid to services provided (Ahmad, Brosio, and Pöschl 2015). The ownership titling difficulties can also be finessed, because the benefit tax can be based on occupancy rather than ownership (unless the property is vacant).[4] Linking property taxes to public services is also current practice in the United Kingdom. Former Prime Minister Margaret Thatcher abandoned the traditional property tax because of difficulties in establishing ownership and keeping valuation changes current.[5] Valuation requirements

[4] Establishment of ownership is relevant for China but also Senegal and India.

[5] The United Kingdom raised more with the property tax (4.0 percent of GDP) than the United States with the traditional property tax (about 3.5 percent of GDP). See the IMF's (2014) *Government Finance Statistics Yearbook 2013.*

are no longer binding in a system that links property use to the cost of local services. However, an accurate map of properties is needed.

Satellite imagery can prove a useful tool and is now highly developed and readily available in most parts of the world. Satellite mapping of properties cannot be easily evaded, so governments can bypass the corruption that takes place in appraising property areas and structures. Another new area for research, being examined even in sub-Saharan Africa (see Ahmad, Brosio and Gerbrandy 2018), is the use of blockchain technology to register property transactions. With extensive property records, governments will be better able to detect evasion of both property and income taxes. Blockchain technology also has useful applications in monitoring forestry and natural resources, as well as stopping illegal logging and mining.

A close link remains, however, between own-source taxes, transfers, and expenditures. This is partly related to the resource envelope, but also the incentives local officials face. Local officials need own-source revenue handles if they are to be held accountable for local spending that comes with hard budget constraints. If municipalities are able to access deficit-filling transfers, the positive incentive effects of the proposed tax system will not materialize. The transfers generate perverse incentives, as local governments are loath to improve revenue collections for fear of losing reliable revenue that carries no local political costs. This perpetuates the culture of "fiscal dentistry"—transfers to fill deficits—that was once pervasive in India at all levels (Rao 2002).

In an assessment for China based on a six-city sample, Ahmad and others (2020) show that a simple area- and location-based tax on occupancy linked to basic services (including basic education) or benefits (including for informal sector workers) can raise revenues quickly (with a target of 2 percent of city GDP), significantly improve income distribution (demonstrated by major reductions in the Atkinson inequality measure, appropriately weighted), and anchor the system of municipal bonds, thus reducing financial risks. Given the location basis for setting tax rates, Guangzhou, the most economically advanced city, generates a much higher rate per square meter than the smaller and less well-off cities. This higher rate also sends taxpayers appropriate signals about the relative costs of migrating to the congested metropolitan areas along China's eastern coast.

Yet, for a beneficial property tax system to work most effectively, the cost of public services should include a provision for informal sector workers, and the revenue base should be standardized according to an equalization framework that provides similar levels of services at similar levels of tax effort. As with any tax and transfer reform, the political economy aspects are critical. The reform must not create incentives that increase workers' migration into the informal sector in metropolitan areas. The benefit-tax agenda consequently needs to be developed with the aim of creating smaller employment hubs—or "poles of development" as proposed in Senegal (World Bank 2016).

An occupancy-based property tax would also enable informal households to more easily access credit and essential public services, including preventive health care, strengthening the ability of urban areas to withstand future pandemics. In providing a basis for informal sector households to integrate with the established citizenry, establishment of an occupancy-based property tax is crucial for emerging market and developing economies.

Kireyev and Mansoor (2016), in keeping with the revenue potential estimates from the World Bank, propose a target of 2 percent of GDP from a property tax in Senegal. This is probably feasible in the medium term, but as Ahmad, Brosio, and Gerbrandy (2018) argued for Senegal and Tanzania, a target of 1 percent of GDP should be easier to meet at least initially. Administration of the tax could be facilitated with a new streamlined tax administration structure for the property tax based on satellite imagery and blockchain technology. However, linking the property tax with basic public services is critical in generating political acceptability.

Tax-Benefit Links at Different Levels of Government

A considered proposal for the property tax to finance local operations will likely include several components:

1. The area- and location-based tax on housing would not preclude the value-based approach for other types of property, such as for commercial enterprises.
2. The value-based property tax should apply to commercial properties, as the market is typically vigorous and the political economy constraint of low-income households in expensive neighborhoods does not apply.
3. All property sales should be subject to the value-based transfer tax, or stamp duty, as in China and the United Kingdom.
4. The area-based tax would be based on occupancy. An occupancy-based property tax would provide migrant households and informal sector workers with benefits, enabling them to apply for loans and access basic services for which proof of residence is required. Area-based and value-based property taxes, thus, should not be seen as mutually exclusive.
5. The beneficial aspect of the tax is critical and needs to be carefully calibrated. Providing benefits solely to poorer migrants might not be politically acceptable to the broad population of taxpayers, even if it reduces inequality. As seen in the China simulations, a wider benefit for all households would be inequality reducing and likely to reduce political resistance.

An occupancy-based beneficial property tax of the sort described would be attractive to all residents, including migrants and informal sector workers. By definition, targeting city revenues about 1–2 percent of local GDP would generate a significantly higher tax per square meter in richer cities, such as Dakar or Mexico City, than in smaller interior cities. Higher taxes would send a market-based signal to workers and temper incentives to migrate to already congested and polluted metropolitan areas.

Cities need a proper system of local own-source revenues before they are able to sustainably borrow for investment without adversely affecting the interests of migrants and informal sector workers. It is important to align incentives for a clean environment with employment generation in clean, compact, and connected hubs.

It is also important to recognize that public-private partnerships and municipal bond systems generate local liabilities, and repayment schedules need to be linked to own-source revenue generation. Otherwise, liabilities might be hidden until there is a crisis, and accentuate risks, as during the 2008–10 financial crisis in Europe (Ahmad, Bordignon, and Brosio 2016).

CONCLUSION

Two dimensions of informality are addressed in this chapter: (1) firms "cheating" to evade taxation on transactions, wages, and profits; and (2) workers engaging in often invisible activities, not paying taxes but also excluded from most public services and benefits.

The first type of informality is greatly facilitated by the second—that is, people willing to work without formal contracts or benefits generate rents for firms, but at a cost of greater inefficiency and loss of public revenues. The second, more typical sort of informality, while generating employment for migrants, also generates inefficiencies, low standards of living, and significant inequalities. Informal workers and their families are excluded from basic services and are vulnerable to shocks and disease, including pandemics such as COVID-19.

The focus on national tax instruments is driven by the need to raise revenues to finance basic general government spending needs and create a unified economic space while reducing the cost of doing business and generating information. The political economy context of reform involves an assessment of gainers and losers and entails a link with multilevel finance, ensuring that no subnational jurisdiction or significant group suffers net losses. Subnational tax instruments, closely linked to the delivery of basic services and SDGs, form a beneficial nexus that also helps address traditional informality.

There is increasing evidence that inappropriately designed policy prescriptions result in what Levy (2008) termed "good intentions, bad outcomes." These policies are often borrowed from the most advanced economies to address income redistribution objectives. Yet exemptions and multiple rates in the VAT and complex means-tested benefits, including conditional cash transfers, may not result in the desired objectives while jeopardizing revenue requirements for the SDGs. Such "bad outcomes" were seen in Mexico and partially redressed in the 2013 reforms, as well as in countries like Indonesia and Pakistan.

A key element in generating revenues and also reducing cheating is information on the full value chain from a "clean" VAT without exemptions that affect business-to-business transactions. A clean VAT also reduces the cost of doing business and helps create a level playing field for investments and exports. This was the objective of the 2013 Mexico reforms, with the integration of REPECOS into the VAT (reversing a recommendation from international financial institutions to focus on large taxpayers) and the 2015 China reforms, when the local business tax on services was folded into the VAT on goods administered by the central government. In both countries, revenues increased significantly as the ability to evade income taxes decreased. This tax-on-tax interaction (the VAT tends to be proportional at best, or mildly progressive if basic food items are excluded) is indeed a better mechanism to raise income tax revenues than targeting nonwage sources of personal income that tend to be difficult to track.

The main drawback to centralization of broad tax instruments is that it leaves subnational governments with relatively few tax handles. This, in turn, impedes progress on the SDGs, which could most effectively be met in clean, compact, and connected cities and through local action. A local tax system should not only finance key components of the SDGs but also generate incentives and market-based signals to slow the growth of informal settlements in the urban periphery.

In China, centralization of broad tax instruments has reinforced land value capture methods, such as land sales, to finance local priorities (Wang, Wu, and Ye 2018). Despite some success, land value capture has resulted in growing urban sprawl with the development of megacities, loss of prime agricultural land, and encouragement of off-budget "public" activities of dubious benefit. The metropolises along the eastern coast of China, as with Dakar, Jakarta, Karachi, and Mumbai, continue to draw migrants, often in informal settlements around the formal city boundaries. Local governments relying on shared revenues in the face of the COVID-19 pandemic have faced additional constraints as central governments have reduced national tax rates to address trade and health care shocks—this is true in all countries. In China, local governments have tried to resume land sales.

Property taxes have been suggested as the most appropriate subnational tax handle, but the traditional ownership valuation model has not worked in most emerging market economies (including China and Mexico), generating almost negligible revenues at best. The ownership basis does not suit informal sector migrants, who would gladly pay a tax (Ahmad, Brosio, Gerbrandy 2018) to show proof of residence, to enable their children to go to school, to visit health clinics, or to qualify for business loans. But the tax-benefit linkage is crucial.

Ongoing research in China and Mexico[6] has simulated the effects of a beneficial property tax based on a simplification of the current UK model. Occupants, not owners (unless the property is empty), would pay a tax per square meter, and this would be higher in the richer localities. Given the minimal information requirements, a beneficial property tax could be adopted quickly. Such a tax would improve access to public services and credit, which many informal households would welcome. The similarities between policy measures relevant for different political systems, as in China and Mexico, highlight the importance of own-source revenues and tax-benefit linkages.

---

[6] See Ahmad, Niu, and Xiao (2018) and Ahmad and others (2020) on China, and Ahmad and Viscarra (2020) on Mexico.

Local beneficial property tax options and links with basic health care and education are critical in the agenda to recover from the global pandemic, to address sustainable employment and informality. This would supplement a national tax agenda that addresses incentives to cheat while reducing the cost of doing business and creating a unified economic space for sustainable growth.

REFERENCES

Ahmad, E. 2015. "Multilevel Fiscal Institutions and Mechanisms for Reducing Tax Cheating: The Case of Mexico." In *Institutions of Intergovernmental Fiscal Relations*, edited by J. Kim and H. Blöchliger. Paris: Organisation for Economic Co-operation and Development.

Ahmad, E. 2018a. "Political Economy of Tax Reforms: Improving the Investment Climate, Addressing Inequality, and Stopping the Cheating." G24 Background Paper, Intergovernmental Group of Twenty-Four, Washington, DC.

Ahmad, E. 2018b. "Rebalancing in China—Fiscal Policies for Sustainable Growth." *Singapore Economic Review* 63 (4): 861–84.

Ahmad, E., and A. Mohammed. 2018. "Pakistan, the United States and the Bretton Woods Institutions: a continuing Great Game?" In *Routledge Handbook of Contemporary Pakistan*, edited by A. Pande. Routledge, New York.

Ahmad, E., and N. Stern. 1991. *Theory and Practice of Tax Reforms in Developing Countries*. Cambridge: Cambridge University Press.

Ahmad, E., and H. Viscarra. 2020. "Distribution and Revenue Effects of a 'Beneficial Property Tax' in Mexico." LSE/CUT Program on Financing Sustainable Urban Transitions in China and Mexico, London.

Ahmad, E., M. Bordignon, and G. Brosio. 2016. *Multilevel Finance and the Eurocrisis*. Cheltenham, UK: Elgar.

Ahmad, E., G. Brosio, and J. Gerbrandy. 2018. *Property Taxation: Economic Features, Revenue Potential, and Administrative Issues in a Development Context*. Luxembourg: Publications Office of the European Union.

Ahmad, E., G. Brosio, and C. Pöschl. 2015. "Local Property Taxes and Benefits in Developing Countries: Overcoming Political Resistance?" In *Handbook of Multilevel Finance*, edited by E. Ahmad and G. Brosio. Cheltenham, UK: Elgar.

Ahmad, E., M. Niu, and K. Xiao. 2018. *Fiscal Policy for Sustainable Development in China: Rebalancing in Guangdong*. Singapore: Springer.

Ahmad, E., Q. Gao, and V. Tanzi, eds. 1995. *Reforming China's Public Finances*. Washington, DC: International Monetary Fund.

Ahmad, E., J. Rydge, and N. Stern. 2013. "Structural Change Leads to Tax Reforms Leads to Structural Change." Paper presented at the China Development Research Forum, Beijing, March.

Ahmad, E., M. Niu, L. Wang, and M. Wang. 2020. "Financing Inclusive Urban Transition in China: The Role of a 'Beneficial' Property Tax." LSE/CUT Program on Financing Sustainable Urban Transitions in China and Mexico, London.

Antón, A., F. Hernández, and S. Levy. 2013. *The End of Informality in Mexico? Fiscal Reform for Universal Social Insurance*. Inter-American Development Bank, Washington, DC.

Best, M., H. Kleven, J. Spinnewijn, and M. Waseem, (2015), "Production versus Revenue Efficiency with Limited Tax Capacity." *Journal of Political Economy* 123 (6): 1311–55.

Fuentes Castro, H. J., A. Z., Carrillo, S. B. Cortés, and A. B. del Rivero. 2011. *Estudio de Evasión Fiscal en el Régimen de Pequeños Contribuyentes*. Instituto Tecnológico y de Estudios Superiores de Monterrey.

Gao, Q. 1995. "Problems in China's Intergovernmental Fiscal Relations, Tax-Sharing System, and Future Reform." In *Reforming China's Public Finances*, edited by E. Ahmad, Q. Gao, and V. Tanzi. Washington, DC: International Monetary Fund.

International Monetary Fund (IMF). 2014. *Government Finance Statistics Yearbook 2013.* Washington, DC: IMF.

International Monetary Fund (IMF), Organisation for Economic Co-operation and Development (OECD), United Nations (UN), and World Bank. 2015. "Options for Low Income Countries' Effective and Efficient Use of Tax Incentives for Investment." Report to the G20 Development Working Group, International Monetary Fund, Washington, DC.

Kanbur, R., and M. Keen. 2014. "Thresholds, Informality, and Partitions of Compliance." Working Paper 180136, Cornell University, Department of Applied Economics and Management, Ithaca, NY.

Keen, M., and J. Mintz. 2004. "The Optimal Threshold for a Value-Added Tax." *Journal of Public Economics* 88 (3–4): 559–76.

Kireyev, A., and A. Mansoor. 2016. "Making Senegal a Hub for West Africa." Departmental Paper 15/01, International Monetary Fund, Washington, DC.

Levy, S. 2008. *Good Intentions, Bad Outcomes: Social Policy, Informality, and Economic Growth in Mexico.* Washington, DC: Brookings Institution.

Marshall, A. 1890. *Principles of* London: Macmillan & Co.

Petroleum Revenue Special Task Force (PRSTF). 2012. "Report of the Petroleum Revenue Special Task Force." PRSTF, Abuja, Nigeria.

Rao, M. G. 2002. "Fiscal Decentralization in Indian Federalism." In *Managing Fiscal Decentralization*, edited by E. Ahmad and V. Tanzi. Abingdon-on-Thames, UK: Routledge.

Rao, M. G. 2012. "Property Tax Reform in India." NIPFP Working Paper, National Institute of Public Finance and Policy, New Delhi.

Wang, W., A. Wu, and F. Ye. 2018. "Land Use Reforms: Towards Sustainable Development in China." In *Fiscal Underpinnings for Sustainable Development in China: Rebalancing in Guangdong*, edited by E. Ahmad, M. Niu, and K. Xiao. Singapore: Springer.

World Bank. 2016. "Revue de l'Urbanisation: Villes Émergents pour un Sénégal Émergent." Report ACS14161, World Bank, Washington, DC.

CHAPTER 10

Beyond the COVID-19 Crisis: A Framework for Sustainable Government-to-Person Mobile Money Transfers

Sonja Davidovic, Soheib Nunhuck, Delphine Prady, and Herve Tourpe

BACKGROUND

As the coronavirus disease 2019 (COVID-19) crisis unfolded, countries across the world promptly expanded their social protection systems to provide support to workers and households. On average, countries have spent an additional 1 percent of GDP to expand existing social programs—insurance, assistance, and labor market–related—and have introduced new ones.[1] Additional fiscal outlays have mainly financed the expansion of social assistance systems to cover more than 1.8 billion people worldwide (Gentilini and others 2020).

Government-to-Person Social Transfers during an Unprecedented Crisis

Countries most often chose government-to-person (G2P) monetary transfers, representing about 51 percent of all social measures planned and implemented, with coverage more than doubling to 38 percent of the population, on average, over 5 months (Figure 10.1).

Scalability and reachability of G2P transfers are essential as the COVID-19 crisis requires governments to cast safety nets more broadly than for conventional shock

In this chapter, mobile money is defined as a digital medium of exchange and store of value using mobile money accounts, which are typically offered by a mobile network operator (MNO) or another entity in partnership with an MNO (Chhabra and Das 2019). Mobile money transfers have been instrumental in enabling governments to reach large swaths of population in need of income support during the COVID-19 pandemic, such as workers in the informal economy largely uncovered by existing safety nets. This chapter presents a comprehensive framework for including mobile money solutions in support of strengthened and sustainable social safety nets (Davidovic and others 2020).

[1] For a comparison of the magnitude of fiscal support in selected countries between the COVID-19 crisis and the global financial crisis, see Cassim and others (2020).

Figure 10.1. Existing, Additional, and Total Population Coverage of Monetary Transfers During COVID-19

(Percent of total population)

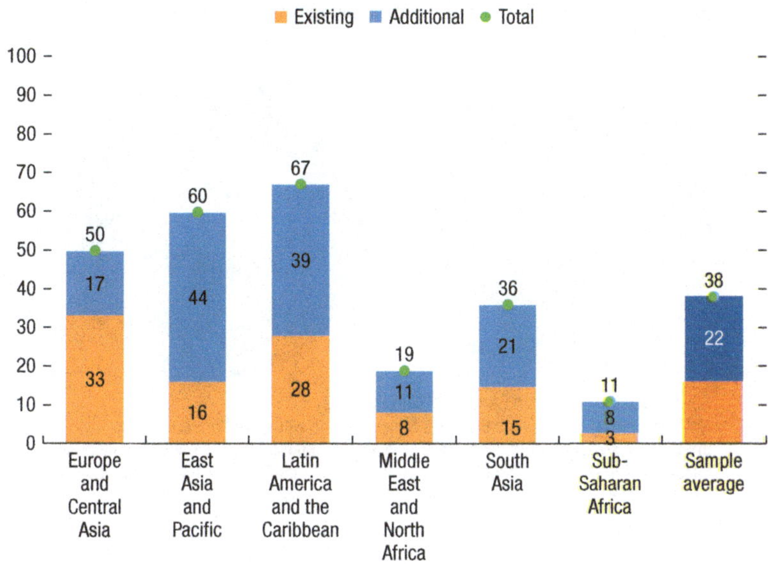

Source: Gentilini and others 2020.
Note: The sample consists of 57 countries. COVID-19 = coronavirus disease 2019.

response. The pandemic and containment measures are affecting all economic sectors, generating large negative income shocks disproportionately across the bottom half of the income distribution (Figure 10.2) and among informal business owners.[2] Many countries have combined benefit programs—monetary and in-kind, digital and analog, old and new—to broaden their support to households with little or no previous links to social protection systems and to maximize their reach.

The rapid expansion of G2P transfers bears several risks, from duplication and high administrative costs to the undermining of well-functioning social programs improperly repurposed for COVID-19 response efforts. For example, the Philippine government established an emergency subsidy program targeting 75 percent of its population and automatically enrolling beneficiaries of the country's flagship conditional cash transfer program, Pantawid Pamilyang Pilipino Program. However, some confusion over rules and unclear communication, combined with changes to the original program's selection and delivery modalities, created social discontent (Fischer, Dadap-Cantal, and Ramos 2020). Therefore, countries that have invested in building scalable and shock-responsive social safety nets are better positioned to face crises such as COVID-19.

[2] In countries with high prevalence of informality (Ayana Aga, Jolevski, and Muzi 2020), an informal business is often the sole source of income for the owner's family, with about 45 percent of businesses making $2 or less per day.

Figure 10.2. Population in Need of Support after a COVID-19–Type Shock

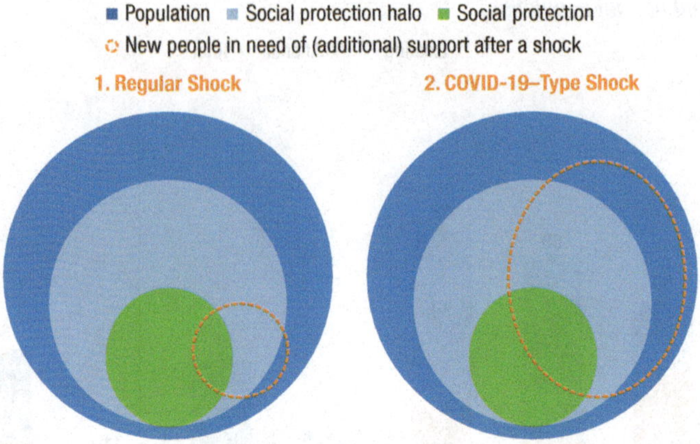

Source: Authors, based on Barca and Beazley 2019.
Note: The social protection halo refers to households whose welfare conditions are close to social programs' eligibility thresholds, making them vulnerable to income shocks and likely to become eligible for support systems. COVID-19 = coronavirus disease 2019.

Many emerging market and developing economies must build on weak and patchy social protection systems and frequently lack crucial information to further expand social protection. Often, existing social programs provide insufficient benefits and have low coverage at the bottom of the income distribution (the percentage of the bottom income quintile population receiving social protection benefits) and provide insufficient benefits (Figure 10.3, panel 1).

Informality further compounds these structural weaknesses (Figure 10.3, panel 2), because governments require verifiable information on employment and income to target public support on the basis of means. Such data are typically only available for workers in the formal sector who are officially registered as employees or are self-employed and potentially liable for payment of income and social security taxes. The lack of data for informal workers therefore restricts governments' ability to effectively target resources to the most affected households. Even in the formal sector, support channels have limited ability to provide employers with liquidity through loans or grants so that they can pay employees throughout the crisis.[3]

[3] Advanced economies also face challenges in providing timely and adequate support for workers and households, particularly gig workers, the self-employed, and independent contractors. Insufficient administrative capacity and complex enrollment processes have delayed the fulfillment of massive simultaneous requests for unemployment and social assistance benefits. For example, in March 2020, the UK Department for Work and Pensions had moved about 9,000 staff to deal with claims and was recruiting more to reduce delays in identification (ID) verification (the UK Secretary of State for the Department for Work and Pensions' oral statement to Parliament on May 4, 2020) and process the 950,000 applications received in one week, compared to a normal flow of about 100,000 applicants in any given two-week period.

Figure 10.3. Coverage of Social Assistance Programs and Share of Informal Economy, by Income Group and Region

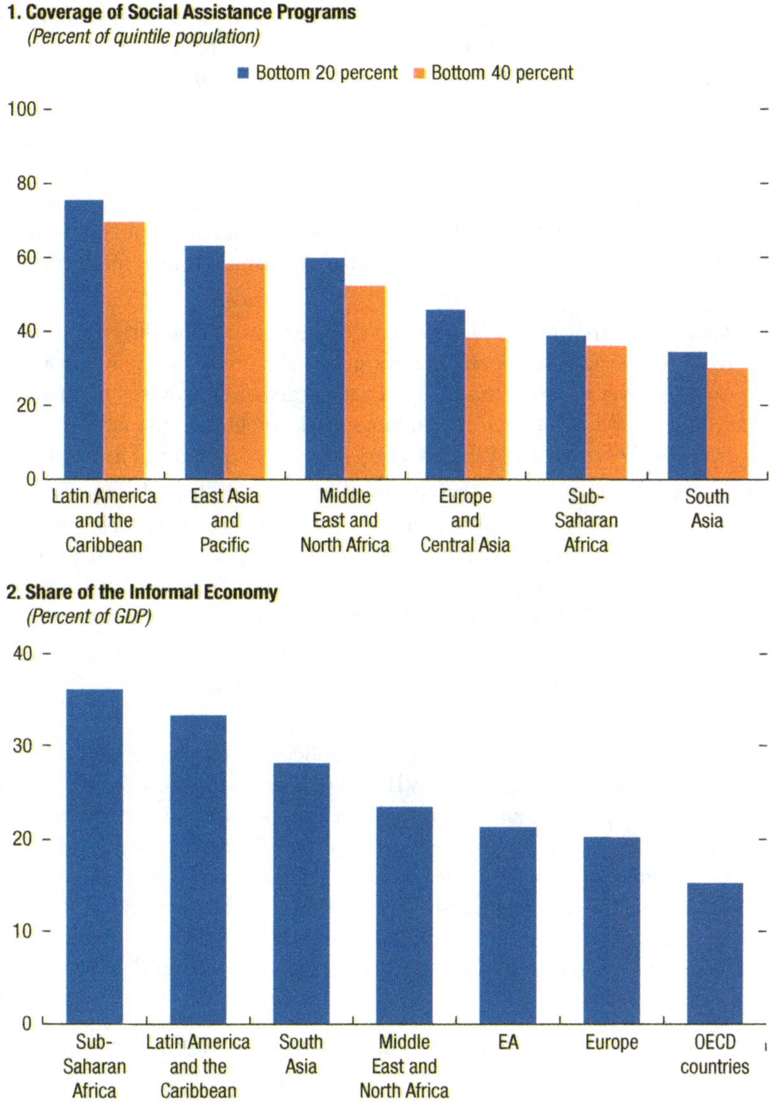

Sources: Medina and Schneider 2018; and World Bank Aspire data.
Note: Panel 1 excludes high-income countries (World Bank classification). OECD = Organisation for Economic Co-operation and Development.

The Importance of Basic Delivery Components

Governments' ability to reach workers and households with lifeline support differs vastly across countries, depending on the availability of basic delivery components (Prady 2020). Three integrated elements are at the core of the delivery of broad and adequate income support: (1) a universal identification (ID) system, (2) socioeconomic data on households, and (3) a mode of benefit delivery (Figure 10.4, panel 1).

Not all countries have the necessary elements to scale up emergency lifeline support. The unavoidable result is short-term prioritization across competing objectives. That is, broad population coverage of lifeline support, fiscal sustainability, and virus containment. We can therefore describe a simple taxonomy of countries by how ready their social assistance programs are to respond to crises (Figure 10.4, panel 2):

- *Ready.* Countries with wide prior coverage for two of the three elements are ready to leverage their delivery infrastructure and provide support at scale. For example, over the past decade, India has integrated its universal biometric ID system, *Aadhaar*, with bank accounts and social programs. Pakistan has a robust national ID system and a social registry covering 87 percent of its population.
- *In-Between.* Many countries have in place some or all of the necessary elements, but the elements may not be comprehensive. For example, Bangladesh and Togo have high mobile money penetration but no robust ID system. The Philippine social registry covers 75 percent of its population, but a reliable ID system is lacking and bank coverage is limited.[4]
- *Not Started.* This category consists mainly of low-income countries with a narrow or no safety net and only rudimentary delivery platforms (for example, Haiti and Lao P.D.R.).

Countries have put in place emergency policies to overcome delivery infrastructure weaknesses during the COVID-19 pandemic, with G2P mobile transfers being key to governments' response, especially in high-informality contexts. Governments are leveraging the high penetration of mobile phones and mobile accounts compared to bank access points[5] to rapidly scale up their monetary support to workers and households (Figure 10.5). Mobile money can be leveraged to reach informal business owners, who tend to use mobile money more often than the average population (Ayana Aga, Jolevski, and Muzi 2020).[6]

[4] The Philippines is developing its national digital ID, starting with 5 million individuals. Because bank coverage is limited, the country will need low-cost touchpoints, such as bank agents, to implement the system.

[5] According to the Global System for Mobile Communications Association (2020a), global averages per 100,000 adults are 11 banks and 33 ATMs, compared to 228 mobile money agents (the small retailers where customers can deposit to or withdraw cash from mobile accounts, buy phone airtime cards, and so on).

[6] World Bank survey data for nine cities in four African countries (Mozambique, Somalia, Zambia, and Zimbabwe) show that between 20 percent (in Nampula, Mozambique) and 82 percent (in Mogadishu, Somalia) of informal businesses use mobile money in their operations. In Mozambique, as measured by the World Bank's Global Findex, twice as many informal business owners use mobile money as the average population.

Figure 10.4. Basic Trinity of Population Reachability

1. Components

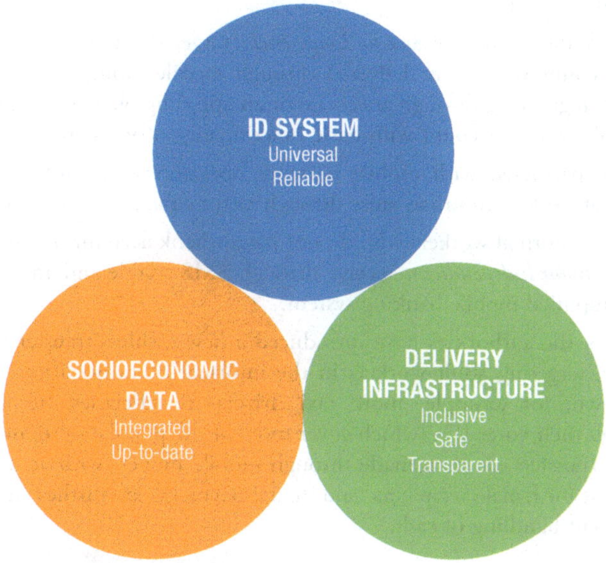

2. Coverage in Selected Countries
(percent)

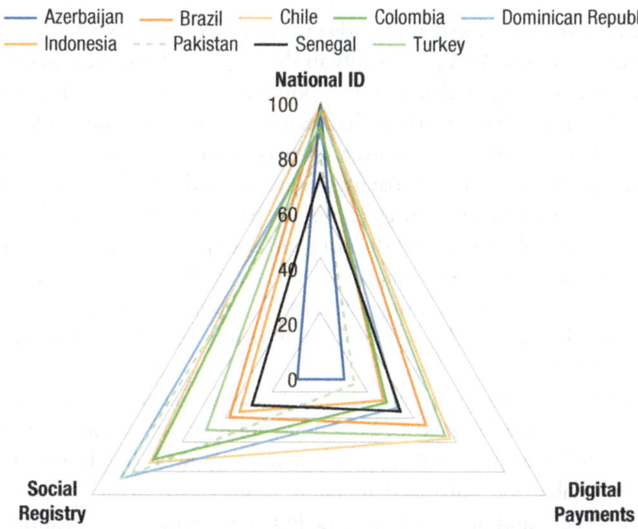

Sources: Leite and others 2017; World Bank Global Findex; and authors.
Note: "Digital payments" refers to the percentage of the population age 15 years and older who report having made a digital payment through mobile money, debit or credit card, mobile phone, or the internet in the past year.

Mobile networks can be used to achieve multiple objectives: (1) disseminate crucial information, (2) collect household and individual data to better target support, and (3) deliver money:

- In Brazil, the temporary *Auxílio Emergencial* targeted mainly at informal and own-account workers is delivered through mobile money accounts, with citizens registering through a website or an app. Eligible workers may open a mobile savings account with basic functionality at one state-owned bank.
- Nigeria partnered with mobile network operators to identify vulnerable informal workers in urban areas through airtime purchase patterns.
- In Peru, informal workers who do not have a bank account but are eligible for the *Bono Independiente* receive through SMS a code and an access link to a simplified mobile banking system.
- In Togo, the authorities have introduced a new cashless transfer program, *Novissi,* targeting adult workers in the informal economy affected by the lockdown, for example, moto taxi drivers. Beneficiaries are identified through their voter IDs (which cover more of the population than national IDs).[7] Transfers are then made through mobile money, with an additional payment for female recipients, and digital payments are further encouraged to prevent handling of cash.

Strong G2P Mobile Transfers for Strong Social Protection Systems

G2P mobile transfers present many advantages relative to other forms of governmental transfers (Table 10.1), especially in the context of social distancing. About 20 percent of emerging market and developing countries use cash for social benefits payments, often because their financial ecosystems remain underdeveloped (Lindert and others 2020). However, in-person cash provision presents many logistic (transportation, security, payment dates), health, and individual challenges (for example, costs to beneficiaries to receive payments at a scheduled time and place) that G2P mobile transfers do not. For example, in Niger, program recipients receiving cash had to travel approximately 2 kilometers (one way), or about half an hour, to receive the transfer, whereas the group receiving transfers through mobile money had to travel less than 0.5 kilometers (less than 10 minutes) (Aker and others 2016).

Mobile transfer platforms promote strong social protection systems that provide equitable and effective coverage for poor households and those vulnerable to poverty. G2P mobile transfers can support inclusive growth (by bringing financial accounts to enable the unbanked to build savings and credit history, empower women financially, and help small and medium enterprises grow within the formal

[7] The Financial Action Task Force (FATF) recently promoted a simplified, risk-based approach to using "trustworthy digital identity for . . . identifying people remotely for both onboarding and conducting transactions" (FATF 2020b).

Figure 10.5. Coverage of Financial Account, Mobile Phone Ownership, and Mobile Money Account, by Region, 2019

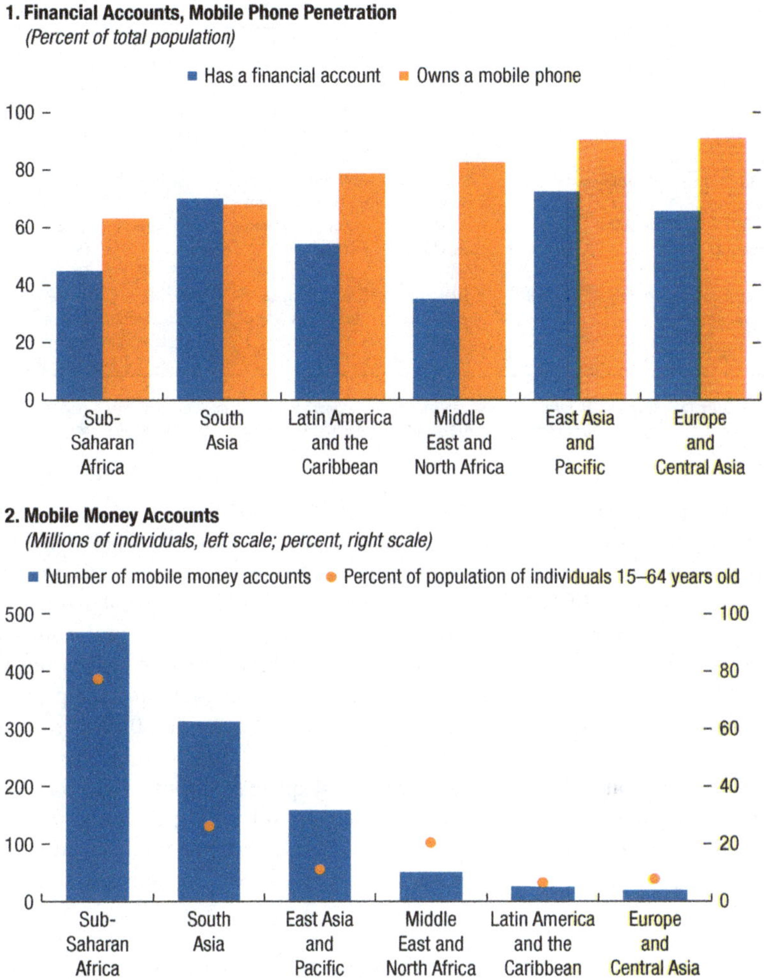

Source: Gelb, Mukherjee, and Navis 2020; and Global System for Mobile Communications Association, State of the Industry Report on Mobile Money 2019.

sector) and efficient government operations (by providing prompt support while maximizing public resources through more transparent and efficient management).[8]

[8] For a discussion on the importance of digital solutions for public finance management, see Una, Allen, and others (2020) and Una, van Eden, and others (2020).

TABLE 10.1.

Channels to Deliver G2P Payments

Format	How/Where to Receive	Where to Save	How/Where to Use	Pros	Cons	Examples
Cash	Post office, agents, bank	Home	Anywhere	Simple, trusted	Risk of waste and theft, human interaction	Ecuador, India
Money order	Post office, bank	Home	Can only be cashed out	Authentication, no bank account	Same as cash	Tunisia
Cash card	Post office, ATM	Home	Can only be cashed out	Authentication, no bank account	Same as cash	Brazil, Philippines
Bank account	Bank, ATM	Bank account	ATM, debit card, checks	Secure, no human interaction	Need bank account	Colombia, Peru, United States
Mobile payment	Remotely	Mobile	Merchants and agents	See "Strong G2P Mobile Transfers" subsection	Need mobile phone, digital literacy	Jordan, Kenya, Uganda, Zimbabwe

Source: G2Px 2020d.
Note: G2Px (2020d) provides further insights on the market aspects for governments to consider when choosing emergency social assistance payment options. ATM = automated teller machine; G2P = government to person.

G2P mobile transfers should be supported by a comprehensive and sustainable ecosystem to fully exploit their advantages. As countries transition from emergency COVID-19 responses to normal operational mode, quick fixes implemented to scale up lifeline programs must be revisited and strengthened to support stronger social protection systems and strategic national goals, such as inclusive growth. Emphasis should be on the scalability of social protection systems, incorporating shock-responsive design features,[9] and limiting program exclusion errors from the outset in a fiscally sustainable manner (in other words, progressive universalism).[10]

Yet G2P mobile transfers cannot provide adequate solutions to all social protection challenges, and they must complement other support programs, for example, in-cash or food distribution systems.[11] G2P mobile transfers can, however, strengthen social protection systems, provided that governments are aware

[9] For example, built-in triggers that can adapt a program to an emergency context to ensure delivery continuity, such as transforming free school-meal programs into cash transfers for the family or in-house food distribution.

[10] For example, in Namibia, the government implemented a new monetary transfer for all adult informal workers and the unemployed, explicitly excluding formal workers and recipients of existing social protection programs. In one week, 579,000 SMS applications were received out of 739,000 adults expected to be eligible (Seekings and Gronbach 2020).

[11] In 2015–16, during the Ebola crisis, only 7 percent of all unconditional cash transfers implemented to provide lifeline supports in Liberia and Sierra Leone were mobile transfers, despite the overwhelming incentive to use digital rather than cash distribution to contain the virus (Dumas, Frisetti, and Radice 2017). A largely inadequate mobile ecosystem—weak infrastructure, lack of awareness among potential beneficiaries, and operational challenges—prevented the use of mobile transfers at scale.

of and follow certain design and implementation steps. In the following section, these steps are detailed within a comprehensive framework that will help governments optimize G2P mobile transfers.

AN END-TO-END FRAMEWORK TO GUIDE EVOLUTION OF MOBILE G2P PAYMENTS

A holistic framework, based on past G2P and mobile payment experiences, can inform short-term measures taken in context of the pandemic crisis to ensure the measures are sustainable, mitigate risks, and allow iterative improvements. This section describes a framework to enable a sustainable G2P monetary transfer through a mobile payment ("mobile G2P") program.[12] The framework is composed of eight building blocks (Figure 10.6) that help stakeholders assess the country's readiness in implementing mobile G2P along foundational enablers. These enablers are explained in detail in Annex 10.1, which describes various implementation paths to increase the maturity of a mobile G2P program, depending on the country's existing conditions.

Figure 10.6. Eight Building Blocks for a Sustainable Mobile G2P Framework

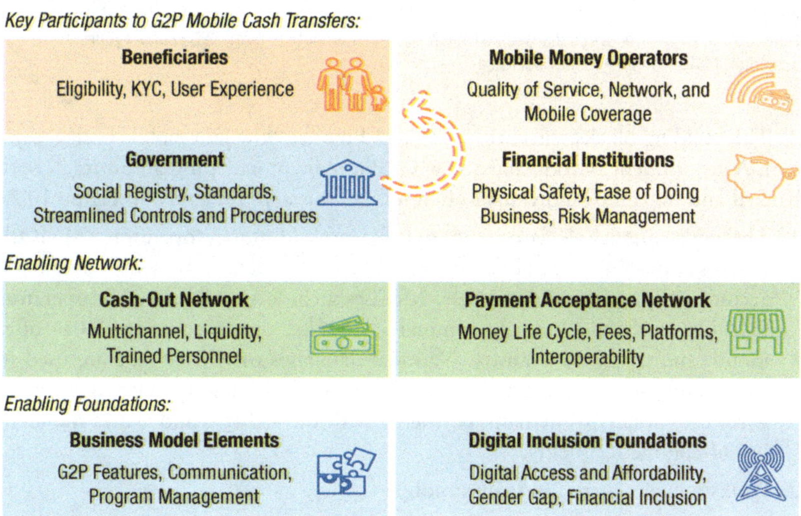

Source: Authors.
Note: G2P = government to person; KYC = know your customer.

[12] The framework builds on the work of many organizations, including the Global System for Mobile Communications Association, the Alliance for Financial Inclusion, and several World Bank initiatives, such as the Consultative Group to Assist the Poor and the World Bank and Gates Association's G2Px. The framework also incorporates the authors' original research in association with Digital Disruptions, a consulting company.

Figure 10.7. How G2P Mobile Cash Typically Flows from Government to the Unbanked and Other Participants

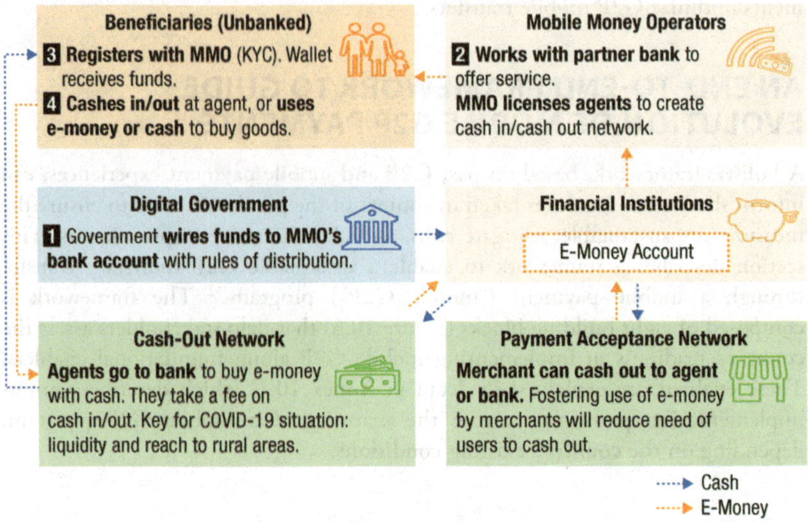

Sources: Digital Disruptions; Global System for Mobile Communications Association; Orange Money; and authors.
Note: COVID-19 = coronavirus disease 2019; G2P = government to person; KYC = know your customer; MMO = mobile money operator.

The building blocks reflect the end-to-end money flow in a mobile G2P ecosystem. A government introducing a new G2P mobile money program to reach both banked and unbanked individuals often follows the steps presented in Figure 10.7:

1. The government selects one or multiple mobile money operators (MMOs), entities allowed to issue electronic money to customers with or without a bank account, through mobile wallets. MMOs include mobile network operators (MNOs, such as Orange), commercial banks, or fintech firms that offer mobile money in the country. National databases or MMO data are used to select applicants who meet the program's eligibility criteria.[13] The government wires the money to the bank partnered with the MMOs and shares the identity of eligible recipients.
2. Banks convert these funds into mobile money.
3. MMOs organize information and outreach campaigns to help beneficiaries apply through an established know-your-customer (KYC) process using the

[13] For example, in Nigeria, the authorities collaborated with MNOs to identify vulnerable informal workers in urban areas through their purchase pattern of airtime. In addition to MMO data, other "proxy registries" can be leveraged to identify workers in the informal economy, such as company and individual member registries held by informal business unions or associations, utility bills, invoices of sales by wholesalers, and local governments' registries of poor households and local informal businesses.

identity plan approved by the government. Recipients are given a mobile wallet containing the amount of mobile cash distributed by the government.[14]

4. From here, beneficiaries can start using their mobile wallet.

Mobile wallet owners can then either cash out the money, typically through a local agent partnering with the MMO, or pay utility bills or purchase goods and services at merchants that accept mobile money. (The latter scenario supports social distancing in the COVID-19 context.) The framework shows the required infrastructure to facilitate mobile payments. The rest of the chapter describes enablers supporting such programs.

A clear understanding of each of the eight interdependent building blocks is critical for a successful mobile G2P program. The building blocks signal to policymakers and regulators where and how to adapt their country's regulatory framework in support of G2P mobile transfers. Each building block influences the success of a mobile G2P program. If any block is not properly managed or designed, the program may face serious risks. For example, failing to properly design and regulate financial institutions and MMOs may diminish unbanked individuals' trust in mobile cash. Likewise, if policymakers fail to incentivize acceptance of mobile money within a sufficient merchant network, many beneficiaries will exchange their mobile money for cash. This could create long lines at cash-out agent offices, endanger social distancing measures, and increase individuals' costs to receive the benefit.

Policymakers should approach the enablers as minimum conditions for the specific maturity of their country's mobile G2P program and plan iterative improvements. As COVID-19 has forced countries to deliver monetary assistance under time pressure, governments with a mature mobile money ecosystem (for example, China, Kenya, and Tanzania) have been able to react faster and more effectively (Rutkowski and others 2020). However, many countries have been able to transfer mobile cash despite the low maturity of their mobile ecosystem, suggesting some enablers are within reach of many emerging market and developing economies. This chapter presents the three maturity stages (Figure 10.8) countries can achieve for each enabler:

1. "Minimum required" enablers can place the mobile G2P program on an easier improvement trajectory.
2. "Good-to-have" enablers allow G2P programs to reach broader segments of a better-identified population to limit certain risks and to achieve economies of scale.
3. "Great-to-have" enablers develop iteratively as technology and adoption patterns change but represent the current state of the art. Today, great-to-have enablers are well illustrated by M-Pesa in Kenya and WeChat Pay and Alipay in China.

[14] A mobile wallet is either a mobile app or a code to access a remote application through SMS or unstructured supplementary service data (see Box 10.2).

Figure 10.8. The Eight Building Blocks Rely on Key "Enablers" That Support Various Degrees of the Mobile Ecosystem's Maturity

MINIMUM REQUIRED	GOOD TO HAVE	GREAT TO HAVE
The **base minimum** a country should strive to implement. An absence of any enabler at that level could jeopardize the success of the program, even in the short term.	Current **best practices** achievable with technologies, skills, and regulation partially accessible to most emerging markets and developing economies, given time and budget.	Achieved only by a few emerging markets and developing economies. This is a **moving target**, given change in technology and best practices.

Key Advantages:

- Faster delivery of relief efforts
- Fosters agility, promotes workarounds to government inefficiencies

→

- More targeted programs and broader reach
- Higher resilience to future shocks
- Platform used for other G2P or P2G services

Key Risks:

- Fraud
- Financial exclusion for lack of identity
- Subpar KYC

→

- Cyber risks
- Data privacy
- Digital divide exclusion

Source: Authors.
Note: G2P = government to person; KYC = know your customer; P2G = person to government.

The framework maturity tables in Annex 10.1 help stakeholders identify their current situation, as well as provide possible evolution strategies.

Building Block 1: Beneficiaries

Our framework promotes a user-centric approach that places beneficiaries at the center of each building block. The design of G2P cash programs must answer three questions: Who is eligible? How do those eligible prove their identity? How can governments maximize adoption by beneficiaries? These three enablers are informed by previous G2P experiences in various countries and by measures introduced during the pandemic crisis.

Eligibility Criteria

Eligibility criteria must rely on information broadly available across the population to minimize inclusion and exclusion errors. Criteria must further be as transparent as possible to minimize the probability that applicants will be rejected during a crisis (for example, basic demographic characteristics, such as age, gender, household composition, or location). Recourse mechanisms should also be in place to limit errors.

Exclusion criteria may be easier to design than inclusion criteria if the risk of exclusion is high. The success of the *Keluarga Harapan* program in Indonesia in 2017 was based on precise data from the Ministry of Social Affairs for mobile money transfers to pregnant and lactating mothers, infants, the elderly, and people with disabilities (Sri Sulastri and Ravi Kumar 2019). Likewise, India clearly communicated exclusion criteria for its COVID-19 transfer program, such as specific professions or individuals paying personal income tax. Absence of reliable citizen registries might force policymakers to use alternative data sources (see Building Block 2) or to make difficult trade-offs (Una, Allen, and others 2020; Una, van Eden, and others 2020).

KYC Requirements

KYC requirements specify which proof of address and proof of identity, such as voter card, national ID card, or health coverage ID, are needed to register for a program. This enabler also describes how to access or spend the mobile money after registration—personal ID number, password, biometric data, and the like.

Some central banks, as in Colombia and Ghana, have also opted to reduce KYC requirements for small payments to ease onboarding of the unbanked and undocumented population. The FATF provides guidance for governments to collaborate with financial institutions and businesses on digital onboarding and simplified customer due diligence during the COVID-19 crisis, while maintaining vigilance against fraud (FATF 2020b).

User Experience

As illustrated in Figure 10.9, for a G2P program to achieve widespread adoption, each step from registration to use of money must be understandable for beneficiaries. In past G2P program rollouts, some governments have not paid enough

Figure 10.9. Designing the Mobile G2P Program around the Beneficiaries

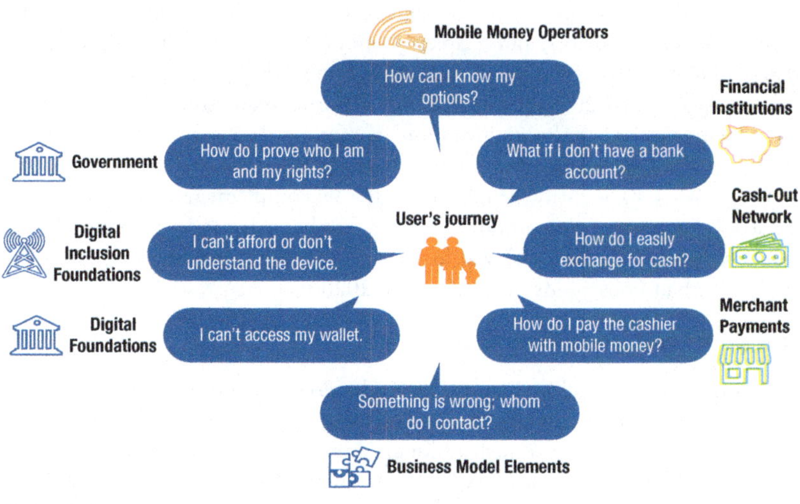

Source: Authors.
Note: Questions and statements in the figure are illustrative. G2P = government to person.

attention to the user experience, leading to mixed results, including the lack of improvement in financial inclusion (Baur-Yazbeck, Kilfoil, and Botea 2019).

Building Block 2: Digital Government

Many emerging market and developing economies lack reliable and broad socioeconomic data—especially in the informal sector—and do not have shock-responsive public finance management systems to aid with crises (IMF 2018). Countries with more complete socioeconomic information can more precisely target households in need of support. Such countries may also have access to advanced technologies, such as digital ID, data analytics, and fraud detection systems to cope with the volume of public funds being remitted. Even imperfect data and technology can be used to ensure that payments are timely, secure, transparent, and adequately controlled and reported. Close collaboration and data-sharing mechanisms across public agencies and with private partners such as MNOs can mitigate the lack of accurate or universal government data on households, especially in the informal sector.

Governments can use the following three enablers to ensure inclusion of individuals in need while limiting public finance risks.

Social Registry

If no reliable database exists or data are only available for a narrow share of the population, individuals should be able to apply for a G2P transfer with simple information, ideally through digital platforms. This information can then be used to enroll eligible individuals into support programs.

For example, Jordan identified households eligible for an emergency cash transfer through the *Takaful* program social register. During the COVID-19 pandemic, the scope of households eligible for emergency assistance expanded beyond *Takaful* recipients, and recipients' online enrollment increased, with beneficiaries allowed to open a mobile wallet or connect their bank account for direct cash transfer (G2Px 2020b). The *Takaful* platform enhanced cash transfer delivery systems through online registration, automatic data verification, improved targeting, and a robust grievance and redress mechanism.

Other ways to identify people in need can complement incomplete social registries, for example, community-based referrals. In Rwanda, for example, the *Ubudehe* "grassroots network" was leveraged to identify the most affected urban and peri-urban households in Kigali (IMF 2020b).

Standards and Open Architecture

Standards and open architecture are the technologies supporting our end-to-end framework and the implementation of mobile money platforms. In Peru, authorities were able to rapidly transfer money through the country's BiM (*Billetera Móvil*) mobile money platform, which is open to financial institutions, MNOs, and fintech firms. The development of standards (Box 10.1) accelerates the

Box 10.1. Emerging Standards and Open Architectures for Mobile Payment

GSMA Mobile Money API

The Global System for Mobile Communications Association (GSMA) and the mobile money industry created a communication standard for mobile money use cases, including domestic and international remittance, merchant payments, bill payments, and interoperability of mobile money accounts across financial institutions. According to GSMA (2020c), this application programming interface enables faster implementation and reduces total cost of ownership in three ways: (1) rapid adoption by partners, (2) ease of support and maintenance, and (3) increased capability for the industry as a whole.

The interface may be used by any stakeholder in the mobile money industry, which can facilitate integration between mobile money providers, for example, mobile money operators, banks, merchants, application developers, and other actors. This standard accelerates countries' mobile payment projects by offering technology best practices, such as RESTful architectural principles to allow scalability, the JavaScript Object Notation data format and the International Organization for Standardization's standards for better interoperability, and virtualization of payment functions to facilitate implementations and upgrades. The application programming interface also provides best-practice security recommendations.

Mojaloop

Mojaloop was developed in 2017 by the Gates Foundation in cooperation with fintech developers within the Level One Project. The goal is to make digital financial services more inclusive and more accessible to the world's poorest populations.

Mojaloop is a publicly available open-source code for creating digital payment platforms, offering functions including a push payment model with same-day settlement and notification from payer to payee; interoperability between all mobile money actors, such as financial institutions and regulated nontraditional financial service providers; adherence to international standards (for example, the payment data standards in ISO 20022); system-wide fraud and security protection; and proportional identity and know-your-customer implementation based on a country's needs, transactions, and the services provided.

In 2018, mobile telecommunications providers Orange and MTN announced a joint venture called Mowali, an implementation of Mojaloop, to enable interoperable payments across Africa. Mowali facilitates financial flows between mobile money users across service providers and countries and could benefit government-to-person programs. The partnership aims to link more than 100 million mobile money accounts and operations in 22 of sub-Saharan Africa's 46 markets.

deployment of open mobile money platforms and related digital financial services and fosters compatibility with card payment and other payment systems (GSMA 2020a).

Streamlined Controls and Effective Procedures

Existing procedures and controls of some countries' core public finance management systems are not designed to deal with emergencies such as COVID-19 and may introduce complexities and delays incompatible with urgent actions. This enabler explores how countries are modifying or temporarily adjusting systems, procedures, and treatment capacities to promote a transparent and effective emergency response (Una, Allen, and others 2020).

Building Block 3: Mobile Money Operators

G2P mobile payments rely on a robust and effective collaboration between the government and MMOs (Box 10.2). In many countries, mobile payment is offered by MNOs, which already have a strong presence for basic voice and data

Box 10.2. How USSD Mobile Wallets Work

In most emerging market and developing economies, mobile services are accessible through a technology called unstructured supplementary service data (USSD). USSD provides text-only services, including financial services, that users can access by dialing a short code on their phone. For example, customers from Orange Money in Liberia would dial *144# to check their mobile wallet balance.

As with short message service, USSD works on standard phones and smartphones without the need to install any app, and a subscription to mobile data is not required. USSD mobile wallets can thus become available in an entire country, for every customer of a service provider, the moment the service is deployed on the network. USSD services are therefore cost-effective and popular, albeit not user friendly.

Box Figure 10.2.1 shows how a user would interact with a mobile wallet before sending mobile money to another person or a merchant.

Box Figure 10.2.1. Process for User to Send Payment through a USSD Mobile Wallet

Source: Global System for Mobile Communications Association website.
Note: USSD = unstructured supplementary service data.

Regulators should note that USSD infrastructure is typically owned and operated by mobile network operators. However, mobile wallets can also be offered by third-party mobile money operators, which are typically banks. In several countries, mobile money operators have been barred from accessing USSD by dominant mobile network operators (Consultative Group to Assist the Poor 2014). In a crisis, policymakers must eliminate this concern to accelerate mobile wallet deployment at a low cost.

services. When nonbanks are sufficiently regulated to provide financial services, as is often the case in Southeast Asia and Africa, they can help accelerate G2P programs. For example, GCash, a Philippine fintech company, was able to rapidly respond to the government's call to enable mobile G2P payments by leveraging its platform and network. Wave Money in Myanmar has greatly facilitated G2P mobile payments while providing users with additional digital and financial assistance. Other nonbank tech companies, such as GrabPay in Malaysia, have been central to the success and speed of government cash transfers.

MMOs often provide payment capabilities, including payment networks or payment rails, previously nonexistent in emerging market and developing economies. In Kenya, M-Pesa emerged from Safaricom's telecommunication network to enable a new form of payment. In Nigeria and Uganda, the fintech company Interswitch provides payment capability for merchants and individuals.

Compared to banks, MNOs and fintech firms also tend to have more mature mobile services, higher customer trust, and better user experience. MNOs also often provide broader agent networks (GSMA 2020a). These advantages have fueled the success of mobile money in many countries, particularly in Africa (M-Pesa in Kenya, Tigo Cash in Tanzania, or fintech firms Paga in Nigeria and Yoco in South Africa) and Asia (Tencent and Alipay in China). In South Asia, mobile money has recently gained traction with an annual growth of 46 percent, the highest across all regions (Chhabra and Das 2019).

Quality of Service

Although many MMOs provide sufficient digital financial services, they may not all qualify for an effective G2P partnership. Governments may clarify the expected services, as well as the required risk-management and reporting requirements. Tigo, an MNO that provides mobile money services in Paraguay and Tanzania, owes its success to high-quality services designed for maximum user adoption (Annex 10.1). Partnering with fintech firms that develop products with well-designed user experiences has led to the successful adoption of G2P programs in Southeast Asia.

Agent Network Coverage

This includes the availability of agents, typically small local retail stores, in urban and rural areas and the quality of service they provide. Nonretail stores—basically independent individuals setting up a temporary stand and acting as agents—also influence some markets. Such coverage is essential when online onboarding and remote support are not available, considering these agents are the "face" of the service.

Mobile Coverage

MNOs' partners must have adequate and reliable mobile coverage (at least 2G and, when feasible, 3G) across a country. Coverage is particularly necessary in harder-to-reach rural areas to prevent exclusion of populations in need. In other words, MNOs must reduce, rather than widen, the "digital divide" (Building Block 8). To overcome inadequate coverage in regions where such services would be commercially unviable for private providers, Zambia issued new policies, changing the digital payment fee structure to boost MMOs' coverage (Baur-Yazbeck 2019).

Mobile Money Regulatory Requirements

MNOs need to ensure that the full equivalent of government-issued outstanding mobile money is invested in safe liquid assets, such as commercial bank deposits and low-risk government securities in regulated financial institutions through trust or escrow accounts. Most countries have adopted regulatory requirements for MMOs to safeguard consumer funds (GSMA 2016).

Building Block 4: Financial Institutions

Financial institutions will receive funds directly from the government and place them in a mobile money account for participants such as MMOs, cash-out agents, and merchants (Figure 10.7). Countries usually have at least one regulated financial institution connected with the government's treasury.

Governments wanting to establish or strengthen their collaborations with participating financial institutions or identify alternative options, such as MMO services, may consider the following enablers.

Branches and ATM Safety

G2P beneficiaries are likely to use banks or ATMs to exchange their government-issued mobile money against cash, even in countries where mobile payments are widely accepted, such as Kenya and Tanzania.[15] During the pandemic, some governments have mandated social distancing measures for banks that make cashing out G2P mobile payments more difficult—and, paradoxically, lead to long queues and waits at scarce cash-out points. A combined policy of easing mobile payments and multiplying and diversifying certified cash-out agents is therefore key to safe and inclusive G2P mobile transfers (see Building Block 5).

Ease of Doing Business and Trust

Governments must assess the ability of participating financial institutions to interact with the population effectively. Customer trust, ease of doing business, user support, and internet presence are important success factors. During the COVID-19 pandemic, Pakistan's central bank requested that banks open their

---

[15] Roessler and others (2019) show that in Tanzania, providing women with free phones improved financial access. However, the women still preferred cash to mobile money for all transactions other than remittances. Acceptance of mobile money was higher for literate participants, highlighting the need for clear and simple communication (Building Block 7).

call centers 24 hours a day, seven days a week to reduce customer visits and to assist with basic operations. In Colombia, some banks use a simplified KYC requirement to provide unbanked beneficiaries with mobile wallets (G2Px 2020a).

Risk Management

Participating financial institutions are accountable for the integrity, security, and privacy of financial and accounting information, as well as for fraud prevention, such as robust KYC policies and anti–money laundering/combating the financing of terrorism (AML/CFT). The risk-management enabler also applies to Building Block 3 for MMOs. To adopt new beneficiaries and to foster mobile payments, the Bank of Ghana authorized mobile money customers to use their existing KYC-protected accounts to register for the country's COVID-19 aid program (Bank of Ghana 2020).

Building Block 5: Cash-Out Network

G2P cash transfer programs use cash-in/cash-out (CICO) networks to allow beneficiaries to safely exchange mobile money for cash. Studies have shown that most beneficiaries withdraw 100 percent of their payment immediately (McKee, Kaffenberger, and Zimmerman 2015). In traditional banking (Building Block 4), CICO locations include direct channels, such as bank branches and ATMs, and indirect channels, such as retail outlets, supermarkets, and pharmacies.[16] These indirect channels are also used by MNOs with a CICO network of their own or managed by a separate agent network.

The following enablers should be considered when assessing whether a country's CICO network is ready to support G2P programs.

Delivery Channel Mix

G2P programs should aim for diversified and dense delivery channels with reach in remote and rural areas. Traditional channels, such as bank branches and ATMs, and governments' direct channels, such as post offices and local authorities, should be complemented by mobile money agents with broad outreach in emerging market and developing economies. Mobile money networks have, on average, 20 times more reach than bank branches (GSMA 2020a). Some governments have incentivized participants to operate in regions with low return on investment. For example, Kenya introduced tiered fees to promote better services in underserved regions during the pandemic (McKay and Mdluli 2020).

Liquidity Management

Projecting estimated cash-out volumes; enlisting the support of banks and third parties, such as agent network managers; and preventing crowd formation have

[16] Although the fee structure of the indirect channels is not treated in this building block, stakeholders should remain aware of its importance. More information on fee structure is provided in Building Block 6.

been essential during the pandemic. Ecuador doubled the number of cash-out access points during the crisis and established payment dates based on the last digits of beneficiaries' IDs (LLorente y Cuenca 2020). Peru used a geolocation system to direct beneficiaries to specific cash-out points at a given time (G2Px 2020c).

Trained Personnel

ATM withdrawals are common, yet mobile money beneficiaries may be interacting with staff who should be trained and knowledgeable about the program, undergo regular audits, and provide adequate customer service. Beyond G2P programs, many emerging market and developing economies have introduced initiatives to improve digital and financial literacy. Such resources could be coordinated to include CICO agents.

Building Block 6: Payment Acceptance Network

A large merchant network, as well as other public and private actors, could further encourage beneficiaries to opt for mobile payments when possible, thus reducing cash out. Businesses should be involved in the design of programs to limit cash out of G2P payments.

Digitization of payment has become a reality in many countries. In 2019, for the first time, more value circulated in the mobile money system than left the system, setting the stage for a broader acceptance by the population to use and save mobile money (GSMA 2020a). In 2018, to cope with cash shortage, the central bank of Zimbabwe, the main mobile operator Econet Wireless, and Mastercard partnered to enable merchants to accept Ecocash mobile money in stores already equipped with card readers. This allowed more than 3,800 merchants to be paid with mobile money. Such public-private partnership is key to reducing the use of cash.

The following enablers integrate payment recipients into the mobile G2P framework, enabling longer-term benefits from mobile money.

Mobile Money Life Cycle

A full digital payment ecosystem must ease the flow of mobile money across government (G), people (P), and businesses (B). In the near term, many countries are focusing on G2P and P2B payments. Annex 10.1 describes advanced models in which P2G, B2G, and B2B payments strengthen a comprehensive digital payment economy.

Fee Structure

A popular measure during the COVID-19 crisis has been the temporary reduction or elimination of mobile money payment fees (both for consumers and merchants).[17] For example, the mobile industry of Ghana worked with the central

[17] The reduction and elimination of charges has taken many forms, from central banks eliminating transaction taxes for person-to-person mobile transfers or taxes paid by merchants on mobile money transactions, to MMOs agreeing to temporarily reduce their charges.

bank to implement free mobile service transactions and promote mobile payments. Similar collaborations between the private sector and central banks in Kenya (Airtel), Uganda (Airtel and MTN), and Rwanda (most banks and MNOs) have facilitated the use of mobile money during the pandemic. Heavier taxation of mobile transactions relative to transactions through the banking system may prove regressive and have unintended consequences (GSMA 2020b).[18]

Payment Platforms and Interoperability

In many countries, mobile money development has been hindered by interoperability issues among banks, mobile wallets, and various payment schemes. Yet mobile money actors and governments are increasingly collaborating on improving interoperability of mobile payments.[19] Before the pandemic, the Philippine central bank implemented the National Retail Payment System, a regulatory framework that requires interoperability among payment service providers—not only banks but also nonbank e-money issuers. This payment system greatly facilitated MMOs' participation in the country's PESONet and InstaPay automated clearinghouses.

Building Block 7: Business Model Elements

A mobile G2P program could benefit from industry best practices for digital solutions. The business model of any product covers not only customer experience and solution advantages but also the distribution channels, marketing strategy, change management, risk management, technology upgrades, and strategic partnerships. When correctly executed with a long-term view, such public-private partnerships can result in a more sustainable and effective service. The various elements of a robust business model are typically interdependent, and a single "broken link" in the chain (for example, poor fraud controls, technology downtime, or a confusing process to open an account) can impair an otherwise well-designed product.

Of the many enablers that define this building block, three are particularly important for sustainable success beyond the short-term objectives of income assistance.

Program Features

Clear and measurable parameters enable better performance tracking and reduce confusion. Examples of program features include eligibility criteria, the transfer amount, frequency, applicable conditions, and the duration. Some countries have

[18] In 2018, a new tax on mobile transactions in Uganda led to street protests. The tax was seen as overwhelmingly affecting the poorest people in the country, who do not have access to banks. Within a few months, P2P values fell by more than 50 percent in favor of cash.

[19] The GSMA Mobile Money application programming interface and Gates Foundation's Mojaloop, described in Box 10.1, are often seen as foundational projects for the future of interoperable payment in developing countries (Martins 2020).

considered conditioning some features to certain behaviors, for example, COVID-19 testing or using a portion of the money to make mobile payments.

Effective and Frequent Communication

Clear, simple, and well-publicized communication is critical to the success of any product. Togo prioritized targeting women in its *Novissi* G2P program and communicated clearly and simply through ads and social media. The effective communication and product management attracted twice as many women as men to the cash transfer scheme.[20]

Program Management

A G2P program can be managed like any other major complex product. Clear definition of roles and responsibilities across building blocks, reporting processes, continuous improvement, and controlled deadlines and budget are basic expectations for product management.

Building Block 8: Digital Inclusion Foundations

The digitalization of payment can leave behind large shares of vulnerable populations (Zimmerman and Baur 2016). Households most affected by the pandemic are often the hardest to reach with technology physically, economically, and culturally (for example, women have less access to communication devices)[21] or from a literacy standpoint. Close coordination with other government agencies and technology, telecommunication, and fintech companies may help countries bridge the digital gap that threatens to leave the most vulnerable segments behind (Davidovic and others 2019).

Digital inclusion involves various stakeholders and is an essential element of a successful mobile G2P program implementation. This building block can also support other development goals, including several of the UN's Sustainable Development Goals for lowering poverty, bridging the gender gap, and reducing inequality. Certain regions, such as sub-Saharan Africa, are more exposed than others to the risk of digital exclusion, despite recent progress (IMF 2020a).

Digital and financial inclusion is a multidimensional and evolving topic that spans beyond the scope of this chapter. Still, two enablers could help policymakers improve the reach of mobile G2P to remote or poor populations.

Digital Access and Affordability

To benefit from mobile G2P, individuals need reliable electricity; affordable, sufficient connectivity; and connected devices, such as a computer or a mobile

[20] The Togolese government frequently updates all data on *Novissi* on its website: https://novissi.gouv.tg/en/.

[21] On average, women are 10 percent less likely to own a mobile phone (GSMA 2020a), with affordability being the most significant barrier to ownership (Lindsey and Wilson 2019).

Figure 10.10. Progress in Digital Access in Sub-Saharan Africa Remains Hindered by High Costs and Lags in Remote Areas
(Enhanced Digital Access Index score)

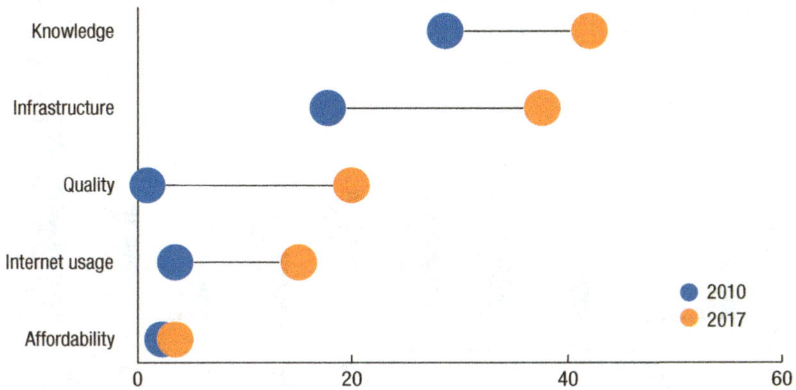

Source: Alper and Miktus 2019.

phone. People also need the knowledge to use the technology and the financial literacy to maximize the benefits of mobile wallet ownership. Alper and Miktus (2019) propose an Enhanced Digital Access Index to measure the ability of a population to access digital services (Figure 10.10). Countries have mandated service providers to reduce electricity and connectivity fees (Malaysia, Panama), strengthen availability and resilience (Argentina, Chile, Qatar, Vietnam), and explore new ways to provide connectivity.[22]

Gender Gap

Over the past seven years, the digital divide between men and women in emerging market and developing economies has widened (Figure 10.11), which is especially challenging when women represent a majority of both the informal sector and caregiving communities particularly affected by COVID-19 (Zimmerman and others 2020).

Emerging market and developing economies should recognize the widening technology gap not only between women and men (International Telecommunications Union 2019) but also with migrants, internally displaced people, and persons with disabilities (United Nations 2020), and design accessibility of mobile G2P accordingly.[23] As part of its antipoverty program *Ehsaas Kafalat*, Pakistan has distributed free smartphones and

[22] In March 2020, South Africa allowed the TV white space spectrum to roll out affordable or free data services, particularly in rural and remote areas (Independent Communications Authority of South Africa 2020).

[23] This enabler can benefit from the work of Zimmerman and others (2020) and other actors who promote the Digitize, Direct, Design Framework to enhance women's economic empowerment through cash transfers.

Figure 10.11. The Internet User Gender Gap in Emerging Markets and Developing Economies, 2013–19
(Percent)

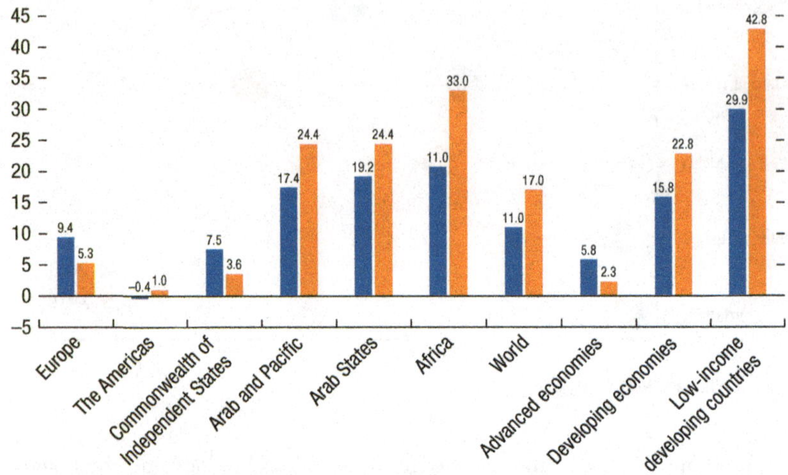

Source: International Telecommunications Union 2019.
Note: International Telecommunications Union estimate. The gender gap represents the difference between the internet user penetration rates for male and female users relative to the rate for male users, expressed as a percentage.

biometrically protected bank accounts to 7 million poor women, significantly facilitating secure access to government money.

LIMITATIONS AND RISKS

The potential of G2P for mobile cash transfers is considerable, but challenges and constraints can limit their effectiveness. Enablers to strengthen the mobile G2P framework can help governments tackle challenges in establishing a mobile G2P payment program under pressure. Larger constraints and limits, however, warrant more attention. Some challenges are structural, such as inadequate infrastructure (including electricity and connectivity) and insufficient digital literacy, whereas others are inherent to digital technology for the transfer of value, such as cyber risks, fraud, and inadequate regulation.

Structural issues will take time and resources to address, yet cyber risks and digital fraud need to be tackled imminently. Policymakers and regulators should ensure that risks are identified, managed, and mitigated to the extent possible to build trust in G2P programs. The risks of accelerating mobile money, including cyber risks and digital fraud, must not outweigh the benefits. For example, most mobile transfers still rely on at least one bank for their custody or escrow account. Such transfers could thus be more sensitive to financial sector shocks if the MNO's partner bank is affected. Conventional social assistance transfers, on the other hand, could be covered under the deposit insurance scheme, if applicable.

Countries may have a varying severity of challenges, from infrastructure development to available fiscal space, requiring different approaches and responses. Emerging market and developing economies with inadequate infrastructure, from electricity to payment rails, have relied on public-private partnerships with MNOs and fintech firms (for example, Interswitch in Nigeria).

Building Block 8 also presents the merits of interagency collaboration on digital connectivity initiatives for G2P programs. With increased deregulation and liberalization of the telecommunication market, countries have explored public-private partnerships, which have gained popularity across the world, particularly in emerging market and developing economies (PPP Knowledge Lab 2020). Such partnerships are significant, yet effective procurement policies and transparent project documentation mitigate the risks of working with the private sector, such as cost overruns and corruption.

Cybersecurity and Digital Fraud

Given the volume of funds and the sensitive nature of beneficiary data, cybersecurity breaches are a risk for G2P platforms. Cybersecurity risks threaten the confidentiality, integrity, and availability of institutional data, applications, processes, and citizens' information. For government agencies and institutions, leaks or misuse of beneficiary data or other consumer fraud could have serious reputational consequences and result in a durable loss of trust. Cybersecurity risks threaten both hardware and software in digital systems (and are often exacerbated during crises, such as the COVID-19 pandemic).

A thorough understanding of cybersecurity and digital fraud risks can help policymakers hold mobile G2P program stakeholders accountable for establishing a robust and secure G2P system. Each of the eight building blocks requires its own governance of cyber and digital fraud risks, from standard protection of infrastructure, applications, and networks to stronger information security. Sharing knowledge and collaborating through interagency information technology taskforces have allowed many low-income developing countries to achieve cyber-resilience objectives within a short time (Una, van Eden, and others 2020).

Likewise, stakeholders should develop business continuity plans to demonstrate shock responsiveness and guard against cyberattacks related to remote work (Leonovich 2020). These plans should identify core business processes and provide alternatives to sustain operations during emergencies.

Regulatory Concerns

A regulatory environment fostering G2P service providers' participation should ensure consumer protection, financial integrity, and financial stability.

Many countries may not have adapted their regulatory and policy framework to allow nonfinancial service providers to participate in payment systems, because of financial integrity or data privacy issues. As discussed, the COVID-19 pandemic has prompted policymakers to reduce the regulatory compliance burden on mobile money issued by telecom or fintech firms. Mobile money customers are thus often not as protected by regulation as customers of regulated financial institutions.

Policymakers can protect financial integrity by remaining vigilant to emerging financial crime related to the pandemic while taking advantage of the flexibility provided by the FATF's risk-based approach (FATF 2020a, 2020b). Flexibility is particularly relevant for countries that do not have reliable identity or socioeconomic data registries. The authorities should require that providers protect customer data, ensure services are easy to use, and comply with pertinent standards for AML/CFT.

In the long term, policymakers should aspire for international agreements on data privacy, cybersecurity, digital ID, cross-border digital currencies, and regulation (Sahay and others 2020). Ongoing collaboration among regulators and service providers enables continuous alignment on risk assessment and ensures a risk-based AML/CFT approach (Alliance for Financial Inclusion 2020). International collaboration and knowledge exchange are welcome developments. For example, INTERPOL has assisted African police in designing proactive strategies to combat organized crime, facilitate information exchange, and enhance investigative skills (INTERPOL 2020).

CONCLUSION

As the COVID-19 crisis unfolded, many emerging market and developing economies expanded mobile money platforms to provide income support at an unprecedented scale. Leveraging the high penetration of mobile phones and mobile accounts relative to banks' access points, governments have expanded or introduced mobile money transfers to reach millions of workers and households that would have otherwise remained beyond reach, particularly in the informal economy.

Analyzing past country initiatives that built social safety nets around mobile transfers, as well as recent emergency responses, this chapter introduced a comprehensive framework to build sustainable G2P mobile programs. Using stylized facts from existing mobile cash transfer efforts and previous G2P and mobile payment initiatives in emerging market and developing economies, the chapter deduced the conditions for a successful G2P mobile program and any associated risks in the form of a comprehensive framework.

Divided into eight building blocks, this framework describes the ecosystem required to fully exploit the advantages of G2P mobile money transfers. The eight building blocks are designed to guide policymakers and regulators in iteratively adapting their countries' regulatory environment, scaling up infrastructure, and choosing the right collaboration partners in support of G2P mobile transfers.

In the longer term, the framework can help policymakers develop stronger social protection systems and contribute to their strategic development goals. Together with other programs, mobile transfer platforms can strengthen social safety nets, allowing for adequate and effective coverage of vulnerable households and workers. Beyond safety nets, G2P mobile transfers can further contribute to inclusive growth by bringing financial accounts to the unbanked, empowering women financially, and helping small and medium enterprises grow within the formal sector. Mobile transfers can also increase the transparency and efficiency of public resource management.

Regardless of the maturity of a country's mobile G2P infrastructure, any G2P solution will introduce risks and reveal constraints that need to be mitigated and managed. Risks will become even more prominent as digitalization progresses and countries introduce more sophisticated technologies into the digital cash ecosystem. Governments should remain cognizant of potential new risks that present themselves as their mobile cash transfer programs mature. Some risks, such as cybersecurity, require immediate attention, whereas others, such as regulation to protect data privacy or mitigate fraud and the violation of financial integrity standards, call for a concerted government effort over the medium term.

ANNEX 10.1. ENABLERS MATURITY MAP

This annex details enablers at each maturity stage across the eight building blocks of a mobile G2P framework. Policymakers can use this maturity map to identify where their countries are currently situated and evaluate options for developing the next evolution along each enabler. The framework is descriptive, not prescriptive; it provides guidance for countries to self-assess their current maturity stage but does not explicitly advise a course of action or decision.

TABLE 10.1.1.

Beneficiaries		
Minimum Required	**Good to Have (Enhanced Scenario)**	**Great to Have (Advanced Model)**
Eligibility Criteria		
Broad eligibility criteria easy to identify, communicate, and implement.	Additional criteria, such as number of children in household and labor type, if available, allow more targeted transfer program.	Ability to include/exclude certain segments, for example, based on income level; articulation with other government benefit programs.
KYC Requirements		
Any form of ID, even if not government issued (tax records, utility bills, health records). Authentication to access mobile wallet often uses personal ID numbers (often used in G2P programs).	Any standardized government ID, such as a voter card, birth certificate, or driver's license. Accept MMOs' KYC and authentication policies (for example, Brazil, Jordan) with certain limits.	National digital ID with streamlined, secure registration (for example, *Aadhaar* in India). Biometric authentication offers additional security. In Pakistan, biometrics promoted use of mobile wallets by women living in poverty.
User Experience		
Most countries have maintained websites to answer questions. Messaging tools, such as WhatsApp in Kenya, have helped provide basic support service.	Countries have worked with MMOs and banks to offer user support. Mobile wallets typically use well-known USSD mobile wallet (Box 10.2).	Smartphones are able to provide superior mobile wallet experience, biometric authentication, and contactless payment. This should not, however, replace USSD, which remains the best option for hardest-to-reach populations.
Typical Risks to Mitigate		
Financial exclusion from the inability to demonstrate identity. Forgery of ID documents.	Inconsistent data across sources. Identity theft.	Cyber crime.
Case Study		
In 2011, the government of Uganda implemented a social cash transfer scheme called Social Assistance Grants for Empowerment (SAGE) to tackle chronic poverty. Two eligibility criteria were used: an index based on demographic indicators (for "vulnerable households," which were low income and lacked labor capacity) and an index geared toward senior citizens, which strictly used age as a factor. The amount and frequency were the same for both: 25,000 Ugandan shillings (about US$10 at that time) per month paid every two months. Over the course of four years, the pilot program reached about 125,000 households and about 560,000 individuals. To register participants, information was gathered from households and entered in a database through a census-style registration system. Beneficiaries were provided a SAGE program card embedded with a SIM card from MTN, the country's largest mobile network operator. Cardholders could withdraw funds at designated pay points after providing identification.		

Source: Authors.

Note: G2P = government to person; ID = identification; KYC = know your customer; MMO = mobile money operator; SIM = subscriber identification module; USSD = unstructured supplementary service data.

TABLE 10.1.2.

Government Digital Tools		
Minimum Required	**Good to Have (Enhanced Scenario)**	**Great to Have (Advanced Model)**
Social Registry		
Existing registries complemented with online self-registration and community-based ID of people in need (for example, local authorities).	Additional KYC requirements. Avoid duplicates and "ghosts" by leveraging other databases (for example, other benefit, programs, social security, tax administration, utilities, school, NGOs, and MNO databases).	Up-to-date and integrated socioeconomic data that allow fully automated validation of self-enrolled individuals by cross-checking reliable internal and external databases.
Standards and Open Architecture		
Assuming data exist, some countries share program data (sometimes just an Excel file shared through secure channels) with government employees authorized to identify program recipients or to audit/manage risks.	G2P and beneficiary data are accessible programmatically and securely across public agencies and with external partners, such as MMOs, through APIs, boosting operational effectiveness and reducing human mistakes.	An open architecture supporting any G2P cash program is used securely, allowing the private sector, such as fintech, research agencies, and third parties to provide additional services. See also Box 10.1.
Streamlined Controls and Effective Procedures		
Identify sources of inefficiencies and overcomplicated processes, procedures, and workflows that would delay G2P program.	Eliminate unnecessary steps, decisions, and intermediaries to improve G2P program delivery. Mitigate risks of such simplification with data collection and reporting from all framework participants.	*Predictive* analysis can improve performance (for example, identifying a population more likely to withdraw on a certain day to improve liquidity management) or reduce risks (for example, agent transaction patterns that flag suspicious activity) by suggesting actions to take.
Typical Risks to Mitigate		
Some individuals may opt out to avoid paying taxes and risk being excluded. Corruption of intermediaries.	Inconsistent data across sources. Privacy breaches may reduce trust in G2P program. Some people may be missed; others may be paid more than once.	Cyber crime. Biased algorithms.
Case Study		
In 2014, Catholic Relief Services began exploring more sophisticated electronic voucher systems for vulnerable populations in northeast Nigeria. The NGO had initially been using paper vouchers, but these were subject to fraud and duplication. In 2016, Catholic Relief launched its Cash and Assets Transfer Management Platform. This includes both back-end software, such as a web-based management system, Android-based apps for vendors or money agents, and data-analysis tools, as well as hardware, such as near-field communications technology, biometric scanners, and smart cards. Once field agents register beneficiaries (and their biometrics) on the platform, beneficiaries receive a smart card. The platform transfers roughly US $5 to US $6 cash to the smart card monthly. Dozens of local vendors accept the card (the implementing partner also recruits vendors). The program has supported roughly 83,000 beneficiaries and involved more than 180 vendors.		

Source: Authors.

Note: API = application programming interface; G2P = government to person; ID = identification; KYC = know your customer; MNO = mobile network operator; NGO = nongovernmental organization.

TABLE 10.1.3

Mobile Money Operators		
Minimum Required	**Good to Have (Enhanced Scenario)**	**Great to Have (Advanced Model)**
Quality of Service		
Partnership with one MMO with proven ability to deliver mobile money to large segment of population. Account opening is straightforward and free.	Data about subscribers and use can be obtained from MMOs, preferably automatically through secure APIs. MMOs can provide additional financial services accessible with G2P money (for example, savings account).	Beneficiaries can select their MMOs, which are interoperable, allowing fund transfer between mobile wallets and with bank accounts.
Agent Network Coverage		
Agents offer cash-out services in rural areas. They should have access to liquidity. They help first-time users navigate basic USSD menus.	Agents conduct basic KYC and offer account-opening services. Services available late and on weekends to flatten peak-hour crowd curves. Answer basic questions about G2P program on behalf of government.	Experienced and dense agent network is available in remote rural areas. Good liquidity management. Agents can answer more questions about the G2P program. MMOs can explain basic financial services, such as savings accounts.
Mobile Coverage		
2G and 3G mobile coverage is available in majority of country.	Service is reliable and affordable.	Available to remote areas, such as mountainous regions, small islands, and low-density areas. Affordable or subsidized for poorest population.[1]
Typical Risks to Mitigate		
Populations hard to reach physically, economically, culturally (for example, women, older population) may not have access to digital payment. Inadequate regulatory rules.	Data privacy. Liquidity.	Financial and digital literacy may limit effectiveness of program.
Case Study		
After a slower-than-expected uptake in the initial years, in 2010, Tanzania private telecom provider Tigo deployed a mobile wallet called Pesa to 12 million users (about half its base of voice and data subscribers), many of whom never had access to financial services before. Tigo Pesa's success relies on compelling services for customers, real-time account activation, cash advance services (through a local bank), and international remittances to other MMOs in neighboring countries. Tigo offers user-friendly merchant payments using mobile money integrated with Mastercard's Masterpass QR-based service. Tigo also counts more than 150,000 agents, many in rural areas, where it tends to dominate larger rival Vodacom. Agents are recruited on strict criteria, cross-referenced, provided financial education, and actively managed to ensure high-quality customer service. Tigo also works with multiple bank partners and "superagents" to ensure agent training; brand and marketing collateral; and liquidity services, including cash delivery. As of 2019, Tigo Pesa contributed nearly one-third of earnings for Tigo Tanzania, estimated at roughly $40 million.		

Source: Authors.

Note: API = application programming interface; G2P = government to person; KYC = know your customer; MMO = mobile money operator; QR = quick-response code; USSD = unstructured supplementary service data.

1 In February 2020, Pakistan began distributing free smartphones and biometrically protected bank accounts to 7 million poor women (Find Biometrics 2020).

TABLE 10.1.4.

Financial Institutions		
Minimum Required	**Good to Have (Enhanced Scenario)**	**Great to Have (Advanced Model)**
Branches and ATM Safety		
Partnership banks must be capable of partnering with MNOs to provide mobile money. Banks should have reasonable ATM coverage in both urban and some rural areas and effective liquidity management. For all three phases represented in this table, social distancing should be mandated.	Branches are available in some rural areas and have flexible operating hours to prevent large crowds. G2P partnership is open to all banks in the country that comply with government criteria. Most operations other than cash out are done over the internet or telephone.	ATMs are functional, and liquidity and appointments are managed through predictive analytics and other automation technologies to prevent long lines. Personnel at branches are well trained and can provide customers with G2P and financial advice. Services are supported by interoperable platforms with MNOs.
Ease of Doing Business and Trust		
Brand is recognized by many beneficiaries and is not distrusted (for example, does not have reputation for fraud). Trust is less an issue when beneficiaries interface with MMOs instead of banks.	Brand is recognized and trusted by most beneficiaries. Customers feel comfortable interacting with branch staff and obtaining information.	Brands of participating banks are strong; recognized by the majority of the population; and trusted to provide high-quality service, including internationally.
Risk Management		
Participating bank adheres to basic internal controls, such as those meant to detect, prevent, and correct threats, particularly financial fraud.	Enhanced controls in place, such as best practices in accounting system access controls, standardized financial documentation, separation of duties, and reasonable AML/CFT/KYC controls. For example, Peru improved its processes to avoid losing funds when cash is not withdrawn by the intended beneficiary or is not withdrawn at all (G2Px 2020c).	Robust internal controls in place, including frequent risk assessment and proactive risk monitoring (for example, early detection systems). Strong AML/CFT/KYC controls.
Typical Risks to Mitigate		
Corruption, fraud. Liquidity. Waste of funds when beneficiary is deceased or doesn't access account. Lack of experience in G2P mobile money management.	Difficulty to control compliance. Clear and quasi real-time reporting on G2P money flows.	Cyber readiness of banks' technology, processes, and personnel.
Case Study		
Several of Peru's largest banks—*Banco Crédito de Perú*, BBVA, Scotiabank, and Interbank—created the ASBANC committee to promote a low-cost banking service for the unbanked and underserved population supported by an interoperable platform. Any bank is eligible to join ASBANC. Policymakers enabled nonbanks to issue electronic money in 2012, allowing for broader financial services participation. The fully interoperable national mobile money platform, called *Billetera Móvil* (BiM), is now supported by financial institutions, the government, and telecommunications companies to serve the unbanked and underbanked. The product allows any customer to open a paperless account on any mobile network with any one of the 34 member banks participating in the consortium. As of December 2019, BiM registered 1.3 million transactions per month, and the government is extending its COVID-19 stimulus through the platform to old and new beneficiaries (Rutkowski and others 2020).		

Source: Authors.

Note: AML/CFT/KYC = anti–money laundering/combating the financing of terrorism/know your customer; ATM = automated teller machine; COVID-19 = coronavirus disease 2019; G2P = government to person; MMO = mobile money operator; MNO = mobile network operator.

TABLE 10.1.5.

Cash-Out Network		
Minimum Required	**Good to Have (Enhanced Scenario)**	**Great to Have (Advanced Model)**
Delivery Channel Mix		
Most countries already have many channels of distribution (banks, ATMs, post offices, cash-out agents). At minimum, government-owned channels, such as local authorities and post offices, are staffed to cope with emergency disbursement.	Countries coordinate or regulate efforts across delivery channels to minimize long lines and better manage liquidity.	Large share of cashless economic transactions with people needing or wanting less and less cash to conduct everyday purchases/payments. Malaysia uses the popular GrabPay mobile wallet to transfer cash to citizens. A total of 70 percent pay GrabPay merchants without cashing out.
Liquidity Management		
Financial institutions and government-owned channels maintain adequate cash reserves to meet demand for cash withdrawals.	Coordination across channels, communication to beneficiaries, and scheduling of time slots lower the risk of long lines and of liquidity problems (as in Peru).	Merchant acceptance of mobile money greatly reduces the need to cash out, which simplifies the issue of liquidity.
Trained Personnel		
Countries have trained personnel at main access points to answer G2P program questions and provide basic redress mechanisms in case of disputes. Even in advanced economies, this can be difficult in times of crisis because of massive flows of applications and demands.	All personnel across participating channels are trained adequately. Internal controls are in place for government personnel who typically do not handle cash.	Well-designed products (including mobile apps, updated websites, and SMS alerts) limit the need for people to interact with cash-out personnel. Still, advanced and unscheduled internal controls limit bad service, fraud, or surcharges.
Typical Risks to Mitigate		
Corruption. Manual mistakes. Subpar services. Liquidity.	Liquidity. Unregulated access to cash-out point.	Low digital literacy may limit the effectiveness of some technology solutions.
Case Study		
In Colombia, private bank *Banco Davivienda* created the *DaviPlata* mobile platform in 2011 in response to a government call to cost-effectively disburse money to lower-income households. An essential component for success was sufficient cash-out points managed by the parent bank. To complement its 600 branches and 1,600-ATM network, *Banco Davivienda* leveraged 5,000 store access points (2.5 times more access points than its direct channels). Moreover, this growth specifically targeted underserved communities; within three years, banking agents covered more than 700 new municipalities that were previously not served by the branches and ATMs, demonstrating that mixed channels of delivery are essential (Consultores 2015).		

Source: Authors.

Note: ATM = automated teller machine; G2P = government to person; SMS = short message service.

TABLE 10.1.6.

<table>
<tr><th colspan="3">Payment Acceptance Network</th></tr>
<tr><th>Minimum Required</th><th>Good to Have (Enhanced Scenario)</th><th>Great to Have (Advanced Model)</th></tr>
<tr><td colspan="3">Mobile Money Life Cycle</td></tr>
<tr><td>Some "essential" businesses, such as those providing water, electricity, food (grocery), and medicine (pharmacy), are registered as merchants and accept mobile money to provide P2B services.</td><td>Wider merchant acceptance. Some government services also accept mobile money to introduce P2G payment (for example, taxes, public transportation, schools).</td><td>Most micro and small businesses, including informal ones, are registered. These include local market vendors, taxi drivers, bars and restaurants, and (small) convenience stores. Businesses can use the same platforms to transact among themselves (B2B) and with the government (B2G).</td></tr>
<tr><td colspan="3">Fee Structure</td></tr>
<tr><td>For essential services, countries have waived fees for registration and transactions and lowered charges for "essential" merchants, for a fixed period.</td><td>Countries have waived charges for customers and lowered or waived fees for small-value transactions (for example, under US $10) across a wide range of merchants for a fixed period.</td><td>Fees are applied more strategically to aim for specific, localized goals (for example, Kenya applied tier fees to encourage MNOs to provide services in underserved regions). Taxation of mobile transactions should aim to avoid creating arbitrage (Global System for Mobile Communications Association 2020b).</td></tr>
<tr><td colspan="3">Payment Platforms and Interoperability</td></tr>
<tr><td>A merchant registered under a certain mobile money plan can accept payments from a beneficiary from any other mobile money plan (that is, one-to-many plan).</td><td>A merchant registered under any mobile money plan can accept beneficiary payments from any other mobile money plan (that is, many-to-many plan).</td><td>A merchant registered under any payment plan (mobile money or bank) can accept beneficiary payments from any other payment plan (that is, many-to-many and across plans).</td></tr>
<tr><td colspan="3">Case Study</td></tr>
<tr><td colspan="3">In June 2018, Econet Wireless, Zimbabwe's leading mobile operator, launched a merchant payment business through its mobile money platform, EcoCash. Because of persistent shortages of physical cash in the country, Zimbabwe's central bank has strongly promoted moving toward a cash-lite economy. The EcoCash Business Wallet is a separate mobile money wallet for businesses that is covered by insurance and allows larger transaction limit amounts compared to an individual wallet (roughly two to three times larger, depending on the size of business). All businesses, both formal and informal, are eligible, and additional services include payroll services and supplier payments. Customers would dial a separate USSD shortcode to access the service, which allows it to work on a 2G handset. EcoNet has also developed a smartphone app to serve the growing population with smartphone devices. EcoCash is not currently interoperable with other mobile money plans (although EcoNet owns most of the mobile money market). EcoNet also enabled consumers to pay with card-based schemes through Mastercard's Masterpass QR services, available at roughly 3,800 merchants, with either their smartphones or feature phones. However, EcoCash has not yet been integrated with bank-based point-of-sale terminals.</td></tr>
</table>

Source: Authors.

Note: B2B = business to business; B2G = business to government; MNO = mobile network operator; P2B = person to business; QR = quick-response code; P2G = person to government; USSD = unstructured supplementary service data.

TABLE 10.1.7.

Business Model Elements		
Minimum Required	**Good to Have (Enhanced Scenario)**	**Great to Have (Advanced Model)**
Program Features		
Some countries have opted for a minimal one-time, unconditional electronic transfer for easily identifiable beneficiary segments.	In many cases, transfer amounts are fixed and occur with a set frequency and last over a defined period.	Transfer amounts vary by beneficiary segment (for example, employment type, gender, age) using up-to-date data. Duration is tied to measurable effects and market conditions. Crisis context is supported by trustable data.
Effective and Frequent Communication		
Countries usually document features through their websites and media: beneficiary eligibility; documents and requirements (including conditions); transfer amount and frequency; and how, where, and how quickly funds are transferred.	Additional financial education and marketing collateral developed, including at cash-out access points. Basic customer support by USSD to check balances and most recent transactions.	Marketing and customer support are available in local languages of the beneficiaries and local authorities. Extensive customer support to address customer queries and resolve disputes.
Program Management		
Ensure basic processes, procedures, and reporting along financial, operations, and technology functions are in place across all stakeholders: government, bank, MNO, and any intermediaries (such as technology vendors or marketing agencies) for effective transfer.	Consider tactics for effectiveness of programs and risk reduction (for example, vetting stakeholders, ensuring sufficient liquidity in specific areas of country). Develop and control deadlines and budgets.	To optimize performance, continuously align objectives of stakeholders, frequently share operational data and best practices, recommend adjustments in business model elements, and proactively identify and mitigate risks to program.
Case Study		
In 2019, Togo began its digital National ID program for Togolese citizens and noncitizen residents. National ID includes even those who do not have birth certificates. After the program obtains biometrics to ensure that each individual is counted only once, a card is provided as proof of ID that enables people to apply for all government and financial services, among others. Furthermore, the Togolese government is also establishing "e-KYC" to facilitate the ability for public and private sector entities to verify identity digitally, rather than rely on verification of a physical document by personnel. At the core is a central registry that holds the data of Togo's 7 million plus citizens and residents. In response to COVID-19, the government launched a G2P program called *Novissi*. The core product features include a monthly transfer of 10,500 CFAF (about US $18) for men and 12,250 CFAF (about US $21) for women, and close to US $35 for motorbike taxi drivers. The Togolese government has also communicated clear eligibility requirements (for example, being 18 years of age; both citizens and residents are eligible) and ID requirements (for example, a voter card is sufficient) and has encouraged beneficiaries to make payments electronically where possible. Registration is by simple USSD code across all networks (*#855) and, conveniently, is the same toll-free number for general customer inquiries (855), making it easier for beneficiaries to remember.		

Source: Authors.

Note: COVID-19 = coronavirus disease 2019; CFAF = CFA franc; G2P = government to person; ID = identification; KYC = know your customer; MNO = mobile network operator; USSD = unstructured supplementary service data.

Digital Inclusion Foundations

The three enablers in Table 10.1.8 are out of reach and out of scope for a G2P program. However, close coordination with stakeholders will help countries further define and prioritize the business model (Building Block 7) and digital inclusion (Building Block 8), as well as coordinate work with other government agencies to maximize the effect of mobile G2P payments and boost the effect of mobile platforms beyond G2P (see the end-to-end framework section).

TABLE 10.1.8.

Digital Inclusion Foundations		
Minimum Required	**Good to Have (Enhanced Scenario)**	**Great to Have (Advanced Model)**
Digital Access and Affordability		
Working with MMO data and government agencies in charge of infrastructure and digital inclusion, G2P program managers identify where mobile G2P can and cannot be implemented in the short term and adapt the program accordingly.	Many countries rapidly mandated that internet and energy providers ensure availability and affordability of services during the pandemic (Argentina, Chile, Malaysia, Panama, Qatar, Vietnam).	All countries suffer from some domestic digital divide because of affordability, internet and electricity coverage, or education. See the Enhanced Digital Access Index (Alper and Miktus 2019) as an example of the tools available to measure and reduce digital divide.
Gender Gap		
Stakeholders should assess the possible negative effect of digital payment for women in emerging market and developing economies, given that they represent a large portion of the informal sector, and the digital divide between genders has been widening in the past seven years (International Telecommunications Union 2019). Also, at a minimum, countries should collect gender-disaggregated information on the G2P program for future improvement.	Programs designed to address gender gaps can have long-term benefits for women's empowerment (G2Px 2020d). In Pakistan and Togo, mobile G2P has explicitly targeted impoverished women.	The Digitize, Direct, Design Framework from Chamberlin and others (2019) can guide the design of mobile G2P for women's economic empowerment.
Typical Risks to Mitigate		
Digital exclusion of the population hardest to reach physically and economically. Digital exclusion of populations with low literacy. Gender gap in financial access.		

Source: Authors.

Note: G2P = government to person; MMO = mobile money operator.

REFERENCES

Aker J. C., R. Boumnijel, A. McClelland, and N. Tierney. 2016. "Payment Mechanisms and Antipoverty Programs: Evidence from a Mobile Money Cash Transfer Experiment in Niger." *Economic Development and Cultural Change* 65 (1).

Alliance for Financial Inclusion (AFI). 2020. "Policy Framework for Leveraging Digital Financial Services to Respond to Global Emergencies: Case of COVID-19." AFI, Kuala Lumpur, Malaysia.

Alper, E., and Michal Miktus. 2019. "Digital Connectivity in sub-Saharan Africa: A Comparative Perspective." IMF Working Paper 19/210, International Monetary Fund, Washington, DC.

Ayana Aga, G., F. Jolevski, and S. Muzi. 2020. "Insights from Enterprise Surveys: Including the Informal Economy in Policy Responses to COVID-19." *Let's Talk Development* (blog), World Bank, May 14. https://blogs.worldbank.org/developmenttalk/insights-enterprise-surveys-including-informal-economy-policy-responses-covid-19.

Bank of Ghana. 2020. "Monetary Policy Committee Press Release." Press release, March 18. https://www.bog.gov.gh/wp-content/uploads/2020/03/MPC-Press-Release-March-2020-3.pdf.

Barca V., and R. Beazley. 2019. "Building on Government Systems for Shock Preparedness and Response: The Role of Social Assistance Data and Information Systems." Australian Government, Department of Foreign Affairs and Trade.https://www.dfat.gov.au/about-us/publications/Pages/building-government-systems-for-shock-preparedness-and-response-the-role-of-social-assistance-data-and-information-systems.

Baur-Yazbeck, S. 2019. "A New Generation of Government-to-Person Payments Is Emerging." *CGAP Blog*, Consultative Group to Assist the Poor, October 1. https://www.cgap.org/blog/new-generation-government-person-payments-emerging.

Baur-Yazbeck, S., C. Kilfoil, and I. Botea. 2019. "The Future of G2P Payments: Expanding Customer Choice in Zambia." Consultative Group to Assist the Poor, Washington, DC.

Cassim, Z., B. Handjiski, J. Schubert, and Y. Zouaoui. 2020. "The $10 Trillion Rescue: How Governments Can Deliver Impact." *McKinsey and Company* (blog), June 5. https://www.mckinsey.com/industries/public-and-social-sector/our-insights/the-10-trillion-dollar-rescue-how-governments-can-deliver-impact#.

Chamberlin, W., L. Kellison, J. Klugman, and J. Zimmerman. 2019. "Enhancing Women's Economic Empowerment through Digital Cash Transfers: Digitize/Direct/Design—The D3 Criteria." Consultative Group to Assist the Poor, Washington, DC.

Chhabra, E., and B. Das. 2019. "Mobile Money Spreads to Asia." *IMF Blog*, September 30. https://blogs.imf.org/2019/09/30/mobile-money-spreads-to-asia.

Consultative Group to Assist the Poor (CGAP). 2014. "Mobile Payments Infrastructure Access and Its Regulation: USSD." CGAP Working Paper, Consultative Group to Assist the Poor, Washington, DC.

Consultores, M. 2015. "DaviPlata: Taking Mobile G2P Payments to Scale in Colombia." *CGAP Blog*, Consultative Group to Assist the Poor, July 1. https://www.cgap.org/blog/daviplata-taking-mobile-g2p-payments-scale-colombia.

Davidovic, S., E. Loukoianova, C. Sullivan, and H. Tourpe. 2019. "Strategy for Fintech Applications in the Pacific Island Countries." Asia and Pacific Department Paper 19/14, International Monetary Fund, Washington, DC.

Davidovic, S., S. Nunhuck, D. Prady, and H. Tourpe. 2020. "Beyond the COVID-19 Crisis: A Framework for Sustainable Government-to-Person Mobile Money Transfers." IMF Working Paper 20/198, International Monetary Fund, Washington, DC.

Dumas, T., A. Frisetti, and H. W. Radice. 2017. "Harnessing Digital Technology for Cash Transfer Programming in the Ebola Response: Lessons Learned from USAID/Office of Food for Peace Partners' West Africa Ebola Responses (2015–2016)." USAID and CaLP, Washington, DC.

Financial Action Task Force (FATF). 2020a. "Guidance on Digital ID." Financial Action Task Force, Paris.

Financial Action Task Force (FATF). 2020b. "Statement by the FATF President: COVID-19 and Measures to Combat Illicit Financing." Press release, April 1. https://www.fatf-gafi.org/publications/fatfgeneral/documents/statement-covid-19.html.

Find Biometrics. 2020. "Pakistan Launches Biometric Cash Transfer Program for Impoverished Women." Press release, February 3. https://findbiometrics.com/biometrics-news-pakistans-prime-minster-launches-biometric-cash-transfer-program-impoverished-women-020303.

Fischer A. M., E. L. Dadap-Cantal, and C. G. Ramos. 2020. "Ephemeral Universalism in the Social Protection Response to the COVID-19 Lockdown in the Philippines." *Developing Economics* (blog), July 3.

G2Px. 2020a. "COVID-19 G2P Cash-Transfer Payments: Country Brief—Colombia." World Bank, Washington, DC.

G2Px. 2020b. "COVID-19 G2P Cash-Transfer Payments: Country Brief—Jordan." World Bank, Washington, DC.

G2Px. 2020c. "COVID-19 G2P Cash-Transfer Payments: Country Brief—Peru." World Bank, Washington, DC.

G2Px. 2020d. "Key Considerations and Policy Options for Emergency Social Assistance Payments." World Bank, Washington, DC.

Gelb A., A. Mukherjee, and K. Navis. 2020. "Citizens and States: How Can Digital ID and Payments Improve State Capacity and Effectiveness?" Center for Global Development, Washington, DC.

Gentilini, A., and D. Orton. 2020. "Social Protection and Jobs Responses to COVID-19: A Real-Time Review of Country Measures." World Bank, Washington, DC.

Global System for Mobile Communications Association (GSMA). 2016. "Safeguarding Mobile Money: How Providers and Regulators Can Ensure that Customer Funds are Protected." Global System for Mobile Communications, London.

Global System for Mobile Communications Association (GSMA). 2020a. "The Causes and Consequences of Mobile Money Taxation: An Examination of Mobile Money Transaction Taxes in Sub-Saharan Africa." Global System for Mobile Communications, London.

Global System for Mobile Communications Association (GSMA). 2020b. "Mobile Money Recommendations to Central Banks in Response To COVID-19." Global System for Mobile Communications, London.

Global System for Mobile Communications Association (GSMA). 2020c. "Why Is There a Need for GSMA Mobile Money API Specification? A Comparison with Other Industry Standards." Global System for Mobile Communications, London.

Independent Communications Authority of South Africa (ICASA). 2020. "ICASA Engages with Licensees to Open Their Services to All South Africans as the Country Fights the Scourge of the COVID-19 Pandemic." Press release, March 19. https://www.icasa.org.za/news/2020/icasa-engages-with-licensees-to-open-their-services-to-all-south-africans-as-the-country-fights-the-scourge-of-the-covid-19-pandemic.

International Criminal Police Organization (INTERPOL). 2020. "Mobile Money and Organized Crime in Africa." INTERPOL, Lyon, France.

International Monetary Fund (IMF). 2018. "Digital Government." In *Fiscal Monitor: Capitalizing on Good Times*. Washington, DC, April.

International Monetary Fund (IMF). 2020a. "Digitalization in Sub-Saharan Africa." In *Regional Economic Outlook: Sub-Saharan Africa—COVID-19: An Unprecedented Threat to Development*. Washington, DC, April.

International Monetary Fund (IMF). 2020b. "Rwanda: Request for Disbursement under the Rapid Credit Facility—Press Release, Staff Report, and Statement by the Executive Director for Rwanda." IMF Country Report 20/207, International Monetary Fund, Washington, DC.

International Telecommunications Union (ITU). 2019. "Measuring Digital Development. Facts and Figures 2019." Interactive Report, ITU, Geneva. https://www.itu.int/en/ITU-D/Statistics/Pages/facts/default.aspx.

Leite P. G., G. Philippe, T. George, C. Sun, T. Jones, and K. A. Lindert. 2017. "Social Registries for Social Assistance and Beyond: A Guidance Note and Assessment Tool." World Bank Discussion Paper 1704, World Bank, Washington, DC.

Leonovich, P. 2020. "Pandemic Preparedness for Financial Institutions." Monetary and Capital Markets, Special Series on COVID-19, International Monetary Fund, Washington, DC.

Lindert K., T. G. Karippacheril, I. Rodriguez Caillava, and K. Nishikawa Chavez. 2020. *Sourcebook on the Foundations of Social Protection Delivery Systems.* Washington, DC: World Bank.

Lindsey, D., and A. Wilson. 2019. "'Affordability': How Mobile Operators Can Improve the Affordability of Their Services for Women to Help Close the Mobile Gender Gap." *GSMA Blog*, Global System for Mobile Communications Association, October 15. https://www.gsma.com/mobilefordevelopment/blog/how-mobile-operators-can-improve-the-affordability-of-their-services-for-women-to-help-close-the-mobile-gender-gap.

LLorente y Cuenca (LLYC). 2020. "Ecuador: Navigating the COVID-19 Crisis and Outlook." Technical Note, LLYC, Mexico City.

Martins, B. 2020. "Interconnecting Mobile Money Providers: Why Is Interoperability Testing So Important?" *GSMA Blog*, March 17. https://www.gsma.com/mobilefordevelopment/blog/interconnecting-mobile-money-providers-why-is-interoperability-testing-so-important.

McKay, C., and G. Mdluli. 2020. "Kenya's Expansion of G2P Becomes Lifeline during COVID-19 Crisis." *CGAP Blog*, Consultative Group to Assist the Poor, April 29. https://www.cgap.org/blog/kenyas-expansion-g2p-becomes-lifeline-during-covid-19-crisis.

McKee, K., M. Kaffenberger, and J. M. Zimmerman. 2015. "Doing Digital Finance Right: The Case or Stronger Mitigation of Customer Risks." CGAP Focus Note 103, Consultative Group to Assist the Poor, Washington, DC.

Medina, L., and F. Schneider. 2018. "Shadow Economies around the World: What Did We Learn over the Last 20 Years?" IMF Working Paper 18/17, International Monetary Fund, Washington, DC.

PPP Knowledge Lab. 2020. "Establishing the PPP Framework." https://pppknowledgelab.org/guide/sections/5-establishing-the-ppp-framework.

Prady, D. 2020. "Reaching Households in Emerging and Developing Economies: Citizen ID, Socioeconomic Data, and Digital Delivery." Special Series on Fiscal Policies to Respond to COVID-19, International Monetary Fund, Washington, DC.

Roessler, C., K. Jahari, and N. Myamba. 2019. "Mobile Phone Ownership and the Uptake and Usage of Digital Financial Services by Women in an Emerging Economy: Evidence from a Field Experiment in Tanzania."

Rutkowski, M., A. Garcia Mora, G. L. Bull, B. Guermazi, and C. Grown. 2020. "Responding to Crisis with Digital Payments for Social Protection: Short-Term Measures with Long-Term Benefits." *Voices* (blog), World Bank, March 31. https://blogs.worldbank.org/voices/responding-crisis-digital-payments-social-protection-short-term-measures-long-term-benefits.

Sahay, R., U. Eriksson von Allmen, A. Lahreche, P. Khera, S. Ogawa, M. Bazarbash, and K. Beaton. 2020. "The Promise of Fintech: Financial Inclusion in the Post COVID-19 Era." IMF Department al Paper 20/09, International Monetary Fund, Washington, DC.

Seekings, J., and L. Gronbach. 2020. "COVID-19 Grant: We Can Learn from Namibia." *University of Cape Town* (blog), May 4. https://www.news.uct.ac.za/article/-2020-05-04-covid-19-grant-we-can-learn-from-namibia.

Sri Sulastri, A., and TVS Ravi Kumar. 2019. "Deepening Financial Inclusion through Cash Transfers: The Case of PKH in Indonesia." *MicroSave Consulting Blog*, November 13. https://www.microsave.net/2019/11/13/deepening-financial-inclusion-through-cash-transfers-the-case-of-pkh-in-indonesia.

Una, G., R. Allen, S. Pattanayak, and G. Suc. 2020. "Digital Solutions for Direct Cash Transfers in Emergencies." Special Series on Fiscal Policies to Respond to COVID-19, International Monetary Fund, Washington, DC.

Una, G., H. van Eden, A. Singh, F. Bardella, and A. Verma. 2020. "Enhancing Digital Solutions to Implement Emergency Responses." Special Series on Fiscal Policies to Respond to COVID-19, International Monetary Fund, Washington, DC.

United Nations (UN). 2020. "Report of the Secretary General: Roadmap for Digital Cooperation." United Nations, New York.

Zimmerman, J. M., and S. Baur. 2016. "Understanding How Consumer Risks in Digital Social Payments Can Erode Their Financial Inclusion Potential." CGAP Brief, Consultative Group to Assist the Poor, Washington, DC.

Zimmerman, J. M., M. A. May, E. Kellison, and J. Klugman. 2020. "Digital Cash Transfers in the Time of COVID-19: Opportunities and Considerations for Women's Inclusion and Empowerment." World Bank, Washington, DC.

CHAPTER 11

Macroprudential Policies and Financial Inclusion: Good Intentions and Unintended Consequences

Corinne Deléchat, Lama Kiyasseh, Margaux MacDonald, and Rui Xu

INTRODUCTION

Financial inclusion is a pillar of the agenda to boost inclusive growth in emerging markets and developing economies. As a multidimensional concept, financial inclusion can be defined as ease of access to (or lack of barriers to), availability of, and use of formal financial services by all members of the economy (Sarma 2008; Camara and Tuesta 2014).[1]

Financial inclusion has thus become a goal of public policy and typically aims to reduce financial exclusion and resort to informal financial services, such as moneylenders.[2] Worldwide, about 67 percent of bank regulators are tasked with promoting financial inclusion (Klapper and Singer 2015). In a similar vein, the Financial Action Task Force (FATF) supports formal financial inclusion to enhance transparency and traceability of transactions by reducing use of cash or informal financial services (FATF 2011).

Greater degrees of formal financial inclusion, that is, lower financial exclusion, however, may not necessarily reduce use of informal financial services. Many studies document that formal and informal services tend to coexist as complements, rather than substitutes, although the gradual increase in formal financial inclusion tends to decrease both exclusion and use of informal financial services

The authors thank Deniz Igan, Futoshi Narita, Machiko Narita, Romain Bouis, Lucyna Gornicka, Purva Khera, Erlend Nier, Amine Mati, the IMF African Department's Research Advisory Group, and seminar participants at the IMF and the Western Economic Association Annual Conference 2019 for helpful comments. Beatrice Quartey and Jacques Treilly provided editorial assistance.

[1] In this chapter, *formal financial services* are any financial institution or mobile-based form of financial access, including microfinance institutions, post offices, credit unions, and cooperatives.

[2] Informal financial services include resort to family and friends or any type of informal credit or savings club, as well as moneylenders.

(Aryeetey 1994, 2008; Soyibo 1996; De Koker and Jentzsch 2013; Pradhan 2013; World Bank 2017).

In this chapter, we investigate the determinants of informal and formal financial inclusion in emerging market and developing economies. We are particularly interested in examining whether monetary and financial policies interact with individuals' choice of financial services. The contributions of our chapter to the existing literature are twofold:

1. We use the World Bank Global Findex Database 2017 microdata worldwide sample to construct a new granular categorization of the various ways individuals combine access to formal and informal financial services. We find that individuals tend to use formal and informal financial services as complements. Mobile banking, in particular, combines with both formal and informal financial services, highlighting its role in bridging informal and formal finance. To our knowledge, ours is one of the first studies to analyze the determinants of formal and informal financial access in a large cross-section of countries, examining mobile banking access separately.
2. We study the relation between monetary and financial sector policies, including macroprudential measures, using the IMF 2016–17 Macroprudential Policies Survey and individuals' use of formal and informal financial services. Although there are intuitive reasons monetary policy or measures aimed at increasing financial stability would influence financial inclusion (and vice versa), this topic remains little explored in the literature. We are particularly interested in the potential relation between macroprudential policies (which affect formal financial services and their users) and the persistence of resort to informal financial services. Such persistence would be consistent with empirical findings that macroprudential policies "leak" by creating incentives for individuals or firms to move from formal toward informal or unregulated financial services (Aiyar, Calomiris, and Wieladek 2014; Ayyagari, Beck, and Martinez Peria 2018; Alam and others 2019).

Our findings suggest that central banks and bank regulators should pay more attention to the interactions between monetary and financial sector policies and financial inclusion. Macroprudential policies, in particular, are significantly related to individuals' use of informal financial services, relative to formal services and no financial access, after controlling for individual and country characteristics. In sub-Saharan Africa, the region with the highest prevalence of informality and the least financial development, we find that macroprudential policies have a particularly strong relationship with lack of financial access. Across all emerging market and developing economies, however, macroprudential policies show the strongest effects in countries with more developed financial systems.

The rest of the chapter briefly reviews the related literature; presents our definitions of formal and informal financial access and key stylized facts; presents the empirical approach, choice of variables, and empirical results; and offers conclusions and implicaitons for policy.

RELATED LITERATURE

Our research links to the literature on formal and informal financial inclusion and their determinants.

Formal versus Informal Financial Inclusion and Mobile Banking

Theoretical and empirical studies mostly focusing on a single country highlight the importance of social capital (Guiso, Sapienza, and Zingales 2004), contract enforcement (Giné 2011; Karaivanov and Kessler 2018), and information asymmetries (Jain 1999; Armendáriz and Morduch 2005; Dabla-Norris and Koeda 2008; Madestam 2014; Mookherjee and Motta 2016) in explaining simultaneous resort to formal and informal financial services.

Empirical studies of the drivers of financial inclusion find that resort to informal financial services is highly persistent, with policy interventions aimed at increasing formal financial inclusion having limited success (Demirgüç-Kunt and Klapper 2012a; De Koker and Jentsch 2013; Allen, Qian, and Xie 2019; Allen and others 2016; Klapper and Singer 2015; Zins and Weill 2016).[3] One explanation is that the reasons people resort to informal finance (accessing emergency funds and developing social networks) make it difficult for them to connect with the formal financial sector (Johnson, Malkamäki, and Niño-Zarazua 2010).

Mobile banking is often seen as a bridge between formal and informal finance; however, evidence suggests that the individual-level determinants of mobile banking are the same as for formal banking and different from those for informal finance, raising questions about mobile banking as a path out of informal finance (Zins and Weill 2016). It is therefore not surprising that government interventions aimed at increasing access to cheaper credit have not reduced use of informal finance (Giné 2011).

Monetary and Financial Sector Policies and Financial Inclusion

The literature on monetary policy and financial inclusion is sparse, although there are three intuitive reasons for why financial inclusion relates to monetary

[3] The IMF's Financial Access Survey provides information on access to and use of financial services for 189 countries and spans more than 10 years containing 121 time series on financial access and use. Beck, Ross, and Levkov (2007); Honohan and Beck (2007); and Mookerjee and Kalipioni (2010) analyze financial inclusion using supply-side measures. On the demand side, the FinScope data sets stem from extensive, nationally representative demand-side surveys conducted in more than 30 countries and focusing on sub-Saharan Africa. Providing a battery of financial inclusion indicators, the World Bank's Global Findex Database is based on Gallup polls and covers 150 countries using representative samples of 1,000 individuals per country. A growing number of empirical studies rely on Findex data, for example, Allen and others (2016); Demirgüç-Kunt and Klapper (2013); Demirgüç-Kunt and Klapper (2012b); and Deléchat and others (2018).

policy. First, monetary policy focused on core inflation may be ineffective in countries with less financial inclusion, because these regions tend to be agricultural and thus food prices are particularly important. Second, interest rate policies are likely to become more effective regarding quantities (money supply) in countries with more informal—that is, cash based—financial transactions. Third, a central bank's interest rate rule may depend on the level of inclusion; the better the financial inclusion, the more effective the interest rate tools, and monetary policy can better focus on inflation stabilization versus output stabilization (Yetman 2017).

Qin, Zhong, and Zhang (2014) find that in China, informal credit lending rates are highly receptive to monetary policies and that informal lending is substitutive to bank savings in the short term but complementary to bank lending in the long term. This finding suggests that the bank lending channel also operates through the informal financial sector.

Another issue for central bankers and financial market supervisors is the relation between financial stability and financial inclusion. On the one hand, evidence has shown that better inclusion improves a bank's deposit bases and thereby deepens and diversifies the finanical system (Hannig and Jansen 2010; Han and Melecky 2013). On the other hand, Sahay and others (2015) find that financial stability is at risk when access to credit is expanded without supervision.

The structure and health of the financial sector might also be associated with financial inclusion, but evidence is somewhat mixed. Owen and Pereira (2018) find that greater banking industry concentration is associated with more access to deposit accounts and loans, provided that the market power of banks is limited. Yet Mengistu and Perez-Saiz (2018) find the opposite true in a sample of sub-Saharan African countries. Sarma and Pais (2011) find that high numbers of nonperforming loans and high capital-to-asset ratios are associated with lower formal financial inclusion.

Macroprudential policies could also interact with financial access.[4] By acting on formal financial intermediaries and households relying on formal credit, macroprudential policies could unintentionally push credit activity toward the informal sector. Ayyagari, Beck, and Martinez Peria (2018) show that borrower-targeted macroprudential policies are robustly and negatively associated with growth in long-term firm financing. Aiyar, Calomiris, and Wieladek (2014) find, when examinig a relevant reference group of regulated banks, that regulated banks reduce lending in response to tighter capital requirements but that unregulated banks increase lending in response to tighter capital requirements. Alam and others (2019) find that the tighter the loan-to-value ratio, the smaller

[4] Macroprudential policies aim to limit systemic risk by absorbing systemic shocks and can be directed at financial institutions, thus affecting the supply of credit (for example, countercyclical capital buffers, liquidity tools), or at borrowers, thus affecting the demand for credit (for example, loan-to-value ratios or debt-to-income ratios) (IMF 2013).

the per-unit effect on household credit, possibly because strong tightening could encourage people to seek credit from abroad or from nonbank lenders. Ben Hassine and Rebei (2019) show that informality weakens the effect of macroprudential policies in emerging markets.

Three main findings emerge from this brief literature survey. First, financial access takes multiple forms for the same individuals. The choice of formal or informal financial access is influenced by personal characteristics but also by country-level factors, including measures of institutional quality. Second, the literature suggests that because individuals mix formal and informal financial services, joint study of the determinants of formal and informal financial access would be useful. Third, given the still scarce literature, how monetary and financial sector policies, including macroprudential policy tools, are related to formal financial inclusion should be examined. Central banks in countries with large informal sectors (emerging market and developing economies in general, but sub-Saharan Africa in particular) would benefit, given their joint objectives of expanding financial inclusion and ensuring macroeconomic and financial stability.

KEY STYLIZED FACTS OF FORMAL AND INFORMAL FINANCIAL ACCESS

To classify respondents as having formal or informal access, we interpret their answers to questions about financial services as revealing their access to and use of financial services.

Definitions of Formal and Informal Financial Access

Our categorization of financial inclusion is based on the World Bank Global Findex Database 2017. The data are from a nationally representative survey of more than 150,000 adults in 150 economies, including 34 in sub-Saharan Africa (Demirgüç-Kunt and Klapper 2012a, 2012b; Demirgüç-Kunt and others 2018, 2020). The Global Findex database builds on similar 2011 and 2014 surveys by including questions on the use of financial technology (fintech), mobile phones, and the internet to conduct financial transactions.

The 2017 Findex questionnaire asked 48 questions, with additional follow-up questions depending on the answer given to certain questions. Questions such as the following examples were aimed at obtaining information about access to a particular type of financial services:

- *Do you currently have an account at a bank or another type of formal financial institution? Yes or no?* We classify a positive answer to this question as indicating that the respondant has formal financial access.

Questions could also indirectly reveal access, for example:

- *In the past 12 months, has an employer paid your salary or wages in any of the following ways? (1) You received payments directly into an account at a bank or another type of formal financial institution; (2) You received payments through a mobile phone*. We consider a positive answer to (1) as revealing that the respondent has an account at a formal financial institution, and a positive answer to (2) as revealing that the respondent has access to mobile financial services.

We examine each individual's responses to all questions and first classify them into one of five mutually exclusive categories. Our criteria for each category are as follows:

1. Complete exclusion: answers negatively to all questions regarding the use of formal, informal, and mobile services.
2. Informal access only: answers positively to any question regarding the use of informal services and answers negatively to all questions regarding the use of formal and mobile services.
3. Formal access only: answers positively to any question regarding the use of formal services and answers negatively to all questions regarding the use of informal and mobile services.
4. Formal and informal access: answers positively to any question regarding the use of formal or informal services and answers negatively to all questions regarding the use of mobile services.
5. Any mobile access: answers positively to any question regarding the use of mobile services, in combination with either no resort to formal and informal financial services, or to both formal and informal financial services, or to only formal or informal services.

Our categorization of individuals combines the extensive and intensive margins of financial service access. That is, we combine pure access or account ownership with intensity of use. There are benefits to taking this approach. First, combining the extensive and intensive margins also allows us to directly answer the question on access to financial services, particularly the role of monetary and macroprudential policies in access. Second, as with any survey data, individuals may make errors when responding to the Findex questions. For example, they may respond *no* to a direct question about having a formal account but may respond *yes* to having their wages paid to a bank account. By combining the extensive and intensive margins, we do not falsely exclude individuals from the extensive margin of access.

In the econometric analysis, we further collapse the index into three categories: (1) complete exclusion, (2) access to informal financial services only, and (3) access to formal or mobile banking. In this exercise, we treat access to mobile services as equivalent to access to formal financial services, because both are often considered as such in policy and research literature. In robustness checks, we show that personal characteristics associated with use of mobile and formal financial services are similar, so we believe this is a reasonable assumption.

Figure 11.1. Financial Inclusion around the World

(All respondents, percentage of population age 15 years and older)

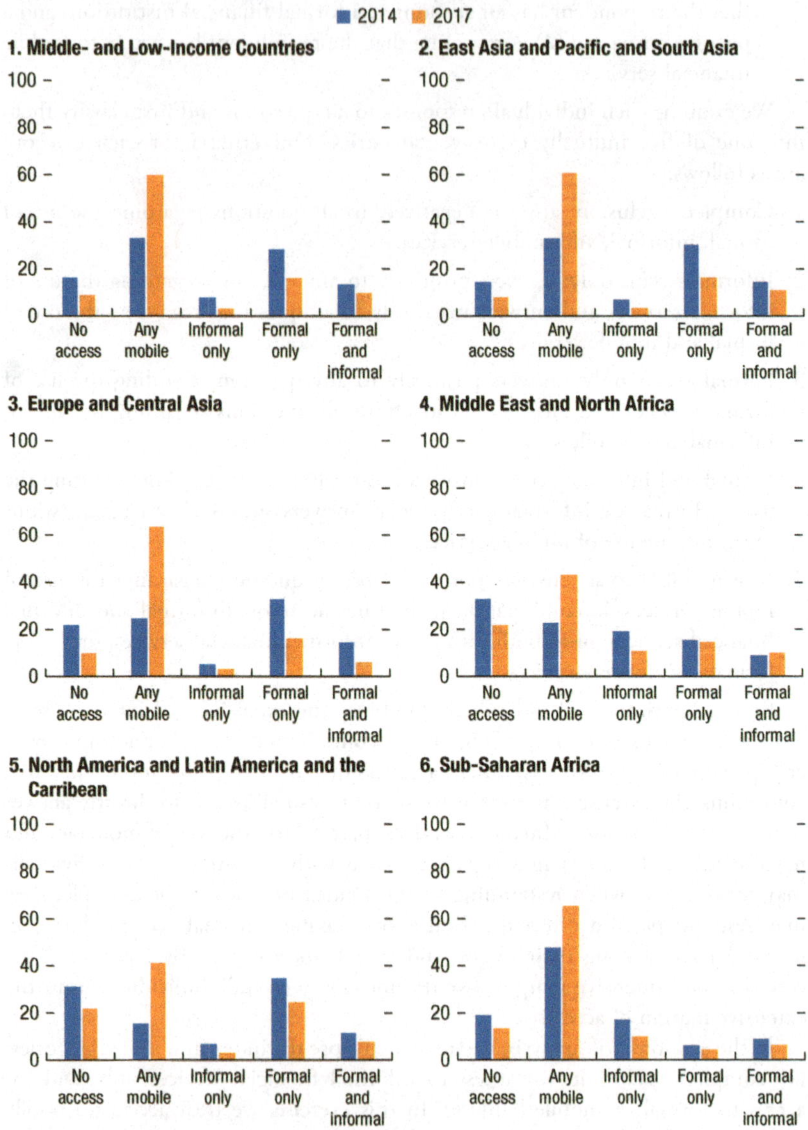

Sources: IMF, World Economic Outlook database; World Bank, Findex 2014, 2017; World Bank, World Development Indicators; and author estimates.

Note: Data represent middle- and low-income countries only and are weighted by individual survey weights and country population.

Figure 11.2. Financial Inclusion in Sub-Saharan Africa
(All respondents, percentage of population age 15 years and older)

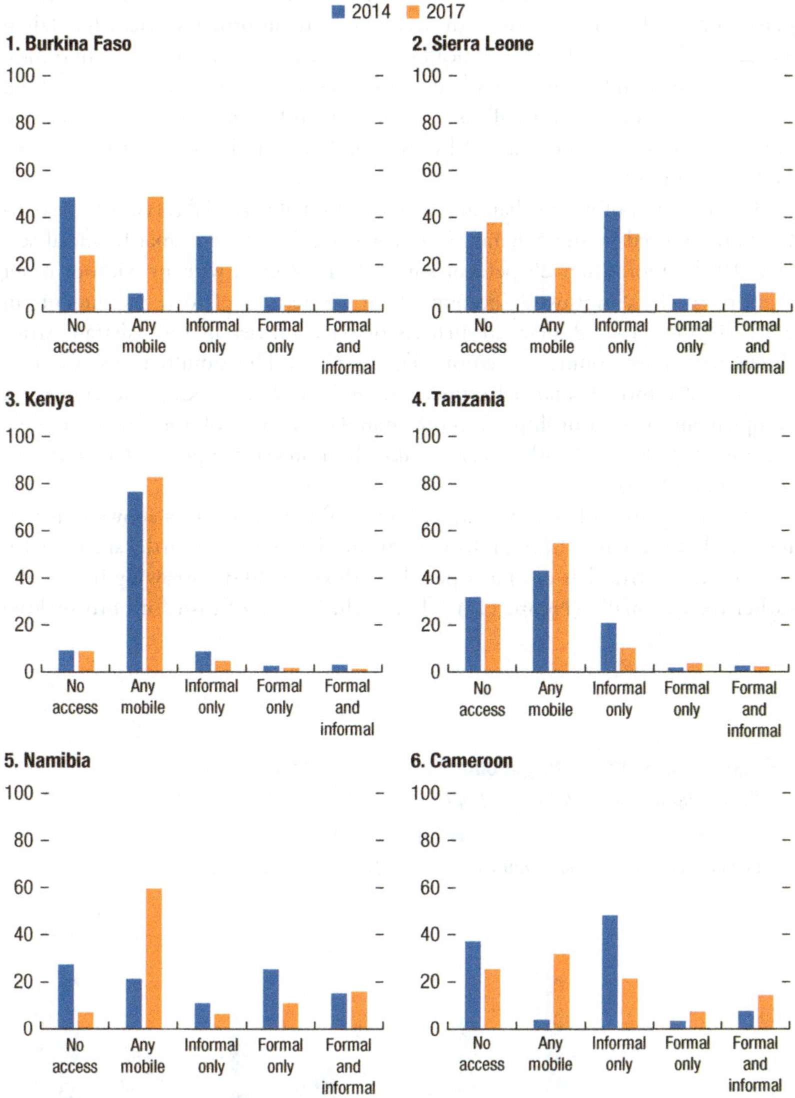

Sources: IMF, World Economic Outlook database; World Bank, Findex 2014, 2017; World Bank, World Development Indicators; and author estimates.
Note: Data are weighted by individual weights.

Facets of Financial Access

Financial access has improved between 2014 and 2017. The number of indviduals completely excluded or with access only to informal services has fallen worldwide (Figure 11.1), practically disappearing in advanced economies. Whereas the number of individuals with access only to traditional banking (that is, those in the "formal" or "formal and informal" categories) has also fallen, this has been outweighed by the number of individuals with access to mobile technology.

The adoption of mobile banking to access formal financial services is particularly pronounced in sub-Saharan Africa, where access to informal financial services fell by more than 25 percent since 2014. Mobile, with or without other types of services, meanwhile accounted for 65 percent of total respondents in 2017 (Figure 11.1). A detailed analysis of six countries in sub-Saharan Africa shows wide cross-country variation (Figure 11.2). The simultaneous resort to formal and informal financial services by individuals is striking and suggests a complementary relationship. A more granular analysis of the use of mobile accounts together with other services also illustrates a complementary relationship (Figure 11.3).

Examining uses of, rather than access to, financial services shows that savings and borrowing through formal means has changed little since 2014. Sub-Saharan Africa has the most people both saving and borrowing informally rather than formally (Figure 11.4). The exclusive use of cash for both making

Figure 11.3. Decomposing Mobile Financial Access
(All respondents, percentage of population age 15 years and older)

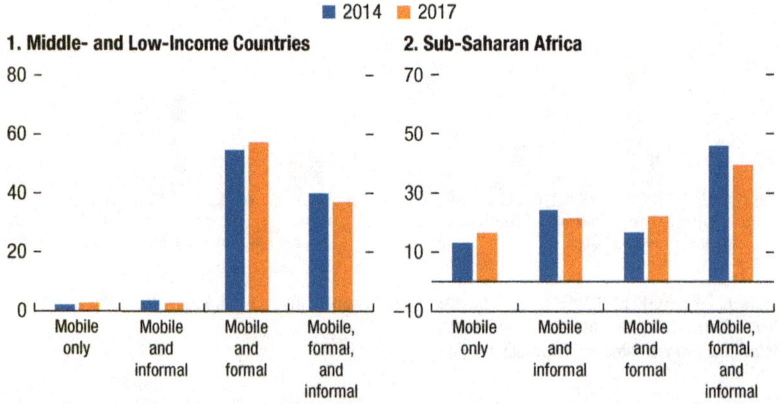

Sources: IMF, World Economic Outlook database; World Bank, Findex 2014, 2017; World Bank, World Development Indicators; and author estimates.
Note: Data are weighted by individual weights and country population.

Figure 11.4 Savings and Borrowing: 2014 and 2017, by Region

(All respondents, percentage of population age 15 years and older)

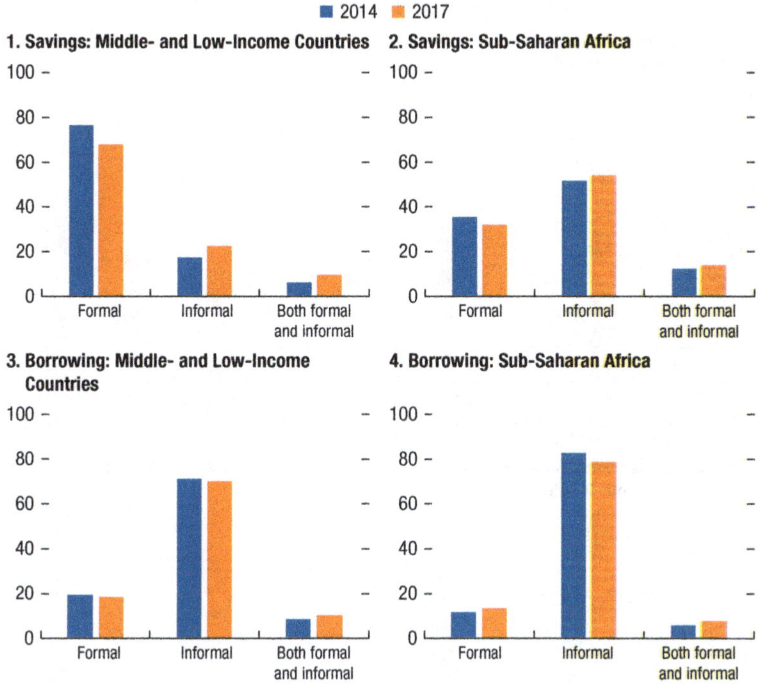

Sources: IMF, World Economic Outlook database; World Bank, Findex 2014, 2017; World Bank, World Development Indicators; and author estimates.

Note: Data represent middle- and low-income countries only and are weighted by individual survey weights and country population.

and receiving payments has become less common; users have moved toward accounts and mobile banking, indicating an increase in financial access (Figure 11.5). The stagnation in formal borrowing and saving is worrisome; their micro and macro benefits have been found to be the strongest relative to individuals having only a bank account. This stagnation also suggests that formal financial institutions may not adequately serve the needs of large parts of sub-Saharan Africa's population.

DRIVERS OF FORMAL AND INFORMAL FINANCIAL ACCESS

The first step in our analysis refines our definitions of access to formal, informal, and mobile financial services. We collapse our index into three categories: (1) complete exclusion, (2) access to informal financial services only, and (3) access to formal or mobile financial services. This last category also includes any combination of access to formal, mobile, and informal financial services.

Figure 11.5. Payments and Transfers: 2014 and 2017
(All respondents, percentage of population age 15 years and older)

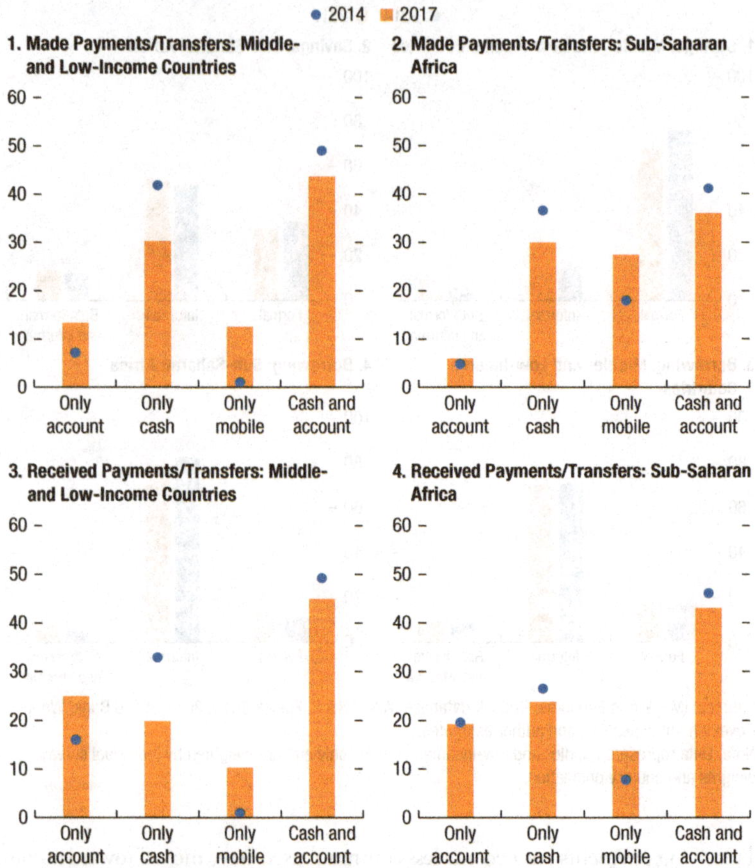

Sources: IMF, World Economic Outlook database; World Bank, Findex 2014, 2017; World Bank, World Development Indicators; and author estimates.
Note: Data are weighted by individual weights and country population.

Empirical Strategy

To estimate the role of each explanatory variable as determinants of these three levels of access, we estimate a multinomial logistic regression:

$$\Pr(excluded) = \frac{e^{X\beta^{(exclude)}}}{e^{X\beta^{(exclude)}} + e^{X\beta^{(informal)}} + e^{X\beta^{(formal-mobile)}}}$$

$$\Pr(informal) = \frac{e^{X\beta^{(informal)}}}{e^{X\beta^{(exclude)}} + e^{X\beta^{(informal)}} + e^{X\beta^{(formal-mobile)}}} \quad (1)$$

$$\Pr(formal-mobile) = \frac{e^{X\beta^{formal-mobile}}}{e^{X\beta^{(exclude)}} + e^{X\beta^{(informal)}} + e^{X\beta^{(formal-mobile)}}}$$

where function $F(z) = \frac{e^z}{1+e^z}$ is the related cumulative logistic distribution; X is our set of explanatory variables for personal, macroeconomic, financial, and monetary and structural characteristics at the individual and country levels; and the dependent variable is a three-way index valued at 0 for complete exclusion, 1 for informal access, and 2 for formal or mobile access (or any combination).

We assume outcomes to be unordered, which means we do not assume exclusion to be "less" than informal, or informal to be "less" than mobile or formal access. Although these outcomes could be ordered, the inclusion of mobile financial services and the simultaneous use of multiple types of financial services makes the ordering more ambiguous than it would be otherwise. We cluster the standard errors at the country level to correct for correlation across individuals within the same country.

In the multinomial logit model, we choose "informal access only" as the referent group and estimate a model for no access relative to informal access and a model for formal access relative to informal access. The multinomial logit essentially runs two logit models: one on formal access versus informal access and the other on no access versus informal access. The coefficient should be interpreted as follows: for a unit change in the explanatory variable, the logit of formal access (or no access) relative to informal access is expected to change by the parameter estimate while holding all other variables in the model constant.

We also estimate two models analogous to equation (1), with the left-side variable being the probability of saving informally, on the one hand, and the probability of borrowing informally, on the other, considering the determinants of access to formal savings and borrowing may be different and may be confounded in our baseline regression. These estimates aim to discover the specific channels through which financial inclusion and financial or macroprudential variables are related.

Our next step is to investigate the specific determinants of access to mobile financial services. We define an individual as having access to mobile financial services if he or she is identified as having access to any mobile financial service (see Annex Table 11.1.1 for questions that fall into these categories). With this definition, we estimate the following simple logistic regression:

$$\Pr(mobile = 1) = \frac{e^{z(\beta_0+\beta_1 X)}}{1+e^{z(\beta_0+\beta_1 X)}}, \tag{2}$$

where function $F(z) = \frac{e^z}{1+e^z}$ is the related cumulative logistic distribution and X is our set of explanatory variables.

Our analysis is conducted using the 2017 Findex microdata and other independent variables for 2017 (or 2016, depending on data availability). The analysis is limited to a simple but large cross-section, because the three successive Findex surveys (2011, 2014, 2017) have not been conducted with the same individuals. Data aggregation would be possible only at the country level, which would collapse the rich individual data and further complicate identification of the model.

Choice of Explanatory Variables

The choice of explanatory variables follows the literature reviewed here. Variable definitions and sources, as well as summary statistics, can be found in Annex Tables 11.1.3 and 11.1.4, respectively.

Individual Characteristics

From the Global Findex Database 2017, we use the following as individual characteristics: ***gender, age, education level, income quintile,*** and a ***proxy for being in the workforce*** (that is, an indicator variable based on the Findex question concerning whether the person has received wages in the past 12 months).[5] We expect being female, younger, less educated, poorer, and unemployed to be negatively associated with formal financial inclusion and mobile inclusion.

Country-Level Controls

For parsimony and to avoid multicollinearity, we use a reduced number of country-level controls, namely the log of real GDP per capita as a proxy for development; the size of the informal economy, measured as the share of the informal sector in GDP from Medina and Schneider (2018); and an indicator variable taking the value of 1 if average inflation is 12 percent and above in the year of the Findex survey (countries with 12 percent inflation and above are in the 90th decile of inflation in our sample), as a measure of macroeconomic stability. An index of regulatory quality from the World Bank Worldwide Governance Indicators, as presented by Kaufmann, Kraay, and Mastruzzi (2003), controls for the quality of institutions. Last, we include controls for financial sector development, including the ratio of domestic credit to GDP as a proxy for financial depth, the mobile regulatory support index from GSMA Mobile Money Metrics,[6] an indicator variable taking the value of 1 if the country has an inflation-targeting regime, and an indicator variable taking the value of 1 if the country has a credit bureau or registry. We expect financial sector development to be positively associated with formal financial inclusion.

Monetary Policy

We control in all regressions for whether a country has an inflation-targeting regime, which is typically associated with more financial development. We also examine additional variables related to monetary policy. We expect higher real interest rates to be negatively associated with formal financial inclusion. We also include an indicator variable taking the value of 1 if interest rate controls are in place in the country. Although the literature finds that interest rate controls tend

---

[5] The individual characteristics variable is generally considered a proxy for formal employment, because most self-employed individuals are in the informal sector. Workers employed by informal firms could also receive wages, however. Nonetheless, given that one reason for involuntary exclusion is lack of income, individuals receiving wages are more likely to be financially included.

[6] Bahia and Muthiora (2019) show that supportive mobile banking regulation is highly correlated with mobile money adoption.

to increase the cost of credit and reduce financial access that are opposite to the intention, several countries in the world still have interest controls in place (Munzele Maimbo and Henriquez Gallegos 2014; Alper and others 2019).

Financial Sector Health and Structure

To assay financial sector health and structure, we use a measure of banking sector concentration, with greater concentration expected to be associated with less formal financial inclusion (Mengistu and Perez-Saiz 2018). We then use the log of the bank-capital-to-total-assets ratio, a measure of financial sector health, which we expect to be positively associated with formal financial inclusion (World Bank 2017).

Macroprudential Policies

We use data based on the worldwide 2016–17 IMF Annual Macroprudential Policies Survey. The data set catalogs the use of macroprudential tools by individual countries in 2016–17, with 141 countries reporting 1,313 measures for an average of 9.3 measures by country (9.9 for advanced economies and 9.1 for emerging market and developing economies). For sub-Saharan Africa, about 11 out of 44 countries resort to macroprudential policy instruments, for an average of 6 measures per country (IMF 2018).[7]

We use an indicator variable for each of the 15 macroprudential measures in the survey, which takes the value of 1 if the measure is reported to be active. Then we test whether the presence of each of the following policies is correlated with the choice of financial access: (1) limit on leverage ratio, (2) forward-looking loan provision, (3) cap on credit growth, (4) other broad-based measures, (5) household sector capital requirement, (6) cap on credit growth to the household sector, (7) loan restrictions or borrower eligibility criteria, (8) cap on loan-to-value ratio, (9) cap on loan-to-income ratio, (10) cap on debt-service-to-income ratio, (11) limit on amortization periods, (12) restrictions on unsecured loans, (13) other, (14) loan-to-deposit ratio, and (15) loan-to-deposit ratio differentiated by currency.

Because for many individual tools the variation is limited, we group macroprudential measures following the classification in Alam and others (2019), including all, demand (that is, targeted at borrowers), and supply measures (that is, targeted at financial institutions). The supply measures are further subdivided into three categories: (1) general-, (2) capital-, and (3) loan-supply tools.[8] For

[7] Information on the IMF Annual Macroprudential Policies Survey is available at https://www.elibrary-areaer.imf.org/Macroprudential/Pages/Home.aspx/.

[8] The "loan-targeted" group consists of the "demand" and the "supply-loans" instruments. "Demand" instruments are the limits to the loan-to-value ratio and the limits to the debt-service-to-income ratio. "Supply-loans" measures are limits to credit growth, loan-loss provisions, loan restrictions, limits to the loan-to-deposit ratio, and limits to foreign currency loans. "Supply-general" instruments are reserve requirements, liquidity requirements, and limits to foreign exchange positions. "Supply-capital" instruments are leverage limits, countercyclical buffers, conservation buffers, and capital requirements.

each country, we count the number of macroprudential measures in each group as a rough estimate of "intensity" of use of macroprudential tools, then estimate the correlation between intensity and each individual's choice of financial services. We are interested in testing whether measures targeted at formal financial institutions (supply measures) are associated with less formal versus informal financial inclusion.

Regional Controls

We control for regional heterogeneity by adding regional indicator variables (East Asia and Pacific, Europe and Central Asia, Latin America and the Caribbean, Middle East and North Africa, South Asia, and sub-Saharan Africa).

Results

Baseline Estimates

Individuals' financial access is strongly associated with personal, macro, and structural characteristics. Table 11.1 reports the multinominal logit regression results specified in equation (2), showing both the emerging market and developing economies sample and the the sub-Saharan Africa sample. The column labeled "No Access" shows determinants of exclusion from financial services relative to informal financial services only, and the column labeled "Formal Access" shows formal and mobile banking access relative to informal access.

- *Individual characteristics.* Being female is negatively associated with having no access and with formal access, suggesting women tend to use informal financial services more often than men. Having only primary education and low income have significant negative association with formal access. Having wage income improves both informal and formal financial access.
- *Country-level controls.* Access to formal financial services is positively and significantly associated with GDP per capita, a measure of development, but has little correlation with other country-level variables. In sub-Saharan Africa, regulatory support for mobile money also has positive association with formal financial access.
- *Monetary policy.* The monetary policy regime, captured by an indicator variable for whether a country targets inflation, is positively associated with formal access and negatively associated with no access. Such associations are consistent with inflation targeting being common in more developed financial markets, although the estimates are not statistically significant.[9] In sub-Saharan African countries, tighter monetary policy, measured by the real interest rate, is associated with less formal financial access.

[9] Results for the inflation-targeting variable are robust to the use of an alternative monetary policy regime control of whether countries have an exchange rate peg. These results are available upon request.

TABLE 11.1.

Multinomial Logit Regressions with Baseline Controls			
	Emerging Markets and Developing Economies		**Sub-Saharan Africa**
Variable	**No Access (vs. Informal Access)**	**Formal (vs. Informal Access)**	**No Access (vs. Informal Access)**
Female	–0.085**	–0.236***	–0.121**
	(0.041)	(0.064)	(0.053)
Primary education	0.055	–0.823***	0.110**
	(0.051)	(0.060)	(0.056)
Low income	0.101**	–0.441***	0.195***
	(0.040)	(0.040)	(0.044)
Age	–0.023***	0.041***	–0.020***
	(0.005)	(0.006)	(0.005)
Age^2	0.000***	–0.000***	0.000***
	(0.000)	(0.000)	(0.000)
Receive wage	–0.486***	0.305***	–0.574***
	(0.049)	(0.065)	(0.073)
High inflation (12 pc)	0.218	0.251	0.132
	(0.163)	(0.199)	(0.184)
Regulatory quality (estimate)	0.283	0.365	–0.005
	(0.194)	(0.232)	(0.290)
Mobile money regulatory support	0.003	0.012	–0.008
	(0.007)	(0.009)	(0.011)
Domestic private credit/GDP	–0.001	0.007	–0.003
	(0.003)	(0.006)	(0.004)
Inflation targeter	–0.175	0.236	–0.157
	(0.156)	(0.291)	(0.252)
Log(GDP per capita)	0.106	0.342***	0.056
	(0.081)	(0.103)	(0.103)
Size of informal sector	–0.001	–0.009	–0.006
	(0.007)	(0.011)	(0.013)
Credit registry or bureau	–0.206	–0.075	–0.050
	(0.158)	(0.239)	(0.194)
Constant	0.688	–2.163**	1.767
	(0.884)	(1.091)	(1.169)
Regional dummies	Yes	Yes	No
No. of observations		67,354	
Pseudo R^2		0.102	

Source: Author estimates.
Note: The reference group is informal access only. The multinomial logit estimates two models, that is, one logit model for no access relative to informal access and one logit model for formal access relative to informal access.
$^{**}p < 0.05$; $^{***}p < 0.01$.

Addition of Monetary and Financial Variables

After establishing the baseline control variables, we explore the relationship between monetary policy and financial market structure on financial inclusion. We add these monetary and financial variables one by one to the baseline specification, considering the high correlation between them. The results, as presented in Table 11.2, suggest that macroprudential policies are significantly associated with individuals' choice of financial services.

- *Financial market structure.* Financial inclusion is significantly associated with banking sector competition. In particular, more concentration in the banking sector is associated with more individuals having no access to financial services in sub-Saharan Africa. This could be because less-developed financial markets also tend to be more concentrated, or because higher lending costs are related to lower competition in the banking sector. For sub-Saharan Africa, Mengistu and Perez-Saiz (2018) find that more competition is related to better formal financial access.

TABLE 11.2.

Multinomial Logit Adding Financial and Monetary Variables

	Emerging Markets and Developing Economies		Sub-Saharan Africa	
Variable	**No Access (vs. Informal Access)**	**Formal (vs. Informal Access)**	**No Access (vs. Informal Access)**	**Formal (vs. Informal Access)**
All control variables	Yes	Yes	Yes	Yes
Interest rate controls	0.444*	0.280		
	(0.234)	(0.366)		
Real interest rate	–0.000	–0.005	0.003	–0.021***
	(0.004)	(0.009)	(0.004)	(0.005)
Log(bank concentration) (%)	–0.047	–0.430	0.461***	–0.172
	(0.258)	(0.434)	(0.175)	(0.393)
Log(bank capital/total assets) (%)	0.176	–0.344	–0.566	–0.160
	(0.679)	(0.830)	(0.824)	(0.812)
Macroprudential Measures				
Limit on leverage ratio	–0.568***	–0.681***	–0.895***	–0.544**
	(0.170)	(0.247)	(0.129)	(0.222)
Cap on credit growth	–0.274	–0.602*	–1.352***	–1.049***
	(0.196)	(0.329)	(0.322)	(0.317)
Broad-based measures	–0.362***	–0.374*	–0.668***	–0.295
	(0.113)	(0.203)	(0.112)	(0.266)
Loan restrictions or borrower eligibility criteria	–0.405***	0.016	–0.377**	–0.213
	(0.119)	(0.164)	(0.165)	(0.215)
Loan-to-deposit ratio	–0.426***	–1.245***	–0.690***	–0.789***
	(0.144)	(0.255)	(0.221)	(0.163)
Macroprudential Count, by Group				
All macroprudential measures	–0.081***	–0.064*	–0.118***	–0.064
	(0.024)	(0.034)	(0.026)	(0.044)
Macroprudential: demand side	–0.021	0.113	0.260**	0.453
	(0.093)	(0.168)	(0.127)	(0.298)
Macroprudential: supply side	–0.109***	–0.099***	–0.145***	–0.097***
	(0.024)	(0.034)	(0.025)	(0.033)
Macroprudential: supply loans	–0.151***	–0.145**	–0.190***	–0.118
	(0.044)	(0.063)	(0.048)	(0.080)
Macroprudential: supply general	–0.228***	–0.162**	–0.394***	–0.260***
	(0.076)	(0.081)	(0.065)	(0.100)
Macroprudential: supply capital	–0.278**	–0.289	–0.506***	–0.438**
	(0.126)	(0.204)	(0.170)	(0.220)
Regional dummies	Yes	Yes	No	No

Source: Author estimates.

Note: These financial sector structure, monetary policy, and macroprudential variables are added to the full list of control variables one by one. These variables are highly correlated and thus should not be included together.

$^{*}p < 0.10$; $^{**}p < 0.05$; $^{***}p < 0.01$.

- *Macroprudential policies.* Supply-side macroprudential policies, including limits on leverage ratio, cap on credit growth, and loan-to-deposit ratio, as well as aggregate indicators of supply-side measures (loans, general, and capital-based) are negatively and significantly associated with having access to formal financial services. Demand-side policies, however, are not significantly associated with choice of financial services. These results can be interpreted as supporting the hypothesis that macroprudential measures targeted at formal financial institutions are easier for people to evade than macroprudential measures targeted at individuals. In other words, macroprudential measures targeted at formal financial institutions may motivate individuals to resort to informal financial services in emerging market and developing economies.

We also present the marginal effects of the baseline personal control variables and the macroprudential variables on the probability of having formal financial access in Figure 11.6 to indicate the relative size of the effect of each dependent variable on the type of financial access. This figure indicates the effect of macroprudential variables is only slighlty smaller than that of personal characteristics.

Figure 11.6. Margin Plots of Baseline Multinomial Logit Regressions

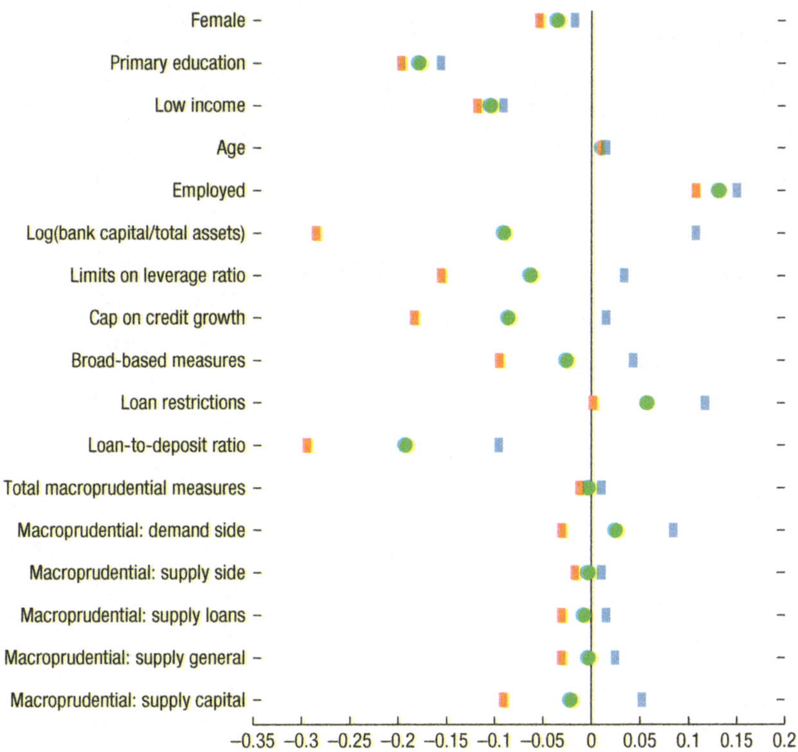

Source: Author estimates.

Note: Green dots indicate coefficient estimates. Orange bars are the lower-bound 90 percent confidence interval, and blue bars are the upper-bound 90 percent confidence interval.

Mobile banking, identified as the main driver of improved financial access in sub-Saharan Africa from 2014 to 2017, is also affected by personal, monetary, and financial factors. Using a simple logit regression to determine the probability of any mobile use, in Table 11.3 we estimate the coefficients for the same macroprudential variables as shown in Table 11.2. The coefficients are similar to those in the multinomial logit on formal and mobile access, with a few exceptions. Mobile money regulatory support is associated with a significant increase in mobile banking access in both samples. The results in Table 11.3 show that certain supply-side macroprudential measures have a strong and negative association with mobile banking in sub-Saharan Africa (caps on credit growth and loan-to-deposit ratios). This may be because mobile banking is complementary to formal banking. (In much of sub-Saharan Africa, mobile financial services have to be backed by a formal bank account.)

TABLE 11.3.

Logit Regressions with Baseline Controls: Mobile

Variable	Emerging Markets and Developing Economies	Sub-Saharan Africa
Female	–0.191***	–0.151***
	(0.040)	(0.043)
Primary education	–0.756***	–0.952***
	(0.092)	(0.082)
Low income	–0.525***	–0.540***
	(0.039)	(0.058)
Age	0.032***	0.033***
	(0.006)	(0.007)
Age^2	–0.000***	–0.000***
	(0.000)	(0.000)
Receive wage	0.552***	0.586***
	(0.054)	(0.082)
High inflation (>12 percent)	–0.334	–0.350
	(0.253)	(0.328)
Regulatory quality (estimate)	–0.081	0.562
	(0.270)	(0.446)
Mobile money regulatory support	0.026***	0.044**
	(0.009)	(0.020)
Domestic private credit/GDP	–0.004	–0.005
	(0.003)	(0.005)
Inflation targeter	0.162	0.565
	(0.232)	(0.360)
Log(GDP per capita)	0.233*	0.198
	(0.124)	(0.185)
Size of informal sector	–0.012	0.001
	(0.012)	(0.023)
Credit registry or bureau	0.477	0.164
	(0.297)	(0.338)
Constant	–4.730***	–4.850*
	(1.344)	(2.569)
Regional dummies	Yes	No
No. of observations	67,354	27,829
Pseudo R^2	0.162	0.112

Source: Author estimates.
Note: *$p < 0.10$, **$p < 0.05$, ***$p < 0.01$.

In addition to the type of financial access, the Findex survey inquires about how people borrow and save, which enables separate analyses. Applying the same multinominal logit regression on our borrowing index, defined as complete exclusion (only informal borrowing, and formal borrowing or formal plus informal borrowing, and with the three categories defined analogously for our saving index), we estimate the model using the same control variables and monetary and financial variables. Our analyses on borrowing and saving also allow us to test the economic relevance of the previous results using our grouping of the Findex variables. Tables 11.4 and 11.5 present the results.

TABLE 11.4.

Multinomial Logit Regressions with Baseline Controls

	Borrowing		Saving	
Variable	No Access (vs. Informal Access)	Formal (vs. Informal Access)	No Access (vs. Informal Access)	Formal (vs. Informal Access)
Female	0.034	–0.008	–0.369***	–0.443***
	(0.025)	(0.047)	(0.066)	(0.078)
Primary education	0.083*	–0.313***	0.213***	–0.683***
	(0.046)	(0.092)	(0.064)	(0.085)
Low income	0.020	–0.246***	0.310***	–0.474***
	(0.038)	(0.059)	(0.039)	(0.057)
Age	–0.028***	0.090***	–0.050***	–0.005
	(0.005)	(0.009)	(0.007)	(0.010)
Age^2	0.000***	–0.001***	0.001***	0.000
	(0.000)	(0.000)	(0.000)	(0.000)
Receive wage	–0.495***	0.298***	–0.600***	0.196**
	(0.039)	(0.067)	(0.058)	(0.082)
High inflation (>12 percent)	0.218*	0.228	0.101	0.316*
	(0.126)	(0.217)	(0.200)	(0.178)
Regulatory quality (estimate)	0.057	0.419***	–0.296	–0.101
	(0.170)	(0.151)	(0.243)	(0.257)
Mobile money regulatory support	0.000	–0.008	0.015*	0.016*
	(0.005)	(0.007)	(0.009)	(0.009)
Domestic private credit/GDP	–0.000	0.003	–0.001	0.005
	(0.002)	(0.003)	(0.003)	(0.004)
Inflation targeter	–0.258*	–0.205	0.203	0.066
	(0.141)	(0.220)	(0.225)	(0.239)
Log(GDP per capita)	0.136	–0.175*	0.235*	0.416***
	(0.089)	(0.091)	(0.131)	(0.149)
Level of informality (Medina and Schneider 2018)	–0.001	–0.001	–0.003	–0.001
	(0.006)	(0.008)	(0.009)	(0.011)
Credit registry or bureau	–0.146	–0.090	0.163	0.509**
	(0.130)	(0.217)	(0.240)	(0.216)
Constant	0.703	–0.222	1.074	–3.604
	(0.808)	(0.939)	(1.341)	(1.501)
Regional dummies	Yes	Yes	Yes	No
No. of observations		67,354		67,354
Pseudo R^2		0.055		0.0992

Source: Author estimates.

Note: The reference group is informal access only. The multinomial logit estimates two models, that is, one logit model for no access relative to informal access and one logit model for formal access relative to informal access.

$^{*}p < 0.10$; $^{**}p < 0.05$; $^{***}p < 0.01$.

TABLE 11.5.

Multinomial Logit Regressions with Baseline Controls				
	Borrowing		Saving	
Variable	No Access (vs. Informal Access)	Formal (vs. Informal Access)	No Access (vs. Informal Access)	Formal (vs. Informal Access)
All control variables	Yes	Yes	Yes	Yes
Interest rate controls	0.177	–0.191	0.703**	0.740*
	(0.222)	(0.230)	(0.331)	(0.421)
Real interest rate	0.003	0.007	0.022	0.020**
	(0.004)	(0.008)	(0.015)	(0.009)
Log(bank concentration) (%)	0.016	0.476	–0.184	–0.539
	(0.161)	(0.302)	(0.338)	(0.392)
Log(bank capital/total assets) (%)	0.509*	0.262	–1.161	–1.781
	(0.291)	(0.500)	(1.061)	(1.157)
Macroprudential Measures				
Limit on leverage ratio	–0.329**	–0.265	–0.676***	–0.688***
	(0.165)	(0.214)	(0.172)	(0.248)
Cap on credit growth	–0.095	–0.139	0.018	–0.256
	(0.162)	(0.280)	(0.281)	(0.330)
Broad-based measures	–0.299***	–0.025	–0.339**	–0.033
	(0.096)	(0.197)	(0.155)	(0.183)
Loan restrictions or borrower eligibility criteria	–0.273**	0.034	–0.134	0.400**
	(0.109)	(0.142)	(0.201)	(0.162)
Loan-to-deposit ratio	–0.171	–0.484*	–0.544***	–0.968***
	(0.131)	(0.248)	(0.185)	(0.319)
Macroprudential Count, by Group				
All macroprudential measures	–0.057***	–0.055*	–0.051	0.003
	(0.021)	(0.029)	(0.034)	(0.040)
Macroprudential: demand side	–0.100	–0.009	0.175	0.250
	(0.080)	(0.115)	(0.159)	(0.169)
Macroprudential: supply side	–0.070***	–0.078**	–0.082**	–0.013
	(0.025)	(0.035)	(0.035)	(0.042)
Macroprudential: supply loans	–0.077*	–0.103**	–0.107*	–0.063
	(0.041)	(0.052)	(0.055)	(0.063)
Macroprudential: supply general	–0.161**	–0.111	–0.161	0.052
	(0.063)	(0.085)	(0.098)	(0.093)
Macroprudential: supply capital	–0.198	–0.244*	–0.233	–0.024
	(0.127)	(0.143)	(0.179)	(0.251)
Regional dummies	Yes	Yes	No	No

Source: Author estimates.

Note: These financial sector structure, monetary policy, and macroprudential variables are added to the full list of control variables one by one. These variables are highly correlated and thus should not be included together.

$^*p < 0.10$; $^{**}p < 0.05$; $^{***}p < 0.01$.

By comparing Table 11.4 with Table 11.1 and Table 11.5 with Table 11.2, we can trace whether a specific factor influences financial access through the borrowing channel, the savings channel, or both.

- *Individual characteristics.* Most individual characteristics affect borrowing and saving choices in the same way they affect overall financial access. One noteworthy difference is in gender: women are more likely to save through informal channels but not to borrow informally.
- *Country-level controls.* Separating borrowing from saving shows more nuanced effects of country controls. For instance, better regulatory quality is now asso-

ciated with a higher probability of formal borrowing. Mobile money regulatory support is positively related to formal financial access, but for mobile regulation, this is only through the savings channel. Higher GDP per capita is similarly associated with formal borrowing mostly through the savings channel.

- *Macroprudential policies.* Supply- and demand-side macroprudential measures both tend to increase informal borrowing by suppressing the populations with no access. Yet only supply-side policies in aggregate are associated with less formal borrowing. Because most macroprudential policies target borrowing rather than saving, they have little influence on the savings channel. Some supply-side policies, however, are still associated with less formal saving (limit on leverage and loan-to-deposit ratios).

"Leaks" in Macroprudential Policies

Despite its exploratory nature, the empirical analysis so far has highlighted fairly consistent and statistically significant associations between the use of macroprudential measures and formal financial access, including how individuals save and borrow. This significance holds after we control for individual- and country-level characteristics. However, policymakers in emerging market and developing economies must better understand how macroprudential policies "leak," because leaks could imply the policies are ineffective. Furthermore, macroprudential policies could also help drive the persistence of resort to informal financial services; this runs counter to the goal of fostering access to formal financial services.

We find that the effect of macroprudential policies changes according to the level of financial development in a country. Table 11.6 reports estimates for our baseline regression on the full sample of countries, splitting the sample into higher- and lower-than-average financial development.[10] By splitting the sample, we are able to estimate the differential effect of country-level controls and macroprudential policies on financial access according to level of financial development, rather than estimate the average effect when we simply control for financial development.

The negative association of macroprudential policies with access to formal financial services is primarily in countries with more financial development especially for specific supply-side macroprudential variables, namely limit on leverage ratio, broad-based measures, and loan-to-deposit ratio. This negative association is consistent with the finding in Cizel and others (2019) that the leaks are stronger for more advanced economies and where quantity of credit is restricted. In countries with little financial development, macroprudential measures are instead associated with greater odds of informal access relative to no access, while individuals' banking choices show little to no movement from formal to informal.

Tight and Loose Macroprudential Policies

In Deléchat and others (2020), we also dig deeper into the role of macroprudential policies by using the integrated Macroprudential Policy database constructed

[10] The index of financial development constructed by Svirydzenka (2016) provides a relative ranking of 176 countries on the depth, access, and efficiency of their financial institutions and financial markets.

TABLE 11.6.

Multinomial Logit Regressions with Baseline Controls, by Level of Financial Development

	Emerging Markets and Developing Economies			
	No Access (vs. Informal Access)	Formal (vs. Informal Access)	No Access (vs. Informal Access)	Formal (vs. Informal Access)
Variable	High Financial Development		Low Financial Development	
All control variables	Yes	Yes	Yes	Yes
Interest rate controls	–2.220	–1.056	0.523	0.222
	(1.561)	(0.757)	(0.368)	(0.558)
Real interest rate	–0.002	0.028	0.006	–0.011**
	(0.011)	(0.020)	(0.004)	(0.005)
Log(bank concentration) (%)	–0.110	4.190**	0.568***	–0.042
	(1.459)	(1.784)	(0.186)	(0.429)
Log(bank capital/total assets) (%)	7.086***	–1.371***	–1.907***	1.131
	(0.204)	(0.519)	(0.538)	(0.908)
Macroprudential Measures				
Limit on leverage ratio	–2.183***	–2.632***	–0.450**	–0.152
	(0.337)	(0.853)	(0.225)	(0.254)
Cap on credit growth	1.148	–1.236	–0.236	–0.158
	(1.098)	(1.166)	(0.334)	(0.487)
Broad-based measures	–1.095	–3.414*	–0.486***	–0.135
	(1.361)	(1.766)	(0.140)	(0.260)
Loan restrictions or borrower eligibility criteria	–0.721***	–0.002	–0.426***	–0.074
	(0.074)	(0.159)	(0.158)	(0.206)
Loan-to-deposit ratio	2.551	–4.486*	–0.602***	–1.056***
	(3.127)	(2.710)	(0.180)	(0.237)
Macroprudential Count, by Group				
All macroprudential measures	–0.210***	–0.084	–0.109***	–0.056
	(0.035)	(0.053)	(0.029)	(0.049)
Macroprudential: demand side	–0.544***	0.077	0.265**	0.350
	(0.094)	(0.167)	(0.131)	(0.234)
Macroprudential: supply side	–0.304***	–0.281**	–0.143***	–0.084**
	(0.061)	(0.132)	(0.026)	(0.042)
Macroprudential: supply loans	–0.379***	–0.236*	–0.182***	–0.093
	(0.077)	(0.126)	(0.050)	(0.081)
Macroprudential: supply general	–0.913**	–2.171***	–0.399***	–0.176*
	(0.373)	(0.266)	(0.066)	(0.095)
Macroprudential: supply capital	–1.481***	0.078	–0.264*	–0.358*
	(0.444)	(0.350)	(0.136)	(0.205)
Regional dummies	Yes	Yes	Yes	Yes

Source: Author estimates.

Note: These financial sector structure, monetary policy, and macroprudential variables are added to the full list of control variables one by one. These variables are highly correlated and thus should not be included together. Results for the baseline coefficients in these high and low levels of informality sample regressions are available upon request.

*$p < 0.10$; **$p < 0.05$; ***$p < 0.01$.

by Alam and others (2019). We show that the strictness of macroprudential measures also appears relevant for financial inclusion. On the demand side, a higher average level of the loan-to-value ratio is associated with greater finanical inclusion, consistent with the idea that higher caps on the loan-to-value ratio allow more individuals to access loans. On the supply side, tighter countercyclical capital buffers, tighter limits on credit growth, foreign currency loans, and loan-to-deposit ratios are all associated with lower formal access and higher incidence of no access. These findings are consistent with our baseline results, where we find that most of the effect of macroprudential policies on formal financial access comes from supply-side measures.

CONCLUSIONS

Financial inclusion continues to be a goal of public policy in low-income countries. The micro- and macroeconomic benefits of greater financial inclusion are by now well established—allowing individuals to smooth their consumption, efficiently allocating productive resources across the economy, empowering women, reducing poverty and inequality, and supporting growth, among other things. Given these benefits, many countries and international organizations, such as the Financial Action Task Force, have rightly set greater financial inclusion as an important objective.

Across emerging market and developing economies, financial inclusion has been improving thanks largely to the adoption of mobile financial services. For example, although sub-Saharan Africa continues to have the highest rates of informal finance, since 2014, its share of total access to financial services has declined by 7.8 percent. In place of informal banking, mobile money and mobile banking have grown in use. Mobile accounts now make up 17.4 percent of all financial services access on the entire continent. The growth of the mobile financial services industry has given millions of the world's poorest people access to formalized accounts, greatly facilitating payment transactions.

The goal of financial inclusion, including access to mobile financial services, still has not been met. Although access greatly increased between 2014 and 2017, a large share of individuals in sub-Saharan Africa are still excluded from the formal financial sector. The rates are lower, albeit still elevated, for financial exclusion in other emerging market and developing economies globally. Access to bank accounts has increased worldwide, yet too few individuals use the accounts for borrowing and saving. Furthermore, in many countries mobile financial services may only include mobile money, which does not necessarily provide the same benefits of formal financial services that full-fledged mobile banking would. To further increase the use of formal savings and borrowing instruments worldwide, developing mobile-based savings and borrowing instruments along with an appropriately supportive regulatory framework could be most effective. Developing mobile-based savings and borrowing instruments along with an appropriately supportive regulatory framework could be the most effective way to continue to boost financial inclusion worldwide.

Macroprudential policies and the health of the financial sector seem to play a role in financial inclusion. Our results are some of the first to show a robust association between financial inclusion and monetary, macroprudential, and financial sector policies and conditions. In particular, supply-side (institution-based) macroprudential policies seem to be associated with more use of informal finance and with less use of formal and mobile services. The association between limits on credit growth and greater use of informal financial services relative to formal ones is particularly strong. These results do not establish causality, yet they suggest a significant relationship between certain policies and individual-level use of certain types of financial services. Although the precise channel for resort to informality remains to be investigated, including the likely complex interactions between the size of the informal sector and financial development, the unintended consequences of macroprudential policies appear to be more persistent for countries at higher levels of financial development.

The key policy implication emerging from these initial findings is that central bankers and bank regulators ought to at least consider the interactions between monetary and financial sector policies and financial inclusion. Given possible negative spillover effects from many macroprudential and financial sector policies, policymakers may need to consider the potential effects of these policies on financial inclusion before implementing them. At the same time, policies to support financial inclusion, including by increasing financial and digital literacy and regulatory support to mobile banking, should be even more actively pursued.

ANNEX 11.1.

ANNEX TABLE 11.1.1.

Findex Questionnaire Mapping to Index

2017 Question ID	Question Definition	Index Classification: Informal	Mobile	Formal
account	Has an account		Yes	Yes
account_fin	Has an account at a financial institution			Yes
account_mob	Has a mobile money account		Yes	
fin2	Has a debit card			Yes
fin5	Used mobile phone or internet to access financial institution account		Yes	
fin7	Has a credit card			Yes
fin17a	Saved in past 12 months: using an account at a financial institution			Yes
fin17b	Saved in past 12 months: using an informal savings club	Yes		
fin19	Has loan from a financial institution for home, apartment, or land			Yes
fin22a	Borrowed in past 12 months: from a financial institution			Yes
fin22b	Borrowed in past 12 months: from family or friends	Yes		
fin22c	Borrowed in past 12 months: from an informal savings club	Yes		
fin27a	If sent domestic remittances: through a financial institution			Yes
fin27b	If sent domestic remittances: through a mobile phone		Yes	
fin29a	If received domestic remittances: through a financial institution			Yes

(continued)

ANNEX TABLE 11.1.1. *(continued)*

Findex Questionnaire Mapping to Index

2017 Question ID	Question Definition	Index Classification: Informal	Mobile	Formal
fin29b	If received domestic remittances: through a mobile phone		Yes	
fin31a	If paid utility bills: using an account			Yes
fin31b	If paid utility bills: through a mobile phone		Yes	
fin34a	If received wage payments: into an account			Yes
fin34b	If received wage payments: through a mobile phone		Yes	
fin39a	If received government transfers: into an account			Yes
fin39b	If received government transfers: through a mobile phone		Yes	
fin40	If received cashless government transfers: first account			Yes
fin41	If received cashless government transfers: opened to receive payments			Yes
fin43a	If received agricultural payments: into an account			Yes
fin43b	If received agricultural payments: through a mobile phone		Yes	
fin27c1	If sent domestic remittances: in cash	Yes		
fin27c2	If sent domestic remittances: through a money transfer service		Yes	
fin29c1	If received domestic remittances: in cash	Yes		
fin29c2	If received domestic remittances: through an MTO		Yes	
fin34c2	If received wage payments: to a card			Yes
fin35	If received cashless wage payments: first account			Yes
fin36	If received cashless wage payments: opened to receive payments			Yes
fin47a	If received self-employment payments: into an account			Yes
fin47b	If received self-employment payments: through a mobile phone		Yes	

Source: Authors.

ANNEX TABLE 11.1.2.

Financial Access Index Definition

Index Value	Label	Question Response Criteria
0	No access	Answers **no to every** formal, mobile, and informal question
1	Informal only	Answers yes to **any** informal question **and** answers **no to every** formal and mobile question
2	Mobile only	Answers yes to **any** mobile question **and** answers **no to every** formal and informal question
3	Informal and mobile	Answers yes to **any** mobile **or** informal question **and** answers **no to every** formal question
4	Formal only	Answers yes **to any** formal question **and** answers **no to every** informal and mobile question
5	Formal and informal	Answers yes **to any** formal **or** informal question **and** answered **no to every** mobile question
6	Formal and mobile	Answers yes **to any** formal **or** mobile question **and** answers **no to every** informal question
7	Formal and informal and mobile	Answers yes **to any** formal **or** mobile **or** informal question

Source: Authors.

ANNEX TABLE 11.1.3.

Definitions and Data Sources of Variables

Name	Definition	Source
Female	Dummy variable equal to 1 if respondent is female	World Bank, Findex 2014, 2017
Primary education	Respondent education level is "completed primary or less"	World Bank, Findex 2014, 2017
Low income	Within-economy household income quintile is "poorest 20%"	World Bank, Findex 2014, 2017
Age	Respondent is age 15 years or older	World Bank, Findex 2014, 2017
Receive wage	Respondent receives wage payments	World Bank, Findex 2014, 2017
High inflation (>12 percent)	Dummy variable equal to 1 inflation in respondent's country is 12 percent or higher	World Bank, World Development Indicators
Regulatory quality (estimate)	Aggregate score for getting credit and protecting minority investors as well as the regulatory quality indices from the indicator sets for dealing with construction permits, getting electricity, registering property, enforcing contracts, and resolving insolvency	World Bank, Doing Business Survey
Mobile money regulatory support	Index based on six aggegated metrics: authorization, consumer protection, transaction limits, know your customer, agent network, investment and infrastructure environment	Mobile Money Regulatory Index, Groupe Spéciale Mobile Association
Domestic private credit/GDP	Domestic credit to private sector (percent of GDP)	World Bank, World Development Indicators
Inflation targeter	0 (no) or 1 (yes)	Annual Report on Exchange Arrangements and Exchange Restrictions
Log(GDP per capita)	GDP per capita	World Bank, World Development Indicators
Size of informal sector	Measured as share of GDP	Medina and Schneider 2018
Credit registry or bureau	Dummy variable equal to 1 if country had a credit registry (public) or bureau (private)	Monetary and Capital Markets Department, IMF
Interest rate controls	0 (no) or 1 (yes)	Annual Report on Exchange Arrangements and Exchange Restrictions
Real interest rate	Value of real interest rate	Annual Report on Exchange Arrangements and Exchange Restrictions
Log(bank concentration) (%)	Measure of concentration in the banking system (percent)	World Bank, Global Financial Development Database
Log(bank capital/total assets) (%)	Percent of bank capital to total assets	World Bank, Global Financial Development Database
Limit on leverage ratio	0 (no) or 1 (yes)	Macroprudential Policy Survey
Cap on credit growth	0 (no) or 1 (yes)	Macroprudential Policy Survey
Broad-based measures (macroprudential)	0 (no) or 1 (yes)	Macroprudential Policy Survey

(continued)

ANNEX TABLE 11.1.3. ***(continued)***

Definitions and Data Sources of Variables

Name	Definition	Source
Loan restrictions or borrower eligibility criteria	0 (no) or 1 (yes)	Macroprudential Policy Survey
Loan-to-deposit ratio	0 (no) or 1 (yes)	Macroprudential Policy Survey
All macroprudential measures	Count of all macroprudential measures (demand side and supply side), by country	Macroprudential Policy Survey
Macroprudential: demand side	Count of measures classified as a cap on loan-to-value ratios, cap on loan-to-income ratio, and cap on debt-service-to-income ratios, by country	Macroprudential Policy Survey
Macroprudential: supply side	Count of measures classified by supply-loans, supply-general, and supply-capital, by country	Macroprudential Policy Survey
Macroprudential: supply loans	Count of measures classifed as forward-looking loan loss provision requirement, cap on credit growth, cap on credit growth to the household sector, loan restrictions or borrower eligibility criteria, restrictions on unsecured loans, loan-to-deposit ratio, and loan-to-deposit ratio differentiated by currency, by country	Macroprudential Policy Survey
Macroprudential: supply general	Count of measures classified as limit on amortization periods, other broad-based measures to increase resilience, and other measures, by country	Macroprudential Policy Survey
Macroprudential: supply capital	Count of measures classified as household sector capital requirements and limits on leverage, by country	Macroprudential Policy Survey

Source: Authors.

ANNEX TABLE 11.1.4.

Means and Standard Deviations of Variables

Variable	Mean	Standard Deviation	No. of Observations
Female	1.54	0.50	150,923
Primary education	0.35	0.48	150,938
Low income	0.35	0.48	150,938
Age	41.91	17.92	150,483
Receive wage	3.06	1.33	150,923
High inflation (>12 percent)	0.13	0.33	150,938
Regulatory quality (estimate)	0.05	0.97	150,923
Mobile money regulatory support	75.12	10.49	74,553
Domestic private credit/GDP	63.04	46.63	140,920
Inflation targeter	0.27	0.44	150,923
Log(GDP per capita)	8.35	1.48	150,923
Size of informal sector	27.75	12.00	140,926
Credit registry or bureau	0.82	0.39	148,878
Interest rate controls	0.11	0.32	150,923
Real interest rate	7.13	12.07	95,167
Log(credit to government and state-owned enterprises/GDP) (percent)	1.92	1.16	137,323
Log(bank concentration) (percent)	4.15	0.34	120,707
Log(bank capital/total assets) (percent)	2.15	0.37	91,618
Limit on leverage ratio	0.21	0.41	150,938
Cap on credit growth	0.10	0.30	150,938
Broad-based measures (macroprudential)	0.45	0.50	150,938
Loan restrictions or borrower eligibility criteria	0.56	0.50	150,938
Loan-to-deposit ratio	0.10	0.30	150,938
All macroprudential measures	2.87	2.59	150,938
Macroprudential: demand side	0.64	0.84	150,938
Macroprudential: supply side	2.23	2.01	150,938
Macroprudential: supply loans	1.14	1.20	150,938
Macroprudential: supply general	0.62	0.78	150,938
Macroprudential: supply capital	0.48	0.61	150,938

Source: Authors.

ANNEX TABLE 11.1.5.

Names of Countries in the Database

Countries in Sample (Macroprudential Policy Survey)		Countries in Sample (Integrated Macroprudential Policy Database)	
Sub-Saharan Africa (19)	**Emerging Markets (49)**	**Sub-Saharan Africa (14)**	**Emerging Markets (40)**
Benin	Argentina	Benin	Argentina
Botswana	Armenia	Botswana	Armenia
Burkina Faso	Bangladesh	Burkina Faso	Bangladesh
Central African Republic	Benin	Côte d'Ivoire	Benin
Chad	Bolivia	Ghana	Botswana
Côte d'Ivoire	Botswana	Kenya	Brazil
Ghana	Brazil	Mali	Burkina Faso
Kenya	Burkina Faso	Mozambique	Cambodia
Madagascar	Cambodia	Niger	Colombia
Mali	Central African Republic	Nigeria	Côte d'Ivoire
Mozambique	Chad	Senegal	Dominican Republic
Namibia	Colombia	South Africa	El Salvador
Niger	Côte d'Ivoire	Uganda	Georgia

(continued)

ANNEX TABLE 11.1.5. ***(continued)***

Names of Countries in the Database			
Countries in Sample (Macroprudential Policy Survey)		**Countries in Sample (Integrated Macroprudential Policy Database)**	
Sub-Saharan Africa (19)	**Emerging Markets (49)**	**Sub-Saharan Africa (14)**	**Emerging Markets (40)**
Nigeria	Dominican Republic	Zambia	Ghana
Rwanda	El Salvador		Haiti
Senegal	Georgia		Honduras
South Africa	Ghana		India
Uganda	Guatemala		Jordan
Zambia	Haiti		Kenya
	Honduras		Kyrgyz Republic
	India		Malaysia
	Jordan		Mali
	Kenya		Mongolia
	Kyrgyz Republic		Morocco
	Madagascar		Mozambique
	Malaysia		Nepal
	Mali		Niger
	Mongolia		Nigeria
	Morocco		Pakistan
	Mozambique		Paraguay
	Myanmar		Philippines
	Namibia		Romania
	Nepal		Russian Federation
	Nicaragua		Senegal
	Niger		South Africa
	Nigeria		Thailand
	Pakistan		Tunisia
	Paraguay		Uganda
	Philippines		Vietnam
	Romania		Zambia
	Russian Federation		
	Rwanda		
	Senegal		
	South Africa		
	Thailand		
	Tunisia		
	Uganda		
	Vietnam		
	Zambia		

Source: Authors.

REFERENCES

Aiyar, S., C. W. Calomiris, and T. Wieladek. 2014. "Does Macroprudential Regulation Leak? Evidence from a UK Policy Experiment." *Journal of Money, Credit and Banking* 46 (1): 181–214.

Alam, Z., A. Alter, J. Eiseman, G. Gelos, H. Kang, M. Narita, E. Nier, and N. Wang. 2019. "Digging Deeper: Evidence on the Effects of Macroprudential Policies from a New Database." IMF Working Paper 19/66, International Monetary Fund, Washington, DC.

Allen, F., M. Qian, and J. Xie. 2019. "Understanding Informal Financing." *Journal of Financial Intermediation* 39 (July): 19–33.

Allen, F., A. Demirgüç-Kunt, L. Klapper, and M. S. Martinez-Peria. 2016. "The Foundations of Financial Inclusion: Understanding Ownership and Use of Formal Accounts." *Journal of Financial Intermediation* 27 (July): 1–30.

Alper, E., B. Clements, N. Hobdari, and R. Moyà Porcel. 2019. "Do Interest Rate Controls Work? Evidence from Kenya." IMF Working Paper 19/119, International Monetary Fund, Washington, DC.

Armendáriz, B., and J. Morduch. 2005. *The Economics of Microfinance*. Cambridge, MA: MIT Press.

Aryeetey, E. 1994. "Financial Integration and Development in Sub-Saharan Africa: A Study of Informal Finance in Ghana." Working Paper 78, Overseas Development Institute, London.

Aryeetey, E. 2008. "From Informal Finance to Formal Finance in Sub-Saharan Africa: Lessons from Linkage Efforts." *AERC/IMF African Finance for the 21st Century*. Unpublished manuscript, Institute of Statistical, Social and Economic Research, University of Ghana.

Ayyagari, M., T. Beck, and M. S. Martinez Peria. 2018. "The Micro Impact of Macroprudential Policies: Firm-Level Evidence." IMF Working Paper 18/267, International Monetary Fund, Washington, DC.

Bahia, K., and B. Muthiora. 2019. "The Mobile Money Regulatory Index." London, GSMA Intelligence.

Beck, T., L. Ross, and A. Levkov. 2007. "Big Bad Banks? The Impact of US Branch Deregulation on Income Distribution." NBER Working Paper 13299, National Bureau of Economic Research, Cambridge, MA.

Ben Hassine, M., and N. Rebei. 2019. "Informality, Frictions, and Macro-Prudential Policy: Evidence from Tunisia." IMF Working Paper 19/255, International Monetary Fund, Washington, DC.

Camara, N., and D. Tuesta. 2014. "Measuring Financial Inclusion: A Multidimensional Index." BBVA Research Paper 14/26, Banco Bilbao Vizcaya Argentaria, Madrid.

Cizel, J., J. Frost, A. Houben, and P. Wierts. 2019. "Effective Macroprudential Policy: Cross-Sector Substitution from Price and Quantity Measures." *Journal of Money, Credit and Banking* 51 (5): 1209–35.

Dabla-Norris, E., and J. Koeda. 2008. "Informality and Bank Credit: Evidence from Firm-Level Data." IMF Working Paper 08/94, International Monetary Fund, Washington, DC.

De Koker, L., and N. Jentzsch. 2013. "Financial Inclusion and Financial Integrity: Aligned Incentives?" *World Development* 44 (April): 267–80.

Deléchat, C., L. Kiyasseh, M. MacDonald, and R. Xu. 2020. "Drivers of Financial Access: The Role of Macroprudential Policies." IMF Working Paper 20/74, International Monetary Fund, Washington, DC.

Deléchat, C., M. Newiak, R. Xu, F. Yang, and G. Aslan. 2018. "What Is Driving Women's Financial Inclusion across Countries?" IMF Working Paper 18/38, International Monetary Fund, Washington, DC.

Demirgüç-Kunt, A., and L. Klapper. 2012a. "Financial Inclusion in Africa: An Overview." Policy Research Working Paper 6088, World Bank, Washington, DC.

Demirgüç-Kunt, A., and L. Klapper. 2012b. "Measuring Financial Inclusion: The Global Findex Database." Policy Research Working Paper 6025, World Bank, Washington, DC.

Demirgüç-Kunt, A., and L. Klapper. 2013. "Measuring Financial Inclusion: Explaining Variation in Use of Financial Services across and within Countries." *Brookings Papers on Economic Activity* 2013 (1): 279–340.

Demirgüç-Kunt, A., L. Klapper, D. Singer, S. Ansar, and J. Hess. 2018. *The Global Findex Database 2017: Measuring Financial Inclusion and the Fintech Revolution*. Washington, DC: World Bank.

Demirgüç-Kunt, A., L. Klapper, D. Singer, S. Ansar, and J. Hess. 2020. "The Global Findex Database 2017: Measuring Financial Inclusion and Opportunities to Expand Access to and Use of Financial Services." *World Bank Economic Review* 34 (Supplement): 2–8.

Financial Action Task Force (FATF). 2011. "FATF Guidance: Anti-Money Laundering and Terrorist Financing Measures and Financial Inclusion." FATF, Paris.

Giné, X. 2011. "Access to Capital in Rural Thailand: An Estimated Model of Formal vs. Informal Credit." *Journal of Development Economics* 96 (1): 16–29.

Guiso, L., P. Sapienza, and L. Zingales. 2004. "The Role of Social Capital in Financial Development." *American Economic Review* 94 (3): 526–56.

Han, R., and M. Melecky. 2013. "Financial Inclusion for Stability: Access to Bank Deposits and the Deposit Growth during the Global Financial Crisis." Policy Research Working Paper, World Bank, Washington, DC.

Hannig, A., and S. Jansen. 2010. "Financial Inclusion and Financial Stability: Current Policy Issues." ADBI Working Paper 259, Asian Development Bank Institute, Tokyo.

Honohan, P., and T. Beck. 2007. *Making Finance Work for Africa*. Washington, DC: World Bank.

International Monetary Fund (IMF). 2013. "Key Aspects of Macroprudential Policy." IMF Policy Paper, Washington, DC.

International Monetary Fund (IMF). 2018. "The IMF's Annual Macroprudential Policies Survey: Objectives, Design, and Country Responses." IMF Policy Note, Washington, DC.

Jain, S. 1999. "Symbiosis vs. Crowding-Out: The Interaction of Formal and Informal Credit Markets in Developing Countries." *Journal of Development Economics* 59 (2): 419–44.

Johnson, S., M. Malkamäki, and M. Niño-Zarazua. 2010. "The Role of Informal Groups in Financial Markets: Evidence from Kenya." Bath Papers in International Development and Wellbeing 7, Centre for Development Studies, University of Bath, Bath, UK.

Karaivanov, A., and A. Kessler. 2018. "(Dis) Advantages of Informal Loans: Theory and Evidence." *European Economic Review* 102 (C): 100–28.

Kaufmann, D., A. Kraay, and M. Mastruzzi. 2003. *Governance Matters III: Governance Indicators for 1996–2002*. Washington, DC: World Bank.

Klapper, L., and D. Singer. 2015. "The Role of Informal Financial Services in Africa." *Journal of African Economies* 24 (Supplement 1): i12–i31.

Madestam, A. 2014. "Informal Finance: A Theory of Moneylenders." *Journal of Development Economics* 107 (March): 157–74.

Medina, L., and F. Schneider. 2018. "Shadow Economies around the World: What Did We Learn over the Last 20 Years?" IMF Working Paper 18/17, International Monetary Fund, Washington, DC.

Mengistu, A., and H. Perez-Saiz. 2018. "Financial Inclusion and Bank Competition in Sub-Saharan Africa." IMF Working Paper 18/256, International Monetary Fund, Washington, DC.

Mookerjee, R., and P. Kalipioni. 2010. "Availability of Financial Services and Income Inequality: The Evidence from Many Countries." *Emerging Markets Review* 11 (4): 404–08.

Mookherjee, D., and A. Motta. 2016. "A Theory of Interactions between MFIs and Informal Lenders." *Journal of Development Economics* 121 (July): 191–200.

Munzele Maimbo, S., and C. A. Henriquez Gallegos. 2014. "Interest Rate Caps around the World: Still Popular, But a Blunt Instrument." Policy Research Working Paper 7070, World Bank, Washington, DC.

Owen, A. L., and J. M. Pereira. 2018. "Bank Concentration, Competition, and Financial Inclusion." *Review of Development Finance* 8 (June): 1–17.

Pradhan, N. 2013. "Persistence of Informal Credit in Rural India: Evidence from 'All-India Debt and Investment Survey' and Beyond." RBI Working Paper Series WPS (DEPR): 05/2013, Department of Economic and Policy Research, Reserve Bank of India, Mumbai.

Qin, D., X. Zhong, and X. Zhang. 2014. "How Much Informal Credit Lending Responded to Monetary Policy in China? The Case of Wenzhou." *Journal of Asian Economics* 31–32 (April–June): 22–31.

Sahay, R., M. Čihák, P. N'Diaye, A. Barajas, R. Bi, D. Ayala, Y. Gao, A. Kyobe, L. Nguyen, C. Saborowski, K. Svirydzenka, and S. R. Yousefi. 2015. "Rethinking Financial Deepening: Stability and Growth in Emerging Markets." IMF Staff Discussion Note 15/08, International Monetary Fund, Washington, DC.

Sarma, M. 2008. "Index of Financial Inclusion." ICRIER Working Paper 215, Indian Council for Research on International Economic Relations, New Delhi.

Sarma, M., and J. Pais. 2011. "Financial Inclusion and Development." *Journal of International Development* 23 (5): 613–28.

Soyibo, A. 1996. "Financial Linkage and Development in Sub-Saharan Africa: The Role of Formal Financial Institutions in Nigeria." ODI Working Paper, Overseas Development Institute, London.

Svirydzenka, K. 2016. "Introducing a New Broad-Based Index of Financial Development." IMF Working Paper 16/5, International Monetary Fund, Washington, DC.

World Bank 2017. *The Global Findex Database*. Washington, DC. https://globalfindex.worldbank.org/index.php/#data_sec_focus.

Yetman, J. 2017. "Adapting Monetary Policy to Increasing Financial Inclusion." Paper presented at the ISI World Statistics Congress on Financial Inclusion, Marrakech, Morocco, July 17–21.

Zins, A., and L. Weill. 2016. "The Determinants of Financial Inclusion in Africa." *Review of Development Finance* 6 (1): 46–57.

CHAPTER 12

Financial Inclusion, Bank Competition, and Informal Employment in Sub-Saharan Africa

Azanaw Mengistu and Hector Perez-Saiz

INTRODUCTION

Economists have discussed for decades the importance of the financial sector to economic growth and development (Levine 2005). Well-developed financial systems that provide individuals with valuable and affordable financial products are key to channeling funds between savers and investors, facilitating payments and money transactions, and helping manage risks in the economy. Despite much debate still on which specific channels connect the financial system to economic growth, broad consensus indicates that countries with more financial development tend to grow more rapidly. Hence, the issue of financial inclusion in low- and middle-income countries has captured the interest of academics and policymakers.

In this chapter, we study how competition and financial soundness in the financial industry affect financial inclusion in sub-Saharan Africa. We use detailed individual-level survey data, combined with key country-level indicators of bank competition and financial soundness, to study the effect of competition and various bank balance sheet variables on access to key financial products (bank accounts, credit and debit cards, and bank loans), by adult individuals and by individuals in the informal economy.

In our empirical model, we use the World Bank Global Findex, a large individual-level database that consistently measures adults' use of financial services across countries and over time. In our empirical model, we include a rich set of individual-level demographic variables, various country-level competition and bank balance sheet variables, and other country-level variables for sub-Saharan Africa for 2011, 2014, and 2017. Contrary to other studies that consider financial inclusion at a more aggregate level, the Global Findex enables a more granular analysis at an individual level so that we can control for individual demographic characteristics. The database also allows us to identify individuals who are part of the informal economy, that is, individuals who do not receive a formal salary from employers. By focusing on sub-Saharan Africa only, we use a homogeneous sample of countries that share common characteristics.

We first study the effect of competition on financial inclusion. The industrial organization literature, through various game-theoretic models, shows that more concentration typically reduces competition, which increases prices and reduces output or welfare (Tirole 1988). In recent decades, bank competition across countries has significantly changed after a gradual deregulation (Vives 2011). More competition increases the supply of financial products, reduces the rates and fees paid, expands the number of financial providers and the network of bank branches, and increases the quality and variety of products offered (Vives 2016), with a positive effect on financial inclusion. The effect of bank concentration in Africa has frequently been studied by researchers and policymakers (Love and Peria 2012; Beck and Cull 2014; Mecagni, Marchettini, and Maino 2015).

We measure financial inclusion by considering individual-level indicators of adoption of bank accounts, debit cards, or credit cards. To measure competition, we use four well-known indicators used broadly in the banking literature: the C5 indicator, the H-statistic, the Lerner index, and the Boone indicator.[1]

Which variables are appropriate to measure competition in an industry is a well-known question in the empirical literature. The degree of competition in an industry is related to the "conduct" of firms in the market, but not necessarily to the degree of concentration in the industry. A market with a single firm could still be "contestable" because the mere presence of potential entrants is enough to reduce the monopoly power of the incumbent (Baumol, Panzar, and Willig 1988). Furthermore, high costs in the provision of financial products, as shown in Allen and others (2016), could simply be caused by other factors not directly related to competition (such as higher input costs or lower economies of scale). Which variables are appropriate to measure competition is therefore a relevant question to characterize the conduct of firms.

In our empirical results, we generally find that competition has a statistically significant effect on the adoption of accounts, debit cards, and credit cards by individuals in sub-Saharan Africa. We combine analysis of the simple C5 indicator with the other competition indicators, which have a more direct behavioral interpretation in terms of competitive behavior and the conduct of firms. We also find a significant relationship between individuals who do not have a bank account because they think it is expensive and the degree of competition. This result suggests that the high cost of bank accounts may be attributed to a lack of competition instead of to other exogenous factors. We also find similar results when we consider only individuals who are part of the informal economy, which tends to be important in sub-Saharan Africa. Our results are robust when controlling for detailed individual-level variables and using other variables related to financial inclusion, such as GDP or financial depth, as well as country and year fixed effects.

[1] For a review of measures of competition used in banking, see Degryse, Morales Acevedo, and Ongena 2014.

We also study the relationship between key bank balance sheet variables and borrowing by individuals. Balance sheet weaknesses may affect the ability of banks to supply credit, restricting individuals' borrowing capacity.[2] One dimension of balance sheet strength is measured through the level of regulatory capital. There is not clear consensus about the implications of higher capital ratios on the supply of credit (Admati and others 2011; Hanson, Kashyap, and Stein, 2011). Banks can increase their capital ratios by increasing their levels of regulatory capital, which increases their resiliency and their ability to take risks and supply credit. Banks, conversely, may decide to increase their capital ratios by restricting credit. The effect of liquidity on lending is also debatable. Although banks with more liquid assets are more resilient against shocks, they may hold liquid assets to the detriment of lending (Cornett and others 2011).

The effect of changes in bank capital on bank credit supply greatly determines the link between the financial system and real activity. Quantifying this relationship has therefore been an important research question (Berrospide and Edge 2010; Gambacorta and Marques-Ibanez 2011; Kapan and Minoiu 2013; Bridges and others 2014; Gropp and others 2016; Brun, Fraisse, and Thesmar 2017). Most of the literature has focused on the effect of bank capital requirements on lending to the corporate sector. Few studies have considered consumer lending, but these studies typically found that higher capital reduces consumer lending less than corporate lending (Bridges and others 2014) and even increases the probability that banks accept mortgage applications (Michelangeli and Sette 2016). This chapter contributes to our understanding of the effect of bank balance sheet variables on individuals' borrowing, a key determinant of financial inclusion in Africa.

In a second set of results, we find a statistically significant relationship between key bank balance sheet variables and borrowing by individuals, although this relationship is not robust when considering country fixed effects or when considering informally employed individuals only. Without country fixed effects, we find that borrowing by individuals is positively affected in countries with higher Tier 1 capital ratios and more liquid financial systems. We also find that more liquid financial systems are more procyclical (that is, more positively affected by larger GDP growth). We find a similar procyclical effect when considering financial systems with higher Tier 1 capital ratios. In other words, stronger financial systems (in terms of higher capital or liquidity) are more procyclical (give more credit when GDP growth is larger). However, once we add country fixed effects, some procyclical effects disappear. We therefore conclude that the effect of higher Tier 1 capital ratios and more liquid financial systems on borrowing is not undisputed. Tier 1 capital ratios tend to be higher in sub-Saharan Africa compared with

[2] This "bank-lending" channel is part of a broader concept called the "credit channel of monetary policy" (Bernanke and Gertler 1987, 1995; Bernanke and Blinder 1988; Kashyap and Stein 2000; Bernanke 2007; Jiménez and others 2012, 2014).

other regions, which may solely be a result of buffers constructed to prevent losses in highly unstable financial systems (Beck and others 2011). In sub-Saharan Africa, where it is costly for banks to raise capital, capital ratios may be raised by constraining lending (Bernanke and Lown 1991).

This chapter contributes to the empirical literature that links financial sector development and economic growth (King and Levine 1993). Financial inclusion can help reduce poverty and inequality by helping people invest, smooth their consumption, and manage financial risks; however, the relationship between financial inclusion and economic growth is not yet well understood, and research on the topic has been limited (Demirgüç-Kunt, Klapper, and Singer 2017). It is important to understand that financial depth and financial inclusion are two different concepts. In general, financial depth concerns aggregate variables, such as the volume of loans or deposits relative to GDP. Meanwhile, financial inclusion refers to how accessible the financial sector is to various population segments, depending on their income, race, gender, age, and so on.

For example, a financial sector could be considered to be developed from the standpoint of the ratio of loans to GDP but negatively ranked in inclusion because a few individuals borrow most of the loans.[3] Allen and others (2016) is the closest reference to our analysis and uses a similar individual-level database from 123 countries for 2011 to find a significant relationship between political stability, legal rights, and other institutional variables on financial inclusion. Deléchat and others (2018) uses a similar database to show the effect of institutional factors on women's financial inclusion.

In this chapter, we describe our data sources, study the relationship between competition and financial inclusion, study the relationship between balance sheet variables and financial inclusion, and conclude with a summary and consider policy implications.

DATA SOURCES

Our analysis relies on the World Bank Global Findex database for 2011, 2014, and 2017; the IMF Financial Soundness Indicators; and the World Bank Global Financial Development database.

Global Financial Inclusion Database

We use the Global Findex database (Demirgüç-Kunt and Klapper 2013), launched by the World Bank in 2011 and updated in 2014 and 2017. The Global Findex covers more than 140 economies, representing more than 97 percent of the world's population. Global Findex data are collected at the individual level,

[3] Studies on financial inclusion in sub-Saharan Africa include Karlan and Morduch 2009, Ahokpossi and others 2013, Allen and others 2013, Mlachila and Moheeput 2014, and Yontcheva and Alter 2016.

through a survey by Gallup, covering approximately 150,000 nationally representative and randomly selected individuals ages 15 years and older (Demirgüç-Kunt and others 2015).

The focus of our analysis is sub-Saharan African countries, so we restrict our sample to this region. Observations total nearly 105,000, with approximately 35,000 in each year. Table 12.1 shows summary statistics that suggest Findex respondents vary greatly. Respondents' ages range from 15 to 99 years. The average age is 34.3 years old, and the median is 30 years old. The median person in the sample has completed primary education, and the female-to-male ratio is 1.5. For income distribution, the poorest 20 percent constitute 15 percent of the sample and the richest 5 percent constitute 28 percent of the sample (not shown).

To measure informal employment, we use a wage variable indicator equal to 1 if the adult individual does not receive a wage from an employer. This definition of informal employment is consistent with guidelines provided by the International Labour Organization (2013). When we use this definition, approximately 85 percent of individuals in the sample are informal workers. The informal employment variable is only available for 2014 and 2017 in the sample.

In our database, 36 percent of individuals have a bank account. Those with a debit card are 18 percent of the sample, and 5 percent have a credit card. Among the people who do not have bank account, 21 percent report not having an account because it is too expensive. Also, 7 percent report having borrowed money from a financial institution in the past year.

Although the Global Findex includes variables related to mobile payments and other new financial technologies (fintech), we do not consider these services in our study. First, these services are still in development, mainly used for sending money, and have a limited use as saving or credit instruments (Maino and others 2019). Second, measuring competition in the fintech industry is difficult, and limited data are available. Last, with the exception of several countries in eastern and southern Africa, most of these new services are not successful in the continent. Therefore, we limit our study to more traditional banking products, such as bank accounts, cards, and loans.

Financial Soundness Indicators Database

We use the IMF Financial Soundness Indicators database at the country level, combined with the Findex, to obtain insight on the financial soundness of banking institutions in sub-Saharan Africa. Financial soundness indicators are compiled to monitor the health and soundness of financial institutions and markets and of their corporate and household counterparts. However, the database suffers from missing data, because it only contains 24 countries from sub-Saharan Africa. The main variables available are institutions that take deposits, asset quality, nonperforming loans to total gross loans, earnings and profitability of the banking sector, return on assets and equity, capital adequacy, and liquidity ratios. Table 12.2 shows the complete list of variables.

TABLE 12.1.

Selected Summary Statistics of Data Sources

Variable	Mean	Minimum	P1	P25	P50	P75	P99	Maximum
Demographic Variables								
Age	34.3	15	15	23	30	42	79	99
Education	1.53	1	1	1	1	2	3	5
Female	1.50	1	1	1	1	2	2	2
Income quantile	3.26	1	1	2	3	5	5	5
Informality indicator	0.85	0	0	1	1	1	1	1
Financial Inclusion Indicators								
Has bank account	0.36	0	0	0	0	1	1	1
Has debit card	0.18	0	0	0	0	0	1	1
Has credit card	0.05	0	0	0	0	0	1	1
Does not have account because it is expensive	0.21	0	0	0	0	0	1	1
Borrowed last year	0.07	0	0	0	0	0	1	1
Competition Indicators								
Boone indicator	−0.06	−0.5	−0.5	−0.11	−0.05	−0.01	0.2	0.2
C5 indicator	81.39	52.08	52.08	69.16	83.73	92.52	100	100
H-statistic	0.49	0.06	0.06	0.39	0.49	0.6	0.83	0.83
Lerner index	0.28	0.1	0.1	0.23	0.28	0.32	0.48	0.48
Bank Indicators and Growth								
Liquidity coverage ratio	29.34	10.61	10.61	21.84	29.14	36.66	53.71	53.71
Tier 1 ratio	15.82	2.18	2.18	13.4	16.19	18.57	30.77	30.77
GDP growth	4.77	−6.43	−6.43	3.19	4.7	6.36	13.6	13.6

Sources: IMF, International Financial Statistics database; World Bank, Global Findex database; and World Bank, Global Financial Development database.

TABLE 12.2.

Financial Soundness Indicators

Variable	Description
Deposit takers	Deposit-taker institutions
Asset quality	Asset quality
Nonperforming loans to total gross loans	Calculated by using the value of nonperforming loans as the numerator and the total value of the loan portfolio (including nonperforming loans and before the deduction of specific loan loss provisions) as the denominator
Earnings and profitability	Earnings and profitability
Return to assets	Calculated by dividing net income before extraordinary items and taxes by the average value of total assets over the same period
Return to equity	Calculated by dividing net income before extraordinary items and taxes by the average value of capital over the same period
Capital adequacy	Capital adequacy
Capital to risk-weighted assets	Calculated using total regulatory capital as the numerator and risk-weighted assets as the denominator

Source: IMF, Financial Soundness Indicators database.

Note: For each variable, type is percent and format is numeric.

Global Financial Development Database

The World Bank Global Financial Development database provides extensive data on financial system characteristics for 206 economies (Čihák and others 2012). Table 12.3 shows some variables included. The main explanatory variables of interest here measure bank competition. We use the C5 indicator (higher C5, less competition), the H-statistic (higher H, more competition), the Lerner index (higher, less competition), and the Boone indicator (higher, more competition).

The Global Financial Development database also contains variables that measure access to banking, such as bank accounts per 1,000 adults and bank branches per 100,000 adults. The indicators that measure the depth of the banking sector include the ratios of private credit to deposit money banks, deposit money banks' assets to GDP, and central bank assets to GDP. The resilience and stability of banks are indicated by variables related to the ratios of nonperforming loans to gross loans, bank capital to total assets, and bank credit to bank deposits. Macroeconomic variables, including GDP and GDP per capita, are the other variables we control for and are included in the database.

We now describe in detail the four indices that measure the level of bank competition, which are our main explanatory variables related to competition. Degryse, Morales Acevedo, and Ongena (2014) provide more detailed information about the use of various competition variables in the financial industry.

C5 Indicator

The C5 indicator is equal to the combined market share of the five largest financial institutions in the country. It is the simplest indicator of competition. The industrial organization literature shows, through game-theoretic models of collusion, that more concentration tends to increase prices and reduce output or welfare (Tirole 1988). Concentration, however, is an imperfect measure of competitive behavior. For example, the Bertrand model without differentiated goods or the contestable market theory (Baumol, Panzar, and Willig 1988) shows that it is possible to have a perfectly competitive market in which price is equal to marginal cost, even with a monopolistic or a duopolistic market structure. Other measures of competition more related to the conduct of firms are therefore necessary to complement the C5 indicator.

Panzar-Rosse H-Statistic

The H-statistic captures the elasticity of bank interest revenues to input prices, where input prices include the price of deposits, personnel, equipment, and fixed capital.[4] As proposed originally by Panzar and Rosse (1987), the H-statistic is defined such that the higher its value, the more competitive the banking system.

---

[4] For more information, see "Banking Competition" in the World Bank's *Global Financial Development Report 2019/2020* (https://www.worldbank.org/en/publication/gfdr/gfdr-2016/background/banking-competition/).

TABLE 12.3.

Selected Explanatory Variables in the Global Financial Development Database

Variable	Description
Bank accounts per 1,000 adults	Number of depositors with commercial banks per 1,000 adults
Bank branches per 100,000 adults	Number of commercial bank branches per 100,000 adults
Loans requiring collateral	Percentage of loans where a formal financial institution requires collateral to provide the financing
Value of collateral needed for a loan (% of the loan amount)	Value of collateral needed by a formal financial institution for a loan or line of credit as a percentage of the loan value or the value of the line of credit
Private credit by deposit money banks to GDP (%)	Financial resources provided to the private sector by domestic money banks as a share of GDP
Deposit money banks' assets to GDP (%)	Total assets held by deposit money banks as a share of GDP
Central bank assets to GDP (%)	Total assets held by deposit money banks as a share of GDP
Bank net interest margin (%)	Accounting value of bank's net interest revenue as a share of its average interest-bearing (total earning) assets
Bank lending-deposit spread	Difference between lending rate and deposit rate; lending rate is the rate charged by banks on loans to the private sector, and deposit interest rate is the rate offered by commercial banks on three-month deposits
Bank concentration (%)	Assets of three largest commercial banks as a share of total commercial banking assets
Bank deposits to GDP (%)	Total value of demand, time, and saving deposits at domestic deposit money banks as a share of GDP
H-statistic	Measure of the degree of competition in the banking market; higher H-statistic means more competition
Lerner index	Measure of market power in the banking market; higher Lerner means less competition
Boone indicator	Measure of degree of competition based on profit-efficiency in the banking market; higher value (less negative) means less competition
Bank *z*-score	Captures the probability of default of a country's commercial banking system
Bank nonperforming loans to gross loans (%)	Ratio of defaulting loans (payments of interest and principal past due by 90 days or more) to total gross loans (total value of loan portfolio)
Bank capital to total assets (%)	Ratio of bank capital and reserves to total assets
Bank credit to bank deposits (%)	Financial resources provided to the private sector by domestic money banks as a share of total deposits
Bank regulatory capital to risk-weighted assets (%)	Capital adequacy of deposit takers; ratio of total regulatory capital to its assets held, weighted according to risk of those assets
Liquid assets to deposits and short-term funding (%)	Ratio of the value of liquid assets (easily converted to cash) to short-term funding plus total deposits
Provisions to nonperforming loans (%)	Provisions to nonperforming loans
Stock price volatility	Stock price volatility is the average of the 360-day volatility of the national stock market index
GDP (current US dollars)	GDP (current US dollars)
GDP per capita (constant 2005 US dollars)	GDP per capita (constant 2000 US dollars)
Population (total)	Population, total

Source: World Bank, Global Financial Development database.

Note: For each variable, type is continuous and format is numeric.

A monopoly situation yields an H-statistic that can be negative or zero, whereas monopolistic competition yields values between 0 and 1, and perfect competition is greater than 1 (Bikker and Haaf 2002; Claessens and Laeven 2004).

Lerner Index

The Lerner index is defined as the difference between output prices and marginal costs (relative to prices) and is equal to the inverse of the elasticity of demand for the case of a perfect monopoly and equal to zero for a perfect competitive market. Higher values of the Lerner index therefore indicate less bank competition. For industry structures between competition and monopoly, the value of the Lerner index depends on the reaction of a bank to competitors' strategic choices. The stronger this reaction, the lower the degree of competition and the higher the Lerner index (Shaffer 1993).

Boone Indicator

The Boone indicator (Boone 2008) reflects the effect of efficiency on profits, calculated as the elasticity of profits to marginal costs. The indicator mainly measures that more efficient banks achieve higher profits. The more negative the Boone indicator, therefore, the greater the competition in the market. The Boone indicator ranges from –0.5 to 0.2, and the average value for our sample countries is close to zero at –0.06.

Our sample demonstrates that the H-statistic and Lerner indices show average statistics indicating low bank competition among the sub-Saharan African countries represented in our database.

When compared with other simpler measures (such as C5), the H-statistic, the Lerner index, and the Boone indicator provide a step forward in measuring competition. Calculating these three competition indicators, however, requires large amounts of data; all use input prices or costs of production at the bank level, which may not be available for researchers in nonadvanced economies, especially the sub-Saharan Africa region.

Financial Access and Bank Competition in Sub-Saharan Africa

Table 12.4 shows summary statistics of variables measuring financial access by global region. Financial account ownership in sub-Saharan Africa is significantly lower compared with more advanced economies. In sub-Saharan Africa, there are 346 bank accounts per 1,000 adults, compared with 1,522 accounts in advanced economies and 591 in emerging markets and low-income developing countries. Other measures of financial access, such as number of bank branches or ownership of credit or debit cards, are also lower in sub-Saharan Africa.

Table 12.4 shows that sub-Saharan Africa does comparatively better in mobile payment use. In the region, 25 percent of adults use a mobile bank account, compared with 85 percent of adults in advanced economies and 29 percent in nonadvanced economies.

TABLE 12.4.

Selected Summary Indicators

Indicator	Sub-Saharan Africa	Africa	Advanced Economies	Nonadvanced Economies	Descriptor
Bank accounts (per 1,000 adults)	345.8	346.0	1,522.2	590.9	
Credit cards (percent adults with)	3.7	3.7	46.5	9.2	
Debit cards (percent adults with)	14.4	14.3	78.3	26.2	
Mobile payments (percent adults using)	24.9	23.2	85.0	29.2	
Bank branches (per 100,000 adults)	7.5	7.8	35.7	14.3	
Boone indicator	−0.08	−0.05	−1.27	−0.05	Higher value (less negative), less competition
H-statistic	0.46	0.49	0.63	0.55	Higher H, more competition
Lerner index	0.32	0.32	0.28	0.32	Higher Lerner, less competition
C5 indicator	82.12	82.21	83.99	76.6	Higher C5, less competition

Source: World Bank, Global Findex database.

When comparing competition indicators measured using the Boone indicator, the H-statistic, and the Lerner index, we find that the degree of competition in the sub-Saharan African banking sector is lower (than in advanced economies). Yet, if we measure competition using C5, the two world regions are similar.

COMPETITION AND FINANCIAL INCLUSION

The objective of our analysis is to use the detailed panel of individuals provided by Findex to focus on two separate research issues. First, we want to understand how various country-level bank competition indicators affect having an account, a debit card, or a credit card. Second, we want to understand how measures of financial soundness at country level affect borrowing by individuals.

Empirical Model

To estimate the effect of competition, we consider a simple probit model where $y_{i,c,t} = 1$ is an indicator that individual i in country c and year t adopted a certain financial product. We further assume that $Pr(y_{i,c,t} = 1) = Pr(y^*_{i,c,t} > 0)$, where

$$y^*_{i,c,t} = \alpha_1\, compet_{c,t-1} + \alpha_2 X_{i,c,t} + \alpha_3 Z_{c,t} + \alpha_t + \alpha_c + \varepsilon_{i,c,t}, \quad (1)$$

where the term $compet_{c,t-1}$ is a lagged variable of competition constructed using the C5, the Boone indicator, the H-statistic, or the Lerner index; $X_{i,c,t}$ is a vector of individual-level variables; $Z_{c,t}$ is a vector of country-level variables; α_t is year fixed effects; and α_c is country fixed effects. We also use model (1) to determine how competition affects the costs of bank accounts. Whether the expense is the reason individuals do not have a bank account is a question in the Findex survey.

From this model, we can test the validity of the market power hypothesis by considering the sign of parameter α_1 in model (1), with Hypothesis 1 as $\alpha_1 > 0$ (greater competition increases the probability of having a financial product).

Country and year fixed effects play a relevant role in identifying the parameters of interest in model (1). Country fixed effects allow control of time-invariant, country-level variables that may influence an individual's decision to adopt a financial product. We estimate a short panel (two years) with approximately 1,000 individuals per country-year. Our individual-level data include rich demographic variables that may affect the decision to buy a financial product or obtain access to credit.

Results for the Full Sample of Individuals

We present results related to the estimation of model (1) that show the effect of bank competition variables on individuals' adoption of bank accounts, debit cards, and credit cards by individuals in sub-Saharan Africa. We first present the results when using the full sample (formally and informally employed individuals). Table 12.5 shows the effect of competition variables on individuals' adoption of bank accounts. Given the definition of every competition indicator, a positive effect of competition on the adoption of bank accounts (that is, if competition in the market increases, adoption increases) would imply that the estimated parameter is negative for the C5 indicator, negative for the Boone indicator, positive for the H-statistic, and negative for the Lerner index. In all regressions we use three country-level indicators: the ratio of private credit to GDP, the GDP in US dollars, and GDP per capita. The three indicators should be positively related to financial depth, which could be related to financial inclusion because financial inclusion tends to be higher in more advanced economies with more developed financial systems.[5] These variables also help control for other factors not included in the other regressors.

We start our econometric analysis with the simplest competition indicator, the C5 indicator of concentration, and we find an intuitive negative coefficient for C5 in column (1). In column (2), we find that the effect of the C5 indicator in countries with a more developed financial system (measured as the ratio of credit to GDP) is positive. This is an interesting result, because it shows that competition indicators for financial inclusion tend to be less important in countries with more financial depth.

In columns (3) to (5), we add additional variables to better measure competition (the Boone indicator, the H-statistic, and the Lerner index), and we interact

[5] Financial inclusion tends to be higher in more advanced economies with more developed financial systems, although this may not always be the case (Karlan and Morduch 2009).

TABLE 12.5.

Individuals Who Have a Bank Account and Bank Competition

	No Country Fixed Effects					Including Country Fixed Effects				
Indicator	**(1)**	**(2)**	**(3)**	**(4)**	**(5)**	**(6)**	**(7)**	**(8)**	**(9)**	**(10)**
C5 indicator	−1.084***	−1.380***	−1.633***	−0.257**	−1.324***	−1.531***	−1.224***	−1.703***	−4.742***	−3.782***
	(0.0341)	(0.0745)	(0.0629)	(0.122)	(0.169)	(0.133)	(0.268)	(0.298)	(0.560)	(0.507)
C5 Indicator × Credit/GDP		0.00955***					−0.0146			
		(0.00217)					(0.0109)			
Boone indicator			32.57***					−22.74***		
			(2.428)					(6.633)		
C5 Indicator × Boone Indicator			−7.708***					5.286***		
			(0.571)					(1.567)		
H-statistic				9.006***					−23.68***	
				(1.464)					(5.503)	
C5 Indicator × H-Statistic				−2.090***					5.805***	
				(0.331)					(1.269)	
Lerner index					−4.823*					−39.42***
					(2.601)					(7.575)
C5 Indicator × Lerner Index					1.197**					9.202***
					(0.601)					(1.789)
Credit/GDP	0.0147***	−0.0271***	0.0175***	0.0153***	0.0177***	0.00332	0.0670	−0.00168	−0.00496	−0.00600
	(0.000421)	(0.00952)	(0.000542)	(0.000581)	(0.000617)	(0.00307)	(0.0478)	(0.00427)	(0.00400)	(0.00492)
GDP per capita	0.143***	0.146***	0.0632***	0.189***	−0.0118	−1.593***	−1.625***	−2.445***	−2.496***	−3.455***
	(0.00859)	(0.00862)	(0.0113)	(0.0131)	(0.0168)	(0.204)	(0.205)	(0.298)	(0.324)	(0.359)
GDP	−0.0394***	−0.0591***	0.00624	−0.0446***	0.0243***	0.791***	0.801***	0.645***	0.340***	1.145***
	(0.00616)	(0.00741)	(0.00805)	(0.00859)	(0.00936)	(0.0748)	(0.0752)	(0.113)	(0.108)	(0.186)
Respondent age		0.00929***	0.0106***	0.0106***	0.0110***	0.00999***	0.01000***	0.0118***	0.0120***	0.0118***
		(0.000384)	(0.000493)	(0.000505)	(0.000531)	(0.000396)	(0.000396)	(0.000507)	(0.000523)	(0.000549)
Female		0.123***	0.112***	0.102***	0.114***	0.148***	0.148***	0.116***	0.113***	0.125***
		(0.0111)	(0.0143)	(0.0146)	(0.0153)	(0.0114)	(0.0114)	(0.0146)	(0.0150)	(0.0157)

(continued)

TABLE 12.5. ***(continued)***

Individuals Who Have a Bank Account and Bank Competition

	No Country Fixed Effects					Including Country Fixed Effects				
Indicator	**(1)**	**(2)**	**(3)**	**(4)**	**(5)**	**(6)**	**(7)**	**(8)**	**(9)**	**(10)**
Primary education or less		−0.181	−0.381***	−0.224	−0.324**	−0.271**	−0.271**	−0.341**	−0.204	−0.271*
		(0.118)	(0.145)	(0.141)	(0.157)	(0.120)	(0.120)	(0.148)	(0.145)	(0.158)
Secondary education		0.432***	0.277*	0.408***	0.335**	0.386***	0.386***	0.349**	0.491***	0.410***
		(0.118)	(0.145)	(0.140)	(0.156)	(0.120)	(0.120)	(0.148)	(0.145)	(0.158)
Tertiary education or more		1.119***	1.189***	1.104***	1.277***	1.222***	1.222***	1.291***	1.360***	1.351***
		(0.122)	(0.151)	(0.144)	(0.163)	(0.125)	(0.124)	(0.154)	(0.149)	(0.166)
Education: missing		−0.238	−0.0980	−0.161	−0.111	−0.296*	−0.297*	−0.420*	−0.264	−0.192
		(0.164)	(0.241)	(0.234)	(0.393)	(0.171)	(0.171)	(0.248)	(0.245)	(0.391)
Poorest 20%		−0.772***	−0.834***	−0.817***	−0.802***	−0.803***	−0.803***	−0.875***	−0.857***	−0.862***
		(0.0184)	(0.0240)	(0.0244)	(0.0256)	(0.0188)	(0.0188)	(0.0245)	(0.0251)	(0.0263)
Second 20%		−0.606***	−0.697***	−0.690***	−0.694***	−0.625***	−0.625***	−0.726***	−0.717***	−0.739***
		(0.0175)	(0.0229)	(0.0232)	(0.0245)	(0.0179)	(0.0179)	(0.0233)	(0.0239)	(0.0252)
Middle 20%		−0.467***	−0.506***	−0.496***	−0.491***	−0.485***	−0.484***	−0.531***	−0.525***	−0.529***
		(0.0166)	(0.0212)	(0.0216)	(0.0227)	(0.0170)	(0.0170)	(0.0217)	(0.0222)	(0.0234)
Fourth 20%		−0.298***	−0.313***	−0.306***	−0.307***	−0.305***	−0.305***	−0.324***	−0.317***	−0.328***
		(0.0157)	(0.0198)	(0.0201)	(0.0212)	(0.0160)	(0.0160)	(0.0202)	(0.0207)	(0.0217)
No. of observations	62,863	62,863	38,992	37,987	33,989	62,863	62,863	38,992	37,987	33,989
Year fixed effects	Yes	Yes	Yes	Yes	Yes	Yes	Yes	Yes	Yes	Yes
Country fixed effects	No	No	No	No	No	Yes	Yes	Yes	Yes	Yes
Expected sign: C5 indicator	−	−	−	−	−	−	−	−	−	−
Expected sign: Boone indicator			−					−		
Expected sign: H-statistic				+					+	
Expected sign: Lerner index					−					−

Sources: IMF, International Financial Statistics database; World Bank, Global Findex database; and World Bank, Global Financial Development database.

Notes: Probit regressions and bank competition. Robust standard errors are in parentheses.

*$p < 0.1$; **$p < 0.05$; ***$p < 0.01$.

them with the simple C5 indicator. Again, bank concentration may not be a strong indicator of competitive behavior.[6] The Boone indicator, H-statistic, and Lerner index have a stronger behavioral interpretation related to the competitive behavior of the industry. In column (4), we find that adoption of accounts increases in markets that are more competitive (higher H-statistic indicator) for a given level of concentration of C5. In addition, the interaction of the two indicators has a negative effect on adoption.

In columns (3) and (5), respectively, we consider the Boone and Lerner indicators. In all columns, the effect of the C5 indicator is negative, and the effect of the Lerner indicator in column (5) is consistent with hypothesis 1. We do not find an intuitive effect of the Boone indicator consistent with our hypothesis in column (3).

The effect of the credit-to-GDP ratio (financial depth) and other economic development (GDP) variables on financial inclusion is positive and statistically significant in most specifications. This suggests a link between financial inclusion and financial depth.

In columns (6) to (10), we repeat the analysis and include country fixed effects. Some results change considerably, probably because we use a short panel with country-level variables and country fixed effects, which may add collinearity effects if the country-level variables vary slightly. With country fixed effects, the estimated effect of ratio of credit to GDP on adoption becomes statistically insignificant, the effect of GDP per capita becomes negative, and the effect of GDP becomes positive and significant. In all cases, the effect of concentration has an intuitive negative sign. When including the effect of the Boone and Lerner indicators, we find intuitive effects consistent with hypothesis 1, whereas the effect of the H-statistic has the expected opposite sign.

Several intuitive results are discovered regarding the effect of individual-level variables (education, gender, age, and so on) on the probability of having a bank account. In all specifications, older individuals, female individuals, and well-educated individuals (secondary education or higher) are more likely to have a bank account. Also, poor individuals (the poorest 20 percent) are less likely to have a bank account. The results are also robust for other products (debit and credit cards), which we present in the following tables.

Table 12.6 shows the estimated parameters for a probit regression where the endogenous variable is an indicator equal to 1 if the individual responds in the survey that he or she does not have an account because accounts are too expensive. We use this probit model to understand whether there is a statistical relationship between accounts being expensive and the banking industry being uncompetitive. This relationship is not obvious. Industries that are more competitive do not necessarily have lower prices for the products offered because other exogenous

[6] For example, a simple duopoly market can be competitive if the two firms compete on prices (Bertrand competition). Also, a monopoly can set a perfectly competitive price if the market is "contestable" (Baumol, Panzar, and Willig 1988).

TABLE 12.6.

Individuals Who Do Not Have Accounts Because They Are Too Expensive

	No Country Fixed Effects					Including Country Fixed Effects				
Indicator	**(1)**	**(2)**	**(3)**	**(4)**	**(5)**	**(6)**	**(7)**	**(8)**	**(9)**	**(10)**
C5 indicator	0.222*** (0.0372)	−0.213*** (0.0756)	−0.218*** (0.0665)	−0.723*** (0.124)	−0.0645 (0.181)	0.494*** (0.137)	1.535*** (0.329)	0.798*** (0.295)	0.876 (0.594)	3.708*** (0.563)
C5 Indicator × Credit/GDP		0.0154*** (0.00234)					−0.0459*** (0.0131)			
Boone indicator			19.43*** (2.624)					32.26*** (7.322)		
C5 Indicator × Boone Indicator			−4.510*** (0.615)					−7.861*** (1.728)		
H-statistic				−10.39*** (1.526)					−13.48** (6.004)	
C5 Indicator × H-Statistic				2.425*** (0.345)					2.991** (1.381)	
Lerner index					−1.750 (2.792)					31.67*** (8.426)
C5 Indicator × Lerner Index					0.0806 (0.644)					−7.787*** (1.977)
Credit/GDP	−0.00938*** (0.000460)	−0.0768*** (0.0103)	−0.0110*** (0.000548)	−0.00948*** (0.000614)	−0.00861*** (0.000653)	0.0182*** (0.00358)	0.222*** (0.0583)	−0.00826 (0.00573)	0.00551 (0.00532)	0.0110* (0.00629)
GDP per capita	−0.0795*** (0.0100)	−0.0751*** (0.00998)	−0.0386*** (0.0125)	−0.117*** (0.0154)	−0.0861*** (0.0183)	−0.421** (0.208)	−0.544*** (0.210)	−0.980*** (0.297)	−1.213*** (0.327)	−1.320*** (0.356)
GDP	0.0289*** (0.00710)	0.00180 (0.00800)	0.0392*** (0.00899)	0.0233** (0.00959)	0.00362 (0.0106)	0.0324 (0.0797)	0.0582 (0.0802)	0.0424 (0.115)	0.231** (0.115)	0.0620 (0.195)
Respondent age	−0.00272*** (0.000407)	−0.00267*** (0.000408)	−0.00229*** (0.000515)	−0.00253*** (0.000528)	−0.00241*** (0.000560)	−0.00316*** (0.000420)	−0.00313*** (0.000420)	−0.00269*** (0.000529)	−0.00271*** (0.000542)	−0.00245*** (0.000572)
Female	0.0152 (0.0118)	0.0155 (0.0118)	0.0202 (0.0149)	0.0123 (0.0151)	0.0178 (0.0159)	0.0173 (0.0121)	0.0171 (0.0121)	0.0187 (0.0152)	0.00844 (0.0154)	0.0188 (0.0162)

(continued)

TABLE 12.6. ***(continued)***

Individuals Who Do Not Have Accounts Because They Are Too Expensive										
	No Country Fixed Effects					Including Country Fixed Effects				
Indicator	**(1)**	**(2)**	**(3)**	**(4)**	**(5)**	**(6)**	**(7)**	**(8)**	**(9)**	**(10)**
Primary education or less	0.513***	0.512***	0.332*	0.420**	0.330*	0.472***	0.474***	0.258	0.353**	0.323
	(0.146)	(0.146)	(0.174)	(0.168)	(0.194)	(0.150)	(0.150)	(0.178)	(0.173)	(0.201)
Secondary education	0.238	0.235	0.0654	0.142	0.0532	0.169	0.172	−0.0555	0.0422	0.00486
	(0.146)	(0.146)	(0.173)	(0.168)	(0.194)	(0.150)	(0.150)	(0.178)	(0.173)	(0.201)
Tertiary education or more	−0.299**	−0.306**	−0.523***	−0.429**	−0.592***	−0.389**	−0.388**	−0.668***	−0.544***	−0.689***
	(0.151)	(0.152)	(0.182)	(0.174)	(0.204)	(0.155)	(0.155)	(0.187)	(0.180)	(0.211)
Education: missing	0.384**	0.359*	0.297	0.487*	−0.442	0.402**	0.400**	0.243	0.434*	−0.483
	(0.190)	(0.190)	(0.285)	(0.249)	(0.551)	(0.196)	(0.196)	(0.290)	(0.257)	(0.571)
Poorest 20%	0.329***	0.329***	0.371***	0.347***	0.350***	0.337***	0.338***	0.380***	0.358***	0.353***
	(0.0190)	(0.0190)	(0.0240)	(0.0243)	(0.0258)	(0.0193)	(0.0193)	(0.0245)	(0.0247)	(0.0262)
Second 20%	0.265***	0.265***	0.314***	0.267***	0.315***	0.269***	0.269***	0.317***	0.271***	0.313***
	(0.0188)	(0.0188)	(0.0238)	(0.0241)	(0.0254)	(0.0191)	(0.0191)	(0.0243)	(0.0245)	(0.0259)
Middle 20%	0.227***	0.228***	0.272***	0.252***	0.277***	0.230***	0.230***	0.277***	0.262***	0.280***
	(0.0183)	(0.0183)	(0.0232)	(0.0234)	(0.0247)	(0.0187)	(0.0187)	(0.0236)	(0.0238)	(0.0252)
Fourth 20%	0.165***	0.165***	0.211***	0.184***	0.205***	0.162***	0.163***	0.209***	0.183***	0.200***
	(0.0177)	(0.0177)	(0.0223)	(0.0225)	(0.0238)	(0.0180)	(0.0180)	(0.0227)	(0.0229)	(0.0242)
No. of observations	62,863	62,863	38,992	37,987	33,989	62,863	62,863	38,992	37,987	33,989
Year fixed effects	Yes	Yes	Yes	Yes	Yes	Yes	Yes	Yes	Yes	Yes
Country fixed effects	No	No	No	No	No	Yes	Yes	Yes	Yes	Yes
Expected sign: C5 indicator	+	+	+	+	+	+	+	+	+	+
Expected sign: Boone indicator			+					+		
Expected sign: H-statistic				−					−	
Expected sign: Lerner index					+					+

Sources: IMF, International Financial Statistics database; World Bank, Global Findex database; and World Bank, Global Financial Development database.

Notes: Probit regressions and bank competition. Robust standard errors are in parentheses.

*$p < 0.1$; **$p < 0.05$; ***$p < 0.01$.

factors, such as changes in the costs of inputs, could affect prices without affecting the level of competition in the industry.[7]

Estimated parameters in Table 12.6 show that individuals are generally less likely to report that they do not have an account because it is expensive in countries where the banking industry is more competitive. For the case of country fixed effects, we find intuitive signs of the competition coefficients for the C5, Boone, H-statistic, and Lerner indicators. Without country fixed effects, the results are less consistent with hypothesis 1. Therefore, we find a direct relationship between prices and competition, consistent with our hypothesis.

Table 12.7 presents estimates similar to Table 12.5 but for debit cards. The sign of the probit estimates for the competition indicators is generally consistent with hypothesis 1 but somewhat less robust than for bank accounts. The estimates for the interaction terms for competition variables are generally similar to those for accounts.

We also find that the effect of financial depth (measured with the ratio of credit to GDP) on GDP per capita and financial inclusion is in general positive. A similar result is obtained for credit cards.

Table 12.8 presents similar estimates to Table 12.5 for the adoption of credit cards. The signs of the probit estimates for the competition indicators are generally less consistent with hypothesis 1 than for accounts or debit cards. The effect of financial deepening or GDP per capita is, in general, positive.

In summary, the empirical results generally show an economically and statistically significant effect of competition on the adoption of bank accounts and debit cards, although not for credit cards. We combine the use of concentration indicators (C5) with other variables that have an easier behavioral interpretation (Boone, H-statistic, and Lerner). In general, we find that concentration matters in explaining financial inclusion, but concentration indicators need to be complemented with other indicators of competition that have a clearer behavioral interpretation. These results are, in general, robust after controlling for individual variables, other country-level variables, and country and year fixed effects.

We also find a statistically and economically significant relationship between less banking competition and bank accounts being too expensive for many individuals. This may be because more competition translates directly to banks offering lower prices for bank accounts. These results contribute to a better understanding of the importance of bank competition and industry deregulation to increase financial inclusion in sub-Saharan Africa.

Results for Adults in the Informal Economy

We repeat the previous regressions for individuals in the informal economy. We define them as individuals 18 years of age or older who do not receive a wage.

---

[7] For example, in an extreme case, the equilibrium price of a perfectly competitive industry with perfectly elastic supply function only depends on the marginal cost of production; prices may depend on purely exogenous factors, such as exchange rates, costs of materials, and labor.

TABLE 12.7.

Individuals Who Have a Debit Card and Bank Competition

	No Country Fixed Effects					Including Country Fixed Effects				
Indicator	(1)	(2)	(3)	(4)	(5)	(6)	(7)	(8)	(9)	(10)
C5 indicator	−0.508***	−0.699***	−0.789***	1.529***	−1.706***	−0.889***	−1.907***	0.353	2.523***	−3.667***
	(0.0355)	(0.0827)	(0.0700)	(0.137)	(0.180)	(0.170)	(0.297)	(0.363)	(0.677)	(0.628)
C5 Indicator × Credit/GDP		0.00557**					0.0516***			
		(0.00221)					(0.0123)			
Boone indicator			19.31***					0.284		
			(2.867)					(7.090)		
C5 Indicator × Boone Indicator			−4.465***					0.174		
			(0.675)					(1.675)		
H-statistic				20.79***					40.05***	
				(1.577)					(6.738)	
C5 Indicator × H-Statistic				−4.904***					−9.062***	
				(0.358)					(1.552)	
Lerner index					−20.45***					−60.57***
					(2.812)					(9.576)
C5 Indicator × Lerner Index					5.050***					14.37***
					(0.653)					(2.253)
Credit/GDP	0.0108***	−0.0134	0.0113***	0.00970***	0.0142***	0.0185***	−0.203***	0.00740*	−0.00457	0.00522
	(0.000389)	(0.00959)	(0.000499)	(0.000534)	(0.000651)	(0.00326)	(0.0528)	(0.00424)	(0.00401)	(0.00535)
GDP per capita	0.269***	0.271***	0.211***	0.372***	0.0982***	1.121***	1.242***	0.251	1.649***	−0.618
	(0.00958)	(0.00963)	(0.0128)	(0.0146)	(0.0198)	(0.246)	(0.249)	(0.376)	(0.417)	(0.475)
GDP	0.0497***	0.0365***	0.117***	0.107***	0.173***	−0.199**	−0.234***	−0.148	−0.254**	0.620***
	(0.00615)	(0.00801)	(0.00822)	(0.00878)	(0.00998)	(0.0799)	(0.0801)	(0.129)	(0.123)	(0.214)
Respondent age	0.00736***	0.00741***	0.00732***	0.00671***	0.00720***	0.00839***	0.00836***	0.00815***	0.00747***	0.00767***
	(0.000441)	(0.000441)	(0.000568)	(0.000588)	(0.000623)	(0.000457)	(0.000457)	(0.000588)	(0.000607)	(0.000645)
Female	0.0976***	0.0979***	0.0602***	0.0515***	0.0660***	0.140***	0.141***	0.0880***	0.0831***	0.0910***
	(0.0128)	(0.0128)	(0.0164)	(0.0168)	(0.0180)	(0.0132)	(0.0132)	(0.0169)	(0.0174)	(0.0185)
Primary education or less	−0.351***	−0.352***	−0.0718	−0.0690	−0.0192	−0.407***	−0.408***	0.0223	0.0110	0.0443
	(0.135)	(0.134)	(0.176)	(0.181)	(0.196)	(0.142)	(0.142)	(0.181)	(0.186)	(0.196)

(continued)

TABLE 12.7. ***(continued)***

Individuals Who Have a Debit Card and Bank Competition

	No Country Fixed Effects					Including Country Fixed Effects				
Indicator	**(1)**	**(2)**	**(3)**	**(4)**	**(5)**	**(6)**	**(7)**	**(8)**	**(9)**	**(10)**
Secondary education	0.362***	0.359***	0.726***	0.731***	0.796***	0.307**	0.307**	0.808***	0.808***	0.833***
	(0.134)	(0.134)	(0.176)	(0.181)	(0.196)	(0.141)	(0.142)	(0.181)	(0.186)	(0.196)
Tertiary education or more	1.049***	1.045***	1.492***	1.435***	1.596***	1.112***	1.112***	1.605***	1.626***	1.618***
	(0.137)	(0.136)	(0.179)	(0.183)	(0.200)	(0.144)	(0.144)	(0.184)	(0.189)	(0.200)
Education: missing	−0.0870	−0.100	0.369	0.236	0.203	−0.324	−0.318	−0.0695	−0.0371	0.139
	(0.188)	(0.188)	(0.263)	(0.266)	(0.411)	(0.209)	(0.209)	(0.272)	(0.277)	(0.398)
Poorest 20%	−0.789***	−0.790***	−0.862***	−0.854***	−0.856***	−0.831***	−0.831***	−0.933***	−0.917***	−0.914***
	(0.0222)	(0.0222)	(0.0291)	(0.0297)	(0.0317)	(0.0231)	(0.0231)	(0.0301)	(0.0308)	(0.0328)
Second 20%	−0.646***	−0.647***	−0.717***	−0.719***	−0.733***	−0.685***	−0.685***	−0.783***	−0.778***	−0.789***
	(0.0205)	(0.0205)	(0.0270)	(0.0276)	(0.0296)	(0.0211)	(0.0211)	(0.0277)	(0.0283)	(0.0304)
Middle 20%	−0.504***	−0.505***	−0.554***	−0.551***	−0.567***	−0.537***	−0.538***	−0.611***	−0.609***	−0.618***
	(0.0188)	(0.0188)	(0.0241)	(0.0248)	(0.0265)	(0.0195)	(0.0195)	(0.0251)	(0.0257)	(0.0275)
Fourth 20%	−0.334***	−0.334***	−0.351***	−0.341***	−0.348***	−0.357***	−0.358***	−0.387***	−0.378***	−0.383***
	(0.0170)	(0.0170)	(0.0217)	(0.0223)	(0.0238)	(0.0175)	(0.0175)	(0.0224)	(0.0230)	(0.0244)
No. of observations	62,863	62,863	38,992	37,987	33,989	62,863	62,863	38,992	37,987	33,989
Year fixed effects	Yes	Yes	Yes	Yes	Yes	Yes	Yes	Yes	Yes	Yes
Country fixed effects	No	No	No	No	No	Yes	Yes	Yes	Yes	Yes
Expected sign: C5 indicator	−	−	−	−	−	−	−	−	−	−
Expected sign: Boone indicator			−					−		
Expected sign: H-statistic				+					+	
Expected sign: Lerner index					−					−

Sources: IMF, International Financial Statistics database; World Bank, Global Findex database; and World Bank, Global Financial Development database.

Notes: Probit regressions and bank competition. Robust standard errors are in parentheses.

$^*p < 0.1$; $^{**}p < 0.05$; $^{***}p < 0.01$.

TABLE 12.8.

Individuals Who Have a Credit Card and Bank Competition

	No Country Fixed Effects					Including Country Fixed Effects				
Indicator	**(1)**	**(2)**	**(3)**	**(4)**	**(5)**	**(6)**	**(7)**	**(8)**	**(9)**	**(10)**
C5 indicator	0.116**	0.312**	−0.0873	1.037***	0.136	−0.810***	−0.491	1.242**	1.252	−1.757
	(0.0504)	(0.125)	(0.106)	(0.247)	(0.275)	(0.259)	(0.403)	(0.604)	(1.090)	(1.090)
C5 Indicator × Credit/GDP		−0.00529*					−0.0162			
		(0.00306)					(0.0162)			
Boone indicator			12.39***					2.824		
			(4.054)					(11.10)		
C5 Indicator × Boone Indicator			−2.635***					−0.232		
			(0.947)					(2.614)		
H-statistic				9.310***					18.39	
				(2.617)					(12.11)	
C5 Indicator × H-Statistic				−2.070***					−3.932	
				(0.593)					(2.772)	
Lerner index					−6.404					−39.02**
					(4.450)					(16.39)
C5 Indicator × Lerner Index					1.992*					9.882***
					(1.023)					(3.826)
Credit/GDP	0.00554***	0.0284**	0.00223***	0.00331***	0.00140*	0.0161***	0.0857	0.0175***	−0.000748	0.0286***
	(0.000495)	(0.0132)	(0.000657)	(0.000687)	(0.000815)	(0.00404)	(0.0697)	(0.00585)	(0.00535)	(0.00737)
GDP per capita	0.220***	0.218***	0.296***	0.304***	0.333***	−0.0749	−0.122	−1.358**	−0.767	−1.234
	(0.0136)	(0.0137)	(0.0181)	(0.0205)	(0.0262)	(0.338)	(0.341)	(0.602)	(0.645)	(0.881)
GDP	−0.0435***	−0.0292**	−0.00275	−0.0398***	−0.00940	−0.469***	−0.456***	−0.548**	−0.652***	0.0455
	(0.00780)	(0.0115)	(0.0102)	(0.0120)	(0.0126)	(0.121)	(0.121)	(0.226)	(0.182)	(0.316)
Respondent age	0.00429***	0.00424***	0.00651***	0.00582***	0.00601***	0.00520***	0.00521***	0.00745***	0.00667***	0.00658***
	(0.000614)	(0.000615)	(0.000806)	(0.000827)	(0.000872)	(0.000623)	(0.000623)	(0.000822)	(0.000837)	(0.000889)
Female	0.115***	0.114***	0.0892***	0.0831***	0.0840***	0.117***	0.117***	0.0960***	0.0888***	0.0911***
	(0.0184)	(0.0184)	(0.0242)	(0.0246)	(0.0264)	(0.0188)	(0.0188)	(0.0247)	(0.0251)	(0.0269)
Primary education or less	−0.457***	−0.453***	−0.424**	−0.478**	−0.346*	−0.336**	−0.335**	−0.254	−0.269	−0.272
	(0.167)	(0.167)	(0.201)	(0.199)	(0.209)	(0.167)	(0.167)	(0.202)	(0.200)	(0.209)

(continued)

TABLE 12.8. ***(continued)***

Individuals Who Have a Credit Card and Bank Competition

Indicator	No Country Fixed Effects					Including Country Fixed Effects				
	(1)	(2)	(3)	(4)	(5)	(6)	(7)	(8)	(9)	(10)
Secondary education	−0.0550	−0.0490	0.117	0.0545	0.193	0.0957	0.0960	0.299	0.286	0.259
	(0.166)	(0.166)	(0.200)	(0.197)	(0.208)	(0.167)	(0.167)	(0.201)	(0.199)	(0.207)
Tertiary education or more	0.466***	0.473***	0.729***	0.668***	0.862***	0.623***	0.623***	0.928***	0.917***	0.942***
	(0.168)	(0.168)	(0.202)	(0.199)	(0.211)	(0.168)	(0.168)	(0.203)	(0.201)	(0.211)
Education: missing	−0.0782	−0.0617	−0.403	−0.509	−0.128	0.0126	0.0110	−0.310	−0.310	−0.173
	(0.239)	(0.239)	(0.383)	(0.382)	(0.515)	(0.241)	(0.241)	(0.384)	(0.381)	(0.514)
Poorest 20%	−0.496***	−0.496***	−0.576***	−0.560***	−0.521***	−0.499***	−0.498***	−0.600***	−0.576***	−0.538***
	(0.0331)	(0.0331)	(0.0460)	(0.0461)	(0.0492)	(0.0337)	(0.0337)	(0.0464)	(0.0467)	(0.0497)
Second 20%	−0.347***	−0.347***	−0.441***	−0.427***	−0.389***	−0.351***	−0.351***	−0.463***	−0.441***	−0.402***
	(0.0290)	(0.0290)	(0.0401)	(0.0402)	(0.0433)	(0.0295)	(0.0295)	(0.0406)	(0.0409)	(0.0439)
Middle 20%	−0.352***	−0.352***	−0.425***	−0.416***	−0.385***	−0.362***	−0.362***	−0.448***	−0.436***	−0.403***
	(0.0276)	(0.0276)	(0.0370)	(0.0375)	(0.0403)	(0.0281)	(0.0281)	(0.0377)	(0.0381)	(0.0409)
Fourth 20%	−0.257***	−0.257***	−0.289***	−0.289***	−0.266***	−0.260***	−0.260***	−0.296***	−0.293***	−0.272***
	(0.0242)	(0.0242)	(0.0314)	(0.0320)	(0.0346)	(0.0246)	(0.0246)	(0.0320)	(0.0325)	(0.0351)
No. of observations	62,863	62,863	38,992	37,987	33,989	62,863	62,863	38,992	37,987	33,989
Year fixed effects	Yes	Yes	Yes	Yes	Yes	Yes	Yes	Yes	Yes	Yes
Country fixed effects	No	No	No	No	No	Yes	Yes	Yes	Yes	Yes
Expected sign: C5 indicator	−	−	−	−	−	−	−	−	−	−
Expected sign: Boone indicator			−					−		
Expected sign: H-statistic				+					+	
Expected sign: Lerner index					−					−

Sources: IMF, International Financial Statistics database; World Bank, Global Findex database; and World Bank, Global Financial Development database.

Notes: Probit regressions and bank competition. Robust standard errors are in parentheses.

$^{*}p < 0.1$; $^{**}p < 0.05$; $^{***}p < 0.01$.

This definition is consistent with the guidelines provided by the International Labour Organization (2013). The Findex database only provides this wage indicator variable for 2014 and 2017. However, the four competition variables are not available from most countries for 2017. Therefore, the regressions for informally employed individuals mainly use observations from 2014, which reduces the number of observations available and subsequently also reduces the length of the panel, making it more difficult to estimate the effects of country-level variables when we include country fixed effects. Because of this, in the regressions for the informal economy, we do not use country fixed effects.

Table 12.9 shows the results for adoption of bank accounts. For brevity, we omit the individual-level demographic results. The results are generally consistent with previous results, and we find that greater competition leads to wider

TABLE 12.9.

Individuals Who Have a Bank Account and Bank Competition

	No Country Fixed Effects				
Indicator	**(1)**	**(2)**	**(3)**	**(4)**	**(5)**
C5 indicator	−1.297***	−1.938***	−1.867***	−0.982***	−2.309***
	(0.0510)	(0.109)	(0.115)	(0.178)	(0.260)
C5 Indicator × Credit/GDP		0.0206***			
		(0.00309)			
Boone indicator			34.31***		
			(4.591)		
C5 Indicator × Boone Indicator			−8.044***		
			(1.056)		
H-statistic				7.345***	
				(2.212)	
C5 Indicator × H-Statistic				−1.440***	
				(0.502)	
Lerner index					−10.95***
					(3.827)
C5 Indicator × Lerner Index					2.290**
					(0.892)
Credit/GDP	0.0163***	−0.0736***	0.0216***	0.0201***	0.0306***
	(0.000631)	(0.0135)	(0.00110)	(0.00112)	(0.00119)
GDP per capita	0.0908***	0.0941***	0.0213	0.0470**	−0.466***
	(0.0124)	(0.0124)	(0.0182)	(0.0228)	(0.0399)
GDP	−0.0316***	−0.0708***	0.0153	−0.0981***	0.158***
	(0.00966)	(0.0111)	(0.0143)	(0.0159)	(0.0197)
No. of observations	29,139	29,139	14,743	13,229	11,463
Year fixed effects	Yes	Yes	Yes	Yes	Yes
Country fixed effects	No	No	No	No	No
Expected sign: C5 indicator	−	−	−	−	−
Expected sign: Boone indicator			−		
Expected sign: H-statistic				+	
Expected sign: Lerner index					−

Sources: IMF, International Financial Statistics database; World Bank, Global Findex database; and World Bank, Global Financial Development database.

Notes: Probit regressions and bank competition. Robust standard errors are in parentheses.

$^{**}p < 0.05$; $^{***}p < 0.01$.

adoption of bank accounts. The signs of the C5, H-statistic, and Lerner index indicators are consistent with our hypothesis, whereas the sign of the Boone indicator has an intuitive sign. We also find that financial depth and higher GDP per capita increase the probability of individuals adopting an account.

In Tables 12.10 and 12.11, we show the effects of bank competition on the adoption of debit and credit cards. The results are similar to the full sample case, and we find that the effect on competition is more consistent with hypothesis 1 for debit cards than for credit cards. The ratio of credit to GDP and GDP per capita also have an intuitive positive effect on adoption of debit and credit cards.

In summary, the empirical results found for informally employed individuals confirm the results for the entire sample and generally show an economically and

TABLE 12.10.

Individuals Who Have a Debit Card and Bank Competition

	No Country Fixed Effects				
Indicator	**(1)**	**(2)**	**(3)**	**(4)**	**(5)**
C5 indicator	−0.539***	−1.050***	−0.629***	1.841***	−3.167***
	(0.0534)	(0.127)	(0.120)	(0.219)	(0.323)
C5 Indicator × Credit/GDP		0.0145***			
		(0.00335)			
Boone indicator			11.04**		
			(5.279)		
C5 Indicator × Boone Indicator			−2.465**		
			(1.222)		
H-statistic				27.18***	
				(2.492)	
C5 Indicator × H-Statistic				−6.207***	
				(0.569)	
Lerner index					−38.23***
					(4.833)
C5 Indicator × Lerner Index					9.101***
					(1.143)
Credit/GDP	0.0114***	−0.0514***	0.0122***	0.00910***	0.0245***
	(0.000584)	(0.0145)	(0.000958)	(0.000929)	(0.00146)
GDP per capita	0.255***	0.258***	0.229***	0.398***	−0.228***
	(0.0144)	(0.0145)	(0.0226)	(0.0263)	(0.0490)
GDP	0.0551***	0.0219*	0.117***	0.0550***	0.303***
	(0.00983)	(0.0124)	(0.0152)	(0.0157)	(0.0226)
No. of observations	29,139	29,139	14,743	13,229	11,463
Year fixed effects	Yes	Yes	Yes	Yes	Yes
Country fixed effects	No	No	No	No	No
Expected sign: C5 indicator	−	−	−	−	−
Expected sign: Boone indicator			−		
Expected sign: H-statistic				+	
Expected sign: Lerner index					−

Sources: IMF, International Financial Statistics database; World Bank, Global Findex database; and World Bank, Global Financial Development database.

Notes: Probit regressions and bank competition. Robust standard errors are in parentheses.

*$p < 0.1$; **$p < 0.05$; ***$p < 0.01$.

TABLE 12.11.

Individuals Who Have a Credit Card and Bank Competition

	No Country Fixed Effects				
Indicator	**(1)**	**(2)**	**(3)**	**(4)**	**(5)**
C5 indicator	0.0517	−0.0608	0.188	1.874***	−1.497***
	(0.0818)	(0.201)	(0.217)	(0.397)	(0.549)
C5 Indicator × Credit/GDP		0.00298			
		(0.00493)			
Boone indicator			9.246		
			(9.806)		
C5 Indicator × Boone Indicator			−2.339		
			(2.207)		
H-statistic				17.57***	
				(4.230)	
C5 Indicator × H-Statistic				−4.095***	
				(0.959)	
Lerner index					−28.50***
					(8.508)
C5 Indicator × Lerner Index					7.304***
					(2.011)
Credit/GDP	0.00752***	−0.00535	0.00792***	0.00624***	0.0169***
	(0.000825)	(0.0213)	(0.00149)	(0.00142)	(0.00252)
GDP per capita	0.148***	0.148***	0.201***	0.238***	−0.181**
	(0.0230)	(0.0231)	(0.0343)	(0.0477)	(0.0877)
GDP	−0.0279*	−0.0356*	0.0335	0.0360	0.203***
	(0.0143)	(0.0193)	(0.0228)	(0.0237)	(0.0365)
No. of observations	29,139	29,139	14,682	13,168	11,440
Year fixed effects	Yes	Yes	Yes	Yes	Yes
Country fixed effects	No	No	No	No	No
Expected sign: C5 indicator	−	−	−	−	−
Expected sign: Boone indicator			−		
Expected sign: H-statistic				+	
Expected sign: Lerner index					−

Sources: IMF, International Financial Statistics database; World Bank, Global Findex database; and World Bank, Global Financial Development database.

Notes: Probit regressions and bank competition. Robust standard errors are in parentheses.

$^{*}p < 0.1$; $^{**}p < 0.05$; $^{***}p < 0.01$.

statistically significant effect of competition on the adoption of bank accounts and debit cards, although not for credit cards.

FINANCIAL INCLUSION AND BANK BALANCE SHEET VARIABLES

We now study how relevant bank balance sheet variables affect financial inclusion, more precisely, the borrowing capacity of individuals. By estimating the importance of this bank-lending channel, we estimate how key balance sheet variables (such as Tier 1 capital ratios, or liquidity ratios) affect the probability of individual borrowing and how these variables interact with the economic cycle.

Empirical Model

To estimate individuals' borrowing capacity, we first consider a simple probit model in which borrowing depends on the following latent variable:

$$\begin{aligned} Borrow\ i,c,t^{*} &= \beta\ 1\ GDPgrow\ c,t-1 + \beta\ 2\ Tier1\ c,t-1 + \beta\ 3\ LAR\ c,t-1 \\ &+ \beta\ 4\ Tier1\ c,t-1 \times GDPgrow\ c,t-1 + \beta\ 5\ LAR\ c,t-1 \\ &\times GDPgrow\ c,t-1 + \beta\ 6X\ i,c,t + \beta\ t + \beta\ c + \varepsilon\ i,c,t \end{aligned} \qquad (2),$$

where $GDPgrow_{c,t-1}$ is the lagged value of GDP growth for country c in period $t-1$, $Tier1_{c,t-1}$ is the lagged average Tier 1 ratio for the country, and $LAR_{c,t-1}$ is the average liquid asset ratio (liquid assets to total assets).

The dependent variable in the probit model is an indicator variable equal to 1 if the individual has borrowed in the past 12 months from a financial institution. The variable allows us to estimate the relationship between new loans obtained by individuals and lagged bank balance sheet variables. The parameters of interest in this regression are the terms $\beta_1 - \beta_5$, which represent the effect of lagged balance sheet variables, economic growth, and their interactions on the probability that an individual borrows from a bank. As in the previous model (1), in model (2) we use a vector of individual-level variables, other country-level variables, and fixed effects.

As discussed in the introduction, the existing literature has not found undisputed results regarding the relationship between an individual's borrowing and his or her country's balance sheet strength. In our model, $\beta_2, \beta_3 > 0$ would be consistent with the view that borrowing increases in countries with stronger financial systems (more liquid or more capitalized). Also, $\beta_4, \beta_5 < 0$ would imply a certain degree of countercyclicality in the credit. That is, stronger financial systems (in terms of higher capital or liquidity) provide less credit when GDP growth is high, so stronger banks are more countercyclical.

A limitation of our empirical strategy is that we are not able to separately identify supply from demand-side determinants of adoption of financial products or borrowing. To separately identify these effects, we would need access to accepted and rejected credit and bank product applications, as in Jiménez and others (2012, 2014). Instrumental variable estimation methods might also be useful to separately identify supply from demand effects, but valid instruments are usually difficult to find, given data constraints in sub-Saharan Africa.

Empirical Results

In the second set of results, we want to understand how bank balance sheets affect the borrowing capacity of individuals. By estimating the importance of this bank-lending channel, we can determine how Tier 1 capital ratios and similar balance sheet indicators affect the probability of borrowing.

As mentioned, the literature does not provide conclusive results on the effect of bank capital on lending. In addition, we are not able to disentangle demand-side from supply-side effects, given the limitations of our data. Also, we expect a certain degree of cyclicality, namely, that borrowing is constrained in countries with lower GDP growth and with less capitalized or less liquid financial systems.

Table 12.12 presents the results of the probit model. Contrary to the probit estimates on competition, results changed considerably when country fixed effects were used. When considering no country fixed effects, we find, as shown in column (1), that countries that have financial systems with higher capital ratios generate a positive effect on borrowing. Also, a higher liquid asset ratio has a positive effect on borrowing in the next period. When we include Tier 1 capital ratios (column 3), we still obtain a positive (and larger) effect of the Tier 1 ratio, but the effect of the liquid asset ratio is not statistically significant.[8]

Second, we consider interaction effects among GDP growth, Tier 1, and liquid asset ratios in specifications (4) through (7). When considering the interaction terms, we generally find a procyclical effect with respect to capital and liquidity. In column (4), we find that higher GDP growth increases credit more in financial systems with higher liquidity ratios. That is, more liquid banks are more procyclical—they lend more. We also find a similar effect of Tier 1 capital in column (5): borrowing increases in countries with high GDP growth and higher capital ratios, so more capitalized banks are more procyclical. When combining the two interactions for liquidity and capital, only the Tier 1 interaction with GDP has a positive sign, whereas the liquidity interaction term has a negative sign.

In columns (8) through (14), we repeat the same regressions but include country fixed effects. Some of the results previously found are no longer present. The individual effects of capital and liquidity are less robust. Interaction terms with GDP have insignificant or opposite effects to the regressions run without fixed effects. We conclude from these results that the effect of bank balance sheet variables on individuals' borrowing is not undisputed.

As with the regressions for accounts, debit cards, and credit cards, we find similar intuitive results regarding the effect of demographic variables on borrowing. In all specifications, older individuals, female individuals, and well-educated individuals (tertiary education or more) are more likely to borrow. Also, poor individuals are less likely to borrow.

When we repeat the results for informally employed individuals (not shown), we do not find undisputed results. Some of the results are not robust and are different from the full sample results.

[8] Higher Tier 1 capital ratios could also have an opposite effect. Tier 1 capital ratios tend to be higher in sub-Saharan Africa compared with other regions. Higher capital ratios may reflect an unstable financial system that is buffered to cover for future loses (Beck and others 2011). In sub-Saharan Africa, where banks incur high costs to raise capital, high capital ratios could constrain lending, such as in a "credit crunch" (Bernanke and Lown 1991).

TABLE 12.12.

Country and Year Fixed Effects for Individuals Who Borrowed in the Past Year and Bank Balance Sheet Variables

	No Country Fixed Effects						
Indicator	**(1)**	**(2)**	**(3)**	**(4)**	**(5)**	**(6)**	**(7)**
GDP growth	0.0264***	0.0259***	0.0259***	0.00621	−0.0514***	0.00621	−0.0435***
	(0.00384)	(0.00368)	(0.00383)	(0.00911)	(0.0132)	(0.00911)	(0.0135)
Tier 1	0.0194***		0.0182***		−0.00943*		−0.0221***
	(0.00202)		(0.00209)		(0.00529)		(0.00592)
LAR		0.00160*	0.000159	−0.00266		−0.00266	0.00867***
		(0.000919)	(0.000967)	(0.00214)		(0.00214)	(0.00255)
LAR × GDP Growth				0.000778**		0.000778**	−0.00204***
				(0.000332)		(0.000332)	(0.000485)
Tier 1 × GDP Growth					0.00537***		0.00847***
					(0.000891)		(0.00113)
Respondent age	0.00647***	0.00651***	0.00667***	0.00655***	0.00655***	0.00655***	0.00679***
	(0.000541)	(0.000547)	(0.000548)	(0.000548)	(0.000542)	(0.000548)	(0.000551)
Female	0.102***	0.0996***	0.100***	0.0997***	0.101***	0.0997***	0.0991***
	(0.0177)	(0.0178)	(0.0178)	(0.0178)	(0.0177)	(0.0178)	(0.0179)
Primary education or less	0.262	0.269	0.266	0.267	0.271	0.267	0.279
	(0.259)	(0.258)	(0.260)	(0.258)	(0.257)	(0.258)	(0.257)
Secondary education	0.616**	0.628**	0.618**	0.625**	0.633**	0.625**	0.640**
	(0.259)	(0.258)	(0.260)	(0.258)	(0.257)	(0.258)	(0.257)
Tertiary education or more	1.017***	1.054***	1.015***	1.050***	1.038***	1.050***	1.040***
	(0.260)	(0.259)	(0.261)	(0.260)	(0.258)	(0.260)	(0.258)
Poorest 20%	0.351	0.343	0.347	0.340	0.366	0.340	0.366
	(0.331)	(0.329)	(0.331)	(0.329)	(0.329)	(0.329)	(0.329)
Second 20%	−0.473***	−0.465***	−0.471***	−0.466***	−0.472***	−0.466***	−0.469***
	(0.0315)	(0.0316)	(0.0317)	(0.0316)	(0.0316)	(0.0316)	(0.0318)
Middle 20%	−0.320***	−0.316***	−0.321***	−0.316***	−0.318***	−0.316***	−0.319***
	(0.0283)	(0.0284)	(0.0285)	(0.0284)	(0.0283)	(0.0284)	(0.0285)
Fourth 20%	−0.232***	−0.226***	−0.231***	−0.227***	−0.230***	−0.227***	−0.228***
	(0.0260)	(0.0262)	(0.0262)	(0.0262)	(0.0260)	(0.0262)	(0.0262)
No. of observations	45,903	44,903	44,903	44,903	45,903	44,903	44,903
Other country variables	Yes	Yes	Yes	Yes	Yes	Yes	Yes
Year fixed effects	Yes	Yes	Yes	Yes	Yes	Yes	Yes
Country fixed effects	No	No	No	No	No	No	No

(continued)

TABLE 12.12. *(continued)*

Country and Year Fixed Effects for Individuals Who Borrowed in the Past Year and Bank Balance Sheet Variables

	Including Country Fixed Effects						
Indicator	**(8)**	**(9)**	**(10)**	**(11)**	**(12)**	**(13)**	**(14)**
GDP growth	0.00448	0.00295	0.00481	0.0579***	0.0419*	0.0579***	0.0738***
	(0.00748)	(0.00709)	(0.00747)	(0.0147)	(0.0236)	(0.0147)	(0.0248)
Tier 1	0.00319		0.00554		0.0208*		0.0107
	(0.00586)		(0.00598)		(0.0123)		(0.0125)
LAR		−0.00702*	−0.00786*	0.00590		0.00590	0.0109**
		(0.00408)	(0.00417)	(0.00518)		(0.00518)	(0.00551)
LAR × GDP Growth				−0.00204***		−0.00204***	−0.00362***
				(0.000498)		(0.000498)	(0.000713)
Tier 1 × GDP Growth					−0.00263*		0.00256
					(0.00159)		(0.00184)
Respondent age	0.00697***	0.00711***	0.00711***	0.00716***	0.00698***	0.00716***	0.00717***
	(0.000556)	(0.000563)	(0.000563)	(0.000563)	(0.000556)	(0.000563)	(0.000563)
Female	0.112***	0.111***	0.111***	0.110***	0.112***	0.110***	0.110***
	(0.0181)	(0.0182)	(0.0182)	(0.0182)	(0.0181)	(0.0182)	(0.0182)
Primary education or less	0.367	0.369	0.367	0.382	0.364	0.382	0.382
	(0.260)	(0.261)	(0.261)	(0.260)	(0.260)	(0.260)	(0.261)
Secondary education	0.707***	0.706***	0.704***	0.719***	0.704***	0.719***	0.718***
	(0.260)	(0.261)	(0.261)	(0.260)	(0.260)	(0.260)	(0.260)
Tertiary education or more	1.127***	1.123***	1.119***	1.136***	1.124***	1.136***	1.133***
	(0.261)	(0.262)	(0.262)	(0.261)	(0.262)	(0.261)	(0.262)
Poorest 20%	0.468	0.463	0.463	0.470	0.465	0.470	0.476
	(0.332)	(0.333)	(0.333)	(0.332)	(0.332)	(0.332)	(0.332)
Second 20%	−0.484***	−0.482***	−0.483***	−0.482***	−0.484***	−0.482***	−0.483***
	(0.0323)	(0.0325)	(0.0325)	(0.0325)	(0.0323)	(0.0325)	(0.0325)
Middle 20%	−0.334***	−0.335***	−0.335***	−0.335***	−0.334***	−0.335***	−0.336***
	(0.0288)	(0.0290)	(0.0290)	(0.0290)	(0.0288)	(0.0290)	(0.0290)
Fourth 20%	−0.244***	−0.243***	−0.243***	−0.242***	−0.244***	−0.242***	−0.243***
	(0.0265)	(0.0267)	(0.0267)	(0.0267)	(0.0265)	(0.0267)	(0.0267)
No. of observations	45,903	44,903	44,903	44,903	45,903	44,903	44,903
Other country variables	Yes	Yes	Yes	Yes	Yes	Yes	Yes
Year fixed effects	Yes	Yes	Yes	Yes	Yes	Yes	Yes
Country fixed effects	Yes	Yes	Yes	Yes	Yes	Yes	Yes

Sources: IMF, International Financial Statistics database; World Bank, Global Findex database; and World Bank, Global Financial Development database.

Notes: Probit regressions and bank competition. Robust standard errors are in parentheses. LAR = liquid asset ratio.

$^{*}p < 0.1$; $^{**}p < 0.05$; $^{***}p < 0.01$.

CONCLUSION

In this chapter, we studied how competition and financial soundness in the financial sector affect financial inclusion in sub-Saharan Africa. We used detailed individual-level survey data, combined with key country-level indicators of bank competition and financial soundness to study the effect of competition and the strength of several bank balance sheet variables on the adoption of key financial products.

Our results generally show a positive and significant effect of competition on the adoption of various financial products. We did not find clear results when considering the effect of balance sheet variables on borrowing by households. These results may help policymakers in sub-Saharan Africa and other regions to be aware of the importance of the key features of the banking sector necessary to promote financial inclusion. This could lead to regulations that may have positive effects on economic growth and long-term economic development.

Two remarkable forces of change could increase competition in the banking sector, with positive effects on financial inclusion. First, new and efficient technologies are being developed to transform the sector with new products, processes, and providers (fintech).[9] Second, financial markets are increasingly interconnected across the world, and sub-Saharan Africa is not an exception. Both forces are instrumental in fostering an optimistic outlook regarding future improvements in financial inclusion.

Although mobile payments are successful in several eastern African countries, we expect that fintech will progressively cover other financial services, such as loans and saving accounts. More granular data are necessary to understand how these services are transforming the industry. Policymakers can take advantage of fintech and other developments to foster competition and improve financial inclusion. Given the economic, social, and political advances that sub-Saharan Africa has achieved, we believe that the financial sector offers opportunities for growth in the future. The potential to improve financial inclusion is high.

REFERENCES

Admati, A. R., P. M. DeMarzo, M. F. Hellwig, and P. C. Pfleiderer. 2011. "Fallacies, Irrelevant Facts, and Myths in the Discussion of Capital Regulation: Why Bank Equity Is Not Socially Expensive." GSB Research Paper 2063, Stanford University, Stanford, CA.

Ahokpossi, C., K. Ismail, S. Karmakar, and M. Koulet-Vickot. 2013. "Financial Depth in the WAEMU: Benchmarking against Frontier SSA Countries." IMF Working Paper 13/161, International Monetary Fund, Washington, DC.

Allen, F., A. Demirgüç-Kunt, L. F. Klapper, and M. S. Peria. 2016. "The Foundations of Financial Inclusion: Understanding Ownership and Use of Formal Accounts." *Journal of Financial Intermediation* 27: 1–30.

---

[9] For example, distributed ledger technologies, mobile payments, virtual currencies, crowdfunding, robo-advice, and others (Maino and others 2019).

Allen, F., E. Carletti, R. Cull, J. Qian, L. W. Senbet, and P. Valenzuela. 2013. "Resolving the African Financial Development Gap: Cross-Country Comparisons and a Within-Country Study of Kenya." NBER Working Paper 18013, National Bureau of Economic Research, Cambridge, MA.

Baumol, W. J., J. C. Panzar, and R. D. Willig. 1988. *Contestable Markets and the Theory of Industry Structure*. New York: Harcourt Brace Jovanovich.

Beck, T., and R. Cull. 2014. "Banking in Africa." In *The Oxford Handbook of Banking*, 2nd edition, edited by A. N. Berger, P. Molyneux, and J. O. S. Wilson. Oxford: Oxford University Press.

Beck, T., S. Munzule Maimbo, I. Faye, and T. Triki. 2011. *Financing Africa: Through the Crisis and Beyond*. Washington, DC: World Bank.

Bernanke, B. S. 2007. "The Financial Accelerator and the Credit Channel." Paper presented at the Atlanta Federal Reserve Bank Conference on the Credit Channel of Monetary Policy in the 21st Century, Atlanta, GA, June 14–15.

Bernanke, B. S., and A. S. Blinder. 1988. "Credit, Money, and Aggregate Demand." *American Economic Review* 78 (2): 435–39.

Bernanke, B. S., and M. Gertler. 1987. "Banking and Macroeconomic Equilibrium." In *New Approaches to Monetary Economics: Proceedings of the Second International Symposium in Economic Theory and Econometrics*, edited by W. A. Barnett and K. J. Singleton. Cambridge: Cambridge University Press.

Bernanke, B. S., and M. Gertler. 1995. "Inside the Black Box: The Credit Channel of Monetary Policy Transmission." *Journal of Economic Perspectives* 9 (4): 27–48.

Bernanke, B. S., and C. S. Lown. 1991. "The Credit Crunch." *Brookings Papers on Economic Activity* 2: 205–47.

Berrospide, J. M., and R. M. Edge. 2010. "The Effects of Bank Capital on Lending: What Do We Know, and What Does It Mean?" *International Journal of Central Banking* 6 (4): 5–54.

Bikker, J. A., and K. Haaf. 2002. "Competition, Concentration and Their Relationship: An Empirical Analysis of the Banking Industry." *Journal of Banking and Finance* 26 (11): 2191–214.

Boone, J. 2008. "A New Way to Measure Competition." *Economic Journal* 118 (531): 1245–61.

Bridges, J., D. Gregory, M. Nielsen, S. Pezzini, A. Radia, and M. Spaltro. 2014. "The Impact of Capital Requirements on Bank Lending." Working Paper 486, Bank of England, London.

Brun, M., H. Fraisse, and D. Thesmar. 2017. "The Real Effects of Bank Capital Requirements." ESRB Working Paper 47, European Systemic Risk Board, Frankfurt.

Čihák, M., A. Demirgüç-Kunt, E. Feyen, and R. Levine. 2012. "Benchmarking Financial Systems around the World." Policy Research Working Paper 6175, World Bank, Washington, DC.

Claessens, S., and L. Laeven. 2004. "What Drives Bank Competition? Some International Evidence." *Journal of Money, Credit and Banking* 36 (3): 563–83.

Cornett, M. M., J. J. McNutt, P. E. Strahan, and H. Tehranian. 2011. "Liquidity Risk Management and Credit Supply in the Financial Crisis." *Journal of Financial Economics* 101 (2): 297–312.

Degryse, H., A. Morales Acevedo, and S. Ongena. 2014. "Competition in Banking." In *The Oxford Handbook of Banking*, 2nd edition, edited by A. N. Berger, P. Molyneux, and J. O. Wilson. Oxford: Oxford University Press.

Deléchat, C., M. Newiak, R. Xu, F. Yang, and G. Aslan. 2018. "What Is Driving Women's Financial Inclusion across Countries?" IMF Working Paper 18/38, International Monetary Fund, Washington, DC.

Demirgüç-Kunt, A., and L. F. Klapper. 2013. "Measuring Financial Inclusion: Explaining Variation in Use of Financial Services across and within Countries." *Brookings Papers on Economic Activity* (Spring): 279–340.

Demirgüç-Kunt, A., L. Klapper, and D. Singer. 2017. "Financial Inclusion and Inclusive Growth: A Review of Recent Empirical Evidence." Policy Research Working Paper, World Bank, Washington, DC.

Demirgüç-Kunt, A., L. Klapper, D. Singer, and P. Van Oudheusden. 2015. "The Global Findex Database 2014: Measuring Financial Inclusion around the World." Policy Research Working Paper 7255, World Bank, Washington, DC.

Gambacorta, L., and D. Marques-Ibanez. 2011. "The Bank Lending Channel: Lessons from the Crisis." *Economic Policy* 26 (66): 135–82.

Gropp, R., T. Mosk, S. Ongena, and C. Wix. 2016. "Banks Response to Higher Capital Requirements: Evidence from a Quasi-Natural Experiment." *Review of Financial Studies* 32 (1): 266–99.

Hanson, S. G., A. K. Kashyap, and J. C. Stein. 2011. "A Macroprudential Approach to Financial Regulation." *Journal of Economic Perspectives* 25 (1): 3–28.

International Labour Organization. 2013. *Measuring Informality: A Statistical Manual.* Geneva: International Labour Organization.

Jiménez, G., S. Ongena, J. Peydró, and J. Saurina. 2012. "Credit Supply and Monetary Policy: Identifying the Bank Balance-Sheet Channel with Loan Applications." *American Economic Review* 102 (5): 2301–26.

Jiménez, G., S. Ongena, J. Peydró, and J. Saurina. 2014. "Hazardous Times for Monetary Policy: What Do Twenty-Three Million Bank Loans Say about the Effects of Monetary Policy on Credit Risk-Taking?" *Econometrica* 82 (2): 463–505.

Kapan, T., and C. Minoiu. 2013. "Balance Sheet Strength and Bank Lending during the Global Financial Crisis." IMF Working Paper 13/102, International Monetary Fund, Washington, DC.

Karlan, D. S., and J. Morduch. 2009. "Access to Finance." *In Handbook of Development Economics*, volume 5, edited by D. Karlan and J. Morduch. Amsterdam: Elsevier.

Kashyap, A. K., and J. C. Stein. 2000. "What Do a Million Observations on Banks Say about the Transmission of Monetary Policy?" *American Economic Review* 90 (3): 407–28.

King, R. G., and R. Levine. 1993. "Finance and Growth: Schumpeter Might Be Right." *Quarterly Journal of Economics* 108 (3): 717–37.

Levine, R. 2005. "Finance and Growth: Theory and Evidence." In *Handbook of Economic Growth*, volume 1A, edited by R. Levine. Amsterdam: Elsevier.

Love, I., and M. S. Peria. 2012. "How Bank Competition Affects Firms' Access to Finance." *World Bank Economic Review* 29 (3): 413–48.

Maino, R., A. Massara, H. Perez-Saiz, P. Sharma, and A. Sy. 2019. "FinTech in Sub-Saharan African Countries: A Game Changer." IMF African Department Paper 19/04, International Monetary Fund, Washington, DC.

Mecagni, M., D. Marchettini, and R. Maino. 2015. "Evolving Banking Trends in Sub-Saharan Africa." IMF African Department Paper 15/10, International Monetary Fund, Washington, DC.

Michelangeli, V., and E. Sette. 2016. "How Does Bank Capital Affect the Supply of Mortgages? Evidence from a Randomized Experiment." BIS Working Paper 557, Bank for International Settlements, Basel, Switzerland.

Mlachila, D., and A. Moheeput. 2014. "Does Openness Matter for Financial Development in Africa?" IMF Working Paper 14/94, International Monetary Fund, Washington, DC.

Panzar, J. C., and J. N. Rosse. 1987. "Testing for 'Monopoly' Equilibrium." *Journal of Industrial Economics* 35 (4): 443–56.

Shaffer, S. 1993. "A Test of Competition in Canadian Banking." *Journal of Money, Credit and Banking* 25 (1): 49–61.

Tirole, J. 1988. *The Theory of Industrial Organization*. Cambridge, MA: MIT Press.

Vives, X. 2011. "Competition Policy in Banking." *Oxford Review of Economic Policy* 27 (3): 479–97.

Vives, X. 2016. *Competition and Stability in Banking*. Princeton, NJ: Princeton University Press.

Yontcheva, B., and A. Alter. 2016. "Financial Inclusion and Development in the CEMAC." IMF Working Paper 15/235, International Monetary Fund, Washington, DC.

Index